Contemporary Agricultural Research from Global Perspectiv

Proceedings of Second International Seminar of Chinese Agricultural-Sage Culture

Chief Editor: Li Changwu Xue Yanbin

全球视角下的当代农业问题研究

第二届中华农圣文化国际研讨会论文集

◎ 李昌武 薛彦斌 主编

中国农业科学技术出版社
China Agricultural Science and Technology Press

图书在版编目（CIP）数据

全球视角下的当代农业问题研究：第二届中华农圣文化国际研讨会论文集／李昌武，薛彦斌主编．—北京：中国农业科学技术出版社，2011.3
ISBN 978－7－5116－0413－2

Ⅰ.①全… Ⅱ.①李…②薛… Ⅲ.①农业问题－世界－国际学术会议－文集 Ⅳ.①F31－53

中国版本图书馆CIP数据核字（2011）第045591号

责任编辑 徐 毅
责任校对 贾晓红

出 版 者 中国农业科学技术出版社
北京市中关村南大街12号 邮编：100081
电 话 (010)82106638(发行部) (010)82106631(编辑室)
(010)82109703(读者服务部)
传 真 (010)82106636
网 址 http://www.castp.cn
印 刷 者 北京华忠兴业印刷有限责任公司
开 本 787 mm×1 092 mm 1/16
印 张 34
字 数 810千字
版 次 2011年3月第1版 2011年3月第1次印刷
定 价 72.00元

《全球视角下的当代农业问题研究》

编 委 会

组成员

王宏伟　寿光市政府党组成员，办公室主任，第二届中华农圣文化节领导小组成员

刘水明　寿光市委宣传部副部长，市广播电视台台长，市广播影视集团董事长，第二届中华农圣文化节领导小组成员

李群成　寿光市委宣传部常务副部长，第二届中华农圣文化节领导小组成员

李泮德　寿光市财政局局长，第二届中华农圣文化节领导小组成员

张文升　寿光市文化局局长，第二届中华农圣文化节领导小组成员

李　燕　寿光市市直机关党工委书记，第二届中华农圣文化节领导小组成员

周杰三　寿光日报社社长，第二届中华农圣文化节领导小组成员

张树强　寿光市体育局局长，第二届中华农圣文化节领导小组成员

杨维田　寿光市农业局局长，第二届中华农圣文化节领导小组成员

张允生　寿光市科技局局长，第二届中华农圣文化节领导小组成员

张春荣　寿光市旅游局局长，第二届中华农圣文化节领导小组成员

潘广科　寿光市文联主席，第二届中华农圣文化节领导小组成员

张丁奇　寿光市科协主席，第二届中华农圣文化节领导小组成员

杨秀英　寿光市妇联主席，第二届中华农圣文化节领导小组成员

苗光彬　寿光市团市委书记，第二届中华农圣文化节领导小组成员

王建文　寿光市建设局副局长，生态农业观光园管理处主任，第二届中华农圣文化节领导小组成员

王启龙　寿光市蔬菜高科技示范园管理处副主任，菜博会组委会办公室常务副主任，第二届中华农圣文化节领导小组成员

于福生　菜博会组委会办公室党支部书记、副主任，第二届中华农圣文化节领导小组成员

刘美霞　寿光市监察局副局长，菜博会组委会办公室宣传部长，第二届中华农圣文化节领导小组成员

张鹏伟　寿光市新闻出版管理办公室主任，第二届中华农圣文化节领导小组成员

武治强　寿光市圣城街道党工委书记，第二届中华农圣文化节领导小组成员

王安文　寿光市洛城街道党工委书记，第二届中华农圣文化节领导小组成员

主　编

李昌武　薛彦斌

副主编

肖万里　李运祝　张　菲

参编人员

王爱丽　徐友信　高俊平　范世杰

肖志文　周永胜

前　言

本论文集是第二届中华农圣文化国际研讨会的论文结集，共收录了57位与会专家与学者的论文66篇，内容涵盖了农学思想、设施园艺、有机农业、现代生物工程、海洋生物、畜牧业、生态环保、农业发展、农业经济和农业文明史等众多方面，特别是中国现代农业发展、现代生物工程、有机农业和环境保护等方面，为传统农学思想注入了现代内涵，为我们提供了全新世界视角。

第二届中华农圣文化国际研讨会由中国（寿光）国际蔬菜科技博览会中华农圣文化节领导小组主办，潍坊科技学院承办，寿光市《齐民要术》研究会协办。中华农圣文化国际研讨会是中国（寿光）国际蔬菜科技博览会的重要组成部分，旨在弘扬传统农业文化，传播现代农学思想，促进农业国际交流与合作，推动现代农业的发展与进步。

研讨会于2011年4月25～27日在山东省寿光市举行。寿光市是中国蔬菜之乡，位于山东半岛中部，渤海莱州湾南畔，总面积2 070km^2，辖14处镇（街道），975个行政村，人口102万，是中国优秀旅游城市、国家园林城市、国家卫生城市、国家环保模范城市、全国县域经济综合实力百强县（市）、山东省文明城市，是保持共产党员先进性教育活动的联系点。寿光市历史悠久，公元前148年置县，是夏代斟灌国、西周纪国的建都地，史传汉字鼻祖仓颉在此创造了象形文字，境内现已发现龙山文化、纪国故城等150处历史遗址。寿光资源丰富，中南部地下水资源丰沛，土质肥沃，宜于粮食、蔬菜等多种农作物生长；北部地下卤水储量40亿m^3，原盐年产量300万t，是全国三大重点原盐产区之一和重要盐化工基地。寿光市农业文化光辉灿烂，早在北魏时期，寿光籍著名农学家贾思勰便总结了包括寿光以及黄河中下游地区的种植、养殖经验，写成了世界上第一部堪称农业百科全书式的农学巨著《齐民要术》，这部农学巨著对我国和世界农业生产产生了深远影响。贾思勰被后人尊为农圣。改革开放以来，寿光市三元朱村党支部书记王乐义于1989年带头试验成功了冬暖式蔬菜大棚，掀起了一场蔬菜反季节栽培技术的“绿色革命”和“银色革命”，寿光成为了全国最大的“菜园子”和“菜篮子”。

本次研讨会由潍坊科技学院具体承办，会议地点设在潍坊科技学院国际学术会议中心。潍坊科技学院是一所经教育部批准成立的全日制普通本科高等院校，校园现占地 160hm^2，建筑面积 76 万 m^2，总资产 15 亿元，教学科研仪器设备总值 1.3 亿元，馆藏图书 136.3 万册，教职工 1 562人，另有外籍教师 33 人，全日制在校生 24 627 人。现设 11 个院系，17 个本科专业，41 个专科专业。学院建有生命科学研究院、蔬菜花卉研究所、植物病虫害防治研究所、作物育种与生物技术研究所、生态与植保研究所、微生物研究所、中日化妆品研究所、中日保健茶研究所、中日有机肥研究所、渤海精细化工研究所、水产养殖研究所、计算机软件研发中心、贾思勰研究中心等 15 个科研机构。学院与美国、日本、韩国、乌克兰、印度等国家和地区在合作办学、学术交流、合办公司、教师引进、教材购入、互派留学生等多个领域进行合作，先后成立了中印计算机软件学院，中印国际交流学院，中印中文学院，中印软件培训学校，山东中印环球软件公司；与乌克兰、韩国合作进行了 2 +2 本科教育项目，与韩国东西大学合作举办了应用韩语专业专科教育项目，与韩国合作成立了生产现代、起亚汽车电子线路厂；与美国微软公司合作成立了微软 IT 学院，与日本的东京大学联合成立了中日生命科学研究院、中日有机肥研究所、中日有机肥厂、山东美高斯麦化妆品有限公司；与东欧 10 所友好大学签订了合作办学协议，举办了大学校长论坛，并成立了潍坊科技学院斯拉夫研究院；与台湾东南科技大学、朝阳科技大学等 5 所台湾省高校签订了合作办学协议，向其派出了两批研修生。2010 年 4 月，学院成功举办了首届中华农圣文化国际研讨会，来自 11 个国家的 200 多位专家、学者参加了研讨会，在国内外引起了广泛关注。同时，在校园内建设了寿光市软件园、学院科技园。软件园现已发展为山东省服务外包示范基地、山东省服务外包人才实训基地、山东省重点服务外包人才培训机构。

本次研讨会邀请的与会代表，有来自日本、韩国、以色列、斯里兰卡、印度、我国台湾省等国家和地区的著名农学、园艺、农业经济、海洋生物、生物工程等方面的专家；有国内高等院校、科研机构的知名农学、园艺、农业经济等方面的学者；有海外留学归国学者，还有实践经验丰富的地方企事业单位的负责同志。不同国家、不同身份的代表，会为我们提供不同的视角、不同的声音、不同的思想，内容更加丰富，论述更加多样，交流更加广泛，体现出当今世界农业的前沿思想、最先进的农业技术。

论文集体现了各位专家的严谨学风、渊博学识和深刻的思想，但由于时间仓促，编者水平有限，本论文集在编排、印制上难免有不当之处，恳望各位专家惠予指正，也敬请广大读者多提宝贵意见。

最后，向对本次研讨会的筹备给予指导和关怀的各位领导，对本次研讨会给予支持的社会各界人士和同仁表示最衷心的感谢。

编　者

2011 年 3 月

Preface

This proceeding is collection of Papers of the Second International Seminar of Chinese Agriculture-Sage Culture. It includes 66 papers of 57 experts and scholars of the Seminar, covering agronomy thought, facilities and gardening, organic farming, modern bio-engineering, marine biology, animal husbandry, ecological environment protection, agricultural development, agricultural economy and history of agriculture civilization and etc. Especially, papers on China modern agriculture development, modern bio-engineering, organic agriculture and environmental protection, has contrbuted modern connotation to traditional agriculture ideology, providing us with a new angle of viewing world.

The Second International Seminar of Chinese Agriculture-Sage Culture is organized by the Leading Group of International Seminar of Chinese Agriculture-Sage Culture of the 12th China (Shouguang) International Vegetable Sci-Tech Fair, undertaken by Weifang University of Science and Technology and co-organized by Qi Min Yao Shu Seminar. It is an important part of the 12th China (Shouguang) International Vegetable Sci-tech Fair, with the aim of developing traditional agriculture culture, spreading modern agronomy thought, boosting international exchange and collaboration in agriculture and promoting development and advancement of modern agriculture.

The Seminar will be held from 25th of April to 27th of April, 2011 in Shouguang, Shandong. Shouguang is Vegetable Hometown of China, it locates in the middle of Shandong Peninsula and on the south of Laizhou Bay, Bohai Sea, and it has a total area of 2 070 Square Kilometers with a population of 1.02 million and 975 villages under its jurisdiction; it is China Excellent Tourism City, National Gardening City, National Sanitation City, National Model City of Environment Protection, Top 100 Comprehensive Economic Strength Counties (Cities) in China, Socialist Civilization Advanced City in Shandong Province, it is also a optional training-city of keeping advancement of Chinese Communist Party members. Shouguang has a glorious history dated back long ago. Named as a county in 148 B. C, Shouguang has been taken as the capital of Zhenguan State in Xia Dynasty and Ji State in Western Zhou Dynasty; It is said that Cangjie, the author of Chinese characters, created Chinese characters in Shouguang; it also has more than 150 cultural ancient heritages here, such as Longshan Culture and ancient city of Ji State. Shouguang is rich in natural resources. It has abundant groundwater resources in central and southern area, fertile soil, it is a ideal place for grain, vegetables and other crops grow; it has 4 billion cubic meters underground brine reserve and a crude salt production of three million tons which is one of the top-three key crude salt production bases in China as well as national important base of salt and chemical industry. Agricultural Culture in Shouguang is splendid. In North Wei Dynasty, famous agronomist Jia Sixie whose hometown is Shouguang, summed up farmer' s experience of planting, breeding and etc in the place of Shouguang as well as agricultural experience of middle and lower reaches of the Yellow River region, wrote the first world famous *Qi Min Yao Shu*, which is like an encyclopedia of agriculture masterpiece and it has profound impact on agriculture production in China and the world. He is regarded as Agriculture-Sage by all Chinese descendants. Since China's reform and opening-up, Wang Leyi, Party Secretary of Sanyuanzhu Village, Shouguang, succeeded in creating winter greenhouse plantation in 1989 and launching a "Green Revolution" and "Silver Revolution" in counter-season vegetable cultivation technology in China, and since then Shouguang has become the largest "Vegetable Garden" and "Vegetable Basket" of China.

The Seminar will be undertaken by Weifang University of Science and Technology and the seminar locates Its International Academic Conference Center. Weifang University of Science and Technology is a full-time university approved by National Ministry of Education. It has an area of 160hm^2, a floor space of 760 square meters, a total fixed assets of RMB1. 5 billion among which 130 million RMB is for lab equipments; there are 1. 363 million books in the library; and now it has 1 562 teachers and 33 foreign teachers and 24 627 full-time students. Now it has 11 departments, 17 undergraduate courses, 41 three-year-courses, and It has research institutes, such as Life Sciences Research Institute, Vegetable and Flower Research Institute, Research Institute of Plant Pest and Disease Control, Crop Breeding and Biotechnology Research Institute, Ecology and Plant Protection Research Institute, Research Institute of Microbiology, Research Institute of

China-Japan Cosmetics, China-Japan Health Tea Research Institute, China-Japan Organic Fertilizer Research Institute, Bohai Research Institute of Fine Chemicals, Aquaculture Research Institute, Computer Software Development Center and Jia Sixie Research Center, all together 15 research groups or institutes. Weifang University of Science and Technology has started education cooperation, academic exchange, enterprise cooperation, foreign teacher recruiting, textbook introduction, students exchange with USA, Japan, Korea, Ukraine and India, etc. it has successively established Sino-Indian Computer Software School, Sino-India International Exchange School, Sino-India Chinese Language School, Sino-India Software Training School, Shandong Sino-India GTT co., Ltd, it has alsocooperated with Ukraine and Korea for 2 +2 undergraduate project as well as Applied Korean course project with Korean Dongseo University, a plant of modern electronic circuit for Hyundai and Kia motors. It has also established China-Japan Life Science Research Institute, China-Japan Organic Fertilizer Research Institute and factory and Shandong Mycosme Cosmetics Co. Ltd with Tokyo University; it has signed friendly cooperation agreement with 10 eastern European universities and held Presidents' Conference and established Slavic institute; the university also signed education cooperation project with 5 Taiwan high education universities in Tiwan province and sent 2 groups of students to have a short time study in their universities. The first International Seminar of Chinese Agriculture Sage Culture was successfully held on April of 2010 and more than 200 experts and scholars have attended the seminar and attracted concern from China and abroad.

What's more our university has built Shouguang Software Park and University Sci-tech Park. Shouguang Software Park has been awarded as Outsourcing Model Base, Talent Outsourcing Practical Training Base and Key Talent Outsourcing Training Base of Shandong Province.

This seminar has invited famous experts in agronomy, horticulture, ocean biology and bio-engineering from Japan, Korea, Israel, Sri Lanka, India, Tai Wan province of china and scholars from national high education universities and research institutes within China and overseas, it also has experts who has rich experience in enterprises and government bureaus, representatives from different country. The seminar will provide us a different angle of view, different sound and thought in which more wide, rich and diversified opinions and communication can be found and shared. The seminar will embody the forefront thinking on agriculture and the most advanced agriculture technologies in current world.

This proceeding shows the result of rigorous study, profound knowledge and deep thought by all experts who are present at seminar. However due to the limit time and level of editors, the proceeding inevitably has some inappropriateness in the editing, layout and printing, corrections and advice are welcomed from professionals and all readers.

Finally, we thank governing leader for their guidance and care during edition of this proceeding. Similarly, last but not least, we give our heart felt thanks all colleagues and all sides of society who has offered their help in editing this proceeding.

Editors

2011. March

目　录

Contents

Open Field and Protected Agriculture: Status and Trends of Vegetables and Ornamental industry

Abed Gera①

(*Head, Institute of Plant Protection, Agricultural Research Organization, The Volcani Centre, Bet-Dagan* 5250 *Israel*)

Abstract: According to recent figures about 800 million tones of vegetables were produced worldwide in 2009. The increase in vegetable production was mainly due to bigger harvests. The leading varieties are tomatoes, cabbage and cucumbers, and sweet pepper, melon and strawberries. China's vegetable production accounts 55 percent of the world total.

The ornamental horticulture industry has become a major international economic sector, and generating extensive interest from farmers, researchers, investors and development planners. Worldwide sales of ornamental horticulture products had reached over $50 billion.

Greenhouses with soilless cultural systems could address several of the serious challenges facing the vegetable and ornamental industry worldwide and could provide a new industry to Shandong producers. In addition to protecting crops in enclosed controlled environment, greenhouses extend the growing season and ensures high profitability and sustainability of an agricultural enterprise. Although, some of the greenhouse culture technologies are currently exist, they need to be evaluated and refined for Shandong use. Detailed information available on production of greenhouse tomatoes, sweet peppers, cucumbers, and strawberries will be discussed. Already, this protected agriculture technology is in use in several places in the world, including Spain, Turkey, Morocco, Holland, the US, Canada, and Mexico. These countries face some of the same challenges as does Israel vegetable and ornamental industry.

The contribution of plant protection research and development, Integrated Pest Management in the floriculture and horticulture industries will be extensively discussed.

Key words: Vegetables; Ornamentals; Greenhouse; Field crops; Plant protection

① Abed Gera，男，教授，以色列农业研究组织植物保护研究所所长。E－mail：abedgera@ volcani. agri. gov. il

1 Introduction

There are 115 countries in the world that produce greenhouse vegetables commercially. The estimates of the total worldwide vegetable production area in greenhouses vary widely: Some estimated the world greenhouse vegetable production area 0.4 ~ 1.2million hectares (hm^2). Some of these greenhouses are covered with plastic and others with glass. In northern Europe, glass-covered greenhouses are the majority, however the Americas and in Asia only small percentage.

The Netherlands is the traditional exporter of greenhouse grown flowers and vegetables all over the world. With about 90 000ha under cover, the Dutch greenhouse industry is probably the most advanced in the world. The area under greenhouses in Spain has been estimated to be around 70 000hm^2 and Italy 20 000hm^2 used mostly for growing vegetable. Israel is the largest exporter of cut flowers and has wide range of crops under greenhouses (12 000hm^2) and Turkey has an area of 10 000hm^2 under cover for cultivation of cut flowers and vegetables. The United States of America has a total area of about 5 000hm^2 under greenhouses mostly used for floriculture. Egypt has about 2 000hm^2 greenhouses consisting mainly of plastic covered tunnel type structures. However, in Asia, China is the 4th largest documented greenhouse vegetable operation in the world. The development of greenhouse technology in China has been faster than in any other country in the world. With a modest beginning in late seventies, the area under greenhouses in China has increased to 60 000hm^2 in recent years.

According to recent figures released by the AMI, 800 million tones of vegetables were produced worldwide in 2009. The increase in vegetable production was mainly due to bigger harvests, while the? area under cultivation remained essentially the same as in 2008. The three leading varieties, tomatoes, head cabbage and cucumbers, account for about 30% of the total production volume. China's vegetable growing area and production estimated to 14.67 million hectares and 440 million tons, accounting for 35% and 55% of the world total respectively.

More than 4% of the world' s vegetable production is traded internationally. Europe is the region that imports the most, fresh vegetables. Within Europe, Spain is the leading fresh vegetable exporter. The major greenhouse crops include: tomato, cucumber, lettuce, sweet peppers, melons, eggplant, strawberry, culinary herbs, and nursery plant material. Many other crops are grown in limited area.

By all accounts, the ornamental horticulture industry has become a major international economic sector, reaching substantial proportions and generating extensive interest from farmers, researchers, investors and development planners on every continent. Analysts at the Hollandws Rabobank estimated that by 2 000 worldwide sales of ornamental horticulture products had reached over $50 billion. Estimates of market size by other sources vary somewhat from these figures, but all agree that the market is very large and expanding. In the case of ornamental horticulture products, virus research plays an important role in a dynamic competitive market.

2 Israeli Agriculture

Since Israel attained its independence in 1948, the total area under cultivation has increased from 165 000hm^2. to some 435 000hm^2. During the same period, agricultural production has expanded 16-fold, more than three times the rate of the population growth.

Despite the decline in its importance relative to other economic branches, agriculture has been growing in absolute terms and still plays an important part in Israel's economy, representing today some 2.0% of the Gross Domestic Product and about 3.5% of exports. Agricultural inputs produced in Israel are valued today at over $2 billion, of which 70% are exported.

Agriculture is of major national importance; in certain areas, such as the Arava and the Jordan Valley, it provides the sole means of livelihood for the population. In 1996 approximately 73 500 people were involved in farming, constituting about 3.0% of the country's workforce.

In monetary terms, Israel produces almost 70% of all its food requirements. It imports much of its grain, oilseeds, meat and fish, sugar, coffee and cocoa. However, these imports are offset by exports of agricultural produce valued at around $800 million and $600 million worth of processed foods per annum. Today, just under a quarter of the income of Israel's farmers derives from the export of fresh produce, including items such as flowers, avocados, out-of-season vegetables and certain exotic fruits grown for export.

Israel's varied climatic, topographical and soil conditions (from sub-tropical to arid, from 400m below sea level to 1 000m above and from sand dunes to heavy alluvial soils) made it possible to grow a wide range of agricultural produce. The success of the country's agriculture stems from the determination and ingenuity of farmers and scientists who have dedicated themselves to developing a flourishing agriculture in a country which is more than half desert, thus demonstrating that the real value of land is a function of how it is used.

3 Mechanization and Agrotechnology

In order to lower costs, increase yields, improve quality and save manpower, innovative agricultural machinery and electronic equipment have been locally designed and manufactured, and are widely used. Intensive experimentation on the drawing board and in the field has resulted, inter alia, in the development of heavy-duty soil preparation machinery; advanced tillage, planting, harvesting and transplanting equipment adaptable to intensive farming; and diverse irrigation systems, ranging from sprinklers to computerized drip irrigation. Automated machinery for the grading, packing, storing and transporting of produce. Locally-developed agrotechnologies include computerized fertigation, which injects fertilizers through the irrigation system, and advanced temperature and humidity control methods, which provide healthy environments for flowers, out-of-season vegetables and fruits.

4 High-Tech Farming

Economists discussing the country's farming choices sometimes draw an analogy between a kilogram of exported tomatoes, which might fetch around five dollars, and a kilo of hybrid tomato seeds, which today may be selling abroad for $7 000. High-tech farming, it is suggested, is the only way to survive. Indeed, market forces at home and abroad, and a scarcity of land, labor and water are forcing major changes on Israeli agriculture. Increasingly, there is a shift from extensively-farmed, mass-produced crops to intensive growing of niche products based on scientific and technological R&D, such as hybrid seeds of virus-resistant tomatoes or tissue-culture propagated banana-tree and vegetatively-propagated ornamentals. The country's farmers face increasing competition.

As in other countries, Israeli agriculture has been forced to employ fewer and fewer people. The work force shrank almost 40% between 1960 (121 000) and 1996 (73 500). However, these growers are producing and exporting more. In the early 1950s one full-time agricultural employee fed 17 people. In 1996, one full-time worker produced food for 90 persons.

5 Agriculture-by Branches

5.1 *Vegetables*

Growing vegetables has become an art in Israel-based on choosing the right hybrid varieties, fertilizers and irrigation methods, selecting greenhouse covers designed for specific crops and employing innovative post-harvest treatments. Vegetables account for about 17% of Israel's total agricultural production. In 2000, the country's farmers produced some 1.7 million tons, of which about 150 000 tons were exported. In 2009 2.26 million tons of vegetables were produced. 1.25 million tons were sold in the local market, 610 thousand tons were exported and 400 thousand tons were sold to factories for processing.

Technologically advanced methods are employed, including soil-less greenhouses with climate control systems. Some 50 000 hectares of vegetables are grown in greenhouses. While tomatoes growing in the open field reach yields of up to 80 tons per hectare, an average 200 ~ 300 tons can be grown in greenhouses under controlled climatic conditions. Israel exploits the sunshine and high temperatures to grow high quality vegetables during the competitors' off-seasons.

In the last few years, new varieties of some crops, notably tomatoes and melons, have been adapted for growth in the desert with saline water irrigation. These are marketed under the brand name "Desert Sweet".

5.2 *Field Crops*

With scarce water, Israel's field crop farmers have been concentrating on new varieties that produce the same or higher yields, with less or no irrigation. Moreover, that irrigation increasingly consists of recycled wastewater.

Some 220 000 hectares are devoted to field crops in Israel. Of these, 160 000 hm^2. are rain-fed winter crops such as wheat for grain and silage, hay, legumes for seeds and sunflower for oil. The remainder is planted with summer crops such as cotton, sunflowers, chickpeas, green peas, beans, corn, groundnuts and watermelon for seeds, mostly irrigated. Almost the entire cotton crop of 28 500hm^2. is drip irrigated, using mainly recycled wastewater.

5.3 *Floriculture*

Floriculture started to develop in Israel in the early 1960' s mainly for export to Europe. In the early 1970 only about 5 million stems were exported. However in the early 2000 export reached 1.3 billion stems and a value of $200 per year.

The mild climate in the winter with strong sunlight, intelligent farmers, good coordination with extension specialists, researchers and authorities, efficient transport and marketing organizations, and the necessity to find additional high value crops for the farmers were instrumental to the rapid growth of the industry.

The ornamental industry is most dynamic and new species are rapidly being introduced. This will require a constant effort to provide the growers with high quality propagation material. Concurrent with cultivation of additional ornamentals, identification and control of their viruses will be necessary.

Individual farms, averaging less than a hectare, are small by international standards, but highly profitable. The expertise of the farmers contributes to the high quality and wide variety of flowers (over 100). These include cut flowers such as roses, gypsophila, carnations, solidago, limonium, gerbera, anemone and ornamental plants. New, acclimatized varieties introduced from other countries account for about 50% of Israel's flower exports. These varieties include "summer flowers" from Europe, acclimatized so that they can be picked and exported during Europe's winter season and flowers indigenous to the southern hemisphere.

Although the number of flower growers has decreased by some 50% in recent years (from 5 000 to 2 700), production has risen steadily to around 1.4 billion flowers a year. This is due to technological advances and an intensive system of production. About half of all the flowers are grown in advanced, computerized greenhouses and some 12% under netting.

Today, most flowers are sold by the individual growers directly to buyers in the flower auctions of the Netherlands, Belgium, Germany and elsewhere. Handling and shipping by Agrexco, the joint government-growers export company, which has special air and sea terminals in Israel and in Europe, ensures quality and timely arrival at the markets. The Flower Production and Marketing Board provides each grower with daily results of sales. Some of the more innovative growers are connected on-line with the auctions and follow transactions in real time.

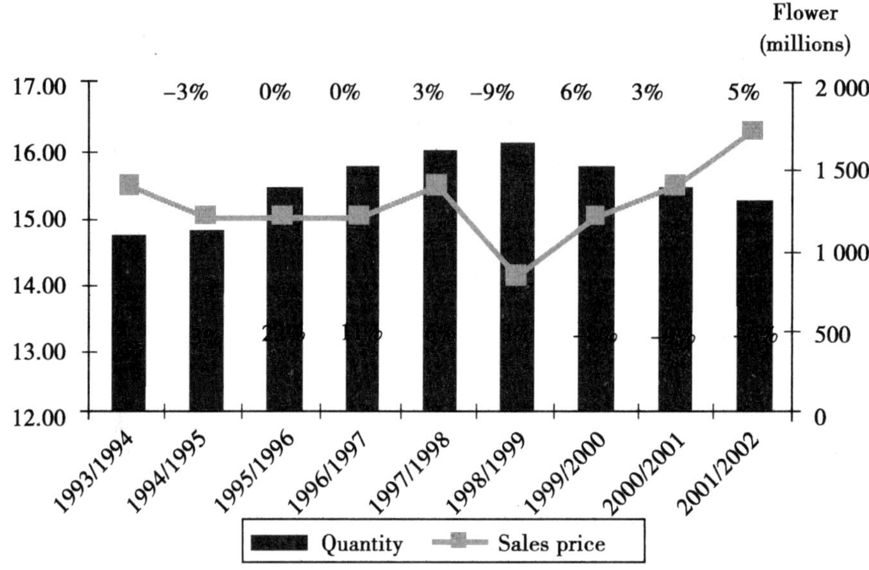

Israeli Flower Export Evolution

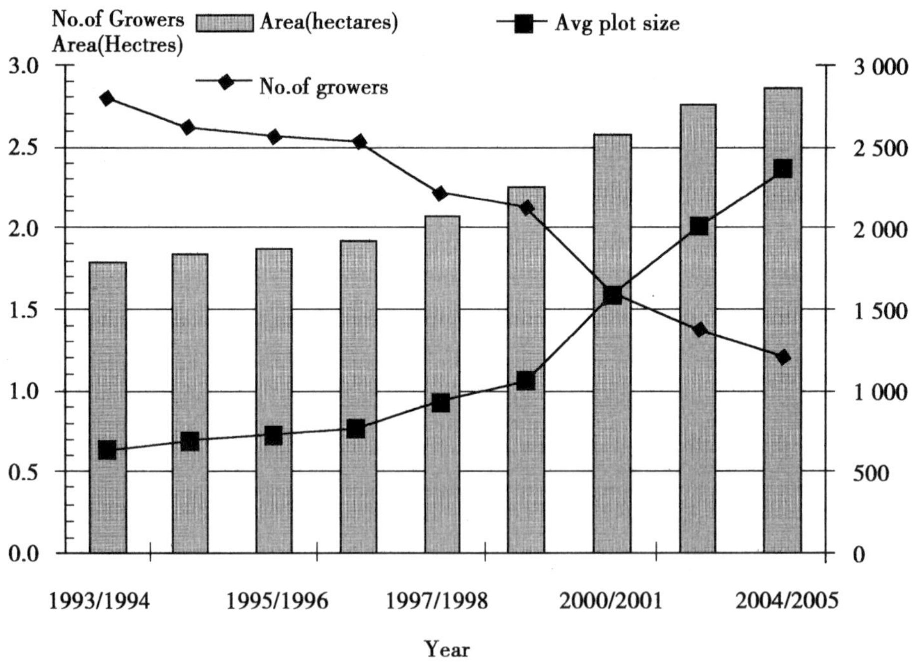

Trends in Israeli flower production

Ornamental plants are a rapidly growing industry. Over $250 million of different ornamental plants, either as rooted or un-rooted cuttings, or in pots in various stages of growth, are exported worldwide, but predominantly to Europe. Most of these plants serve as the starting materials for European house-and garden plant nurseries, who may gain a season or even a year by having the initial stages of growth carried out in Israel's warmer climate. Much of this industry is based on person-to-person contractual arrangements.

The contribution of plant protection research and development, Integrated Pest Management in the floriculture and horticulture industries will be extensively discussed. With continuing R&D investment, export sales are likely to continue growing.

References

[1] Hickman, Gary W. World Greenhouse Vegetable Production Statistics-2010 Edition. web site: www. cuestaroble. com. 2010

[2] Hickman, Gary W. World Greenhouse Vegetable Production Statistics-2011 Edition. web site: www. cuestaroble. com. 2011

[3] Gera, A. and, Zeidan, M. New and emerging virus disease in ornamental crops in Israel. Acta Hort: 2006, 722: 175 - 181

[4] Global seed Sector 2020 Outlook: Major Vegetable Crops, 2nd edition, 2010

[5] Loebenstein, G., Hammond, J., Gera, A., Derks, T. and Van Zaayen, A. (Editors). Proceedings of the 9th International Symposium on Virus Disease of Ornamental Plants. Acta Horticulturae: 1966: 432, 231

Global Warming, its Effect on Dormancy of Deciduous Fruit Trees, Risks and Solutions

Amnon Erez①

(*Emeritus Plant Sciences Institute*, *The Volcani Center*
P. O. Box 6 *Bet Dagan*, 50200 *Israel*)

Abstract: The expected global warming may affect markedly deciduous fruit growth and production in various locations around the globe. Reduced effective winter chilling may pose new problems in areas that never experienced problems in bud breaking. Understanding the multiple effects of temperature on dormancy development led to development of temperature models. The Dynamic model was found to follow closely the actual effect of temperature on bud dormancy. The best approach to remedy the situation is by breeding towards lower chilling requiring cultivars. Good basis for that work is the cultivars bred in warm countries having low chilling requirements. Other approach is to use dormancy-breaking chemicals oOr physical means on existing cultivars. Various cultural means are described that could reduce the actual chilling requirements of deciduous fruit trees.

Key words: Chilling; Abnormal development; Dormancy breaking chemicals; Dynamic model

1 Introduction

Temperate fruit crops are spreading continuously to warm countries. Marked increase in production is noted in many subtropical and tropical countries. One of the major limitations of production in warm countries is overcoming the dormancy period typical of all temperate zone fruit trees. We have now good means to monitor chilling by using models like the Dynamic model that can give relatively accurate results as to actual chilling available in various regions. No doubt, overcoming dormancy is the most critical element in growing temperate fruit crops in warm climates lacking the chilling required to overcome dormancy naturally. The threat of global warming may spread this phenomenon to hitherto cooler locations.

---

① Amnon Erez，男，博士，以色列国家植物科学研究所教授，E－mail：erezamn@ gmail. com

2 Dormancy, The phenomenon

Dormancy of buds of perennial fruit trees is a basic phase in the annual cycle of trees originated in temperate climate developed ecologically to resist winters too cold for development. Dormancy was natures' development to enable survival of the perennial plant through a climatically hostile period (Erez 2000). Dormancy allows adaptation of the plant to its environmental conditions by coordinating growth and development to the appropriate annual periods and by preparing the plant to the unfavorable conditions enabling it to accumulate reserves mostly carbohydrates, dropping the sensitive organs, developing organs to protect the meristems and resist harsh conditions by developing cold hardiness characteristics. Once in the dormant state, the tree evolved a time measuring mechanism that enables it to decide when the environmental conditions are appropriate for growth renewal. The basic limits in these plant strategies is the irreversible direction of events, i. e. once a decision is taken the sequence of events must proceed forward. This strategy means that there is no place for mistakes. The basic decisions for the plant regarding dormancy are: dormancy induction and dormancy release. In the first decision, the critical element is not to respond too late as this may result in damage to unprepared tissues, while in the second decision the critical element is not to respond too early and get unduly early bud break that will be damaged by late frosts. On the other hand, too early dormancy induction and too late bud break will affect the tree by reducing its maximal developmental potential.

3 The climatic requirements of dormant buds

Two climatic elements affect the dormant bud and hence its response: light and temperature.

Although under experimental conditions light could show a considerable effect, temperature is, with no doubt, the major element in the climatic requirement of the dormant bud. Even though chilling may first enhance dormancy induction, it soon becomes the major element that is controlling the development of the dormant bud (Coville 1920, Samish 1954). Once dormancy is induced, low temperature exposure is needed for overcoming this state and allowing growth resumption. From many studies done, it is quite clear that the optimum low temperature effect is around 6 ~ 8℃ (Erez and Lavee, 1971, Richardson et al 1974). Temperature efficiency drops towards the lower and higher temperatures. As to the threshold of effect it was shown that 14℃ has no chilling effect (Erez and Couvillon 1987), As to the lower end of the curve, temperatures lower than 0℃ may have little effect if at all. But the effect of temperature is more complex as an interaction of temperatures was found when low temperatures are cycled with higher ones. Erez et al (1979a) and Couvillon and Erez (1985), showed that alternating high-low temperatures in a daily cycle negate chilling at temperatures of 19℃ and higher. The chilling negation by high temperatures was found to depend on the level of the temperature and the duration in the cycle. The longer the duration and the level of the high temperature in a daily cycle, the stronger the negating effect (Couvillon and Erez 1985). Also the length of the cycle was found to be critical. Short cycles like daily cycles were the most negating while with longer ones the negating effect disappeared (Erez et al. 1979b). This was interpreted as evidence that there is a fixation effect of chilling after a certain period of time that was calculated to be of ca 30 hours at 6℃.

An additional effect to temperature was found for moderate temperatures. A synergistic effect for cycling non-active moderate temperatures and chilling was shown (Erez and Couvillon 1987). This was demonstrated with peaches with temperatures of 15℃ when cycled with cold temperatures. Summarizing chilling requirements in peaches and apples have revealed 3 effects of temperature. (1) A positive effect with an optimum of 2 ~ 8℃; (2) A chilling negation effect at temperatures > 19℃; (3) A moderate temperature effect at temperatures of 13 ~ 16℃ that by themselves have no chilling effect but when cycled with lower temperatures have a strong positive effect.

Even small changes in the maximum daily temperature in winter without changing the low night temperatures may affect dormancy breaking. By knowing the chilling requirement of a cultivar and measuring the cumulative chilling in specific location evaluation of the level of dormancy completion can be predicted. The Dynamic model that was developed for the peach incorporates all the effects mentioned above (Fishman et al 1987). It was found to follow well the temperature effects on the dormant buds.

4 The problems of an incomplete dormancy release

The impact of an incomplete dormancy release is very heavy on a modern fruit production system. Incomplete dormancy release affects tree behavior in 3 main aspects: A low level of bud break; a late bud break; and lack of uniformity of leafing and bloom. Each of these parameters has a special significance with various crops in various growing locations.

(1) Early bud break

This is especially important for getting precocious cultivars that their return depends very much on their time of ripening. Early maturation has a special premium value. Early bloom may be important for advancing bloom for cross pollination purposes or to avoid a specific problem that may occur later, or to spread the bloom and hence ripening time over a wider period especially if a single cultivar has been raised.

(2) High level of bud break

For obtaining high yield and good foliage cover, a high level of bud break is needed. Also when fruit set conditions are not optimal this full bloom conditions may improve setting. In young trees this is one of the ways to get early bearing by breaking the extreme vigor due to many competing vegetative sinks that will grow moderately produce short vegetative growth or spurs and by this differentiate easier to floral buds the next year.

(3) Uniform budbreak

This parameter of good dormancy breaking is very important in the modern orchard that depends on various treatments that should be applied at a specific stage of fruit development like chemical thinning. If the fruit is not developing uniformly, the efficiency of the subsequent treatments will be reduced. Furthermore, in non-uniform bloom, the late bloom wave has always a low chance for setting due to competition with stronger established sinks thus leading to a reduced yield.

With stone fruit species, a major sensitivity is manifested to extreme high temperatures in warm climates. Typically mummified fruit in peaches is seen with certain cultivars after exposure to a relatively warm winter. Another typical response is the formation of multiple styles in a flower where normally one style is produced. No wonder that repairing the poor bud break in warm climates resulting from incomplete dormancy became the major concern of growing temperate fruit crops in warm climates.

Global warming is becoming a major concern. Indications of changing temperature and increasing trmperature are numerous. Luedeling et al (2009) forcast increased problems to deciduous fruit crops that are grown on a huge scale in California. They predict increased difficulties in production due to reduce in chilling accumulation in winter leading to poor bud break in present cultivars.. A second paper by Xuebin et al (2005) relates to the middle east stating that similar effects of warming trends that will result in reduced chilling accumulation in winter.

5 Other negative high temperature effects

Apart from the direct effect of climate warming on reduced chilling accumulation, two other negative indirect effects are evident:

5.1 Abnormal development of the reproductive organ

Specific effects on the reproductive development are found especially in stone fruit species. Under extreme high temperature during flower bud initiation period, drop of flower primordia will occur (Peaches). Also in sweet cherries and peaches malformations in flower buds and formation of doubles are enhanced by high temperatures during spring and summer leading to reduced yields. Effective pollination period is shortened by high bloom temperatures. High temperatures during bloom and fruitset may reduce or even prevent setting. Partial chilling may dispose buds in peaches to drop or if followed by high temperatures in winter will enhance mummies formation. In Apples, high temperatures [short heat spells] post anthesis reduces the cell division period leading to smaller fruits.

5.2 Excessive vegetative growth

Enhanced vegetative growth competes stronger with the reproductive sink. All stages of reproductive development are negatively affected by high temperature (above a certain threshold): reduced flower bud differentiation and hence delay of fruiting, reduced fruit set, increase in fruitlet drop, reduced fruit quality due to excessive shading, and increase in chilling requirements of buds on vigorous growth.

6 Means to compensate for lack of enough chilling

The term "breaking bud dormancy" requires clarification. The fact that a bud is breaking and either a flower or a vegetative growth is emerging does not secure a normal development and functioning. Typically abnormal floral development may lead to small flowers with smaller than usual petals, double pistils and even triple and quadruple pistils that may produce twin fruits, poor anther development with few pollen grains, abnormal ovule development leading to mummies: fruit develops normally but freezes and kept as such as small fruit size till harvest. It seems that also nectar production is affected by poor levels of bud break leading to poor bee attraction and hence to a poor fruit set with cross pollination requiring species. Another pattern may be an excess June drop resulting from aborted embryo questioning whether the embryo formed was a normal one. With vegetative buds, a typical rosette formation testifies to a non complete dormancy release. Fuchigami and Nee (1987) and Nee and Fuchigami (1992) suggested that the breaking of rest involves 2 distinct processes: bud release and stem elongation.

6.1 The genetic approach

Since chilling requirements are genetic traits of every variety, breeding of plant material towards reduced chilling requirements is the straight forward approach to withstand lower chilling exposure. Also selection of cultivars more resistant to heat in the reproductive organs is important. Breeders in warm locations like Florida, Texas and California in the US, Brazil South Africa and Queensland in Australia have developed many lines of low chilling requiring cultivars of various fruit tree species (Byrne et al. 2000, Hauagge and Cummins 2000). Even under reduced exposure to chilling there are means to improve the situation and obtain optimal levels of bloom and leafing. In addition when chilling is not sufficient, chemical sprays of dormancy breaking agents may be applied to improve bud break.

6.2 The Chemical approach

Use of chemicals can sometimes improve performance of the tree even when chilling seems enough. The 3 effects of proper breaking of dormancy are: early, uniform and high level of bud break. With apple or pear, apical dominance under insufficient chilling gets much stronger due to earlier bud break of the apical bud having a much lower chilling requirement.

Chemical treatment can compensate for lack of chilling up to 1/3 of the requirement depending on the chemical used (Erez 1987). Experience with such chemicals was accumulated over the years in countries with marginal winter chilling that insisted on growing such crops. Especially developed was the research in this line in Israel South Africa, southern Brazil and eastern Australia.

Poor bud break in spring is detrimental to growth and fruit production in deciduous fruit tree species. In case specific cultivars are continued to be grown the following means are available for improving bud break under marginal conditions.

With most of the dormancy breaking chemicals it was found that they may be phytotoxic to flower buds that are always more sensitive than other plant organs. This may lead to loss of yield after treatment.

a. Oils

This group of chemicals is the oldest used commercially. The powerful combination with uncouplers of the dinitrophenols group gained acceptance since the mid thirties (Samish 1945, Erez and Zur 1981) and it is still used in a few countries world wide. Apart from their effect to break dormancy oils are being used also as an insecticide and a miticide.

The increase awareness to human phytotoxicity, led in the last decade to look for alternatives to dinitro ortho cresol as an adjuvant to the oil either by another substitution or by replacing the oil altogether. Certain dinitro compounds are not that toxic and may be accepted as replacement like Carathane known as Waicap in South Africa (Honeyborne and Rabe 1993).

The effect of oil-DNOC is via respiration therefore its effect is strongly affected by the prevailing temperatures at and during the week following spray. It was shown that high day-time temperature is essential for a good effect (Erez 1979). This situation explains the sensitivity after treatment to excessive temperatures and to water logged soil. Under normal situation the phytotoxic risk is low enabling spray even at the stage of bud swell. It was shown that at this stage swelling terminal buds are inhibited (by DNOC) and this may increase the potential of the laterals to break.

b. Cyanamide

No doubt cyanamide became the leading dormancy breaking chemical. The discovery that the hydrogen cyanamide, which easily can be sprayed in a solution, acts as a rest breaking agent (Shulman et al. 1983) opened the way to a wide series of trials on many deciduous species to test its efficiency.

It is extremely effective in grape vines (Shulman et al. 1983) and in kiwi fruit (Hampton and Parker 1992) but also in apple, plum, apricot, high chilling requiring peach (Erez, 1987, De Benito 1990) pears (Lin and Lin 1992) raspberry (Snir 1983) and fig (Weizman et al. 1985). From the very beginning it was evident that vegetative buds respond easily to cyanamides. As to flower buds it seems that the more protected ones (grapes, kiwi) are not damaged, while the less protected (like in simple buds of stone fruits) are. Damage to flower buds was reported for various species (Nee and Fuchigami 1992, George and Nissen 1993). Interestingly, sweet cherries are by far less sensitive to cyanamides probably due to a better protection of the bud initials than other stone fruit species and responds favorably to the chemical (Snir and Erez 1988, Nicolas and Bonnet 1993).

As to pome fruits, it was found that flowers within the mixed bud were damaged and the bud opened as a vegetative bud leading to yield reduction.

Contradicting results were obtained between years and location with similar species and even cultivars. The main cause for the varied result seems to reside in the level of dormancy of the buds. Resistance to the phytotoxic effect of the chemical declines fast with release of dormancy. Thus in order to avoid damage to flower buds, it is essential to avoid late application unless it is evident that dormancy was not released. This is one of the main reasons why it is so important to monitor the development of dormancy in the buds prior to treatment.

Another important aspect of use of cyanamide is for the purpose of advance maturation. Reports from Southern France (Nicolas and Bonnet 1993) indicate advance of maturation of the precocious CV. Burlat by 7 to 10 days when Dormex at 2.5% was applied 50 days prior to normal bloom. In Israel we have indicated an advance of bloom by 12 days with Rainier (Snir and Erez 1988). George and Nissen (1993) report on 19 day harvest advancement by hydrogen cyanamide in peaches.

Possible competition between vegetative and reproductive development may develop especially when using chemicals like cyanamide that will advance leafing. Excessive vegetative bud break may have negative effects on fruit set due to sink competition.

c. Effects of oil-cyanamides

Petri et al. (1990) reported on the efficiency of the combination oil-hydrogen cyanamide in breaking apple bud dormancy. They report on the relative efficiency of different oil-hydrogen cyanamide combinations in apple during a 3-year period. In this work, best results were obtained with 2% oil and 0.25% hydrogen cyanamide. North (1992), examined in South Africa various combinations of oil-hydrogen cyanamide and found a few combinations with low cyanamide concentrations to be as or better than oil-DNOC. In Israel the combination of 4% oil and 0.25% hydrogen cyanamide was as or better in breaking apple bud dormancy during a 3 year trial (Ringwald, 1994). It was also found that tank mix application of these two components is as efficient as separate applications in apple (Ringwald, 1994). Petri and Pola (1992) have shown that oil-cyanamide treatment keeps its effect to break apple bud dormancy also under low temperatures as against oil-DNOC treatments. To summarize, toxicity of hydrogen Cyanamide is dormancy-stage dependent. With more resistant species, this chemical is excellent and with optimal timing it may have a major impact on production and on the crop economy. With more susceptible species it may be too risky to use and a reduced concentration in combination with other chemicals is recommended.

d. KNO_3

This chemical was showing a rather mild effect even with a concentration of 10%. It was effective in increasing bud break especially of flower buds (Erez et al. 1971, Erez 1987, George and Nissen 1993). It was used in combinations with other chemicals mostly to enhance the effect. From recent work it seems that poor penetration could be one of the causes for the mild effects.

e. Growth regulators.

Gibberellic acid and cytokinins break bud dormancy. (Erez 1987, Wang et al. 1986, Lloyd and Firth 1993) But the concentration needed are 100 to 400 mg/kg of GA and benzyl adenine (Erez 1987) rendering these rather expensive chemicals non economical. Trials with the artificial cytokinin dithiazuron showed very strong effects (Erez et al 2006)

f. Growth retardants

The introduction of paclobutrazol as a growth retardants in fruit tree orchards, revealed beside its vegetative growth retardation also a specific effect on advance bud break. This characteristic was found with trees treated in the former growing season (Erez 1985, George et al. 1992, George and Nissen 1992, 1993). The cause for the effect seems to reside in the biosynthesis inhibition of GA, a chemical known to increase vegetative vigor and depth of dormancy.

g. Armobreak

A unique group of fatty amines was introduced recently by Akzo-Nobel, a Dutch firm claiming the agent has an enhanced cuticle penetration carrying with it other chemicals. The agent named Armobreak may change the situation in a few ways: First it may reduce the cost of treatment by lowering the concentration of expensive rest breaking agents like hydrogen cyanamide and by that it may reduce phytotoxicity of the chemical. It may boost the effect of a mild agent like KNO_3 and allow relatively safe and powerful combinations, and it may bring the cost of presently too expensive materials, like GA, down to become commercial.

First reports on a combined effect of KNO_3 with Armobreak on apples came from South Africa (North 1992) indicating a strong enhanced KNO_3 effect. These data were confirmed by experiments carried out in Israel since 1994. Enhanced effects of added chemicals to Armobreak was evident with Gibberellic acid on vegetative buds in nectarines and with hydrogen cyanamide on both floral and vegetative buds in peach and vegetative buds in apricots. (Erez 1995).

6.3 The physical approach-Evaporative cooling

Whenever night temperature is reduced below 13℃, a potential of chilling accumulation exists. In many subtropical marginal locations, night temperatures are cool enough to break dormancy but day temperature exceeds, sometime by far, 19℃ leading to complete chilling negation. As in other recommended practices, the only field means to lower bud temperature is by evaporative cooling using over the orchard sprinkling (Gilreath and Buchanan 1981, Erez and Couvillon 1983, Nir et al 1988). The over the tree sprinkling is thermostatically controlled and operation is intermittently. It was shown experimentally that bud temperature may be dropped from 24℃ to 16℃ and by that prevent chilling negation by high daytime temperatures. Use of water to cool plant canopy is limited first by water availability second by its quality and thirdly by a relatively dry day time to allow evaporative cooling.

7 Other means to improve bud break

On top of the genetic chilling requirement of the cultivar, certain elements influenced by orchard management have a strong modulating effect that is not stressed enough in the literature. Four such factors are mentioned:

7.1 Control of tree vigor

Means that will reduce tree vigor were found to improve bud break. The more vigorous the growth, the deeper the ED (Saure 1985). As a result, generally young trees express a higher chilling requirement than older ones. Thus an advantage to dwarfing vigor controlling rootstocks is found under marginally warm growing conditions, on top of other advantages they have under temperate-zone climates. It is thus common to see under marginal conditions better bud break in poorly kept orchards that lack in vigor in comparison to very well irrigated and fertilized orchards. Thus special attention should be focused on restricting vegetative growth in warm locations as this element is a major factor in enabling control of its bud dormancy.

7.2 Branch orientation

An old practice of manipulation tree branches led to the observation that horizontally oriented branch breaks buds much easier than more vertically oriented one. This effect definitely stems from the change in balance of hormones in the buds and from the reduced vigor if bending is done during the growing period. It also may involve a reduced correlative inhibition effect that otherwise on a vertical branch prevent bud break of most of the laterals leading to poor bud break. Apical dominance is a major concern in warm winter climates. With upright branches, earlier break of the terminals, due to their lower chilling requirements, will induce a strong apical dominance and by that to further reduce level of lateral bud break. Bending branches to horizontal position will induce an earlier flower bud differentiation and reduce vegetative competition by reducing growth vigor,

7.3 Time and type of pruning

Heading back under marginal winter conditions, especially if applied early (mid winter), will enhance the uppermost one or two buds. This is due to an additional dormancy breaking effect of the wound. This will lead to a resumption of apical dominance preventing the other laterals that are lagging behind to open. The latter the pruning the less is its negative effect on bud break of the laterals. Summer pruning having a much reduced invigorating effect is more desirable in warm locations.

7.4 Time of leaf drop

A few reports in the literature (Walser et al 1981) indicate an effect of time of leaf drop on depth of dormancy. Early defoliation leads to reduced chilling requirement and vice versa, delay in leaf drop will delay bud break as a result of a higher chilling requirement. A possible cause for that is the move out of the leaves and into the buds of chemicals that control the depth of dormancy. Chemical defoliation in early autumn is therefore beneficial providing it is not applied too early to causing autumn bud break unintentionally.

8 Conclusions

Although the threat of global warming negative effect on growing deciduous fruit-tree species is real and scaring, there are various means available to compensate for reduced accumulation of winter chilling and for excessive heat. Breeding for low chilling cultivar is the first and safest approach. Use of appropriate genetic material available mostly in warm countries growing these species, can replace present high chilling requiring cultivars. In addition, chemical and physical means are available that can compensate for partial lack of chilling. These chemicals have other side effects that may be beneficial for fruit growers like advancing bloom and enabling better coincidence of bloom between cultivars for cross pollination and improving bloom uniformity. Other cultural means were stressed that affect markedly the actual chilling requirements of the buds. The dynamic model was found adapted for monitoring chilling in various sites thus following the actual effect of change of climate on deciduous trees bud dormancy.

References

[1] Byrne, H. D., Sherman, W. B. and Bacon, T. A. Stone fruit genetic pool and its exploitation for growing under warm winter conditions. In: Temperate Fruit Crops in Warm Climates. A. Erez (Ed) Kluwer Academic Publishers Dordrecht p. 2000: 157 – 230

[2] Coville F. V. The influence of cold in stimulating the growth of plants. Journal of Agricultural Research. 1920: 20, 151 – 160

[3] Couvillon G. A., and Erez, A. Effect of level and duration of high temperatures on rest in the peach. Journal of the American Society for Horticultural Science 1985: 110, 579 – 581

[4] De Benito, J. Dormex, Nuevos horizontes para la fruiticultura. Fruiticultura Profesional. 1990: 30, 119 – 121

[5] Erez A. The effect of temperature on the activity of oil + dinitro-cresol spray to break the rest of apple buds. HortScience 1979: 14, 141 – 142

[6] Erez A. Growth control of peaches by paclobutrazol. Acta Horticulturae 1985：160, 217 -224

[7] Erez A. Chemical control of bud break. HortScience. 1987：22, 1240 -1243

[8] Erez, A. Means to compensate for insufficient chilling to improve bloom and leafing. Acta Horticulturae. 1995：395, 81 -95

[9] Erez, A. Bud dormancy：phenomenon, problems and solutions in the tropics and subtropics. In：Temperate Fruit Crops in Warm Climates. A. Erez (Ed) Kluwer Academic Publishers Dordrecht. 2000, 17 -48

[10] Erez A., and Couvillon G. A. Evaporative cooling to improve rest breaking of nectarine buds by counteracting high daytime temperatures. HortScience. 1983, 18：480 -481

[11] Erez A., and Couvillon G. A. Characterization of the influence of moderate temperatures on rest completion in peach. Journal of the American Society for Horticultural Science. 1987, 112：677 -680

[12] Erez A., Couvillon G. A., and Hendershott, C. H. Quantitative chilling enhancement and negation in peach buds by high temperatures in a daily cycle. Journal of the American Society for Horticultural Science. 1979a, 104：536 -540

[13] Erez A., Couvillon G. A., and Hendershott C. H. The effect of cycle length on chilling negation by high temperatures in dormant peach leaf buds Journal of the American Society for Horticultural Science. 1979b, 104：573 -576

[14] Erez A., Fishman S., Linsley-Noakes G. C. and Allan P. The dynamic model for rest completion in peach buds. Acta Horticulturae. 1990, 276：165 -174

[15] Erez A., and Lavee S. The effect of climatic conditions on dormancy development of peach buds：I. Temperature. Journal of the American Society for Horticultural Science. 1971, 96：711 -714

[16] Erez A., Lavee, S., and Samish, R. M. Improved methods to control rest in the peach and other deciduous fruit species. Journal of the American Society for Horticultural Science. 1971, 96：519 -522

[17] Erez, A. Yablowitz, Z. Aronovitz, A and Hadar, A. Dormancy breaking chemicals：Efficiency with reduced phytotoxicity. Acta Hort. 2006, 772：105 -112

[18] Erez A., and Zur A. Breaking the rest of apple buds by narrow-distillation-range oil and dinitro-o-cresol. Scientia Horticulturae. 1981, 14：47 -54

[19] Fishman S., Erez A., and Couvillon G. A. The temperature dependence of dormancy breaking in plants：Mathematical analysis of a two-step model involving a cooperative transition. Journal of Theoretical Biology 1987b, 124：473 -483

[20] Fuchigami, L. H. and Nee, C. Degree growing stage model and rest breaking mechanisms in temperate woody perennials. HortScience. 1987, 22：836 -44

[21] George, A. P. and Nissen, R. J. Effects of water stress, nitrogen and paclobutrazol on flowering, yield and fruit quality of the low chill peach cultivar, 'Flordaprince' Scien-

tia Horticulturae. 1992, 49: 197 - 209

[22] George, A. P. and Nissen, R. J. Effects of growth regulants on defoliation, flowering, and fruit maturity of the low chill peach cultivar Flordaprince in subtropical Australia. Australian Journal of Experimental Agriculture. 1993, 33: 787 - 795

[23] George, A. P., Nissen, R. J. and Baker J. A. Effects of hydrogen cyanamide in manipulating budburst and advancing fruit maturity of table grapes in south-eastern Queensland. Australian Journal of Experimental Agriculture. 1988, 28: 533 - 538

[24] Gilreath, P. R. and Buchanan, D. W. Floral and vegetative bud development of 'Sungold' and 'Sunlite' nectarine as influenced by evaporative cooling by overhead sprinkling during rest. Journal of the American Society for Horticultural Science. 1981, 106: 321 - 324

[25] Hampton, E. and Parker, B. Cyanamide essential for kiwifruit economics. The Orchardist. 1992, 8: 49 - 54

[26] Hauagge, R. and Cummins J. N. Pome fruit genetic pool for production in warm climates. . In: Temperate Fruit Crops in Warm Climates. A. Erez (Ed) Kluwer Academic Publishers Dordrecht. 2000: 267 - 304

[27] Honeyborne G. E. and Rabe E. Evaluation of two mineral oil based artificial rest breaking compounds on Golden Delicious apples. Deciduous Fruit Grower. 1993, 43: 206 - 210

[28] Luedeling, E., Zhang, M. and Girvetz, E. H. Climatic changes lead to declining winter chill for fruit and nut trees in California during 1950 - 2099. Plos one. 2009: 4 (7)

[29] Lin, H. S. and Lin, C. H. Enhancement of budbreak of container-grown 'Shinseiki' pear in Taiwan's lowlands by split application of cyanamide. Gartenbauwissenschaft. 1992, 57: 235 - 237

[30] Lloyd, J. and Firth, D. J. Effect of hydrogen cyanamide and promalin on flowering, fruit set and harvest time of 'Flordaprince' peach (Prunus persica (L.) Batsch) in subtropical Australia. Journal of Horticultural Science. 1993, 68: 177 - 183

[31] Nee, C. and Fuchigami, L. H. Overcoming rest at different stages with hydrogen cyanamide. Scientia Horticulturae. 1992, 50: 107 - 113

[32] Nicolas, J. et Bonnet, E. Cerises, Avance de Maturite avec Cyanamide Hydrogene. Trois Annees döessais. L' Arboriculture Fruitiere. 1993, 458: 17 - 20

[33] North, M. S. Alternative rest-breaking agents to DNOC/oil for apples. South African Plant and Soil. 1992, 9: 39 - 40

[34] Nir, G., Klein, I., Lavee, S., Spieler, G. And Barak, U. Improving grapevine budbreak and yields by evaporative cooling. Journal of the American Society for Horticultural Science. 1988, 113: 512 - 517

[35] Petri, J. L. and Pola, A. C. Influencia de temperaturas baixas e altas na eficiencia do oleo mineral mais cianamida hidrogenada na quebra de dormencia da maciera. Revista Brasiliera Fruiticultura. 1992, 14: 133 - 136

[36] Petri, J. L. Pola, A. C. and Stuker, H. Effect of mineral oil and hydrogen cyanamide on dormancy breaking of apples. 23rd International Horticultural. Congress. 1990, 2: 4326

[37] Richardson E. A. Seeley S. D. and Walker D. R. A model for estimating the completion of rest for "Redhaven" and "Elberta" peach trees. HortScience. 1974, 9: 331 -332

[38] Ringwald, S. Alternatives for oil-DNOC which is used for bud breaking spray on apple trees. M. Sc. thesis, Hebrew University Jerusalem. 1994: 65pp. (In Hebrew with an English summary)

[39] Samish, R. M. The use of dinitro cresol mineral oil sprays for the control of prolonged rest in apple orchards. Journal of Pomology and Horticultural Science. 1945, 21: 164 - 179

[40] Samish R. M. Dormancy in woody plants. Annual Review of Plant Physiology. 1954, 5: 183 -203

[41] Saure, M. C. Dormancy release in deciduous fruit trees. Horticultural. Reviews. 1985, 7: 239 -300

[42] Shulman, Y., Nir, G. Fanberstein, L. and Lavee S. The effect of cyanamide on the release from dormancy of grapevine buds. Scientia. Horticulturae. 1983, 19: 97 -104

[43] Snir, I. and Erez, A. Bloom advancement in sweet cherry by hydrogen cyanamide. Fruit Varieties Journal. 1988, 42: 120 -121

[44] Snir, I. Chemical dormancy breaking of red raspberry. HortScience. 1983, 18: 710 -713

[45] Walser, R. H., Walker, D. R. and Seeley, S. D. Effect of temperature, fall defoliation and gibberellic acid on the rest period of peach buds. Journal of the American Society Horticultural Science, 1981, 106: 91 -94

[46] Wang, S. Y., Steffens, G. L and Faust M. Breaking bud dormancy in apple with a plant bioregulator, Thidiazuron. Phytochemistry. 1986, 25: 311 -317

[47] Weizman, Z., Erez, A., Gur, A. and Shulman, Y. Breba figs-a commercial orchard: 1. Enhancement of flower bud break by cyanamide. (In Hebrew with English summary). Hassadeh. 1985, 66: 503 -505

[48] Xuebin Zhang et al. (26 authors) Trends in Middle East climate extreme indices from 1950 to 2003. Jour. Geophys. Res. 2005, 110: D22104, 12 PP

Utilization of Treated Effluents for Irrigation in Modern Agriculture

Nirit Bernstein①

(*Nirit Bernstein*, *Institue of Soil*, *Water and Environmental Sciences*, *Agricultural Research Organization* (*ARO*), *The Volcani Center*, *P. O. Box* 6, *Bet Dagan*, 50250, *Israel*)

Abstract: The use of wastewater for agricultural irrigation is steadily increasing world-wide and due to shortages of fresh water is common today in many regions throughout the world. Irrigation with treated effluents incorporate benefits to modern agricultural by reducing demands for fertilizers inputs as a result of the higher concentrations of macronutrients in these water. At the same time, inhibiting effects on the irrigated crops may source from the higher concentrations of salts, bicarbonate, boron, heavy metals, and pH level present in the treated effluents. The use of treated wastewater for agricultural irrigation may result in human exposure to pathogens, creating potential public health problems. Although the concentration of human pathogens decrease during the wastewater reclamation process, the secondary treated effluents most commonly used for irrigation today still contain bacterial human pathogens. National and global regulations where developed and aplied to facilitate optimal and safe production.

Key words: Effluents; Food-safety; Irrigation; Salinity

1 Introduction

Water is the most valuable resource in arid and semi-arid regions, where local population growth increases the demand for food, including crops and plant products. This heightened demand can be met by modern irrigated agricultural systems. Water availability is the limiting factor for the required spread of extensive irrigated production in arid and semi-arid regions of the world. Therefore, maintained or increased productivity requires the utilization of marginal water for irrigation. Due to their availability and relatively low cost, treated sewage effluents are be-

① Nirit Bernstein，女，以色列农业研究组织（ARO）土壤、水分和环境科学研究所教授。E-mail：Nirit@agri. gov. il

coming the main source of alternative marginal water for agricultural irrigation. Environmental protection considerations for minimizing discharge also encourage the use of wastewater for agricultural purposes. The use of wastewater for agricultural irrigation is, therefore, increasing steadily world-wide, and is practiced today in almost all arid regions of the world (Scott et al., 2004). Numerous countries have established water resource planning policies based on maximal re-use of urban wastewater.

Treated effluents may have detrimental effects on the irrigated crops (Feigin et al., 1991). In particular, the high salinity levels in the effluents can restrict plant growth (Lazof and Bernstein, 1998; Bernstein and Kafkafi, 2000), decrease biomass production (Neves-Piestun and Bernstein, 1991; Bernstein et al., 1993a, b; Neves-Piestun and Bernstein, 1995) and reduce yield quality (Bernstein et al., 2006). Nevertheless, many successful agricultural production systems that utilize this water have been developed (Feigin et al., 1991; Bernstein et al., 2006; Friedman et al., 2007). Despite the economic and ecological advantages associated with the use of treated wastewater for irrigation, its use also carries risks to public health and the environment. Pathogenic microorganisms present in the treated wastewaters can pose a health risk to farmers, contaminate the irrigated crops and/or be carried along to the consumers. Additionally, these microorganisms may persist in the soil and be transported to surrounding areas together with the agricultural drainage. The sanitation quality of treated wastewater is therefore a key issue in their reuse for agricultural irrigation.

Many countries throughout the world and global organizations have developed regulations for agronomic utilization of the effluents for irrigation, which facilitate safe utilization. Treated effluents are thereby successfully and safely used for irrigation of modern agriculture.

2 Wastewater Purifications Practices

To be suitable for irrigation according to modern countries regulations, raw wastewater has to undergo a series of purification steps, physical, biological and chemical. A typical scheme of a wastewater treatment plant is depicted in Figure 1. The quality of reclaimed wastewater depends on the degree of treatment. In municipal wastewater treatment plants, raw municipal wastewater undergoes preliminary, primary, secondary, and in some cases, additional treatment to yield treated effluent and a concentrated stream of solids in liquid, called sludge. The sludge is treated as required for utilization or disposal, and additional treatment of effluent may be needed to accommodate specific water reuse opportunities.

Generally, tertiary treated water that has undergone a disinfection stage is considered to be safe for irrigation of all crops, including vegetables that are consumed raw. Primary and secondary treated waters are of variable microbial quality and may be adequate for restricted irrigation of specific crops that are not consumed raw.

It should be emphasized that while in developed countries most of the wastewater used for

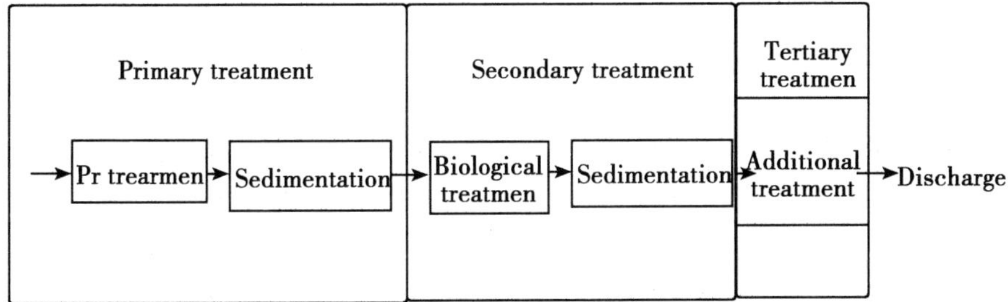

Figure 1 Flowchart of a conventional wastewater treatment plant

irrigation are treated, raw wastewater is the only water source available for agricultural purposes in a number of developing countries (Hussain et al., 2001; Carr et al., 2004). It has been estimated that at least one-tenth of the world's population consumes foods produced by irrigation with wastewater (Smit and Nasr, 1992). Homsi (2000) estimated that about 10% of all wastewater in developing countries is treated, while WHO/UNICEF (2000) estimated that the median percentage of wastewater effectively treated is 35% in Asia, 14% in Latin America and the Caribbean, 90% in North America and 66% in Europe.

3 Effect of Efflunet Irrigation on Crops

In effluent-based irrigation, effects of the effluent irrigation on agronomic crop production should be taken into account. The irrigation effluent water may have beneficial as well as deleterious effects on the irrigated crop. Although treated municipal wastewaters are usually applied as a source of irrigation water for crops, they are also a source of plant nutrients, especially nitrogen. The concentration of nutrients in wastewaters depends on the water source, the quality of the wastewater, and the type and degree of wastewater treatment. Usually, each stage in the wastewater treatment process reduces the concentration of both nitrogen and phosphorus. Typically, conventionally treated municipal wastewaters contain from 10 to 40 mg of nitrogen per liter and from a few to 30 mg of phosphorus per liter (Asano et al. 1985). Potentially, these nutrients in the wastewater may replace some of the crop requirement for fertilization. The application rates of the water may meet or, in some cases, exceed the nitrogen and phosphorus fertilizer needs of many crops throughout the cultivation period. Moreover, plants require varying amounts of nutrients at different stages of development, and the timing of irrigation may not correspond to when plant nutrients are needed. Wastewater applications at times when the plant needs are low can potentially lead to contamination of ground water.

In additional to micro and macronutrients, treated effluents may contain higher levels of several other chemical constituents, such as total soluble solids (TSS), salts (mainly Na, Cl and bicarbonates), heavy metals and organic matter, than in the potable water which may affect as well plant performance and commercialized yield production (Feigin et al., 1991;

Bernstein et al. , 2006; Friedman et al. , 2007). Wastewater constituents that can degrade water quality for irrigation include salts, nutrients and trace contaminants.

The soluble cations and anions found in effluents which are of concern in agricultural systems, usually include potassium, sodium, calcium, magnesium, chloride, sulfate, nitrate, bicarbonate, selenate, and boron (as boric acid and borate). All of these are absorbed by plants and may contribute to the nutritional status of the plant, or result in toxic effects. Above concentrations of about 0.7 mg/liter in irrigation waters, boron may be toxic to sensitive plants (Maas, 1990). Consequently, to prevent damage to crops, caution must be exercised to insure that the boron concentrations in soils irrigated with treated wastewater do not exceed this critical level for sensitive crops. Similar to conventional irrigation, salts in treated wastewater need to be managed to prevent salinity damage to crops. Concentrations of salts in treated effluents can vary widely, and irrigation regimes with effluents need to take into account the need for leaching to prevent salt build-up in the soil, and consequently damage to crops and the soil and.

4 Potential Health Risks Associated with Effluent Irrigation

A variety of human pathogens have been identified in sewage water (Armon et al. , 2002). Although the high numbers of human pathogens present in non-treated sewage decrease successively at each step of the wastewater reclamation process (Steen et al. , 2000), the secondary treated effluents which are the effluents most commonly used for irrigation still contain fecal coliforms that may pose a threat to public health (Maynard et al. , 1999; Armon et al. , 2002). There is a risk of direct contamination of crops by human pathogens present in the treated effluents used for irrigation, as well as indirect contamination of crops through contaminated soil at the agricultural site.

Over the last few years, outbreaks of foodborne illnesses have been increasingly linked to the consumption of contaminated fruits and vegetables and irrigation with wastewater (Blumenthal et al. , 1989). Therefore, the potential transmission of infectious diseases by pathogenic agents is the most common concern associated with the agricultural use of treated wastewaters (Shuval et al. , 1986).

A variety of regulations and recommendations have been developed around the world for sanitation quality of effluents to be used for irrigation of food crops. These regulations are aimed at protecting consumers from possible exposure to pathogens. For example, the World Health Organization (WHO) has recommended a guideline of not more than 1 000 fecal coliforms (FCs) per 100 ml for water used for the unrestricted usage for irrigation of all crops, with special emphasis on the removal of helminth eggs (to a concentration of no more than one egg per liter) during effluent treatment (WHO, 1989). The U. S. Environmental Protection Agency (US EPA) guidelines require that there be no detectable FCs per 100ml (US EPA, 1973). California' s wastewater reclamation standard is 2.2 coliforms/100ml, and the Israeli regulations for effluents for 'unrestricted irrigation' in agriculture is ≤10 FCs/100ml (IMH, 2001).

Different countries have developed various approaches for the sanitation of effluents prior to their use in agricultural irrigation, in order to protect public health and the environment. Economics are generally the major factor affecting the choice of regulatory strategy. While most developed countries have adopted conservative, low-risk standards based on a high technology/high cost approach, a number of developing countries have developed a low technology/ low cost approach based on the WHO recommendations (US EPA, 2004). Recently, the notion that better health protection can be achieved not only by employing strict water quality limits, but also by adopting other practices that could provide additional barriers against crop exposure to the pathogens has been gaining acceptance (Fine et al., 2006). An example of such an approach is the standard issued by the Israeli Ministry of Health (IMH, 2001; Shelef and Halperin, 2002). These standards set a low coliform limit of less than 10 *E. coli*/100ml for reclaimed water that can be used for irrigation of vegetables which will be eaten raw, in the absence of any additional barriers. At the same time, additional barriers, either physical ones such as buffer zones between the wastewater and the aboveground part of the plants and inedible peels or shells, or others, such as high heat treatment of the produce prior to eating, are required if water of a lower quality is to be utilized for irrigation. The development of the physical barrier concept relies on the accepted notion that potential health risks to consumers from the consumption of agricultural produce irrigated with contaminated water stem primarily from the attachment of human pathogens to plants via the plant's aboveground organs, and not internalization via the root system. However, recent studies suggest that human pathogens can also associate with the underground parts of the plants (Gagliardi and Karns, 2002; Natvig et al., 2002), penetrate internal plant tissues via the root (Bernstein et al., 2007a, c; Guo et al., 2002; Solomon et al., 2002), translocate and survive in edible, aerial plant tissues (Samish et al., 1962; Guo et al., 2002; Bernstein et al., 2007a). The practical implications of these new findings for food safety are not yet known, but no doubt reflect the pathogenic microorganisms' ability to penetrate the plant roots, translocate to aboveground parts, and survive and multiply in water, soil and the harvested edible crop through the marketing chain.

5 Contamination of Crops by Internalization of Bacterial Human Pathogenas into Roots

The contamination of fresh produce by human pathogens can occur in the field or post-harvest. Until recently, it was generally accepted that potential health risks to consumers from edible agricultural produce irrigated with contaminated water, source primarily from the direct attachment of human pathogens to the aboveground parts of plants, and not to the root system. However, recent studies suggest that human pathogens may also be associated with underground plant organs (Gagliardi and Karns, 2002; Natvig et al., 2002); may internalize plant tissues through roots (Gue et al., 2002; Solomon et al., 2002; Bernstein et al., 2006; Franz et al., 2006; Bernstein et al., 2007) or seeds (Natvig et al., 2002; Warriner et al., 2003; Islam et al., 2004), and be translocated to the edible, aerial plant organs, where they can persist (Samish et al., 1962; Gue et al., 2002).

The use of contaminated irrigation water, such as treated effluents, and the applications of raw or composted manure to agronomic production systems may introduce human pathogens to the roots of agricultural crops. A range of human pathogens are capable of surviving extended periods of time in soils, manure (Kudva et al., 1998) and water, where they can act as inoculum for the contamination of crop roots.

Today, a growing body of evidence is available to demonstrate the internalization of *E. coli* and *Salmonella* into plants via the root system and their translocation to the aboveground plant organs. *E. Coli* was reported to internalize roots of several dicotyledonous plants including lettuce (Solomon et al., 2002; Wachtel et al., 2002a), tomato (Guo et al., 2002) and *Arabidopsis thaliana* (Cooley et al., 2003). In lettuce (Solomon et al., 2002) and spinach (Warriner et al., 2003), *E. Coli* cells were found to penetrate the vascular system, probably facilitating their long-distance transport in the plant. Fewer studies have investigated the uptake of *Salmonella* by roots. The studies available report internalization of *S. enterica* into the roots of lettuce (Bernstein et al., 2007a) and tomato (Guo et al., 2002).

While most studies involving internalization of pathogenic bacteria focused on dicot plants, recent studies identified this phenomenon in roots of monocots. We have recently reported internalization of *E. coli* into hydroponic maize plants (Bernstein et al., 2007c). *E. coli* was introduced into the growth medium of a hydroponic maize system at a concentration of 9.3×10^6 CFU/ml and was detected 48 h later in the shoot. Another study used FISH/CSLM to demonstrate that *S. enterica*, found as an endophyte on barley roots, spread to subjacent rhizodermis layers and the inner cortex of the root, and reached the plant shoot (Kutter et al., 2006). Although foodborne enteric disease in humans is generally associated with consumption of plant tissues from dicot plants (eg., spinach, lettuce, alfalfa, radishes), contaminated monocots (such as corn) might also pose a safety hazard by (re-) introduction of pathogens into the food chain through animal feed.

Interestingly, not all studies of root internalization have identified bacterial penetration and some of the available reports are contradictory. For example, internalization of *S. enterica* was reported in hydroponically-grown tomato (Guo et al., 2002), while in another study with soil-grown lettuce, no internalization of the bacterium was observed after 21 days of exposure to contaminated soil (Franz et al., 2005). In a recent study with lettuce grown in a potting medium, we observed internalization of *S. enterica* via the root and its spread to aboveground plant organs in 33-day-old plants, but not in 17-or 20-day-old plants (Bernstein et al., 2007a). The observed differences in penetration of the plant roots could be due to variations in developmental stages of the plants, growth media characteristics, concentration of the pathogen, genetic background of the specific strain used, as well as interactions with the rhizosphere community.

Very little information is currently available concerning the factors that govern those interactions between human pathogens and plants that affect the uptake of bacteria by roots and their subsequent translocation in the plant. Similarly unknown is the variability within the root population of a single plant, in terms of permeability to enteric pathogens and resistance to bacterial loading and transport in the apoplast. Therefore, reported inconsistencies regarding contamination of vegetables by foodborne pathogens via the root system may also be due to variability in the physiological traits of the different roots existing in the plant at different developmental stages. The fact that, in the above-mentioned study, the bacterium (*S. enterica*) internalized 33-day-old plants, but not 17-or 20-day-old plants (Bernstein et al., 2007a), suggests a plant development-dependency of the process. Results from studies of *E. coli* also suggest that the interaction of the bacteria with spinach plants is dependent on the developmental stage of the plant at the time of introduction (Warriner et al., 2003). This dependency points to variability in the susceptibility to penetration of roots of different ages, or of different root types formed at different stages of plant development. The timing and the concentration of the pathogen may also influence its potential for root internalization (Solomon et al., 2002), and the penetration may be bacterial specific (Kutter et al., 2006; Dong et al., 2003; Jablasone et al. 2005).

6 Concluding Remarks

Numerous countries throughout the world utilize treated effluents for modern agricultural irrigation. National and global agronomic guidelines and regulations were developed to guide productive and safe agronomic production under utilization of treated effluents. Cultivation with the treated effluents incorporate beneficial effects, related to conservation of fertilizers resources due to the micro and macronutrients available in the treated effluents. At the same time, inhibiting affects on crops may be induced by the higher levels of salts present in the treated water compared to potable water. Agronomic practices should be adjusted to prevent accumulation in the soil and thereby damage to crops by the salts present in the effluents. Risk assessments for the use of wastewater for irrigation in developed countries should incorporate recent knowledge regarding waterborne pathogens and their persistence in water, soil and the crop.

References

[1] Armon, R., D. Gold, M. Brodsky and G. Oron. Surface and subsurface irrigation with effluents of different qualities and presence of *Cryptosporidium* oocysts in soil and on crops. Water Sci. Tech. 2002, 46: 115 – 122

[2] Asano, T. Irrigation with reclaimed municipal wastewater . Water and Agriculture. 1985, 15: 273 – 282

[3] Bernstein, N., A. Bar Tal, H. Friedman, P. Snir, R. Ilona, A. Chazan and M. Ioffe. Application of treated wastewater for cultivation of roses (*Rosa hybrida*) in soil-less cul-

ture. Scientia Horticultura. 2006, 108: 185 - 193

[4] Bernstein, N, U. Kafkafi. Root growth under salinity stress. In: Waisel Y, Eshel A, Kafkafi U, eds. Plant roots-the hidden half. Marcel Dekker, Inc., 2000, 787 - 805

[5] Bernstein, N., A. Löuchli and W. K. Silk. Kinematics and dynamics of sorghum (*Sorghum bicolor* L.) leaf development at various Na/Ca salinities. I. Elongation growth. Plant Physiol. 1993a, 103: 1107 - 1114

[6] Bernstein, N, S. Sela, S. Neder-Lavon. Assessment of contamination potential of lettuce by Salmonella enterica serovar Newport added to the plant growing medium J. Food Protec. In Press 2007a

[7] Bernstein, N., S. Sela and S. Neder-Lavon. Effect of irrigation regimes on persistence of *Salmonella enterica* serovar Newport in small experimental pots designed for plant cultivation. Irrigation Sci. In Press 2007b

[8] Bernstein, N., S. Sela, R. Pinto and M. Ioffe. Evidence for internalization of *Escherichia coli* into the aerial parts of maize via the root system. J. Food Prot. 2007c, 70: 471 - 475

[9] Bernstein, N., W. K. Silk and A. Läuchli. Growth and development of sorghum leaves under conditions of NaCl stress. Spatial and temporal aspects of leaf growth inhibition. Planta. 1993b, 191: 433 - 439

[10] Blumenthal, U. J., D. D. Mara, A. Peasey, G. Ruiz-Palacios and R. Stott. Guidelines for the microbiological quality of treated wastewater used in agriculture: recommendations for revising WHO guidelines. Bulletin of the World Health Organization. 1989

[11] Cooley, M. B., W. G. Miller and R. E. Mandrell. Colonization of Arabidopsis thaliana with Salmonella enterica and Enterohemorrhagic *Escherichia coli* O157: H7 and Competition by Enterobacter asburiae. Appl. Environ. Microbiol. 2003, 69: 4915 - 4926

[12] Dong, Y., A. L. Iniguez, B. M. Ahmer, E. W. Triplett. Kinetics and strain specificity of rhizosphere and endophytic colonization by enteric bacteria on seedlings of Medicago sativa and Medicago truncatula. Appl Environ Microbiol. 2003, 69: 1783 - 90

[13] Feigin, A., I. Ravina and J. Shalhevet. Irrigation with treated sewage effluents. Management for Environmental protection. Advanced Series in Agricultural Sciences 1991, 17. Pub Springer-Verlag

[14] Fine, P., R. Halperin, E. Hadas. Economic considerations for wastewater upgrading alternatives: An Israeli test case. J. Environ. Manag. 2006, 78: 163 - 169

[15] Franz, E, A. D. van Diepeningen, O. J. de Vos and A. H. C. van Bruggen. Effects of cattle feeding regimen and soil management type on the fate of *Escherichia coli* O157: H7 and *Salmonella enterica* Serovar Typhimurium in manure, manure-amended soil, and Lettuce. App. Environ. Microbiol. 2005, 71: 6165 - 6174

[16] Franz, E, A. A. Visser, A. D. Van Diepeningen, M. M. Klerks, A. J. Termorshuizen and A. H. van Bruggen. Quantification of contamination of lettuce by GFP-expressing *Escherichia coli* O157: H7 and *Salmonella enterica* serovar Typhimurium. Food Microbi-

ol. 2006, 24: 106 – 112

[17] Friedman, H., N. Bernstein, M. Bruner, I. Rot, Z. Ben-Noon, A. Zuriel, R. Zuriel, C. Finkelstein, N. Umiel, A. Hagiladi. Application of secondary-treated effluents for cultivation of sunflower (*Helianthus annuus L.*) and celosia (*Celosia argentea L.*) as cut flowers. Scientia Horti. 2007, 115: 62 – 69

[18] Gagliardi, J. V. and J. S. Karns. Persistence of *Escherichia coli* O157: H7 in soil and on plant roots. Environ. Microbiol. 2002, 4: 89 – 96

[19] Guo X., M. W. van Iersel, J. Chen, R. E. Brackett and L. R. Beuchat. Evidance of association of *Salmonella* with tomato plants grown hydroponically in inoculated nutrient solution. Appl. Environ. Mocrobiol. 2002, 68: 3639 – 3643

[20] Homsi, J. The present state of sewage treatment. International report. Water Supply 2000, 18: 325 – 327

[21] Hussain, I. L. Raschid, M. A. Hanjra, F. Marikar and W. van der Hoek. A framework for analyzing socio-economic, health and environmental impacts of wastewater use in agriculture in developing countries. *IWMI Working Paper no.* 26. International Water Management Institute (IWMI), Colombo, Sri Lanka, 2001: 31

[22] IMH., Irrigation with effluents standards, The Israeli Ministry of Health principles for giving permit, for irrigation with effluents (treated waste water), English translation by the Palestinian Hydrology Group and Ramy Halperin, Israeli Ministry of Health. Jerusalem, Israel 2001

[23] Jablasone, J. K. Warriner and M. Griffiths. Interactions of *Escherichia coli* O157: H7, Salmonella typhimurium and *Listeria* monocytogenes with plants cultivated in a gnotobiotic system. Int. J. Food Microbiol. 2005, 99: 7 – 18

[24] Kudva, I. T. K. Blanch and C. J. Hovda. Analysis of Escherichia coli O157 – H7 survival in ovine or bovine manure and manure slurry. Appl. Environ. Microbiol. 1998, 64: 3166 – 3174

[25] Kutter, S, A. Hartmann and M. Schmid. Colonization of barley (Hordeum vulgare) with Salmonella enterica and Listeria spp. FEMS Microbiol. Ecol. 2006, 56: 262 – 271

[26] Lazof, D. B. and N. Bernstein. The NaCl-induced inhibition of shoot growth: The case for disturbed nutrition with special consideration of calcium nutrition. Adv. Bot. Res. 1998, 29: 113 – 189

[27] Maynard, U. S. Ouki and S. Williams. Tertiary lagoons: a review of removal mechanisms and performance. Water Research. 1999, 33: 1 – 13

[28] Natvig, E. E. S. C. Ingham, B. H. Ingham, L. R. Cooperband and T. R. Roper. *Salmonella enterica* serovar typhimurium and *Escherichia coli* contamination of root and leaf vegetables grown in soils with incorporated bovine manure. Appl. Environ. Microbiol. 2002, 68: 2737 – 2744

[29] Neves-Piestun. B. G. and N. Bernstein. Salinity-induced inhibition of leaf elongation is not mediated by changes in cell-wall acidification capacity. Plant Physiol. 2001, 125:

1419 – 1428

[30] Neves-Piestun, B. G. and N. Bernstein. Salinity induced changes in the nutritional status of expanding cells may impact leaf growth inhibition in Maize. Func. Plant Biol. 2005, 32: 141 – 152

[31] Samish, Z., R. Etinger-Tulczynska and M. Bick. The microflora within the tissue of fruits and vegetables. J. Food Sci. 1962, 28: 259 – 266

[32] Scott, C. A. N. I. Faraqui and Raschid-Sally, L. 2004. Wastewater Use in Irrigated Agriculture: Coordinating the Livelihood and Environmental Realities. Pub. Wallingford, UK: CABI 2004

[33] Shelef G and R. Halperin. The development of wastewater effluent quality requirements for reuse in agricultural irrigation in Israel. Regional Symposium on Water Recycling in Mediterranean Region, International Water Association (IWA), Iraklio, Greece. 2002, 1: 443 – 449

[34] Shuval, H., A. Adin, B. Fattal, F. Rawitz and Y. Perez. Wastewaer irrigation in developing countries. World Bank Technical 1986: 51

[35] Smit, J., J. Nasr. Urban agriculture for sustainable cities: using wastes and idle land and water bodies as resources. Environ. Urban. 1992, 4: 141 – 152

[36] Solomon, E. B., S. Yaron and K. R. Matthews. Transmission of *Escherichia coli* O157: H7 from contaminated manure and irrigation water to lettuce plant tissue and its subsequent internalization. Appl. Environ. Microbiol. 2002, 68: 397 – 400

[37] Steen, P van-der, A. Brenner, Y. Shabta and G. Oron. Improved fecal coliform decay in integrated duckweed and algal ponds. Water Sci. Tech. 2000, 42: 363 – 370

[38] U. S. EPA. Water Quality Criteria. National Academy of Sciences Report to the United States Environmental Protection Agency. Washington DC. 1973, 350 – 366

[39] U. S. EPA. Guidelines for Water Reuse. U. S. Environmental Protection Agency. EPA/625/R-04/108. 2004: 241 – 286

[40] Wachtel, M. R., Whitehand and R. E. Mandrell. Association of *Escherichia coli* O157: H7 with pre-harvest leaf lettuce upon exposure to contaminated irrigation water. J. Food Prot. 2002a, 65: 18 – 25

[41] Warriner, K. F. Ibrahim, M. Dickinson, C. Wright and W. M. Waites. Interaction of *Escherichia coli* with growing salad spinach plants. J. Food Prot. 2003, 66: 1790 – 1797

[42] WHO. 1989. Health Guidelines for the Use of Wastewater in Agriculture and Aquaculture. Report of a Scientific Grou. Technical Report No. 778. Geneva, Switzerland, 1989

[43] WHO/UNICEF. 2000. Global Water Supply and Sanitation Assessment 2000 Report. World Health Organization, United Nations Children's Fund: Genevas; 2000: 80

Essential Oils as Allelochemicals and their Potential Use as Bioherbicides

Nativ Dudai①

(*Division of Aromatic Plants*, *Agricultural Research Organization*, *Newe Ya'ar Research Center*, *P. O. Box* 1021, *Ramat Yishay*, *Israel*)

Abstract: Allelopathic activity of aromatic plants has been described frequently. Essential oils inhibit germination and growth of various plants. Residues of leaves of aromatic plants in soil inhibit the growth and the emergence of seedlings. We have developed a good quantitative assay to test for the inhibitory activity of volatiles on seed germination and have screened dozens of essential oils and their components. The major active allelochemicals were found to be aldehydic and ketonic monoterpenes, having a α-β unsaturated double bond, such as citral, (geranial and neral) and pulegone. Exposure of seeds for 4h to the compounds was enough to cause inhibition of the rate of germination and of seedling development in wheat, *Amaranthus palmeri* and *Brassica nigra*. Using histochemistry, we observed that citral is absorbed by wheat seed through the abscission layer, and that it reaches highest concentration in the embryo, where it accumulated in the aleurone, scutellum and parts of the endosperm. After exposure of wheat seeds to pure components of essential oils, GC-MS analysis of extracts of the seeds showed the presence of new products in the endosperm and embryo. These were probably formed by the metabolic detoxification of the inhibitors by the seed. The derivatives of the toxic compounds usually found in the seeds were less toxic than the original compound. Detoxification occurs in both embryo and endosperm during the first day of imbibition. In field studies, in which known amounts of residues of aromatic plants were mixed with soil in which wheat seeds sown, some components of the essential oil and their derivatives were found in the seed embryo and endosperm. The agrotechnology aspects will be discussed and further work of formulation and application of essential oils as bio-herbicides will be present.

Key words: Essential oils; Allelochemicals; Bioherbicides

① Nativ Dudai，男，博士，以色列 Newe Ya'ar 研究中心芳香植物分类农业研究所教授。研究方向：芳香植物与生物除草剂。E－mail：nativdud@ gmail. com

1 Introduction

The inhibition of growth of plants by other plants in their vicinity has been known for a long time. The chemical interaction between plants, which can cause enhancement or inhibition of growth, has been named allelopathy (Molisch, 1937; Rice, 1984).

Most of the germination and growth inhibitors produced by perennial angiosperms identified by Rice (1984) were phenolic compounds or derivatives of cinnamic acid. Other authors also found coumarins, flavonoids, alkaloids, cyanoglycosides, proteins, and amino acids among the inhibitory compounds (Friedman and Waller, 1983; Putnam, 1985; Waller, 1989).

Allelopathic activity of aromatic plants has been described frequently. (Sigmund, 1924; Went, 1942; Bonner, 1950; Asplund, 1968; Chou, 1986, 1989; Muller, 1986; Reynolds, 1987). Muller et al. (1964) and Muller (1965) reported that in the vicinity of aromatic shrubs, such as whiteleaf sage (*Salvia leucophylla* Greene) or California sagebrush (*Artemisia californica* Less.), there were no annual plants within a diameter of 90 cm, and the presence of annuals was very limited within 2 ~ 6m. Muller et al. (1964) and Friedman et al. (1977) found that volatile foliage compounds were the active ingredients causing the repression of growth in the vicinity of the *Salvia* and *Artemisia* species. Inhibition of germination and growth of various plants by essential oils has been not infrequently reported. Volatile terpenes are the main components of essential oils (Fischer, 1986; Muller, 1986; Elakovich, 1988). This ecological phenomenon provides a competitive advantage to aromatic plants in their natural environments.

These reports suggest that allelochemicals could be a viable alternative to herbicides for weed control in agriculture. Such a viable alternative has long been sought to counter their potential damage to human health and to the environment.. The aim of this article is to give an overview of our study regarding this topic during the last 15 years.

2 In vitro experiments

We have developed a good quantitative assay to test for the inhibitory activity of volatiles on seed germination and have screened dozens of essential oils and their components (Dudai et al. 1999). We detrmined that wheat seeds (*Triticum aestivum* L.) are a good model for this assay. The seeds were germinated in glass scintillation vials, 25ml, on three layers of filter paper (Whatman No. 1), saturated with 1.5ml of distilled water. Vials containing 20 seeds were incubated at 27 °C in the dark. The volatile substances causing inhibition of germination were applied in the gaseous phase by loading (using a calibrated glass microcapillary) on a piece of filter paper, which was attached to the inner side of the cover of the vial. The vials were closed hermetically. Amounts of up to 2μl of oil were applied in this way. The oil per vial (1μl) was equivalent to 40nl/ml. Experiments were repeated in five replicates. After 48 h the seeds were counted for germination percentage. The major components of the oils were identified by gas chromatography and gas chromatography-mass spectrometry (GC-MS). For most of the essential oils, 50% inhibition of the germination was observed in the range of concentrations between 28 ~ 100nl/ml in the gaseous phase.

The major active allelochemicals were found to be aldehydic and ketonic monoterpenes, having a α-β unsaturated double bond, such as citral (geranial and neral) and pulegone.

Essential oils from three species with high inhibitory activity were selected for further study. The major components of these oils represent different types of monoterpenes: phenolic (carvacrol) in *Origanum syriacum*; ketonic (pulegone) in *Micromeria fruticosa*; aldehydic (geranial and neral) in *Cimbopogon citratus*. The germination of various plant species, including wheat, responded differently to the three essential oils, but all were strongly inhibited when applied at 20 ~ 80nl/ml. In experiments which examined the effect of the length of exposure time of the seeds to the inhibitors during imbibition, it was found that exposure for a little as 4h is enough to cause some inhibition both of the germination rate and in the seedling development. This effect increases as the length of the exposure time increases. The increasing inhibition with time can be ascribed to increasing absorption of the inhibitory compound by the seed.

3 The active ingredients are metabolized by the inhibited seed

A critical question is: how much oil is absorbed by the seed, especially by the embryo, when exposed to the inhibitor? A number of techniques were used to attempt to estimate the very low amounts of the compounds present in the embryo. We tried to use the radioactive monoterpene, geraniol, and also developed a system for quantitative measurement of citral in the seeds based on the Schiff reaction (Dudai et al. 2004a). We also determined the amount of active compounds in the seed and embryo using gas-chromatographic analysis combined with mass spectrometry (Dudai et al. 2000). The amounts of citral were only 1.3 ~ 2.6 n mole per embryo and 5 ~ 11 n mole per endosperm. By histochemical localization in the grain we observed that the highest concentration is in the embryo, but it also accumulated in the aleurone, scutellum and parts of the endosperm. It seems that citral is absorbed by the grain mainly through the abscission tissue.

When the inhibitor supplied to the seeds was citral, GC-MS showed the presence of new compounds in the treated seeds. These new compounds appeared to arise by reduction or oxidation of citral. The appearance of geraniol, nerol, geranic acid and neric acid was observed. These compounds were detected both in the endosperm and the embryo. The new monoterpenes did not appear when using boiled seeds, indicating that the formation of these substances is due to biological activity and not spontaneous. Transformation of citral to oxidation and reduction derivatives took place in an aseptic system when seeds were disinfected by treatment with hypochlorite. Under these conditions mainly reduction products were detected. When wheat seeds were used without disinfection the resultant derivatives arose due to the activity both of the seed and of contaminant microorganisms. Derivatives of citral were less toxic than citral itself. This appears to result from metabolic processes which may be regarded as a kind of detoxification. We examined the kinetics of the biotransformation. The biotransformation occurs in both the embryo and the endosperm already at the beginning of imbibition. The citral and its metabolites accumulated during the first day of imbibition, and their amount either remained constant or thereafter decreased (Dudai et al. 2000).

Citronellal, another aldehydic monoterpene, was metabolized in a similar manner, with the formation citronellol and citronellic acid. Non-terpenoid aldehydes such as vanillin and decanal also yielded the corresponding oxidation and reduction products vanillyl alcohol and vanillic acid and decanol and decanoic acid, respectively. The results suggest that there is a general mechanism in the seed for metabolizing aldehydes. The phenolic monoterpene carvacrol was metabolized to thymoquinone and hydrothymoquinone (Dudai et al. 2000).

The ketone monoterpene carvone was reduced to (E) + (Z) -dihydrocarvone and (E) + (Z) -carveol. (E) -dihydrocarvone was reduced to neo-dihydrocarveol and dihydrocarveol . Similary, the ketonic monoterpene pulegone was converted to isopulegol and menthone (Dudai et al., 2004). This suggests the existence of a nonspecific mechanism, which can result in the reduction of ketones. In the same way, artemisia ketone was reduced to artemisia alcohol. The monoterpene alcohol carveol was reduced to dihydrocarveol, which further was reduced to carvomenthol or oxygenated to carvenone. Oxygenation also occurred in the cases of linalool (to 8-acetoxylinalool), α-terpineol (to sobrerol) and the hydrocarbone terpenes γ-terpinene, p-cymene, and δ-3-carene (Dudai et al. 2004b). The number of quite different substances, which are either reduced or oxidized, might indicate that non-specific enzyme systems are involved. The degradation of essential oils requires the activity of several enzyme systems. Thus, reductive processes might be catalyzed by non-specific dehydrogenases (Plapp et al., 1993) and oxidation might be due to the presence of cytochrome P-450 type enzymes, which today are known to be present in plant tissues and are involved in the biosynthesis of terpenes (Mihaliak et al., 1993; Halkier, 1996). The amount of monoterpene either remained constant or decreased. There is high correlation between the inhibition of germination of the compounds and the amount of total metabolites determined in the seed. This suggests that the catabolism of monoterpene is part of a detoxification process, and that the degree of inhibition is related to the ability of the seed to metabolize the monoterpene. The presence of low amounts of monoterpenes may be due to higher rates of metabolism and not the result of lower uptake.

4 Residues of leaves of aromatic plants in soil inhibit the growth and the emergence of seedlings

In pot experiments, in which leaves of the three selected species were incorporated into the top layer of the soil, there was marked inhibition of growth and emergence of both wheat and tomato. Dried leaves, from which the essential oils were removed by steam distillation, were used as a control. The observations support the view that allelopathic interactions between the species examined as test plants do indeed occur. Allelopathic activity of monoterpenes showed some selectivity towards different test plants. For example, *Micromeria fruticosa* leaves did not effect germination and growth of tomato, but significantly inhibited the emergence of wheat (Dudai, unpublished data).

5 Allelochemicals are released by leaf residues in soils, and are absorbed and metabolized by the inhibited wheat seed

Most of the studies on allelopathic effects of aromatic plants described the inhibition of seed germination and development of neighboring plants under field conditions and quantified the volatile compounds present in these plants when applied under laboratory or field conditions. The fate of the volatile compounds in the soil environment in these types of experiments is not clear. In order to confirm allelopathic effect it must be shown that the allelochemicals are released from the plant tissues, reach the target seed and induce inhibition or stimulation effect (Willis 1985).

In our study (Dudai et al. 2009) we followed the release of the volatiles known to be present in the tissue of the white micromeria leaves and determined which of them reached the target seeds. We further tested whether they are metabolized in the target tissue, and how this could lead to inhibition of seed germination. The germination of the seeds and subsequent development of the seedlings were inhibited by the addition of the leaves to the soil. The degree of inhibition was found to be concentration dependent, and the extent of inhibition was higher in the sandy soil than the clay. Volatile components from white micromeria and their derivatives were found in the soil and in the seeds. Soil sterilization inhibited the degradation of the volatiles but its effect on seedling emergence was not significant. We suggest that the active compounds pulegone and isomenthol are the probable cause of the inhibitory effects. Taken together, these observations support the notion that allelopathic interactions do indeed occur when leaves, which are shed and remain in the field, release allelochemicals that may accumulate in the soil. The chemicals released are then absorbed by the seeds and inhibit their germination and subsequent growth. Allelochemical interactions in the soil depend both on the soil type as indicated by the differences between clay and sandy soil in sterilized soils and on biotic factors such as the soil microflora. The use of mulches using leaves of aromatic plants could potentially be used as selective herbicidal agents. Their selectivity will depend on the soil, on the microflora and on the chemical composition of the seeds and their ability to take up and to metabolize the volatile compounds released from the leaf mulch.

6 Mode of action of the allelopatic activity of essential oil

For the study of the physiology of the inhibition, the activity of the isolated major compounds of the essential oils, citral, pulegone and carvacrol, was tested. Apparently monoterpenes containing oxygen, in an unsaturated carbonyl group were the most active, i. e., citral, pulegone, carvone, piperitone.

Our hypothesis was that the inhibitory monoterpenes might cause damage to the membranes. We therefore studied their effect on the leakage of electrolytes from wheat seeds during imbibition. No significant increase of the leakage of the following ions: Na^+, K^+, Ca^+ and Mg^+ was observed from intact seed, in the presence of pulegone, carvacrol or citral (Dudai, unpublished data). Some effects were observed when very high concentrations of these substances were used-10 ~ 20 fold of the inhibiting concentrations (Table 1). Since we got total inhibition of the germination in concentrations of only 40 ~ 80nl/ml, these results can not explain the membrane damage as the primary mechanism of the strong inhibition of germination by the monoterpenes.

Table 1 K^+ leakage from wheat seeds germinated in Petri dish after exposure for 24h to various amount of carvacrol, citral or pulegone in the gaseous phase

Inhibitor	Concentration (nl/ ml)	K^+ leakage (% of control)
Carvacrol	0	100
	80	100
	200	106
	400	109
	800	119
	1 200	131
	1 600	150
	2 000	144
Citral	0	100
	80	116
	200	122
	400	133
	800	144
	1 200	155
	1 600	167
	2 000	189
Pulegone	0	0
	2 000	124

The leakage of the control was was 0.56 mg from 20 seeds.

In further work it was found that microtubules of Arabidopsis seedlings were disrupted within minutes after exposure to very small concentrations of citral in the gaseous phase, whereas actin filaments remained intact. The effect of citral on plant microtubules was both time-and dose-dependent, and recovery was possible only if the exposure war short, no more then several minutes, and occurred only many hours later. (Chaimovitsh et al. 2010). Similar results were observed in divided cells of germinated wheat seedling (Chaimovitsh et al., paper in preparation).

7 Essential oils potential to be used as bio-herbicides

Most investigations on allelopathy have characterized the phenomenon but have not considered applications in agriculture. In order to examine a possible practical application, essential oil suspended in water with 0.5% v/v of a surfactant was sprayed on the surface of the soil after sowing. Our results showed that essential oils not only inhibit germination and growth of plants in Petri dishes but also in soil. The most active tested essential oil was the aldehyde from lemon grass, and it was therefore chosen for study. Inhibition of wheat, *Amaranthus palmeri*, and *Brassica nigra* seeds by the essential oil was generally more effective in loam or loess than in clayey soil (Table 2). The inhibition of germination decreased as the sowing depth increased.

Table 2 Effect of lemon grass essential oil suspension on emergence of Wheat and palmer amaranth seed in three soils[a]

Species	Concentration (%)	Emergence (% of control)		
		Loess	Loam	Clay soil
Wheat	0.0	100 A[b]	100 A	100 A
	0.5	16 B	31 B	62 B
	1.0	11 C	10 BC	9 B
	1.5	0 C	0 C	0 C
	2.0	0 C	0 C	0 C
Amarant	0.0	100 a	100 a	100 a
	0.5	12 b	4 b	55 b
	1.0	12 c	0 b	12 b
	1.5	0 c	0 b	10 c
	2.0	0 c	0 b	0 c

[a]Seeds were sown at 1 mm depth. Values were determined 8 days after sowing.

[b]Within columns, different letters for wheat (upper case) and for palmer amaranth (lower case) next to the values indicate values significantly different at $P < 0.05$.

8 Conclusion

The results of the study show that there are differences in the sensitivity of the various species. There are also differences in potency of the essential oils. Seeds that germinated in the presence of essential oils usually did not develop normally. The growth of their radicles and coleoptiles was inhibited compared with the control. Fifty percent inhibition of growth occurred at a lower oil concentration than for germination, and radicle growth was somewhat more sensitive than coleoptile growth (Dudai et al. 1999). The fact that, in a given species, germination is only partly inhibited by a given essential oil does not imply that the germinated seeds will develop into a normal seedling. It seems probable that growth inhibition prevents the normal penetration of the root into the soil. After leaf fall in summer, in dense populations of *Origanum syriacum* and *Micromeria fruticosa*, almost no other plants develop near the aromatic plants. In pot experiments, in which leaves of these species were incorporated into the top layer of the soil, there was marked inhibition of growth and germination (Dudai et al. 209). The observations support the view that allelopathic interactions do indeed occur. These data suggest that essential oils could be used to inhibit emergence of weeds. Further studies, especially on formulation of essential oils for application, are still required to apply this technique to agriculture.

References

[1] Asplund, R. O. Monoterpenes: relationship between structure and inhibition of germination. Phytochemistry 1968, 7: 1995 – 1997

[2] Bonner, J. The role of toxic substances in the interaction of higher plants. B*ot. Rev.* 1950, 16: 51 – 65

[3] Chaimovitsh, D., Abu-Abied, M., Belausov, E., Rubin, B., Dudai, N. and Sadot, E. Microtubules are an intracellular target of the plant terpene citral. The Plant Journal 2010, 61: 99 – 408

[4] Chou, C. H. The role of allelopathy in subtropical agroecosystems in Taiwan, 57 – 73, *in* A. R. Putnam and C. S. Tang (eds.). The Science of Allelopathy. Wiley-Interscience, New York 1986

[5] Chou, C. H. The role of allelopathy in phytochemical ecology, pp. 1989: 19 – 38, *in C*. H. Chou and G. R. Waller (eds.). Phytochemical Ecology: Allelochemicals, Mycotoxins and Insect Pheromones and Allomones. Institute of Botany, Academia Sinica Monograph Series No. 9, Taipei, Taiwan 1989

[6] Dudai, N., Mayer, A. M., Poljakoff-Mayber, A., Putievsky, E. and Lerner, H. R. 1999

[7] Essential oils as allelochemicals and their potential use as bio-herbicides. J. Chem. Ecol. 25: 1079 – 1089

[8] Dudai, N., Larkov, O., Putievsky, E., Lerner, H. R. Ravid, U., Lewinsohn, E. and Mayer, A. M. Biotransformation of constituents of essential oils germinating wheat seeds. Phyochemistry. 2000, 55: 375 - 382

[9] Dudai, N., Larkov O. and Lewinsohn E. Simple colorimetric measurement of citral in lemon scented essential oils using Schiff's reagent In: Act. Hort. (ISHS) 2004a, 629: 499 - 504

[10] Dudai, N., Ben-ami, Chaimovich, R. and Chaimovitsh, D. Essential oils as allelopathic agents: bioconversion of monoterpenes by germinating wheat seeds. In: *Act. Hort.* (ISHS) 2004b, 629: 505 - 508

[11] Dudai, N., Chaimovitsh, D., Larkov, O., Ficsher, R., Blaicher, Y. and Mayer, A. M. Allelochemicals released by leaf residues of *Micromeria fruticosa* in soils, Their uptake and metabolism by inhibited wheat seed. Plant and Soil 2009, 314: 311 - 317

[12] Elakovich, S. D. Terpenoids as models for new agrochemicals, pp. *in* H. G. Cutler (ed.). Biologically Active Natural Products - Potential Use in Agriculture. American Chemical Society, Washington, D. C 1988, 250 - 261

[13] Fischer, N. H. The function of mono and sesquiterpenes as plant germination and growth regulators, 1986, 203 - 218, *in* A. R. Putnam and C. S. Tang (eds.). The Science of Allelopathy. Wiley-Interscience, New York

[14] Friedman, J., and Waller, G. R. Seeds as allelopathic agents. J. Chem. Ecol. 1983, 9: 1107 - 1117

[15] Friedman, J., Orshan, G., and Ziger-Cfir, Y. Suppression of annuals by *Artemisia herbaalba* in the Negev Desert of Israel. J. Ecol. 1977, 65: 413 - 426

[16] Halkier, B. A. Catalytic reactivities and structure/function relationships of cyto507 chrome P-450 enzymes. Phytochemistry 1996, 43: 1 - 21

[17] Mihaliak, C. A., Karp, F. and Croteau, R. Cytochrome P-450 terpene hydroxylases. In: Lea P. J. (ed.) Methods in Plant Biochemistry vol. 9. Academic Press Limited, London. 1993, 261 - 279

[18] Molisch, H. Der Einfluss einer Pflanze auf die Andere—Allelopathie. Verlag G. Fischer, Jena 1937

[19] Muller, C. H., Muller, W. H., and Haines, B. L. Volatile growth inhibitors production by aromatic shrubs. Science 1964, 143: 471 - 473

[20] Muller, W. H. Volatile materials produced by *Salvia leucophylla*: Effect on seedling growth and soil bacteria. *Bot. Gaz.* 1965, 126: 195 - 200

[21] Muller, W. H. Allelochemical mechanisms in the inhibition of herbs by chaparral shrubs, *in* A. R. Putnam and C. S. Tang (eds.). The Science of Allelopathy. Wiley-Interscience, New York 1986, 189 - 199

[22] Plapp, B. V., Green, D. W. and Sun, H. Substrate specificity of alcohol dehydrogenases. In: Weiner, H. (ed.), Enzymology and Molecular Biology Of Carbonyl Metab-

olism. Plenum Press, New York. 1993: 391 -400

[23] Putnam, A. R. Weed allelopathy, *in* S. O. Duke (ed.). Weed Physiology, Vol. 1. CRC Press, Boca Raton, Florida 1985, 131 -150

[24] Reynolds, T. Comparative effect of alicyclic compounds and quinones on inhibition of lettuce fruit germination. *Ann. Bot.* (*London*) 1987, 60: 215 -223

[25] Rice, E. L. Allelopathy, 2nd ed. Academic Press, Orlando, Florida. Sigmund, W. 1924. Ueber die Einwirkung von Stoffwechselendprodukten auf die Pflanzen. *Biochem. Z.* 1984, 146: 389 -419

[26] Waller, G. R. Allelochemical action of some natural products, *in C.* H. Chou and G. R. Waller (eds.). Phytochemical Ecology: Allelochemicals, Mycotoxins and Insect Pheromones and Allomones. Institute of Botany, Academia Sinica Monograph Series No. 9, Taipei, Taiwan 1989, 129 -154

[27] Went, F. W. The dependence of annual plants on shrubs in Southern California deserts. *Bull. Torrey Bot. Club* 1942, 69: 100 -114

[28] Willis RJ The historical basis of the concept of allelopathy. J Hist Biol 1985, 18: 71 -102

クリ果実における糖とデンプン含有量の品種間差違，並びに，加工グリの不良品発生要因*

本間貴司[1①] 原弘道[1] 阮樹安[2] 陳喜忠[2]
王志運[3] 井上栄一[4] 月橋輝男[1]
（1 茨城大学農学部，2 遼寧省経済林研究所，3 遼寧省岫岩県林業局）

摘　要： チュウゴクグリの品種特性を把握するために，主要品種の可溶性糖含有量，デンプン含有量，水分量，その他固形物含量について品種間の相違を検討した.また，アミロプラスト（デンプンを蓄積する細胞内小器官）の蓄積状態をSEMで観察した.

さらに，市販加工栗の不良果実の果肉組織をSEMで観察し，不良果実の発生要因を考察した.

得られた結果は以下の通りである.

①チュウゴクグリの生体重当たりの可溶性糖含量は2.68%～8.01%（平均4.53%），デンプン含量は20.61%～33.16%（平均24.6%），水分含量は44.55%～54.40%（平均50.3%）であった.

②糖濃度の品種間差違は大きく，その変動係数は33%に達した.

③糖濃度が低い果実でも，その他の固形物含量は多い.したがって，食味を判断するためには，加熱後の分析データを使用しなければならない.

④果実組織におけるデンプン蓄積は，日本グリと同様に，果実周辺部から果実中央部方向へ順次進行した.

⑤山東省で育成された‘華光’は，糖含量，デンプン含量ともに他品種よりも多く，果実中心部細胞でもデンプン蓄積密度は高かった.このデータは，‘華光’が，貯蔵性に優れた品種であることを示唆している.

⑥白色・緑色の果実や水分過多の果実は不良品とされるが，いずれの果実でも，細胞内容物の収縮が顕著に観察された.

⑦細胞内容物の収縮は，加熱時にデンプンの糊化による膨潤が不十分であったことが原因と思われ，デンプンの蓄積が不十分であったことが示唆される.

⑧収穫時に，未熟果やデンプン貯蔵の不十分な果実を排除することによって，不良果実の混入・発生を減少させることが出来ると思われる.

キーワード：クリ糖；デンプン；品種間差違発生要因；不良果実

* 本報告の一部は，園芸学会2003年度秋季大会（日本）で発表した.

① 本間貴司，男，日本茨城大学农学部教授。研究方向：食品加工。E－mail：enghiro1071@yahoo. co. jp

中国国内には板栗（*Castanea mollissima* BL.），錐栗（*C. henryi Pehd*. et Wils.）および芽栗（*C. seguinii* Dode）が分布するが栽培種の殆どは板栗であり（呉，1984；姜，1995；明，2000；張，2004），チュウゴクグリ（Chinese Chestnut）と称される.

日本へ輸出された果実は，焼き栗として販売され，「甘栗」あるいは「天津甘栗」と称されることが多い.

チュウゴクグリの品種について，江蘇植物研究所は1957年から板栗資源の調査を行い，板栗の品種は500種存在するとしているが，その殆どは実生選抜であった.山東省果樹研究所には7種300の品種・系統が保存され，接木繁殖による系統維持と交配による育種が行われている（林ら，1991；明桂冬，2000）.

チュウゴクグリが「中国産甘栗」として日本へ輸入されたのは1910年に始まったと言われる.

中国からの積み出し港が天津であったことから，「天津甘栗」として商品化され，戦争による中断があったものの，戦後1949年には再開され，その後は両国政府間の対立で貿易が中断した時にも，周恩来総理（当時）による「友好配慮物資として輸出供給をする」との政策によって，日本への輸入が継続された，日中民間友好貿易の象徴的商品であった（中田，1987）.

近年は渋皮剥皮と加熱処理，いわゆる一次加工を中国国内で行った後に冷凍して輸出され，日本国内で再加熱，パック詰めなどの二次加工をした製品が増加している.しかしながら，色調や食味のばらつき，特に水分過多の果実や白色，緑色などを呈する，いわゆる，不良果実の存在は長年にわたっての懸案事項である.

クリは自家不和合性が強く（松原・牧，1940），クリ果実の可食部位は受精によって形成された胚である.このため，クリは遺伝的にヘテロ性が強く，果実品質は同一品種であっても樹内，園内の変動が大きいとされる.チュウゴクグリは長い間，実生による繁殖が行われてきたために，変動はさらに大きいものであろう.

クリ果実の諸形質に及ぼす花粉の影響については，果実の大きさ（梶浦，1936），結果歩合（梁取，1961），渋皮の剥皮性（大崎ら，1942；飯森ら，1943；Jaynes，1963；Mackeyら，1983；田中ら，1992）などが，キセニア現象として報告されている.このうち，果実重量，果肉色についてはチュウゴクグリについても検討されており，キセニア現象の存在を確認しながらもその発現程度は軽微であるとしている.

なお，渋皮の剥皮性について，田中・壽（1998，1998）は，渋皮由来のポリフェノールが原因となって接着することを明らかにし，渋皮の剥皮性はメタキセニア現象であることが確定した.

可溶性糖類とデンプンは食味に大きく影響する要因であるが，交配花粉の影響についての報告は少なく，原ら（2000）はニホングリ間の交配試験から，交配品種間で最大20%の変動を観察し，高品質果実の生産対策としての可能性を指摘したが，生産地での実情については不明なことが多い. また, 本間ら（2004）は, 市販甘栗を調査し, 果実の大きさ, 重量, 果形, 糖含量及びデンプン含量にバラツキの多いことを認め, その要因の一つに多品種の混在を指摘している.

本報ではチュウゴクグリの主要品種ならびに中国で育成された日中雑種について, 自然交配ではあるが, 食味品質に関係の深い可溶性糖含量とデンプン含有量, 並びに果肉の微細構造を比較検討を行うとともに, 日本国内で販売されているチュウゴクグリの加工品（剥き甘栗）から, 不良品とされる‘色調の異なる果肉’を選抜して, その微細構造を比較検討し, 不良品の発生要因と対策について考察した.

1　材料および方法

供試果実は2002年9月に山東省果樹研究所植栽のチュウゴクグリ10品種（‘辛荘2号’, ‘浅刺’, ‘燕魁’, ‘燕山紅栗’, ‘垂枝栗’, ‘葉里蔵’, ‘海豊’, ‘華光’, ‘郯城207’, ‘石豊’）, 及び, 遼寧省で育成・選抜したニホングリとチュウゴクグリの交雑種1品種（‘遼栗10号’）から採取した.

採取した果実のそれぞれ1kgを4週間冷蔵し, 平均的な大きさの果実を5個選抜して分析に供試した.

可溶性糖含有量の測定は, 子葉の中央部を液体窒素で凍結後, 振動破砕機で粉砕し, 80%エタノール可溶性成分から高速液体クロマトグラフ（島津製作所製, LC6A; 昭和電工社製, NH-2Pカラム）によって, フルクトース, グルコース, スクロースおよびマルトース含量を測定し, その合計を糖含量とした.

デンプンは, エタノール可溶性成分抽出残査から, Fキット法（ベーリンガーマンハイム製, スターチセット）によって含量を測定した.

微細構造観察用の試料作成は, 糖デンプン分析のために切り取った隣接部位の組織を液体窒素で凍結後に組織用真空凍結乾燥機（丘サイエンス製, ステージ温度－50℃, 10～4 Toor）で乾燥した.

市販甘栗の観察用組織は, 色調の異なる子葉を選抜して, その中央部を同様に凍結乾燥した.

乾燥後の試料は観察用試料台にマニキュアで接着した後, オスミウムプラズマコーター（JEOL製, JOS-100D）で導電処理を行い, さらにマグネトロンスパッタ（JEOL製, JUC-5000）で白金をコーティングして, 走査電子顕微鏡（JEOL製 JSM-T300, 加速電圧10kv）で観察した.

供試した果実の品種・系統を第1表に示した.

第 1 表　供試品種・系統一覧

分類	品種・系統名	来歴および特徴
チュウゴクグリ	辛荘二号	山東省果樹研究所によって選抜（偶発実生）．果実が大きく豊産性．
	浅刺	湖北省原産．詳しい来歴は不明．数百年前の偶発実生と言われている．刺毛は短く発生が粗らく硬い．
	燕山魁栗	河北省原産（偶発実生）．果皮色は赤褐色で果実はやや小ぶり．品質が優れている．
	燕山紅栗	北京 1 号，別名：燕紅．北京昌平県原産．当地の有力品種．果皮色は赤褐色で光沢がある．品質が極めて優れている．
	垂枝栗	山東省原産（偶発実生）．枝が垂れる．収量が少ない．
	葉里蔵	安徽省で発見された偶発実生．当地の有力品種．結果枝先端部の葉の密度が高く，毬果が葉に隠れる．
日中交雑種	海豊	山東省果樹研究所で選抜．母樹不明の接ぎ木苗．品質が優れている．
	華光	山東省果樹研究所で交配育成．品質が優れている．
	郯城 207	山東省果樹研究所で選抜（偶発実生）．果実が大きく品質が優れている．
	石豊	山東省果樹研究所により同省海陽県の実生栗園で選抜（偶発実生）．品質が優れ，貯蔵に適している．
	遼栗 10 号	遼寧省経済林研究所で1980 年に‘丹東栗 10 ~ 12’（ニホングリ）×‘遵化 11’（チュウゴクグリ）の交配実生から選抜．2002 年命名．果実は19g 前後で品質が良い．ニホングリと親和性がある．

2　結果および考察

【可溶性糖類及びデンプンの定量分析結果】

各品種の生体重当たりの可溶性糖含量，デンプン含量および水分含量の割合を第 1 図に，乾物重当たりの可溶性糖含量とデンプン含量及び乾物の割合を第 2 図に示した．

【水分】

第 1 図によれば，供試果実の水分含量は，日中雑種の‘遼栗 10 号’が最も多くて57.3%，チュウゴクグリでは‘葉里蔵’が最も多くて52.5%，‘燕魁’は最も少な異品種は‘燕魁’で44.5%であり，平均水分含量は50.3%，変動係数は5.8%であった．

ニホングリにおける平均水分率は60%前後とされており，表には示していないが，同時期に遼寧省で採取し，冷蔵貯蔵したニホングリの平均水分含量は約 64%であったことから，チュウゴクグリの果実はニホングリと比較して水分含量が少ない特

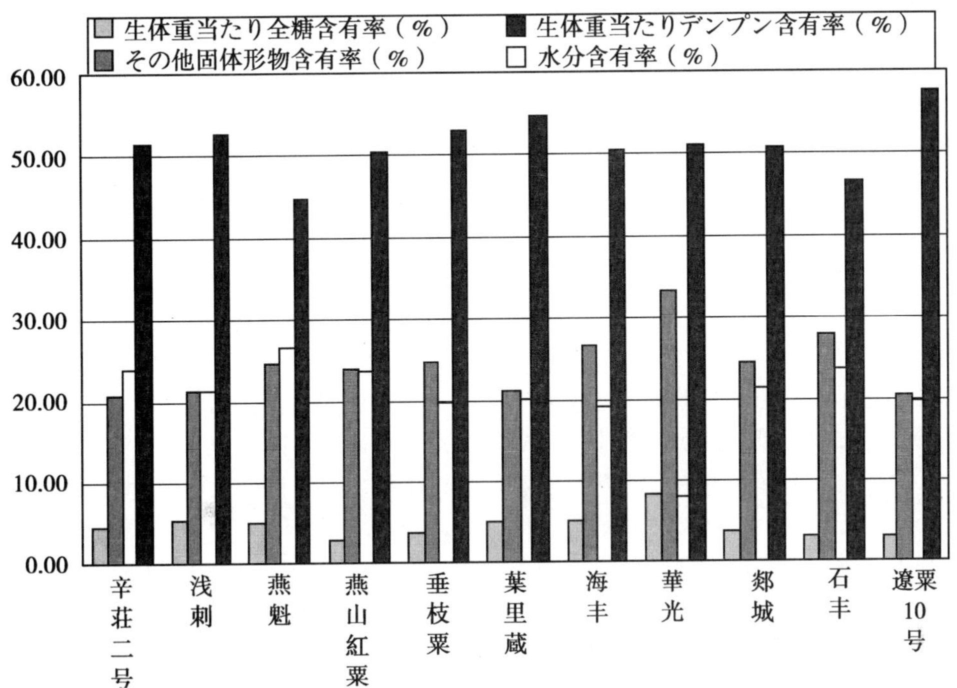

第1図　生体重量当たりの可溶性糖，デンプン、その他固形物，及び水分の含有率

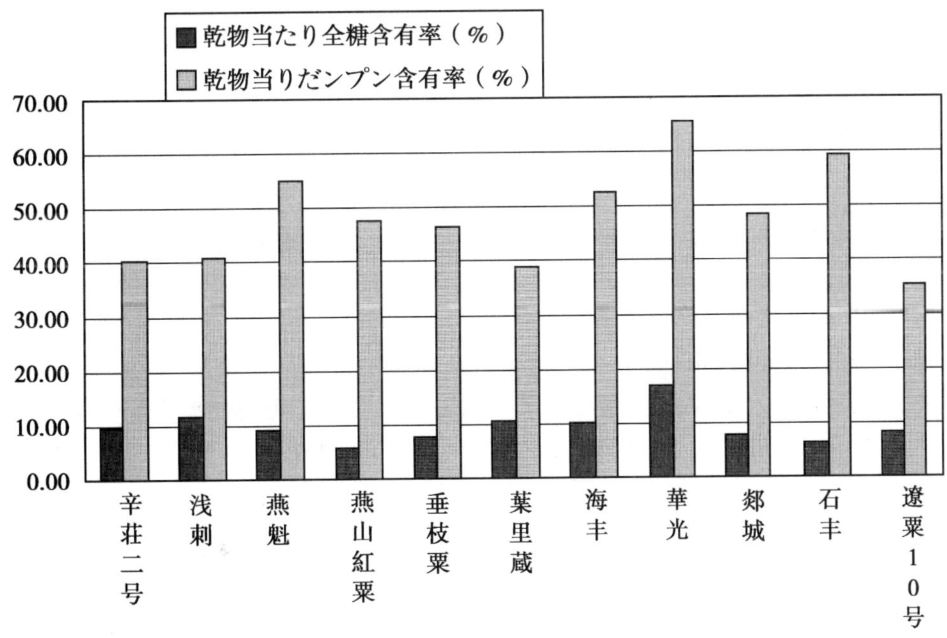

第2図　乾物当たりの全糖，デンプン含有率

徴を有することが示唆される.

【糖】

中国で発行されている品種解説によれば，チュウゴクグリの糖含有量はおよそ10%～20%（測定法不詳）と記載されているが（呉，1984；姜，1995；明，2000；張，2004；王，1993），第2図によれば，乾物重量当たりの平均可溶性糖含有量は9.2%であり，供試した果実の値はやや低かった.

生体重量当たりでも，乾物重量当たりでも，最も高い値を示したのは'華光'の8.01%（乾物当たりでは16.3%），最も低い値を示したのは'燕山紅栗'の2.68%（乾物当たりでは5.4%）であり，乾物当たりの糖含量変動係数は33.4%に達した.

ここで示した可溶性糖含量は生果における分析値であり，加熱工程を経て食するクリの食味には，糖のみが影響するのではなく，後述する貯蔵デンプンや繊維質，その他の固形物分解産物も大きく関与するので，生果の可溶性糖含量が食味の優劣を示しているのではないことに注意しなければならない.

果実の糖含量に品種間の差異が大きいことや貯蔵中の推移にも品種の特徴が存在することはニホングリにおいても知られており（Nomuraら，1995），さらに，原ら（2000）は花粉親の影響によっても15%～20%の変動があることを観察している.

したがって，本報告のデータは絶対値を示すものではないが，供試品種間の相対的な特徴を概観することは，今後の育種あるいは加工品の高品質化に資するものと思われる.

【デンプン】

デンプンの含有量は，品種間での変動係数は生体重当たりで15.2%，乾物重当たりでは17.7%であった.

チュウゴクグリのデンプンの含有率は糖含有量よりも品種間差が小さく，ニホングリとの交雑品種よりもやや高い傾向を示した.これは日本グリやヨーロッパグリでも認められている傾向と同様である（永井ら，1992；Nomuraら，1995；真部，2001；Bernardez et al.，2004；Montana et al.，2004）.

クリ果実は一般に，収穫直後からの冷蔵貯蔵によって可溶性糖含有量が増加し，デンプン含有量は減少する（河野ら，1984，菅原ら，1987；永井ら，1992；Nomuraら，1995）が，これは冷蔵によってデンプン分解酵素が活性化し，貯蔵デンプンを糖に分解することによるものと考えられている.

本研究に供試した果実は自然受粉果実であり，収穫後は約1ヶ月の冷蔵貯蔵を経ているので，デンプン含有量は収穫直後よりも減少し，品種間の差違が小さくなっている可能性（下村，1995）もありながらも，なお，品種間における大きな変動係数が存在することは，品種のもつ特徴を相対的に表していると考えられる.

本間ら（2008）は，日本グリを8ヶ月貯蔵した際に，糖含有量とデンプン含有量が殆ど減少していない果実の存在を認め，収穫時のデンプン蓄積が優れていた結果であること，このような果実は貯蔵性に優れている可能性を指摘している.

一般に，短期間の貯蔵を経たニホングリでは，糖含量の増加とデンプン含量の減少が認められるが，‘華光’は糖含有量とデンプン含有量ともに高い数値を示した.

これは，本間らが指摘した果実と同様な特徴を有しているとも考えられ，年次変動を含めて，より詳細な特性調査が必要であるが，食味のみならず，貯蔵性にも優れた品種である可能性が示唆される.

【その他の固形物成分】

クリの果肉に含まれる糖，デンプン以外の成分として，細胞質や細胞壁に含まれるポリフェノール，脂質，タンパク質，有機酸，ペクチン質及び無機成分が知られている（真部，2001）.

本研究ではそれぞれの画分についての分析を行っていないので，第1図に総量のみを示した.

ニホングリでは蔗糖の含有率のみで食味を判断すると言う意見もある（永井ら，1992）が，ニホングリのその他固形物含量は10%程度であり，チュウゴクグリよりも少ない（データ省略）.

水溶性ペクチン，ヘミセルロースには，甘味を感じさせる働きもあり，その他の成分が多いチュウゴクグリ品種における食味の検討は，加熱後の状態で行う必要があると思われる.

【組織観察】

原ら（1992）は，ニホングリ果実の組織観察を行い，デンプン蓄積は受精によって形成された子葉の背軸側（果実外周部）から，子葉向軸側（果実中心部）へ求心的に進行すること，デンプンを蓄積する細胞内小器官であるアミロプラストの蓄積程度はデンプンの蓄積と果実の比重に密接な関係にあることを指摘している.

そこで，デンプン含有量の最も多い‘華光’と最も少ない‘葉里蔵’について，デンプンを貯蔵する細胞内小器官のアミロプラストに着目し，子葉における蓄積状況をSEMによって観察した.

第3図は‘華光’と‘葉里蔵’の果実外周部細胞のSEM観察像である.

‘華光’では，試料調製時の衝撃による間隙がも認められるが，大型のアミロプラストとその間隙を小・中型のアミロプラストが密に蓄積されており，細胞壁，アミロプラストには多量の細胞基質が付着している.

一方，‘葉里蔵’では，細胞内容物の収縮による間隙が認められ，アミロプラストは‘華光’よりも小型で，蓄積程度も低いことが明らかである.

第4図は果実中心部細胞を比較したものであるが，‘華光’では‘葉里蔵’の外周部と類似の様相を呈しており，小型のアミロプラストが多く，細胞内容物の収縮による間隙が認められ，細胞基質の付着も多い.

一方，‘葉里蔵’では，液胞の痕跡と思われる空隙が多数認められ，アミロプラストの蓄積程度は低い.

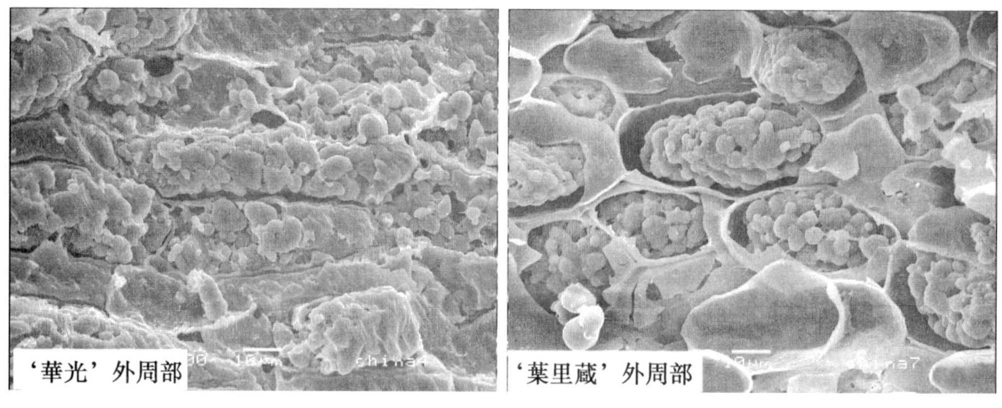

第3図　果実外周部（子葉背軸側）におけるアミロプラストの蓄積状態

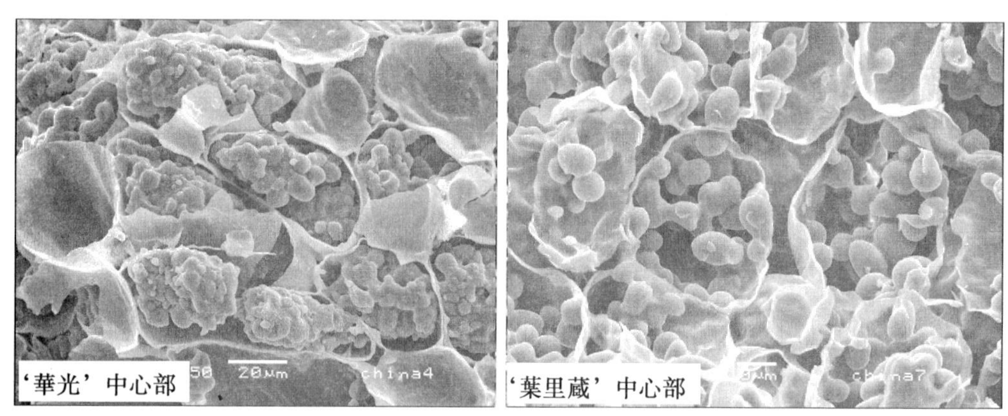

第4図　果実中心部（子葉向軸側）におけるアミロプラストの蓄積状態

原ら（1989）はニホングリの組織観察から，アミロプラストは包膜から突起を出して増殖をしながら，そ

の内部にデンプンを合成して肥大することを明らかにし，また，果実の比重の大きい果実ではアミロプラストの蓄積密度は果実中心部でも高く，デンプン含有量も多いことを指摘している.（原ら，1992）.

‘華光’と‘葉里蔵’の組織観察結果は，‘葉里蔵’よりも‘華光’におけるアミロプラストの蓄積，すなわちデンプンが高密度に蓄積されていることを示しており，チュウゴクグリにおけるデンプン蓄積もニホングリと同様に進行していることは明らかである.

デンプン含有量は加熱時の糊化特性や食感などのテクスチャーに大きく影響する要因であり，甘味を増加させるためには，アミロース等の酵素活性を活発にすること，すなわち，加熱過程において40℃前後を一定時間維持する工夫をすることによって，食味，特に甘味の向上が可能となることが知られている.

【加工品の不良果発生要因】

日本で販売されているチュウゴクグリの加工品においては，一次加工して冷凍された果実を短時間で解凍し，アルミニウムパックに封入するいわゆるレトルトパック製品が多数販売されている.

パックされた製品には，小さいものでは十数個の剥き栗となったチュウゴクグリが入っており，一般には淡褐色を呈しているが，時折，白色や濃緑色を呈する果実，あるいは水分過多の果実が入っており，不良品として扱われる.そこで，果実組織の観察からその原因と対策を検討した.

クリ果実は加熱によって，蓄積されたデンプンが膨潤して細胞内部は網目状構造で満たされるが，デンプン蓄積が不十分な果実では膨潤程度が少ないために，放熱後の収縮によって空隙が生じ，そこに水蒸気や水が残存して過湿気味の食感となる（原ら，1992）.

加工グリは加熱後に冷却・冷凍で貯蔵され，日本へ輸送されてから再度加熱されている.このため細胞内のデンプンは膨潤ののち冷却・凍結による収縮，さらには水蒸気による解凍・軟化と殺菌のための高圧・高温の過程を経過するために，本来の組織構造を維持することが困難であることは容易に想像できる.

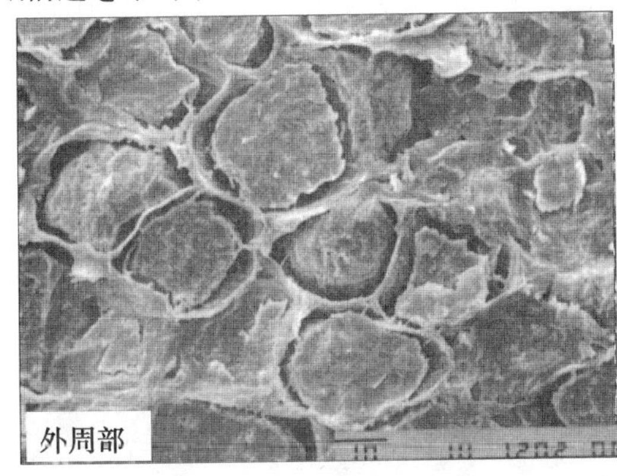

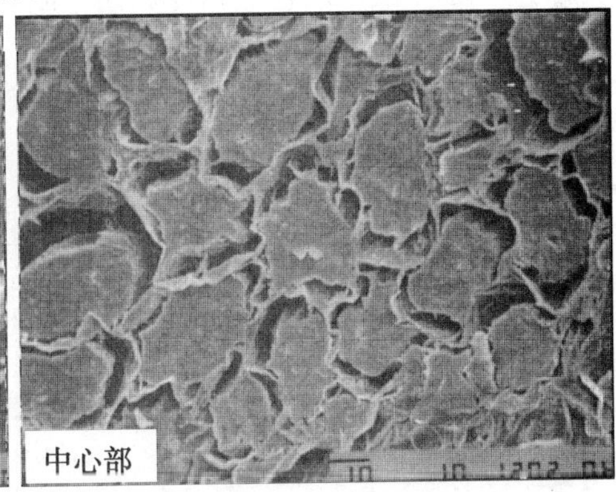

第5図　水分の多かった加工果実の子葉組織

第5図は市販甘栗で水分が多く，食感の悪かった果実のSEM観察像である.

水分の多かった果実では，外周部・中心部ともに，細胞壁は保持されているが，細胞内容物の周囲に空隙が多い.細胞内容物にはわずかに気泡状の孔隙を認めることが出来るが，殆どは凝縮されて固体化されているように見受けられる.これは，加熱時の膨潤が不十分であることを示しており，デンプンの蓄積量不足が原因と考えられる.

このため，加工過程で浸透した水分は，細胞内組織へ吸収されることが出来ずに，収縮して出来た間隙に保持されて水っぽい食感を呈していたものと考えられる.

また，中心部細胞では波打つような細胞壁と扁平な細胞が認められたが，これもデンプンの蓄積が少ないことによる膨潤不足と細胞壁の発達が遅れていることに起因していると考えられる.

第6図は白色を呈する果実の外周部と中心部のSEM観察像である.

外周部では，細胞内容物の収縮による空隙は認められるが，水分の多い果実より

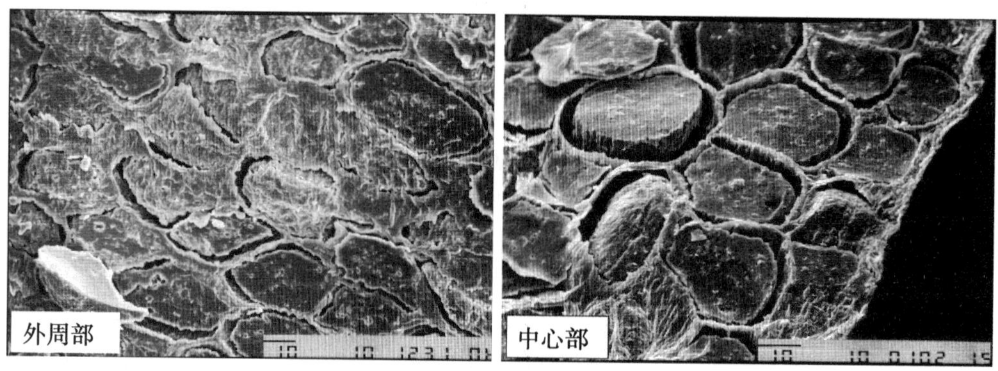

第6図　白色を呈した加工果実の子葉組織

は少なく，細胞内容物には孔隙が多数認められる.

中心部では，水分の多い果実と同様に，収縮による大きな空隙が生じているが，細胞内容物には外周部同様に比較的多くの孔隙を認めることが出来る.

なお，SEM 像を示していないが，暗緑色を呈した果実でも，どうようの傾向が観察された.

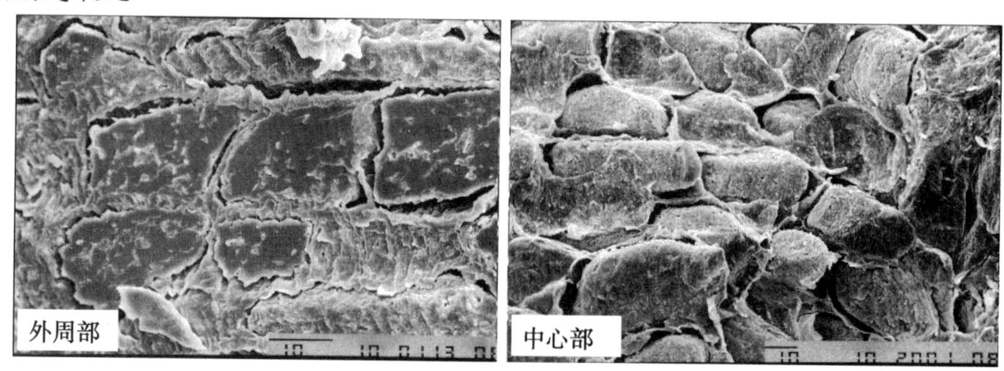

第7図　褐色を呈した加工果実の子葉組織

第7図は，やや褐色を呈した正常と思われる果実の外周部と中心部のSEM 観察像である.

外周部では，収縮による空隙は認められるが，細胞内容物と細胞壁にはデンプンの膨潤によって押しつけられた波状痕跡が残り，細胞内容物にはアミロプラスト包膜の痕跡も認めることが出来る.

中心部では，外周部と同様に収縮による空隙は認められるが，細胞内容物の網目状構造が保持されており，デンプンの膨潤によって出来た骨格構造の強さを認めることが出来る.

以上の観察結果は，水分過多や白色，暗緑色を呈する果実がデンプン蓄積不十分であること，すなわち，未熟果，あるいは日照不足などの生育条件下で生産された果実が加工された可能性を示している.

【対策その他】

未熟果については，日本に輸出されるチュウゴクグリの品質改善について，1980年代から日本との技術交流を通じて，未熟果を打落すような収穫法を禁止した（中田，1987）.

未熟果や生育不良果など，デンプン蓄積が不十分な果実は比重が小さい（原ら，1992）.

果実を輸出していた時代には，輸送過程での蒸れや腐敗を防ぐために，水洗を禁じていたが，中国国内で一次加工をすることが多い現代では，一次加工直前にやや強めの塩水選を行うことによって，比重の小さい果実を排除することは可能であると思われる.

早晩性や品質特性の明らかな品種群によるクリ園が理想ではあるが，広大なクリ圃場で生産されるチュウゴクグリでは，実生樹による膨大な品種系統を分類し，特性を明らかにすることは容易ではない. 日本におけるクリ属の遺伝学的研究に関する報告は多いとは言えない（山本ら，1998；井上ら，2003，2005，2005，2008，2009；寧ら，2004，2005，2006,）が，中国においては，近年，活発な研究活動が行われているようである.（Cao Qing-qin et. al.，2008；Ai Cheng-xiang et. al，2006 他）.

研究成果が生産現場に適用され，クリ産業の隆盛に生かされることを念じて結語とする.

【謝辞】

供試果実の採取に当たっては山東省果樹研究所の皆様にご協力をいただきました. 厚く御礼申し上げます.

参考文献

[1] Ai Cheng-xiang, Yu Xian-mei, Liu Qing-zhong, Zhang Li-si. Extraction and RAPD and SSR Analysis of Genomic DNA in Castanea Plants. Acta Botanica Boreali-Occidentalia Sinica. 2006, 26（3）

[2] 田壽樂・明桂冬・沈廣寧・單公華・張美勇・許林. 5 個板栗品種性状比較研究. 中国果樹. 2008（1）

[3] Cao Qing-gin, Zhen Zhen, Jiang Jie, Liu Yu-fen, Peng Yong-ging, Qin Ling. Chloroplast DNA analysis technology and its aplication in Castanea. J. Fruit Science. 2008, 25（3）

[4] 原弘道・松田智明・松田照男. クリ果実の組織形成と転流・蓄積に関する研究（第 2 報）アミロプラストの発達過程に関する透過型電子顕微鏡観察. 園芸学会雑誌. 1989，58. 別 2

[5] 原弘道・松田智明・月橋輝男. 発育後期の遮光処理が子葉におけるアミロプラストの発達とデンプン蓄積に及ぼす影響. 園芸学会雑誌. 1994，63（2）

[6] 原弘道・原好裕・松田智明.クリ果実の組織形成と転流・蓄積に関する研究（第7報）果実の比重とアミロプラスト密度との関係，並びに蒸しグリの微細構造.園芸学会雑誌.1992，61 別2

[7] 原弘道・岡田和恵・松田智明・井上栄一・月橋輝男.クリ果実の組織形成と転流・蓄積に関する研究（第12報）食味品質に及ぼす果実の比重ならびに父本の花粉の影響.園芸学会雑誌.2000，69（別1）

[8] 原弘道・寧林・都築久仁・井上栄一.アジアのクリの遺伝学的分類（第9報）核および葉緑体SSRマーカーによるクリ加工品の解析.園芸学研究.2007，6（別）1

[9] 本間貴司・原弘道・井上栄一・月橋輝男.甘栗の食味に関する諸要因.園芸学会雑誌，2004，73（別2）

[10] 本間貴司・井上栄一・松田智明・原弘道.クリ果実の長期貯蔵中における品質要因の変化.園芸学研究.2008，7（4）

[11] 本間貴司・井上栄一・松田智明・原弘道.貯蔵中におけるクリ果実の貯蔵物質動態に関する走査電子顕微鏡観察.園芸学研究.2009，8（4）

[12] Eiichi Inoue，Lin Ning，Hiromichi Hara，Shuan Ruan，Hiroyuki Anzai. Development of SSR Marker in Chinese Chestnuts and their Characterization in Diverse Chestnuts Cultivars. J. AMER. SOC. HORT. SCI.，2009，134（6）

[13] 井上栄一・寧林・山本俊哉・阮樹安・松本裕美・安西弘行・原弘道.ニホングリSSRマーカーによる朝鮮半島由来のクリ7品種の解析.園芸学研究.2008，7（4）

[14] 井上栄一・阮樹安・佐野真美・月橋輝男.中国で栽培されているニホングリ（Castanea crenata Sieb. et. Zucc.）の来歴とRAPDマーカーによる分析.園芸学研究.2003，2（4）

[15] 井上栄一・寧林・阮樹安・原弘道.アジアのクリの遺伝学的分類（第4報）チュウゴクグリSSR遺伝子座ICM014におけるヌルアリルの解析.園芸学会雑誌.2005，74（別2）

[16] 井上栄一・寧林・都築久仁・原弘道.アジアのクリの遺伝学的分類（第8報）座から抽出したDNAを用いた生グリの品種識別法の開発.園芸学研究.2007，7（別1）

[17] 井上栄一・倉林樹・寧林・本間貴司・原弘道.アジアのクリの遺伝学的分類（第10報）クリ種間および種内における葉緑体SSR遺伝子座の変異.園芸学研究.2009，8（別2）

[18] 飯森三男・太田敏輝.1943. 支那栗のXeniaに関する研究.園芸学会雑誌.1943，14（3）

[19] Janes，R,A. Biparental Determination of Nut Characters in Castanea. J. Heredity. 1963，54

[20] 梶浦實.栗の受粉に関する研究.園芸学会誌.1936，7（1）

[21] 河野澄夫・小野寺武夫・早川昭・岩元睦夫・太田英明・菅原渉.クリの予冷と低温貯蔵.園芸学会雑誌.1984，53（2）

[22] Keiichi Nomura，Y. Ogasawara，H. Uemukai and M. Yoshida. Change of Sugar Content in Chestnut during Low Temperature Strage. Acta Horticulture. 1995，398

[23] Mackay，J. W. and H. L. Crane. The Immediate Effect of Pollen on the Fruit of the Chestnut. Proc. Amer. Soc. Hort. Sci.，1983，36

[24] 永井耕介・堀本宗清・澤正樹・吉川年彦.クリの低温貯蔵中における糖含量の変化.兵庫中央農技研報.1992，40

[25] 永井耕介.消費者の嗜好に応じたクリの甘さ調節と甘さの基準づくり.農産物流通技術研究会報.1996，196

[26] 真部孝明.クリ果実－その性質と利用－.農文教.東京.2001

[27] 中田慶雄.甘栗読本.青年出版社.東京.1987

[28] 新津宏.栗の授粉に関する実験.園芸学会雑誌.1939，10（4）

[29] 寧林・井上栄一・松本裕美・阮樹安・山本俊哉・安西弘行・原弘道.アジアのクリの遺伝学的分類（第1報）ニホングリSSRプライマーによる朝鮮半島由来のクリ遺伝資源の解析.園芸学会雑誌.2004，73（別2）

[30] 寧林・井上栄一・阮樹安・安西弘行・原弘道.アジアのクリの遺伝学的分類（第2報）チュウゴクグリ'淺刺'におけるSSRマーカーの開発.園芸学会雑誌.2005，74（別1）

[31] 寧林・阮樹安・原弘道・井上栄一.アジアのクリの遺伝学的分類（第3報）チュウゴクグリSSRマーカーによるニホングリ品種の親子関係の検証.園芸学会雑誌.2005，74（別2）

[32] 寧林・阮樹安・原弘道・井上栄一.アジアのクリの遺伝学的分類（第5報）葉緑体SSRマーカーによるクリ遺伝資源の解析.園芸学会雑誌.2006，75（別1）

[33] 明桂冬.板栗栽培技術.北方果樹.2000（4）

[34] 張鉄如編著.板栗無公害高效栽培.北京：金盾出版社.2004

[35] 姜国高編.板栗早實豊産栽培技術.北京：中国林業出版社.1995

[36] 王福堂編著.板栗栽培貯蔵與加工.北京：農業出版社.1993

[37] 大崎守・佐宗久雄.支那栗の渋皮離脱に関する研究.園芸学会雑誌.1942，13（3）

[38] 林伯年・堀内昭作・王近衛・沈徳緒.中国の果樹（11）クリ.農業および園芸.1991，66（12）

[39] 志村勲・金戸橘夫・松永晴夫.クリ果実の肉質と比重について.園芸学会昭和41年度春季大会講演要旨集.1966

[40] 下村正彦.クリ果実の貯蔵による糖上昇.石川県農業研究成果集報.1995，8

[41] 菅原渉・河野澄夫・太田英明.低温貯蔵中における生果の品質変化.日本食品低温保蔵学会誌.1987，13（1）

[42] Toshiya Yamamoto，Takehiko Shimada，Kazuo Kotobuki，Yumiko Morimoto and Masao

Yoshida. Genetic Characterization of Asian Cestnut Varieties Assessed by AFLP. Breeding Science 1998, 48

[43] 田中敬一・壽和夫. ニホングリの渋皮剥皮性に関する要因の組織的・化学的解析. 園芸学会雑誌. 1992, 61 (1)

[44] K. Tanaka and K. Kotobuki. The Role of Phenolic Substances in the Adhesion between the Pelicle and Kernel of Japanese Chestnut Under Experimental Conditions. J. Japan Soc. Hort. Sci. 1998, 67

[45] K. Tanaka and K. Kotobuki. Partial Purification, Estimated Chemical Structure, and the Adhesive Property of Castahesion between pellicle and Kernel of Chestnut. J. Japan Soc. Hort. Sci. 1998, 67

[46] 吴耕民 编著. 中国温带果樹分類学. 北京: 農業出版社. 1984

[47] 梁取作次. これからのクリ栽培. 東京: 産業図書. 1961

Varietal Differences of Sugar and Starch Content in Chestnuts, and the Incidence Factor of Defective Product in Processed Chinese Chestnuts

Takashi Honma[1] Hiromichi Hara[1] Shu-an Ruan[2]
Xi-zhong Chen[2] Zhi-yun Wong[3] Eiichi Inoue[4] Teruo Tsukihashi[1]

(1 *Agriculture department of ibaraki University*, 2 *Jin Ji Lin institute of Liaoning Province*, 3 Forestry Bureau of Xiu Yan City of Liaoning Province)

Abstract: This paper has dealt with the types of Chinese chestnuts, and the connection of between the tastes of Sino-Japanese chestnuts hybrid cultivated in China and its soluble sugar content, starch content and tiny structures of its pulp. It has also given an analysis on reasons of rotten peeled Chinese chestnuts sold in Japanese market and the measures to prevent it from happening.

Key words: Chestnuts; Sugar; Starch; Varietal Differences; Incidence Factor; Defective Product

新興蔬菜:有機菇類生產

陳昇明[①]
（明道大學生物科技學系，台灣彰化 523）

摘 要： 菇類是利用生物技術栽培的一種「新興蔬菜」。本文報告菇類之生物特性：菇類用途，菇類食用價值與菇類保健效果；台灣菇類的種類、行銷與生產量；全球菇類之生產量等。而且，探討台灣有機菇類之栽培技術，有機菇類之生產流程與驗證制度等。有機菇類對於開發中國家的經濟重要性，一併予以討論。
關鍵詞： 新興蔬菜；有機菇類；有機栽培

1 前言

食用菇類（edible mushroom）是一種營養豐富含有保健養分的「新興蔬菜」，它含有高單位的蛋白質、氨基酸、維生素和稀有元素等（Bano and Rajarathnan，1986；Breene，1990）。近年來，菇類已經大量栽培生產使它成為一種新興的「菇類作物」（Royse，1997）。中国台灣省、日本、泰國等各地百貨公司或超級市場，常見生鮮菇類與蔬菜一起擺放於冷藏櫃，供銷費者選購（明道，2009）；然而，菇類產品的數量日益增多，種類也更多樣性。台灣超級市場菇類的消費量相當大，冷藏櫃中放置菇類的數量與蔬菜相當，有超越葉菜類之勢。由此顯示，菇類已經深受到消費者的喜愛，成為一種新興良質的生鮮蔬菜。在台灣，全年都可以從超級市場購買到各色的生鮮菇類。菇類在市場的優點是價格穩定，貯藏容易，不受到天候變化，例如：雨季或颱風的影響，能夠供應消費者的需要。建立菇類穩定行銷的原動力，應歸功於我們能夠利用菇類的室內環控栽培法。這種方法不但可以維持菇類穩定的生產量，而且可以生產清潔、優質的有機菇類。台灣有菇機類因為品質優良價格好，頗受銷費者歡迎；因此，有機菇類將如同其他有機農產品成為未來農業生產的主流（陳，1999）。本文以台灣省菇類產業發展為例，探討菇類作物的種類、特性、應用價值，以及有機菇類生產技術等，藉以促進有機菇類作物之生產與推廣。

---

① 陳昇明，男，德國哥廷根大學博士，中興大學名譽教授。明道大學生物科技學系講座教授兼農業暨生物科技研究中心主任。研究方向：农业生物工程与食品加工。E - mail：smtschen@ mdu. edu. tw

2 菇類的用途

栽培菇類有以下幾個重要的用途。(1) 菇類是一種烹飪食物，是現代蔬菜，栽培菇類可以增加食物生產；(2) 菇類含有豐富的營養成份，食用菇類可以獲得良好的食品營養（莊，1996）；(3) 菇類是一種保健食品，栽培菇類可以供應健康保養的食品，例如：菇類含有活性多醣類、各種維生素、鍺等微量元素、抗氧化物質等，有益健康（Hawksworth，2001）；(4) 菇類可以利用農業廢棄物栽培生產，因此栽培菇類可以消化廢棄物，有益於環境保護（Dundar and Yildiz，2009）。由於以上理由促使菇類生產逐年增加，市場快速擴大，台灣菇類栽培已經成為一種農業生物科技產業，具備專業精良的生產技術（陳，2007）。

3 菇類的食用價值

台灣有許多因為宗教信仰或健康因素而長期素食者，他們都是菇類重要的消費者，從菇類獲得補充身體內必要氨基酸與其他重要營養素，以及生物活性代謝物質（Chang，1996）。菇類含有高單位的必要氨基酸，最高者幾乎與牛肉相當，由此可見菇類是一種富有營養的食物。菇類與各種食物所含必要氨基酸含量的相對比值列舉述如下（Chang and Hayes，1978）。(1) 豬肉、雞肉、牛肉 100；(2) 牛奶 99；(3) 菇類 98 ~ 72（平均 85）；(4) 馬鈴薯、蠶豆 91；(5) 玉米 88；(6) 胡瓜 86；(7) 花生 79；(8) 菠菜、黃豆 76；(9) 高麗菜 72；(10) 蘿蔔 69；(11) 胡蘿蔔 53；(12) 蕃茄 44。

4 食用菇類的保健效果

菇類含有生物活性代謝物質，可以增進身體的免疫力，具有相程度的食療功效，因此被視為高級的保健食品（Chang，1996；Fukushima，et al. 2001；王等人，2008）。我們舉出幾種常見的菇類加以說明（Hawksworth，2001），例如：洋菇具有促進人體消化與消除壓力的作用；香菇有強身與提高免疫力的作用；蠔菇有促進肌肉與關結放鬆的作用；木耳有增進健康與促進血液循環的作用；杏鮑菇有強身與提高免疫力的作用等。

5 台灣省食用菇類與市場價格

台灣省栽培的菇類多半屬於中溫菇，生長適宜溫度在℃25℃左右。菇類傳統栽培的生產季節主要在秋天到次年春夏之交。夏天，因為天氣炎熱傳統菇舍停止生產，菇類的總生產量減低。在台灣，菇類是重要的火鍋食材，夏季火鍋食物不如冬天盛行，菇類的消費量下降。公元 2009 年 8 月，我們在台灣的超級市場從事生鮮菇之市場調查，探討各種生鮮菇類的售價，以每台斤（600 公克）新台幣表示其價格（明道，2009）。結果顯示洋菇（*Agaricus campestris*）的價格最高，120 元。其次價格排行次序如下：白精靈菇

(*Agrocybe cylindracea*) 100 元；草菇 (*Volvariella volvacea*) 90 元；柳松菇 (*Agrocybe cylindracea*) 90 元；美白菇 (*Hypsizigus marmoreus*) 90 元；黑珍珠菇 (*Pholiota nameko*) 90 元；香菇 (*Lentinus edodes*) 85 元；杏鮑菇 (*Pleurotus eryngii*) 70 元；蠔菇 (*Pleurotus ostreatus*) 70 元；珊瑚菇 (*Pleurotus cornucopiae*) 55 元；木耳 (*Auricularia polytricha*) 50 元；鮑魚菇 (*Pleurotus ostreatus*) 50 元；金針菇 (*Flammulina velutipes*) 45 元。一般而言，生鮮菇的價格與產量有相關性，產量少的菇種價格較高。在台灣，除了上述的菇類之外，尚有酒杯菇 (*Clitocybe maxima*)、雞腿菇 (*Coprinus comatus*)、阿魏菇 (*Pleurotus ferulae*) 等，雖然有零星的生產，但是尚未達到市場規模。白木耳 (*Tremella fuciformis*) 與巴西磨菇 (*Agaricus blazei*) 則主要以乾燥菇類銷售。總而言之，台灣菇類研究與栽培技術很成熟，市面上出現的菇類品種約有二十多種 (陳，2009)。

6 台灣省食用菇類之生產量

公元 2004 年，台灣生鮮菇類年產量為 115 000公噸，生產總值共計新台幣 63 億元 (莊，2003)。所有菇類當中以香菇的產量為最大宗，年產量 40 000公噸，占第一位 (34. 8 %)。其次是金針菇，年產量 32 000公噸占，第二位 (27. 8%)；第三位是木耳，年產量 14 000公噸 (12. 2%)；第四位是秀珍菇 (與同屬菇類)，年產量 12 000公噸 (10. 4%)；其他食用菇類年產量為 12 000公噸 (10. 4 %)。

7 全球食用菇類之生產量

食用菇類是歐美各國佳餚重要的素材，許多名貴的西餐料理都以食用菇類入菜。因此，食用菇類烹調成為一種重要的廚藝，其中以法國菜和義大利菜最為著稱。公元 1997 年，全世界生鮮食用菇類的總生產量共計 6 158仟公噸 (Royse，1997)。其中洋菇的年產量有 1 956仟公噸，是第一位占總生產量之 31. 8%；其次是香菇，它的年生產量是 1 564仟公噸，是全世界第二位占總生產量之 25. 4%，第三位是秀珍菇 (包含同類的杏鮑菇、鮑魚菇、蠔菇等)，年產量 876 仟公噸，占總生產量之 14. 2%；第四位是木耳，年生產量 485 仟公噸占總生產量之 7. 9%；第五位是金針菇，年產量 285 仟公噸，占總生產量之 4. 6%；第六位是草菇，年產量 181 仟公噸，占總生產量之 3. 0%；第七位是白木耳年產量 130 仟公噸，占總生產量之 2. 1%；其他菇類年產量則 681 仟公噸，占總生產量之 11%。由以上統計數字可以了解，洋菇是世界最普及的食用菌銷售量最大。

相較世界菇類和台灣菇類的生產量，我們發現，洋菇是世界產量最大的食用菌，占總生產量之 31. 8%。然而，台灣產量最大的食用菌是香菇，占總生產量之 34. 8%，洋菇生產量只占 4. 3%，差別很大。由以上數字顯示，東西方人士對菇類喜好有別。洋菇是西方社會最重要的食用菇類；然而香菇卻是東方最重的食用菇類。洋菇雖然原本不是東方食物，假如透過烹飪專家設計配製適合東方口味的洋菇菜餚，相信洋菇的銷售量應該有更大的發展空間。

8 有機菇類栽培材料與具備要件

目前，菇類的栽培方法依照其營養習性可歸納為兩種：（1）利用禾本科植物的莖稈栽培的草生菇類，使用主要培養基質有稻草、麥稈、牧草等。生產的菇類例如：洋菇、草菇、巴西蘑菇等（Royse，1997）；（2）利用段木或鋸木屑栽培的木生菇類，使用的培養基質原料，常見樹種有相思樹、芒果、龍眼、其他雜木等。生產的菇類例如：香菇、蠔菇、木耳、金針菇、杏鮑菇等。不論是使用何種栽培材料，必須是符合有機農業認證規範條件，例如，禁止使用基因改造菌種，不含化學肥料、化學農藥以及其他違反有機栽培的資材等；而且栽培場地、原物料、生產與管理、產品的儲藏與運輸等都必須保留詳細完整的紀錄。

近年，台灣實施有機菇類生產農場驗證制度，茲列舉有機菇類驗證檢驗之主要項目與內容供參考（慈心，2008）。

（1）菇類栽培方式：栽培方式調查；生產計畫。（2）菌種、種子及其處理：菇類應使用有機菌種，除非在種子市場無法購得。（3）生長介質：列出產瓶培養基之成份；列出太空包培養基之成分；列出土生菇栽培的生長介質成分；土生菇；植菌孔；堆肥使用。（4）埋土生產區的管理：產品管理；自然資源管理。（5）生產管理：養分管理；病蟲害管理；水源；投入資材。（6）產品處理：產品採收；採收後處理；作物貯存；運輸。（7）紀錄管理：保持符合有機標準的所有農場活動及作業的紀錄至少 2 年。（8）有機作物年產量及銷售紀錄：銷售方式；標籤及標章。

9 有機菇類生產作業流程

有機菇類生產方式可以分為兩種：一為傳統網室栽培法，另一種是密閉環控室栽法。前者栽培設施因為沒有溫控設備，氣溫隨著外界氣候而變動，因此菇類生產量不穩定。後者的栽培設施因為附設有溫度、濕度、通氣、空氣循環等自動控制系統。這種方式的菇類生產，可以全年無休，而且品質優良，產量穩定，生產力強，是現代有機菇類生產的主流。

一般而言，有機菇類的生產作業流程之檢驗過程分為以下 9 個步驟。

（1）取得原菌種：養菇場必須取得菇類原菌種做為栽培母菌，通常是購自於菌種公司或研究機構。

（2）菌種繁殖：將原菌種接種於菇菌培養基大量繁殖，例如：穀類培養基等，以備栽培之用。

（3）太空包製作：培養菇菌用的基質盛入塑膠袋或塑膠瓶稱為太空包，它是栽培菇的容器。通常各家菇場依自己習慣製作不同大小的太空包。太空包使用前必須經過滅菌，以便接種菇菌後得以維持純粹培養。

（4）菌絲生長：太空包接種菇菌之後，必須放置於室溫（約 25℃）環境下讓菌絲生長。待太空包中菌絲充分生長之後，將長滿菌絲的太空包（菇菌包）移至栽培室菇架上，開始栽培管理。

（5）栽培管理：栽培室內的菇架是由金屬材質建構而成的多層立體空間，專供菇菌包擺放立體栽培之用。栽培管理時期，菇類栽培室的溫度設定較菌絲期為低，濕度則較高，而通氣量較大，以便促進菇菌生長發育。

（6）刺激出菇：有些菇類菌絲在出菇（形成子實體）時，必須經過刺激處理，處理方法主要分為溫度處理與機械處理二種。刺激的方法和刺激條件常因菇類的種類不同而異。

（7）採收包裝：菇朵發育完成之後就可以採收。菇類採收時通常為迎合市場需要在菇朵尚未完全展開前進行採收，而且利用真包裝保持菇類新鮮度。

（8）儲運：採收菇類產品必須立即儲藏於清潔無汚染的冷藏庫，並且使用冷藏貨車將生鮮菇類運至超級市場的冷藏櫃。菇類的行銷過程必須一路保持菇類生鮮為原則。

（9）廢料處理：生產有機菇類後遺留下來的廢料，必須依照環境保護原則應予妥善處理，不得任意拋棄污染至環境。

參考文獻

[1] 王貞文，陳昇明，許惠恆．靈芝對糖尿病患者降血糖之輔助治療。內科學誌，2008，19：54－60

[2] 明道大學農生中心．台灣菇類價格排行，菇類天地，[F]http://tw.myblog.yahoo.com/kulei523/2009

[3] 莊老達．菇類產銷與輔導策施。農政與農情，2003，138：1－2

[4] 莊苓萍．食用菇的營養價值。食品工業月刊，1996，9：30－38

[5] 陳文德．我國有機農業之發展策略與方向。有機栽培應用技術．1999，1－9。行政院農業委員會農業試驗所

[6] 陳昇明（主編）．大型真菌研討會論文集．明道大學．2007

[7] 陳昇明．台灣食用菌新品種與新技術介紹．首屆海峽兩岸食用菌技術與產業發展研討會．九江，江西．2009

[8] 慈心有機農業發展基金會．有機菇類驗證申請書．2008

[9] Bano，Z. and Rajarathnam. S. Vitamin values of *Pleurotus* mushrooms Qualitas Plantarum Plant Foods for Human Nutrition. 1986，36（1）：11－16

[10] Breene，W. M. Nutritional and medicinal value of specialty mushrooms. J. Food Protect.，1990，53：883－894

[11] Chang，R. Functional properties of edible mushrooms. Nutr. Rev. 1996，54：91－93

[12] Chang，S. T. and W. A. Hayes. The Biology and Cultivation of Edible Mushrooms. London Academic Press，1978

[13] Dundar，A. and A. Yildiz. A comparative study on *Pleurotus ostreatus*（Jacq.）P. Kumm. cultivated on different agricultural lignocellulosic wastes. Turk. J. Biol.，2009，33：171－179

[14] Fukushima，M.，T. Ohashi and Y. Fujiwara. Cholesterol-lowering effects of maiitake

(*Grifola frondosa*) fiber, shiitake (*Lentinus edodes*) fiber, and enokitake (*Flammulina verlutipes*) fiber in rats. Exper. Biol. Med. 2001, 226: 758 -765

[15] Hawksworth, D. L. . Mushrooms: the extent of the unexplored potential. Intl. J. Medicinal Mushrooms, 2001, 3: 333 -337

[16] Royse, D. J. . Specialty mushrooms and their cultivation. Hort. Rev. 1997, 19: 59 -97

[17] Tschen, J. S. M. , Organic mushroom production in Taiwan. International Seminar on Organic Agriculture and Bio Dynamic Farming. Changhua, Taiwan, 2010

A New Vegetable: Organic Mushroom Production

Johannes Scheng-Ming TSCHEN

(*Department of Biotechnology*, *Mingdao University*, *Pitou*, *Changhua in Taiwan Province* 5235)

Abstract: Mushroom is a "new vegetable" cultivated by use of biotechnology. This paper presents biological characteristics of mushroom: The usefulness of mushroom, edible value, and health of mushroom; Taiwanese mushroom, its marketing and amount of production; world mushroom production, etc. The study reports also cultivation technique of organic mushroom in Taiwan, procedure of organic mushroom production and its recognition. The economic importance of mushroom production in developing countries will be discussed.

Key words: New vegetable; Organic mushroom; Organic cultivation

蛋白质芯片技术在农产品及食品安全检测中的应用研究进展*

刘帅帅[1,2]① 周德庆[2]
（1 中国海洋大学食品科学与工程学院，青岛 266003；
2 中国水产科学研究院黄海水产研究所，青岛 266071）

摘 要：蛋白质芯片技术是采用微阵列方法，对样品蛋白进行高通量、高灵敏度、高特异性的分析技术。目前这一技术已经被广泛应用到生命科学研究的各个领域，本文主要阐述了蛋白质芯片技术在食品质量安全检测领域的国内外应用与研究现状，旨在为蛋白质芯片技术研究提供参考，进而推动该技术在食品质量安全领域中的应用。

关键词：蛋白质芯片；微阵列；食品安全；检测；研究进展

蛋白质作为生命功能的最终执行者，其功能已越来越受到人们的重视。深入研究蛋白质的结构、功能以及它们之间的相互作用，已扩展到生命科学的各个方面，蛋白质芯片（Protein chip）技术亦应运而生。蛋白质芯片又称蛋白质微阵列（Protein microarray），是20世纪90年代继基因芯片之后发展起来的一项研究蛋白质的高新技术，蛋白质芯片是将已知蛋白点印在固定于不同种类支持介质上，制成由高密度的蛋白质或多肽分子组成蛋白微阵列，其中，每个分子的位置及序列是已知的，将待测蛋白质与该芯片进行孵育反应，用未经标记或标记（荧光物质、酶或化学发光物质等标记）的生物分子与芯片上的探针进行反应，然后通过特定的扫描装置进行检测，由计算机分析处理显示结果。

目前，蛋白质芯片的研究主要集中在简化操作过程，增加特异性等方面上，已取得了一定的成果。Macbeath 等[1]用一层牛血清蛋白铺在玻片表面，以提供亲水性表面，防止点于其上的探针蛋白变性，然后将探针蛋白点阵（1 600点/cm^2）于牛血清白蛋白膜表面，与微阵列进行孵育的蛋白质、酶作用的底物小分子物质分别标有不同颜色的荧光基团，反应结束后采用通用的激光聚焦扫描分析系统进行检测，成功解决了固体表面蛋白质活性的问题，而且使得操作过程得到很大的简化。张义浜等[2]研究表明，经过PEG 化磷脂膜修饰的二氧化硅表面，可以显著抑制蛋白的非特异性吸附，并通过功能

* 基金项目：公益性行业（农业）科研专项（No.：200903055）资助

① 刘帅帅，男，中国海洋大学食品科学与工程学院硕士研究生，研究方向：农产品食品安全。E-mail：liushuai3036@126.com

化的 PEG 分子有效固定配基及其抗体。Marta Bally 等[3]用微粒子荧光标签对荧光信号放大进行了测试，用可控的持续的微粒子流促进抗生蛋白链菌素包被荧光微粒子，并特异性结合到牛血清白蛋白点上，用电子显微镜观察和定量。

1 蛋白质芯片的检测技术原理与分类

蛋白质芯片的检测技术分为两种，第一种是间接检测法，也叫探针标记检测法。它使用同位素或荧光等物质标记探针，通过相应的仪器，如放射显像仪、电荷偶合芯片扫描仪或激光共聚焦芯片扫描仪对信号进行检测，从而获得相关的生物学信息。标记物主要包括荧光物质、化学发光物质、酶及同位素等。目前在蛋白质芯片检测中应用最广的是荧光染料标记，该方法原理简单、使用安全，且有很高的分辨率，缺点在于易产生蛋白质间的非特异性作用，且由于标记物的加入可能会降低分析的准确度。

第二种叫直接检测法，也叫无探针标记检测法，是目前研究的热点。它直接对捕捉到的目的蛋白进行检测，最常用的是表面加强激光解吸离子化-飞行时间质谱法[4]；SELDI 是目前发展最快和应用最广泛和成熟的一种蛋白质芯片技术。随着芯片技术、质谱分析技术及生物信息学的进一步发展，该检测技术会越来越成熟，可以更加快速、高灵敏性、高特异性和全自动化地进行蛋白质质谱分析[5]。检测折射指数变化的表面等离子体共振法[6]也是一种很有发展前景的技术；现在越来越多的人将科研方向转移到该检测技术的研究上来。Lee 等[7]将 SPR 应用到蛋白质芯片技术中，能简单快速地检测到抗谷氨酸脱羧酶抗体，可用于早期糖尿病的辅助诊断。余兴龙等[8]将空间相位调制与 SPR 传感结合，使发生 SPR 时引起的反射光的相位变化转化为干涉条纹的位置变化，通过分析干涉条纹的位置变化即可获得反射光的相位变化，从而解析出相关生物信息。Hiroyuki 等[9]发现一种新型的方法制备以蛋白质为基质的水凝胶，即 3D NPH（三维纳米结构的蛋白质水凝胶），由蛋白质聚合体混合物的纳米粒构成，它的点用小量的蛋白质聚合体混合物溶液修饰，溶液在很短的时间内交联并使 3D NPH 也形成像海绵状的薄薄的一层松弛交联，提高了 SPR 蛋白质芯片的敏感度。光学蛋白质芯片技术、原子力显微镜[10]等在蛋白质检测方面也有着各自的优势。刘芳芳等[11]为获得丰富的特异识别分子和实现无标记、高灵敏度检测，利用噬菌体展示技术，选择在 PⅢ 蛋白上展示 12 肽的噬菌体 M13 作探针，采用羧基-氨基共价耦联法制备噬菌体展示蛋白质芯片的无标记检测。韩欢欢等[12]将微印刷技术与银增强法相结合，建立了一种蛋白质阵列芯片制备与检测的新方法。通过定量分析证明了蛋白质可以被均匀地转印至固相载体表面，此新方法应用于蛋白质阵列上具有灵活、灵敏及成本低廉等特点。

2 蛋白质芯片在农产品及食品安全领域的主要应用

所谓食品安全（food safety），是指食品无毒、无害，符合应当有的营养要求，对人体健康不造成任何急性、亚急性或者慢性危害。根据世界卫生组织的定义，食品安全是食物中有毒、有害物质对人体健康影响的公共卫生问题。近几年来，食品安全问题越来越引起人们的重视，已成为当今社会关注的热点之一。由于蛋白质芯片技术具有快速、平行、微型化、自动化和高通量的特点，能够在一次实验中对大量样本中的目的蛋白质同时进行检测，这引起了食品安全科技工作者的浓厚兴趣，越来越多的食品安全专家尝试将该技术引入到食品安全检测上来，实践证明，蛋白质芯片在食品安全分析方面具有较好的应用前景。食品中营养成分，有毒、有害的化学物质的分析，污染的致病微生物、生物毒素、农药兽药残留、转基因食品、食品原料的检测，食品毒理学的研究等都可以用蛋白质芯片来完成。

2.1 在病原微生物检测上的应用

病原微生物是食品生物性污染的最主要因素，也是引发人体食源性疾病的主要原因。传统的培养分离检测方法耗时费力，已不能满足目前食品质量与安全控制体系的要求。而蛋白质芯片技术在微生物的监测、检测、分离、鉴定分类等方面拥有巨大的应用前景。蛋白质芯片技术在微生物领域的应用目前主要表现在两个方面。第一，开展微生物蛋白质组学研究，揭示蛋白质作用新的机理，开发未知蛋白质资源；第二，利用已知蛋白质分子的性质，通过蛋白质与其他生物活性分子的相互作用，实现对不同微生物的检测[13]。在对微生物特别是病原微生物的检测上，已取得很好的研究结果。Grow 等[14]利用表面增强拉曼散射芯片技术，根据各生物体（革兰氏阳性李斯特菌、革兰氏阴性军团菌、芽孢杆菌的芽孢和隐孢子虫卵囊）拉曼散射指纹图谱，检测病原体及所含毒素。Stokes 等[15]采用配备微流体传输系统的二维感光芯片，利用集成电路原理与免疫诊断技术检测出大肠杆菌 O157:H7。Howell 等[16]通过微接触印迹法将靶细菌对应的特异性抗体通过物理吸附固定在硅烷修饰的玻片上，利用抗体和细菌的特异性结合捕获细菌；他们使用 Nikon TE2300 光学显微镜和扫描探针显微镜分别检测了大肠杆菌（E. coli）O157：H7 菌株和肾沙门氏杆菌（Renibacteriums salmoninarum，RS），证明抗体蛋白质芯片对细菌具有高度的特异性、灵敏性和亲和力。Nanduri 等[17]用 pIII 蛋白上展示有单抗 scFv 的噬菌体 Lm P4：A8 为探针，检测了单核细胞增生李斯特氏菌（Listeria. monocytohenes），检测限可达 2×10^6 CFU/ml。

Park 等[18]利用微生物孢子既可以长期稳定保存，又可以接受外界刺激萌发的性质，结合类似噬菌体展示的技术，在芯片上构建了重组苏云金芽孢杆菌（Bacillus thuringiensis，BT）芽孢微图案的活性蛋白质芯片，并阐述了芯片表面重组 BT 孢子图案的成功萌发过程，作为这种原理的证据，在孢子表面展示了增强的绿色荧光蛋白，表明蛋白质芯片也适用于微生物致病因子及其机理的研究。

2.2 在农兽药残留检测上的应用

农兽药残留是农兽药使用后残存于食品中的微量农兽药原体、有毒代谢物、降解物和杂质的总称。农产品中高农兽药残留不仅是化学性危害的主要因素，而且对人体具有潜在的慢性危害。近年来，农兽药残留问题成为我国农畜产品出口屡屡受阻的主要障碍。2005 年，生物芯片北京国家工程研究中心研制成功了世界上第一个能够监测肉类中兽药残留的生物芯片系统。兽药残留蛋白芯片检测系统可同时检测动物组织中的多种残留，实现了多种兽药残留的高通量快速筛查，提高了检测效率。目前，此芯片系统已可对包括瘦肉精、磺胺二甲嘧啶、链霉素在内的多种重点兽药进行检测。Zuo 等[19]构建了一种可同时检测食品中 3 种兽药残留的小分子微阵列，检测时间不超过 2h，待测样品检测与加标回收实验结果表明所构建的微阵列具有良好的可靠性。左鹏等[20]用蛋白质芯片法快速定量检测食品中氯霉素和磺胺二甲嘧啶残留，并同现行的免疫学测定方法进行了比较。

抗生素是由微生物（包括细菌、真菌、放线菌属）或高等动植物在生活过程中所产生的具有抗病原体或其他活性的一类次级代谢产物，在食品特别是动物性食品及制品中，抗生素类残留对人体健康有影响已引起关注。现已普遍认为其对人体造成的过敏和变态反应、细菌耐药性和菌群失调有关。Knecht 等[21]报道了一种可快速、自动、平行检测牛奶中 10 种抗生素残留的蛋白质微阵列，该阵列采用间接竞争 ELISA 模式，通过灵敏的 CCD 照相记录反应过程中产生的化学发光信号，单个组分检测所用时间少于 5min，10 种组分的检测限在 0.12 ~32μg/L 之间，这表明蛋白质微阵列将有可能用于更多抗生素的平行检测，从而对乳品质量进行监控。

Belleville 等[22]以小分子的农药敌草腈的代谢物 2，6-二氯苯甲酰胺和阿特拉津为对象，以 IC50 值为指标，建立了新型的检测方法。目前，已经在芯片上实现的检测兽药品种包括：磺胺二甲基嘧啶、链霉素、恩诺沙星和克伦特罗，检测对象包括了鸡肉、鸡肝、猪肉、猪肝和牛奶等。蛋白质芯片用于农兽药残留检测具有前处理简单，灵敏度高，特异性好，检测速度快，检测通量高，质控体系严密等优点[23]。

2.3 在转基因食品检测上的应用

自 1994 年美国第一个转基因植物产品-转基因番茄获得 FDA 的批准进入市场以来，全球转基因作物数量飞速增加。目前，仅美国市场上就有 4 000种食品来自基因工程产品。我国培育成功的转基因烟草、番茄、棉花等均已经大规模种植。转基因作物大豆、玉米等种植面积逐年增加，转基因食品在取得巨大经济效益同时，其安全性问题已引起社会各界的广泛关注。常用的转基因作物检测方法主要有 PCR 检测法、Southern 杂交法、Northern 杂交法、Western 杂交法和 ELISA 法等。这些方法在检测时具有明显的单一性、假阳性高和周期长等缺点。利用转基因食品因含有转基因技术导入的外源基因和外源基因在受体内的表达产物，外源基因最终是以蛋白质或多肽形式得以表达，通过对蛋白质芯片设计不同探针阵列、使用特定分析方法可使该技术在此方面具有较高应用价值，是未来转基因食品安全检测的主要发展方向，不断发展和完善蛋白质芯片技术可对转基因食品进行定性检测[24]。对转基因食品的检测和鉴定不仅是满足消费者知情权的需要，而且是食品法规的必然要求。为了加强对农业转基因生物的安全管理，2002 年 1 月，我国农业部颁布了《农业转基因生物标识管理办法》，规定自 2002 年 3 月 20 日起，凡是列入标识管理目录并用于销售的农业转基因生物，必须进行标识；未标识和不按规定标识的，不得进口或销售。

2.4 在食品原料控制与检测上的应用

作为食品原料的农作物和动物等发生病害后，也会给人类带来的危害，特别是用带有疾病的动植物加工成食品后，可直接对人类的产生危害。对动植物疾病的检测，能够减少给人类带来的危害。传统的 EL ISA 方法操作复杂，PCR 的方法有相当的漏检率，而且难以满足对大量样品的同时检测。蛋白质芯片技术的出现为解决这个问题指明了研究方向。

在农业上，蛋白质芯片可用来筛选高产、抗虫、抗病、经济价值高的作物。利用蛋白质芯片本身优点，可更详细了解作物各种酶的功能，各种因素如干旱、肥力、光质、光量、植物激素、除草剂等对作物的影响，从而通过各种处理使作物向期望方向发展，加快食品原料作物新品种培育。OMSV 病毒（糙皮侧耳球形病毒）是引发糙皮侧耳（Pleurotus ostreatus）顶枯病的主要原因，这种病毒偶尔的暴发就会导致严重的病害以及重大的经济损失。Sang-Woo Kim[25] 等人用蛋白质芯片技术尝试制备了与 OMSV 病毒蛋白 RAN 聚合酶域（RPD）特异性结合的单克隆抗（mAbs）并进行筛选。方法是在玻片上用 RPD 蛋白进行修饰，从对 RPD 具有免疫的并携带骨髓瘤细胞的老鼠的脾细胞融合后得到 87 个杂种细胞，培养破碎取上清液，将其点在制好的芯片上。结果用 Alexa488 染料检测，用免疫球蛋白作为二级抗体。在 87 个样中，13 个荧光信号强度明显，以后免疫印迹表明 mAbs 与 RPD 的特异性结合符合与荧光信号强度的对应，表明该技术可用来筛选单克隆抗体，对预防 OMSV 病毒对人类造成经济和健康危害提供技术支持。

在畜牧业，Joos 等[26]将 18 种动物疾病相应的标志性抗原固定在芯片上，将待测样品经特殊的处理后加入反应体系，然后加入酶标二抗，加底物显色。根据显色位置的不同可判断出为何种抗体阳性，从而诊断出相应的疾病。

3 展望

尽管近年来对蛋白质芯片技术研究获得了很大的发展和进步，但是，如何获得种类众多的用于芯片制备的蛋白质依然是蛋白质芯片应用的主要瓶颈之一。近年来，无细胞蛋白质表达系统再次受到关注。无细胞蛋白质合成系统是一种以外源 DNA 或 mRNA 为模板，利用细胞抽提物中的蛋白合成机器、蛋白折叠因子及其他相关酶系，通过添加氨基酸、T7 聚合酶和能量物质等来实现蛋白质表达的体外系统[27]。无细胞表达系统非常适合用于蛋白质芯片技术[28~30]。利用无细胞表达系统制备蛋白质芯片能有效解决传统蛋白质芯片技术面临的诸如蛋白质的高效表达与纯化、蛋白质的固定、蛋白质稳定性的保持等难题，并发挥了芯片技术高通量、高灵敏、检测快捷等优点。蛋白质在芯片表面的有效固定与蛋白质活性的保持等内容是蛋白质芯片技术发展的关键。采用纳米生物技术与无细胞表达系统，已经可以在生物芯片表面通过植入基因的方式制备相关的蛋白质芯片，从而为蛋白质芯片的原位制备开辟了新的方向[31]。限制蛋白质芯片广泛应用的另一个瓶颈是检测准确度不高，原因是在一定程度上受限于所选择的抗原或抗体的来源、纯度与特异性，蛋白质种类繁多，而一种蛋白质具有高亲合性的抗体也可以低亲和性地结合其他相似蛋白上，使蛋白质芯片技术的优势得不到充分发挥。

食品安全是一门专门探讨在食品加工、存储、销售等过程中确保食品卫生及食用安全，降低疾病隐患，防范食物中毒的一个跨学科领域。随着社会的不断进步和发展，人们对食品安全提出了更高的要求，而危害人们健康甚至生命的重大食品安全事故屡有发生，建立准确、灵敏、快速的卫生检验方法对于食品安全具有重要的意义。蛋白质芯片技术在食品安全的检验中与传统方法相比具有巨大的优势。如何将这两者更好的结合，为人类的健康作出更大的贡献，是摆在食品科技工作者面前的重要课题。它的优势是其他方法不能比拟的，相信随着芯片技术的发展和完善，像无细胞表达系统等新的科技成果的转化和应用，其他相关学科如纳米技术、材料科学和表面科学的发展，这些问题终将得到解决。蛋白质芯片作为一种重要的检测工具和技术平台，定会在食品的生产、流通、检测等方面发挥越来越重要的独特作用，必将为生命科学的发展提供更有力的技术支持。

参考文献

[1] Macbeath G, Scheriber S L. Pringting Proteinas microarray for high-through put function determintion [J]. Science, 2000, 289: 1760 - 1763

[2] 张义浜，陈艳艳，靳刚. PEG 化磷脂膜在蛋白质芯片表面修饰中的应用 [J]. 材料工程，2008 (10): 0208 - 0210

[3] Marta Bally, Raghuram Dhumpa, Janos Vörös. Particle flow assays for fluorescent protein microarray applications [J]. Biosensors and Bioelectronics, 2009, 24: 1195 - 1200

[4] David A Hall, Jas on Ptacek, Michael Snyder. Protein Microarray Technology [J]. Mech Ageing Dev, 2007, 128 (1): 161 - 167

[5] 马可，仉红刚. SELDI 蛋白质芯片检测技术 [J]. 中国生物工程杂志，2008，28 (8): 118 - 122

[6] Mc Donnell J M. Surface Plasmon Resonance: Towards an Understanding of the Mechanisms of Biological Molecular Recognition [J]. CurrOp in ChemBiol, 2001, 5: 572 - 577

[7] Lee J W, Sim SJ, Cho SM, et al. Characterization of a self-assembled monolayer of thiol on a gold surface and the fabrication of a biosensor chip based on surface Plasmon resonance for detecting anti-GAD antibody. Biosens Bioelectron [J], 2005, 20 (7): 1422 - 1427

[8] 余兴龙，闫硕，定翔等. 基于 SPR 传感的空间相位调制蛋白质芯片检测方法 [J]. 仪器仪表学报，2009，30 (6): 1134 - 1139

[9] Hiroyuki, Tanaka. Enhancement of sensitivity of SPR protein microarray using a novel 3D protein immobilization [J]. Colloids and Surfaces B: Biointerfaces, 2009, 70: 259 - 265

[10] Kaur J, Singh KV, Schmid A H, et al. Atomic force spectroscopy based study of antibody pesticide interactions for characterization of immunosensor surface [J]. Biosens Bioelectrn, 2004, 20 (2): 284 - 293

[11] 刘芳芳，罗昭锋，定翔. 噬菌体展示蛋白质芯片的无标记检测 [J]. 清华大学学

报（自然科学版），2008，48（11）：1935－1939
[12] 韩欢欢，于晓波，吕任极，等.一种蛋白质阵列芯片新技术的研究 [J].分析试验室，2008，27（2）：107－109
[13] 顾军，刘作易，张春秀. 蛋白质芯片在微生物学领域的应用进展 [J]. 微生物学杂志，2006，26（6）：0064－0067
[14] Grow A E，Wood LL，Clayco mb JL，et al. New biochip technology for label-free detection of pathogens and their toxins [J]. J Microbiol Met hods，2003，53（2）：221－233
[15] Stokes D L，Griffin G D，VoDinh T，et al. coli using a microfluidics based antibody biochip detection system [J]. Fresenius J Anal Chem，2001，369（324）：295－301
[16] Howell S W，Inerowicz H D，Regnier FE，et al. Patterned protein microarrays for bacterial detection [J]. Langmuir，2003，19（2）：436－439
[17] Nanduri V，Bhunia A K，Tu S，et al. SPR biosensor for the detection of L. monocytogenesus-ing phage-displayed antibody [J]. Biosensors and Bioelectronics，2007，23：248－252
[18] Park T J，Lee K B，Lee SJ，et al. Micropatterns of spores displaying heterologous proteins [J]. J Am Chem，2004，126（34）：10512－10513
[19] Zuo P，Ye BC. Small Molecule Microarrays for Drug Residue Detection in Foodstuffs [J]. Journal of Agriculture and Food Chemistry，2006，54：6978－6983
[20] 左鹏，叶邦策.蛋白芯片法快速测定食品中氯霉素和磺胺二甲嘧啶残留 [J].食品科学，2007，28，（2）：254－257
[21] Knecht B G，Strasser A，Dietrich R，et al. Automated Microarray System for the Simultaneous Detection of Antibiotics in Milk [J]. Analytical Chemistry，2004，76：646－654
[22] Belleville E，Dufva M，Aamand J，et al. Quantitative microarray pesticide analysis [J]. Journal of Immunological Methods，2004，286：219－229
[23] 李振兴，林洪，杜亚楠. 蛋白质芯片在食品安全方面的应用 [J]. 海洋湖沼通报，2007（1）：130－136
[24] 陈东海，刘云焕. 蛋白质芯片技术在食品研究方面展望 [J]. 粮食与油脂，2005，2：9－11
[25] Sang-Woo Kim，Min-GonKimb，Hyo-AmJung b. An application of protein microarray in the screening of monoclonal antibodies against the oyster mushroom spherical virus [J]. Analytical Biochemistry，2008，374：313－317
[26] Joos TO，Schrenk M，Hopfi P，et al. A microarray enzyme-linked immunosorbent assay for autoimmune diagno stics [J]. Elect rop horesis，2000，21（13）：2641－2650
[27] 洪励上，苏志宁. 无细胞蛋白表达系统研究进展 [J]. 科技经济市场，2009（6）：14－15
[28] Endoh T，Kanai T，Sato Y T，et al. Cell-free protein synthesis at high temperatures u-

sing the lysate of a hyperthermophile [J]. Biotechnol, 2006, 126 (2): 186 - 195
[29] Mikami S, Kobayashi T, Yokoyama S, et al. A hybridoma-based in vitro translation system that efficiently synthesizes glycoproteins [J]. Biotechnol, 2006, 127 (1): 65 - 78
[30] He M Y, Stoevesandt O, Taussig M J. In situ synthesis of protein arrays [J]. Curr Opin Biotechnol, 2008, 19 (1): 4 - 9
[31] 章杰，刘琼明，许丹科. 无细胞系统原位制备蛋白质芯片及其应用 [J]. 生物化学与生物物理进展，2009，36 (4): 391 - 397

Application Progress on Protein Chips Detection Technology in Food Safety Detection

LIU Shuai-shuai[1,2] ZHOU De-qing[2]

(1 *College of Food Science and Engineering*, *Ocean University of China*, *Qingdao* 266003; 2 *Yellow Sea Fisheries Research Institute*, *Chinese Academy of Fishery Sciences*, *Qingdao* 266071)

Abstract: The protein chip technology is microarray methods, high throughput, high sensitivity and high specificity of the analysis techniques for the protein samples. At present, this technique has been widely applied to various fields of life science research. In this review, the application and research situation? of protein chip technology in food quality and safety at home and abroad is expatiated, aiming at providing references for protein chip technology, further promote the application of this technique in food safety research.

Key words: Protein chip; Microarray; Detection; Food safety; Research progress

环境激素对水产品安全性的影响及监控*

苏静怡[1,2]① 周德庆[2]

(1 中国海洋大学食品科学与工程学院，青岛 266003；

2 中国水产科学研究院黄海水产研究所，青岛 266071)

摘 要： 本文介绍了环境激素的定义、种类和来源，重点阐述了环境激素对生物和人的危害以及对水产食品安全性的影响，提出了防控环境激素污染而应采取的相关措施及对策。

关键词： 环境激素；水产品；安全性；污染；监控

1 环境激素的定义、种类和来源

20世纪90年代，人们对环境问题开始给予高度关注。1992年，当时作为美国副总统候选人的戈尔写了一本名为《地球平衡》的书，其主要内容涉及地球变暖、臭氧层破坏、热带雨林减少等全球范围内的环境问题，这本书在当时大为畅销。而最早在全球呼吁环境激素问题的，当属1996年美国生物学者T. 科尔泊恩。在他执笔的《我们被偷走的未来》(*Our Stolen Future*) 一书中，除了谈及戈尔副总统所谈论的上述问题外，还着重讨论了以前被忽视的环境毒性物质对内分泌系统的影响，认为这些物质可能影响到包括人类在内的各种生物的生殖功能、生殖器健康以及性行为。接着敲响环境激素警钟的是英国BBC广播电视公司，一直从事BBC科学节目制作的D. 卡布里也于1997年出版了一本书，名为《雌性化的自然》(*The Feminization of Nature*)，书的副标题中有“环境激素污染的恐怖”字样，作者作为科学新闻记者，以记实的手法增强身临其境之感，披露了很多研究人员的困难及尚未公开的一些事情。

1.1 环境激素的定义

1977年，日本学者就提出“环境激素”这个名词，但是没有引起广泛注意。1996年，美国环境记者戴安·达玛诺斯在西方首先提出了“环境激素”这个名词。她认为“环境激素”并不直接作为有毒物质给生物体带来异常影响，而是以激素样的面貌对生物体起作用，即使数量极少，也能让生物体的内分泌失衡，而出现种种异常现象，由此

* 基金项目：公益性行业（农业）科研专项（No.：200903055）资助

① 苏静怡，女，中国海洋大学食品科学与工程学院硕士生。E - mail：sujingyi1987@yahoo.com. cn

“环境激素”也译作“环境荷尔蒙”，学术上也命名为“内分泌干扰物”。人们原来知道人体内有 8 类激素，所以也有人把“环境激素”称为“第九类激素”。

世界卫生组织给环境激素所下的定义是“使内分泌功能发生变化并因此对个体及子孙或者集团产生有害影响的外因性化学物质或者混合物”。由此可以看出，环境激素是继臭氧层破坏、温室效应之后，又一世界环境大问题。臭氧层破坏、温室效应对生态环境影响是渐进型的，对人类社会影响尚有时空上的距离，也给人类社会留有解决问题的时间，并且随着严格控制其破坏程度，可望缓解或维持现状。而环境激素一经产生，就直接危害野生动物和人类社会。许多专家学者甚至表示，环境激素已发展到威胁人类生存的程度。科尔泊恩告戒人们：“合成化学物质中存在着一些即使极其微量也会对人体产生影响的物质，而这种影响可能极其巨大，甚至波及一生。”当前环境激素污染不仅是世界环境问题，更是食品、医学、遗传学、生态学等学科应共同关注的问题。

1.2 环境激素的种类

已经实用化的几万甚至十几万化学物质中，大约 70 种有环境激素的嫌疑。1996 年，美国环保局列出 60 种；1996 年，美国疾病防治中心列出 48 种；1996 年，美国《我们被盗的未来》一书列出 50 种；1997 年，世界野生动物基金会（WWF）把上述 50 种扩展为 68 种；1997 年，日本环境厅《关于外因性扰乱内分泌化学物质问题的研究班中间报告》列出 65 种。而在日本学者筏义人著作的《环境激素与健康》中，罗列出 81 种确定和有重大嫌疑的疑似环境激素。现在能够确定的是环境激素物质的主要是人工合成的化学物质。总体上环境激素可分为已经很明确即使很微量也表现毒性的物质，以及我们身边存在的有环境激素嫌疑的化合物两类。

属于前者的是：（1）含有多个氯原子的脂溶性有机氯化合物（二噁英、PCB、DDT、HCH）；（2）天然及合成的雌激素（植物雌激素、DES、炔雌醇）（也有一些研究机构称环境激素也包括天然或合成的激素药物，如雌三醇、雌酮、已烯雌酚、雌二醇等，被用作药物及饲料添加剂；还包括来自豆科植物及白菜、芹菜等植物的植物性激素。但这些激素与世界卫生组织所定义的环境激素在定义外延含义上略有出入）；有机锡（三丁基锡）等，几乎可以确信，它们是环境激素。与此相对的没有确切证据证明它们会扰乱人的内分泌系统，但却有重大嫌疑的主要是塑料类物质和洗涤剂，它们属于分子中不含氯原子，脂溶性也比前者低的非氯有机化合物，如 P-壬酚、双酚 A、增塑剂和苯乙烯等。

1.3 环境激素的主要来源

对人体产生影响的环境激素主要来源是大气、水、食品包括水产品、母乳、家庭用品和药物及医疗器械。水产食品是最让人担心的，因为如果浮游生物吃了海水中的环境激素后被小鱼吃掉，小鱼被大鱼吃掉，而人又会吃掉鱼，于是环境激素就会从浮游生物转移到人体内，通过食物链产生了生物浓缩，由此对人类的身体健康产生非常大的影响。

1.4 环境激素与性激素的区别

环境激素表现出类似雌激素的生理作用，所以，很多环境激素被称为“类雌激素物质”。环境激素不表现出男性激素即雄激素的作用，而是表现出抗雄激素作用。抗雄激素就是妨碍雄激素的作用的激素，这种作用被称为拮抗作用。雌激素和雄激素有着相似的化学结构，可是有的环境激素表现出类雌激素的作用，有的环境激素表现出抗雄激素的作用。环境激素会与激素的受体结合，从而影响正常激素与受体的结合。

环境激素与性激素的区别在于环境激素分子内含有苯环，易溶于体内脂肪，不易分解，即使极其微量也表现出生物学作用。环境激素与性激素一样，都是小分子。性激素以外的激素除了甲状腺激素，一般都是蛋白质，与环境激素无论是在结构上还是大小上，以及对脂肪的溶解难易上，都有很大的不同。环境激素表现出类似雌激素的生理作用，所以很多环境激素被称为“类雌激素物质”。但是，环境激素分子因为不具有酶容易分解的酯键和酰胺键，在有机体内难分解，会一直保存下去。

2 环境激素对生物体和人的作用与危害

一般来说，激素在生物体内发挥作用大致可以分为以下 5 步：（1）内分泌腺分泌激素；（2）通过液体输送到目的地；（3）与靶细胞上的受体相结合；（4）向靶细胞发出遗传基因指令；（5）引起靶细胞产生特殊效应——调节控制各种物质代谢和生理功能。

环境激素就具有类似激素的作用，尽管它们在环境中浓度极小，但是一旦进入人体和动物体内，一方面有些能与雌激素受体结合，对生物的神经系统产生毒害，导致雌激素的合成、传输异常，作用于生物体的生殖腺，影响性激素的分泌；另一方面，其他一些进入体内的环境激素还能进一步与生物体 DNA 特定的片段结合，使 DNA 序列或构象发生变化，干扰内分泌系统的正常功能。

2.1 对动物的危害

20 世纪 70 年代，化学合成物质对生物的危害，特别是对生物雄性生殖系统的危害开始被发现。最早发现是一些鱼类的生殖器官始终不能发育成熟，雌雄同体率增多，雄性退化、种群退化、处于濒危灭绝状态，野生动物中最早出现“阴盛阳衰”现象，数量锐减。环境激素是一部分野生动物濒危的重要原因。1999 年 4 月，日本建设省公布一项调查结果显示，7 条河流中的雄鲤鱼有 1/4 雌性化。在日本，还发现了可能是有机锡引起某些雌性的贝类长出了阴茎，个体数减少的现象——这种现象出现在被调查的 100 处海岸中。而最有名的事件是位于美国佛罗里达州一个湖中的鳄鱼的变异：自从该淡水湖中的诱导体泄漏事故后，鳄鱼的数量急剧减少，而且雄性的阴茎都普遍变小，雌性的卵都不成熟。美洲狮睾丸发育不良，精子数正在减少。五大湖中鲑鱼甲状腺肥大，个体数也在减少。密歇根湖美国燕鸥卵的孵化率下降，个体数减少。作为美国国鸟的白头鹰发生雄性退化，甚至无法区分雌雄。同样，在其他国家，英国河川中一种鲤鱼出现雌雄同体化；雄性红鳟鱼雌性化，且个体数减少。1998 年，研究人员发现有多只北极熊生殖器官变异。而非洲雄豹、雄狮早已是雄风不在。如此等等，不胜枚举。动物的这些生理功能变异，导致个体数量减少，势必加速物种的灭绝。

2.2 对人类的危害

上述变异的情况不但发生在动物身上，也有关于人类的异常现象，如有研究发现人类精子数减少，异常精子增加。

《我们被偷走的未来》首先介绍了哥本哈根大学 1992 年的调查结果。人的精子平均水平，1940 年时每毫升精液 1.13 亿个，1990 年下降到每毫升只剩 6 600万个，与此同时，精液量也减少了 25%。而且这个报告证实，不仅精子数量减少，很多男性还存在隐睾和尿道萎缩的问题。这本书中还介绍了法国的研究小组的研究结果。他们不相信哥本哈根大学的调查结果，于是自己进行调研。该调查证实，1945 年出生的男性 30 岁时的精子数为平均每毫升 1.02 亿个，1962 年出生的男性 30 岁时的精子数为平均每毫升 5 100万个，而且精子的运动性以及正常精子数都显著降低。按照这个势头下去，到 2005 年，1975 年出生的 30 岁男性的精子数约为每毫升 3 200万个，这是 1925 年出生的男性的精子数的 1/4。

苏格兰的研究也表明，1970 年以后出生的人比 1959 年以前出生的人精子数明显下降。如果胎儿期暴露在污染的化学物质下，那么到成人后，他的精子形成就受到严重影响。据报告，伦敦市以泰晤士河为水源的居民不孕男人的精子量，1984—1989 年比 1978—1983 年急剧减少，而不以泰晤士河为水源的居民则无此现象。在巴黎和芬兰虽没有发现精子数的变化。但是芬兰其他的研究小组报告认为经过 30 年尸检精巢精子形成的病理过程中，发现每年的精子形成低下已经很明显，除精子数下降、精液量减少外，精子正常形态率、活动率都呈明显下降趋势。目前，在西方发达国家，约有 20% 的夫妇苦于没有孩子。在我国，北京（医科）大学公共卫生学院环境卫生教研室在安徽省的一个农药厂做过检测，30 个生产工人的精液与正常工种的同龄人对比，精液量少，精子密度减小，活性降低，畸形率高。

环境激素不但对男性生殖能力造成危害，也带来了男女生殖系统病变。男女生殖系统癌症发病率增高，生殖系统异常的新生儿增多。

精巢癌是年轻男人中常见的恶性肿瘤，在老年人中少见。丹麦男性精巢癌患者中，占 1% 的人有生命危险，而且情况还在恶化；北欧各国、波罗的海沿岸各国、澳大利亚、新西兰、英国、日本等此癌的发病率也在增加；美国 50 岁以下每年以 2% ~4% 的比率上升，绝大部分地区都有精巢癌增多的倾向。根据美国的疾病统计，1990 年以来，前列腺癌增加达 3 倍之多，由每年的 10 万人增加到 31 万余人。它是美国男人癌症中仅次于肺癌的第二号杀手，是第六号死亡原因，同时也是日本男人第八号死亡原因，每年约有 5 000人死于此。

环境激素还会使女性患子宫内膜症及不孕症的几率增加，导致免疫系统失调，癌症发病率上升，尤其是子宫癌和乳腺癌。很多环境激素是脂溶性低分子，它们可以透过血脑屏障而引发疾病。这是因为细胞膜的内部是脂溶性的，表面只是稀稀疏疏的水溶性物质，因此，脂溶性的外来物质就可以物理性的通过了。环境激素还会通过母乳将化学污染传给下一代，使儿童发生多动症、学习障碍等。

综上所述，环境激素之所以危险，不仅是因为它们致癌，还因为它们对后代的生育和生殖也有危害。

虽然各国几乎都存在这样的问题，但是也有人说，这是由于这半个世纪以来发生巨变的性行为及抽烟、喝酒等习惯所导致。同时，也会有人质疑，说合成化学物质危险，真的有确凿的证据吗？清楚的证实其因果关系了吗？到底哪种物质是危险的，哪种物质又是安全的？其实，对于环境激素和人体癌症和生育生殖疾病之间的明确因果关系现在并没有确切的证据可以证实。但是对于上面的一连串疑问，《我们被偷走的未来》的作者科尔伯恩这样回答："有人直言不讳地说：'正确的判断一定要有确凿的证据'这种人只配'白白地等待'。在现实的世界里，人和野生生物都暴露在数十种污染物质中。这些化学物质重复着复杂的协同作用和拮抗作用，在有些情况下，暴露时间比暴露量更重要。在极其复杂的现实里，不能指望取得什么严密的因果关系……现在，不能期望对于人类面临的状况，有什么万全的处方或正好合适的对策。现在文明全面依赖于化石燃料和合成化学物质。"

2.3 环境激素对人类的危害途径

如果在食物和饮用水中混入有害物质的话，它就会经口进入消化道。在那里，它或是直接，或是在消化道酶的作用下进行分解后，主要被小肠壁的上皮细胞吸收到血管。如果是环境激素那样的高脂溶性低分子的话，就可以从细胞间质或细胞膜物理性地扩散开。进入血液中的水溶性物质直接由血液流载走，而脂溶性化合物则与血液中的血清蛋白或球蛋白等蛋白质结合，这种蛋白质被称为结合蛋白质。但是，被吸收的脂溶性物质并不都与蛋白质结合，有一部分是不结合的。只有这些非结合物质才能通过细胞膜。

除了从消化器官，物质还可以随着呼吸进入气管从而进入体内。外来物质一直到达肺部，并经那里的肺泡壁进入到血管。能从皮肤侵入体内的物质有限，只能是硝化甘油之类的微溶于水、易溶于油的物质。皮肤的表面通常都有角质层，阻止外来物质的入侵。

以血液为代表，我们的体内有免疫防御网络的重要成员——抗体、淋巴结、吞噬细胞等在守卫着，会对侵入体内的异物进行处理。侵入体内的病毒和病菌等就是靠这个免疫系统排除的。

然而，在这些免疫系统不能将侵入物质识别为异物时，侵入物质就会从消化道通过门静脉进入肝脏内。因为胞饮作用这一机理，外来物质很容易被运到肝细胞内接受化学处理。如果这是异常物质的话，就在肝脏里实现无毒化，这就叫肝脏的解毒作用见图1。

3 水产动物生长环境中环境激素现状

近20年以来，曾多次发现鲸和海豚大批冲上海滩"集体自杀"事件。日本学者岩田久人等在海豚尸体中检测出三丁基锡和三苯基锡等有机锡。有机锡的毒性主要表现为

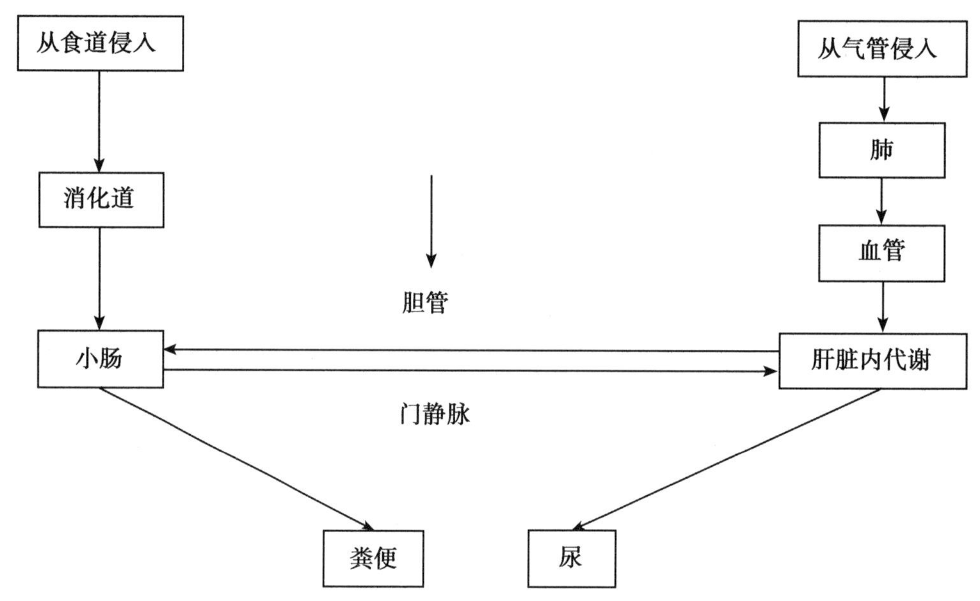

图1 肝脏对侵入体内物质的代谢和排泄

损害动物的神经细胞和内脏。动物脑细胞受损害之后，丧失了方向感。而鲸和海豚具有集体追逐头领行动的习性。当其中有一两头鲸（或海豚）因中毒而失去辨别方向的能力，冲上海滩时，其他的也会盲目跟进。一旦在海滩上搁浅，便无法回到大海，从而表现为“集体自杀”。有机锡是一种船底涂料和渔网防腐剂。海船每年均需涂一次这种涂料，一只集装箱船一次要用1.5万L有机锡涂料。鲸和海豚喜欢追逐海船，因而易于中毒。同时，另有报道，美国近海海域的雄性海鸥雌性化，甲状腺癌变增加，个体数减少。在美国的，荷兰的海豹和加拿大的白海豚免疫机能低下，个体数减少。这些事件都可以说明海洋中也存在着环境激素。

根据《世界技术研究与发展》杂志1999年的一则新闻报道，日本通产省工业技术院资源环境研究所在日本近海海域发现了微量环境激素——壬基酚。这家研究所从1995年开始对茨城县至宫城县的太平洋沿岸、津轻海峡西侧的日本海、积丹半岛的北海道沿岸等距离海岸数10~200km海域的海水水质情况进行了全面调查。调查结果表明，在被调查的所有海域内均发现有可导致动物内分泌障碍的化学物质壬基酚。不过，近海海水中的环境激素浓度大大低于内河河水中的含量。每升海水中的壬基酚含量分别为：太平洋沿岸海域$0.093\times10^{-3}\mu g$、日本海沿岸海域$(0.002\sim0.145)\times10^{-3}\mu g$、北海道沿岸海域$(0.011\sim0.058)\times10^{-3}\mu g$。研究人员还对水深5 000m以上的积丹半岛和日本海北部的西伯利亚海沟不同水深的海水情况进行了调查。调查发现，在水深1 000m左右的海水区域，壬基酚的含量最高。壬基酚主要源于塑料添加剂和洗涤剂，天然物质中几乎不存在。研究人员认为，日本近海海水中的环境激素含量还不至于对人的健康造成影响，但必须引起足够的重视。

4 国内外对水产品环境激素的控制

日本环境厅发表“环境激素战略规划公告”，对今后的方针政策作了综述。美国国家环保局和美国国家环境保健科学研究所已经成为美国环境激素研究的中枢机构，于1998 年开始实施内分泌干扰物筛选计划，对年产量超过4.5万t的15 000种化学品进行调查，1998 年完成简易试验法的预分析筛选，2003 年以后进行特定环境激素的动物实验。欧洲各国也普遍建立政府行为的研究中心，实施环境激素的研究计划。一些国际组织成立了环境激素专门委员会。联合国协同化学品安全国际规划署和联合国经济合作与开发组织的专家委员会联合成立了环境激素专家委员会。1998 年，欧洲议会以压倒多数通过从欧洲市场逐步淘汰干扰激素的化学品，501 名议员中仅有 4 人反对。欧盟已经禁止生产和销售用聚氯乙烯制造的儿童玩具。

环境激素问题已经成为国际上环境科学领域中的热门研究课题。发达国家以巨大的投入，研究环境激素的种类、污染途径、主要污染源、生态危害、分子作用机理、污染控制和防治对策。壬基酚和辛基酚已经被美国环境保护署列为70 种激素干扰素化学物质之一，在欧盟的优先物质清单中，壬基酚也被列为一种荷尔蒙干扰素。由于壬基酚和辛基酚对环境和健康潜在的危害已被广泛论证，各国已开始着手立法管制壬基酚和辛基酚的生产和使用。在欧盟水框架指令中，壬基酚被列为“优先有害物质”，这意味着在2020 年之前，欧盟成员国将最终完全停止向环境中排放壬基酚。

目前，国内的法律法规还没有对这些环境激素的产品使用和排放进行管理，也没有检测排放、产量控制和质量控制及毒性设定有相关规定。到目前为止，环境激素对人类健康的危害评价缺乏基本的数据。各国政府和民间研究机构目前正集中精力进行这方面的研究。

5 环境激素的监控对策

环境激素的来源多，几乎遍布我们生活的每个角落。概括起来，环境激素主要来源于以下 6 个方面：大气、水、食品、母乳、家庭用品和药物、医疗器械。

在呼吸时，最有可能进入体内的环境激素是二噁英类。他们大部分是从垃圾焚烧炉的烟囱中排出来的。家庭产生的一般垃圾和工业废弃物的焚烧是二噁英类的主要释放源，不过，在工厂制造工业产品和农药等时，也有为副反应产物生成的二噁英和 PCB。由于不完全燃烧产生的二噁英极多，所以，4 个家庭焚烧垃圾而产生的二噁英就相当于在公共焚烧设施焚烧 200t 垃圾。焚烧垃圾和塑料制品，释放出二氯化物或二氧化物，易于空气中其他离子生成环境激素类物质，通过沉降进入土壤和水体，再次形成危害。焚烧产生的二氯化物、二氧化物对人类生殖系统有直接影响。

我们通常只饮用瓶装水和自来水，所以，对于水来说，令人担心的不是人，而是水生生物。人们在日常生活中使用的洗涤剂、消毒剂进入水体，抑制微生物活动，降低水体自净能力，使毒素发生积累，污染水源。任何生物在自然界共生，如果野生生物被环境激素所污染，接下来就会影响到人。

对于食品而言，环境激素残留在农产品上，被人类直接食用；含有环境激素的牧草及添加激素配合饲料被畜禽利用，给人类提供含有激素的肉、蛋、奶。环境激素通过植物、动物等食物链，进行生物浓缩，进入人体，尤其是母体脂肪中残留，体内残留浓度十倍增加，通过胎盘传递给子女。母乳中所含的二噁英类比牛奶多。因为母亲脂肪组织内所蓄积的二噁英类会在乳腺细胞生物合成母乳时成大约 10 倍的被浓缩到母乳脂肪层中。于是母亲体内的二噁英类，近一半被转移到了婴儿身上。在所有食品中最令人担心的是水产品。因为人是食物链最高一级，环境激素由于食物链而产生的富集作用最终都会被食用水产品的人摄入体内，它在体内的浓度会一下被放大。

家庭里使用着各种塑料容器、食品包装用保鲜膜、氯乙烯材料的管道、塑料玩具、聚碳酸酯奶瓶等，这些聚碳酸酯透明材料又耐高温，还抗冲击、不易破裂。但是聚碳酸酯是由双酚 A 合成的，而在合成过程中并不是所有的双酚 A 分子都被编入了高分子链中，一般无论怎样都会有极少量的低分子原料不能被编入高分子链中保持原有形态残留在被合成的高分子内。这部分双酚 A 分子会在上述家庭用品的使用中逐渐溶出，危害人体健康。虽然含量非常少，但正如前面所提到，这些化学物质即使微量也会对人体产生影响，而这种影响可能非常巨大，甚至波及一生。

药物和医疗器械在使用后的废弃处理，如果没有严格的规定，处理不当的话，也会产生环境激素。因为血液包、点滴设备、体内插管等都是用含苯二甲酸氢酯的塑化氯乙烯制成的。另外，美国发表了关于在蛀齿填料中萃取出环境激素的论文。不过稍后也有牙科材料专业的研究人员澄清说并没有从蛀齿填料中检测到双酚 A。

环境激素无处不在，所以，并不是都禁止使用就可以一了百了，同时，我们不能消极地采取禁用措施，而是要从以下几个方面多管齐下。

第一，废弃物的焚烧要尽可能在接近完全燃烧的条件下进行。焚烧时生成的二噁英类，至少在完全燃烧的状态下可以防止它的产生。所以要尽可能的将焚烧炉大型化，将废弃物尽量完全燃烧。禁止居民家庭焚烧垃圾和塑料制品。

第二，加快调查塑料等产品中溶出的物质的生殖毒性。环境激素最让人担心的是对胎儿和新生儿的影响。因为很微量的环境激素作用于胎儿和新生儿，可能就跟药物的作用完全相同。而目前我们只是把一般毒性、致癌性、与染色体异常有关的变异原性等作为问题，而不把生殖毒性考虑在内。

第三，进行风险评估。无论什么药，都有一定的副作用。这个世界上不存在任何完全安全的东西。例如，食盐对人体是安全的，但是如果一次吃掉一斤食盐，人也会一命呜呼。所以，要考察危险程度和有益程度的平衡性的危险性评估极为重要。制定危险度，不仅要专家参与，还必须有承认不同价值观的一般人参与。

第四，开发替代材料。开发新的较为安全的材料来替代有环境激素嫌疑的材料。

第五，让科学研究更灵活变通，更人性化。工业界因为环境激素影响人类健康的因果关系并不明确，所以还没有叫停产品制造的打算。但是环保团体又担忧，已经有很充分的证据了，如果还置之不理，男性精子继续减少，生殖危害不断增大，人类就会走向灭亡。但是，在我国目前有关环境激素的研究还不多，因为这不并是开发新型产品这样高产出高回报的研究，甚至会触动一些生产厂家的利益。所以，目前对环境激素的研究既没有时间也没有经费，但这是事关人类健康的事情，科学研究应以整个人类的利益为终极目标，在我国这项研究不能止步不前。

对于我国的水产品中环境激素的控制，我们也要做到以下几点。

（1）从水产品、水产的源头开始控制。①加强宣传教育，强化环保意识，严格控制造纸厂、化工厂等工厂的废液排放。目前我国与发达国家相比，在控制环境的污染方面还存在着较大的差距。②建立健全法律法规和制度，使鱼饲料等可能含有环境激素或能产生环境激素的渔业生产资料尽量少用，或用高效无公害的物质来替代目前有毒有害的渔业生产资料，使环境激素污染最大限度地降低。③制定严格的环境质量标准，梳理水产品生产各环节的环境激素，杜绝水产品养殖基地及周边大气污染源和水污染源。④建立全国乃至全球的环保网络，从根本上治理水、土和空气污染，以确保水产品生产有个优良的生态环境。

（2）在水产品加工、包装和贮运过程中控制环境激素的污染。

食品加工、包装和贮运过程中控制环境激素的污染的最有效办法就是实行规范化的加工、包装和贮运，在食品加工、包装和贮过程中进行规范化管理。目前来说，主要是实行 GMP 生产规范、HACCP 的质量控制体系和 ISO9000 质量保证体系的方法。

（3）在水产品消费过程中控制环境激素的污染。

我国国民对环保的参与在观念上、机制上、深度上和广度上还存在一定的差别，所以要加强环境教育与宣传，提高人们的环境意识，让公众了解环境激素的真实面目，在水产品的消费过程中自觉采取适当的措施来减轻环境激素的危害。

政府当务之急是应尽快摸清当前使用和排放有毒有害物质的情况，特别是需要建立化工产品从“出生”到“死亡”的档案表，并加速出台管理规定来逐步减少、限制并最终停止有毒有害化学物质的使用和排放。

参 考 文 献

[1] 王毓秀，张利民，邹敏. 化学农药与环境激素［J］. 农村生态环境，1999，15（4）：37 -41

[2] 郝明德，刘晓宏. 环境激素的危害及预防方法［J］. 世界农业，1999，9：245

[3] 刘晓庚. 环境激素对食品安全的危害及防治［J］. 食品科学，2003，124：8

[4] 孟海涛，王丽君，由京周，陈明，任仁. 环境激素类农药的危害［J］. 职业卫生与应急救援，2003，09

[5] 香山不二雄. 环境激素问题研究现状［J］. Seikatsu To Kankyo，1997：24

[6] 郝明德，刘晓宏. 环境激素与环境保护型农业. 农业现代化研究，1997，07

[7] 周少奇，林云琴. 环境激素污染研究进展. 环境污染与防治，2004，126（1）

[8] 江田汉，杨晓明. 赖玉平. 环境激素问题浅析. 中国环境管理，2001，（1）

[9] 赵劲松，袁星. 环境激素对鱼的影响. 环境科学研究，2001，14（3）

[10] 任仁. 环境激素的种类和污染途径. 大学化学，2001，10

[11] Lawrence H. Keith. Environmental endocrine disruptors. Pure&Appl. Chern, 1998: 2319 - 2326

[12] 筱义人. 环境激素与健康. 健康新时代系列 [M]. 科学出版社

Environmental Hormone Effects and its Monitors on Security of Aquatic Products

1 SU Jing-yi 2 ZHOU De-qing

(1 *Food Science and Engineering College of China Ocean University*, 266003 *Qingdao*;
2 *Yellow Sea Fishery Institute of Chinese Academy of Fishery Sciences*, 266071 *Qingdao*)

Abstract: This paper deals with the definition, genres and sources of Environmental Hormone and particularly its effects on biology, human and securities of aquatic products. Upon this, the paper proposes some measures on how to prevent and monitor the pollution by Environmental Hormone.

Key words: Environmental Hormone; Aquatic Products; Securities; Pollution; Monitoring

龙头鱼中甲醛的产生机理研究

孙　永　周德庆
（中国水产科学研究院黄海水产研究所，青岛　266071）

摘　要：从龙头鱼中获得了肾脏提取物，在体外模拟体系中，该提取物能够将氧化三甲胺分解为甲醛和二甲胺，通过响应面分析，发现该提取物反应最适条件为50℃，pH=7，能够被三氯乙酸灭活而丧失分解氧化三甲胺的能力，该提取物在不同的温度和pH条件下呈现酶的特性，且分解产物甲醛和二甲胺的含量比例关系稳定，保持在1.6~1.8之间。在一定程度上解释了龙头鱼中甲醛的产生原因，表明龙头鱼中的甲醛可以自身产生。

关键词：龙头鱼；氧化三甲胺酶；甲醛；二甲胺；响应面

甲醛（FA）在食品中属于禁用化学物质，如原农业行业标准NY5073-2001《无公害食品 水产品中有毒有害物质的限量标准》对甲醛安全限量规定为“不得检出”，但是标准在具体的实施应用中遇到问题，引起了一些争端或困惑，甚至造成了经济损失。究其原因，在于该标准制定时没有认识到一些水产品可自身产生甲醛，从而造成只要检测到甲醛就是人为添加的错觉，该标准的制定缺乏科学性和严谨性。作为水产品有机渗透压调节物质重要组成部分的氧化三甲胺（TMAO）广泛存在于海产水产品中（Yancey et al. 1982）。龙头鱼（Harpadon nehereus），俗称水潺、九吐鱼，属硬骨鱼纲灯笼鱼目狗母鱼科龙头鱼属，在我国主要分布在浙江和福建沿海，鱼体柔软，呈乳白色，主要栖息于大陆架深水域，但常至河口域觅食，为中小型底栖鱼类，主要以小型鱼类及甲壳类为食（WHITEHEAD 1984）。研究发现捕获后的龙头鱼在排除人为添加的可能性之后，其体内甲醛含量非常高，随着贮藏时间的增加最高可达500mg/kg，干品甚至可以达到2 000mg/kg（钟惠英等 2006）。TMAOase被认为是水产品中内源性甲醛产生的主要原因，这方面的研究国外已有报道，国内仅见一些综述性文章（马敬军等 2004；宋丹阳等 2007），深入探讨甲醛产生机理的研究工作开展得较少。本文从水产品本底甲醛产生的生化机理方面研究了与甲醛产生相关的因素，以期阐明水产品产生甲醛的机理，甄别水产品中人为添加甲醛和本底甲醛，从而为水产品甲醛标准的制定提供科学的依据。

1 材料与方法

1.1 材料与试剂

龙头鱼：在浙江舟山捕获上岸后，立即加冰封箱运至实验室处理，肾脏取出后，放置在塑料密封袋中于 -80℃保藏备用；氧化三甲胺，Fluka 公司；Trisbase，Biosharp 公司；Triton X100，Solarbio 公司；其余试剂均为分析纯。

1.2 仪器与设备

DELTA 320 pH 计，Mettler-Toldedo；Sigma 3k15 高速冷冻离心机，Sigma；LD5-10 低速离心机，雷勃尔；723A 分光光度计，上海精密科学仪器有限公司；SHA-B 水浴恒温震荡器，金坛精达仪器制造厂；T18 basic 高速匀浆机，IKA。

1.3 试验方法

1.3.1 龙头鱼肾脏提取物制备

龙头鱼肾脏样品于4℃冰箱解冻2h，以1∶5比例加入提取液（20mmol/L Trisbase-醋酸，0.1mol/L NaCl，0.1% Triton X100，pH =7.0），高速匀浆机破碎1min（每次不超过10s），4℃条件下20 000g离心1h，取上清液备用。以上过程均在4℃条件下操作。

1.3.2 反应体系

参考 KIMURA 等人（2000）的的反应体系，4.5ml 反应液（20mmol/L TMAO，100mmol/L Trisbase-醋酸，pH = 7.0）中加入 0.5ml 肾脏提取物开始反应，最后以1ml10%三氯乙酸（TCA）中止反应，20 000g 条件下离心 30min，分别取 1ml 溶液测定甲醛和二甲胺含量。

1.3.3 酶促反应体系中甲醛和二甲胺含量的测定

甲醛含量采用乙酰丙酮显色法测定，1ml 反应液以蒸馏水补齐至 10ml，加入 1ml 乙酰丙酮显色，沸水浴中加热 10min，流水冷却后在 413nm 波长下测定甲醛含量。

二甲胺含量按 Dyer 等人（1945）建立的方法测定，略有改动，1ml 反应液以蒸馏水补齐至 5ml，加入 1ml 铜氨试剂和 10ml 5%二硫化碳-甲苯溶液，40 ~ 50℃水浴 5min，涡旋混合器混合 5min，静置 5min，加入 1ml10%醋酸溶液，涡旋震荡至甲苯层澄清，取甲苯层，以无水硫酸钠干燥后在 440nm 波长下测定二甲胺含量。

2 结果与分析

2.1 单因素试验

国外许多文献报道，作为水产品中氧化三甲胺生化降解原因的 TMAOase 主要分布在水产品的内脏器官中，Rehbein 等人（1984）报道 TMAOase 大部分存在于肾脏和脾中，但是肌肉中少有发现；Benjakul 等人（2003）从狗母鱼（*Saurida tumbil*）的肾脏中分离出一种部分纯化的 TMAOase，并测定其最适 pH 和温度分别为 7.0 和 50℃。以下分别固定 pH =7 和温度为 50℃ 做单因素试验，测定不同温度和 pH 条件下二甲胺和甲醛产生量的变化，以及二甲胺与甲醛两者之间的关系，结果如图 1 所示。

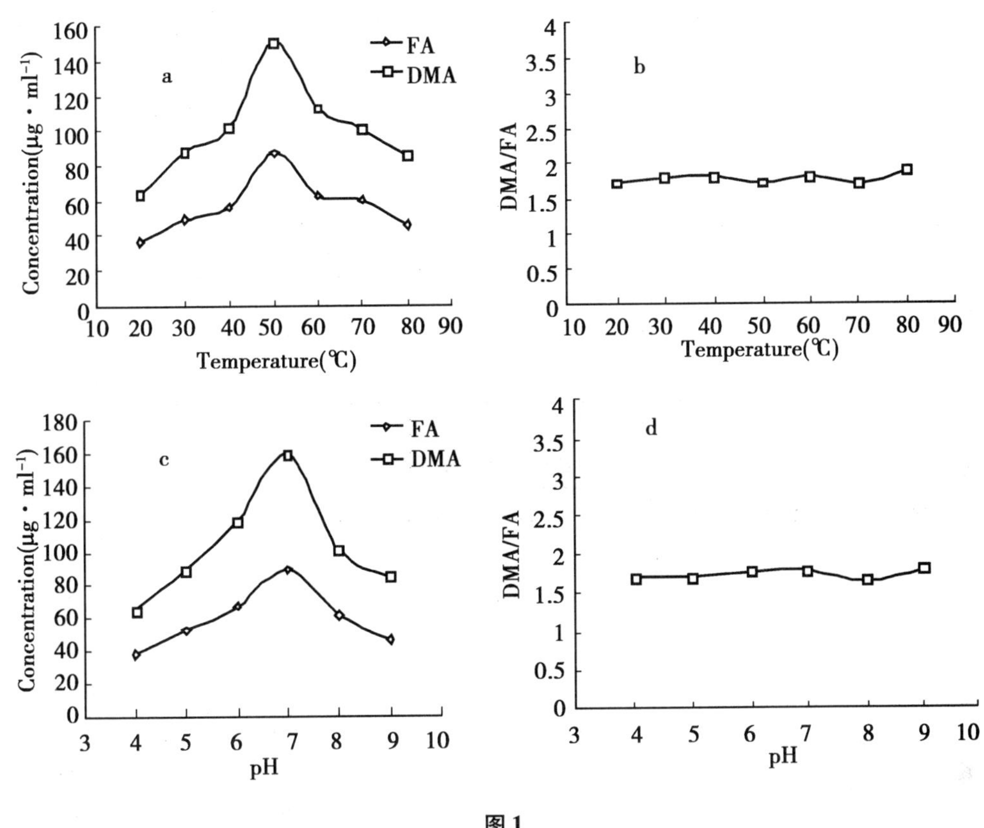

图 1

a. pH =7 时，不同温度下产生的 FA 和 DMA 含量变化；b. DMA 与 FA 含量比值变化；c. 温度为 50℃时，不同 pH 下产生的 FA 和 DMA 含量变化；d. DMA 与 FA 含量比值变化

从图 1a 可以看出，在 pH 为中性条件下，龙头鱼肾脏提取物的活性随着温度改变有较大程度的波动，在 50℃ 之前随着温度的上升活性增大，50℃ 时反应活性最强，50℃之后活性开始下降，从图 1c 可以看出在温度为 50℃时，肾脏提取物的活性随着 pH 变化而变化，在 pH =7 时活性最高，这两组曲线都呈现酶特有的催化特性。

国外有文献报道，TMAOase 能够催化 1mol TMAO 生成 1mol DMA 和 1molFA（CASTELL H. et al. 1971；HEBARD E. et al 1982；MACKIE M. et al. 1974）即：（CH_3）3NO→（CH_3）2NH + HCHO。生成的 DMA 与 FA 的理论质量比值为 1.5，考虑到反应体系中由于提取物的加入而存在一定量的蛋白质，而甲醛能够与蛋白质结合，导致测定的 FA 含量偏低而使 DMA/FA 值偏高。这两组单因素试验中，DMA/FA 均稳定在 1.6 ~ 1.8 之间，如图 1b 和图 1d 所示，说明 DMA/FA 的比值基本符合理论推断。水产品中人为添加的 FA 往往含量较高，与水产品中的 DMA 的比例关系远远超过自然产生的 FA 与 DMA 的比例关系，因此，可以在检测 FA 的同时测定 DMA 的含量，先比较两者之间的关系，再判断水产品中的甲醛是否为人为添加。

2.2 反应体系最适条件的确定

根据单因素实验的结果，本文选取了温度、pH 和反应时间 3 个因素以 Design Expert7.1 软件设计了 Box-Behnken Design 以确定龙头鱼肾脏提取物的最适反应条件。此设计以产生的 FA 含量为响应值做响应面模型，其中温度范围为 20～80℃，pH 范围为 5～9，反应时间为 20～60min，如表 1 所示。根据试验设计所要求的试验条件分别测定了甲醛的响应值，如表 2 所示。

表 1 响应面实验设计

	变量	单位	-1 level	+1 level
A	pH		5	9
B	Temperature	℃	20	80
C	Time	min	20	60

表 2 各处理组的试验结果

处理组	A：pH	B：温度/℃	C：时间/min	FA/μg/ml
1	9	80	40	30.40
2	7	20	60	34.31
3	7	50	40	89.75
4	7	50	40	86.31
5	9	20	40	23.01
6	6	50	20	62.84
7	7	50	40	79.08
8	7	50	40	87.28
9	7	20	20	24.38
10	6	80	40	40.92
11	6	50	60	67.76
12	9	50	20	55.68
13	7	80	60	26.06
14	7	50	40	90.05
15	9	50	60	64.74
16	7	80	20	26.62
17	6	20	40	46.60

2.3 响应模型的分析与验证

采用 Design Expert 7.1 进行分析，得到甲醛生成量与 pH，温度等变量之间的函数关系为：

$$FA = +86.49 - 1.05 \times A - 1.10 \times B + 2.72 \times C + 4.53 \times A \times B + 1.55 \times A \times C - 2.62 \times B \times C - 12.66 \times A_2 - 43.09 \times B_2 - 15.56 \times C2$$

从表3可以看出，此模型的F值为51.39，$p < 0.0001$，达到极显著水平，而失拟项F值为1.25，$p = 0.40 > 0.05$，不显著，说明该模型有较高的可信度。

表3　模型方差分析表

变异来源	平方和	自由度	均方	F值	p	
Model	10 110.72	9	1 123.413	51.390 79	< 0.000 1	极显著
A-pH	1.894 8	1	1.894 8	0.086 678	0.777 0	
B-Temp	9.266 535	1	9.266 535	0.423 9	0.535 8	
C-Time	56.434 75	1	56.434 75	2.581 621	0.152 1	
AB	48.816 44	1	48.816 44	2.233 12	0.178 7	
AC	5.705 938	1	5.705 938	0.261 019	0.625 1	
BC	27.510 03	1	27.510 03	1.258 453	0.298 9	
A2	159.343 9	1	159.343 9	7.289 227	0.030 6	
B2	7 816.798	1	7 816.798	357.581 3	< 0.000 1	
C2	1 020.015	1	1 020.015	46.660 85	0.000 2	
残差	153.021 4	7	21.860 2			
失拟	74.155 67	3	24.718 56	1.253 703	0.401 8	不显著
纯误差	78.865 72	4	19.71643	51.390 79	< 0.000 1	
总变异	10 263.74	16	1 123.413	0.086 678	0.777 0	

经计算，该模型在反应时间固定在40min时，在49.5℃，pH＝6.9时，甲醛产生量最高，即肾脏提取物的反应活性最高，预测值为86.53μg/ml，这与实际值88.83μg/ml的绝对误差仅有2.6%，说明该模型基本反映了温度，pH值和时间三者之间的关系，拟合度较好。

根据实验所得数据由Design Expert 7.1得到的相应面模型由图2所示：

2.4　三氯乙酸（TCA）灭活试验

龙头鱼肾脏提取物用10% TCA变性后加入氧化三甲胺反应体系中，pH＝7，50℃反应40min，与对照组相比没有甲醛和二甲胺产生，如图3所示。

由此可以看出，三氯乙酸处理之后肾脏提取物失去了分解氧化三甲胺生成甲醛和二甲胺的能力，说明在肾脏提取物中起到催化作用的物质属于蛋白质。根据单因素实验以及反应最适条件等反面的数据可以认为肾脏提取物中含有大量能够催化氧化三甲胺分解的酶或者酶系。

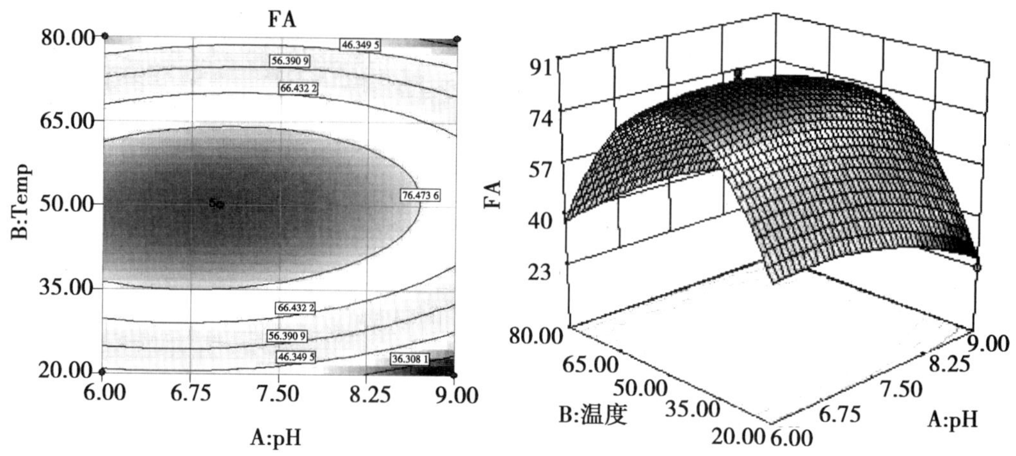

图 2 反应体系中甲醛产生量的响应图

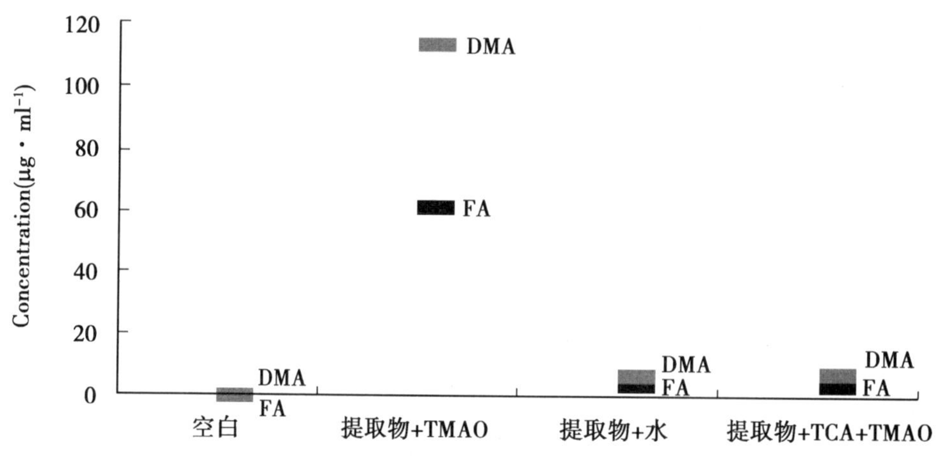

图 3 TCA 灭活后的肾脏提取物对氧化三甲胺体系的作用

3 结论

在体外模拟体系中，龙头鱼肾脏提取物能够将氧化三甲胺分解为甲醛和二甲胺，通过响应面分析，发现该提取物反应最适条件为 50℃，pH = 7，能够被三氯乙酸灭活而丧失分解氧化三甲胺的能力，该提取物在不同的温度和 pH 条件下呈现酶的特性。分解产物甲醛和二甲胺的含量比例关系稳定，保持在 1.6 ~ 1.8 之间，证明氧化三甲胺分解为甲醛和二甲胺。

参 考 文 献

[1] 马敬军，周德庆，张双灵．水产品中甲醛本底含量与产生机理的研究进展．海洋水产研究，2004，25（4）：85 – 89

[2] 刘志标，钟创光. 冷藏龙头鱼甲醛本底含量研究. 广州：中山大学，2006

[3] 宋丹阳，周德庆，杜永芳等. 氧化三甲胺酶研究进展. 食品科学，2007，28（1）：350－353

[4] 钟惠英，申屠基康，梁芹芹等. 龙头鱼 Harpadon nehereus 的甲醛含量调查. 中国食品卫生杂志，2006，18（5）：144－147

[5] AMONA K, YAMADA K, BITO M. Detection and identification of formaldehyde in gadoid fish. Bull Jan Soc Sci Fish, 1963, 29: 695－701

[6] AMONA K, YAMADA K. Studies on biological formation of formaldehyde and dimethylamine in fish and shellfish－Ⅶ. Bull Jan Soc Sci Fish, 1965, 31: 1030－1037

[7] BENJAKUL S, VISESSANGUAN W, TANAKA M. Partial purification and characterization of trimethylamine-N-oxide demethylase from lizardfish kidney, Comparative Biochemistry and Physiology Part B 2003, 135: 359－371

[8] CASTELL H, SMITH B, NEAL W. Production of dimethylamine in muscle of several species of gadoid fish during frozen storage. especially in relation to presence of dark muscle. J Fish Res. 1971, 28: 1－5

[9] DYER, W. J. MOUNSEY, Y. A. Amines in fish muscle. II. Development of trimethylamine and other amines. Fish. Res. Board Can. 1945, 6, 359－367

[10] HARADA K. Studies on enzyme catalyzing the formation of formaldehyde and dimethylamine in tissues of fishes and shells. J Shimonoseki Univ Fish, 1975, 23: 163－241

[11] HEBARD E, FLICK J, MARTIN E, et al.. Chemistry and Biochemistry of Marine Food Products. AVI Publishing Company Westport, Connecticut, 1982, 149－304

[12] Kelly R. H, Yancey P. H. High Contents of Trimethylamine Oxide Correlating With Depth in Deep-Sea Teleost Fishes, Skates, and Decapod Crustaceans. Bio. Bull., 1999, 196（1）: 18－25

[13] KIMURA M, SEKI N, Kimura I. Purification and characterization of trime- thylamine-N-oxide demethylase from walleye Pollock muscle. Fish Sci. 2000b, 66: 725－729

[14] LANDOLT, L. A.; HULTIN, H. O. The removal of trimethylamine oxide and soluble protein from intact red hake muscle by washing. J. Food Pr. Prese. 1981, 5: 227－242

[15] LAPA-GUIMARAES, J.; Eduardo de FELICIO, P.; CONTRERAS GUZMAN, E. S. Chemical and microbial analyses of squid muscle (Loligo plei) during storage in ice. Food Chem. 2005, (91): 477－483

[16] MACKIE M, THOMSON W. Decomposition of trimethylamine oxide during iced and frozen storage of whole and comminuted tissue of fish. Proc. IV International Congress Food Sci. and Technology, 1974, 243－250

[17] NASH, T. The colorimetric estimation of formaldehyde by means of the Hantzsch reaction. Biochem. J. 1953, 55: 416－421

[18] REHBEIN H, SCHREIBER W. TMAOase activity in tissues of fish species from the northeast Atlantic. Comp Biochem Phystol, 1984, 79（3）: 447－452

[19] WHITEHEAD, P. J. P. Harpadontidae. In W. Fischer and G. Bianchi (eds.) FAO species identification sheets for fishery purposes. Western Indian Ocean fishing area 51. FAO, Rome 1984

[20] YANCEY, P. H.; CLARK, M. E; HAND, S. C; R. D. BOWLUS, and SOMERO, G. N.. Living with water stress: Evolution of osmolyte systems. Science 1982, 217: 1214 - 1222

Studies on Decomposing Effects of Kidney Extract from Harpadon Nehereus to Trimethylamine-N-oxide

SUN Yong ZHOU De-qing

(*Yellow Sea Fishery Research Institute*, *Chinese Academy of Fishery Science* 266071, *Qingdao*)

Abstract: A kidney extract was obtained from bombayduck (Harpadon nehereus). Trimethylamine-N-oxide can be decomposed to formaldehyde and dimethylamine by the extract. The optimum catalyzing conditions of the extract were found to be 50℃, pH = 7, and it can be inactivated by the trichloroacetic acid and lose the ability of decomposing trimethylamine-N-oxide. The extract shows typical enzyme properties in different temperature and pH value. There was stable ratio between formaldehyde and dimethylamine which ranged from 1.6 ~ 1.8. All above explain why there was formaldehyde in the bombayduck and proved that some formaldehyde was endogenous.

Key words: Bombayduck; TMAOase; Formaldehyde; Dimethylamine Reponding; Surface CLC number: Document code: A Article IC:

采前喷洒和浇灌1-甲基环丙烯水溶液对西兰花贮藏品质的影响

李秀杰① 王庆国
（山东农业大学，泰安 271018）

摘 要： 以西兰花品种“独舞”为试材，研究了采前喷洒和浇灌1-甲基环丙烯水溶液对其贮藏品质的影响。实验结果表明，采前对西兰花进行喷洒和浇灌400μl/L 1-MCP水溶液处理能减少其失重率，降低可溶性固形物和糖的损失，抑制叶绿素和VC的降解，降低细胞膜相对透性和POD活性，有效的延缓衰老和延长贮藏时间；同一处理条件下采前喷洒处理优于浇灌处理，将西兰花贮藏时间延长了126%，可达到5℃下用1μl/L 1-MCP熏蒸处理6h的效果。

关键词： 1-MCP水溶液；西兰花；采前；贮藏品质

西兰花（Broccoli）又称青花菜或绿菜花，主要食用部位是绿色的肥嫩花球，它营养丰富还有抗癌、延缓衰老等作用，在国际市场上备受消费者青睐。但其采后呼吸旺盛，极易衰老黄化和萎蔫，20℃下1～3d、0℃下3～4周便失去商品价值[1]。西兰花虽然自身产生乙烯很少，但对环境中的乙烯非常敏感。国内外研究表明，10℃条件下，2mg/kg的乙烯可使货架寿命缩短一半。

1-甲基环丙烯（1-MCP）为近年来发现的一种新型乙烯受体抑制剂，具有在常温下稳定、使用剂量低、安全、高效等特点，因而受到广泛的应用和研究，在延缓果蔬成熟衰老方面受到越来越多的重视。已有大量研究表明，用1-MCP熏蒸处理西兰花能显著提高其贮藏品质[1,2,3,4]，在5℃下用1mg/kg浓度的1-MCP熏蒸6h就能将西兰花的贮藏时间延长200%[1]。但目前1-MCP最常用的使用方式是将其粉末或溶液注入到放置待贮藏果蔬的密封容器或空间中，使其以气体形式释放出来，浓度达到10～1 000nl/L或更高，熏蒸1～24h[5]。这种使用方式的缺陷在于不仅需要人力进行二次操作，对密封容器要求较高，而且运输所需时间会导致1-MCP保鲜效果随滞后处理时间的延长而减弱[8]。国外已有研究表明采后用不同浓度1-MCP水溶液浸醮处理番茄[7]、鳄梨[8]、李子[9]、苹果[10]均能提高贮藏品质和货架期。苹果在采前1周喷洒250mg/kg 1-MCP水溶液能显著提高贮藏品质（罗门哈斯专利）。但国内外尚未有1-MCP水溶液用于西兰花采

---

① 李秀杰，女，山东农业大学食品科学与工程学院硕士研究生。研究方向：果蔬采后生理与贮藏。E－mail：lixiujie－2007@163.com。

前的报道，为此，我们进行这方面的研究和探讨，以期为西兰花的贮藏保鲜和 1-MCP 水溶液的采前应用研究提供理论和技术参考。

1 材料与方法

1.1 试验材料与设计

试验用西兰花为晚熟品种“独舞”，产自山东省肥城市边院镇高庄。

选择长势一致，成熟度、大小、色泽均一的西兰花地块，分成 4 个小区，分做如下 4 个处理：处理 1，采前喷洒 1-MCP 水溶液，简称 S。量取山东营养源食品科技有限公司生产的鲜峰^R 1-MCP 稳定溶液（专利号：CN200610069625. 9）20ml，缓慢加入 1 000 ml 水中，现用现配成水溶液，用气相色谱测定，间接法进行计算 1-MCP 浓度大约为 400μl/L。分别在采前 5 和 2d 用该水溶液喷洒西兰花花球；处理 2，采前用 1-MCP 水溶液浇灌，简称 I。采前 5d 和 2d 分别用 1 – MCP 水溶液对西兰花根部进行两次浇灌处理；CK_1，正常生长的西兰花，采前、采后均不用 1-MCP 处理；CK_2，采后 5℃ 条件下，在密封的泡沫箱里用 1μl/L 1 – MCP 熏蒸处理 6h。上述 4 种处理的西兰花，采摘后，均放入加冰泡沫箱内，4h 内运至山东营养源食品科技有限公司冷库，入库预冷至 5℃。处理 S、I 和 CK_1 的西兰花，分别装入 PE 保鲜袋内，每 4 个西兰花一袋，袋口折叠，进行贮藏，贮藏温度 5℃。处理 CK_2，熏蒸后再贮藏，贮藏条件与 S、I 和 CK_1 相同。每 5d 对下述感观指标和成分指标测定 1 次，每次测定设 3 个平行。

1.2 测定指标及方法

1.2.1 可溶性固形物（%）

用日本 ATAGO 公司生产的 POCKET REFRACTOMETER PAL-1 进行测定。

1.2.2 可溶性糖

用苯酚硫酸法。

1.2.3 叶绿素

采用紫外分光光度计法。

1.2.4 VC 含量

采用 2，6 – 二氯靛酚滴定法。

1.2.5 丙二醛（MDA）

采用硫代巴比妥酸比色法[11]。

1.2.6 细胞膜相对透性（%）

参照郭香风的电导仪法[12]。

1.2.7 过氧化物酶（POD）

将样品用冷冻的研钵研磨后准确称取 1. 00g，加入 10ml 磷酸缓冲溶液在冰箱内提取 2h 后过滤得粗酶液。然后分别取 1ml 缓冲溶液、1. 0ml 质量分数为 2% 的 H_2O_2、1. 0ml0. 05mol/L 愈创木酚溶液和 0. 6ml 稀释酶液，于 470nm 波长下测定其吸光值，以缓冲溶液作为对照，以每分钟内 A_{470}变化0.01 为1 个过氧化物酶活性单位进行计算[13]。

1.2.8 失重率（%）

采用称重法，失重率 = （贮前重量 - 贮后重量）/贮前重量 ×100%。

1.2.9 感官指标评定

参照徐斐燕的方法[14]，稍作修改。按照西兰花的新鲜度包括色泽、气味、表面状况、手感硬度等按9 分制法进行评分。9 分：非常新鲜（刚采收），色泽深绿，花球紧凑结实，硬度好，无异味；7 分：较为新鲜，色泽深绿，花球较紧凑，硬度较好，无异味；5 分：还可以（商品界限），色泽绿色，无黄化（花蕾切口稍有黄化），花球稍松散，硬度降低，无异味；3 分：较差，黄化面积30%以下，花球较为松散，硬度较差，稍有异味；1 分：非常差，黄化面积达50%以上，花球松散脱落，有霉斑和腐坏味。

1.3 数据处理方法

数据计算、做图和分析采用 Excel 2003 和 SPSS 11.0。

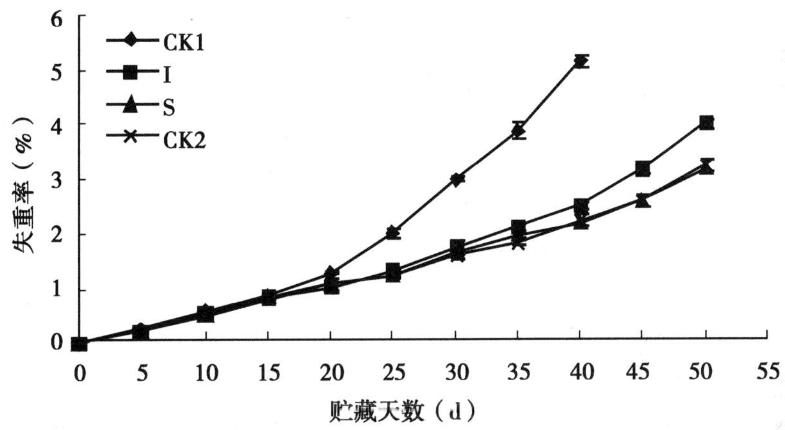

图1 西兰花失重率随贮藏时间的变化

2 结果与分析

2.1 不同1-MCP 处理对西兰花失重率的影响

由图1 可知，3 组经1-MCP 处理过的西兰花失重率较对照组 CK_1 明显降低。CK_1 组西兰花贮藏至第15d 失重损失开始明显加剧，贮藏至第25d 西兰花失重率已达2.00%，40d 严重黄化时失重率达到5.10%。浇灌处理的西兰花在贮藏至35d，失重率大于喷洒处理和熏蒸处理，失重率的差异随着贮藏时间的延长逐渐扩大。喷洒处理和熏蒸处理抑制失重效果最佳且两种处理无显著差别（$P>0.05$）。

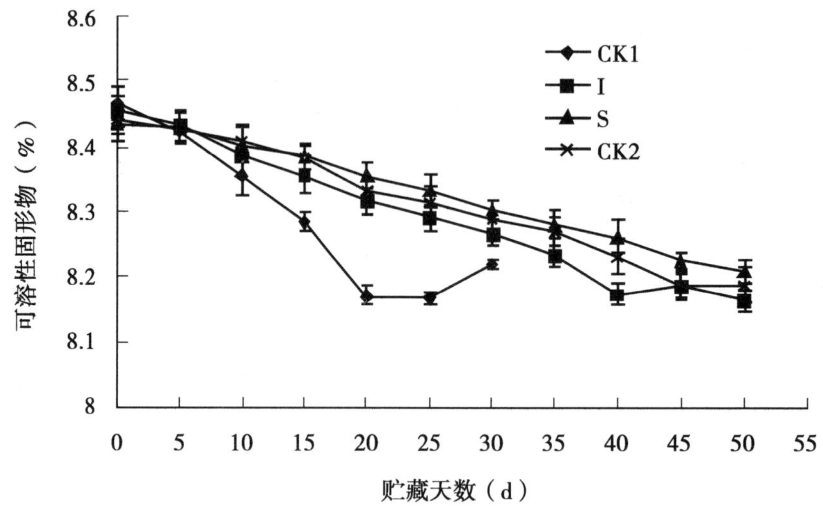

图2　西兰花可溶性固形物含量随贮藏时间的变化

2.2　1-MCP处理对西兰花可溶性固形物含量的影响

由图2可知，西兰花的可溶性固形物含量在贮藏过程中总体呈下降趋势，这可能是由于植物组织的呼吸作用消耗基质所致。而 CK_1 和浇灌处理的西兰花贮藏后期变化不大或略有上升，这可能由于两者失水多，可溶性物质相对浓缩引起。喷洒和熏蒸处理，可溶性固形物一直下降。综观各处理贮藏开始和试验结束的可溶性固形物含量，虽呈下降趋势，但变化并不很大，变化范围在8.47%～8.17%。在贮藏的前30d，CK_1 的可溶性固形物含量变化范围较大。其他3组西兰花可溶性固形物含量变化较为平缓，这说明经过1-MCP处理有利于减少组织物质消耗，保持风味，延缓西兰花衰老。但喷洒、浇灌和熏蒸各处理间差异并不显著（$P > 0.05$），这说明不同的1-MCP处理方式对西兰花可溶性固形物含量没有显著影响。

2.3　1-MCP水溶液采前处理对西兰花可溶性糖含量的影响

由图3可知，各处理的西兰花，贮藏前10d，可溶性糖变化不明显，随后以不同速度上升，然后又下降。CK_1 组西兰花，可溶性糖上升和下降最快。贮藏至30d，经1-MCP处理的可溶性糖含量明显高于 $CK_{1.}$。贮藏至后期，喷洒和熏蒸处理的可溶性糖高于浇灌处理的。可溶性糖是采后果蔬生物代谢的重要基质，其变化速度反映了生物代谢的强度，为了延长贮藏时间，在保证不伤害的前提下，应尽量降低采后果蔬代谢强度。采前喷洒或浇灌1-MCP处理的西兰花可溶性糖的变化减缓，有效抑制了淀粉的转化和可溶性糖降解，这从侧面反映了这一处理可以延长西兰花的保鲜时间。

2.4　采前1-MCP处理对叶绿素含量变化的影响

如图4所示，不同处理的西兰花叶绿素含量随贮藏时间的延长都逐渐下降。CK_1 组

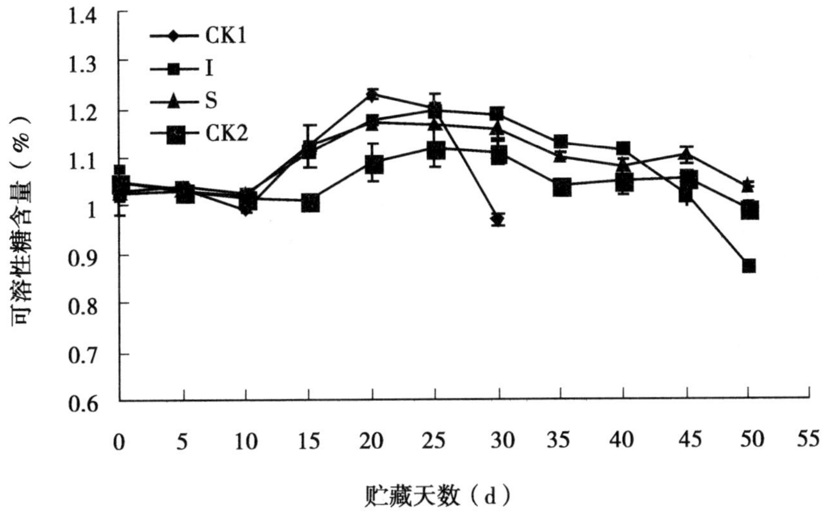

图3　西兰花可溶性糖含量随贮藏时间的变化

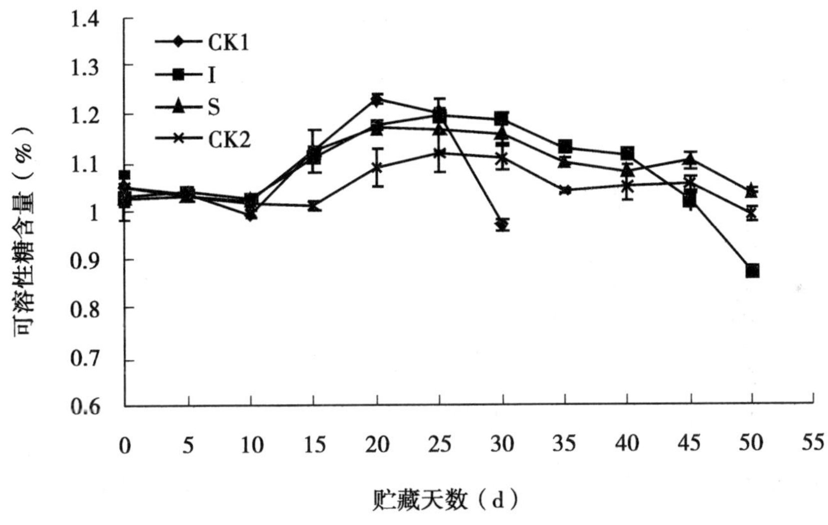

图4　西兰花叶绿素含量随贮藏时间的变化

叶绿素含量在贮藏过程中下降最快，在贮藏第30d后叶绿素含量仅为727.64μg/g，仅占初始含量的36.83%，下降了63.17%；而同期，采前浇灌的叶绿素含量为1 502.47 μg/g，降为初始含量的75.55%，下降了24.45%；采前喷洒和采后熏蒸的，分别下降了18.47%和16.93%。贮至50d，采前浇灌的叶绿素含量降为875.54μg/g，降至初始值的44%.03；采前喷洒和采后熏蒸的叶绿素含量分别为1 285.94 μg/g 和1325.89 μg/g，仍明显高于采前浇灌的和CK_1西兰花中贮藏30d叶绿素的含量。这些结果表明，采前浇灌和喷洒均可以很好延缓采后西兰花叶绿素的降解，采前喷洒的效果与采后熏蒸的差异不显著（$P>0.05$）。

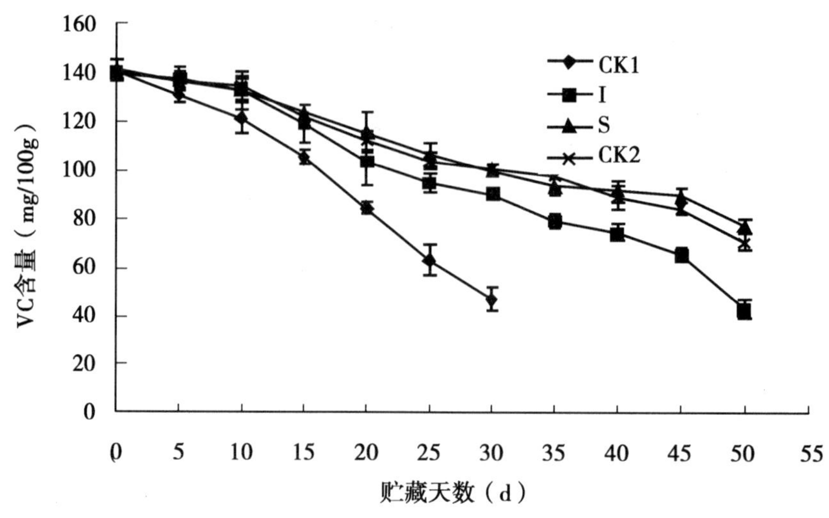

图5 西兰花 VC 含量随贮藏时间的变化

2.5 采前1-MCP 处理对采后 VC 含量变化的影响

西兰花中 Vc 含量非常丰富。它既是人体比不可少的营养成分，也是一种天然的抗氧化物质，能提高 SOD 的活性，抑制脂质过氧化反应，保证生物体的正常代谢。由图5 可见，在整个贮藏过程中，西兰花中 V_C 的含量都是呈下降趋势。其中，CK_1 组 V_C 含量下降最快，其含量明显低于其他3 组，贮藏30d 后其 V_C 含量降低了63.62%，浇灌、喷洒和熏蒸三组处理同期 VC 含量仅降低了35.53%、29.12%、28.49%。贮藏50d 后浇灌处理 V_C 含量明显低于喷洒和熏蒸处理，因此喷洒和熏蒸处理对西兰花的 V_C 有更好的保持作用，且采前喷洒处理与采后熏蒸在对 V_C 的保持效果上差异不显著（$P>0.05$），可达到采后熏蒸的效果。

2.6 不同1-MCP 处理对细胞膜透性的影响

细胞膜相对透性可以反映细胞膜的完整性和稳定性，一定程度上反映了细胞受伤害的程度。国内外关于细胞膜相对透性的研究，通常用电导率的变化作为一个重要指标。由图6 可知，在贮藏过程中，西兰花的细胞膜相对透性随贮藏时间的延长而增大。CK_1 组的细胞膜相对透性在贮藏20d 后急剧上升。其他3 组用1-MCP 处理的，透性也增加，但增加速度明显低于 CK_1，且贮至50d，透性仍低于 CK_1。采前喷洒和采后熏蒸处理的，细胞膜透性明显低于浇灌处理的（$P<0.05$）。国内外研究表明，随着果蔬的衰老，细胞膜透性往往增加。本研究表明，采前喷洒和浇灌1-MCP 水溶液均延缓了细胞膜透性的增加，这也说明两种处理对防止西兰花衰老具有一定效果。

2.7 1-MCP 处理对 MDA 含量变化的影响

丙二醛（MDA）是膜脂过氧化产物之一，其含量的增加是膜结构损伤的重要标志。由图7 可知，西兰花在贮藏过程中 MDA 积累，其含量总体上都呈上升趋势。CK_1 组上

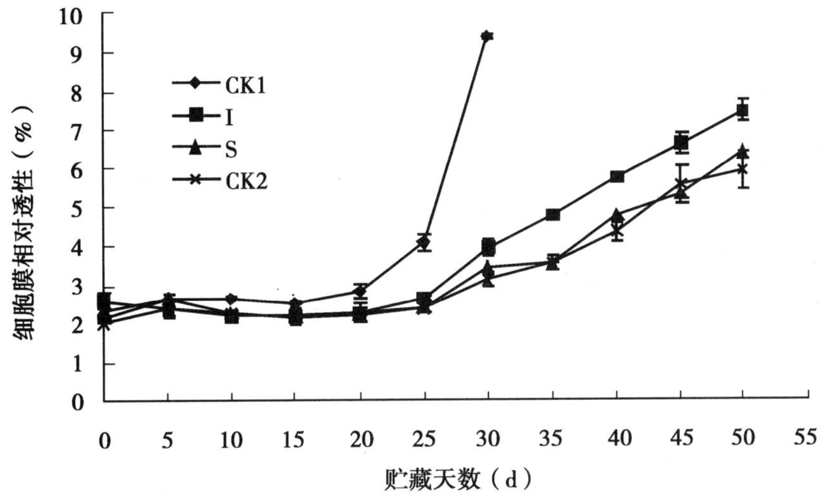

图6 西兰花细胞膜透性随贮藏时间的变化

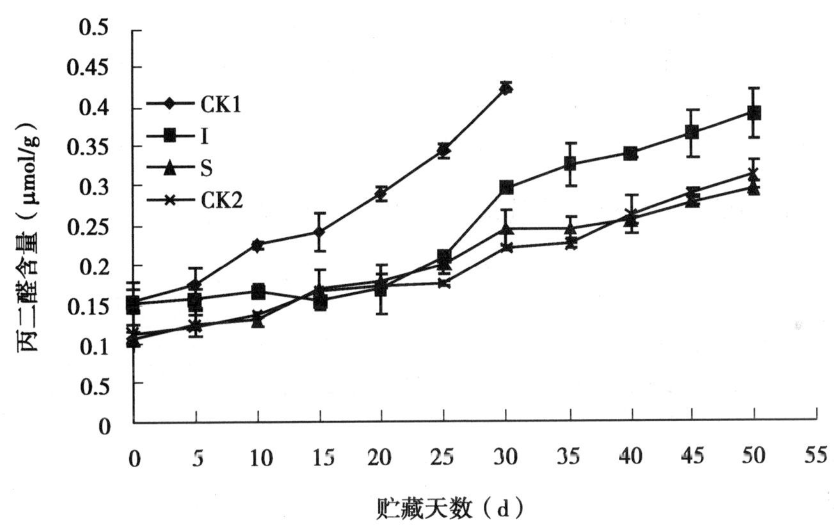

图7 西兰花丙二醛含量随贮藏时间的变化

升趋势明显大于其他3组。喷洒和浇灌处理MDA含量在整个贮藏期内呈缓慢增加趋势，增幅较小，对MDA的积累起到一定抑制作用，从而延缓了花蕾细胞的膜脂过氧化和衰老。浇灌处理的较CK_1也能对MDA积累起到一定抑制作用，但抑制效果不如喷洒和熏蒸处理。

2.8 采前1-MCP处理对过氧化物酶（POD）活性的影响

由图8可知，西兰花在贮藏过程中POD活性总体呈上升趋势。CK_1组在贮藏至15d开始急剧上升，25d POD活性达到最高，然后又明显下降。其他处理贮藏前期、中期持续上升，后期（35d后）变化平缓，但后期浇灌处理的POD活性明显大于喷洒和熏蒸

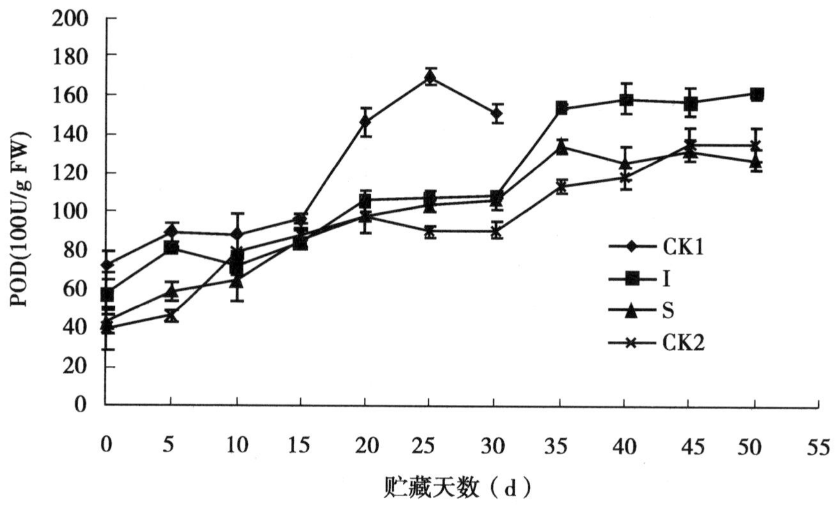

图8 西兰花 POD 活性随贮藏时间的变化

处理，喷洒和熏蒸处理的 POD 活性交替升高，相差不大，贮藏的整个过程都低于 CK_1 和浇灌处理。POD 是植物体内清除过氧化氢的酶类，它对于维持活性氧代谢平衡，保持膜结构，延缓果蔬衰老具有重要作用。以上结果表明，衰老刺激了 POD 活性的变化，而喷洒和熏蒸处理延缓了 POD 活性的增加，在一定程度上又抑制了西兰花的衰老，。

2.9 1-MCP 水溶液不同处理对西兰花感观品质的影响

表1 西兰花感观评定随贮藏时间的变化

贮藏时间/（d）	感官评定/（分）			
	CK_1	采前浇灌（I）	采前喷洒（S）	采后熏蒸（CK_2）
0	9	9	9	9
5	8.33±0.07	8.42±0.14	8.54±0.07	8.5±0.13
10	8.08±0.19	8.17±0.07	8.20±0.14	8.25±0.13
15	6.93±0.21	7.38±0.25	7.67±0.14	7.71±0.14
20	6.46±0.44	7.29±0.07	7.50±0.13	7.54±0.19
25	4.63±0.13	7.13±0.13	7.25±0.13	7.33±0.07
30	3.38±0.13	6.58±0.44	6.71±0.44	6.67±0.26
35		6.13±0.13	6.65±0.17	6.46±0.07
40		5.42±0.14	6.42±0.19	6.25±0.13
45		4.75±0.25	5.71±0.14	5.46±0.07
50		3.48±0.15	5.33±0.07	5.04±0.19

由表1可知，贮藏至第20d，1-MCP 水溶液喷洒和浇灌处理以及 1-MCP 熏蒸处理的西兰花，感观品质明显优于对照 CK_1。试验中观察到，CK_1 西兰花在贮藏至23d 达到商

品品质底限，之后逐渐失去食用价值，且最先出现霉斑和腐烂。浇灌处理（I）的西兰花在贮藏到43d后也失去商品价值，但贮藏期较对照 CK_1 延长了87%。喷洒（S）和熏蒸处理 CK_2 的西兰花感官品质最好，分别在第52d和50d达到商品底限，贮藏期较对照延长了126%和117%。这些结果表明，采前喷洒和浇灌1-MCP水溶液，均较好地保持了西兰花的感官品质，采前喷洒达到了采后熏蒸的保鲜效果。

3 结论与讨论

（1）采前用400μl/L 1-MCP水溶液对西兰花进行喷洒和浇灌能减少失重，降低可溶性固形物和糖的损失，抑制叶绿素和VC降解，保持细胞膜的完整性，降低POD活性和MDA含量，有效抑制花蕾中各种营养成分的降解，显著提高其采后贮藏品质，延长贮藏时间。（2）400μl/L 1-MCP水溶液采前两次喷洒处理对西兰花贮藏品质的提高优于浇灌处理，能将贮藏时间延长126%，可达到5℃下用1μl/L 1-MCP熏蒸6h的效果。

在冷链还不发达的国家和地区，西兰花在采后的挑选分级运输和销售等各个环节都可能处于较高的温度条件，采前对其进行1-MCP处理可以提高品质，有利于其贮藏时间的延长，且可以避免采后熏蒸处理的许多烦琐操作。但有关1-MCP水溶液用于采前的研究才刚刚起步，1-MCP稳定水溶液的配置、更多果蔬采前处理的可行性、采前处理的最佳时间和浓度以及采前处理的作用机理还需进一步的研究。

参考文献

[1] V. V. V. Ku, R. B. H. Wills. Effect of 1-methylcyclopropene on the storage life of broccoli [J]. Postharvest Biology and Technology, 1999, 17: 127－132

[2] 李志强，汪良驹，王文辉，朱云娜. 1-甲基环丙烯延缓果实衰老的生理效应及其应用［J］. 植物生理学通讯，2007，43（1）：201－206

[3] 汪俏梅，郭得平，Kyikyi Win，袁晶. 1-甲基环丙烯延缓青花菜衰老的效应及机理［J］. 园艺学报，2004，31（2）：205－209

[4] Fan X, Mattheis J. P. Yellowing of broccoli in storage is reduced by 1-methylcyclopropene [J]. Hortsci. 2000, (35): 885－887

[5] Sun Tay Choi, Donald J. Huber. Influence of aqueous 1-methylcyclopropene concentration, immersion duration, and solution longevity on the postharvest ripening of breaker-turning tomato fruit [J]. Postharvest Biology and Technology, 2008, 49: 147－154

[6] 袁晶，徐志豪，许亚俊，汪俏梅. 1-MCP对青花菜贮藏效果的影响［J］. 浙江农业学报2005，17（1）：31－34

[7] Sun Tay Choi, Donald J. Huber. Influence of aqueous 1-methylcyclopropene concentration, immersion duration, and solution longevity on the postharvest ripening of breaker-turning tomato fruit [J]. Postharvest Biology and Technology, 2008, 49: 147－154

[8] Sun Tay Choi, Pavlos Tsouvaltzis, Chai Il Lim, Donald J. Huber. Suppression of ripening and induction of asynchronous ripening in tomato and avocado fruits subjected to

complete or partial exposure to aqueous solutions of 1-methylcyclopropene [J]. Postharvest Biology and Technology, 2008, 48: 206 -214

[9] G. A. Manganaris, C. H. Crisosto, V. Bremer, D. Holcroft. Novel 1-methylcyclopropene immersion formulation extends shelf life of advanced maturity ‘Joanna Red’ Plums [J]. Postharvest Biology and Technolo. gy, 2008, 48: 429 -433

[10] Argenta, Fan. Xuetong, Mattheis. James. Responses of 'Golden Delicious' apples to 1-MCP applied in air and water [C]. Annual Meeting Horticultural Society, 2006

[11] 赵世杰，史国安，董新纯．植物生理学实验指导 [M]. 北京：中国农业科技出版社，2002

[12] 郭香凤，向进乐，李秀珍，张国海，史国安．贮藏温度对西兰花净菜品质的影响．农业机械学报 [J]，2008，39 (2)：201 -204

[13] 中国科学院上海植物生理研究所主编．现代植物生理学实验指南 [M]. 北京：科学出版社，1999

[14] 徐斐燕，蒋高强，陈健初．臭氧在鲜切西兰花保鲜中应用的研究 [J]. 食品科学，2006，27 (5)：254 -257

Effect of Sprayable and Irrigable Aqueous Solution of 1-methylcyclopropene Treatment Applied Preharvest on the Storage Quality of Broccoli

LI Xiu-jie WANG Qing-guo

(*Shandong Agricultural University*, *Tai'an* 271018)

Abstract: In this study, effect of sprayable and irrigable aqueous solution of 1-MCP treatment applied preharvest on the storage quality of broccoli “duwu” was evaluated . Results indicated that preharvest application of aqueous solution of 1-MCP on broccoli decreased weight loss, reduced the loss of soluble solids and water-solubility sugar content, inhibited decomposing of chlorophyll and ascorbic acid, lowered membrane permeability and peroxidase activitie, delaying senescence and extending storage life of broccoli. Under the same condition, sprayable 1-MCP treatment was more effective than irrigable treatment, which resulted in 126% extension in storage life and compared to 1μl/L gas treatment for 6h at 5℃ to induce similar physiological responses.

Key words: Aqueous solution of 1-MCP; Broccoli; Preharvest; Storage quality

乙醇和1-MCP熏蒸对中华寿桃贮期冷害发生的影响*

陆振中[1]① 徐 莉[2] 王庆国[1]

(1 山东农业大学食品科学与工程学院，泰安 271018；
2 山东省果蔬食用安全工程技术研究中心，济南 251400)

摘 要： 以中华寿桃为试材，研究了乙醇（300μl/L）和1-甲基环丙烯（1-MCP）（1μl/L）处理对其贮藏过程中冷害发生的影响。试验结果表明，1-MCP、乙醇熏蒸处理既明显地抑制了中华寿桃因低温冷害导致的果肉褐变，又能保持其风味、脆度。冷害导致的褐变与多酚氧化酶活性以及总酚含量的变化相关，贮藏过程中，多酚氧化酶活性呈先上升后下降的峰型变化，两种处理均降低了该酶活性的上升速度，延迟了峰值出现的时间，果实总酚含量也相对较高。1-MCP和乙醇处理还能有效地抑制可滴定酸含量的降低和丙二醛含量的增加。

关键词： 中华寿桃；冷害；乙醇；1-甲基环丙烯（1-MCP）

桃属于蔷薇科（Rosaceae）核果类植物。中华寿桃（*Prunus persica* L.）是我国培育出的极晚熟优质品种[1]。果实个大，汁多味美，芳香诱人，色泽艳丽，营养丰富，广为人们所喜爱。中华寿桃成熟期在每年的9月中下旬，正值高温季节，采后极易软化腐烂变质，因此时令性很强。中华寿桃采后在常温下存放，极易腐烂、褐变，而在低温条件下又极易发生冷害，冷害后的桃果实风味和质地劣变，失去商品价值和食用价值，严重影响了果实的内在品质和商品价值。

乙醇是植物生长过程中的次生代谢产物之一，具有杀菌和抑制微生物生长的作用。适量的外源乙醇处理可减少果蔬采后的病害和腐烂率[2,3]；乙醇还有减轻春雪桃低温贮藏过程中冷害的作用，大概是因为其诱导产生某些耐冷性蛋白质[4]，从而延缓了果实冷害的发生。

1-MCP，是近年来常用的乙烯受体抑制剂，具有安全无毒、低量、高效等优点。1-MCP能强烈阻断内源乙烯与受体的结合，抑制组织器官的呼吸作用和乙烯的催熟作

* 基金项目：国家十一五科技支撑项目“农产品贮藏期间的冷害控制技术”，项目编号2006BAD22B05－06

① 陆振中，男，山东农业大学食品科学与工程学院硕士研究生，研究方向：果蔬采后生理与贮藏。E－mail：wqgyyy@126.com

用[5]；还可以阻断香蕉内乙烯反馈调节的生物合成[6]。有研究表明，适宜浓度的1-MCP处理可显著地降低油桃的乙烯释放水平[7]。经1-MCP处理的富士苹果，短期贮藏中果实的内源乙烯浓度几乎为零[8]。在中华寿桃贮藏方面，只有刘红霞[9]等报道1-MCP可抑制果实硬度和可滴定酸含量下降，抑制或者减轻冷害的效果还未见报道。笔者对乙醇、1-MCP抑制中华寿桃冷害和品质变化进行了系统的研究，以期为该品种提供一种安全、有效的贮藏保鲜措施。

1 材料和方法

1.1 试验材料

试验用中华寿桃，于2008年9月26日采自山东省沂源县果园，当地海拔300m左右。采摘后，挑选大小均匀，无机械伤、无病虫害、无畸形的果实，单果套网套，装入塑料周转箱5h后，常温运至山东营养源实验冷库。该批果实单果重300g左右，固形物含量9.5%～13.6%。

1.2 试验处理

乙醇处理：用1 000μl/L的scholar（咯菌睛）溶液浸蘸中华寿桃以杀灭其表面携带的微生物，然后将果实放在吸水纸上晾干。放入泡沫箱，每个泡沫箱放置桃果实8kg左右，在纱布上滴上乙醇，然后用塑料筐扣在泡沫箱的底部，使桃果实不直接接触乙醇，迅速把泡沫箱密封，把泡沫箱放置在20℃的恒温室内熏蒸10h，开箱后套上网套，装入PE保鲜袋，同时装入乙烯吸收剂两包（每包重40 g）。放入－1～0℃冷库预冷贮藏，完全预冷后将袋口折叠，压紧防止被冷风吹开。

1-MCP处理：同上装箱后，把泡沫箱密封，用微量进样器注入一定量的1-MCP溶液，然后用胶带迅速密封进样口，把泡沫箱放置在20℃的恒温室内熏蒸8h，开箱后套上网套，装入PE保鲜袋，同时装入乙烯吸收剂两包（每包重40 g）。放入－1～0℃冷库预冷贮藏，完全预冷后将袋口折叠，压紧防止被冷风吹开。

每个处理条件设3个重复，每个重复处理果实约15kg。将各处理进行理化指标全程测定，在贮藏后期，进行感官评价，获取最直接的感官信息。

1.3 测定指标及方法

1.3.1 硬度

用Wagner硬度计，测定10个果实的硬度，取平均值。在每个果实中间最大横径处，去皮，取4个点测定硬度。

1.3.2 可滴定酸的测定[10]

将桃果实去皮切丝匀浆，称取5g匀浆加去离子水定容到100ml，取10ml加入两滴酚酞，用0.01mol/L的NaOH滴定（以苹果酸计），重复3次。

1.3.3 多酚氧化酶活性（PPO）的测定[11]

吸光值法测定，取样方法同1.3.2，以每分钟内吸光值变化0.001为1个酶活力单位，计算多酚氧化酶的活性。

1.3.4 多酚物质含量的测定[12]

用福林酚法测定，标准曲线以没食子酸为标准物质绘制。

1.3.5 丙二醛含量的测定[11]

用三氯乙酸提取然后加硫代巴比妥酸煮沸法测定。

1.3.6 感官评价评分标准

感官评价标准参见表1。

表1 感官评价标准

评定指标	评定标准
褐变程度	0分：无褐变；1分：轻微褐变，褐变面积10%以下，仍有较好的商品价值；2分：褐变明显，褐变面积10%～20%，有一定商品价值；3分：褐变面积20%～30%，无商品价值；4分：褐变面积30～50%；5分：褐变面积在50%以上
风　味	4分：桃子风味浓郁，味美多汁；3分：桃子风味较浓，果汁丰富；2分：有桃子风味，口感果汁较少；1分：桃子风味很淡，口感果汁很少；0分：无桃子风味，无果汁
香　味	3分：香味浓；2分：较浓；1分，香味淡；0分：无桃子香味
脆　度	3分：脆；2分：较脆；1分：稍软；0分：较软

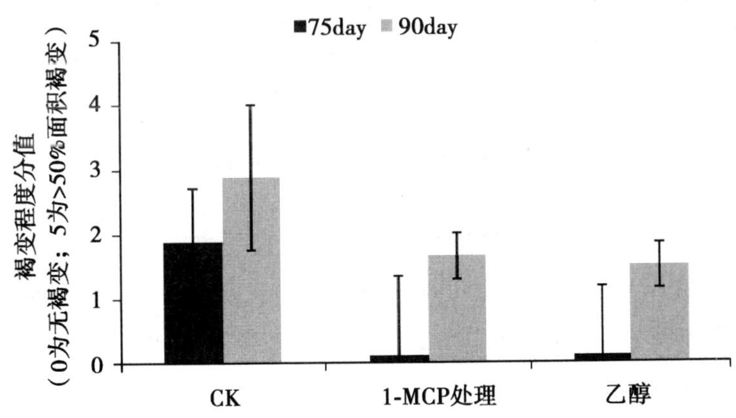

图1 不同熏蒸处理条件对桃果实褐变的影响

2 结果与分析

2.1 不同处理对桃果实褐变程度的影响

从图1可以看出，贮藏到第75d，对照褐变分值已接近2分（褐变面积10%～20%），表明褐变已比较明显。1μl/L 1-MCP、300μl/L 乙醇单独处理的桃果实褐变分值接近0

分。此时，这两组处理的桃果实褐变程度与对照相比，差异均为极显著（$P<0.01$），但两组处理之间并无显著差异（$P>0.05$）。贮藏到第90d，对照褐变程度接近3分，已无商品价值，褐变面积20%～30%。两组熏蒸处理的褐变程度分值均为1.8分，且这两组处理之间差异不显著（$P>0.05$）。上述试验结果表明，低温贮藏前，乙醇、1-MCP熏蒸处理均可以较好地抑制桃果实贮藏中的果肉褐变。

2.2 不同处理对桃果实风味的影响

在贮藏至第75d时，对试验桃果实的风味进行了评定，从图2可以看出，各处理果实的风味均好于对照（1.8分）。其中，1μl/L 1-MCP处理为3.1分，300μl/L乙醇处理为2.8分，两处理得分均明显高于对照，且差异显著（$P<0.05$）。贮至90d时，1μl/L 1-MCP、300μl/L乙醇熏蒸处理的风味分值分别为2.3分和2.2分，均高于对照（0.75分），且差异极显著（$P<0.01$），但两组处理之间差异不显著。所以，乙醇和1-MCP处理可以较好地保持桃果实在贮藏期间的风味。

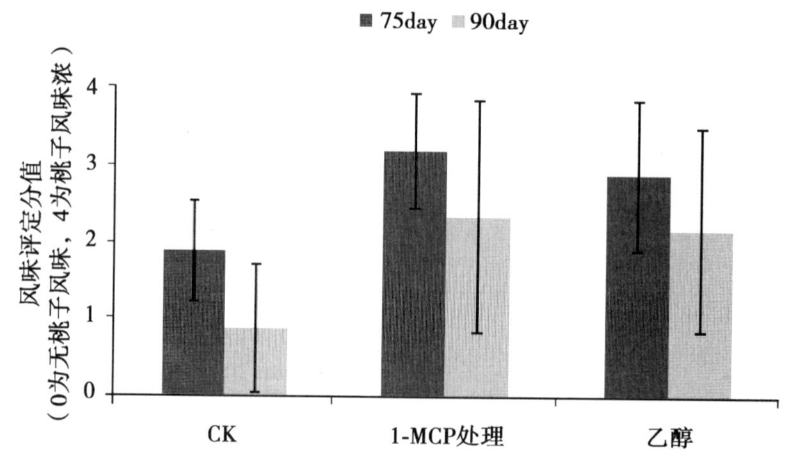

图2 不同熏蒸处理条件对桃果实风味的影响

2.3 不同处理对桃果实香味的影响

从图3可以看出，中华寿桃在贮藏到第75d时，各种处理的桃果实香味分值均高于对照，但差别并不明显。贮藏到第90d时，对照，乙醇和1-MCP两组处理分值与对照无明显差异，香味分值均已接近于1分（香味淡）。

2.4 不同处理对桃果肉脆度的影响

从图4可以看出，中华寿桃贮藏到第75d时，1μl/L 1-MCP、300μl/L乙醇熏蒸处理的食用脆度评定分值分别为1.96分、1.88分，均为“较脆”或以上，而对照为1.2分，已接近“稍软”不脆的状态，两组处理的脆度明显要好于对照（$P<0.05$）。贮藏到第90d时，对照的食用脆度分值已降至0.72分，1μl/L 1-MCP和300μl/L乙醇处理的评定分值分别为1.5分和1.33分，表明脆度均显著高于对照（$P<0.01$）。试验结果

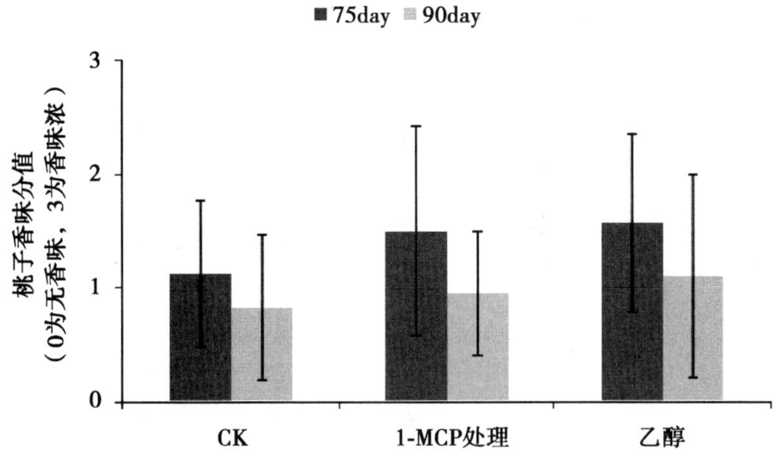

图3 不同熏蒸处理条件对桃果实香味的影响

说明，两组处理均可以明显地保持桃果实的食用脆度。

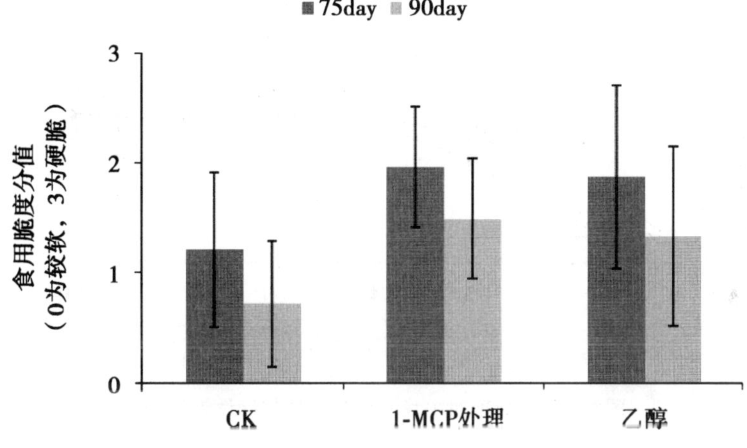

图4 不同熏蒸处理条件对桃果实食用脆度的影响

2.5 不同处理对桃可滴定酸含量变化的影响

酸是果实的重要呈味物质，也是果实代谢的重要基质，试验测定了中华寿桃贮藏过程中可滴定酸的含量变化，结果参见图5。

从图5可以看出，在贮藏过程中，中华寿桃的可滴定酸含量总体呈现逐渐降低的趋势。对照在前期变化平缓，贮藏中后期变化较大。而1μl/L的1-MCP和300μl/L乙醇两组处理变化较平缓。从贮藏中后期（60～90d）可滴定酸的含量来看，两处理组可滴定酸含量均高于对照组，这说明两组处理对于长期贮藏中桃果实可滴定酸的保持具有较好作用。

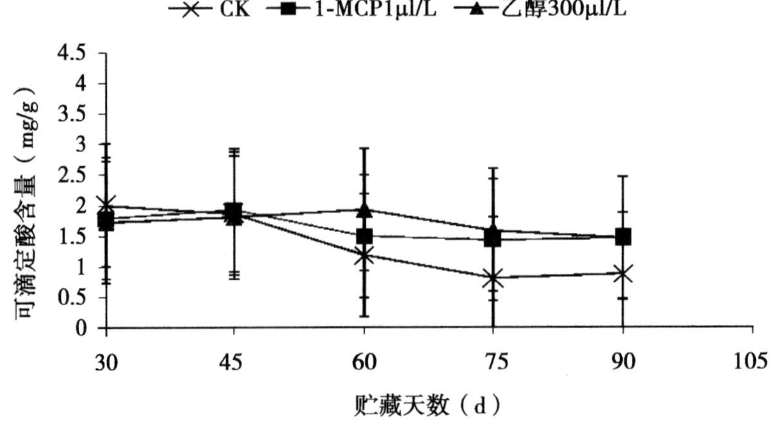

图5　不同熏蒸处理条件对桃果实可滴定酸含量的影响

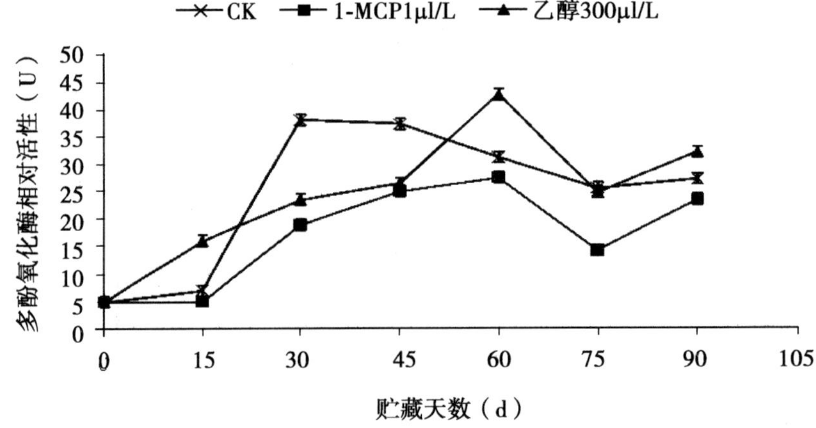

图6　不同处理对中华寿桃多酚氧化酶活性的影响

2.6　不同处理对中华寿桃多酚氧化酶活性及多酚含量的影响

多酚氧化酶存在于植物细胞质体和微体内，植物组织感病或在逆境条件下造成伤害时，多酚氧化酶活性明显升高，起到保卫作用[13]。在组织褐变过程中，多酚氧化酶往往直接催化氧化酚类成醌，再进行一系列反应，最后形成褐色物质，导致褐变发生。从图6可以看出，中华寿桃多酚氧化酶活性呈先升高后下降的趋势。对照在贮藏15d后，大幅上升至最高值，然后小幅下降，而1μl/L 1-MCP和300μl/L乙醇处理，总体上升速度明显小于对照，至60d达到最高值，然后下降。因此，1μl/L 1-MCP和300μl/L乙醇两处理降低了中华寿桃多酚氧化酶活性上升的速度，延迟了达到最高值的时间。

由图7所示，各处理的总酚含量在贮藏过程中均呈下降趋势，但1μl/L 1-MCP和300μl/L乙醇处理的下降幅度小于对照。对照贮至90d时，总酚含量由45.68μg/g下降到11.36μg/g，降低了34.32μg/g。而1μl/L 1-MCP和300μl/L乙醇处理组分别下降了22.73μg/g、14.51μg/g。结合1-MCP和乙醇处理对褐变影响以及总酚含量的变化可知，

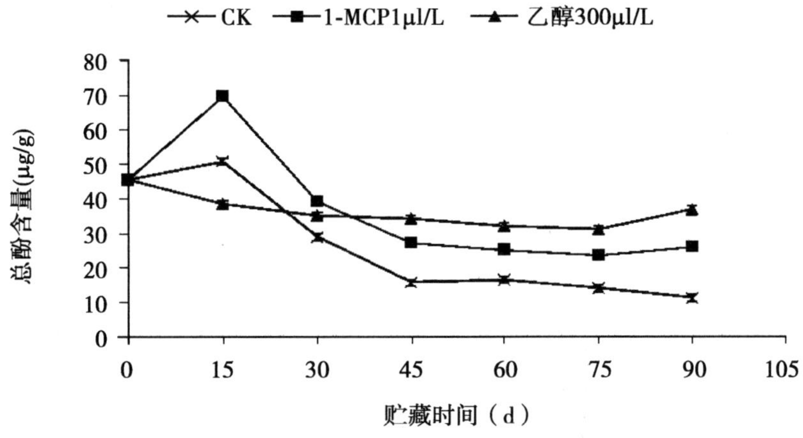

图7　不同处理对中华寿桃总酚含量的影响

褐变出现早，褐变重，总酚含量越低。这可能是由于褐变过程消耗多酚类物质引起。

2.7　不同处理对桃果实丙二醛含量的影响

植物器官衰老时或在逆境条件下往往发生膜脂过氧化，丙二醛（MDA）是其产物之一。通过测定丙二醛的含量可以判断果实衰老程度。从图8可以看出，随着贮藏时间的延长，各处理的丙二醛含量总体呈上升趋势。对照丙二醛含量高于1μl/L 1-MCP和300μl/L乙醇处理组，贮至90d时，上升幅度最大，而1μl/L 1-MCP和300μl/L乙醇处理组虽有上升，但上升幅度明显小于对照，两组熏蒸处理之间差异不显著（$P<0.05$）。

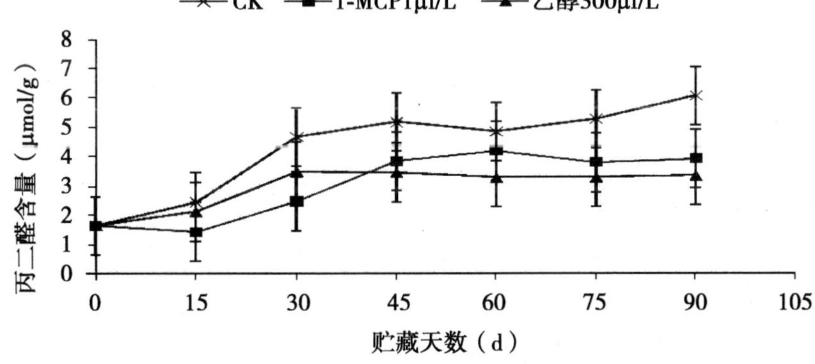

图8　不同熏蒸处理条件对桃果实丙二醛含量的影响

3　结论

上述试验结果表明，1-MCP、乙醇熏蒸处理均可明显地抑制果实低温冷害导致的果肉褐变。降低了多酚氧化酶活性的上升速度，延迟了峰值出现的时间，这两组的果实总酚含量也相对较高。1-MCP和乙醇处理也有效地保持了可滴定酸含量，抑制了丙二醛含量的增加，在抑制中华寿桃的冷害发生方面有较好的效果。乙醇和 1-MCP 为近年来使用的果蔬保鲜剂，可以保持果实品质，延缓商品价值下降。并且符合国家食品安全标准，适合当前生产和市场的需求。在此研究基础上，进一步开发研制真正适用于中华寿桃的保鲜剂实现大规模生产贮藏，将具有十分广阔的发展前景。

参 考 文 献

[1] 刘明，吴绍行，丁国琦. 极晚熟桃新品种—中华寿桃 [J]. 中国果树，1999 (3)：7 -8，10

[2] 段学武，蒋跃明，张昭其. 乙醇和乙醛在采后园艺作物保鲜中的作用 [J]. 植物生理学通讯，2003，39 (3)：289 -293

[3] 于建娜，张利莉，高疆生等. 鲜食葡萄无公害保鲜技术应用进展 [J]. 塔里木大学学报，2006 (2)：37-40，63

[4] Frenkel C，Erez A，enninger M R. Ethanol-induced cold-tolerance in chilling-sensitive crops [M] St Joseph：ASAE，1995：512 -522

[5] Golding J B，Shearer D，Wyllie S G，et al. Application of 1-MCP and propylene to identify ethylene dependent ripening process in mature banana fruit [J]. Postharvest Biol Techol，1998，14：87 -98

[6] Fan X，Argenta L，Mattheis J P. Interactive effects of 1-MCP and temperature on "Elberta" peach quality [J]. Hort Scinece，2002，27 (1)：134 -138

[7] 王俊宁，饶景萍，李落叶等. 1-MCP 处理对油桃果实硬度、呼吸及乙烯合成的影响 [J]. 西北植物学报，2002，22 (5)：1171 -1175

[8] Fan X T，Matthesis J P. Methy jasmonate promotes apple fruit degreening indepently of ethylene action [J]. Hort Sci，1999，34 (2)：310 -312

[9] 刘红霞，姜微波，罗云波. 1-MCP 处理对采后中华寿桃品质的影响 [J]. 中国食品学报，2003，3 (3)：55 -59

[10] 冯国庆，周丽丽，赵玉梅等. 果树贮运学试验指导 [M]. 北京：中国农业大学出版社，1991

[11] 中国科学院上海植物生理研究所主编. 现代植物生理学实验指南 [M]，北京：科学出版社，1999，317 -318

[12] 严守雷，王清章，彭光华. 藕节中总酚含量的福林法测定 [J]. 华中农业大学学报，2003，22 (4)：412 -414

[13] Luza J G，Van Gorsel R，Polito V S，et al. Chilling injury in peaches：A cytochemical and ultrastructural cell wall study [J]. Amer Soc Hort Sci，1992，117 (1)：114 -118

Influences of Ethanol and 1-MCP on Chilling Injury of Zhonghuashou Peach During Storage

LU Zhenzhong[1] XU Li[2] WANG Qingguo[1]

(1 College of Food Science and Engineering, Shandong Agricultural University, Tai'an 271018;
2 Shandong Research Centre for Safety Engineering and Technology of Fruits and Vegetables, Jinan 251400)

Abstract: In order to inhibit the chilling injury and prolong the storage life, Zhonghuashou peaches were treated with 1-MCP and ethanol, then stored at (-1 ~ 0)℃. The results showed that 300μl/L ethanol, 1μl/L1-MCP significantly inhibited the flesh browning caused by chilling injury and had good effect on keeping taste, crispness and preventing woolliness. The browning was associated with the changes of PPO activity and total phenols. During storage, PPO activity first went up, then went down, a peak appeared. 1-MCP and ethanol treatments reduced the rising slope compared with control, and retarded the time when peak value occurred. 1-MCP and ethanol treatments also had good effects in keeping titratable acid and restrained the increase of malondialdehyde.

Key words: Zhonghuashou peach; Chilling injury; Ethanol; 1-MCP

莲藕采后生理生化特性研究

徐 莉[①] 王庆国

（山东农业大学食品科学与工程学院，泰安 271018）

摘 要： 以新鲜莲藕为试验材料，对不同品种的莲藕在贮藏过程中的生理生化特性进行了研究。结果表明，贮藏过程中表皮白度逐渐下降，但藕肉白度变化不大；多酚氧化酶活性和多酚含量变化均呈现出先上升后下降的趋势；纤维素含量对藕的脆度变化有一定的影响；综合白度变化、脆度和腐烂率等因素来考察，三个品种中以济南大卧龙品质最优。

关键词： 莲藕；采后；白度；生理生化

莲藕（*Nelumbo nucifera gaertn*），原产中国和印度，我国湖南、湖北、浙江、江苏、福建、广东、山东等省普遍栽培[1~2]。莲藕含有丰富的蛋白质、碳水化合物、淀粉、钙、铁、抗坏血酸、多种氨基酸，另外还含有生物碱、胡萝卜素、尼克酸、核黄素、硫胺素等化合物以及锰、钛、铜等元素[3]。莲藕性平味甘，补中养神，益气力，止渴，止血，清血，降血压，既可生食又可熟食，可以加工成藕片、藕段、藕粉等[4]。我国莲藕栽种面积很大，已达 20 万 hm^2 以上，占水生蔬菜种植总面积的 1/3 以上[5]，但莲藕采后易于腐烂，品质下降较快，特别容易褐变，本研究主要对莲藕采后与其褐变及耐贮性有关的生理生化性质进行了分析，并比较了不同品种的莲藕在贮藏过程中品质变化的情况。

1 材料与方法

1.1 材料

试验选用 3 个品种：济南大卧龙、北京白莲藕、鄂莲四号，均采自济南吴家堡镇，采收后选择无机械伤、病害的新鲜莲藕（保持完整地藕节）为实验材料，运回实验冷库(5 ~6℃，相对湿度 90% ~95%)，预冷 12 ~ 18h 后，清洗干净，置于 PE 薄膜袋中，放于库中贮藏。

---

① 徐莉，女，山东农业大学食品科学与工程学院硕士研究生，研究方向：果蔬采后生理与贮藏。E - mail：lilibaby521@163.com

1.2 仪器与设备

色差计（Model CR-300，Minolta，Tokyo，Japan），Beckman Allegra 64R 高速冷冻离心机，UV-2000 分光光度计，烘箱，TA. XT2i 质构分析仪，岛津 UV-2450PC 紫外可见分光光度计。

1.3 方法

1.3.1 莲藕白度测定

用色差计（Model CR-300，Minolta，Tokyo，Japan）测定，以标准白度（L = 97.06，a = 0.04，b = 2.01）对色差计进行校准，测定表皮和藕肉白度变化情况。以下列公式来表示白度值 WI（Whiteness Index）：$WI = 100 - [(100 - L)^2 + a^2 + b^2]^{1/2}$。[6]

1.3.2 含水量测定

采用烘箱烘干法。

1.3.3 纤维素含量测定

采用重量法。

1.3.4 多酚氧化酶活性测定

采用吸光值法[7]。

1.3.5 莲藕多酚含量测定

采用福林法[8]。

标准曲线的制定：先配制不同浓度的没食子酸，然后取 1ml，加入 1ml 去离子水、0.5ml 已稀释两倍的福林试剂，1.5ml10% $NaCO_3$，用水定容至 10ml，室温下反应 2h，于 760nm 下测定吸光度，由吸光度对浓度进行回归，求得标准曲线。

样品总酚含量的测定：取样品 5g，加入 5ml 去离子水，研磨后加入 70% 丙酮 25ml 浸提 6h，4000r/min 离心 10min。取上清液 1ml，加入反应液（同制定标准曲线）反应 2h 后，稀释适当倍数后于 760nm 下测定吸光度，查标准曲线，求出含量。

1.3.6 莲藕脆度测定

采用 TA-XT2i 物性测定仪测定，测定条件设置如下。

Setting Measure Force in Compression; Mode : Return To Start; Pre Test Speed: 8.0mm/s; Test Speed: 5.0mm/s; Post Test Speed : 8.0mm/s; Distance : 5.0mm/s; Acquisition Rate = 200pps; Probe: P/0.25S

用破碎力 Force（g）来表示其脆度，破碎力为曲线中第一个峰值，破碎力越小表明其脆度越大[9]。

1.3.7 腐烂率变化

采用重量法，腐烂的重量占总重的百分比。

2 结果与分析

2.1 莲藕白度、多酚氧化酶（PPO）活性以及多酚含量变化情况

2.1.1 莲藕白度变化情况

莲藕采后，极易褐变，使莲藕白度下降，严重的影响莲藕的感观品质。莲藕褐变主要是由于组织中的多酚氧化酶将酚类物质氧化成醌，再进一步聚合形成褐色和黑色素，造成褐变。另外，多酚类物质氧化缩合也会造成组织褐变。莲藕在贮藏过程中白度变化情况如图1、2所示。

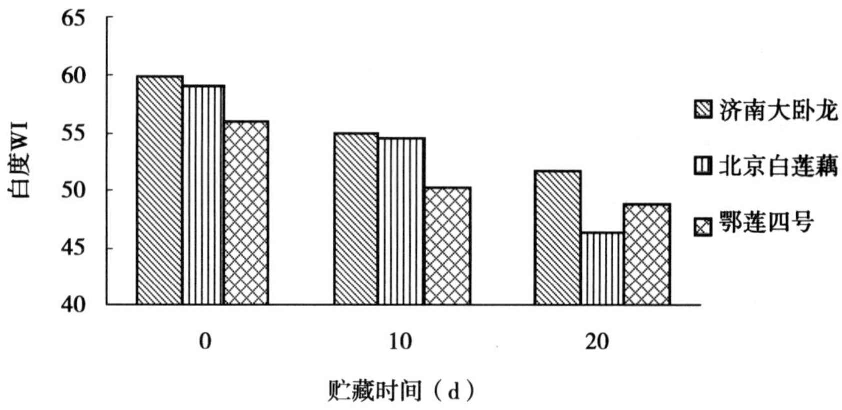

图1 贮藏过程中莲藕表皮白度变化情况

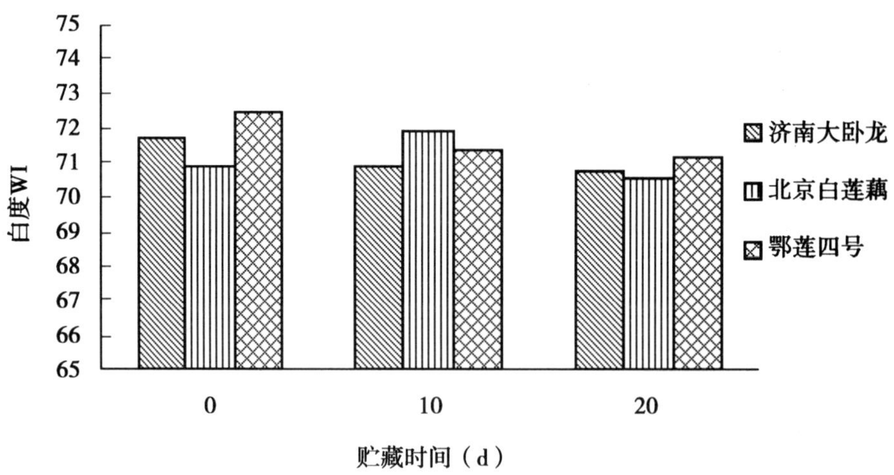

图2 贮藏过程中莲藕肉部白度变化情况

从图1、图2中可以看出，莲藕表皮白度明显小于肉部。贮藏过程中，表皮白度下降比肉部白度下降快，贮藏后莲藕表皮白度比贮藏前降低了10左右，而肉部仅降低了大约1，这是由于表皮暴露于外部，易于被空气中的氧气氧化而发生褐变，另外，外部表皮由于摩擦或碰撞更易于组织损伤导致感官品质下降。比较不同品种的莲藕，由图1可知，济南大卧龙表皮白度最高。而且在贮藏过程中，北京白莲藕表皮白度下降最快，WI值从59.015 09下降至46.355 38（下降了12.659 71），而大卧龙和鄂莲四号下降较慢，WI值分别下降了8.136 58和7.059 54。由图2可知，3个品种藕肉白度相差不大，而且贮藏过程中变化不大。

2.1.2 莲藕多酚氧化酶（PPO）活性变化情况

多酚氧化酶属氧化还原酶[10]，活性位点含有Cu，在有氧存在的情况下，它能催化酚类物质形成醌，醌类物质聚合而导致褐变。由图3可以看出，在贮藏前期，各品种莲藕的PPO活性均呈上升趋势，到第10d达到高峰，而后逐渐降低。

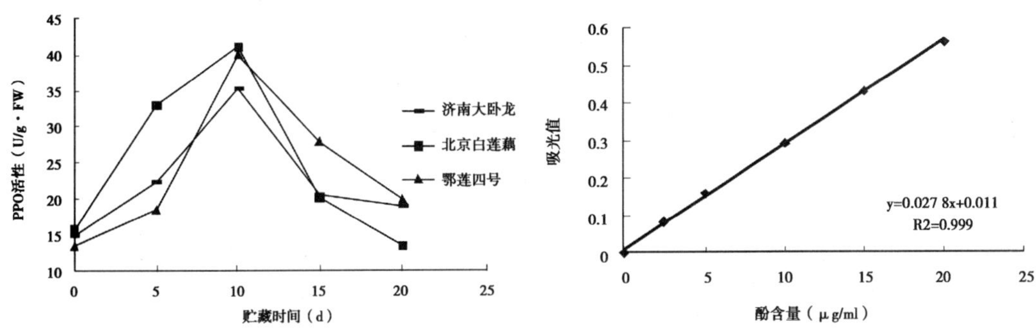

图3 莲藕贮藏过程中PPO活性变化情况 **图4 酚含量与吸光值的关系**

2.1.3 莲藕多酚含量变化情况

有研究表明[11]，没食子酸为莲藕多酚的主要成分，故选择没食子酸为标准品。没食子酸与福林试剂反应后的溶液经190～900nm波长范围内扫描，在760nm处有明显的吸收峰。图4为由没食酸为标准物配制的标准曲线，结果表明没食子酸浓度在0～20μg/ml范围内与其吸光值呈良好线性关系，线性回归方程为 $y=0.027\,8x+0.011$，相关系数为0.998。

从图5、图6中可以看出，藕节中酚含量高于肉中，贮藏过程中，酚含量变化呈现先上升后下降的趋势，第10d含量达到最高。由图5可知，3个品种的酚含量相近，而且在贮藏过程中变化规律一致，变化数量相差不大。分析图6，北京品种在第10d酚含量明显高于其他两个品种，而其余时间相差不大。

2.1.4 褐变与PPO活性及多酚含量的关系分析

莲藕褐变与组织所含的酚类物质以及多酚氧化酶有密切关系，莲藕在贮藏过程中，不论表皮还是肉质，其白度都是逐渐降低的，尤其是表皮变化更明显，出现了明显的表皮褐变。PPO活性和酚含量呈现了相似的规律性，即先上升后下降的趋势。已有研究表明[12]，总酚和游离酚之间存在动态平衡，酶反应的底物是游离酚，但当底物减少时，

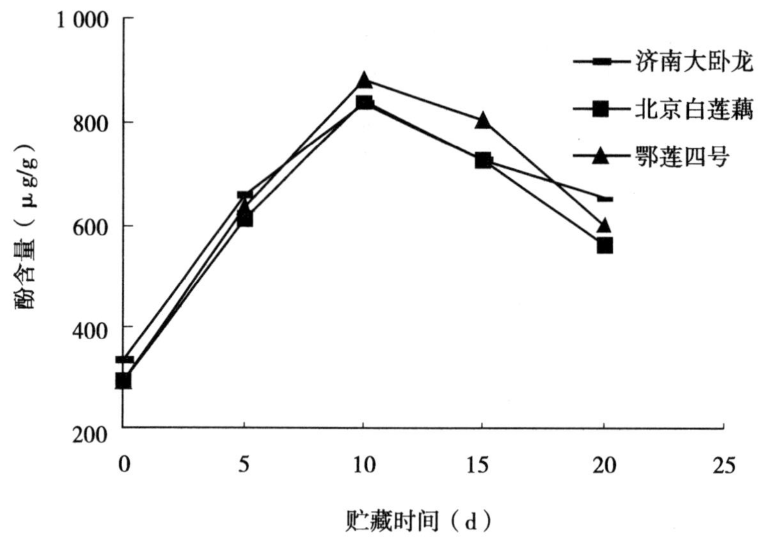

图5 贮藏过程中藕肉总酚含量变化情况

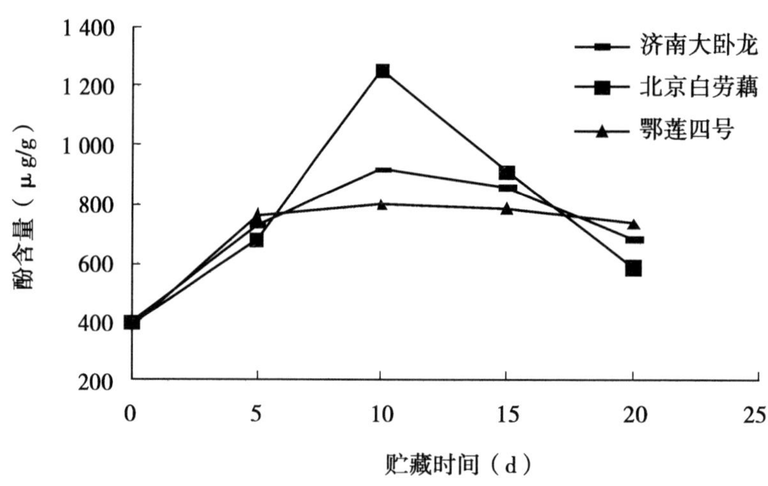

图6 贮藏过程中藕节总酚含量变化情况

总酚会转化为游离酚，因此，总酚起主导作用。所以，研究时以总酚为衡量指标，而不应以游离酚。贮藏前期，白度下降与PPO活性升高有一定的相关性；而贮藏后期，白度下降与酚含量下降呈一定的负相关性，但关于对褐变起主导作用的因素及机理需进一步深入细致的研究。

2.2 水分含量变化情况

莲藕含水量大，采后由于改变了其生长环境，极易失水而导致品质下降。从表1可以看出，鄂莲四号含水量最高，而且贮藏过程中含水量下降速度较另外两个品种慢。

表1 贮藏过程中莲藕含水量变化情况

贮藏天数（d）	0	5	10	15	20
济南大卧龙	81.020 45%	80.413 27%	79.704 84%	75.941 63%	75.917 5%
北京白莲藕	80.059 38%	79.678 17%	77.643 56%	77.873 2%	76.638 9%
鄂莲四号	81.242 22%	80.958 43%	80.900 00%	80.283 37%	79.020 9%

2.3 纤维素含量及脆度变化情况

表2 贮藏过程中莲藕纤维含量变化情况

品种	贮藏天数（d）				
	0	5	10	15	20
济南大卧龙	0.574 9%	0.608 9%	0.655 2%	0.684 3%	0.728 1%
北京白莲藕	0.649 6%	0.711 2%	0.764 0%	0.842 5%	0.987 7%
鄂莲四号	0.699 0%	0.776 6%	0.781 1%	0.820 0%	1.027 0%

从表2可以看出，随着贮藏时间的延长，莲藕纤维含量呈上升趋势。在整个贮藏过程中，大卧龙纤维含量最低，而且含量增加最慢，贮藏20d仅增加了0.108 2%，而北京品种和鄂莲四号分别增加了0.338 1%和0.328 0%。

组织结构和细胞排列对藕的品质包括脆度、硬度、粗糙感等有较大的影响[13]，而纤维素是细胞壁的重要组成部分，所以和藕的脆度有一定的关系。由图7结果可以看出，大卧龙脆度最大，鄂莲四号脆度最小，与粗纤维含量表现出正相关性。

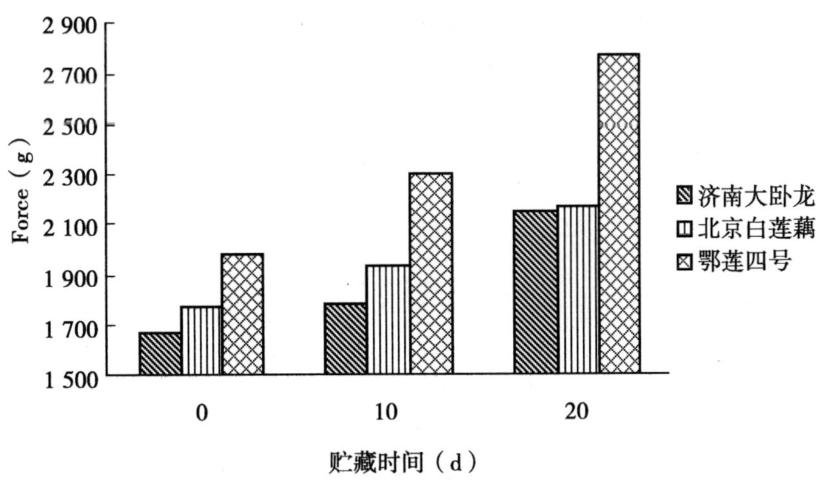

图7 贮藏过程中莲藕脆度变化情况

2.4 腐烂率变化情况

表 3 贮藏过程中腐烂率变化情况

品种	贮藏天数（d）		
	15	20	25
济南大卧龙	0.478 7%	0.975%	4.734 8%
北京白莲藕	0.88%	2.653%	3.719 5%
鄂莲四号	0.836 5%	3.719 5%	6.216 7%

北京白莲藕和鄂莲四号从贮藏第 11d 开始出现腐烂，大卧龙从第 13d 开始出现腐烂，腐烂主要表现为表面出现腐烂斑，有黄色或绿色菌斑，藕节处明显出现霉菌；随着腐烂程度的加重，逐渐向内部扩展，使藕肉质腐烂，表现出褐色或灰色，并出现异味。比较表 3 结果，可以看出，鄂莲四号腐烂最严重，而且腐烂速度比另外两个品种都快。

3 结论

（1）济南大卧龙表皮白度最高，贮藏过程中，北京白莲藕表皮白度下降最快，大卧龙和鄂莲四号下降较慢，但 3 个品种藕肉白度相差不大，而且贮藏过程中变化不大。

（2）多酚氧化酶活性和酚含量变化情况均呈现出先上升后下降的趋势。

（3）比较 3 个品种，济南大卧龙脆度最高，纤维素含量最低，纤维素含量对脆度有一定的影响。

（4）从白度变化、脆度和腐烂率方面来考察，3 个品种中以济南大卧龙品质最优。

参 考 文 献

[1] 于新等．藕采后生理及保鲜技术研究进展［J］．广州食品工业科技，2002，18（3）：58－61

[2] 许金蓉等．不同品种莲藕生理生化特性研究［J］．广州食品工业科技，2003，19（4）：24－27

[3] 许金蓉等，莲藕（地下膨大茎）贮藏及其生理生化研究进展［J］．氨基酸与生物资源，2003，25（2）：4－7

[4] 李传宝．白莲藕品种及栽培技术［J］．中国种业，2004，3：56－57

[5] 郑寨生等．水生蔬菜生产现状及其前景分析［J］．当代蔬菜，2005（10）：4－5

[6] H. P. Vasantha Rupasinghe, Jeanine Boulter-Bitzer, Taehyun Ahn, Joseph A. Odumeru. Vanillin inhibits pathogenic and spoilage microorganisms in vitro and aerobic microbial growth in fresh-cut apples [J]. Food Research International 39 (2006) 575－580

[7] 中国科学院上海植物生理研究所主编．《现代植物生理学实验指南》［M］．科学

出版社
[8] 严守雷，王清章，光华．藕节中总酚含量的福林法测定［J］．华中农业大学学报，2003，22（4）：412－414
[9] 范柳萍等．真空油炸胡萝卜脆片基本特性的研究［J］．食品与生物技术学报，2005，24（6）：49－52
[10] 韩涛，李丽萍．果实和蔬菜中多酚氧化酶的作用［J］．北京农学院学报，1998，13（2）：115－124
[11] 金悠．莲藕早期褐变原因及保鲜研［D］．华中农业大学食品科学技术学院，1999
[12] 郁志兴等．鲜切果蔬酶促褐变底物的分析确定［J］．食品科学，2002，23（4）：41－44
[13] 苗如意等．大白菜组织结构感官与评定指标的关系［J］．园艺学报，1996，23（4）：355－358

Studies of Biochemistry and Physiology of Lotus root After-Harvest

XU Li　WANG Qingguo

(*College of Food Science and Engineering*, *Shandong Agricultural University*, *Tai'an* 271018)

Abstract: In this paper, biochemistry and physiology of various of lotus root after-harvest were investigated. The result showed that during storage, the WI value of lotus epidermis were in a tendency to decrease, but the change in WI value of lotus root were not obvious; Change of Polyphenol oxidase activity and phenols content of lotus root were tend to increase and then decrease during storage; The fibre content of lotus root can affect the change of brittlement; Take the factor of WI value and brittlement and decomposed rate of lotus root into account, the quality of JN Dawolong was the best in the three breeds.

Key words: Lotus root; Whiteness Index; Physiological

切割牛蒡保鲜技术的研究

徐　莉[①]　王庆国

（山东农业大学食品科学与工程学院，泰安　271018）

摘　要：以新鲜牛蒡为试材，对保鲜剂的种类、浓度和包装方法等进行了综合试验。结果表明，在0～3℃的贮藏温度下，经1.5%柠檬酸+0.5%抗坏血酸+0.5%氯化钙复合保鲜液浸渍处理后，用厚0.08mm厚的聚乙烯袋进行真空包装，贮存30d，品质保持良好。

关键词：切割牛蒡；保鲜；真空包装

牛蒡，菊科，牛蒡属，2～3年生草本植物，英文名称为Great burdock，是一种天然营养植物，被视为强身健体，防病治病的保健蔬菜，近年来，在我国实现了大面积的种植，其产品主要出口日本和韩国。牛蒡有较厚的表皮，食用时首先要去皮再进行切割，切割后的牛蒡很容易褐变，严重地影响其外观品质。牛蒡褐变主要是因为牛蒡中含有大量的儿茶酚和酪氨酸等酚类化合物，切割后这些化合物在牛蒡中存在的多酚氧化酶（PPO）的催化作用下，被空气氧化成醌、邻醌，再进一步氧化聚合生成褐色至黑色素（或类黑精）[1]。另外，切割后的牛蒡在贮藏过程中还存在营养物质流失、因微生物侵染造成的腐败变质等问题。因此，研究如何保持贮藏期间的品质以及获得较长的保质期对切割牛蒡非常重要。目前，国外保鲜技术可使切割后的牛蒡在低温（4～5℃）下保鲜期达30天以上，能够满足国际市场的需求，而在国内尚达不到此水平，用护色液处理后，经真空包装在0～3℃贮藏，保质期仅有3周左右。本研究通过使用不同保鲜剂和包装方式处理切割牛蒡，以确定最佳保鲜方案。

1　材料与方法

1.1　材料

牛蒡（产自山东诸城），直径15～23mm，长度60～80cm。

① 徐莉，女，山东农业大学食品科学与工程学院硕士研究生，研究方向：果蔬采后生理与贮藏。E-mail：lilibaby521@163.com

1.2 试剂

柠檬酸，抗坏血酸，L-半胱氨酸，氯化钙，焦磷酸钠，磷酸二氢钙，六偏磷酸钠，EDTA，草酸，氢氧化钠，95%乙醇等皆为分析纯；牛肉膏，蛋白胨为生化试剂。

1.3 主要试验仪器

UV-2000型分光光度计（上海尤尼柯仪器有限公司），DZQ-800L真空气调包装机（上海龙井电器有限公司），高压蒸汽灭菌锅（山东省新华医疗器械厂），无菌操作台（济南空气净化消毒设备厂），臭氧发生器（实验室自备）。

1.4 试验方法

牛蒡→采收→运输→入库→清洗→去皮→消毒→漂洗→切片→保鲜液处理→甩干→包装→贮存

选择无裂纹、病斑、机械伤，粗细均匀的新鲜牛蒡为原料，用清洁的水洗净。经不锈钢刀去皮后浸于50mg/kg的NaClO溶液中约5min，然后取出用清水漂洗干净，再用不锈钢刀斜切（厚0.3~0.5cm），切好片的牛蒡迅速浸渍于保鲜液中约5min。各组保鲜液如表1所示。

表1 保鲜剂成分及含量

保鲜剂编号	保鲜剂浓度（%）							
	柠檬酸	抗坏血酸	焦磷酸钠	氯化钙	L-半胱氨酸	磷酸二氢钙	六偏磷酸钠	EDTA
A1	0.5	0.5		0.5				
A2	1.0	0.5		0.5				
A3	1.5	0.5		0.5				
B1	0.5		0.5	0.5				
B2	1.0		0.5	0.5				
B3	1.5		0.5	0.5				
C1	0.5			0.5	0.2			
C2	0.5			0.5	0.5			
D1	1.0							
D2	1.5							
E1		0.02				0.05	0.04	0.03
E2		0.04				0.10	0.08	0.06

从保鲜液中取出后经离心脱水后进行包装，分下述3种包装：①直接包装放入0.03mm厚的PE（聚乙烯）袋中扎口。②充臭氧包装放入0.03mm厚的PE（聚乙烯）

袋中，充入一次5mg/kg臭氧，臭氧由臭氧发生器制备，浓度测定参照马毅红[2]测定方法，然后扎口。③真空包装放入0.08mm厚的PE（聚乙烯）袋中，用真空气调包装机进行抽真空包装。最后于0～3℃冷库贮藏，在贮藏期间定期进行观察和测定。

1.5 测定项目及方法

1.5.1 感官品质评定

实验室人员（7人）组成的评判小组按表2所示的感官品质评定标准进行综合评定。

表2 切割牛蒡感观评定标准

等级	得分	色泽	褐变面积	质地	风味
一	9～10	全呈正常白色	—	硬	正常
二	7～9	大部分白或灰白，部分稍发暗黄，圈浅黄	—	硬	正常
三	5～7	浅褐或灰色，圈浅褐	<1/5	硬	正常
四	3～5	暗黄、浅褐或灰色，圈褐色，部分边浅褐	<1/3	硬	正常
五	1～3	深灰色、褐色或部分发黑，圈棕色，边褐	>1/3	较硬	稍微异味

1.5.2 褐变程度（BD）测定

采用吸光度法。将牛蒡浸入50%的乙醇中浸提20h，提取液经过滤后，滤液于420nm处比色，以吸光度A_{420}来表示BD，平行测定3次，结果取平均值。吸光度越大，则BD越大。

1.5.3 维生素C含量测定

采用2，6-二氯酚靛酚滴定法[3]，平行测定3次，结果取平均值。

1.5.4 微生物指标测定

测定牛蒡片表面的微生物总数[4]，采用平板计数法。

2 结果与分析

2.1 保鲜剂筛选

2.1.1 不同保鲜剂对切割牛蒡表面褐变的影响

牛蒡切割后，在贮藏过程中，以开始明显褐变天数为评判标准，颜色变化情况以评判小组感官评判为准，对于用0.03mm厚PE袋包装的牛蒡，每天记录一次表面褐变情况，结果如表3所示。

表 3 不同保鲜剂对 0.03mm 厚 PE 包装的牛蒡褐变的影响

保鲜剂编号	贮藏期（d）							明显褐变时间/（d）
	1	2	3	4	5	6	7	
对照	±	+	+ +					2
A1	-	-	±	+	+ +			4
A2	-	-	-	±	+	+ +		5
A3	-	-	-	±	+	+	+ +	5
B1	-	-	±	+	+ +			4
B2	-	-	±	+	+ +			4
B3	-	-	-	±	+	+ +		5
C1	-	-	-	-	±	+	+	6
C2	-	-	-	-	±	±	+	7
D1	-	-	±	+	+ +			4
D2	-	-	±	±	+	+ +		5
E1	-	±	+	+ +				3
E2	-	±	+	+ +				3

注：“ - ”表示牛蒡呈本色；“ ± ”表示开始褐变；“ + ”表示较明显褐变；“ + + ”表示严重褐变

从表 3 可以看出，各种处理的牛蒡随贮藏时间的延长，褐变越来越严重。比较处理和对照，处理的褐变程度均低于对照。比较不同的保鲜剂，以 C1 组复合保鲜剂对褐变的抑制效果最好，贮藏 5d，未出现褐变。较好组为 C2 组复合保鲜剂，贮藏 4d，牛蒡表面颜色保持良好。最差组为 E1 组和 E2 组复合保鲜剂，第 2d 就开始出现褐变。比较同一成分的保鲜剂，在不影响产品品质的条件下，一般浓度越大，对褐变的抑制效果越好。对于经臭氧处理的牛蒡，保鲜剂对褐变的作用效果与上述结果一致。对于真空包装的牛蒡，在贮藏期间测定了各组褐变程度（BD）变化的情况，如图 1 所示。

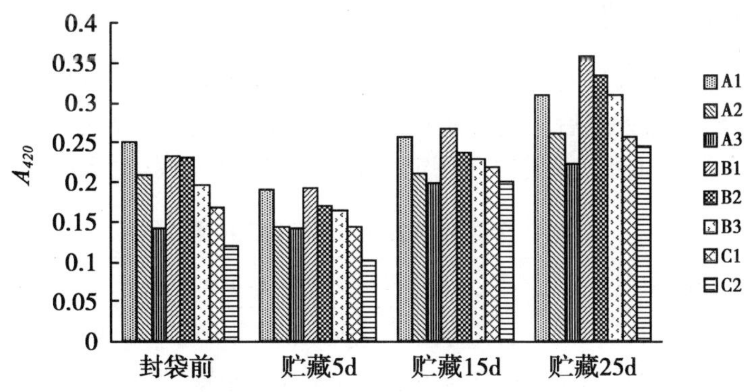

图 1 真空包装的牛蒡在贮藏期间褐变程度（BD）变化情况

从图 1 可看出，在真空包装的牛蒡中，褐变最轻的为 A3 组，即用 1.5% 柠檬酸 + 0.5% 抗坏血酸 + 0.5% $CaCl_2$ 复合保鲜剂处理的，较轻的组为 A2、C2、C1 组。分析图 1 中各组 BD 大小和变化情况可知，在贮藏过程中，各种处理的牛蒡 BD 均增大，其中，BD 一直较小的组为 A2、A3、C1、C2 组。贮藏到第 5d 时，BD 大小顺序为 C2 < A3 <

A2 < C1 < B3 < B2 < A1 < B1；贮藏到第 15d 时，BD 大小顺序为 A3 < C2 < A2 < C1 < B3 < B2 < A1 < B1；贮藏到第 25d 时，BD 大小顺序为 A3 < C2 < C1 < A2 < A1 < B3 < B2 < B1。从变化情况来看，起初 C2 组较小，但随贮藏时间的延长，增大幅度较大，而 A3 组增大幅度较小，致使到中后期 A3 组 BD 小于 C2 组，在各组中值最小，即褐变程度最轻。由此看来，在短期（1 周）内贮藏，用 C2 组处理效果好，但长期贮藏，用 A3 组效果好。从整个贮藏过程来看，用 A3 组处理抑制褐变效果最好，即最佳保鲜剂组合为：1.5% 柠檬酸 + 0.5% 抗坏血酸 + 0.5% $CaCl_2$。较好保鲜剂组合为 1.0% 柠檬酸 + 0.5% 抗坏血酸 + 0.5% $CaCl_2$、0.5% 柠檬酸 + 0.2% L-半胱氨酸 + 0.5% $CaCl_2$、0.5% 柠檬酸 + 0.5% L-半胱氨酸 + 0.5% $CaCl_2$。另外，从图上可以看出，入库贮存 5d 后的褐变程度均小于封袋前的封袋前，牛蒡处在常温下），这说明低温可以明显抑制褐变。

综上所述，对于用 0.03mm 厚 PE 袋包装的牛蒡，最佳保鲜剂组合为 0.5% 柠檬酸 + 0.5% L-半胱氨酸 + 0.5% $CaCl_2$，对于真空包装的牛蒡，最佳保鲜剂组合为 1.5% 柠檬酸 + 0.5% 抗坏血酸 + 0.5% $CaCl_2$。

2.1.2 不同保鲜剂对切割牛蒡硬度的影响

从感官评定来看，不论处理组还是对照组，贮藏过程中，牛蒡一直都保持着较高的硬度。即使外观品质已明显变劣，硬度也保持较高，这说明保鲜剂对硬度的影响较小。在保鲜剂中加入 $CaCl_2$ 的目的主要是来保持产品的硬度，但感官评定结果说明，使用和不使用 $CaCl_2$ 对硬度的影响很小。

2.1.3 维生素 C 含量测定结果

每 100g 新鲜牛蒡中含维生素 C 2.5mg。试验中，在牛蒡去皮、切割后测得每 100g 牛蒡中含维生素 C 仅为 0.478mg，在贮藏 3d 后，用同样方法再测时已基本测不出。这说明，牛蒡在切割过程中，维生素 C 已损失了大部分，贮藏一段时间后，维生素 C 含量已很少，损失非常严重。

2.2 包装方式筛选

对于保鲜护色效果较好的几组保鲜液处理的牛蒡，比较其用不同的包装方式处理后颜色变化情况，经感官评定后，记录其开始褐变（评定分值 6 ~ 7 分）时间、明显褐变（评定分值 4 ~ 6 分）时间、保质期（评定分值 7 分以上）如表 4 所示。

表 4 不同包装方式的感官评定结果

保鲜剂编号	开始褐变时间（d）			明显褐变时间（d）			保质期（d）		
	PE 包装	充 O_3PE 包装	真空包装	PE 包装	充 O_3PE 包装	真空包装	PE 包装	充 O_3PE 包装	真空包装
A2	4	3	20	5	5	26	3	2	20
A3	4	4	30	5	5	35	3	3	30
C1	5	5	19	6	7	24	4	4	18
C2	5	6	20	7	7	25	4	5	19

从表4中可以看出，真空包装的牛蒡比其他包装的保鲜效果好，开始褐变时间、明显褐变时间都较晚，保质期较长。用0.03mm厚PE袋包装的牛蒡中，充臭氧与不充臭氧的差别不大，说明使用臭氧效果不明显。用1.5%柠檬酸+0.5%抗坏血酸+0.5% $CaCl_2$ 复合保鲜剂处理后经真空包装的牛蒡贮藏30d颜色、风味保持良好，与其他组相比，保质期最长，可达30d。

为进一步比较不同包装方式对褐变的影响，贮藏5d后，测得各种包装牛蒡的褐变程度（用吸光度大小表示）如表5所示。

表5 贮藏5d后不同包装牛蒡的褐变程度（BD）

保鲜剂编号	褐变程度/A_{420}		
	直接包装	O_3 处理	真空包装
对照	1.230	0.998	0.231
A1	1.004	0.806	0.189
A2	0.761	0.749	0.143
A3	0.758	0.726	0.141
B1	0.579	0.586	0.192
B2	0.704	0.650	0.170
B3	0.721	0.659	0.164
C1	0.629	0.589	0.144
C2	0.561	0.558	0.102
D1	0.865	0.632	—
D2	0.893	0.621	—
E1	0.782	0.623	—

注：“-”表示D、E组处理的牛蒡没有使用真空包装

贮藏5d后，比较各组的褐变程度，真空包装的褐变程度明显小于直接包装的和充臭氧包装的，进一步说明了真空包装对褐变抑制效果好。所以，在贮藏过程中隔绝氧气非常重要，真空包装时，氧气和空气一起排除，包装材料使产品和外界大气屏蔽，氧气不能进入包装袋中，氧化被彻底防止[5]，从而减少了牛蒡表面的褐变，延长了产品的保质期。在用0.03mm厚PE袋包装的各组中，充臭氧包装的牛蒡褐变程度略小于直接包装的，说明臭氧对抑制褐变也有一定的作用。但数值差别不大，所以，从抑制褐变来说，臭氧作用效果不明显。

2.3 臭氧对切割牛蒡品质的影响

2.3.1 臭氧对切割牛蒡感官品质的影响

从前面的结果分析中可看出，用臭氧处理和不用臭氧处理的牛蒡在感官品质保持上差别不大，说明臭氧处理效果不明显。

2.3.2 臭氧对微生物的影响

试验中对于用0.03mm厚PE袋包装的牛蒡，在贮藏前（处理后未进库）和贮藏1

周后测得牛蒡表面的微生物数目，以此来检验臭氧对微生物的影响。在贮藏前各种处理的牛蒡表面均未检测出微生物，贮藏 1 周后测得各组牛蒡的表面微生物数目如表 6 所示。

表 6 贮藏 1 周后用 0.03mm 厚 PE 袋包装的牛蒡表面微生物数目

保鲜剂编号	微生物数目（个/g）	
	未经臭氧处理	经臭氧处理
A1	6.689×10^3	3.860×10^3
A2	6.450×10^3	3.450×10^3
A3	5.998×10^3	2.930×10^3
B1	3.13×10^3	2.032×10^3
B2	2.558×10^3	1.281×10^3
B3	2.615×10^3	1.037×10^3
C1	1.920×10^3	1.189×10^3
C2	1.730×10^3	ND
D1	1.789×10^4	9.014×10^3
D2	1.765×10^4	8.650×10^3

注：“ND” 表示未检测出

贮藏 1 周后，用臭氧处理组比未用臭氧处理组数目要少，可见，臭氧在抑菌方面起到了一定的作用。臭氧氧化能力强[6]，能与微生物细胞中的多种成分发生反应，使微生物细胞结构受到破坏而杀灭微生物。

3 讨论

臭氧作为一种冷杀菌技术，现已在食品领域得到了广泛的应用。试验中，臭氧对灭菌起到了一定的作用，但处理组与未处理组微生物数目都在 $10^3\sim10^4$ 数量级，差别不显著，这或许是因为试验中只在开始充入了一次臭氧，臭氧有一定的衰变期，杀菌作用不能在整个贮藏过程中一直稳定持续，可能后期杀菌作用已较弱，从而造成杀菌不彻底。若改善方法，如增加充入次数，或许可以提高灭菌效果，但有待进一步试验证明。

牛蒡中含有丰富的维生素 C，但切割过程会造成维生素 C 的大量损失。由于维生素 C 极易被空气中的氧气所氧化，所以减少或避免氧气氧化就非常重要。但目前，尚无有效的方法来解决切割过程中维生素 C 的损失问题。如果加工过程可保证在无氧环境（如 N_2 环境）中进行，就可以很好的减少氧化损失，但实际应用中会增加生产成本。

本试验中，主要采用保鲜剂处理来防止褐变，但目前应用的保鲜剂都属于化学物质，考虑到切割牛蒡的食用安全性问题，使用天然的褐变抑制剂具有更强的优越性，其开发必将成为未来的发展方向。

4 结论

经过保鲜剂和包装方式筛选后，切割后的牛蒡经下列保鲜方案：牛蒡→去皮→消毒→切割→浸于 1.5% 柠檬酸 +0.5% 抗坏血酸 +0.5% $CaCl_2$ 复合保鲜液中 5min→甩干→装入 0.08mm 厚 PE 袋→进行抽真空包装→0～3℃贮藏，贮藏 30d 感观品质最好。贮藏 30d 后，测得产品表面的微生物数目为 225 个/g，日本[7]目前对鲜切菜制定的微生物管理基础为贮藏后一般活菌数应在 10^5 个/g 以下，所以，本试验中产品微生物数目不超标。因此，将此方案确立为最佳保鲜方案。

参 考 文 献

[1] 周志才等．牛蒡中多酚氧化酶活性及其影响因素研究 [J]．烟台大学学报，1998 (1)：62－65

[2] 马毅红．一种简单快速测定臭氧浓度的方法 [J]．惠州大学学报，2000，20 (4)：35－37

[3] 王宪泽主编．生物化学实验技术原理和方法 [M]．北京：中国农业出版社，2002

[4] 牛天贵，张宝芹编著．食品微生物检验 [M]．北京：中国计量出版社，2004

[5] 高愿军，熊卫东主编．食品包装 [M]．北京：化学工业出版社，2005

[6] 高翔，陆兆新，张立奎等．臭氧在鲜切西洋芹保鲜中应用的研究 [J]．食品科学，2003，24 (12)：131－134

[7] 何建军等．真空包装冷藏生鲜净菜莲藕的研制 [J]．湖北农业科学，2002 (6)：1－3

Studies on the Technology of Storage for Fresh-cut Great burdock

XU Li　WANG Qingguo

(*College of Food Science and Engineering*, *Shandong Agricultural University*, *Tai'an* 271018)

Abstract: During the experiment, the fresh Great burdock was treated with different kinds and different concentration of fresh-keeping reagent and different package. It showed that the Fresh-cut Great burdock which was treated with 1.5 % Citric acid +0.5% Ascorbic acid +0.5% $CaCl_2$ and vacuumized with 0.08mm polythene package could be well preserved for 30 days.

Key words: Fresh-cut Great burdock; Fresh- keeping; Vacuumize

1-MCP 采前喷施对泰山早霞苹果品质的影响

李红震① 王庆国

（山东农业大学食品科学与工程学院，泰安 271018）

摘 要： 泰山早霞苹果是一种极早熟品种，它具有外观美、风味浓、品质优及早果性、丰产性强等特点。但其采后货架期极短，常温下 4～5d 即绵化（以硬度计），商品价值明显降低。本研究探讨了 1-MCP 处理防治泰山早霞苹果采后绵化、延长货架期的技术，试验结果表明：采前 8d 喷施 1-MCP，对果实着色影响较小，货架放置时，明显抑制了果实硬度的下降，延缓乙烯的释放，延缓可滴定酸和可溶性固形物的升高。采前喷洒处理，抑制早霞苹果绵化是可行的，但其效果需要通过选择适宜使用时间进一步提高。

关键词： 泰山早霞；1-MCP；绵化

"泰山早霞"是从苹果种子繁殖的砧木苗中选育出的极早熟苹果新品种，果实宽圆锥形，平均单果质量 138.6g，果面光滑，底色淡黄，果面着均匀鲜红彩条，果肉白色，酸甜适口，具有成熟极早，外观美，风味浓，品质优及早果性，丰产性强等特点[1]。但"泰山早霞"苹果同时也存在着货架期短，极易出现绵化，腐烂的现象。1-MCP（1-甲基环丙烯），是一种新型的乙烯受体阻断剂，可与果蔬组织中的乙烯受体发生不可逆的结合，阻断乙烯与受体的结合，因此，能抑制乙烯的作用[2,3]，延缓其后熟和衰老进程[4]，1-MCP 能不同程度地抑制苹果[5]、香蕉[6,7]、梨[8]、番茄[9]等跃变型果蔬以及非跃变型果实如草莓[10]、甜橙[11]等中乙烯的产生和释放。泰山早霞苹果成熟期早，采后一般不需较长时间贮藏，而是直接上市销售，过去采后库房内用 1-MCP 熏蒸延长货架期的措施较为繁琐。本实验目的在于研究探讨 1-MCP 采前喷洒提高泰山早霞苹果采后货架品质、延长货架期的可行性，为该品种的推广提供技术支持。

1 实验材料与方法

2.1 材料

聊城冠县泰山早霞苹果，2010 年 7 月 8 号采摘，常温下运输至山东营养源食品科

① 李红震，男，山东农业大学食品科学与工程学院硕士研究生。研究方向：果蔬采后生理与贮藏。E－mail：maitiankeeper@163.com

技有限公司实验室。1-MCP 溶液：含量 2%。

2.2 方法

将 1-MCP 稳定溶液稀释 100 倍，分别于采前 8d、12d 用喷雾器喷洒树冠。试验设 3 个处理。处理 1，采前 12d 喷洒 1 次；处理 2，采前 8d 1 次；处理 3：采前 8d、12d 各喷洒 1 次。苹果采收后，当日取部分未经喷洒的苹果，用 1-MCP 常温熏蒸 10h。以采前不喷洒，采后不熏蒸为对照。每个处理 1.5kg，每个处理重复 3 次。货架条件为 20℃常温敞口放置。

2.3 测定指标

单果重；色差采用 Model CR-300，Minolta，Tokyo，Japan 的色差计；乙烯释放量采用上海科创色谱仪器有限公司生产的气相色谱测定仪测定，各处理分别取果实约为 1.5kg，室温条件下密封 12h 后抽取气体测定乙烯含量；以单位鲜重（FW）的果实在单位时间内释放的乙烯的量表示果实的乙烯释放速率，单位 μl/（kg · h），检测器为：FID 检测器；柱温：60℃；进样口温度：100℃；检测器温度：120℃；气体样品进样 1ml。硬度采用意大利 Wagner Instruments 生产的 Wagner FT30 硬度计测定；可溶性固形物采用日本 ATAGO 的 Pocket refractometer Pal-1 手持糖量计；可滴定酸测定采用碱滴定法。重复 3 次测定，取平均值。采用 Excel 软件对检测数据进行统计分析与制图。采用 SPSS 软件进行差异显著性分析。

3 结果分析

3.1 1-MCP 处理对泰山早霞苹果色差的影响

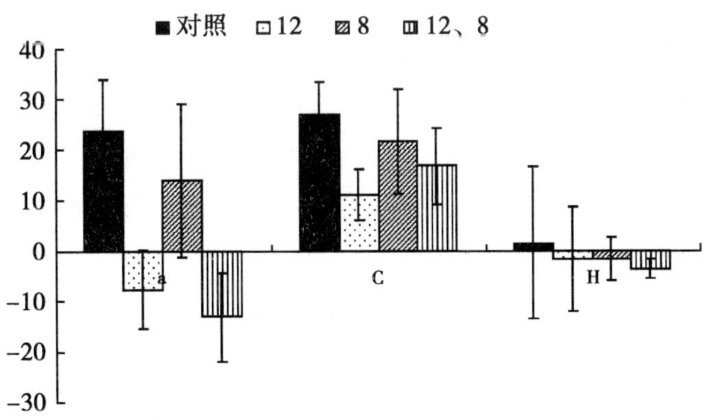

图 1 采前 1-MCP 处理对泰山早霞苹果颜色的影响

注：12 代表采前 12d 喷施 1 次；8 代表采前 8d 喷施 1 次；12、8 代表采前 12d 和 8d 连续喷施。以下各图表相同表示

每个处理中随机选取鲜切苹果 10 个，用色差计（Model CR-300，Minolta，Tokyo，Japan）苹果表面的颜色（CIE L*、a*、b*），测定前以标准白度（L* =97.06，a* =0.04，b* =2.01）对色差计进行校准。其中，L*表示光亮度值（数值 0 ~ 100），a*表示红（+a）绿（-a）色值，b 表示黄（+b）蓝（-b）色值。由测得的结果计算 C*、H*值。

$$C = \tan - 1\left(\frac{b^*}{a^*}\right) \quad H = \sqrt{a^{*2} + b^{*2}}$$

实验中观察到，果实采摘时，对照果已接近于完全转红，采前 8d 处理也已经接近于全部转红，a 值显示与对照没有显著性差异。而采前 12d 处理和采前 12d 及 8d 处理则显著的抑制了果实转红，a 值显示有明显差异（P <0.05）。C 值也表现出相同的规律。采前 8d 喷施 1 次不会影响果实的转红。这与观察到的事实是一致的。常温放置 5d 后，各处理组果实颜色没有显著变化。

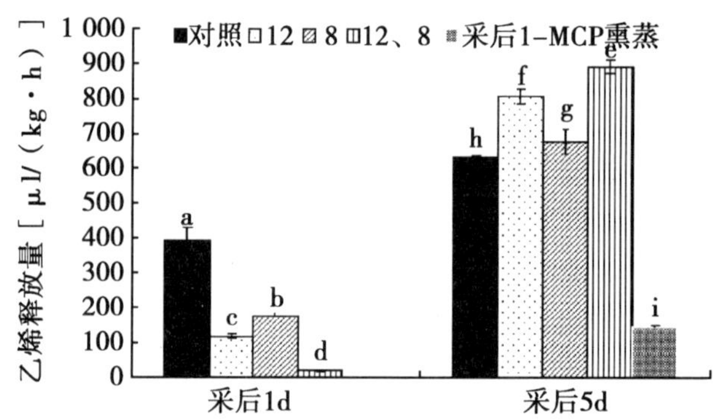

图 2 1-MCP 处理对泰山早霞苹果乙烯释放量的影响

3.2 1-MCP 处理对泰山早霞苹果乙烯释放量的影响

已知研究表明，1-MCP 可显著抑制和减少果实乙烯的合成，延迟果实乙烯高峰的出现[12~14]。SPSS 数据分析知，采摘 1d 测定时，对照与各处理组之间差异性显著，处理果乙烯释放量明显小于对照果。两次喷施乙烯释放量最小，其次为采前 12d 喷施，而采前 8d 处理，乙烯释放量则要高于采前 12d 及两次喷施。常温放置 5d 后，喷施处理乙烯释放量大于采前对照组，但小于采后熏蒸对照组，从数据分析知，采前喷施处理在一定程度上很好的控制了乙烯释放，明显的抑制了乙烯的生成，与采前对照及喷施处理差异性显著（图中不同的小写字母代表差异显著，P <0.05）。

3.3 1-MCP 处理对泰山早霞苹果硬度的影响

采后 1d 测定时，对照果实硬度明显低于喷洒处理，对照与各处理组之间差异性显著；处理组间，采前 8d 喷施硬度明显低于采前 12d 及两次喷施处理。常温放置 5d 后，采前对照苹果硬度显著降低，绵化严重；采前对照与采前 12d 及二次喷施处理有明显差异。处理组硬度仍然明显小于采后熏蒸处理，且差异性显著。而此时硬度比较与采后 1d 测定时，较好的保持果实的硬度（图中不同的小写字母代表差异显著，P <0.05）。

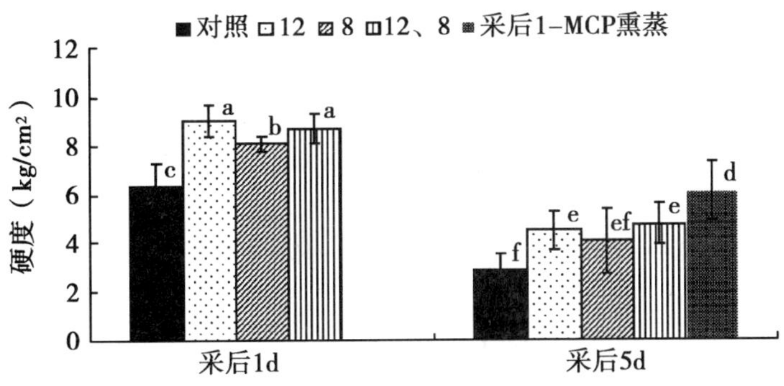

图3 1-MCP 对泰山早霞苹果硬度的影响

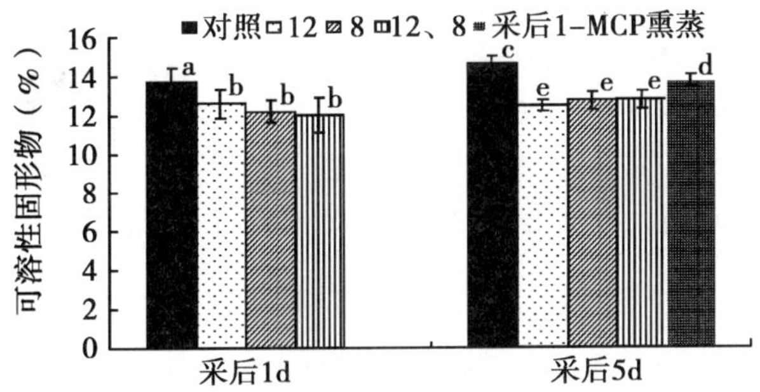

图4 1-MCP 处理对泰山早霞苹果可溶性固形物含量的影响

3.4 1-MCP 处理对泰山早霞苹果可溶性固形物的影响

由测定数据及数据分析知，采后 1d 测定时，采前对照可溶性固形物含量最高，与喷洒处理差异性显著；而处理组间差异性不显著。常温放置 5d 后，采前对照可溶性固形物升高，与处理组之间有明显的差异（$P<0.05$）；喷施处理组之间差异性不明显；喷施处理组可溶性固形物含量低于采后熏蒸处理，差异性显著（图中不同的小写字母代表差异显著，$P<0.05$）。

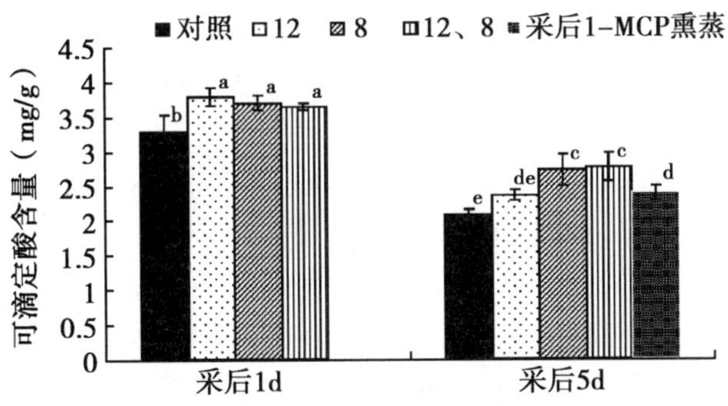

图5 1-MCP 处理对泰山早霞苹果可滴定酸含量的影响

3.5 1-MCP 处理对泰山早霞苹果可滴定酸的影响

大量试验结果说明，果实的可滴定酸（TA）含量随着贮藏和货架期的延长逐渐降低[15~17]。从图中及分析数据知，采后 1d 测定时，喷洒处理组可滴定酸含量明显高于采前对照处理；对照与处理组差异性显著，而喷洒处理之间差异性不显著。常温放置 5d 后，采前对照可滴定酸含量最低，仅和 12d 喷洒 1 次没有明显差异（图中不同的小写字母代表差异显著，$P<0.05$）。

4 结论

采前 1-MCP 喷施需要选择确定适宜的时间和次数，使用较早会影响果实后期膨大和着色。采前 8d 进行 1-MCP 溶液喷施处理，对果实着色及单果重影响较小；果实在常温放置 5d 后，没有出现腐烂，与对照较好的保持了果实品质，货架期也较长，但处理效果明显不如采后熏蒸。通过进一步研究后，在一定程度上可代替采后熏蒸处理。而采前 12d 及连续两次处理很大程度上抑制了果实的成熟，不适合在实际生产中应用。

参 考 文 献

[1] 陈学森，辛培刚. 极早熟苹果新品种“泰山早霞” [J] 园艺学报. 2008. 35 (1)：148

[2] Sisler E C, Serek M. Inhibition of ethylene responses by 1-Methylcyclopropene and 3-Methylcyclopropene [J]. Plant Growth Regulation, 1999, 27 (2)：105-111

[3] Jiang Yueming, Joyce D C, Macnish A J. Extension of the shelf life of banana fruit by 1-Methylcyclopropene in combination with polyethylene bags [J]. Postharvest Biology and Technology, 1999, 16：187-193

[4] Sisler EC. Serek M . Inhibitors of ethylene responses in plants at the receptor level：recent developments 1997 (03)

[5] 韩冬芳，马书尚，王鹰. 1-MCP 对新红星苹果乙烯代谢和贮藏品质的影响 [J] 园艺学报. 2003 (01)

[6] 苏小军，蒋跃明，张昭琪. 1-甲基环丙烯对低温贮藏的香蕉果实后熟的影响 [J] 植物生理学通讯. 2003 (05)

[7] Golding J B Application of 1-MCP and propylene to identify ethylene-dependent ripening processes in mature banana fruit 1998 (01)

[8] 李正国. EI-Sharkawy I. Lelieve J M. 温度、丙烯和 1-MCP 对西洋梨果实乙烯合成和乙烯受体 ETR1 同源基因表达的影响 [J]. 园艺学报. 2000 (05)

[9] 孙希生，王志华，李志强. 1-MCP 对番茄采后生理效应的影响 [J]. 中国农业科学. 2003 (11)

[10] Jiang Y M. Joyce D C. Terry L A 1-MCP treatment affects strawberry fruit decay 2001 (23)

[11] Porat R. Weiss B. Cohen L Effects of ethylene and 1-methlcyclopropene on the postharvest quality of " shamouti" oranges 1999 (02)

[12] Fan X T, Mattheis J P, Blankenship S. Development of apple superficial scald, soft scald, core flush, and greasiness is reduced by MCP [J] -J A Food Chem, 1999, 47 (8): 3063 -3068

[13] Fan X T, Mattheis J P. Impact of 1-methylcyclopropone and methyl jasmonate on apple volatile production [J]. J A Food Chem, 1999, 47 (7): 2847 -2853

[14] Song J, Tian M S, Dilley D R, et o1. Efect of 1-MCP on fruit ripening and volatile production [J]. Hort Sci, 1997: 32: 536

[15] 孙希生，王文辉，李志强. 1-MCP 对新红星苹果保鲜效果的影响 [A] 中国园艺学会第九届学术年会论文集 [C]. 北京：中国科学技术出版社，2001: 51 -55

[16] 孙希生，王文辉，李志强. 1-MCP 对砀山酥梨保鲜效果的影响 [J] 保鲜与加工，2001，1 (6): 14 -17

[17] 郭燕，马书尚，朱玉涵等. 1-MCP 对不同成熟度粉红女士苹果贮藏生理和品质的影响 [J] 果树学报，2007: 415 -418

Effects of Pre-harvest 1-MCP Spray on Postharvest Quality of Taishan Zaoxia Apple

LI Hong-zhen WANG Qing-guo

(*College of Food Science and Engineering*, *Shandong Agriculture University*, *Taian* 271018)

Abstract: Taishan Zaoxia is an extra early mature apple cultivar with characteristics of good appearance, delicious flavour, good quality, early fructification and high productivity, but its postharvest shelf life is very short. It will become mealy after 4 ~5 days at normal temperature (measured by hardness), which can obviously decrease its commercial value. This paper investigated the effect of pre-harvest 1-MCP spray on inhibiting postharvest mealiness and prolonging shelf life of Taishan Zaoxia apple. The results showed that 1 - MCP sprayed 8 days before harvest did not affect coloring of the fruit . During shelf life, significantly inhibited the decrease in fruit firmness and delay the release of ethelene, delayed titratable acidity and soluble solids increased. Spray before harvest is feasible, but its effect needs to be improved by choosing optimum spray time.

Key words: Taishan Zaoxia; 1-MCP; Meal

山药切割生理生化特性研究

范文广① 王庆国
（山东农业大学食品科学与工程学院，泰安 271018）

摘 要：本文以新鲜山药为试验材料，对不同品种的山药在贮藏过程中的生理生化特性进行了研究。结果表明，贮藏过程中各种山药褐变程度变大；切割后出现两个呼吸高峰；多酚氧化酶出现先上升后下降的趋势，过氧化物酶是逐渐上升的趋势，苯丙氨酸解氨酶呈现上升趋势，其中，毛山药和当地山药上升趋势比较明显。从综合考虑，毛山药适合鲜切贮存。

关键词：山药；鲜切；生理生化

山药为薯蓣科薯蓣属植物，原产亚洲、西非和南非等地区。在我国方、西北、西南等地区种植普遍[1]。目前，国内较为常见的品种有怀山药山药、土山药[2]。山药中含有大量蛋白质、各种维生素和有益的微元素、黏质多糖等，是营养价值很高的食品[3]。此外，山药还含有尿囊、山药素、皂苷、胆碱等药用成分健脾胃、补肺、固肾、益精等功效有强身健体及医疗保健作用[4~5]但山药鲜切后易于腐烂，品质下降较快，特别容易褐变，本研究主要对山药鲜切后与其褐变及耐贮性有关的生理生化性质进行了分析，并比较了不同品种的山药在贮藏过程中生理生化特性。

1 材料与方法

1.1 材料

试验选用4个品种：佛手山药（湖北武穴），花山药（山东潍坊），毛山药和牛腿山药（山东泰安），采收后选择无机械伤、病害的新鲜山药（保持完整的枝体）为实验材料，运回实验室，经浓度为200μl/L次氯酸钠水溶液（保持低温）清洗后，再用清水冲洗并吸干表面水分，装于干净的聚乙烯袋中，于2~3℃冷库中放置备用。

1.2 仪器与设备

Beckman Allegra 64R高速冷冻离心机（美国BECKMAN公司）、UV-2000分光光度

---

① 范文广，男，山东农业大学食品科学与工程学院硕士研究生。研究方向：果蔬采后生理与贮藏。E-mail：fanwenguang_ 88@163. com

计（海尤尼柯仪器有限公司）、超级恒温水浴锅（常州国华电器有限公司）。

1.3 实验方法

1.3.1 处理

将原料从冷库中取出，用不锈钢刀切成厚5mm的薄片，迅速放入浓度为50μl/L次氯酸钠的水溶液中浸泡5min，离心脱水后，将切片平放入塑料筐中，并将切片同筐一起放入准备好的塑料箱内，放上层纱布，并放置一小风扇，保持表面相对干燥，1h后，装入PVC袋中，贴上标签，放入2~3℃的冷库中贮藏。

1.3.2 测定方法

1.3.2.1 呼吸强度：采用滴定法测定。

1.3.2.2 多酚氧化酶活性测定：采用吸光值法[6]测定。

1.3.2.3 过氧化物酶活性测定：采用吸光值法[6]测定。

1.3.2.4 苯丙氨酸解氨酶酶活性测定

取样品5.0g，加入20ml巯基乙醇缓冲液，研磨后用纱布过滤，滤液经12 000r/min，4℃条件下离心15min，上清液即为粗酶液。酶活性测定的反应体系包括：2ml缓冲液，2ml L-苯丙氨酸和1ml酶液，在37℃下反应1h后于290nm测定吸光值。以每分钟内A_{290}变化0.01为1个PAL酶活性单位（U）。

1.3.2.5 褐变度测定

取样品5g，用20ml乙醇（95%）浸提24h，在420nm下，测定吸光值，吸光值越大，褐变越厉害。

2 结果与分析

2.1 山药呼吸强度变化情况

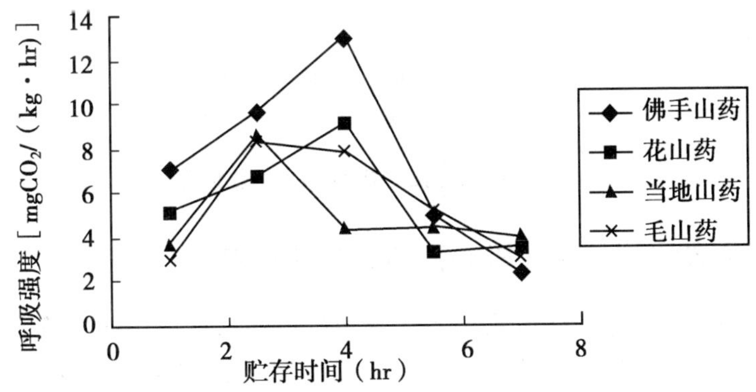

图1 山药贮藏过程中一天内的呼吸强度变化情况

2.1.1 一天内各种山药的呼吸强度

由图1可知，4种山在鲜切后都会出现一个呼吸高峰，佛手山药和花山药，大约在

4h 左右出现呼吸高峰；毛山药和当地山药在 2h 左右出现呼吸高峰。从图 1 上，可以看出佛手山药呼吸强度是 4 种山药中最大的。切分导致果蔬组织代谢加剧最明显的表现和特征是呼吸增强，伤呼吸增强，出现了第一次的呼吸高峰。

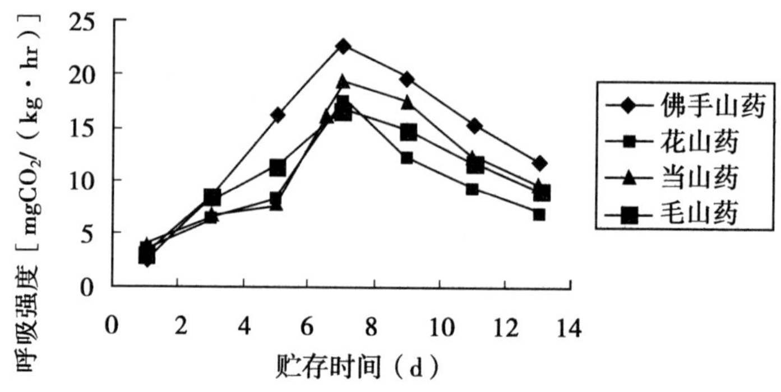

图 2 山药贮藏过程中呼吸强度变化情况

2.1.2 鲜切后各种山药的呼吸强度

由图 2 可以看出，4 种山药出现第二次呼吸高峰大约都在鲜切后 7d 左右，可以看出佛手山药的呼吸强度最大，而毛山药最小。鲜切山药在贮存过程中，出现了第二次呼吸高峰。

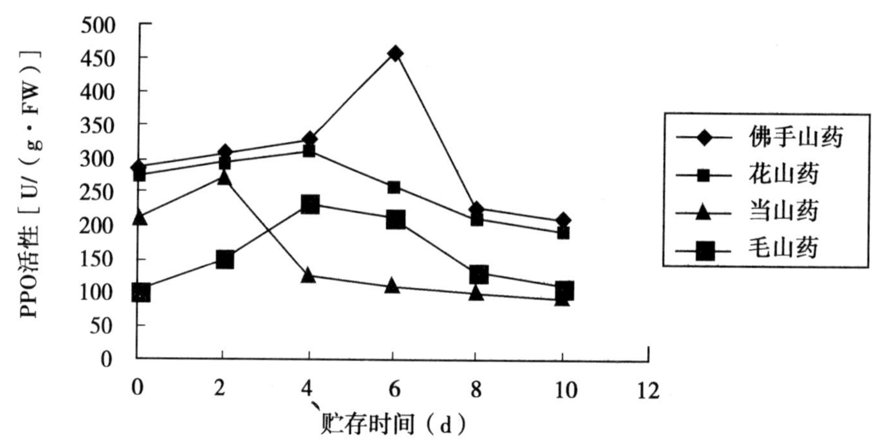

图 3 贮藏过程中 PPO 活性变化情况

2.2 山药多酚氧化酶（PPO）活性变化情况

贮藏过程中鲜切山药 PPO 活性变化情况如图 3 所示，由图可知，佛手山药和花山药在前期活性很大，逐渐升高。佛手山药活性在第 6d 时达到高峰；花山药在活性第 4d 时达到高峰；毛山药活性在鲜切初期，活性最低，在第 4d 时达到高峰；当地山药 PPO 活性在第 2d 时达到高峰。从整个过程看，佛手山药和花山药的 PPO 活性高于当地山药和毛山药。PPO 活性增加可能与切分胁迫导致新 PPO 的合成有关，也可能与切分促使结合态酶的释放有关，还有可能是切分导致 PPO 与酚底物区域化分布的打破促进了酶的活化[7]，其确切机理有待进一步研究。

2.3 山药过氧化物酶（POD）活性变化情况

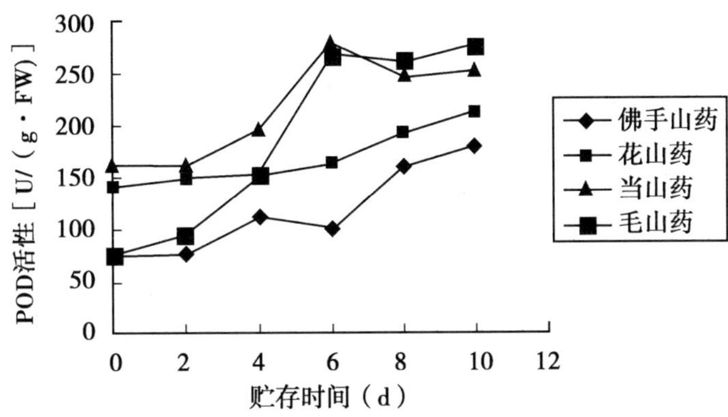

图4 贮藏过程中切割山药 POD 活性变化情况

由图4可知，POD 活性在贮藏前期变化较小，基本上呈现缓慢上升的趋势。随着贮藏时间的延长，到贮藏中期的时候，活性升高，4种山药趋势差不多。贮藏期间鲜切山药 POD 活力的增加可能与切分造成较多的伤口有关，因为研究表明机械伤可诱导 POD 活力的增加[8]，贮藏期间极高的 POD 活力可促进鲜切山药组织的褐变。

2.4 切割山药苯丙氨酸解氨酶（PAL）活性变化情况

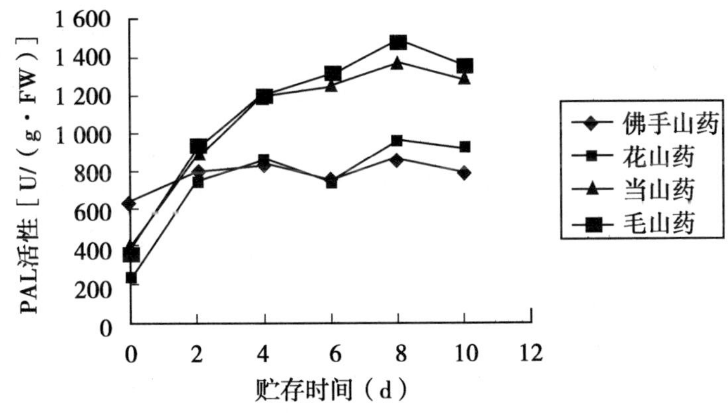

图5 贮藏过程中切割山药 PAL 活性变化情况

贮藏过程中切割山药 PAL 活性变化情况如图5所示，从图中可以看出，毛山药和当地山药变化趋势基本一致，PAL 活性一致升高，活性比较大，在8d 时达到最高，而后降低。佛手山药和花山药 PAL 活性稍微升高，变化趋势不大。报道指出 PAL 与酚的合成有密切关系，其活力大小可作为褐变发生潜力的指标[9]。

2.5 切割山药褐变情况

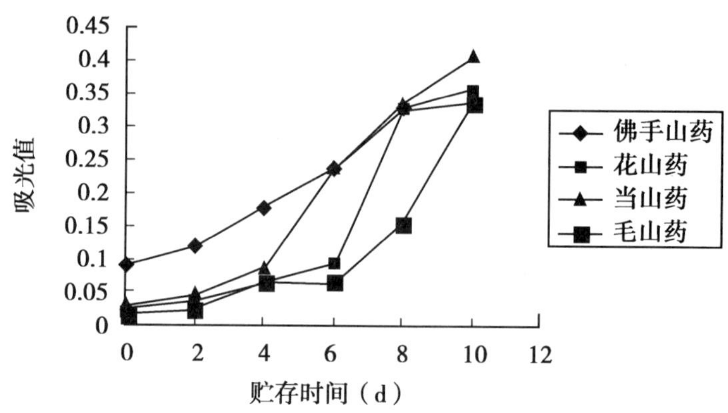

图6 贮藏过程中切割山药褐变情况

贮藏过程中山药褐变如图6所示，由图中看出4种山药的褐变度都是随着贮存时间的延长，而变大。佛手山药褐变度一直是最大的，毛山药褐变度是最小的。贮藏结束时都有加速趋势。

3 结论

有人研究认为，贮藏期间鲜切山药的呼吸的增强不是褐变发生的主要和直接原因，通过本文研究发现，褐变度和呼吸强度有一定的关系，呼吸强度越大的山药，褐变程度越大，分析可能是鲜切加速了物质的降解，活化了三羧酸循环和电子传递链[10]，加速了 O_2 的消耗，增加了 CO_2 的产生，呼吸产生的热能和生物能对褐变是否有作用还得进一步的研究。

山药经去皮、切分后褐变缓慢上升，后期呈加速上升趋势。鲜切山药贮藏后期褐变速度加快可能与鲜切山药组织衰老，导致细胞按室分工功能的破坏，酶与底物接触加速酚的氧化有关。

研究发现，山药经去皮、切分后很容易褐变，主要是因为山药组织中的多酚氧化酶（PPO）更容易将酚类底物氧化并进一步聚合生成有色物质而导致褐变[11]。POD的变化和褐变度的变化分析有相关性，表面POD活力与褐变关系密切，有研究表明切分后 O_2^- 的形成，诱导POD活力增加。PAL可以作为褐变的一个指标，经研究发现，毛山药和当地山药的PAL活性，上升比较迅速，而佛手山药和花山药上升比较缓慢，可能与山药内含有的酚量有关系，PAL活力的增加与褐变程度不呈正相关，期待进一步的研究。

参 考 文 献

[1] 黄泰康．常用中药成分与药理手册［M］．中国医药科技出版社，1999

[2] 谢宗万．中药材品种论述［M］．上海科技出版社，1984：193

[3] 丁赢．赵云岚，刘铁成等．山药穿山龙［M］．中国中医药出版社，2001

[4] 贡树铭．药食同源的枸杞和山药［J］．中医古文知识．2000（3）：16～17

[5] 姜德明．抗癌保健佳蔬——山药［J］．吉林蔬菜，2000（2）：40

[6] 李合生．植物生理生化试验原理和技术［M］．高等教育出版社，2000. 46～47

[7] Conn EE1Chemical conlugation and compartmentation: plant adaptation to toxic natural products [M] 1 In: Key TL, KosugeT1Cellular and Molecular Biology of Plant Stress1 New york: AlanR L iss, 1985, 1351～3651

[8] Mohan, R. P Vijayan, P E Kolattukudy. Developmental and tissue-specific expression of a tomato anionic peroxides gene by a minimal promoter, with wound and pathogen induction by an additional 5-flanking region [J]. Plant Mol. 1993, 22: 475～490

[9] Mateos, M., D. Ke, M. Cantwell, et al. Phenolic metabolism and ethanolic fermentation in intact and cut lettuce exposed to CO_2_ enriched atmosphere [J]. Postharvest biology and technology, 1993, (3): 22～1233

[10] Saltveit, M. E., R. F. Kasmire. Changes in respiration and composition of different Length asparagus spears during storage [J]. HortSci, 1985, 20: 1114～1116

[11] 李晓莉等．山药多酚氧化酶特性研究．精细化工．2005，22（7）：527～529

Studies of Biochemistry and Physiology of Yams After-Fresh cut

FAN Wen-guang WANG Qing-guo

(*College of Food Science and Engineering, Shandong Agricultural University, Tai'an* 271018))

Abstract: In this paper, biochemistry and physiology of various of yams after-harvest were investigated. The results showed that during storage, the extent of the browning was in a tendency to increase; two respiratory peaks appear after fresh-cut; change of Polyphenol oxidase activity of yams was tend to increase and then decrease during storage; change of Peroxidase was tendency to increase; change of Phenylalanine ammonia-lyase was tendency to increase tendency to increase, the trend of Mao yam and The local yam was obvious. Take all the factors into the account, the quality of Mao yam was best in the four of breeds to fresh-cut.

Key words: Yams; Freshcut; Physiological

根层水肥调控技术对设施番茄根系生长、产量及氮素淋洗的影响*

李俊良[1①] 张经纬[1] 王丽英[2,3] 金圣爱[1] 陈 清[2]

（1 青岛农业大学资源与环境学院，青岛 266109；
2 中国农业大学资源与环境学院，北京 100193；
3 河北省农林科学院农业资源环境研究所，石家庄 050051）

摘 要： 本文以寿光设施番茄生产体系为对象，研究了根层水肥调控技术（W_2F_S）和增加促根管理的根层综合调控技术（W_2F_R）对番茄产量、根系、氮素利用和土壤无机氮的影响。结果表明，设施番茄根层水肥调控技术与农民传统相比明显节水节肥，灌溉量减少29%，养分投入量$N-P_2O_5-K_2O$较传统施肥措施的施用量分别降低59%、23%、42%和79%、78%、48%；根层综合调控有助于促进番茄苗期的根系生长，分别比传统水肥（W_1F_S）、对照（W_2F_0）和根层水肥调控的（W_2F_S）总根长提高46%、42%、36%，根表面积增加36%、34%、46%，根系体积增加29%、28%、67%，根层综合调控显著提高了氮磷钾肥料的偏生产力（PFP），比传统施肥分别提高了4倍，3.7倍和0.98倍，提高肥料利用效率，降低氮素淋洗风险。

关键词： 水肥一体化；根层养分调控；根层综合调控；设施番茄；氮淋洗

我国是蔬菜生产大国，2008年，蔬菜种植面积17 875千hm^2，蔬菜总产量5.5亿t，分别占世界总量的41.7%和47.7%，其中设施蔬菜种植面积335万hm^2（2009年中国统计年鉴）。蔬菜栽培管理中灌溉与施肥是重要的农艺措施，施肥的增产贡献率达到37%以上。随着对蔬菜高产优质和环境友好的要求越来越高，加上农民对灌溉与施肥没有足够的重视，水分管理和施肥方式比较粗放，过量水肥供应导致根层养分浓度较高，不仅容易导致根系发育弱，分布浅[1,2]，同时，增加了环境污染的潜在风险，例如，土壤硝态氮积累与淋洗造成土壤和地下水的污染[3]，因此，加强对蔬菜生产过程中水分和养分管理，采用合理的水肥技术提高水分和养分利用效率，对于蔬菜产品的优质高产具有重要的意义[4,5,6]。

---

* 基金资助：公益性行业科研专项“最佳养分管理技术研究与应用（200803030），国家水专项（2008ZX07425－001）

① 李俊良，男，博士，教授，青岛农业大学资源与环境学院副院长。研究方向：蔬菜养分管理及水肥一体化研究。E－mail：jlli1962@163. com

近年来，国际上对于蔬菜氮肥推荐技术研究有了很大的发展[7]，但氮素控制方法都是基于农民习惯灌溉条件下根层优化施肥，例如，N-Expert 系统[8]和 KNS 系统[9]等，都是根据根层氮素平衡来调控氮素用量[10]，本研究在水肥一体化的前提下，以冬春茬设施番茄为研究对象，通过对根层水肥调控和根层综合调控对番茄产量、品质和土壤无机氮空间分布的影响，探索设施番茄水肥调控和根层养分管理技术，提高水分和养分利用效率，为实现设施蔬菜最佳养分管理提供依据。

1 材料与方法

1.1 试验设计

试验地点设在山东省寿光市古城街道办罗家村，该地点是典型的寿光市集约化设施番茄种植区。该日光温室为水泥柱和钢架结构，棚龄 10 年，灌溉井深 40m。供试作物为番茄（*Lycopersicum esculentum* Mill），品种为美粉宝石。种植方式为当地典型的栽培模式，一年两季番茄，即 2 ~ 6 月为冬春季、8 月至翌年 1 月为秋冬季，7 月份休闲，不揭棚膜。试验温室面积为 70m × 9m，共 50 畦。2009 年 1 月 24 日定植，平栽定植方式，大小行种植，畦面的畦长 8.2m，宽 1.4m，每畦 40 株。行间距为：株距 40cm，小行距 60cm，大行距 80cm，定植密度为：34 872 株/hm^2；土壤质地为粉质壤土，试验于 2009 年 1 月 18 日取 0 ~ 200cm 基础土壤样品，其基础理化性状见表 1。

表 1　土壤基础理化性状

土壤层次 (cm)	pH	有机质 (g/kg)	土壤无机氮 (mg/kg)	速效 P (mg/kg)	速效 K (mg/kg)
0 ~ 30	7.08	12.41	139.41	118	233
30 ~ 60	8.43	4.22	74.92	101	98
60 ~ 90	8.52	2.20	57.98	35.8	89
90 ~ 120	8.26	2.63	85.02	4.3	71
120 ~ 150	8.52	0.81	58.79	4.5	67
150 ~ 180	8.58	0.40	68.30	5.3	46

试验设置 4 个处理：（1）传统施肥 W_1F_C：菜农习惯灌水施肥处理，灌溉方式为畦灌；（2）对照 W_2F_0：膜下微灌，只施有机肥，不施化学氮肥；（3）根层水肥调控 W_2F_S：膜下微灌，灌溉制度与处理 2 相同；有机肥施入量和方式同处理 2；根据根层氮素实时监控技术，按照任涛研究[11]确定的冬春茬番茄关键需肥期追肥的氮肥推荐原则，在 3 月底和 4 月份追肥 4 次，每次 50kg N/hm^2；（4）根层综合调控 W_2F_R：苗期根际 N、P 养分启动液，结果期追肥 4 次，每次追肥根据氮素实时监控技术，有机肥用量为处理 2 的 50%；具体操作如下：养分启动液技术在番茄移栽后的生长早期注施养分启动液，移栽后第 20d 于番茄根部一侧（5 ~ 10cm）处注施含 170mg N 的启动液 50ml 及

海绿素 50ml（300 倍液）；移栽后 30d 注施 240mg N 的启动液 50ml 及海绿素 50ml（300 倍液）。养分启动液采用速溶性肥料，其氮磷钾（$N-P_2O_5-K_2O$）含量为 13－34－22。氮素管理采用氮素供应目标值，考虑环境养分数量，确定每次的根层氮素追施量。氮素供应目标值：冬春茬番茄在一、二、三穗果膨大期推荐的氮素目标值为 200 kg N/hm^2，第 4、5 穗果膨大期目标值为 150kg N/hm^2[10]（高兵等，2008）。处理 2、3、4 追肥时间及钾肥用量相同（表 2），钾肥每次追施 107 kg N/hm^2，追 4 次。由于土壤基础有效磷含量较高，底肥施用一定量的有机肥，除传统施肥外，处理 2、3 均不施磷肥，处理 4 根层综合调控技术在早期采样养分启动液技术注施少量磷肥作为启动肥料。氮肥用尿素、钾肥用硫酸钾。灌溉量采用定额灌溉的方法。

1.2 测定项目与方法

土壤无机氮测定：采集的鲜土样迅速带回实验室，过 4mm 筛，用 1mol/L KCl 溶液浸提（水：土＝12：100ml），振荡 1h，过滤，用流动分析仪（型号：TRAACS2000）测定滤液中无机氮含量，同时用烘干法测定土壤含水量。

采用硝酸盐试纸条——反射仪方法速测 0.01mol/L $CaCl_2$ 土壤浸提液中 NO_3^-－N 浓度，计算根层土壤硝态氮含量；速测灌溉水中硝酸盐含量，结合灌溉量计算每次灌溉带入的氮量。

氮肥推荐方法：在每次追肥前取 0～30cm 土，采用反射仪速测土壤硝态氮含量，根据氮素供应目标值，确定追施氮量，根据下式计算。

追施氮量＝推荐目标值－根层 NO_3^- －N—灌溉水带入氮素

根系样品采集与测定：番茄生长早期（注射启动液后 20d）以番茄植株为中轴沿行间和垂直行间两个方向，用内径为 8.5cm、高为 15cm 的根钻密集取样，根系样品用水冲洗后，用根系扫描分析仪扫描，测定根长、根表面积、根体积和根系平均直径参数。

产量：在试验小区的中间位置选取两行为测产区（40 株番茄），每次收获时将各计产小区内的果实单独称重、计产。

果实可溶性可溶性固形物的测定：在果实采收后期，于每个重复小区内随机选取 3～4 株番茄，每穗果实采摘成熟度一致 1 枚、榨汁，将果实汁液混匀后用糖分速测仪测定果实可溶性固形物含量（Bir%）。

数据分析：用 SAS（6.0 版）系统 ANOVA 进行数据方差分析。

2 结果与分析

2.1 水肥投入情况

番茄整个生育期灌溉 10 次，移栽时所有处理灌溉量为 60 mm，以后灌溉时传统处理每次的灌溉量是 45 mm，其他处理的每次灌溉量为 30 mm（表 2），在整个单季种植中，采用水肥一体化技术灌溉量为菜农传统灌水量的 71%，可节水 29%，从肥料用量来看，传统施肥措施，单季施肥量总量（$N-P_2O_5-K_2O$）达到（1 046－383－1 020）

kg/hm²，而采用根层水肥调控处理施用肥料总量是（430－293－589）kg/hm²，根层综合调控技术施肥总量为（215－84－533）kg/hm²，采用根层调控处理的化学肥料 N－P_2O_5－K_2O 养分用量较传统施肥措施的施用量分别降低 59%、23%、42%和 79%、78%、48%；可以看出，采用膜下微灌模式，结合根层养分调控和综合调控措施，可以大幅度减少化学肥料投入，但番茄产量差异不显著。

表 2 各处理的水肥投入情况

日期(2009 年)(月－日)	措施	施肥量(kg/hm²)N－P_2O_5－K_2O				灌溉量(mm)			
		W_1FC	W_2F0	W_2FS	W_2FR	W_1FC	W_2F0	W_2FS	W_2FR
1－18	干鸡粪均匀撒施后翻耕	299－121－209	230－93－161	230－93－161	115－46.5－80.5				
1－24	移栽水					60	60	60	60
2－13	养分启动液注射				5.9－15.5－10,海绿素 6L/hm²				
2－14	第 1 次灌水					45	30	30	30
2－25	养分启动液注射				8.4－22.0－14.2,海绿素 6L/hm²				
3－6	第 2 次灌溉					45	30	30	30
3－20	第 3 次灌溉,第 1 次追肥	139－70－139	0－0－107	50－50－107	15－0－107	45	30	30	30
3－30	第 4 次灌溉	96－32－32				45	30	30	30
4－10	第 5 次灌溉,第 2 次追肥	128－40－160	0－0－107	50－50－107	22－0－107	45	30	30	30
4－18	第 6 次灌溉,开始收获	128－40－160				45	30	30	30
4－31	第 7 次灌溉,第 3 次追肥	128－40－160	0－0－107	50－50－107	49－0－107	45	30	30	30
5－10	第 8 次灌溉,第 4 次追肥	128－40－160	0－0－107	50－50－107	0－0－107	45	30	30	30
5－19	第 9 次灌溉					45	30	30	30
6－4	拉秧	1 046－383－1 020	230－93－589	430－293－589	215－84－533	465	330	330	330

在整个单季种植中，采用水肥一体化技术灌溉量为菜农传统灌水量的 71%，可节水 29%，从肥料用量来看，传统施肥措施，单季施肥量总量 N－P_2O_5－K_2O 达 1 046－383－1 020kg/hm²，而采用根层水肥调控技术施肥总量是 430-293-589kg/hm²，根层综合调控技术施肥量仅为 215－84－533kg/hm²，采用调控技术处理的化学肥料 N－P_2O_5－K_2O 养分用量较传统施肥措施的施用量分别减少了 59%、23%、42%和 70%、15%、42%；可见，采用膜下微灌结合根层调控措施，可以有效减少化学肥料的投入，但可以保持产量不降。

2.2 根层调控技术对番茄早期根系生长的影响

表3 番茄生长早期不同处理的根系生长指标

	根长（cm）	根表面积（cm^2）	根平均直径（cm）	根体积（cm^3）
W_1Fc	3 840.24b	518.22b	0.36a	6.26b
W_2F0	4 230.61b	627.59b	0.39a	8.26ab
W_2FS	4 114.43b	615.21b	0.39a	8.22ab
W_2FR	6 019.00a	838.92a	0.39a	10.62a

1. 同一列带有相同字母表示不同处理的产量在0.05水平下差异不显著.

从定植到4月5日温室内0～15cm土壤温度一直在15～17℃，5月1日开始升到20℃以上（自动气象站监测数据）。该阶段是养分需求旺盛期和关键期，但根系活力较弱，因此，只有合理调控根层养分浓度，同时采取促根措施增加根系吸收面积和体积来提高养分吸收效率。采用养分启动液根际施用后第30d的番茄根系生长的结果表明（表3），根层综合调控处理（W_2F_R）的总根长分别比传统水肥（W_1F_S）、对照（W_2F_0）和根层水肥调控的根系（W_2F_S）增长46%、42%、36%，根表面积增加36%、34%、46%，根系体积增加29%、28%、67%，因此，根层综合调控有利于促进番茄早期的根系发育。此外，微灌处理在整体上根系发育好于传统处理，可见，水肥一体化技术也是一种根际调控的措施，促进植物根系生长。说明根层养分的有效性会影响根系的生长和养分吸收。为了加强养分的吸收，可以通过调节根际N、P浓度促进根系的生长[12]。养分启动液的施用有助于增加根际养分浓度梯度，特别在低温条件下，根系发育弱，高磷含量的养分启动液提高了番茄根系对低温胁迫的抵抗能力，同时提高了根际养分的生物有效性。因此，养分启动液技术既是调控根层养分浓度的策略又是一种可以实现促根的根层调控技术。

2.3 水肥调控对设施番茄不同采收期产量及果实品质的影响

番茄移栽较早，移栽后87d（DAT）开始进入采收期，每2～3d采收一次，到收获结束共采收26次。按照采收时间分成前、中、后三个阶段，各阶段番茄产量结果表明（表4），除根层水肥调控和综合调控处理的番茄前期产量高于对照，但与传统水肥处理差异不显著。从总产量结果看，根层水肥调控和综合调控处理与传统水肥管理的产量差异不显著，但从水肥投入量分析，施肥量和灌水量分别是喷灌区的3倍和1.4倍，可见微灌条件下的根层调控技术表现出保持产量不减的前提下，大幅度节约水肥资源。此外，各阶段产量和总产量的结果表明，根际养分综合调控在冬春季番茄生产中的效果显著，特别是生育早期，番茄根系较弱，但是地上部养分需求量大，使其根系养分吸收受到一定的限制，所以，在微灌模式下进行根层养分的局部调控，有利于提高根际养分供应浓度，促进根系发育，同时实现节水节肥，提高了水肥利用效率。

果实可溶性固形物含量是番茄品质的重要指标之一，根际综合调控处理提高了番茄果实中可溶性固形物含量（表4）。番茄的可溶性固形物含量与番茄可溶性糖、VC含量以及番茄红素含量密切相关，固形物含量高的果实耐储藏性要好。

表 4 根层调控对不同采收阶段设施番茄产量及品质的影响

处理	前期 4/25 ~ 5/5	中期 5/6 ~ 5/16	后期 5/17 至收获	总产量 (t/hm^2)	比对照增产 (%)	可溶性固形物含量 (%)
W_1F_C	42.3ab	40.2a	15.6a	98.1ab	2.6	5.2b
W_2F_0	41.0b	39.4a	15.2a	95.6b	—	5.1b
W_2F_S	42.7a	41.0a	15.2a	98.9ab	3.5	5.2b
W_2F_R	43.3a	41.5a	16.2a	101.0a	5.6	5.5a

1. 同一列带有相同字母表示不同处理的产量在 0.05 水平下差异不显著

2.4 根层土壤 Nmin 的动态变化和收获后土壤剖面中的 Nmin 残留

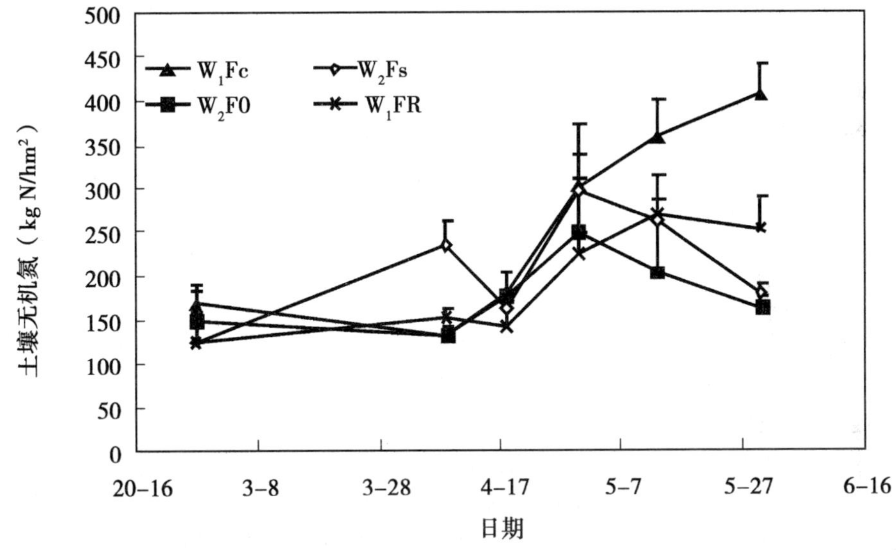

图 1 不同根层调控处理番茄生育期根层土壤无机氮的动态变化

番茄生育期根层土壤无机氮素的动态变化结果表明（图 1），定植后到 4 月 17 日以前，根层水肥调控和根层综合调控两个处理的根层土壤无机氮含量保持在 160 ~ 200kgN/hm^2之间，与推荐的氮素供应目标值基本一致，但农民传统施肥和对照不施氮肥两个处理的根层土壤无机氮含量较低，在 130kgN/hm^2左右，原因是农民传统处理的采用传统大水沟灌的模式，定植后的 4 次灌溉水为 160mm，优化和对照处理的小管出流灌溉量为 120mm，因此，农民传统灌溉多灌 60mm 的水，增加了对根层土壤氮素的淋洗。结果期 6 次追肥，使根层土壤无机氮呈逐渐增加的趋势，整个结果期保持在 300 ~ 400kgN/hm^2 的残留，氮素淋洗的风险很大；根层综合调控处理对土壤无机氮含量的影响不大，结果期土壤 Nmin 一直保持在 150 ~ 250kgN/hm^2 之间，收获后的 Nmin 残留在 250kg N/hm^2，与农民传统施肥相比，氮素淋洗的风险明显降低。可见，根层综合调控技术在高产和养分高效利用方面具有很大的潜力。

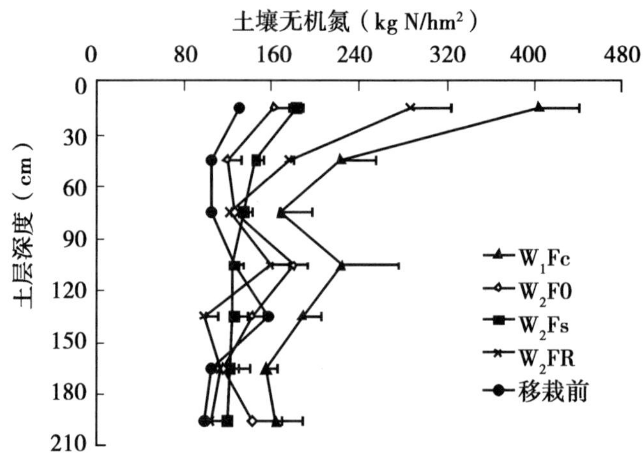

图 2　不同水肥调控处理对番茄收获后土壤剖面无机氮残留量的影响

收获后，各处理 0 ~ 200cm 土层土壤 Nmin 残留含量结果（图 1）表明，农民传统施肥 0 ~ 210cm 土壤无机氮含量均比移栽前有所增加，大水和高氮投入的根层养分供应强度不高，而且大水容易使氮素向下层土壤淋洗。在 0 ~ 90cm 土层内所有处理土壤无机态氮的含量是随着土层加深而在减少，且各层各处理土壤无机态含量均高于移栽前；90 ~ 120cm 土层各处理土壤无机态氮含量仍高于移栽前，说明经过一季的番茄栽培，土壤无机态氮有盈余，下季栽培仍有节肥潜力，而传统施肥处理土壤无机态氮素含量几乎在所有层次（至 210cm）都是最高的，所以相对农民传统的施肥其节肥潜力更大。总体上，随着 N 投入水平的增加，无机氮淋洗状况逐渐加剧；其中，农民传统处理（W_1Fc）土壤中无机氮残留量要明显高于水肥处理（W_2F_0、W_2Fs、W_2F_R）。在 90 ~ 200cm 土层内，微灌处理与移栽前的无机氮含量并没有明显差异，说明硝酸盐并没有向深层淋失，但是传统水肥管理的处理在 0 ~ 200cm 产生明显的硝酸盐积累；在 120 ~ 200cm 土壤中，根层综合调控处理的土壤无机氮含量低于移栽前，因此，根层综合调控整个生育期追肥很少的氮肥，在保证根层氮素供应的同时，较好的根系生长提高了土壤氮素的有效性，减少无机氮的淋失[9]。

2.5　节水节肥效果及经济效益评价

日光温室蔬菜生产具有明显的季节性，因此，不同季节的产品价格也受生产季节的影响。早春由于低温果类蔬菜生长慢，果实收获量小，加上寿光的番茄有很大一部分出口，在采收前期，番茄市场价格高达到 4.4 元/kg，平均价格 3.6 元/kg。从表 5 可以看出，膜下微灌区的总利润要显著高于传统处理，虽然膜下微灌区的灌溉设备费用和电费要高于漫灌区，但是膜下微灌节水节肥，使得每 667m^2 地总利润（以处理四为例）高出漫灌区大约 5 400元，对于农户来说，一年可增加收入 21 600元（按一年两季，每户两棚为例）。另外，在劳动力成本上，水肥一体模式下可以大量降低农民劳动力成本，提高劳动效率；以肥料偏生产力的结果表明，采用水肥一体化模式下，根层调控显著提高的养分的偏生产力。传统模式下肥料的偏生产力分别为 94kg/kg N，256kg/kg P_2O_5，

96kg/kg K_2O，根层综合调控处理的肥料偏生产力为 470kg/kg N，1 204kg/kg P_2O_5，190kg/kg K_2O，分别提高了 4 倍，3.7 倍和 0.98 倍。

表 5 根层调控技术的肥料偏生产力和经济效益

处理	产量 (t/hm^2)	肥料投入 (kg/hm^2) ($N-P_2O_5-K_2O$)	养分偏生产力 (PFP) (kg/kg)	产值 (万元/hm^2)	技术成本 (元)	利润 (万元/hm^2)
W_1F_C	98.1	1 046 - 383 - 1 020	94 - 256 - 96	35.3	86 000	26.7
W_2F_0	95.6	230 - 93 - 589	415 - 1 028 - 162	34.4	19 031	32.5
W_2F_S	98.9	430 - 293 - 589	230 - 338 - 168	35.6	52 478	30.4
W_2F_R	101.1	215 - 84 - 533	470 - 1 204 - 190	36.4	15 040	34.9

注：单位养分 ($N-P_2O_5-K_2O$) 产量 = 产量/肥料投入 ($N-P_2O_5-K_2O$)

3 结论与讨论

本试验条件下，与农民传统模式相比，在保证产量的前提下，基于膜下微灌模式，采用根层水肥调控和根层综合调控可以大幅度地节水节肥。在冬春季温室番茄苗期的低温时期，采用根际注施养分启动液技术，既可以保证苗期养分供应，又显著促进番茄根系发育，提高了肥料的利用效率；根层水肥调控和促根综合调控技术是温室蔬菜最佳养分管理有效的技术措施，实现了水肥高效和环境友好的目标。

鉴于日光温室蔬菜水肥需求量高以及反季节栽培的特点，蔬菜生产中需要频繁的灌溉和施肥，有关蔬菜节水灌溉制度和相关技术研究较多[13]，施肥研究大多在农民传统灌溉条件下的试验研究，但在水肥一体化模式下的根层调控技术应用效果较差。水肥一体化可以有效的解决水肥供应协调的矛盾。试验结果表明，采取根层水肥调控（W_2F_S）的灌水量是传统灌溉量的71%，施肥量是传统的41%，根层综合（W_2F_R）的施肥量较根层水肥调控区（W_2F_S）减少50%，但是番茄产量没有差异，这说明在肥力较高的设施菜地，可以通过根际局部施肥和促根措施进一步降低施肥量，实现高产高效和环境友好。根际是植物、土壤、微生物相互作用的关键区域。通过调控根际过程可是实现对植物生长的影响，能够改善根系生长，增强养分的吸收[14]。在本实验中，通过对番茄生长早期的养分启动液促根技术，作物前期根系的调控措施，明显提高了番茄的根系发育，与 Ma Chin-hua and Manuel [15]的研究结果一致，对提高养分利用效率有重要意义。

土壤中硝酸盐淋失与施肥[16,17,18]和灌水[19]有密切关系，在实验中也可以看出，在大肥大水的情况下，土壤无机氮的淋失较为严重，根层综合调控处理较其他处理在土壤深层的无机氮含量要明显的较少，可以有效的减少氮素的淋失；由于该处理采用营养启动液技术（Starter Solution Technology，SST）[15]，理论上讲营养启动液技术可以有效地减少肥料的投入，增加作物的产量，减少土壤中肥料残留，并且使其养分更加利于被作物吸收[8]，但是，W_2F_S 与 W_2F_R 的产量相差并不大，植株长势也没有显著差异，但根层促根调控提高了根系生长，而且 W_2F_S 处理的果实可溶性固形物含量显著增加，可见，根际调控是有利于作物吸收积累有机物，可以提高果实品质。

参 考 文 献

[1] 张福锁等．根际生态学过程与调控 [M]，中国农业大学出版社．2009：162 ~ 163

[2] Zhang，M.，A. K. Alva，Y. C. Li and D. V. Calvert. Root distribution of grapefruit trees under dry granular broadcast vs. fertigation method. Plant and Soil，1996，183：79 ~ 84

[3] 周艺敏，任顺荣，王正祥．氮素化肥对蔬菜硝酸盐积累的影响 [J]．华北农学报，1989，4 (1)：110 ~ 115

[4] 庄舜尧，孙秀廷．肥料氮在蔬菜中的去向及平衡 [J]．土壤，1997，2：80 ~ 83

[5] Parris K. Agricultural nutrient balances as agri-environmental indicators：An OECD perspective [J]．Environ. Poll.，1998，102：219 ~ 251

[6] Chen Q，Zhang X S，Zhang H Y et al. Evaluation of current fertilizer practice and soil fertility in vegetable production in the Beijing region [J]. Nutr. Cycl. Agroecosyst. 2004，69：51 ~ 581

[7] 陈清，张宏彦，李晓林．德国蔬菜生产的氮肥推荐系统．中国蔬菜，2000 (6)：55-57

[8] 陈清，张宏彦，张晓显等．N-Expert 专家系统在无公害菠菜生产中的应用 [J]．华北农学报，2002，17 (4)：128 ~ 134

[9] Lorenz，H. P.，J. Schlaghecken，G. Engl，A. Maync and J. Zegler. Ordnungsgemäße Stickstoff - Versorgung imFreiland Gemüsebau -KNS system. Rheinland Phalz：Ministerium Fur Landwritschaf，Weinbau und Forsten，1989

[10] 高兵，任涛，李俊良等．灌溉策略及氮肥施用对设施番茄产量及氮素利用的影响 [J]．植物营养与肥料报．2008，14 (6)：1104 ~ 1109.

[11] 任涛．设施番茄生产体系氮素优化管理的农学及环境效应分析 [M]．中国农业大学硕士论文，2007，北京

[12] Scherer，H. W. Ahrens，G. Depletion of non-exchangeable NH_4-N in the soil-root interface in relation to clay mineral composition and plant species. *European Journal of Agronomy* 1996 (5)：1 ~ 7

[13] 郭文忠，陈青云，高丽红等．设施蔬菜生产节水灌溉制度研究现状及发展趋势 [J]．农业工程学报. 2005，21 (S)：24 ~ 27

[14] Römheld，V. & Neumann，G. 2006. The Rhizosphere：Contributions of the soil-Root Interface to Sustainable Soil Systems. In：Uphoff，N. et al. (ed.) Biological Approaches to Sustainable Soil Systems. CRC Press，Boca Raton，FL. P：91 ~ 107

[15] Ma Chin-hua and Manuel C. Fertility Management of the Soil-rhizosphere System for Efficient Fertilizer use in Vegetable Production. Palada. Avrdc - the World Vegetable Center. 2006

[16] 王朝辉，李生秀，田霄鸿．不同氮肥用量对蔬菜硝态氮累积的影响 [J]．植物营养与肥料学报，1998，4 (1)：22 ~ 28

[17] 张维理．我国北方农用氮肥造成地下水硝酸盐污染的调查 [J]．植物营养与肥料

学报，1995，1（2）：80～87

[18] 沈明珠，翟宝杰，车惠茹．不同蔬菜硝酸盐和亚硝酸盐含量分析［J］．园艺学报，1982（4）：41～47

[19] 汤丽玲，陈清，张宏彦等．不同灌溉与施氮措施对露地菜田土壤无机氮残留的影响［J］．植物营养与肥料学报，2002，8（3）：282～287

Effect of Water and Fertilizer Management in Root Zone on the Tomato Root Growth , Yield, and Soil Nitrogen Leaching

LI Jun-liang[1] ZHANG Jing-wei[1] WANG Li-ying[2,3] JIN Sheng-ai[1] CHEN Qing[2]

(1 *College of resources and environment sciences*, *Qingdao Agricultural University*, *Qingdao* 266109; 2 *College of resources and environment sciences*, *China Agricultural University*, *Beijing* 100193, *China*; 3 *Agricultural resources and environment institute*, *Hebei academy of agriculture and forestry science*, *Shijiazhuang* 050051)

Abstract: The technology of water and fertilizer management by micro-irrigation system was conducted in Shouguang greenhouse. It showed that the application amount of water and fertilizer was reduced much more than farmer' s conventional management. The amount of irrigation water was reduced by 29%. The amount of fertilizer ($N-P_2O_5-K_2O$) with optimal water and nutrient management technology and integrated nutrient management in root zone was decreased by 59%, 23%, 42% and 79%, 78%, 48% to maintain yield and quality of tomato. Root zone integrated management improved root growth and development, the root length increased 46%、42%、36%, root surface increased 36%、34%、46% and root volume increased 29%、28%、67%. The partial productivity of fertilizer ($N-P_2O_5-K_2O$) increased 4, 3.7and 0.98 folders with root zone integrated management than conventional management. Water and fertilizer management technology reduced the Nmin residue in root zone soil and soil profile to decrease the risk of N leaching.

Key words: Fertigation; Nutrient management in root zone; Integrated management; Greenhouse tomato; Nitrate leaching.

山東省における野菜の栽培様式と生産の現状

薛彦斌[1①] 桝田正治[2] 村上賢治[2]
（1 維坊科技学院，山東寿光 262700；2 岡山大学，日本岡山 700）

摘 要： 山東省における野菜の栽培様式と生産の現状について調査した。山東省における野菜産業の発展状況、野菜の生産施設の特徴、野菜の四大集中生産区、地区別の野菜作付面積、主要野菜の分布と五大特色野菜を分析していた。
キーワード：野菜；栽培様式；作付面積；生産施設；日光温室

1 はじめに

山東省の略称は「魯」で、中国東部黄河の下流部に位置し、渤海、黄海の両海に接する半島が含まれるため、海岸線は約3 千キロにも達する。面積は約16 万平方キロで、日本国土の40%に相当する。道路、鉄道が発達し、加えて多くの海港と空港が存在する交通至便な地域である。人口は約9 417万人、17 個地級市（省の下級単位、県を管轄する）と140 個県級単位（地級市の下級単位、鎮、郷、街道を管轄し、そのうち、49 個区、31 個県級市、60 個県）があり、省都は済南である。農業人口は、年々減少する傾向にあり2008 年現在で5 860万人となっている（図1）。山東省は古くから中国を代表する農業地域として知られるばかりでなく、カリフォルニアやウクライナと共に世界の三大野菜地帯として知られている。本省の野菜は種類が多く、栽培品種は2 千余り、中国全土の「キッチンプロジェクト（菜藍子 読み方：チャイランズ Cailanzi、野菜の籠、即ち集中の野菜団地と供応基地という意味）」、基地の中でも重要な食料基地として位置付けられている。ここでは山東省における野菜の栽培様式と生産の現状を述べる。

2 山東省における野菜産業の発展状況

2.1 野菜作付面積、総生産量、総生産額

山東省の野菜作付面積、総生産量、総生産額は1991 年から2005 年まで15 年間全国の首位を占めていたが、2006 年、河南省が瓜類の作付面積を積極的に拡大し野菜の作

---

① 薛彦斌，男，博士，研究员，潍坊科技学院副院长。研究方向：农产品贮藏加工与农业产业化。E－mail：yanbin_ xue@ yahoo. com. cn

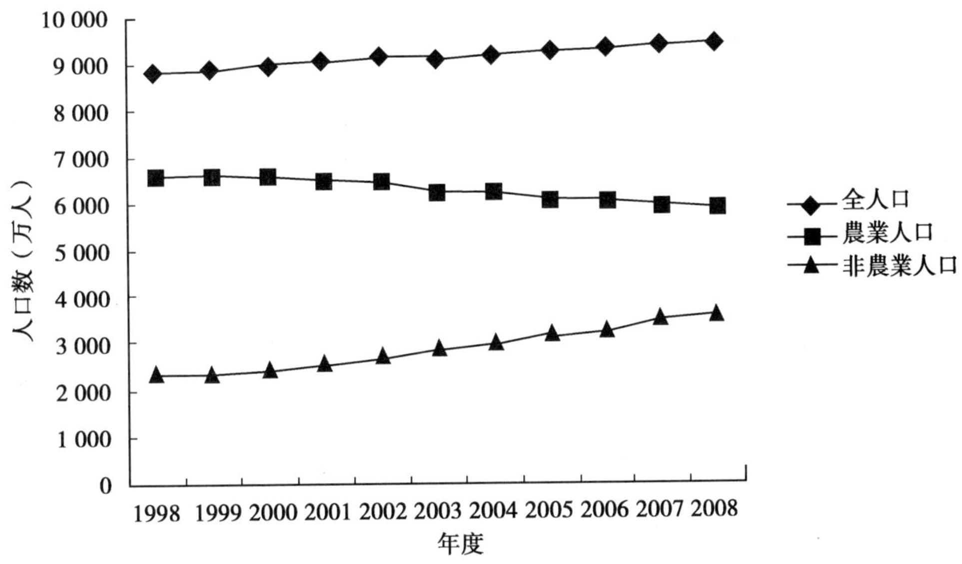

図1　山東省の住民構成

（山東省統計年鑑より）

付面積では山東省を抜き第一位となった。各省間の野菜生産規模と発展速度の差が拡大したものの、トップ5 省間の発展レベルはほぼ等しく、山東省は周辺の河南省、江蘇省、河北省、安徽省間との競争が激しくなりつつある。2008 年全国野菜作付面積が100 万 haを超えた省は9 個あり、上位 10 省の順位はほぼ固定し、交替的に並んでいるが、10 省で全国のほぼ65%、山東省は全国の約 10% を占めている（表 1）。

表 1　上位 10 省の野菜作付面積　（単位：千 hm^2）

順位	2006 年		2007 年		2008 年	
	省名	面積	省名	面積	省名	面積
1	河南	2 076	河南	2 015	河南	2 030
2	山東	2 006	山東	1 965	山東	1 983
3	江蘇	1 287	河北	1 179	江蘇	1 220
4	広東	1 233	江蘇	1 168	河北	1 204
5	四川	1 332	広東	1 110	広東	1 153
6	河北	1 231	湖南	1 108	四川	1 151
7	広西	1 212	四川	1 096	湖南	1 130
8	湖南	1 167	湖北	1 013	湖北	1 106
9	湖北	1 111	広西	1 001	広西	1 035
10	安徽	879	安徽	907	安徽	885

中華人民共和国農業部 2007 年、2008 年、2009 年「中国農業統計年鑑」より

表中のデータは瓜類（菜用瓜と果用瓜）を含む。菜用瓜はカボチャ、ペポカボチャ、キュウリ、トウガン、ニガウリ、ヘチマ、スカッシュなどを含む。果用瓜はスイカ、ネットメロン、マスクメロン、哈密瓜、白蘭瓜、クリスプメロンなどを含む

各省名称の読み方：河南（かなん）、山東（さんとう）、江蘇（こうそ）、広東（こうとう、カントンとも言う）、四川（しせん）、河北（かほく）、広西（こうさい）、湖南（こなん）、湖北（こほく）、安徽（あんき）

（同じ地名は何回も出てくるので、原則としてその新出のところだけに発音を示す）

野菜の生産量は、表2の示したように、山東省が全国第一位で、全国の約15%を占めている。面積と生産量が、河南と山東で入れ替わるのは山東省では施設野菜の割合が他省よりも圧倒的に高く、土地はほとんど2－3毛作であり、年間単位面積の収量が高くなるからである。同様に、東北地区の遼寧省は施設野菜の割合が高く、同省の作付面積は上位10省に入っていないが、生産量は上位8位に入り、作付面積9位の広西省が生産量では上位10省から脱落することになる。

表2　上位10省の野菜総生産量　　（単位：万トン）

順位	2006年		2007年		2008年	
	省名	面積	省名	面積	省名	面積
1	山東	9 564	山東	9 550	山東	9 852
2	河南	7 814	河南	7 661	河南	7 810
3	河北	7 131	河北	6 916	河北	7 163
4	江蘇	4 071	江蘇	3 735	江蘇	3 993
5	湖北	3 267	湖北	2 977	湖北	3 199
6	四川	3 083	湖南	2 966	四川	3 196
7	湖南	2 828	四川	2 823	湖南	2 886
8	広東	2 751	広東	2 458	遼寧	2 607
9	安徽	2 372	安徽	2 456	広東	2 529
10	遼寧	2 264	遼寧	2 399	安徽	2 443

中華人民共和国農業部2007年、2008年、2009年「中国農業統計年鑑」より
表中のデータは瓜類（菜用瓜と果用瓜）を含む
省名称の読み方：遼寧（りょうねい）

表には示していないが、生産額からみると、山東省は連続18年間安定して第1位の位置を堅持している。2008年の山東省野菜生産額は846億元であり、全国の5096億元の約17%に相当している。山東省に次いで河南省、江蘇省、広東省、河北省の4省が上位に位置している。

2.2　野菜生産の特徴—量拡張型から質向上型への転化

2003年と2004年は山東省野菜が数量拡張型から質量向上型への転化年であり、単位面積当たりの生産量と質の向上を追求している。1995年以来、作付面積と生産量は全国をリードし、作付面積は2003年に最大値236万haに達して、当年全国2031

万 haの約 12% を占めた。その後、徐々に減少し、近年 200 万 haのレベルを維持している。生産量は2004 年にピーク10206 万トンに達して、当年全国 60998 万トンの約 17% を占めた（図2）。転化の第一の要因は、20 年間にわたる発展を経て、全国の野菜総量が基本的に飽和に達して、国民平均野菜摂取量が459kg/年・人に達して、世界平均 140キロ/年・人を遙かに超え、世界平均の3. 3 倍になったこと。中国内では山東省は全国野菜生産と流通発展レベルの「風向計」と言われ、人類生存のための農業の初期段階を経過し、発展的現代農業への遷移段階に位置しているように考えられる。第二に、グローバル視角からみると、山東省は典型的な野菜輸出省であり、海外輸出の依存度が高く、2000 年から2003 年までの4 年間は、周知のように山東省をはじめ中国産輸出野菜の農薬残留問題が頻発し輸出産業は不安定となり、外向型の野菜産業の再拡大は阻害を受けこと。これに対して、他の省は外向型野菜が山東省より相対的に少なく影響は少なかったといえる。第三に、国民の食品安全意識、健康保持心理、消費の少量多様化志向も益々増強し、各級政府の検査も強化され、量より質を追求する傾向が高まったこと。

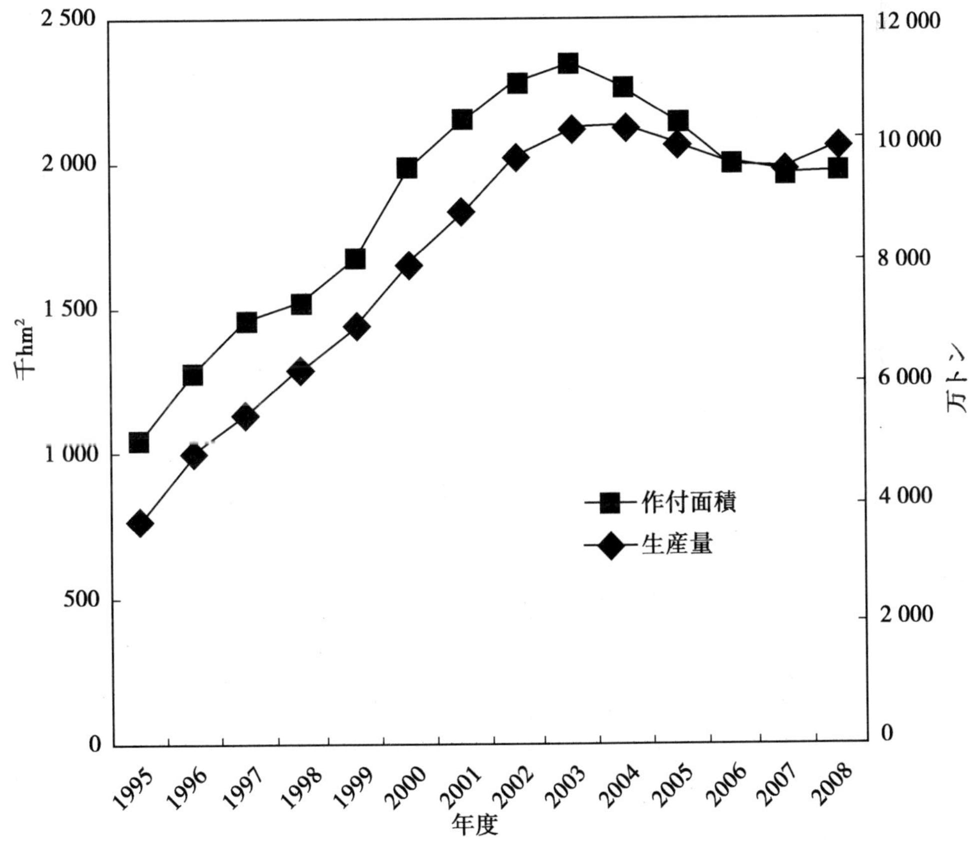

図 2　1995 年以来山東省野菜作付面積と生産量

山東省農業庁　データは2008 年年末まで（瓜類を含む）

3 山東省における野菜の生産施設の特徴

施設野菜の省別割合において山東省は全国一の位置を占めている。山東省2008年作付面積（瓜類を含む）は198万haであり、そのうち、施設面積は73万haに達している。施設では、日光温室（冬暖式大棚）が21万ha、弓円大棚は25万ha、中小弓棚は26万haであり（図3、図4、図5）、露地と施設の割合は63：37となっている。日光温室の栽培対象は果菜類であり、真冬から早春まで室外－10～20℃、無加温で栽培の威力を発揮している。弓円大棚と中小弓棚では出荷期間を端境期に延長して葉菜類、根菜類、瓜菜類を主として栽培している。日光温室の資金投入は大きく、10a当たり8.94～10.48万元を要しているが、収量が高く、キュウリとトマトは10a当たり4.5万キロと2.3万キロに達し、収入は10～11万元であり、当面は施設建設のコストは回収出来ている。

図3 中小弓棚の様子（弓は竹材）

4 山東省における野菜の四大集中生産区

山東省の野菜地域の分業と構造は20年の発展を経て基本的に形成され、56個の野菜大県は四つの集中生産区に分かれている（図6）。

4.1 日光温室による野菜集中生産区

「中国野菜の里」と言われた寿光市（じゅこうし）と維坊市（いぼうし）の他市県区を中心として、済青（さいせい）高速道路（済南と青島間の高速道路）沿線の11個県市区を指している。飛行機の上「銀色の海」と呼ばれる景色が見え、東西狭く長い平原地帯を貫通し、維坊市をはじめ、野菜施設栽培の隣接集中エリアとなり、県級市としての寿光市は日光温室40万個を有し、面積は5.33万ha、生産量は410万トンに達し、山東省の中核の野菜施設生産区となっている（図7、図8）。このエリアは主に維坊市所属の寿光市、昌楽市（しょうがくし）、青州市（せいしゅうし）、高密市（こうみつし）、安丘市（あんきゅうし）、諸城市（しょじょうし）など、緇博市（ツーポーし）所属の臨缁区（リンツーく）、張店区（ちょうてんく）、周村区（しゅうそんく）、垣台県（かきだいけん）など、済南市（さいなんし、チーナンしとも言う）所属の章丘市（しょうきゅうし）などである。野菜は果菜類、瓜菜類を主としているが、種子は海外のイスラエル、オランダ諸国からの優良な品種F1が圧倒的に多くなっている。

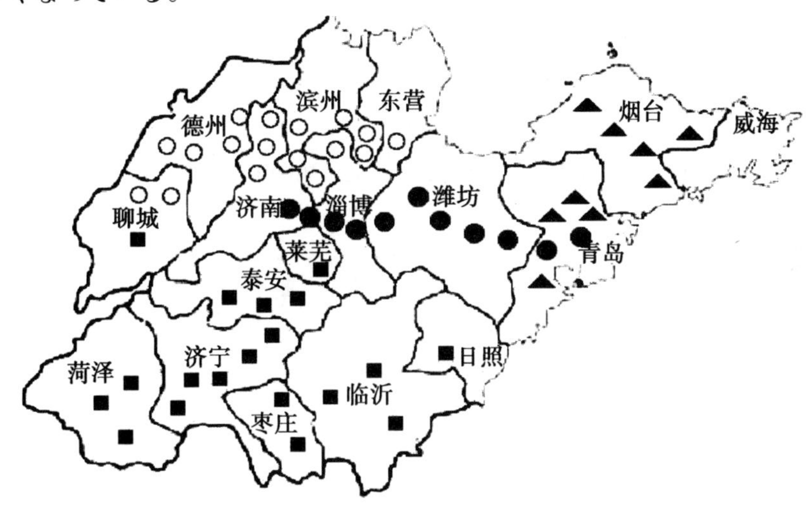

図4　山東野菜の四大集中生産区

●日光温室野菜集中生産区　▲露地野菜生産と加工輸出区

■名品・特品及び弓棚野菜集中生産区　○総合施設栽培及び露地野菜集中生産区

山東省各主要都市の読み方：済南（省都）ちいなん、さいなんとも言う、濰坊いぼう、淄博つーぼー、枣庄 つあおちょわん、東営 とんいん、煙台 いえんたい、済寧 ちーにん、泰安 たいあん、青島ちんたお、威海 うえいはい、日照りーちゃお、莱蕪 らいうー、臨沂 りんい、徳州 とーちょう、聊城 りゃおちょん、濱州 びんちょう、荷澤 おーつおー

4.2　野菜生産と加工輸出区

魯東（山東省の東部）の9個市県区であり、煙台市所属の莱陽市（らいようし）、海陽市（かいようし）、招遠市（しょうえんし）、莱州市（らいしゅうし）、竜口市（りゅうこう）など、青島市所属の即墨市（きぼくし）、膠州市（こうしゅうし）、膠南市（こうなんし）、平度市（へいどし）などである。野菜加工企業と工場が多く、日本、韓国への港口と空港にも近く、交通が便利である。種類は葉菜類、根菜類を主としている。莱陽市の野菜作付面積は2.8万ha、年間生産量は97万トン、

図5　「銀色の海」と呼ばれた寿光市の野菜大棚群
（夕刻にはワラのコモが下りる）

図6　寿光市における近年の自動巻き上げ機
（一部、厚手のシートに変わっているものもある）

野菜年間加工能力は42万トンに達している。野菜加工企業は325個、売上高10億元以上の企業は4個、竜大、魯花、天府、吉竜、春雪、恒潤などの野菜加工企業は有名であり、2008年全市の野菜（冷凍野菜、調理野菜食品）輸出金額は3.8億ドル、国内野菜加工品の販売も80億元に達している。

4.3　名品・特品及び弓棚野菜集中生産区

臨沂市、済寧市、莱蕪市、泰安市、日照市、荷澤市、枣庄市所属の14個市県区：蒼山県（そうさんけん）、金郷県（きんごうけん）、莘県（しんけん）、藤州市（とうしょうし)、沂南県（ぎなんけん)、岱岳区（だいかくく)、平原県（へいげんけん)、泗水県（しすいけん)、単県（たんけん)、陽谷県（ようかくけん)、冠県（かんけん)、肥城市（ひじょうし)、薛城区（せつじょうく)、成武県（せいぶけん）などである。名品？特品は主にニンニク、タマネギ、ショウガなどである。済寧市の金郷県はニンニク作付面積は1.3万ha、輸出量は全国の41%を占めている。

4.4　総合施設栽培及び露地野菜集中生産区

山東省北西部17個市県区であり、秋季遅延出荷、春季繰上出荷向け及び露地野菜、食用菌の集中生産区になっている。徳州市所属の陵県（りょうけん)、武城県（ぶじょうけん)、東営市所属の広饶県（こうじょうけん）などを含んでいる。

5　山東省における地区別の野菜作付面積

野菜の栽培面積の上位5位の市は維坊、済寧、徳州、荷澤、泰安であり、全省の約60%を占めている。特に、維坊市は遙かに全省をリードし、全省の約20%を占めている（表3)。寿光市（維坊市所属)、蒼山県（臨沂市所属)、金郷県（済寧市所属)、岱岳区（泰安市所属）は重点基地と供応大県となっている。

表3　地区別野菜作付面積　（単位：千 hm^2、2008年）

順位	地区名	作付面積	順位	地区名	作付面積
1	維坊	348	10	済南	85
2	済寧	247	11	煙台	79
3	徳州	225	12	莱蕪	48
4	荷澤	213	13	東営	41
5	泰安	176	14	缁博	38
6	臨沂	125	15	日照	25
7	聊城	103	16	威海	23
8	青島	100	17	枣庄	10
9	濱州	98	全省		1 984

山東省農業庁と各地級市農業局のデータにより整理

6　山東省における主要野菜の分布と五大特色野菜

山東省の140個県市区のいずれも野菜が生産でき、その中、25個の典型的特色を持つ野菜生産県市区を挙げる（図7)。

以上の産地のうち、最も有名な山東省特色野菜としては5品目ある（表4)

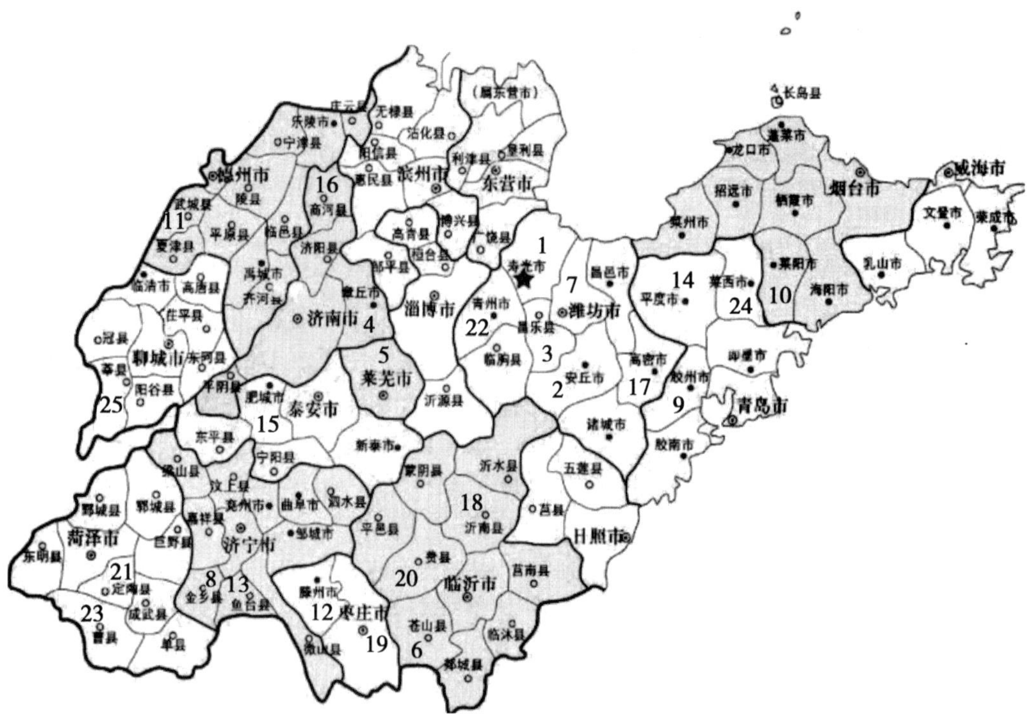

図7　山東省25個県市区の主要野菜分布

1. 寿光市 じゅこうし（維坊市いぼうし所属）　日光温室による果菜類（トマト、キュウリ、ナス、ピーマン）と露地のニンジン、ニラ
2. 安丘市 あんきゅうし（維坊市 いぼうし所属）　ショウガ、ゴボウ、ネギ
3. 昌楽県 しょうがくし（維坊市 いぼうし所属）　スイカ、メロン、ニガウリ
4. 章丘市 しょうきゅうし（済南市 さいなんし所属）　大ネギ、
5. 莱城区 らいじょうし（莱蕪市 ライウーし所属）　ショウガ、ネギ、ペッパー
6. 蒼山県 そうさんけん（臨沂市 りんぎし所属）　ニンニク、ゴボウ、ニンニクの苔
7. 維城区 いじょうく（維坊市 いぼうし所属）　維県ダイコン、
8. 金郷県 きんごうし（済寧市 チーニンし所属）　ニンニク、タマネギ、セロリ
9. 膠州市 こうしゅうし（青島市 チンタオし所属）　ハクサイ、トウガラシ、
10. 莱陽市 らいようし（煙台市 イエンタイし所属）　孤芋、魯芋、ホウレンソウ
11. 武城県 ぶじょうけん（徳州市 トーチョウし所属）　トウガラシ
12. 藤州市 とうしゅうし（枣庄市 ツアオチョワンし所属）　ジャガイモ
13. 魚台県 ぎょだいけん（済寧市 チーニンし所属）　レンコン
14. 平度市 へいどし（青島市 チンタオし所属）　セロリ　ニンニクの苔
15. 肥城市 ひじょうし（泰安市 タイアンし所属）　全国最大の有機野菜県（ブロッコリー、サヤエンドウ、オクラ、アスパラガス、ホウレンソウ、枝豆、グリーン豆、ニンジン）
16. 商河県 しょうかけん（済南市 さいなんし所属）　ホウレンソウ、ニンニク
17. 高密市 こうみつけん（維坊市 いぼうし所属）　トウガラシ、ニラ
18. 沂南県 ぎなんけん（臨沂市 りんぎし所属）　キュウリ
19. 峄城区 ほうじょうし（枣庄市 ツアオチョワンし所属）　インゲン豆
20. 費県 ひけん（臨沂市 りんぎし所属）　スカッシュ
21. 定陶県 ていとうけん（荷澤市 ホーツオーし所属）　ヤマイモ
22. 青州市 せいしゅうし（維坊市 いぼうし所属）　トウガラシ、銀ウリ
23. 曹県 そうけん（荷澤市 ホーツオーし所属）　アスパラガス
24. 莱西市 らいさいし（青島市 チンタオし所属）　メロン、ニンジン
25. 莘県 しんけん（聊城市 リャオチョンし所属）　マッシュルーム

表4 山東省の五大特色野菜

名称	区域構成	主要方向と発展目標	標準化示範基地建設
蒼山ニンニク	主に魯南地区の臨沂市の蒼山県、費県、済寧市の金郷県、嘉祥県（かしょうけん）、魚台県、枣庄市の藤州市、山亭区（さんていく）などに分布している	臨沂市の蒼山、済寧市の金郷県をニンニク基地とし、新品種を育成し、優秀企業によって周辺地区のニンニク産業の発展を推進する	選抜標準：品質が良く、収量が高く、輸出量が大きい優秀ニンニク 建設場所：臨沂市の蒼山県、済寧市の金郷県 建設目標：2010年に面積2万 hm^2、収量15万トン 建設内容と規模：有機ニンニク $333hm^2$、投資は500万元、建設期限は2006—2010年
莱蕪ショウガ	全省に広く分布し、主に莱蕪市の莱城区、泰安市の岱岳区、肥城市、寧陽県（ねいようけん）、枣庄市の藤州市、缁博市の缁川区（ツーセンく）、博山区（はくさんく）、沂源県（ぎげんけん）、維坊市の安丘市、諸城市などに分布している	新品種を育成し、病気抵抗能力を向上し、農薬残留を減少し、作付面積を拡大する。2010年に全省のショウガ面積は6.6万 hm^2 に達する。輸出割り合を拡大し、優秀な企業によって国際市場に進出する	選抜標準：ショウガ成長に適する中性、微酸性の肥沃土壌 建設場所：莱蕪市の莱城区 建設目標：2010年に面積1.3万 hm^2 建設内容と規模：無公害？緑色標準示範基地0.3万 hm^2 を新しく建設し、投資は2500万元、建設期限は2006—2008年
章丘大ネギ	主に済南市の章丘市、歴城区（れきじょうく）、泰安市の岱岳区、莱蕪市、缁博市の臨缁区、周村区、濱州市の邹平県（すうへいけん）などに分布している	済南市の章丘市を重点とし、2010年に面積は1.3万 hm^2。全部標準化栽培し、産品は緑色食品標準に達し、部分は有機食品標準に達する。大ネギぎの総収量は80万トン、年収は6億元、年加工能力は50万トン、生鮮大ネギ、ネギ油、乾燥ネギ及びその他シリーズ製品を形成し、全国最大のネギ製品産地加工中心を建設する	選抜標準：大ねぎ成長に適する中性、微酸性の肥沃土壌 建設場所：済南市の章丘市 建設目標：2010年に面積0.6万 hm^2 大ネギ標準化示範区を建設し、年産冨含セレン大ネギは40万トン。積極的大ネギ加工優秀企業を導入し、加工率は60%以上に達し、年間総産値は4億元を達成する
昌楽スイカ	主に維坊市の昌楽県、臨朐県（りんくつけん）の東部、安丘市の北部、青州市の東部、寿光市の南部などに分布している	新技術を採用し、座果率良くの「金鐘冠竜」、「邵陽花皮無籽」などの中早熟品種を選択する。工場化育苗を普及し、病虫害総合防止技術を実行し、無公害、無汚染スイカを生産する。2010年に作付面積0.6万 hm^2 に達する	選抜標準：維坊市の昌楽県にスイカ栽培に適する地区 建設場所：維坊市の昌楽県 建設目標：2010年に面積0.6万 hm^2 建設内容と規模：緑色大棚スイカは0.6万 hm^2 を新しく建設し、投資は20万元、建設期限は2007—2008年
維県ダイコン	主に維坊市の維城区（いじょうく）、寒亭区（かんていく）、昌楽県、青州市、臨朐県、安丘市などに分布している	2010年に緑色無公害基地は3.33万 hm^2 に増加する	選抜標準：軽粘性、肥水保持性良く、有機質、リン、カリウムなどの元素含量高い土壌に適する 建設場所：維坊市の維城区 建設目標：2010年に緑色無公害大根基地3.3万 hm^2 に新しく増加する 建設内容と規模：緑色無公害大根試験基地は0.3万 hm^2 を新しく建設する。投資は50万元であり、建設期限は2008—2009年

参 考 文 献

[1] 焦自高，何启伟，周绪元，潘子龍．山東省野菜の優勢生産区域の構造と産業の発展目標［J］．中国蔬菜．2007（4）：4～6
[2] 王志暁，趙凱，薛欧．山東省野菜の主生産区の農地流転の影響因子の実証分析［J］．山東農業大学学報．2010（4）：534～538
[3] 朱智強．山東省野菜産業発展の基本特性の分析［J］．北方園芸．2008（8）：222～223

Vegetable Cultivation modes and Production Status in the Shandong Province

Xue Yan-bin[1]　Masuda Masaharu[2]　Murakami Kenji[2]
（1 *Weifang University of Science and Technology*, *Shouguang*　262700；
2 *Okayama University* , *Okayama*　700）

Abstract: This paper has done a research on vegetable cultivation modes and its current production situation. It has also given a depth analysis of development of vegetable industry, vegetable production facility, four vegetable production areas and planting area of different vegetable cultivation place.

Key words: Vegetables; Cultivation modes; Planting area; Production facilities; Sunlight greenhouse

山東省における輸出・流通動向と日本向け野菜生産

薛彦斌[1] ①　桝田正治[2]　村上賢治[2]
（1 維坊科技学院，山東寿光　262700；2 岡山大学，日本岡山　700）

摘　要： 山東省における輸出・流通動向と日本向け野菜生産について調査した。中国に対する山東省の野菜輸出の位置、輸出量と輸出額、海外輸出向けの野菜重点基地県、日本への輸出野菜の加工エリア、日本への主な輸出野菜の種類と代表的品種、日本への主な輸出野菜の種類と代表的品種、近年の対日輸出の新動向を分析していた。
キーワード：輸出量；輸出額；輸出向け生産基地；輸出品目；輸出対象国

はじめに

中国山東省は最近、世界180余の国と野菜貿易関係を建立し、輸出市場も年々拡大している。日本への輸出量は年によりかなりの振幅があるものの、基本的に増加の一途をたどっている。輸出産品は生鮮品、乾燥品、冷凍品、缶詰及び調理加工品など多岐にわたる。ここでは、山東省における野菜輸出の現況と日本向け野菜の動向について述べる。

1　中国に対する山東省の野菜輸出の位置、輸出量と輸出額

山東省は中国一位の野菜輸出大省であり、野菜輸出量は2000年の100万トンから2008年の250万トンに増加し、全国の27%～36%を占めている（表1）。野菜輸出額は4億ドルから18億ドルに増加して全国の13%～27%を占めている（表2）。2008年上位6省の野菜輸出順位は山東、福建（ふくけん）、新彊（しんきょう）、浙江（せっこう）、江蘇、広東であり、山東省の野菜輸出額は遙かに他省を凌ぎ中国全体の3割を占めている（表3）。

① 薛彦斌，男，博士，研究员，潍坊科技学院副院长。研究方向：农产品贮藏加工与农业产业化研究。E－mail：yanbin_ xue@ yahoo. com. cn

表 1　山東省の野菜輸出量と割合　（単位：万トン，%）

年度	中国全土	山東省	割合	年度	中国全土	山東省	割合
2000	314	103	32.8	2005	680	245	36.0
2001	394	106	26.9	2006	749	235	31.4
2002	465	158	33.9	2007	817	294	35.9
2003	548	153	27.9	2008	859	254	29.6
2004	602	211	35.0	2009		未集計	

1. 山東省商務庁、山東省対外経済貿易合作庁、青島税関の各データにより総合整理作成
2. データはその種類の生鮮品、乾燥品、冷凍品、缶詰品及び調理加工品を含む

表 2　山東省の野菜輸出額と割合　（単位：億ドル，%）

年度	中国全土	山東省	割合	年度	中国全土	山東省	割合
2000	20.3	4.43	21.18	2005	44.8	13.00	29.01
2001	23.4	5.60	23.93	2006	49.3	16.70	33.87
2002	26.3	6.42	24.41	2007	53.8	16.19	30.09
2003	34.5	7.99	23.16	2008	58.1	18.06	31.08
2004	37.9	10.42	27.49	2009		未集計	

1. 山東省商務庁、山東省対外経済貿易合作庁、青島税関の各データにより総合整理作成
2. データはその種類の生鮮品、乾燥品、冷凍品、缶詰品及び調理加工品を含む

表 3　2008 年上位 6 省の野菜輸出額と全国の割合　（億ドル，%）

順位	省別	輸出額	全国の割合
1	山東	18.06	31.08
2	福建	10.92	18.80
3	新疆	4.81	8.29
4	浙江	4.20	7.22
5	江蘇	3.38	5.82
6	広東	2.98	5.13

1. 山東省商務庁、山東省対外経済貿易合作庁、青島税関の各データにより総合整理作成
2. データはその種類の生鮮品、乾燥品、冷凍品、缶詰品及び調理加工品を含む

2　海外輸出向けの野菜重点基地県*

中国農業部により確定された東南沿海輸出向け野菜重点区域のなかで山東省基地県は35 個あり、寿光市、昌楽県、青州市、高密市、安丘市、諸城市、肥城市、莱陽市、成武県、莱州市、金郷県、膠州市、膠南市、平度市、臨邑県（りんゆうけん）、東明県（とうめいけん）、莱城区、莱西市、曹県、藤州市、蒼山県、巨野県（きょの

けん)、広饶県、兖州市（えんしゅうし)、長清区（ちょうせいく)、岱岳区、河東区(かとうく)、博興県（はくこうけん)、郯城県（たんじょうけん)、楽陵市（らくりょうし)、牡丹区（ぼたんく)、武城県、夏津県（かつけん)、単県（たんけん)、即墨市を含んでいる. 日本への輸出向けの市県区は主に安丘市、諸城市、莱陽市、金郷県、膠州市、胶南市、平度市、蒼山県、長清区、莱城区、即墨市である

3　日本への輸出野菜の加工エリア

概略、其々の特徴を持つ四つの加工エリアに分かれている。

3.1　膠東半島生産加工区

煙台市の莱陽市を中心として、主に急速冷凍野菜の生産と加工を行っている。冷凍生産品はサトイモ、ホウレンソウ、ブロッコリー、グリーン豆、インゲン豆などである。2010年6月8日、中国野菜冷凍協会が煙台市に成立し、全国23家の理事のうち、煙台市には9個の企業がある。2010年1－4月、山東省の対日冷凍野菜輸出量は2.79万トン、輸出額は2 985万ドルに達している。

3.2　魯中生産加工区

維坊市の安丘を中心として、主に生鮮野菜の生産と加工を行っている。生産品は長ネギ、ショウガ、ニンニク、ニンニクの苔、山芋などである。寿光市はニンニクの苔を生産しないが、生産地の蒼山県、金郷県、平度市、広饶県、江蘇省の射陽県(しゃようけん) などから大量に購入し、寿光市の冷蔵倉庫にて6～8か月間貯蔵したのち、正月或いは真冬に出荷される。貯蔵量は4万トンに達している。寿光市の生鮮ニンジン、カボチャの対日輸出も増えている。済南市所属の槐荫区（かいいんく)、長清区でのタマネギ、莱蕪市所属の莱城区でのショウガは対日輸出の重要野菜となっている。

3.3　魯南生産加工区

臨沂市の蒼山県を中心として、主に生鮮野菜、塩漬産品、乾燥野菜の生産と加工をやって、生産品は生鮮ニンニク、ゴボウ、塩漬ダイコン、乾燥ニンニクの（*前報:「山東省における野菜の栽培様式と生産の現状」図7を参照)。
スライス、ニンニク粉、人参千切、チャイブなどである。

3.4　魯西南生産加工区

済寧市の金郷県と荷澤市の牡丹区を中心として、主に生鮮野菜の生産と加工を行っている。生産品はアスパラガス、タマネギ、ニンニク、レンコンなどである。

4 日本への主な輸出野菜の種類と代表的品種

基本的に、日本輸出依存型、日本不作対応型、日本端境期対応型及び日本国産と山東輸出競合型の四類型に分けられる（表4）。主作目はショウガ、ニンニク、タマネギの「三辛農産品」である。

表4 山東省の対日野菜輸出の主要種類と数量

類型	代表的な輸出種類	2008年の対日輸出総量（万トン）	2008年の対日輸出量（万トン）全体の割合（%）	山東省輸出の主要産地
日本輸出依存型 日本国内生産が殆どなく、需要に応じるために殆ど全量を輸出する	ニンニクの苔など	33	ニンニクの苔：3万トン（9%）	蒼山県（臨沂市所属） 金郷県（済寧市所属） 平度市（青島市所属） 広饶県（東営市所属）
日本不作対応型 冷夏、少雨、台風、地震などの異常により、日本国内生産量が激減した場合、需要を補完するためにスポット的に輸出する	キャベツ、ニンジンなど		キャベツ2万トン（6%） ニンジン2万トン（6%）	莒南県きくなんけん（臨沂市所属） 泗水県（済寧市所属） 寿光市（維坊市所属） 莱西市（青島市所属）
日本端境期対応型 季節的な輸出で、日本国産品との競合は小さい	カボチャ、アスパラガスなど		カボチャ2万トン（6%） アスパラガス1万トン（3%）	寿光市（維坊市所属） 曹県（荷澤市所属） 莒県きくけん（日照市所属）
日本国産と山東産輸出競合型 日本国産品と輸出品の品質差は小さいが、内外価格差が大きいもので、日本国内の作柄に関係なく輸出が行われる	ニンニク、タマネギ、ショウガ、ゴボウ、サトイモなど		ニンニク3万トン（9%） タマネギ3万トン（9%） ショウガ5万トン（15%） ゴボウ1万トン（3%） サトイモ1万トン（3%）	金郷県（済寧市所属） 蒼山県（臨沂市所属） 槐蔭区（済南市所属） 長清区（済南市所属） 莱城区（莱蕪市所属） 安丘市（維坊市所属） 莱陽市（煙台市所属）

1. 山東省商務庁、山東省対外経済貿易合作庁、青島税関の各データにより総合整理作成
2. データはその種類の生鮮品、乾燥品、冷凍品及び調理加工品を含む

近年、山東省から日本への輸出野菜の種類は約50種であり、主にニンニク球、ニンニク苔、ショウガ、タマネギ、ニンジン、ホウレンソウ、サトイモ、ジャガイモ、ゴボウ、ブロッコリーなどである。最近5年間では、施設栽培の貯蔵運送耐性が良好のトマト、ピーマンなどの生鮮品輸出も増加傾向を示している。日本の多くの商社は兼業的「産地開発」を積極的に進行し、日本の品種と栽培技術を導入し、その優良の産品を日本へ逆輸出する現象も少なくない。タマネギの輸出は主に日本の泉州

中甲高黄、OP 黄、OK 黄、紅葉 3 号などの品種である。ニンジンの輸出は主に日本、韓国の改良五寸ニンジン、超級五寸ニンジン、日本新黒田五寸、高冠黒田などの品種である。ホウレンソウの輸出は主に日本大葉、日本全能などの品種である。サトイモの輸出は主に莱陽孤芋、魯芋 1 号などの品種である。ブロッコリーの輸出は主に緑王、緑峰、緑翠などの品種である。

5 近年の対日輸出の新動向

2008 年、山東省の野菜輸出量は年間 214 万トンになっているが、日本への輸出量は年間 33 万トンである。さらに近年は以下の新動向を呈している。

5.1 輸出対象国の多極化

日本政府は2003 年 5 月 30 日に《食品衛生法》を発布し、その中で「肯定列表制度」を導入した。2006 年 5 月 29 日から正式実施し、日本への輸入質量と安全に非常に有効に働いているが、(特定の734 種農業化学品と51 392 個限量標準）は山東省に適応し難く、以来、貨物キャンセルの現象が多くなっている。山東省は積極的に対応し、その制度に対する輸出指南書を作成し、各地の食品安全の養成トレーニングをやって、重点的に生産過程の管理を厳しくチェックし、安全システム認証と食品検査の制度も強化している。同時に、輸出対象国を東南アジア、EU、韓国、アフリカ、中東諸国、南米など制限が緩やかな国に時機を見て輸出し、野菜輸出の損失を最低限に抑えるといった動向を呈している（表5)。

表 5 2008 年山東省野菜の輸出主要対象国

国家と地区	輸出量（万トン）	総輸出量（万トン）	割合（%）
アセアン（東南アジア諸国連合）	65		26
EU（欧州連合）	60		24
韓国	40	254	16
日本	33		13
米国	16		6

1. 山東省商務庁、山東省対外経済貿易合作庁、青島税関の各データにより総合整理作成
2. データはその種類の生鮮品、乾燥品、冷凍品、缶詰品及び調理加工品を含む

5.2 輸出向け産地の内陸化

1990 年代、山東省の輸出野菜基地は殆ど青島、煙台、維坊などの沿海地区に集中していた。特に2006 年以来、沿海労働力の人件費と生産コストの増大、食品多様化の需要などから、山東内陸に浸透し、済寧、臨沂、徳州、荷澤、泰安、聊城、濱州、莱蕪、枣庄などが輸出野菜の新基地となり、各自の特色を持つようになった。設備は年々整備、更新され、管理上 GMP（Good Manufacturing Practiceの略称、良好作業

規範)、HACCP(Hazard Analysis and Critical Control Pointの略称、危害分析重要管理点)、ISO9000(国際間の物資やサービスの流通をスムーズにさせるために、ISO国際標準化機構が定めている品質保証規格のこと)、ISO14000(ISO国際標準化機構が定めた企業や団体などの環境管理を目的とした規格群で、企業や団体が環境負荷を低減させ、地球環境保護の観点から活動を管理していくための世界共通基準ともいえるもの)認証を取得して実施する内陸の生産加工企業も益々増えている。2008年8月、維坊市税関寿光事務所が中国税関総署により批准された「中華人民共和国維坊市税関寿光事務所」これにより「野菜の里」の野菜輸出の通関手続きが地元で取扱ができ非常に便利になった。山東省圏内に輸出地の緒城市、次いで寿光は二番目の輸出県級税関市となった。

5.3 輸出と国内販売平衡化

野菜輸出は初級階段で高利潤時代から現段階の微利益時代に入り、山東省の対日野菜基地は国際国内の両市場を視野に入れ、一部前の輸出基地と企業は目標を1.3億人口の日本市場から13億人口の自国市場に戻して、適時に良好な商機を目指している。最近は、国内向けの企業の方が日本向けの企業より利潤の高い例も少なくない。

5.4 輸出種類の調整化

日照市は近年積極的にアスパラガスの栽培基地を養成し、2008年作付面積1万ha、生産量は9万トンに達し、その中、2万トンは海外輸出し、全国の60%を占めている。日本のアスパラガス、ブロッコリーの輸入国は米国であるが、近年山東省からの輸入が増えている。日本は輸入国として一般に、先ず本国生産者の主要品目に輸入制限を実施させ、日本市場でのショウガ、ニンニク、ネギは中日間の農産物競争品であり、山東省産の対日輸出農産物の全体の80%、70%、68%で両国間に生じやすい貿易摩擦の敏感品目であるといえる。この観点から、伝統的な輸出品目に代わり、一部の企業は主に米国、オーストラリアからの非敏感品目に属するブロッコリー、アスパラガス、ジャガイモなど、制限される可能性が小さい種類を選別し、近距離、安価人件費、低コストなどにおける有利性を利用し、栽培品目構成を調整して良い効果を挙げている。同時に、日本市場の季節端境期を狙い、オフシーズン野菜輸出も有効に働いている。また最近2,3年で、山東市場をしっかりと占領したイスラエル、オランダ諸国からの優良な果菜類のF_1品種、これら野菜の日本への輸出も増えているのが実情といえる。

参考文献

[1] 鄭風芹. 山東省野菜輸出と貿易に対する挑戦と対策についての検討[J]. 甘粛農業. 2006(11): 153~154

[2] 接玉梅, 張吉国, 宋信息. 山東省野菜輸出と貿易の構造についての分析[J]. 農業科技管理2007(5): 20~23

[3] 劉学忠．山東省野菜の国際競争力の影響因子についての分析［J］．農村経済及び科技．2008（4）：34～36

Export and Circulation Trend in Shandong Province and Vegetable Production for Japan

Xue Yan-bin[1] Masuda Masaharu[2] Murakami Kenji[2]
(1 *Weifang University of Science and Technology*, *Shouguang* 262700, *Shandong*;
2 *Okayama University*, *Okayama* 700)

Abstract: This paper has given a research on export, circulation of vegetables and vegetable production for Japan market. It mainly deals with vegetable export position of Shandong province in China, its export volume, turnover, major vegetable export bases. The major vegetable processing areas, types vegetable of export and new export tendency for Japan market is also analyzed in the paper.

Key words: Export volume; Export turnover; Export production base; Export type; Exports the object country

寿光旱地设施蔬菜的生态环境保护与生态食品的安全生产

薛彦斌[1]① 肖万里[1] 杨 洁[2]
(1 潍坊科技学院，寿光 262700；2 寿光市第一中学，寿光 262700)

摘 要： 本文介绍了寿光市蔬菜产业的基本概况，分析了旱地农业区域发展设施农业的适宜性，发展生态农业的必要性，冬暖式大棚蔬菜生产的生态意义，设施蔬菜的生态环境保护与蔬菜质量安全基础，强化蔬菜生态食品质量的安全措施，最后提出了全面提升寿光蔬菜品牌形象和打造生态食品的安全生产的对策的看法和建议，旨在为蔬菜产业今后的科学发展提供理论和实践上的依据。

关键词： 旱地农业；设施蔬菜；生态环境；安全生产

旱地农业是黄河中下游农业的特征之一[1]，“一代农圣”贾思勰的里籍即在山东寿光，他的巨著《齐民要术》在前代农学的基础上，全面、系统地总结了魏晋以来400年间黄河流域旱地农业生产的新经验和新成就。寿光市地处山东半岛中部，渤海莱州湾南畔，位于黄河三角洲高效生态经济区、山东半岛蓝色经济区和胶东半岛高端产业聚集区“三区”交叠的重要节点位置，总面积2 072km^2，辖14处镇（街道），人口102万，是“中国蔬菜之乡”，也是中国最集中连片的设施蔬菜生产基地。寿光是中国最大的蔬菜产业基地，1995年被国务院命名为“中国蔬菜之乡”。寿光蔬菜生产历史悠久。寿光籍农学家、南北朝时北魏太守贾思勰在他的农学专著《齐民要术》中，就对蔬菜生产作了科学而详细的论述。清朝年间，寿光韭黄成为皇宫贡品。改革开放以来，寿光蔬菜产业发展迅速。1989年，寿光市孙家集镇三元朱村党支部书记王乐义率先实验成功了冬暖式大棚蔬菜种植技术，使蔬菜深冬生产成为现实，推动了一场遍及全国的“绿色革命”和“银色革命”，寿光因此成为“中国一号菜园子”。目前，全市蔬菜面积已发展到5.3万hm^2，年产蔬菜40亿kg，收入35亿元，2009年农民人均纯收入8 274元。被誉为“亚洲最大”、“中华之最”的寿光农产品物流园现已成为全国蔬菜集散中心、价格形成中心和信息交流中心之一。2000—2009年，寿光市连续10次成功地举办了中国寿光国际蔬菜科技博览会，每届都是盛况空前，人流如潮。10届博览会共有来自美

---

① 薛彦斌，男，博士，研究员，潍坊科技学院副院长。研究方向：农产品贮藏加工与农业产业化研究。E-mail：yanbin_ xue@ yahoo. com. cn

国、荷兰、日本、韩国等50多个国家和地区以及全国30个省市区的1 400万人到会参观，是当前国内外参加人数最多，举办时间最长的农业盛会，是全国5大农业展会之一，中国唯一的国际性蔬菜专业品牌展会，在世界范围内产生巨大轰动和反响。寿光蔬菜产业的飞速崛起和发展，引起了国内外各界人士的高度重视和广泛关注。胡锦涛总书记在保持共产党员先进性教育活动中，把山东寿光确定为联系点。他在2005年4月7日、8日两天来寿光市调查研究时指出："要进一步做好推进农业产业化经营这篇大文章，特别要打造好'寿光蔬菜'这个农业品牌，促进农业增效，农民增收"。胡总书记的重要讲话既对寿光蔬菜产业的发展提出了明确要求，又对今后的工作的提出了殷切期望，指明了前进方向。

1　旱地农业区域适宜发展设施农业

寿光同山东及华北地区大多数干旱和半干旱地区一样，年降雨量少，地下水位低，是"引黄济青工程"十个节点之一。山东是干旱化程度较为严重的沿海大省，在诸多自然灾害中尤以干旱灾害发生最为频繁，对农业生产的影响也最为严重[2~3]。据资料统计，山东省干旱灾害成灾面积占各种自然灾害成灾总面积的48%，经济损失占各种灾害损失的40.6%[4]。寿光每年降水量只有608mm左右，且集中在夏季，寿光地下水位很低，一般在30m以下。寿光市年平均水资源量为2.3亿m^2，人均水资源量为225m^2，仅为全国平均水平的九分之一，不足山东省人均占有量的2/3。近10年来，寿光市年用水量均在.2.2亿~2.6亿m^2之间，个别年份超过2.8亿m^2，年缺水0.3亿~0.5亿m^2，水资源供需矛盾非常突出。2010年，寿光市将动工修建双王城水库建设工程，农村饮水安全示范县工程、小型农田水利重点县工程、塌河治理工程、北部水网工程和弥河王口拦河闸改建工程等六大水利工程，以解决水资源供需矛盾。2000年，寿光市遇到了近20年来最严重的干旱，全年累计降雨量421.2mm，比历年同期减少201.3mm，特别是1~7月份降雨仅有135.8mm，全市大小17条河道全部断流，2 500多眼机井干涸，地下水位自1975年以来急剧下降，平均下降了13.79m，农田受旱面积7.33万hm^2，其中，绝产0.41万hm^2，有40个村庄，6.3万人人畜饮用水困难，水资源的严重短缺成为制约寿光市农业生产的发展的瓶颈[5]。但是，寿光又具有旱区和半旱区的共同特质即日照充足的优越条件，因此，因地制宜大力发展设施园艺，既是利益的驱动，也是环境所逼、顺应自然条件的必然结果，设施园艺属于典型节水节光型农业，特别是滴灌技术在设施园艺中的大面积成功应用，以及设施园艺的小环境、小气候的保水保湿功能，显示出干旱和半干旱地区普及设施园艺的巨大优越性，同时设施园艺也属于精耕细作型农业，可以生产优质的高附加值的经济作物，与巨大的经济产出相比，适当的先期投入使农民仍然愿意接受，在这方面以色列的干旱农业和设施园艺已为全世界树立了榜样，况且我国还有其他国家不具备的劳动力密集优势和技术优势。而且，蔬菜设施栽培的环境条件与露地栽培相比，相对来说较为密闭，其温、光、水、肥、气等环境条件，更多地依赖人为的控制，设施栽培常采用反季节栽培，环保型蔬菜设施与露地栽培有着不同的环境条件、生理障碍、病虫害及解决途径[6]。建设设施园艺的场地，恰恰要求地下水位较低，排水良好，如果地势低洼，地下水位较高，会导致棚内湿度过大，土壤升温缓慢，蔬菜根系生长不良，易感病害。选用物理性状、耕层疏松、富含腐殖质的肥沃土壤，其优点是吸热性能强，透水透气性好，适耕性强，有利于根系生长[6]。近年全国部分地区套用寿光设施园艺模式不甚成功的原因主要有两个：一是地下水位高，切开墙体后土壤水分过多，生长过程中“烂根”现象严重，地表形成“汤泡菜”现象；二是阴雨天过多，没有寿光的日照和辐射的先天资源。

2 旱地农业区域必须发展生态农业

2.1 寿光旱地设施蔬菜生产赋予生态农业概念新的涵义

设施园艺框架内不是不能搞生态农业，而是理应搞得更好，搞得更有科技含量。按照生态农业的概念，是依据生态学原理来规划、组织和进行农业生产，必须符合下列基本的生态学要求：第一，生产结构的确定，产品布局的安排等都必须切实做到因地制宜，和当地的环境条件相匹配；第二，对自然资源的利用不能超过资源的可更新能力；第三，在能量和物质的利用上，要做到有取有补，维护生态平衡；第四，在利用可更新自然资源的同时，要注意培育和增殖自然资源，使整个生产的发展，走向良性循环。寿光作为全国著名“蔬菜之乡”，发展高效生态农业的意义更为重要，其重点应当放在在原有高效产出的规模效益的基础上，保护设施蔬菜的生态环境，大力提升蔬菜产品的安全性和健康性，推动蔬菜产业化上档升级。

2.2 冬暖式大棚设施蔬菜生产的生态意义

2.2.1 高效利用太阳能

当电力、煤炭、石油等不可再生能源频频告急，能源问题日益成为制约国际社会经济发展的瓶颈时，越来越多的国家开始实行“阳光计划”，开发太阳能资源。太阳能作为一种可再生的新能源，越来越引起人们的关注。中国蕴藏着丰富的太阳能资源，太阳能利用前景广阔。目前，我国太阳能产业规模已位居世界第一，其中农用节能温室即冬暖式大棚的规模也是世界第一。中国生态农业建设的基本内容之一是充分利用太阳能，努力实现农业生产的物质转化。也就是利用绿色植物的光合作用，不断提高太阳能的转化率，加速物流和能流在生态系统中的运动过程，以不断提高农业生产力。寿光冬暖式大棚是农业利用太阳能的杰作，取材、成本、投入、产出和管理都富有中国特色，符合寿光当地气候（日照时间较长）和地理（沃野平畴）特点。据寿光市气象局资料，寿光日照和辐射资源是：全年平均日照时数 2 607.4h，日照率为 59%，年内日照分布不均，以 5 月日照时数最多，为 274.3h，日照率为 59%。0℃以上的日照时数为 2 086.4 h，占全年总日照时数的 80%。10℃以上的日照时数为 1 568.6h，占总日照时数的 60%；年平均太阳总辐射量 124.3kcal/cm^2。5、6 月份最多，为 15.1kcal/cm^2。12 月份最少，为 5.7kcal/cm^2[7]。无论是“三元朱式”、“五台式”、还是“无立柱钢架式”，其共同特点都是白日充分利用光能蓄热，夜间利用墙体和覆盖材料保温，其棚面角度、棚脊高度、跨度、棚膜、墙体厚度的设计保持了较高水平的太阳光入射率和较大的透光面积，经专家测算有关采光效应的相关因素如棚面角、太阳投射角、太阳高度角、赤纬、时角的设计均比较科学，蕴藏了劳动人民的智慧。世界园艺学会前主席、美国普渡大学园艺系教授朱莱斯·简尼克（Jules Janick）是国际园艺界著名权威，他的著作《园艺学》不仅是畅销世界的园艺学经典和名著，一版再版，也是包括中国在内的世界各国大专院校规定的园艺学科报考博士、硕士研究生的重要参考书目和在校研究生课程的必读教材。2002 年，他在一篇《亚洲园艺技术史》论文中客观评价了以中国为代表的亚洲园艺，在评论亚洲现代农业技术时指出："近年来，亚洲农业科学家和技术人员取得了三项将会影响未来的极为突出的成就：节能温室、蔬菜嫁接和杂交水稻"[8]。

2.2.2 节约不可再生能源

（1）节约煤炭。在王乐义发明冬暖式大棚之前，寿光也有取暖式大棚，每个棚一冬要烧 2 ~ 3t 煤，还只能生产叶菜，不能生产果菜。目前寿光有 40 万个冬暖式大棚，如果按照过去取暖式大棚的耗煤比例计算，每年应该耗煤 80 万 ~ 120 万 t，按照中国 2 862个县级行政单位计算，每县平均按照 10 万个大棚粗算，则每年至少需要燃煤 5. 7 亿 ~ 8. 8 亿 t，截至 2009 年末，山西省煤炭保有储量为 2 600多亿 t，如果不计工业和生活用煤，仅仅温室用煤，山西省的煤炭储量仅仅够取暖式大棚的耗煤 295 ~ 456 年的需要。

（2）节约燃料和电力。20 世纪 80 年代以前，我国以首都北京为代表的京津唐地区和以东北三省为代表的"三北地区"市民冬春吃菜大部分来自海南、广东、广西、福建、云南、四川等华南地区，运距远及 2 000 ~ 3 000km，无论公路运输还是铁路运输，都消耗大量汽油、柴油、和电力资源。寿光是我国北方最大、最集中连片的"冬春菜园子"之一，由于纬度适中，形成全国最大的蔬菜产地中心和交易集散中心，有 20 多个省、区、市的瓜菜来此交易。作为我国较早的一条重要鲜活农产品"绿色通道"的源头，每年从寿光运往京津方向的蔬菜有 10 多万 t，从事蔬菜运输经营的车辆有 30 余台，产菜旺季，每天的运菜车辆达 50 余台次。据测算，华北平原冬暖式大棚蔬菜的出现使北方寒冷地带运菜距离缩短 1/3 ~ 2/3，每年至少可节约汽油或柴油 1 200万 t，电力 67 亿 w·h。

3 设施蔬菜的生态环境保护与蔬菜质量安全基础

设施蔬菜的生态环境保护是蔬菜质量安全基础，只有建设良好的设施蔬菜的生态环境，才能保证生产合格的生态食品。设施蔬菜中要推行"减法农业"，严格管制和减少化肥、农药、农膜、除草剂、杀虫剂、激素六大致害因子。最近，海南毒豇豆事件引发了反季节蔬菜争议，作者认为目前反季节蔬菜栽培技术是过硬和达标的，蔬菜是否含有违禁药物或农残超标，关键看菜农的操作，与蔬菜种植的方式如露地栽培还是设施栽培无关。寿光市近年以《农产品质量安全法》为标尺，以标准化生产为抓手，以打造全国最安全的蔬菜产销基地为目标，多措并举，标本兼治，蔬菜质量安全显著提升。在历年来农业部蔬菜质量抽检中，寿光市蔬菜平均合格率均在全国名列前茅，先后荣获"全国农业标准化示范县建设先进单位"、"全国农产品质量安全工作先进单位"、"国家食品安全示范县（市）”、“全国农业综合执法试点县”、“全国农业标准化生产示范县”、“全国农技推广体系建设示范县”、“全国农业信息化建设示范县”、“全国土壤肥料检测工作先进单位”等称号，这说明设施园艺质量安全的关键在管理，这些成绩的取得归根结底来源于严格的制度制定、落实和技术管理措施的贯彻执行。

3.1 源头管制体系

农资市场，即农业投入品市场是蔬菜农药残留超标的源头，寿光对剧毒、高毒、高残留农药的市场进入途径采取可操作性很强的封死对策，加强农资监管，全部取缔了上述农药的销售，从源头上和根本上保证了蔬菜标准化生产水平。寿光市从2006年7月正式启动了农业投入品市场准入制度，市政府先后出台了《农业投入品管理办法》、《关于加强蔬菜生产用药管理的意见》、《关于加强剧毒、高毒、高残留农药销售和使用管理工作的通知》、《蔬菜质量安全管理责任制及考核奖惩责任追究办法》、《关于大力发展无公害蔬菜生产的意见》、《农产品基地准出、市场准入管理办法》等有关文件，并印发到全市的农资经营业户。严禁在蔬菜产区销售和使用剧毒、高毒、高残留农药，推广应用高效低毒低残留农药，严格执行农药使用安全间隔期，尽量减少用药量和使用次数，保证了蔬菜农药残留不超标。

3.2 农业执法监管体系

监管未动，机构先行，必须在组织上落到实处，责权才能分明，寿光成立了市长任组长的农产品质量安全领导小组，建立了部门联席会议制度，设立了农产品质量安全监督管理办公室，按正局级单位管理，专门拿出一名市府副秘书长任办公室主任，有职有权，有车有马，具体负责全市农产品质量安全的监督管理工作。各镇街道相应成立了农产品质量安全监督管理办公室和农业行政执法中队，按照不少于6人的标准配齐了人员，进行了执法培训，统一制作了执法服装，下发了上岗执法证。其主要职能是：负责农产品质量安全监督管理工作，制定和落实农产品质量安全监督管理的考核奖惩；负责农产品质量安全的宣传、培训与指导；负责农业标准化生产基地建设、农产品品牌创建、“三品”（无公害农产品、绿色食品、有机食品）认证的上报及管理；负责农业投入品生产经营和使用的监督管理；负责农产品质量检测计划的制定和落实；负责规范管理农产品交易市场；负责农业龙头企业、农民专业合作社及其他经济合作组织的建设与管理。同时，市政府对各镇街道实行农产品质量安全工作量化考核，各村实行村委负责制，每个村委成员都是农产品质量安全监管员。目前，寿光市形成了一级抓一级、层层抓落实的责任监管体系，为确保农产品质量安全提供了坚强的组织保障。

3.3 蔬菜生产标准体系

先后出台了《蔬菜标准化生产考核奖惩办法》、《蔬菜质量安全管理责任制及考核奖惩责任追究办法》、《关于全面加强蔬菜质量检测的实施意见》等一系列政策性文件，有效地推动了农产品质量安全工作的经常化、规范化。同时，为适应国内外市场对蔬菜质量安全的要求，按照“完整、接轨、配套、简便”的原则，重点围绕蔬菜产、供、销等各个环节，以市场为导向，抓住主导产品，组织有关专家制定了《寿光市农业标准化生产操作规程汇编》和《寿光市农产品生产技术操作规程实用手册》，将农业生产全部纳入标准化体系，彻底解决了无标生产、无标流通、无标销售的问题。

3.4 蔬菜质量监测体系

按照“布局合理、结构科学、服务便捷、满足需要”的要求，投资1 400多万元建设了市农产品质量检测中心，14处镇街道投资200多万元新上了28台高标准检测设备，全部配备了农产品质量流动检测车，农产品企业、基地、市场、超市均建立了蔬菜质量检测室。特别是去年以来，寿光本着“布局合理、方便交易、便于管理”的原则，按照有场所、有法人、有人员、有设备、有台帐、有制度的“六有”标准，对村头地边蔬菜交易市场进行了集中整治，取缔了755处不符合标准的村头地边交易市场，保留的575处市场全部配备了速测设备，形成了全覆盖的检测网络。同时，为全面提高科学监管水平，市、镇（街道）、企业、市场共同投资504万元建设农产品质量安全视频监控与信息管理平台，把寿光市镇街道、“三品”蔬菜生产加工企业、超市、蔬菜交易市场的613处检测室全部纳入视频监控和检测信息采集范围，对全市蔬菜质量进行实时监控、统计、分析、预警与智能化管理。目前，第一期建设的14处镇街道、15处蔬菜生产加工企业、市蔬菜批发市场、50处村头地边市场，已逐步投入运行，初步实现了对蔬菜质量的全方位动态监管，为蔬菜标准化生产提供了可靠依据。

3.5 农民合作组织体系

按照“民办、民管、民受益”的原则，积极发展农民专业合作经济组织，寿光市形成了基地加农户式的稻田燎原模式、连锁式的东方誉源模式和统一购销、统一管理式的洛城绿色食品基地模式等各种模式的合作组织，提高了农民抵御市场风险的能力。目前，寿光市农民专业合作经济组织发展到270个，辐射带动40%的村、10多万农户，为农民持续增收创造了良好条件。同时，扶持壮大了一批重点农业龙头企业，实现了企业增效与农民增收的双赢，全市各类农业龙头企业发展到410家，80%的农户进入了产业化经营体系。

3.6 科技服务推广体系

投资30多万元建设了寿光农业信息网，设立了320家农村信息网络服务站，通过网络视频服务等形式，“面对面”为农民群众提供生产技术指导。目前，已为农民解决生产技术难题16万个，推广标准化生产新技术2 100多项。依托山东农业科技人才市场和潍坊科技学院，以市农技培训中心、镇街道农技服务中心和村综合服务大院作为培训基地，开展了30万农民科技大轮训工程，目前，全市有8.9万农民获得“绿色证书”，2.4万农民取得“农民技术员”资格，130人获“农民科技专家”称号，农民科技素质明显提高。借助市内蔬菜、食用菌等12处科研机构和瑞士先正达等20多处外资农业示范基地，大力引进新技术、新品种，全市农业先进技术和高科技覆盖率分别达到了95%和98%。

4 强化蔬菜生态食品质量的安全保障

4.1 投入品使用制度

全面整顿农资市场，特别是对农药的销售建立定点经营和购销登记制度，规范了农资市场秩序。加大对禁用、限用农药的查处力度，由市农产品质量安全监督管理办公室牵头，农业、工商、质监、公安等部门参加，对剧毒农药的生产、销售、使用等各个环节，定期不定期进行排查，对农药经营业户全部建立排查档案，从源头上杜绝剧毒农药的产生。同时，市政府每年还设立10万元专项举报奖金，对生产、销售、使用违禁农药的行为实行有奖举报，举报情况一经查实，在对举报人保密的前提下严格兑现奖励，坚决杜绝生产、销售、使用违禁农药现象的发生。

4.2 基地准出制度

由农业部门设立基地认定前置条件，对达不到标准的，坚决不予申报，对要求续报的，从严把关。大力推行统一技术培训、统一物资供应、统一配备检测仪器、统一制度规范、统一注册商标“五统一”管理模式，建立指导机构，确定专人负责。到目前，寿光市获得国家“三品”认定的基地达到15处、4.5万 hm^2。同时，寿光还规定，凡蔬菜生产企业、农民专业合作经济组织、自产自销的蔬菜生产者所生产的蔬菜都要持质量检测合格证明办理产地证明，方可上市销售。对销售不合格蔬菜的，由农业部门责令停止销售，并进行无害化处理或者监督销毁。

4.3 市场准入制度

蔬菜批发市场、超市、农贸市场、村头地边市场等市场和蔬菜销售组织、个体购销者等经营者严格执行进货检查验收制度，凡无质量合格证明、产地证明的不得入市销售，并对进场销售的蔬菜质量安全状况进行抽样检测，经检测不合格的，由工商部门责令停止销售，追回已经销售的蔬菜，进行无害化处理或者监督销毁。

4.4 蔬菜检测制度

对蔬菜重点区域、重点产品，坚持自检和抽检相结合，扎实开展好例行监测、监督抽检和质量监控等工作。寿光市农产品质量检测中心负责对全市基地、市场、超市及加工企业进行抽检，每月检测蔬菜样品800个以上，其中，定量检测200个以上。各镇街道检测室对辖区内蔬菜基地、种植户、经销市场不定期进行抽检，每月检测蔬菜样品不少于500个，市、镇两级全年检测蔬菜样品7.8万个。村头地边市场对进入市场销售的蔬菜全部进行普检，确保入市蔬菜质量安全。为进一步摸清寿光市蔬菜质量安全状况，2009年，寿光市制定出台了《蔬菜质量定向定位检测实施方案》，组织开展了对全市蔬菜生产环节的定向定位检测，每月抽签确定两个镇街道的两个村，组织农业行政执法大队、各镇街道执法中队、检测室的工作人员，对被抽中村的大棚菜、露天菜全部进行普检，实现了检测的全覆盖。前期对部分村的蔬菜大棚进行了普检，共抽取蔬菜样品1 530个，速测样品全部合格，定性定量检测样品215个，合格率达到99%。为确保检测工作落到实处，寿光还建立了检测结果通报和责任追究制度，对出现问题的追根溯源，跟踪检测，跟踪执法，有效杜绝了不合格蔬菜的产生。

5 全面提升寿光蔬菜品牌形象

5.1 宣传推广力度

每年组织有关企业和部分蔬菜种植户积极参加中国（北京）国际农产品交易会和上海、青岛、烟台等大城市农产品对接会，宣传寿光蔬菜，推介名优产品，进一步提高了寿光蔬菜知名度。同时，从2000年开始，寿光市连续成功举办了十届中国（寿光）国际蔬菜科技博览会，充分展示寿光蔬菜新品种、新技术、新模式，收到了很好的经济效益和社会效益。第十届菜博会共展出2 000多个新品种、300多项新技术、30多种栽培模式。

5.2 政策扶持力度

凡在寿光市行政区域内从事农产品生产、加工、经营的企事业单位、农村经济合作组织和其他经济组织，对当年新获“中国名牌农产品”、“地理标志产品”、“山东省名牌农产品”的，由市财政一次性分别奖励50万元、20万元、10万元；对当年新获国家有机食品、绿色食品、无公害农产品认证的，由市财政一次性分别奖励1万元、0.5万元、0.5万元；对创建成为国家、山东省、潍坊市农业标准化示范区和农业标准化示范基地的，由市财政一次性分别奖励5万元、2万元、1万元，有力地推进了品牌争创工作。2009年，寿光对获得“中国名牌农产品”称号的“乐义”黄瓜奖励了50万元。全年落实品牌创建奖励资金370万元。

5.3 品牌创建力度

按照“规划一批、培育一批、成熟一批、推出一批”的要求，坚持“独、特”和具有不可复制性原则，以争创地理标志产品和山东名牌农产品为重点，充分挖掘优势蔬菜资源，集中培育一批品牌产品和品牌企业，不断加强农产品品牌认证。目前，已有412种农产品获得优质农产品标志，打造了“乐义”蔬菜、“王婆”香瓜等十几个知名商标，桂河芹菜和寿光独根红韭菜成功申报为国家地理标志产品。同时，依托中国农业大学寿光蔬菜研究院，研发了4个具有自主知识产权的甜瓜品种和2个甜瓜新品种，提高了寿光市蔬菜产业的核心竞争力。

6 生态食品的安全生产的今后对策

6.1 进一步健立完善蔬菜质量检测体系

投资3 000万元建设新检测中心，增强检测能力，扩大检测范围。市财政每年出资

700万元，招聘700名蔬菜质量检测人员，统一管理，全部派驻到蔬菜市场检测室负责质量检测监管，实现检测数据的直接上传、全程监控和实时调度处理。

6.2 深入开展农药市场清理整顿

加大农业执法力度，严厉打击违法犯罪行为，维护农民利益；进一步完善农资直营配送体系，严格农药经营主体和农药产品的市场准入，逐步实现农药经营的定点直营；督导农药经营单位建立进销货台帐，实现农药经营使用的可追溯。

6.3 规划发展标准化程度高、品牌效益明显的新型基地

为全市的标准化生产树立新样板，采取“政府组织、多方投资、科技推动、现代管理、示范带动”的形式，规划建设集蔬菜优良品种试验示范、现代化种苗培育、绿色循环农业示范于一体的万亩现代生态绿色示范园区，通过典型引路、以点带面，带动寿光市优质、高产、高效、生态、安全蔬菜发展。

6.4 搭建国字号现代农业发展新平台

积极争取农业部支持，在寿光建设中国蔬菜产业协会，争创全国农村改革试验区和国家现代农业示范区，为全市蔬菜产业的快速持续发展开拓新空间、搭建新平台。

6.5 进一步推进安全园艺、生态农业发展

制定出台有关政策，通过农资连锁配送企业，采取政府补贴等形式，对基地进行有机肥、生物肥、生物药专供，加快绿色、有机农产品发展步伐。

由上可见，寿光虽位于干旱和半干旱的鲁中平原，但坚持走节水、节光、劳动密集型加技术密集型的设施园艺的道路，蔬菜产业成为农业支柱性产业，成为闻名全国的设施园艺领头羊和风向标。近年又加大对设施蔬菜的生态环境保护与生态食品的安全生产管理的执行力度，使寿光蔬菜质量大幅提升。而且，政府对蔬菜产业向健康型、生态型方向发展的导向作用是巨大的，特别在无公害食品、绿色食品、有机食品的推进过程中所起的作用是不可代替的。由于农业的弱质性、分散性和多功能性，在导向和管理上政府的职能和作为更能充分体现出来。寿光市的大棚准建、基地准出和市场准入制度的实行均体现了政府在农产品质量安全中的独特作用，尤其是部门联合、齐抓共管的机制有别于其他西方国家的管理机制，具有中国特色，行之有效。由政府牵头成立由农业、畜牧、渔业、林业、环保、质监、卫生、药监、工商、公安、新闻等单位组成的食品安全委员会和农产品质量监督小组，建立了定期和不定期联合督查的长效工作机制。同时，财政部门加大了对农业标准化和农产品质量安全监管的资金投入，新闻宣传部门加大舆论监督力度，使寿光全市上下形成了人人关注农产品质量的良好氛围和合力，2008年底，寿光创建成了国家级食品安全示范县。2009年，山东省、全国、潍坊市农产品质量安全工作会相继于3月、5月、7月在寿光召开，三级农产品质量安全工作会在寿光的召开，表明对寿光市蔬菜质量安全工作的肯定和支持。权威的新华社国内动态专刊以“政府制定标尺，农民卡标种菜：寿光市蔬菜质量安全监管探析”为题对寿光蔬菜质量

安全监管情况进行了刊发，农业部内部刊物进行了层层转发，在全国宣传推广蔬菜质量安全寿光模式。寿光蔬菜产业发展的成功为全省乃至全国蔬菜产业的发展提供了借鉴。

参考文献

[1] 李生秀．中国旱地农业．科学出版社，北京：2007：1-450
[2] 薛德强，王建国，王兴堂，龚佃利．山东省的干旱化特征分析．自然灾害学报，2007，6；60-65
[3] 高秉伦．山东省主要自然灾害及减灾对策．北京：地震出版社，1994：49-65
[4] 杨剑英，张保华，郝导华．寿光市抗旱之后的思考．山东水利．2001，5：9-10
[5] 侯喜林，吴志行．无公害蔬菜生产病虫草害综合防治技术．中国蔬菜．2004，1：58-62
[6] 朱振华．寿光棚室蔬菜生产实用新技术．济南：山东科学技术出版社．2001，1-65
[7] 胡国庆．寿光蔬菜．北京：人民出版社，2001，3-12
[8] Janick, J. History of Asian horticultural technology. Acta Hort. 2003, 620: 19-32

Drylalnd Facilities Vegetables in Shouguang: Protection of Ecological Enviroment and Safe Production of Ecological Food

XUE Yan-bin[1] XIAO Wan-li[1] YANG Jie[2]
(1 *Weifang University of Science and Technology*, *Shouguang* 262700)
(2 *Shouguang City First Middle School*, *Shouguang* 262700)

Abstract: This artical intruduces the general situation of vegetalbe industry in Shouguang, analyses the horticulture suitability of regional development in dryland farming and the necessity of developing ecological agriculture. And it elaborates the ecological significance of producing solar greenhouse vegetalbes, the protection of ecological enviroment and the security foundation of quality vegetables and also the safty measures to secure the quality of ecological vegetable food. Finally, it puts forwards views and suggestions on the countermeasures of comprehensively promoting brand image of Shouguang vegetables and safe production of ecological food. It provides both theoretical and practical basis for future scientific development of vegetable industry.

Key words: Dryland farming; Facilities vegetables; Ecological enviroment; Safe production

莱州湾沿海地下卤水精细化工产业战略性开发与技术创新

薛彦斌[1①] 杨 洁[2] 杨树仁[3]

（1 潍坊科技学院，寿光 262700；2 寿光市第一中学，寿光 262700；
3 山东墨锐化学有限公司，寿光 262700）

摘 要：本文就地下卤水的一般特性，山东莱州湾的独特优势，卤水产业发展现状，我国卤水精细化工产业面临的机遇，产业技术的发展特点、趋势，我国卤水精细化工产业存在的差距和不足，示范联盟技术创新活动与国家战略和山东省战略，示范联盟组建对推动产业技术创新的作用等进行了分析和论述，旨在为卤水产业今后的科学发展提供理论和实践上的依据。

关键词：莱州湾；卤水；精细化工；产业；战略性开发；技术创新

潍坊市及其所属的县级市寿光市地处山东半岛中部，渤海莱州湾南畔，位于黄河三角洲高效生态经济区、山东半岛蓝色经济区和胶东半岛高端产业聚集区“三区”交叠的重要节点位置，而且拥有丰富石油、荒地、滩涂和盐卤等优质资源的黄河三角洲，是我国唯一一个尚未全面开发的大河三角洲，黄河三角洲位于渤海南部黄河入海口沿岸地区，包括山东省的东营、滨州和潍坊、德州、淄博、烟台市的部分地区，共涉及 19 个县（市、区），总面积 2.65 万 km^2，占山东省的 1/6，总人口约 985 万。黄河三角洲不仅是胜利油田的所在地，而且还是连接渤海湾经济带和长江三角洲、对接天津滨海新区和上海浦东新区间的重要通道，在我国东部整个经济社会发展战略中有着十分重要的战略地位。可以说，加快实施黄河三角洲大开发战略，不仅是今后推进山东省及环渤海湾地区经济增长的一个新亮点，而且也是我国东部发展战略的一个重要组成部分。

根据山东省国土资源厅提供的资料，山东省地下卤水资源静储量为 80.8 亿 m^3，而且主要分布在海岸带沿线，可开采量为 2.87 亿 m^3/年。调查发现，山东省地下卤水矿床主要分布在黄河三角洲平原区、莱州湾南岸平原区和胶州湾港湾区，呈条带状沿海岸带分布，面积约 3 003km^2，地下卤水总体处于采补平衡，但分布不均匀。卤水有潜力区主要分布在无棣、沾化、垦利、东营和青岛等卤水未开采地区及寿光市羊口镇、道口镇、岔河盐场一线以及寒亭区 S320 省道以南等地区。目前，卤水开采主要集中在莱州

---

① 薛彦斌，男，博士，研究员，潍坊科技学院副院长。研究方向：农产品贮藏加工与农业产业化。E－mail：yanbin_ xue@ yahoo. com. cn

湾南岸的寿光、寒亭、昌邑、莱州，黄河三角洲的沾化、东营区和广饶县。

1 地下卤水的一般特性

地下卤水一般无色透明，局部地区略带微黄色，棕黄色，味咸，稍有苦涩感。莱州湾沿岸地下卤水是形成于晚第四纪的盐矿藏，储量丰富，含盐量高，易于开采，是中国无机盐生产的重要来源。对莱州湾沿岸地下卤水进行的初步调查与研究表明：其卤水来源于海水，可能是蒸发成卤或冰冻成卤，但目前还没有明确结论。莱州湾沿岸地下卤水与海水有着相同的化学组成，主要离子含量与海水中离子含量排序相同。研究证明了莱州湾沿岸地下卤水是海水蒸发成卤而不是冰冻成卤。地下卤水中各主要组分的氯度比值与海水的相应值比较都有一定的变化，说明卤水在形成和赋存的过程中发生了一系列变化，包括浓缩蒸发、离子交换、脱硫酸作用、矿物蚀变等。

2 山东莱州湾的独特优势

莱州湾是渤海三大海湾之一，位于渤海南部，山东半岛北部。西起黄河口，东至龙口的屺姆角。海岸线长319km，总面积9 530km^2。有黄河、小清河、潍河等注入。海底地形单调平缓，水深大部分在10m以内，海湾西部最深处达18m。平均潮差（龙口）0.9m，最大可能潮差2.2m。多沙土浅滩。西段受黄河泥沙影响，潮滩宽6~7km，东段仅500~1 000m。由于潍河、胶莱河、白浪河、弥河，特别是黄河泥沙的大量携入，海底堆积迅速，浅滩变宽，海水渐浅，湾口距离不断缩短。莱州湾冬季结冰，冰厚约15cm。莱州湾滩涂辽阔，河流携带有机物质丰富，盛产蟹、蛤、毛虾及海盐等。是中国重要的渔业、海盐、地下卤水生产区，亦有石油和天然气蕴藏。其沿岸潍坊、东营、龙口港和羊角沟港为山东省重要港口。

莱州湾沿岸地下卤水埋藏深度为0~60m，分3层赋存于第四纪松散砂层中。东部莱州盐场，上部0~10m粉砂层，为潜水卤水层，下部两层中、细砂砾层，厚度分别为10~25m、15~46m，为承压卤水层；西部羊口盐场，3层卤水分别赋存于0~10m、15~22m、35~50m的粉砂层中，卤水浓度东部较西部高，具分带性，自海岸向陆地，分为近岸低浓度带、中间高浓度带和远岸低浓度带。莱州湾卤水浓度为10~17波美度，最高为20波美度，其他地区一般为5~12波美度。波美度为15的卤水中，含溴350g/m^3、硼5.3g/m^3、碘0.4g/m^3。此外，尚含有锂、锶等稀有元素。

3 国内外卤水产业发展现状

山东省莱州湾畔拥有富含溴素的地下卤水资源，储量约为70亿m^3，占山东省整体储量的87%，具有重大的经济价值。同全国其他地区相比较，该地区最突出的优势体现在两个方面：一是卤水中溴素资源丰富，溴素年产量12万t，占全国产量的90%，占世界产量的16%；二是精细化工基础好，淄博、东营等地的大型石化、化工企业为精细化工的发展提供了充足的基础原料。依托这些优势，该地区已经发展成为以溴素深加工、氯精细化工，镁功能材料等为主要特色的国内第一、国际知名的卤水精细化工产业聚集区。目前该地区溴素阻燃剂生产规模达到10万t/年，占全球总产能的25%；溴系列中间体达70多个品种；环保清洗剂（非ODS）溴丙烷产能达到15 000t，占全球产能的60%以上。该地区已经形成了以墨锐化工、新华制药、富康制药、卫东化工、海王化工等为代表的卤水精细化工企业集群，在国民经济建设中起到了举足轻重的作用。

国内青海省在盐湖资源开发方面具有重要影响力。青海盐湖所围绕盐湖综合开发利用，相应开展盐湖地球化学等方面的研究，重点研究青海、新疆、内蒙古、西藏和山西等中国盐湖区和云南、四川等盐矿地区盐类资源的勘查、开采与加工技术。青海盐湖工业集团是该地区的代表性企业，主要依靠察尔汗盐湖的资源优势，建成了中国目前最大的钾肥工业生产基地，近年来在镁资源综合利用方面取得很大进展。但是，有机化工原料运输不便，远离销售市场等因素，严重制约了该地区盐湖精细化工的发展。

国外卤水精细化工产业主要分布在以色列、美国、日本等国家，以跨国公司为主体。以色列主要依托死海丰富的高浓度卤水资源，组建以色列化工集团，对卤水进行综合利用与精细化工的开发，其溴素年产量近30万t，约占世界产量的40%。以色列化工集团业务结构以精细化工为主，涉及溴素阻燃剂、磷系阻燃剂、无机溴化物、水处理剂等四大系列100多个品种，年产值近70亿美元。美国的卤水精细化工产业以科聚亚公司、雅宝公司为主。美国科聚亚公司年产值在35亿美元，业务结构包括聚合物添加剂（阻燃剂）、高性能特种产品、作物保护（农药）等。美国雅宝公司年产值在25亿美元，业务结构包括溴系阻燃剂、镁功能材料等。日本的卤水精细化工产业以东曹公司、日本大八公司等企业为主。总部设在东京的东曹公司是一家多元化的国际化工企业集团，在石化、氯碱和功能产品方面享有盛誉，其在亚洲异氰酸酯业务拓展方面获得成功，拥有40万t/年MDI（二苯基甲烷二异氰酸酯）产能而成为亚洲最大MDI生产商，虽然全球经济危机会影响到全球聚氨酯需求的增长，但是中国烟台万华、德国拜耳和巴斯夫宣布在中国新建一系列大型装置，东曹公司为了加强其市场竞争力，并维持其亚洲第一的地位，公司制定了新的扩能计划，以便于把握市场变化趋势。东曹公司的专利之一是利用海水提取溴素，进行系列溴素阻燃剂、中间体的生产，但限于海水提溴的高成本，规模受限。总部设在大阪的日本大八化学工业近年不断增产塑料用磷系阻燃剂，对日本和中国的工厂合计投资20亿日元，到2011年将生产能力由目前的年产3万2 000t增至4万3 000t。目的是满足来自PC及家电部件的塑料材料对阻燃剂的不断增长的需求。计划两年后将塑料用阻燃剂的销售额由目前的200亿日元增至300亿日元。日本大八公司是磷系阻燃剂的国际第一品牌，近年的年产值一直维持2.5亿美元左右，氯气、三氯化磷、三氯氧磷是其主要原料。

我国的卤水精细化工产业同国外比较，存在较大差距。国外精细化率达65%，而我国精细化率只有40%。国外卤水精细化工公司，年产值几十亿甚至过百亿，业务结构涉及数条产品链数百个品种，产品利润率高，竞争率强，国内公司均难以匹敌。国内各卤水精细化工企业迫切希望，通过技术创新，以精细化工为手段，以高附加值为目标，拉长卤水利用产业链，建立卤水循环经济发展模式，使宝贵的卤水资源得到充分利用，使传统卤水利用产业技术水平得到显著提升。

4 我国卤水精细化工产业面临的机遇

我国卤水精细化工产业的发展也面临着难得的机遇，主要表现在以下 3 个方面。

4.1 国家鼓励节能减排、循环经济、可持续发展，为卤水精细化工产业发展提供了有利的宏观环境

2009 年初，我国出台了《中华人民共和国循环经济促进法》，鼓励资源再利用。2009 年 12 月，《黄河三角洲高效生态经济开发区发展规划》发布上升为国家战略。高效生态经济是指具有典型生态系统特征的节约集约经济发展模式。在产业类型上，形成由清洁生产企业组成的循环经济产业体系。一系列政策的出台，有利于推动传统粗放式卤水利用方式的转变，有利于促进卤水精细化工集约节约利用资源，强化环境保护、发展循环经济局面的形成。

4.2 精细化工在世界范围内的飞速发展，为卤水精细化工产业的发展提供了有利的行业环境

精细化工的发展在世界范围内方兴未艾，在卤水精细化工行业体现出同样的趋势。区别于传统的两碱（纯碱、氯碱），以溴素深加工、氯精细化工、镁功能材料等为特色的卤水精细化工产业将得到更加迅猛发展，并成为卤水利用乃至海洋化工新的增长极，在国民经济中发挥更为重要的作用。

4.3 新兴战略性产业的提出和规划，为卤水精细化工产业的发展指明了方向

卤水精细化工包含有阻燃剂（阻燃材料）、医药等，属于新兴战略性产业中的新型功能材料、新医药领域。我国卤水精细化工行业，在阻燃剂（阻燃材料）、溴系医药方面，具备一定的比较优势和广阔的发展空间，完全可以有所作为。

5 我国卤水精细化工产业存在的差距和不足

经过几十年的技术创新和产业化发展，我国卤水精细化工产业在溴素提取与综合利用、中间体、阻燃剂、水处理剂等领域积累了丰富的产业化技术开发经验。但是，就总体而言，我国的卤水精细化工产业还存在很多不足，主要体现在以下两点。

5.1 关键共性技术开发落后，产业发展缺乏支撑

以色列围绕着开发死海卤水资源，在溴素综合利用方面具有世界领先的水平；日本在利用油田卤水提取溴、电渗析浓缩海水制盐等方面领先世界。国内的天津科技大学、青岛科技大学等科研单位在卤水资源利用的某些方面做了大量工作，取得了较好成绩，

但仍然存在很大差距。例如，电渗析制盐技术，我国虽进行过试验探索，但无成功案例，一些核心关键技术仍被日本旭电化、德山曹达等公司垄断。再如多晶硅的核心生产技术，也为国际光伏巨头所垄断并大肆扩产，目前国际七大厂均有扩产规划。继 2008 年 12 月全球最大的多晶硅生产厂家——美国 Hemlock 公司将多晶硅产能由 1.9 万 t/年提升为 2.9 万 t/年之后，德国瓦克公司表示至 2011 年将在目前基础上扩充 1.3 万 t/年的产能，日本德山曹达将计划在 2013 年从现在的 8 200t 提高到 14 200t。

5.2　产品开发理念、机制、核心技术落后

国外产品研究和开发主要集中于跨国公司，例如，美国雅宝、科聚亚、以色列死海溴等，他们在卤水精细化工的产业链开发方面工艺先进，引领国际技术发展趋势。

国内产品研发主要集中于研究机构和高校，企业在产品研发方面力量薄弱，研发与生产脱节现象普遍存在。具有自主知识产权的新产品少，高附加值产品发展缓慢，基本上是跟在国外公司后面亦步亦趋，产品技术含量较低。

6　产业技术的发展特点、趋势

6.1　产业技术发展特点

进入 21 世纪，世界发达国家的战略重点已从基础化工转向精细化工，精细化工产业已经成为新的增长点。纵观近年国内外卤水精细化工产业科技发展动态，有如下几个特点。

（1）重视对卤水资源综合利用的研究，体现循环经济和可持续发展理念。

（2）重视卤水精细化工产业链的延伸和高附加值精细化工产品技术的开发。

（3）重视安全、环保的理念对新型阻燃剂、环保水处理剂等产品技术开发的导向作用。

（4）重视清洁生产、节能减排技术在卤水精细化工中的应用。

（5）重视交叉高新技术，例如微胶囊化技术、超细化技术、表面改性技术、复配协同技术、交联技术、消烟技术和大分子技术在卤水精细化工中的作用。

（6）注重引进他国资源和先进技术，建立卤水精细化工科技国际合作与交流关系。

6.2　产业发展趋势

卤水精细化工产业技术发展将呈现出如下趋势。

（1）逐步形成卤水精细化工产业链集成技术体系。即卤水精细化工由规模化扩张发展模式逐渐走向上下游一体化的内涵式发展模式，由横向一体化的盲目扩张逐渐走向产业链技术整合、形成卤水元素分离、中间体、终端高附加值精细化工产品、客户解决方案的产业链技术集成体系。

（2）从粗放式利用卤素（溴、氯）元素向集约型利用发展。在溴、氯中间体生产过程中，开发溴、氯循环利用新技术，使卤水资源发挥更大的价值，同时力求实现清洁

和环保的生产过程。

（3）从满足一般的性能要求向满足绿色、环保、高效的趋势发展。卤水精细化工所衍生的阻燃剂和水处理剂历来在保护生命财产安全、环境方面发挥重要作用。随着社会的发展，人们对阻燃剂、水处理剂提出了更高的性能要求，从而促使产品技术开发向着绿色、环保、高效方面发展。

7 示范联盟技术创新活动与国家战略和山东省战略

示范联盟技术创新活动与国家和省战略目标、产业发展政策的关联性主要表现为以下 3 个方面。

（1）“卤水精细化工产业技术创新”相关研究开发领域在《国家中长期科学和技术发展规划纲要（2006—2012 年）》中被列为优先主题。“2. 水和矿产资源—（8）海水淡化—浓盐水综合利用技术等；海洋资源高效开发利用—海水化学资源综合利用技术。”

（2）“卤水精细化工产业技术创新”符合国家发布的《黄河三角洲高效生态经济区发展规划》中的“高技术产业”部分。“加强创新能力建设，大力发展电子信息、生物工程、新材料等产业，培育海洋生物医药、海洋功能食品、海洋工程材料、海水综合利用等海洋高技术产业，加快形成一批高成长、带动力强的骨干企业，开发一批具有自主知识产权的核心产品，建设以新型油田化学品、盐化工为特色的新材料产业基地。

（3）“卤水精细化工产业技术创新”符合《山东省中长期科学和技术发展规划纲要（2006—2020 年）》。“（一）资源与环境—循环生产技术—卤盐化工—工业循环经济中关键技术。”、“（四）海洋技术—海水资源综合利用技术——以潍坊、滨州、东营为研发基地，开展海水化学资源开发技术研究。研制海盐生产工艺及系列盐产品；研究苦卤综合利用技术以及海水提取钾、溴、镁等化学元素新技术，开发以镁、溴为主导的精细化工系列产品；加强海水淡化、海水循环冷却、废弃浓海水制盐、元素提取和深加工技术的研究。海洋精细化工品种达 70 种以上，建立大规模海水化学资源提取、深加工的循环节能模式示范工程。”

可见，“卤水精细化工产业技术创新”符合国家战略，符合山东半岛蓝色经济区建设的指导思想，符合国家产业、环保和能源政策，属于山东省重点扶持的 15 个高新技术产业群范围。

8 示范联盟组建对推动产业技术创新的作用

8.1 聚集国内卤水精细化工领域创新资源，形成持续和稳定的产学研合作

依托天津科技大学、青岛科技大学、四川大学、山东省海洋化工科学研究院、潍坊科技学院等国内在卤水精细化工领域具有优势传统的高校和科研机构，联合新华医药

（寿光）有限公司、寿光市豪源化工有限公司、寿光富康制药有限公司、山东墨锐化学有限公司、山东海王化工股份有限公司、山东裕源集团有限公司、东营春兴盐化有限公司、山东兄弟实业集团、寿光卫东化工有限公司等13家区域海洋精细化工实施企业（其中上市企业2家），组成联盟，充分考虑产、学、研各方的需求和利益，发挥各自技术和产业优势，打造产业技术创新链，以强化联盟集群优势和促进行业发展为共同目标，克服国内同行业现实的无序竞争，形成持续和稳定的产学研合作体。潍坊科技学院与山东墨锐化学有限公司还共同出资成立了山东省卤水利用研发中心。

8.2 着力解决产业技术发展瓶颈

针对多年来我国卤水精细化工产品数量少、性能差、利用粗放、发展缓慢的现实，着重研究溴氯清洁生产、节能减排和循环利用新技术，开发系列氯专用化学品和溴中间体；重点研制和生产高效、环保的、以溴、氯、三氯化磷、三氯氧磷为起始原料的新型高端换代阻燃剂；加强研究环保高效卤系水处理剂的新技术、水处理解决方案；加快开发晶须材料、吸附材料、阻燃材料、晶体材料、电子陶瓷材料等镁系功能材料的生产与应用技术，解决卤水精细化工产业发展过程中的共性技术难题。努力形成高端化、精细化、集约型、内涵式、可持续的发展模式，为卤水精细化工产业的发展提供技术支撑和保障。

8.3 促进产业核心自主知识产权形成

卤水精细化工产业技术创新战略联盟具有国内唯一的资源优势，厚重的产业基础和显著的研发优势，通过解决共性技术难题和新产品新工艺研发，依靠原始创新、集成创新、消化吸收再创新，将快速形成覆盖卤水精细化工产业，占领卤系医药、农药、染料中间体、卤系与磷系阻燃剂、卤系水处理剂和镁系功能材料等产业链环节的自主知识产权体系，极大地促进卤水精细化工产业自主创新能力和产业核心竞争力的提升。

8.4 带动产业经济发展

建设卤水精细化工产业技术创新战略联盟，将从壮大产业规模、加强产业技术研发、集聚高端技术人才、加快科技成果转化和卤水资源高效、有序开发利用等方面形成集群竞争优势，从而带动卤水精细化工产业健康、持续、快速发展。5年内，区域产业产值新增300亿元，形成核心自主知识产权100件，引进培养产业高端技术人才100名。形成具有相当规模和技术优势的莱州湾沿岸卤水精细化工产业带。

参考文献

[1] 娄金华，黄秉杰，周德田．从东部提升的战略高度重新审视黄河三角洲大开发战略．改革与战略．2009，25（8）：105－107

[2] 慈福义，张晖．黄河三角洲高效生态经济区循环经济发展的SWOT分析与战略目标选择．工业技术经济，2009，28（2）：68－71

[3] 李广杰．推进黄河三角洲高效生态经济区建设的路径与对策．生态经济，2009，22

(4)：82－86
[4] 宁劲松，于志刚，江雪艳．莱州湾沿岸地下卤水的化学组成．海洋科学，2005，29(11)；13－17
[5] 韩有松，吴洪发．莱州湾滨海平原地下卤水成因初探．地质评论，1982，28(2)：126－131
[6] 张晖明，丁娟．企业技术创新战略联盟的理论分析．社会科学，2004，8：5－10

Strategic Development and Technological Innovation of Brine Chemical Industry under Coast of Laizhou Bay

XUE Yan-bin[1] Yang Jie[2] YANG Shu-ren[2]
(1 *Weifang Uiversity of Science and Technology*, *Shouguang* 262700
2 *Shouguang City First Middle School*, *Shouguang* 262700
3 *Shandong Moris Chemical Co.*, *Ltd*, *Shouguang* 262700)

Abstract: In this paper, it has analyzed the general characteristics of underground brine; unique advantages of Laizhou Bay in Shandong Province, development and opportunities for China's fine brine chemical industry; Brine Industrial technology development characteristics and its tendency, gaps and deficiency of brine industry are also addressed; Still, the paper also gives a treatment on Model of Coalition Union of Brine Technological Innovation Activities, complying with national strategies and strategies of Shandong Province, and a discourse on the significant meaning of establishment of Model Coalition Union in inspiring technological innovation. The objective of the paper is to provide theoretical basis and practical guidance for the scientific development of brine industry in the future.

Key words: Laizhou Bay; Brine; Fine Chemicals; Industry; Strategic Development; Technology Innovation

Molecular-weight Dependent Antifungal Activity and Action Mode of Chitosan Against *Fulvia fulva* (cooke) Ciffrri

LI Mei-qin ① XUE Yan-bin PEI Hua-li XUE Qi-qin
QIAO Ning LIU Yong-guang YANG Tian-hui
(*Weifang University of Science and Technology*, *Shouguang* 266700)

Abstract: Antifungal activities of chitosans (CTS) with different molecular weights (MW) and different concentrations against *Fulvia fulva* (cooke) ciffrri (*F. fulva*) causing leaf mould in tomato plants were studied *in vitro* and *in vivo*, the action mode and its inhibition at different stages during the life cycle of *F. fulva* were observed. Results showed that; (1) *In vitro*, CTS exhibited strong antifungal activity against *F. fulva*, especially for the medium MW (213 kDa and 499 kDa) CTS. Almost complete inhibition of *F. fulva* conidia germination and mycelia colony radial growth was found when CTS was at concentration of 0.5 and 2 mg ml^{-1} respectively, however, inhibitory effect on sporulation was not very obvious for all CTSs tested in this experiment. *In vivo*, CTS of 213 kDa CTS at 6 mg ml^{-1} concentration produced stronger antifungal effect than others. (2) The morphological study by scanning electron microscope (SEM) showed that CTS could induce the hypha swelling, and the surface of hypha which was treated with low MW (82 kDa) chitosan was smooth, but was rough treated with high MW (1320 kDa) chitosan. The further study using a confocal laser scanning microscopy (CLSM) coupled with fluorescein isothiocyanate (FITC) -fluorescence detection system showed fluorescence of the FITC-labeled chitosans of which MWs were below 500 kDa could enter into the inner of hypha, however, 1320 kDa chitosan was blocked off the outer of hypha.

Key words: Chitosan; Molecular weight; Antifungal activity; Action mode; *Fulvia fulva* (cooke) ciffrri.

---

① 李美芹，女，博士，副教授，潍坊科技学院蔬菜花卉研究所所长。研究方向：生物学。E-mail：mqli901@126.com

1 Introduction

Chitosan (CTS), a high molecular weight cationic polysaccharide, is a β-1, 4-linked polymer of glucosamine (2-amino-deoxy-β-D-glucose), and is formed by the deacetylation of chitin (poly-*N*-acetylglucosamine), an abundant byproduct of the crab and shrimp processing industries. It is inexpensive and nontoxic, and possesses reactive amino groups. Therefore it has been widely used in many different fields, for instances, as an antimicrobial compound in agriculture, as a potential elicitor of plant defense responses, as a flocculating agent in wastewater treatment, as an additive in the food industry, as a hydrating agent in cosmetics, and as a pharmaceutical agent in biomedicine. Recently its use of bioactive substance has attracted much more attention due to its antimicrobial [1~7], antitumor[8~10] activities, and its immune enhancing effects[11].

Leaf mould, caused by the fungus *Fulvia fulva* (cooke) ciffrri, is one of the most common and destructive foliar diseases of tomato grown under humid conditions, especially in the greenhouse, which could kill large portions of the leaves and result in significant yield reduction (20% ~80%)[12]. Cultivars carrying one or more resistance genes are available for use against the disease, but the fact that the fungus mutates easily leads to a limited application of these cultivars, so the use of chemical fungicides is still necessary [13]. Here brings another question; the applications of various fungicides could lead to resistance development and appearance of different cross-resistance groups. Hence, the frequent development of *F. fulva* isolates resistant to common fungicides and the desire to reduce pesticide use have led to efforts to develop alternatives[14].

CTS and its derivative are proved to have strong antimicrobial activity against different groups of microorganisms[1~7], and have attracted much attention as a potential environment safe means in controlling plant disease. Because of the positive charge on the C-2 of the glucosamine monomer below pH =6, CTS is more easily soluble and has stronger antimicrobial activity compared to chitin[15]. As a new, natural antimicrobial agent, CTS is biodegradable, non-toxic, biocompatible, and antimicrobial against a wide range of target organisms. Numerous studies on antifungal activity of CTS and its derivative against plant pathogens have been carried out[16~20], and several fungi were studied[17,21~23], such as *Fusarium accuminatum*, *Cylindrocladium floridamum*, *Botrytis cinerea*, *Fusarium solani* f. sp. *Glycines*, etc. But little research focused on its antifungal activity against *F. fulva* and even less in its mode of action. Since the activity varies with the type of CTS and the target organism and the environment in which it is applied, it is necessary to study the ability of different MW and concentration CTS to kill *F. fulva*.

Different mechanisms have been proposed although the exact mechanisms of the antimicrobial action of chitin, CTS, and their derivatives are still uncertain. For instance, CTS is adsorbed to bacterial walls leading to walls covering, membrane disruption and cell leakage[24~27], while mainly focused on fungal cell wall[28~30] and cell membrane[31,32] and resulted in antifungal activity. Recently, penetrability of fluorescent-labeled CTS oligomers with molecular weight under 8 kDa into living cells of *Escherichia coli* (bacterium) was observed and oligochitosan was suggested to inhibit bacteria from inside of the cell[33~35]. However, little information about action mode of different MW CTS on the fungal hypha has been made. It's necessary to further study the exact action mechanism of different MW CTS on the fungal hypha because the action mode of CTS varies with the difference of CTS MW and the structure of microbe (fungi or bacteria).

In this investigation, experiments were carried out to test the antifungal activity of different concentration CTS with different MW against *F. fulva*, and its inhibition in different development stages, such as spore viability and germination, mycelia growth, sporulation. The possible mechanism of the antifungal activity of different MW CTS was discussed to gain more accurate information on its mode of action.

2 Experimental

2.1 Materials

CTS (85% deacetylated, MW; 1540, 1320, 499, 213, 144, 82, 38, 3 kDa) were acquired using acetic acid hydrolyzes in our laboratory[36]. All other chemicals and reagents used in the present study were of analytical grade (A. R., Sigma Co. ST. Louis, USA).

2.2 Isolation and culture of F. fulva

Fulvia fulva (cooke) ciffrri used in the present study was isolated from infected tomato leaf (cultivated in greenhouse) with leaf mould disease. The diseased leaves were firstly disinfected with 75% (v/v) ethanol for 10 sec, 0.1% (v/v) $HgCl_2$ for 5 min, and then rinsed the treated leaves with sterile-distilled-water (SDW) for 5 times, small pieces (1 ~ 2mm^2) of the boundary tissue between the healthy area and the region showing leaf mould symptoms were removed and placed on potato-dextrose-agar medium (PDA) consisting 200g/L potato infusion, 20g/L dextrose, and 18g/L agar, cultured in the dark at 22.5℃. Single-spore cultures were maintained on PDA for the following use.

2.3 Antifungal assays

Antifungal assay of CTS (MW; 3, 38, 82, 144, 213, 499, 1320, 1540 kDa) was conducted for the radial growth determination of *F. fulva* on PDA. The same quantity CTS solutions (dissolved in 1% (v/v) acetic acid) were added to the different quantity sterile molten PDA to obtain the desired CTS concentration. The pH value was adjusted to 5.6 with 1 M

NaOH, and then distributed to different plates (7. 5 cm in diameter) . Five-millimeter-diameter fungal plug taken from the margin of a freshly growing colony of *F. fulva* were placed on PDA medium supplemented with CTS of different concentrations (0, 0. 125, 0. 25, 0. 5, 1, 2 mg/ml) and MWs, and incubated at 22. 5℃ in the dark. Two control treatments were set up for the experiments, one contained PDA only (abbreviated as CK_W) and the other contained acetic acid but not CTS (abbreviated as CK_H) . The quantity of acetic acid in all treatments was equal except for CK_W to eliminate the influence of solvent. The growth of colony was monitored daily, and the diameter of colony was measured using crossing method when the mycelium of fungi reached the edges of the control plate (CK_W) . Growth inhibition was expressed as the percentage of inhibition of radial growth relative to the control, and EC_{50} (the middle effective concentration) and EC_{90} (the 90% effective concentration) were calculated to evaluate the antifungal activity of different MW CTS on *F. fulva*. All experiments were repeated three times with three replicates.

the percentage of inhibition (%) $= (1 - D_a/D_b) \times 100$

Where D_a is the diameter of the growth zone in the test plates, D_b is the diameter of growth zone in the control plate (CK_W), and the data were average.

EC_{50} and EC_{90} values were calculated according to the toxic regression equation between the logarithm (x) of chitosan concentration and the probability (y) of the percentage of inhibition.

2. 4 Effect of CTS on sporulation

The influence of CTS on control of sporulation was determined. Six mycelium plugs (5 mm in diameter) were cut from the edge of the growing fungal colony on the medium containing 0, 0. 063, 0. 125, 0. 25, 0. 5, 1, 2mg/ml CTS of which MW were 213, 499, 1320 kDa, and immersed in 0. 5 ml of SDW in 1. 5 ml tube containing 0. 05% Triton X-100, and rinsed for 0. 5 min using a medical ultrasonic syringe (KQ-250*E*, KunShan ultrasonic apparatus LTD. , China) . The number of spore was counted using haemacytometer under inverted microscope and calculated the magnitude of sporulation per mm^2 and the inhibition percentage. Experiments were repeated for three times.

2. 5 In vitro assay on activity of CTS against conidia germination of F. fulva

The same concentration of conidial suspensions (about 1×10^6 conidia/ml) supplemented with different concentration (0, 0. 031 3, 0. 062 5, 0. 125, 0. 25, 0. 5 mg/ml) and different MW (38, 213, 499, 1 320kDa) CTS were kept on 6-well microscope concave slides, and were incubated at 22. 5℃ in the dark, in a wet chamber. The numbers of germinated conidia, which was defined as that the germ tube length of conidium was as long as the length of conidium, were counted in three different microscopic fields at a magnification of ×400 under the light microscope (CX31RTSF, OLYMPUS, Tokyo, Japan) after 24 h. A total of 100 spores per replicate were observed. The germination inhibition percentages were calculated. Each experiment was performed two times with three replications.

The germination inhibition percentage (%) = $(1 - Q_2/Q_1) \times 100$

Where Q_1 is the quantity of germination of the control, Q_2 is the quantity of germination of the treatment containing CTS.

2.6 Effect of CTS on hypha growth and morpha

Effect of CTS on hypha growth was conducted for submerged growth determination. Mycelial plugs (5 mm in diameter) of *F. fulva* were cut from the margins of the colony cultured for 5 days on PDA medium, and aerobically cultivated in Potato Dextrose (PD) which is liquid at 25℃ with continuous shaking at 121 rpm (rotary oscillating shaker, ZHWY-2102, Zhicheng analysis apparatus LTD., ShangHai, China). Every treatment was three replicates containing 100 ml PD supplemented with different concentration (0, 0.5, 1, 2 mg ml^{-1}) CTS of which MWs were 82kDa, 499 kDa, and 1 320 kDa. After 20 days, the colony growth was monitored by dry weight determination (after repeated washing with SDW). Growth inhibition was expressed as the percentage of inhibition (relative to the control).

Single-hypha cultured in the PD described as above was isolated and the morphology of hypha was observed under light microscope and scanning electron microscope (SEM) (KYKY2800B, KYKY Technology Development LTD., Beijing, China) to determine the putative mechanism of the action of CTS.

2.7 Preparation of FITC-labeled CTS and observation of their penetrability using confocal laser scanning microscopy

CTS was flocculated when the pH value of different MW CTS solution (10mg/ml, dissolved in 0.1 M CH_3COOH) was adjusted to 6.8 using 0.2 M NaOH, and the FITC-labeled CTS was synthesized by adding 10ml of FITC solution dissolved in dehydrated methanol (2.0mg/ml) to 20 ml of CTS solution, stirring in the dark at ambient temperature. After 15 h, the labeled flocculation was centrifuged at 12 000 g (10min) and washed with methanol/water solution (v/v; 70:30). The washing and flocculation were repeated until no fluorescence was detected in the supernatant when analyzed by fluorescence spectrophotometers (Hitachi F-4 500, Tokyo, Japan, λ_{ex} = 490nm, λ_{em} = 520nm). The FITC-labeled chitosan was redissolved in 10ml of 0.1% CH_3COOH and dialyzed in the dark against 5 L of 70% methanol, the methanol being replaced with fresh 70% methanol every 6 h until no fluorescence in the methanol. Finally the FITC-labeled CTS was freeze-dried, weighted[37].

FITC-labeled CTS at 0.5 mg/ml (dissolved in sterile 1% acetic acid) was incubated with actively growing fungal bead in PD. The fungal bead was picked out after 24 h, and washed by SDW repeatedly until no fluorescence in the water was detected. Hypha was isolated from mycelial fungal pellet, and observed under CLSM (LSM5PASCAL, ZEISS, German) to judge whether the FITC-labeled CTS penetrated into the hypha. Conidia were observed simultaneously according to the method described as above to determine the putative mechanism of inhibition of CTS to conidium.

2.8 In vivo, Field trials to evaluate the inhibitory effect of chitosan on leaf mould

The use of chitosan as a natural antifungal agent against leaf mould in tomato was investigated in greenhouse. Tomato (*Lycopersicon esculentum* Mill.) cv. 'Qianxi' was used as the target plant in the present experiment and cultivated to the stage of the fourth true leaf. The plants were sprayed three times with different concentrations (based on preliminary dose response studies) and different MW (82, 144, 213, 1 320, 1 540kDa) CTS at an interval of 10 days, and the control plants were sprayed with water only. Conidia were harvested from the PDA plates by adding 5 ml SDW containing 0.05% (v/v) Triton X-100 to each plate on which the colony was cultured 20 days and gently rubbing the sporulation mycelial mat with a bent glass rod. The conidial suspension concentration was adjusted to 1×10^6 conidia/ml with the aid of a haemocytometer.

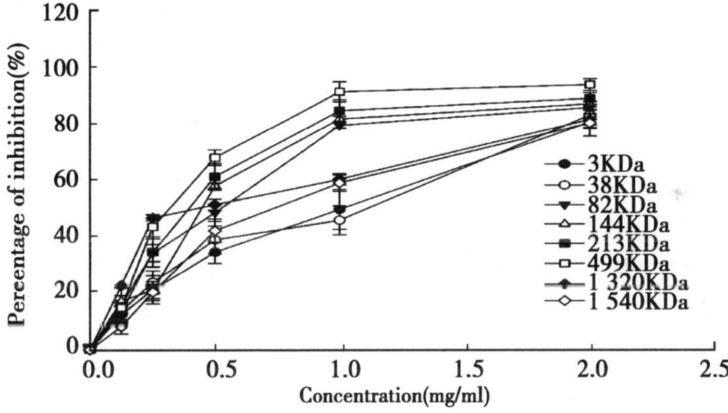

Figure 1 Effect of different MW and concentrations of chitosan on antifungal activity (the inhibition percentage of the mycelial radical growth) of *F. fulva* at pH 5.6. (mean ± SD, n = 9).

24 h after, plants sprayed with CTS and water three times were artificially inoculated with conidial suspension of *F. fulva*, and incubated for another 48 h at 22.5℃ and 90% relative humidity in greenhouse. Two weeks later, the disease was investigated every 5 days, a total of three times. Leaf mould was evaluated on a scale of 0 ~ 7with; 0 = no necrosis, leaf area is completely healthy; 1 = 25% of the leaf area is with symptoms; 3 = 50% of the leaf area is with symptoms; 5 = 75% of the leaf area is with symptoms; 7 = 100% of the leaf area is covered with symptoms. A disease index was calculated as the sum

of the area of the five leaves. Non-treated plants served as the control. Treatments were arranged in a randomized complete block design with three replications, and each treatment was consist of 30 plants.

2.9 Statistical analysis

Results were analyzed with the software package Sigmaplot 8.0 and SPSS13.0 (SPSS Inc., Chicago, IL). Mean values and standard deviations from the different replicates per treatment were calculated, and the significance between the treated group and the control was analyzed by two tailed paired t-test with significance set at $P < 0.01$.

3 Results and Discussion

3.1 Antifungal activity of chitosan as a function of its concentration and MW in vitro

Antifungal activities of CTS with different MW and concentration against *F. fulva* were tested. The colony of *F. fulva* reached the edges of the control plate (CK_W) after 4 weeks cultivation. The inhibition percentage of different concentration and MW CTS was shown in figure 1, their EC_{50} and EC_{90} were calculated (Table Ⅰ). All CTS samples tested in this experiment had antifungal activity, the difference of antifungal activity with the difference of concentration and MW was obvious, and the antifungal activity improved with the increase of concentration, and the middle MW CTS of 499 kDa had strongest inhibition, and its EC_{50} and EC_{90} were 0.318 and 1.204mg/ml respectively (Table Ⅰ). CTS had strong antifungal activity (the inhibition percentage was bigger than 80%) at concentration of 2mg/ml for all tested CTS samples, and at 1mg/ml for 82, 144, 213, 499 kDa CTS, respectively (Fig. 1).

There are several factors, both intrinsic and extrinsic, that affect the antimicrobial activity of CTS, and the concentration and MW are more important factors among these. In this experiment, it demonstrated that CTS with different MW could inhibit the radial growth of *F. fulva* with an optimal effect at concentrations ranging from 0.25 to 2mg/ml, and the middle MW CTS were more effective than others used in this study. It is in accordance with the study of Qin[38], although the CTS and pathogen used in the experiment are different. While in other studies, CTS with MW below 300 kDa, the antimicrobial effect on *Staphylococcus aureus* was strengthened as the MW increased. In contrast, the effect on *E. coli* was weakened[39]. CTS samples with MW from 55 to 155 kDa have antimicrobial activities at the concentration higher than 0.2mg/ml. And the antimicrobial activity of low MW CTS is higher than that of the high MW samples[6]. These diverging results may originate from the differences of CTS and pathogen, because the sensibility is different for the different microorganisms (mould and/or bacteria) for CTS and it is related to the MW of the CTS.

Table 1 Effect of Different Concentration and MW CTS on EC_{50} and EC_{90} Value of Hyphal Radical Growth Inhibition (mean ± SD, n = 9, mg/ml)

Chitosan (MW; kDa)	EC_{50} value	EC_{90} value
3	0.777 ±0.008	4.838 ±0.003
38	0.718 ±0.007	4.802 ±0.009
82	0.442 ±0.008	2.241 ±0.007
144	0.445 ±0.005	2.009 ±0.006
213	0.396 ±0.009	1.677 ±0.008
499	0.318 ±0.003	1.204 ±0.004
1 320	0.438 ±0.006	5.260 ±0.007
1 540	0.704 ±0.009	3.466 ±0.007

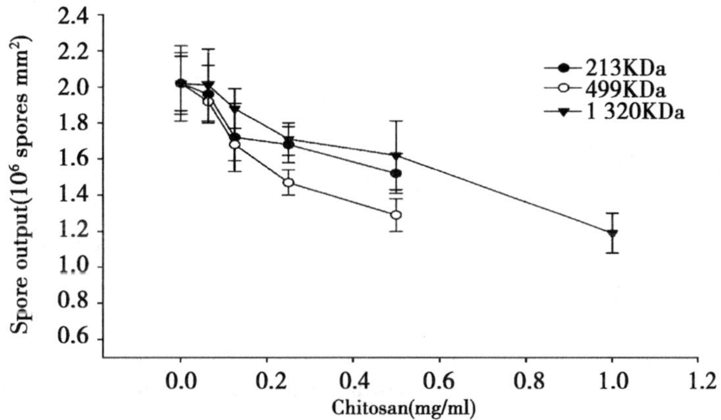

Figure 2 Effect of different MW and concentration chitosan on the sporulation of F. fulva. (mean ± SD, n = 3).

3.2 Efficiency of CTS on the quantity of sporulation

The mycelial plugs on the medium containing 0 ~ 2mg/ml CTS were cultured in the dark at 25℃. After about 20d, there was not sufficient radial growth for the mycelial plugs growing on mediums containing 1, 2mg/ml for 213 and 499 kDa CTS, respectively; and 2mg/ml for 1 320 kDa CTS, so no data were obtained for these treatments. Inhibitory effects of these tested CTS to sporulation were not notable compared to the control (Fig. 2). At the concentration of

0.5mg/ml, the biggest inhibitory percentage was 24.8% and 34.9% for 213 and 499 kDa MW CTS respectively. And at the concentration of 1mg/ml, the biggest inhibitory percentage was 41.1% for the 1 320 kDa CTS.

In this experiment, the method assaying inhibitory effect on sporulation is calculate the quantity of sporulation for every 5 mm diameter of mycelial plug growing on the medium containing different MW and concentration CTS, the inhibitory effect on sporulation was not obvious by this way. However, the total of sporulation on whole colony growing on the medium containing different CTS is still very different, this can be explained by its antifungal activity described as above.

3.3 In vitro activity against conidia germination

In vitro, the effect of CTS on spore germination was studied. Result showed that all CTSs with different MWs could inhibit germination of *F. fulva* conidia (Table 2). A low concentration of 499 kDa CTS (0.034mg/ml) caused 50% inhibition of germination, and almost complete inhibition was observed at 0.25mg/ml of all tested CTSs (Fig. 3). The percentage of spore germination in CK_H was 99.1% after 24 h incubation. Table 2 and Figure 3 showed that the antifungal activity of 499 kDa CTS on *F. fulva* was better than other MWs.

Figure 4 showed various shapes of conidia after 24 h incubation. Compared with the shape of normal spore (Fig. 4 A) and germinated spores (Fig. 4 B) which were not treated with CTS. Conidia which treated with CTS did not germinate and appeared distorted or plasmolyzability (Fig. 4 D) observed under light microscope, and its appearance was covered with a layer of FITC-chitosan further observed with 400x CLSM (Fig. 4 C). Incubation for another 24 h, these results did not change. Inhibition of CTS to spores germination may be related with its solution osmotic potential and adhesion of CTS to spore which led to conidial distortion, affected spore viability.

Table 2 Effect of Different Concentration and MW CTS on the Value of EC_{50} and EC_{90} of Conidia Germination Inhibition (mean ± SD, n = 6, mg/ml)

Chitosan (MW; kDa)	EC_{50} value	EC_{90} value
38	0.083 ± 0.003	0.211 ± 0.003
213	0.070 ± 0.002	0.160 ± 0.003
499	0.034 ± 0.001	0.146 ± 0.001
1 320	0.088 ± 0.003	0.195 ± 0.002

(EC_{50}; median effect concentration, EC_{90}; 90% effect concentration.)

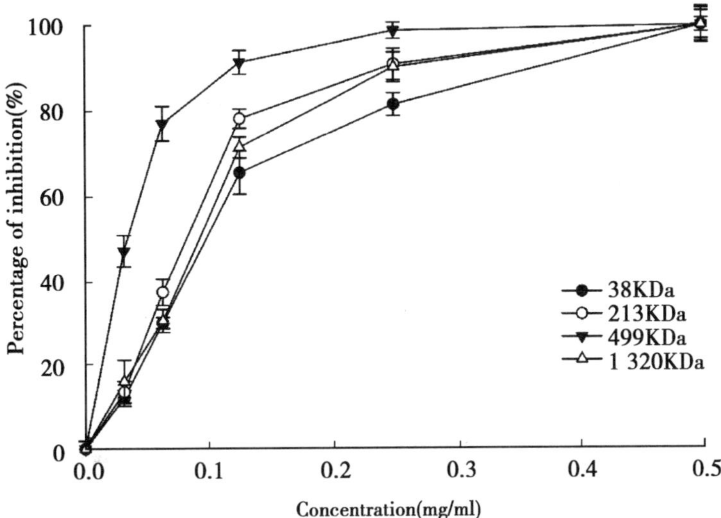

Figure 3 Effect of various MW and concentration of chitosan on the inhibition percentage of conidia germination of *F. fulva.* (mean ± SD, n = 6)

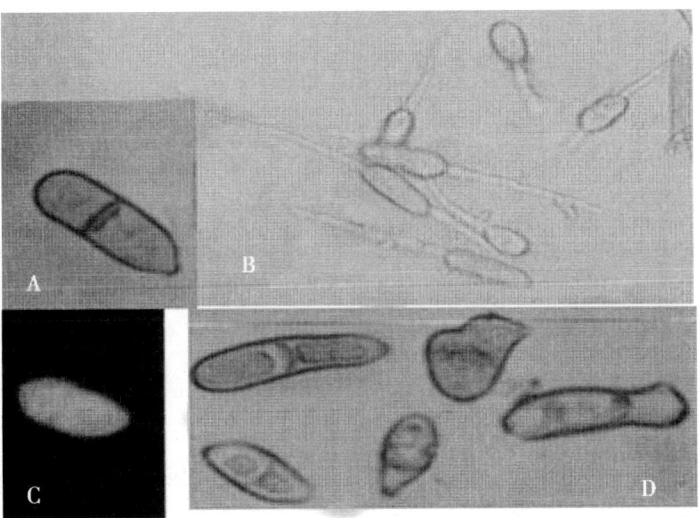

Figure 4 The shapes of normal spore (A) and normal germination spores (B) which did not be treated with chitosan; the shapes of spore treated with chitosan (D); A, B, and D are the images observed under light microscope. The shape of spore treated with FITC-chitosan observed under a confocal laser scanning microscope (C).

3. 4 Effect of CTS on hyphal growth and morpha

Effect of CTS on hyphal growth was determined. After 20 d mycelial disks cultured in PD, the inhibitory effects of all CTSs on hyphal growth at 1 ~ 2mg/ml concentration were obvious (Table 3) . The mycelial plugs formed fungal ball in PD containing 0 and 0. 5mg/ml CTS, but they came into being fragments in the PD supplemented with 1 and 2mg/ml CTS. It was because CTS might destroy the whole mycelia which led to form fragments. The dry weight of *F. fulva* mycelia treated with 1320 kDa CTS was the most weight, and the 499 kDa CTS was the lightest among the three CTSs (Table 3), this result is correlated with antifungal activity which 499 kDa CTS has strongest inhibitor to *F. fulva* among the tested CTS (Fig. 1), especially at the concentration of 1 ~ 2mg/ml.

Hypha cultured in PD supplemented with 0. 5mg/ml 82kDa and 1320 kDa CTS was isolated and examined by light microscope and SEM. The morpha of *F. fulva* hypha growing in the absence of CTS showed typical outline feature of the genus (Fig. 5 A_1 and A_2), but the hypha cultured in PD supplemented CTS showed hypha swelling, distortion, excessive branching, and shorting of mycelial segments observed under light microscope (Fig. 5 B_1 and D_1) . The further observation by SEM showed that the swelling hypha which was cultured in PD containing 0. 5mg/ml 82kDa CTS was smooth in appearance (Fig. 5 B_2), but rough in PD containing 0. 5mg/ml 1 320 kDa CTS (Fig. 5 D_2) .

SEM observation showed the possible action of CTS and its derivatives on different fungi[30,31,40 ~ 43]. CTS and its derivatives induced obvious structural alterations including cell wall loosening, vacuolation, and protoplasm degradation. Moreover, a histochemical assay on *Rhizopus stolonifer* with chitin specified wheat germ agglutinin/ovomucoid - gold complex has suggested that cell wall loosening was the result of upset balance between biosynthesis and turnover of chitin at the hyphal apex[30]. In this study, the results showed that the antifungal action mode of different MW CTS may be different; although all CTS samples could induce the hypha swelling, the surface of mycelia treated with CTS of lower MW was smooth, and it was rough with higher MW CTS.

3. 5 Effect of different MW of FITC-labeled CTS on permeability through hypha

The action mode of different MW CTS was investigated through the research of the permeability of FITC-labeled CTS by laser fault images using CLSM in different depth of mycelium. The stacking of 1 320 kDa CTS to the hyphal surface of *F. fulva* was confirmed, and there was no fluorescence at the inner of hypha (Fig. 6) . It demonstrated that the CTS of 1 320 kDa could not permeate into the inner of hypha. The fluorescence of the FITC-labeled 499 kDa MW CTS at the inside of the *F. fulva* cell was observed (Fig. 7), and the brightness of green fluorescence increased with the increase of depth (Fig. 7 A-G), but weakened from the inner to the surface (Fig. 7 G-L). It demonstrated that the CTS of which MW below 499 kDa could permeate into the inner of hypha.

Table 3 Dry Weight (g) of *F. fulva* Mycelia C ultured in LPD Conta ining different CTS After 20 Days

Concentration of CTS (mg/ml)	82kDa CTS	499kDa CTS	1 320kDa CTS
0 (CKW)	1.608 ±0.15	1.608 ±0.15	1.608 ±0.15
0 (CKH)	1.504 ±0.10	1.504 ±0.10	1.504 ±0.10
0.5	0.422 ±0.03b	0.382 ±0.03b	0.653 ±0.05b
1	0.142 ±0.01b	0.101 ±0.01b	0.309 ±0.03b
2	0.092 ±0.02b	0.053 ±0.02b	0.118 ±0.28b

Compared with CKW b $p < 0.01$

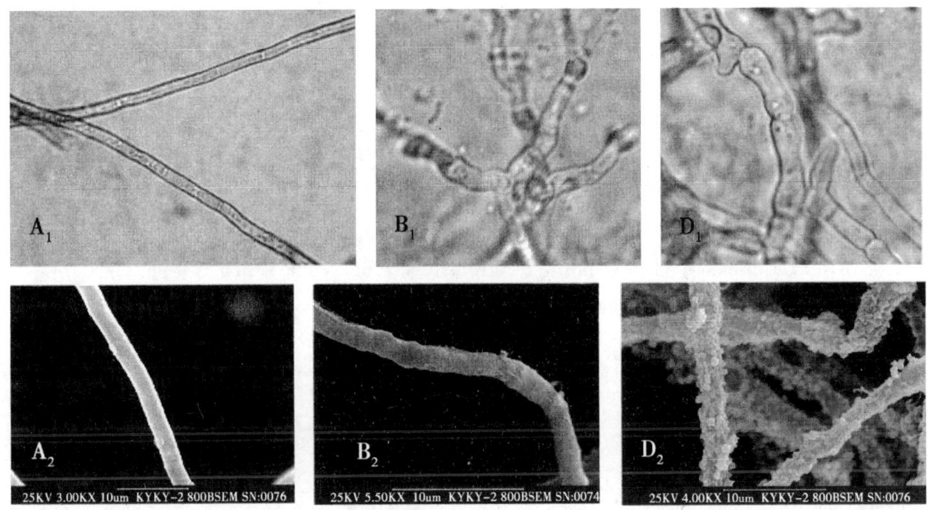

Figure 5 Effect of chitosan on the hyphal morpha under both the light microscope and SEM A_1 is the typical micrographs of the genus of F. fulva not treated with CTS, B_1 and D_1 is the micrographs of *F. fulva* treated with 82 kDa and 1 320 kDa chitosan respectively, which were observed under the light microscope.

A2 is the typical micrographs of the genus of F. fulva not treated with CTS, B2 and D2 is the micrographs of F. fulva treated with 82 kDa and 1 320kDa chitosan respectively, which were observed under the scanning electronic micrographs

It was further confirmed that the antifungal mechanism of different MW CTS was different. The permeation of lower CTS into hypha was also observed (Fig. 7) by CLSM. So the growth of *F. fulva* may be inhibited by CTS from the inside of cell, and the antifungal mechanism of CTS with low MW may be caused mainly by the inhibition of the transcription from DNA[44]. While the higher MW CTS, acted mainly on the outer surface of the mycelia, formed an impervious layer around hypha (Fig. 5 D_2), and directly stunted the development of mycelia. On the other hand, the effective growth inhibition of hypha was assumed to be the prevention of nutrition delivery through cell wall.

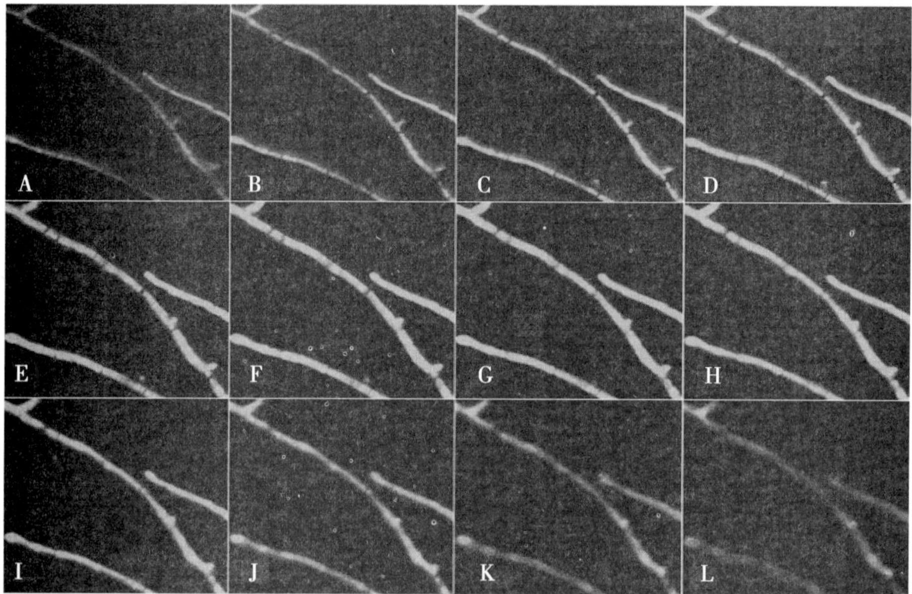

Figure 6　Confocal laser scanning micrographs (×1 000) of hypha treated with 1 320 kDa chitosan. A to H is the different layers of hypha which is from one surface to another surface of the hypha.

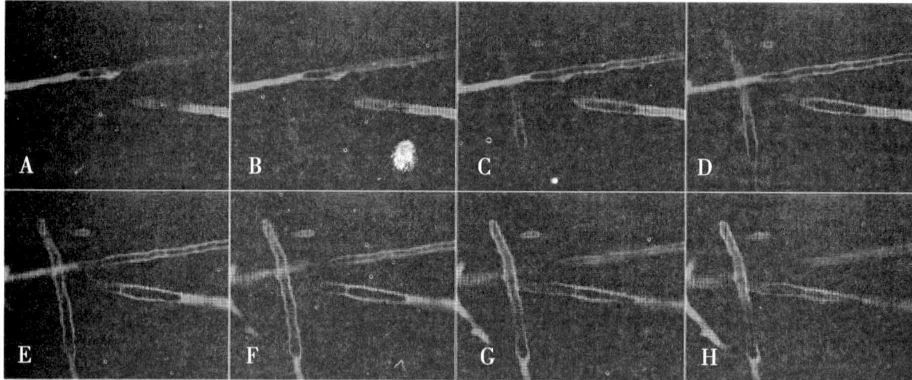

Figure 7　Confocal laser scanning micrographs (×1 000) of hypha treated with 499 kDa chitosan. From A to F is from the surface to the inner, and G to L is from the inner to against surface of hypha.

Penetrability of FITC-labeled CTS oligomer with molecular weight of 9. 3 kDa stacking to the cell wall of *Escherichia coli* was confirmed[35]. This is obviously different from that CTS with 499 kDa can be diffused into inner of mycelia. The main reason may be that MW of CTS and target pathogen were different in this experiment.

3.6 In vivo, the effect of chitosan on leaf mould in the field

The adverse effects on growth of tomato plants causing by CTS were not found in this experiment. Spraying CTS on tomato plants three times before inoculation of conidia caused a decrease in the diseased leaf rates and the disease index which were shown in Table 4. Three times foliar application of the 213kDa CTS at 1 ~ 10mg/ml concentration and different MW CTS at 5mg/ml significantly reduced disease index as compared to the control, and the 213 kDa CTS at 6mg/ml concentration reduced disease index from 29.2 in the control to 11.1, however no very obvious difference in the disease severity among the different MW CTS but at the same concentration of 5mg/ml was observed, 213 kDa CTS was little better than others.

In this study, the reason that the effect of different MW CTS on diseased index was not obvious may be the concentration of 6mg/ml CTS was appropriate for control tomato leaf mould. It' s not exactly accordance with the antifungal activity tested *in vitro*, this maybe correlated with the method of experiment which tomato plants were sprayed three times CTS before inoculated conidia of *F. fulva*. so the reason which CTS could decrease the diseased index was not only the antifungal activity of CTS but also the inducing resistance caused by CTS.

Table 4 The rates of diseased leaf and diseased index of tomato cultivars after leaves sprayed with Chitosan

Chitosan (MW: kDa)	Treatment (mg/ml)	Investigation leaves	Diseased leaf rates (%)	Diseased index
CK	0	295	70.5 ±3.4	29.2 ±1.3
213	0.1	352	67.9 ±3.6	23.2 ±0.9
	1	363	41.7 ±1.9^b	17.1 ±1.1^b
	3	379	44.1 ±1.9^b	16.8 ±1.1^b
	6	413	33.0 ±3.7^b	11.1 ±0.8^b
	10	301	47.3 ±1.9^b	14.6 ±1.2^b
82	5	387	45.8 ±2.3^b	15.5 ±1.4^b
144	5	369	47.3 ±2.0^b	16.2 ±0.9^b
213	5	422	35.4 ±5.2^b	13.5 ±2.4^b
1 320	5	365	49.2 ±2.8^b	18.5 ±1.0^b
1 540	5	329	55.5 ±1.7^b	14.4 ±1.2^b

Note: 1. The data in the table are the average of three times investigation data.

2. Compared with CK ^{b} $P < 0.01$

4 Conclusions

In vitro assay showed that CTS exhibited strong antifungal activity against *F. fulva* at optimal concentration, and the middle MW CTS had stronger antifungal activity than larger or smaller MW CTS tested in the present study, and the inhibition rate enhanced with the increase of CTS concentration. Among the three stages of life cycle of *F. fulva*, CTS showed the strongest inhibition on spores germination, and the weakest inhibitory effect on the sporulation. CTS could significantly reduced the occurrence of tomato leaf mould in the greenhouse, especially for the 213 kDa CTS, at 6mg/ml concentration had better antifungal effect than that of other CTS tested in this experiment.

CTS could induce the mycelia distorted. The stacks of 1 320 kDa CTS to the hyphal surface was found but not of 82 kDa. The further research using CLSM demonstrated that the CTS samples of which MW were lower than 499 kDa could enter into the inner of mycelia, and 1320 kDa CTS was block off outer of the membrane of mycelia. So the action mode of different MW CTS is different. An investigation with CLSM is under carrying out in our laboratory to find the exact action site of different MW CTS.

5 Acknowledgements

The authors are indebted to the financial support from National Natural Science Foundation of China (No. 30270258), National Natural Science Foundation of Shandong province (Y2008F15) and Program for New Century Excellent Talents (NCET-05-0597).

References

[1] Choi, K.; Kim, K. Y.; Yoo, Y. J.; Oh, S. J.; Choi, J. H.; Kim, C. Y. Int J Antimicrob Agents, 2001, 18: 553

[2] Guerra-Sánchez, M. G.; Vega-Pérez, J.; Velázquez-del Valle, M. G.; Hernández-Lauzardo, A. N. Pestic Biochem Physiol, 2009, 93: 18

[3] No, H. K.; Park, N. Y.; Lee, S. H.; Meyers, S. P. Int J Food Microbiol, 2002, 74: 65

[4] Yoshihiko, O.; Mayumi, S.; Takahiro, A.; Hiroyuki, S.; Yoshihiro, S.; Ichiro, N.; Tetsuaki, T. Biocontrol Sci, 2003, 8, 25

[5] Chung, Y. C.; Wang, H. L.; Chen, Y. M.; Li, S. L. Bioresour Technol, 2003, 88, 179

[6] Liu, N.; Chen, X. G.; Park, H. J.; Liu, C. G.; Liu, C. S.; Meng, X. H.; Yu, L. J. Carbohy Polym, 2006, 64, 60

[7] Eweis, M.; Elkholy, S. S.; Elsabee, M. Z. Int J Bio Macromolecules, 2006, 38, 1

[8] Suzuki, K. ; Mikami, T. ; Okawa, Y. ; Tokoro, A. ; Suzuki, S. ; Suzuki, M. Carbohydr Res, 1986, 151, 403
[9] Qi, L. F. ; Xu, Z. R. Bioorg Med Chem Lett, 2006, 16, 4243
[10] Qin, C. Q. ; Du, Y. M. ; Xiao, L. ; Li, Z. ; Gao, X. H. Int J Bio Macromolecules 2002, 31, 111
[11] Seferian, P. G. ; Martinez, M. L. Vaccine 2001, 19, 661
[12] Smith, P. ; Last, F. T. ; Kempton, R. J. ; Gisborne, J. H. Ann Appl Biol 1969, 63, 19
[13] Laterrot, H. Neth J Plant Pathol 1986, 92, 305
[14] Yourman, L. F. ; Jeffers, S. N. Plant Dis 1999, 83, 569
[15] Chen, C. S. ; Liau, W. Y. ; Tsai, G. J. J. Food Prot 1998, 61, 1124
[16] Roller, S. ; Covill, N. Int J Food Microbiol 1999, 47, 67
[17] Ben-Shalom, N. ; Ardi, R. ; Pinto, R. ; Aki, C. ; Fallik, E. Crop Prot 2003, 22, 285
[18] Xu, J. G. ; Zhao, X. M. ; Han, X. W. ; Du, Y. G. Pest Biochem Physiol 2007, 87, 220
[19] Guo, Z. Y. ; Chen, R. ; Xing, R. ; Liu, S. ; Yu, H. H. ; Wang, P. B. ; Li, C. P. ; Li, P. C. Carbohydr Res 2006, 341, 351
[20] Chang, W. T. ; Chen, Y. C. ; Jao, C. L. Bioresour Technol 2007, 98, 1224
[21] Laflamme, P. ; Benhamou, N. ; Bussieres, G. ; Dessureault, M. Can J Bot 1999, 1460
[22] Sharathchandra, R. G. ; Niranjan Raj, S. ; Shetty, N. P. ; Amruthesh, K. N. ; Shekar Shetty, H. Crop Prot 2004, 23, 881
[23] Prapagdee,B. ; Kotchadat, K. ; Kumsopa, A. ; Visarathanonth, N. Bioresour Technol 2007, 98, 1353
[24] Helander,I. M. ; Nurmiaho-Lassila, E. L. ; Ahvenainen, R. ; Rhoades, J. ; Roller, S. Int J Food Microbiol 2001, 71, 235
[25] Yang, F. ; Cui, X. Q. ; Yang, X. R. Biophys Chem 2002, 99, 99
[26] Liu,H. ; Du, Y. M. ; Wang, X. H. ; Sun, L. Int J Food Microbio 2004, 95, 147
[27] Chung, Y. C. ; Su, Y. P. ; Chen, C. C. ; Jia, G. ; Wang, H. I. ; Wu, J. C. G. ; Lin, J. G. Acta Pharm Sin 2004, 25, 932
[28] Bautista- Banos; S. ; Hernandez-Lauzardo, A. N. ; Velazquez-del Valle, M. G. ; Hernandez- Lopez, M. ; Barka, E. ; Bosquez-Molina, E. ; Wilson, C. L. Crop Prot 2006, 25, 108
[29] Allan, C. R. ; Hadwiger, L. A. Exp Mycol 1979, 3, 285
[30] Elghaouth, A. ; Arul, J. ; Asselin, A. ; Benhamou, N. Mycol Res 1992, 96, 769
[31] Elghaouth, A. ; Arul, J. ; Wilson, C. ; Benhamou, N. Physiol Mol Plant Pathol 1994, 44, 417

[32] Zakrzewska, A.; Boorsma, A.; Brul, S.; Hellingwerf, K. J.; Klis, F. M. Eukaryot Cell 2005, 4, 703

[33] Huang, M.; Khor, E.; Lin, L. Y. Pharm Res 2004, 21, 344

[34] Liu, X. F.; Guan, Y. L.; Yang, D. Z.; Li, Z.; Yao, K. D. J Appl Polym Sci 2001, 79, 1324

[35] Tokura, S.; Ueno, K.; Miyazaki, S.; Nishi, N. Macromol Symp 1997, 12, 1

[36] Chen, X. G.; Zheng, L.; Wang, Z.; Lee, C. Y.; Park H. J. J Agric Food Chem 2002, 50, 5915

[37] Huang, M.; Khor, E.; Lim, L. Y. Pharm Res 2004, 21, 344

[38] Qin, C. Q.; Li, H. R.; Xiao, Q.; Liu, Y.; Zhu, J. C.; Du, Y. M. Carbohy Polym 2006, 63, 367

[39] Zheng, L. Y.; Zhu, J. F. Carbohy Polym 2003, 54, 527

[40] Hadwiger, L. A.; Beckman, J. M.; Adams, M. J. Plant Physiol 1981, 67, 170

[41] LaFontaine, P. J.; Benhamou, N. Biocontr Sci Technol 1996, 6, 111

[42] Muzzarelli, R. A. A.; Muzzarelli, C.; Tarsi, R.; Miliani, M.; Gabbanelli, F.; Cartolari, M. Biomacromolecules 2001, 2, 165

[43] Plascencia-Jatomea, M.; Viniegra, G.; Olayo, R; Castillo-Ortega, M. M.; Shirai, K. Macromol Biosci 2003, 3, 582

[44] Hadwiger, L. A.; Fristensky, B.; Riggleman, R. C. Zikakis, J. P. Es., New York; Plenum 1984, 291

玉米弯孢菌叶斑病发病率与严重度关系研究

李金堂①
（潍坊科技学院，寿光 262700）

摘　要： 2005—2006 年，在田间接种条件下对玉米弯孢菌叶斑病发病情况进行系统调查，获得了病害普遍率与严重度间对应关系的数据，利用 SAS 软件分析了两者的关系（I-S 关系）。结果表明，屯玉 1 号和海禾 14 的 I-S 关系均可用互补双对数模型（Complementary Log-log model）描述，两模型参数间的差异不显著，病害在两品种上的 I-S 关系可用下述模型描述：S = exp｛［ln（-ln（1-p））+2.408 5］/1.089 3｝，P、S 分别表示病叶率和病情指数。

关键词： 玉米弯孢菌叶斑病；发病率；严重度；I-S 关系

玉米弯孢菌叶斑病（Curvularia leaf spot of maize）是近年在我国北方玉米产区发生的一种重要病害，该病由弯孢菌［*Curvularialunata*（Wakker）Boed.］引起，病害发展蔓延快，流行频率高。国内学者对玉米弯孢菌叶斑病的研究主要集中于病原生物学、品种抗病性鉴定、病害流行及病害防治等领域[1~5]。病情调查是检验其发病程度、防治效果及估计损失率的主要依据，通常采用严重度或病情指数为指标，这两个指标在实际调查中工作量大，占用大量人力物力，相比之下，病叶率调查则要容易得多，因此利用病叶率间接地估计严重度（病情指数），对于提高病情监测和产量损失估计的效率及准确性具有重要意义。

普遍率（incidence）和严重度（severity）间的关系（简称 I-S 关系）是植病流行学观测技术上的一个重要内容，James 等首先研究了小麦白粉病和叶锈病的 I-S 关系，发现白粉病的 I-S 关系呈指数函数关系[6]，之后国内外学者已先后开展了苹果白粉病[7]、太豆锈病[8]、稻瘟病[9]等一些植物病害的 I-S 关系研究。而对玉米弯孢菌叶斑病的 I-S 关系目前尚未见报道，因此，本文利用试验及调查获得的数据，分析玉米弯孢菌叶斑病的 I-S 关系，为利用普遍率间接估计严重度提供科学依据。

① 李金堂，男，博士，副教授，潍坊科技学院植物病虫害研究所所长。研究方向：植物病理学。E－mail：li_ jintang@ 163. com

1 材料与方法

1.1 试验材料及试验方法

选用玉米生产上的主栽品种屯玉1号和海禾14于2005—2006年进行田间接种试验。设立病情观测圃，每个品种播种一个小区，南北垄向，垄距0.6m，株距0.35m，每个小区20行，每行玉米保苗24~28株，将上年采集的玉米弯孢菌叶斑病病叶及室内培养繁殖的弯孢病病菌撒于观测圃土表作为田间病原菌菌源。自田间玉米植株叶部始见病斑时开始调查病叶率及病情指数，选取有代表性的发病株，定株挂牌，每隔7 d调查1次，分别记载不同品种的单株病叶数和每株不同发病级别的叶片数，病害分级参考玉米小斑病分级标准，按整株0~5级严重度分级标准记载[10]，至病害停止发展为止。并按如下公式计算病叶率（普遍率）和病情指数（严重度）。

病叶率=发病叶片总数/调查叶片总数×100%

病情指数=100×∑（病级叶数×代表数值）/（调查叶片总数×发病最高级别的代表数值）

1.2 数据分析

将通过试验调查获得的每个品种的病叶率及病情指数进行各种转换，如对数、正弦、反正弦等，以获得最佳的拟合效果。数据拟合采用SAS统计软件（Release 8.01，SAS Institute Inc.）进行，以各模型的决定系数R^2、剩余平方和SSE、F值和检验概率（$Pr>F$）作为模型取舍的标准[11~13]。

2 结果与分析

2.1 发病率及严重度调查结果

2005—2006年对每个品种各调查10次，获得了病害普遍率与严重度相互对应的数据，它们的散点图如图1所示。从图中可以看出，在病叶率（普遍率）比较低时，病情指数（严重度）增加较为缓慢，当病叶率达到约80%以上时，随着病叶率的增加，相对应的病情指数增加速度明显加快。从图中还可以看出，病叶率在90%~100%之间时，相对应病情指数的变异幅度剧增。

2.2 数据分析

利用SAS软件对变量（病叶率及病情指数）的不同转换形式拟合后得到描述玉米弯孢菌叶斑病I-S关系的最佳模型为CLL模型（Complementary Log-log model，互补双对数模型），CLL模型形式为：

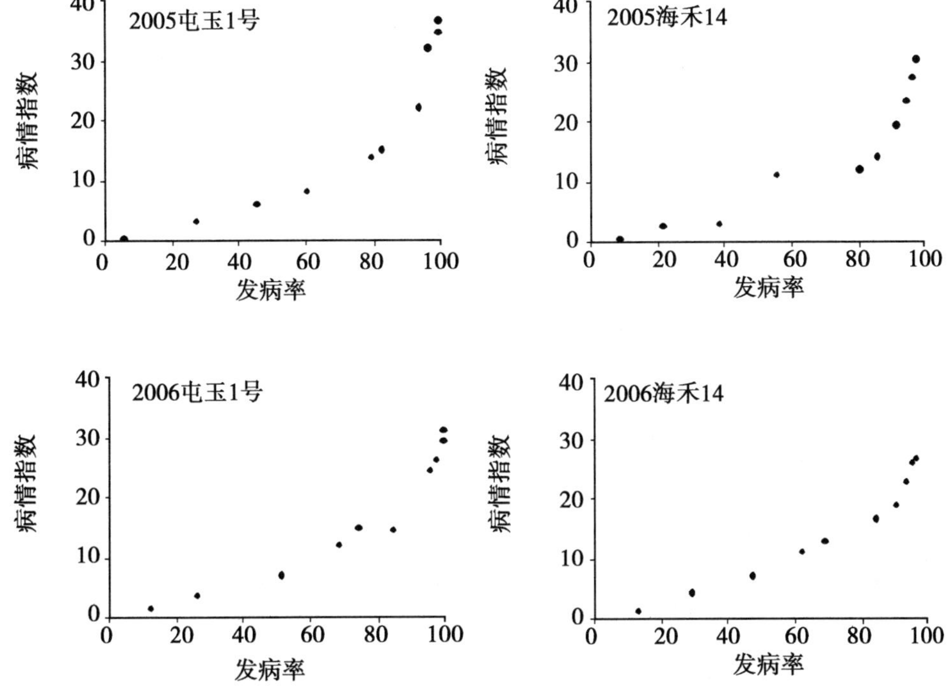

图1 玉米弯孢菌叶斑病普遍率及严重度调查结果

Fig. 1 The investigation results of incidence and severity of Curvularia leaf spot of maize

$$y = a + b \times x \qquad (1)$$

式中Y表示ln（-ln（1-P））；x表示ln（S）；P、S分别代表病叶率和病情指数

两个品种的CLL模型分别如下：

$$屯玉1号：y = -2.6484 + 1.1700x\ (R^2 = 0.9920\ SD = 0.0135) \qquad (2)$$

$$海禾14；y = -2.1979 + 1.0141x\ (R^2 = 0.9634\ SD = 0.0480) \qquad (3)$$

回归方程（2）和（3）的参数差异性比较：对直线方程（2）和（3）的两个参数a（截距）和b（回归系数）进行t检验[14]，结果表明回归方程的截距和回归系数间均无显著差异，其t值分别为1.65和1.36，小于0.05的t临界值2.02。因此对两个品种的数据综合在一起进行曲线拟合，得到玉米弯孢菌叶斑病I-S关系的总模型为：

$$y = -2.4085 + 1.0893x\ (R^2 = 0.9733\ SD = 0.0381) \qquad (4)$$

式（4）的直线图见图2。

式（4）即ln（-ln（1-P））=-2.4085+1.0893ln（S），经过变换得到下式：

$$S = \exp\{[\ln(-\ln(1-p)) + 2.4085]/1.0893\} \qquad (5)$$

式（5）的曲线见图3。

3 结论与讨论

通过SAS统计软件对玉米弯孢菌叶斑病病叶率及病情指数数据不同转换形式拟合

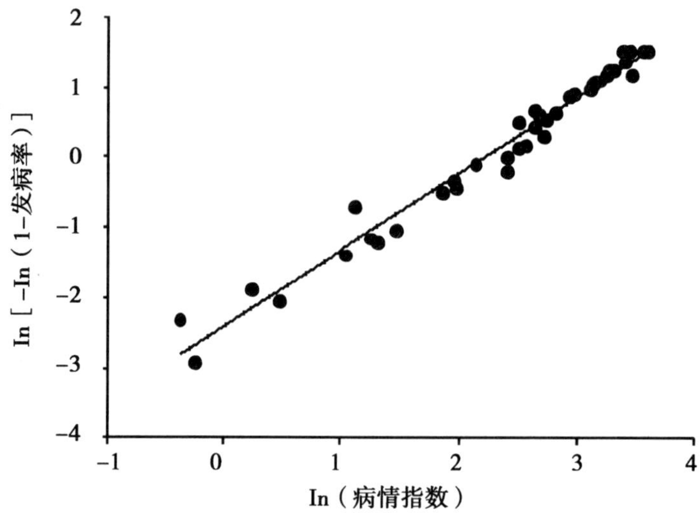

图 2 玉米弯孢菌叶斑病普遍率与严重度关系图

Fig. 2 The relationships between incidence and severity of Curvularia leaf spot of maize

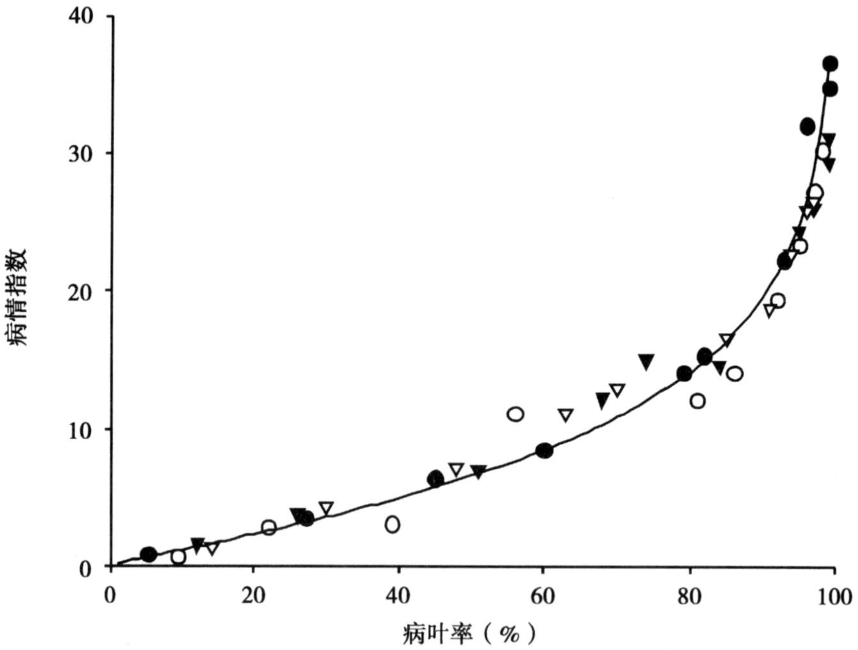

图 3 玉米弯孢菌叶斑病普遍率及严重度的观察值和预测值

Fig. 3 The investigation values and prediction values of incidence and severity of Curvularia leaf spot of maize

后得到描述玉米弯孢菌叶斑病 I-S 关系的最佳模型为互补双对数模型（CLL 模型），其关系式为：

$$S=\exp\{[\ln(-\ln(1-p))+2.4085]/1.0893\}$$

式中，P、S 分别代表病叶率和病情指数。

在实际调查中可利用上式通过病叶率间接估算病情指数的大小，大大节省时间和人力。对一般植物病害来说，普遍率的调查较为容易，而严重度或病情指数的调查则相对要繁琐的多，且经常带有一定的主观误差，不同调查者，甚至同一调查者在不同时期调查都有可能造成较大的误差，且费时、费力难以使农民掌握。为此寻找一种对植物病害迅速、准确且容易推广的监测方法，是植物病害综合管理的重要内容之一。

CLL 模型（Complementary Log-log model，互补双对数模型）实质上是双参数 Poisson 模型的一种直线化形式[15]，在昆虫学中曾被广泛地应用于估计昆虫感染率与昆虫种群密度间关系的研究[16]，后来植病学者将该模型引入到植病流行学领域并用其来描述病害的 I-S 关系，结果表明，CLL 模型是描述病害 I-S 关系的理想模型[17]，本论文的研究也证明了这一点。

本试验通过对玉米弯孢菌叶斑病病叶率及病情指数间关系的研究，进一步证实了利用普遍率预测严重度的可行性，但必须考虑到影响 I-S 关系的因素，如品种、气象条件等。在病害监测中，使用该方法不仅可以节省时间，减少人为误差，也更容易被农民掌握和使用。

参 考 文 献

[1] 戴法超，王晓鸣，朱振东等．玉米弯孢菌叶斑病研究［J］．植物病理学报，1998，28（2）；123－129

[2] 傅俊范，白元俊，孟凡祥等．玉米弯孢菌叶斑病产量损失估计模型的研制［J］．沈阳农业大学学报，2000，31（5）：468－471

[3] 傅俊范，李海春，白元俊等．玉米弯孢菌叶斑病传播梯度模型［J］．植物病理学报，2003，33（5）：456－461

[4] 李金堂，傅俊范，李海春等．寄主生育期、接种条件对玉米弯孢菌叶斑病发生的影响［J］．西北农林科技大学学报，2007，35（6）：147－151

[5] 陈梅英，夏瑛光，陈万先．玉米弯孢菌叶斑病的发生与防治［J］．河南农业科学，2000，（7）：19－20

[6] James WC，Shih CS. Relationship between incidence and severity of powdery mildew and leaf rust on winter wheat［J］. Phytopath，1973，63；183－187

[7] Seem RC，Gilpatrick JD. Incidence and severity relationships of secondary infections of powdery mildew on apple［J］. Phytopath，1980，70；851－854

[8] Imhoff MW，Leonard KJ，Main CE. Analysis of disease progress curves，gradients，and incidence- severity relationships for field and phytotron bean rust epidemics［J］. Phytopath，1982，72；72－80

[9] 黄春艳，商世吉，稻瘟病普遍率与严重度关系初步探讨［J］．植物保护学报，1993，20（3）；237－240

[10] 白金铠，潘顺法，罗畔池．玉米大、小斑病及其防治［M］．上海：上海科学技术出版社，1985

[11] Madden LV, Knoke JK, Louie R. The statistical relationships between aphid trap catches and maize dwarf mosaic virus inoculation pressure. In Plant Virus Epidemiology (Plumb, R. T. and Thresh, J. M. et al.) [M]. Oxford; Blackwell Scientific Publications, 1983

[12] 王振中，林孔勋．花生锈病流行曲线分析[J]．植物病理学报，1986，16(1)；11－16

[13] 彭昭英．世界统计及分析全才 SAS 系统应用开发指南［M］．北京：北京希望电子出版社，2000

[14] 杜荣骞．生物统计学［M］．北京；高等教育出版社，2003

[15] Nachman, G. A mathematical model of the functional relationship between density and spatial distribution of a population. J. Anim. Ecol [J], 1981. 50: 453－460

[16] Kono, T., and Sugino, T. On the estimation of the density of rice stems infested by the rice stem borer. Jpn. J. Appl. Entomol. Zool [J], 1958. 89: 770－781

[17] Xu XM, Madden LV. Incidence and density relationships of powdery mildew on apple [J]. Phytopath, 92; 1005－1014

Study of Relationship Between Incidence and Severity of Curvularia Leaf Spot of Maize

LI Jin-tang

(*Weifang University of Science and Technology*, *Shouguang* 262700)

Abstract: The information of incidence and disease index of Curvularia leaf spot of maize [*Curvularialunata* (Wakker) Boed.] were obtained through inoculation experiments conducted in the field from 2005 to 2006. The relationship between disease incidence and severity (I-S) of Curvularia leaf spot was analyzed by SAS software. Results showed that the I-S relationship of Curvularia leaf spot on tunyu 1 and haihe 14 could be expressed individually by complementary log-log model. There was no significant difference between the parameters of two model. The relationship between incidence and severity could be described by the following model; $S = \exp\{[\ln(-\ln(1-p)) + 2.4085] / 1.0893\}$, in which P and S represented incidence and severity respectively.

Key words: Curvularia leaf spot of maize; Incidence; Severity; Relationship beween incidence and severity

梨黑星病流行时间动态分析

李金堂① 肖万里
（潍坊科技学院，寿光 262700）

摘 要：用不同的流行学模型拟合2002年、2003年莱阳地区梨黑星病（Venturia nashicola）的系统监测数据，结果表明：Logistic模型能较好地描述梨黑星病病叶率随时间的变化动态；Gompertz模型能较好地描述平均病斑数随时间的变化动态。根据Logistic模型，梨黑星病的最佳防治时期是在梨树初花期后的60d内。

关键词：梨黑星病；流行；Logistic模型

梨黑星病（*Venturia nashicola* Tanaka et Yamamoto.）是我国梨树的重要病害，危害严重，流行年份损失巨大。国内外对梨黑星病的研究主要集中在病原生物学[1]、品种抗病性[2~4]、发病规律[5,6]以及防治措施等领域，对梨黑星病发病流行的时间动态研究报道较少。本文通过对莱阳地区梨黑星病连续两年的系统调查数据进行了分析，并构建了能够描述梨黑星病流行时间动态的模型，为病害的测报和防治提供参考。

1 材料与方法

1.1 梨黑星病系统调查

2002年和2003年，在莱阳农学院植保系实验站茌梨园内对梨黑星病的流行动态进行系统监测。监测梨树品种为莱阳茌梨，监测梨园在生长期间的浇水、施肥等按果园常规管理措施进行，但不施用任何杀菌剂。

2002年，在监测梨园内选取10棵生长良好、50年树龄茌梨树，每树分别在东西南北4个方向上，标记两个枝条，每枝20～30片叶。自梨树盛花期，每7～15d调查1次，调查时按叶序记录标记枝条上每个叶片上的病斑数。

2003年，采用随机取样调查，调查时，每树分别东西南北4个方向上，随机选取3个枝条，按叶序记录每个叶片上的病斑数。自盛花期，每7～15d调查1次，每次调查

① 李金堂，男，博士，副教授，潍坊科技学院植物病虫害研究所所长。研究方向：植物病理学。E-mail：li_ jintang@163. com

10 株树。

1.2 数据处理

分别以病叶率和平均病斑数为因变量，所对应的时间（初花期后天数，即病害调查日期与当年梨树初花期日期的间隔天数 d）为自变量。用 Exponent、Logistic、Gompertz 和 Weibull 模型拟合实测数据。数据拟合采用 SAS 统计软件（Release 8.01，SAS Institute Inc.）的 NLINE 过程，以各模型的决定系数 R^2、剩余平方和 SSE、F 值（F value）和检验概率（Pr > F）作为模型取设的标准[7~9]。

2 结果与分析

2.1 梨黑星病流行实测动态

2002 年，梨黑星病病出现最早的时间为初花期后 25d（2002 年梨树的初花期为 4 月 5 日），以后随着时间的增加，病情逐渐加重。发病高峰出现在初花期后 64 ~ 71d；8 月 7 日以后梨树落叶严重，调查停止。2003 年，第一批梨黑星病病斑出现在初花期后 25d（2003 年梨树的初花期为 4 月 17 日），发病高峰出现在初花期后 70 ~ 90d；梨树叶片平均病斑数的增加高峰出现在初花期后 80 ~ 90d，8 月 15 日以后落叶严重，调查结束（图 1）。

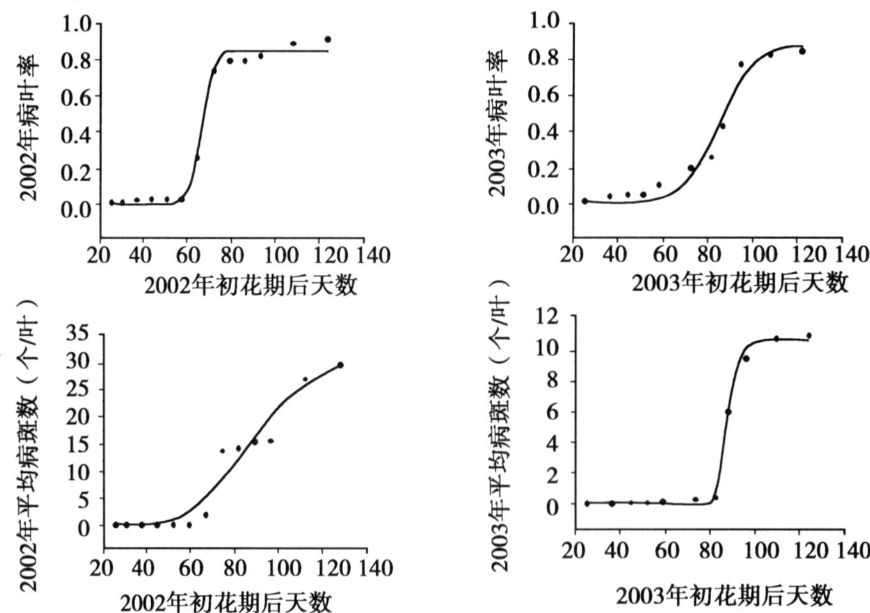

图 1 2002—2003 年病叶率和平均病斑数的拟合模型与实际值

（——拟合模型；·实际值）

2.2 病害流行时间动态曲线拟合

表1为2002年和2003年的数据拟合结果。SAS系统计算了判断模型拟合效果的4个指标：R^2、F value、Pr > F和SSE。其中，前3个指标越大表明模型的拟合效果越好，SSE越小表明模型的拟合效果越好[7~9]。

表1 2002—2003年病叶率与平均病斑数不同模型及其检验

Year	Model	Model Expression	R2	SSE	F Value	Pr > F
2002	Exponontial	X_t =0.094 5 × EXP (0.020 4t)	0.681 3	0.639 0	31.28	<0.000 1
		Z_t =1.058 5 × EXP (0.028 2t)	0.852 4	211.700 0	59.78	<0.000 1
	Logistic	X_t =0.856 0/ {1 + EXP [−0.365 9 × (t −67.082 8)]}	0.992 5	0.015 1	941.36	<0.000 1
		Z_t =30.695 6/ {1 + EXP [−0.079 3 × (t −85.350 1)]}	0.940 5	85.302 7	94.84	<0.000 1
	Gomperts	X_t = EXP [−1818.5 × EXP (−0.113 7t)]	0.965 4	0.069 3	333.58	<0.000 1
		Z_t =33.436 6 × EXP [−EXP (3.679 2 −0.046 6t)]	0.952 6	67.990 8	119.84	<0.000 1
	Weibull	X_t =1 −EXP [− (t/72.614 2) **8.840 6]	0.941 3	0.117 6	194.31	<0.000 1
		Z_t =30.304 9 × {1 −EXP [− (t/92.522 4) **4.666 4]}	0.943 9	80.444 6	100.78	<0.000 1
2003	Exponontial	X_t = 0.039 0 × EXP (0.026 9t)	0.850 9	0.170 8	57.36	<0.000 1
		Z_t =0.241 7 × EXP (0.033 0t)	0.775 4	51.605 8	27.10	0.000 2
	Logistic	X_t =0.890 7/ {1 + EXP [−0.128 1 × (t **84.847 7)]}	0.970 1	0.034 2	180.41	<0.000 1
		Z_t =10.431 6/ {1 + EXP [−0.633 3 × (t −85.5583)]}	0.993 8	1.416 3	681.02	<0.000 1
	Gomperts	X_t = EXP [−197.5 × EXP (−0.065 07t)]	0.952 8	0.054 0	191.02	<0.000 1
		Z_t =10.664 7 × EXP [−EXP (24.927 5 −0.295 4t)]	0.996 8	0.739 2	1 304.75	<0.000 1
	Weibull	X_t =1 −EXP [− (t/94.182 1) **5.245 9]	0.953 0	0.053 8	191.74	<0.000 1
		Z_t =10.407 2 × {1 −EXP [− (t/86.261 5) **51.073 1]}	0.993 5	1.484 1	648.57	<0.000 1

注：t为初花期后天数（d）；X_t 和 Z_t 分别为梨树初花期后td的病叶率和平均病斑数（个/叶）

根据以上标准[7~9]，由表1可知，2002年和2003年病叶率和平均病斑数的最佳模型分别为：

2002年病叶率模型：Xt =0.856 0/ {1 + EXP [−0.365 9 × (t −67.082 8)]}　(1)

2003年病叶率模型；Xt =0.890 7/ {1 + EXP [−0.128 1 × (t −84.847 7)]}　(2)

2002年平均病斑数模型；Zt =33.436 6 × EXP [−EXP (3.679 2 − 0.046 6t)]　(3)

2003年平均病斑数模型；Zt =10.664 7 × EXP [−EXP (24.927 5 −0.295 4t)]　(4)

模型中的Xt，Zt，t分别表示梨树初花期后td的病叶率、平均病斑数（个/叶）和初花期后天数（d）。

由模型（1）～（4）可以看出，模型（1）和（2）为逻辑斯蒂模型（Logistic Model）；模型（3）和（4）为高姆比茨模型（Gompertz Model）。这就说明在梨黑星病的发病流行中，病叶率随时间变化的动态可用逻辑斯蒂模型来描述，而平均病斑数的发生发展则可用高姆比茨模型来描述。

2.3 病害的最佳防治时间

一般来说，对多循环病害，当病情低于0.05时，病害增长速率高，但病害绝对增长量较小，持续时间长，在流行学上，这一时期称为指数增期，也是病害防治的有利时期。当病情超过0.05时，病害绝对量增长迅速，如无有效的防治药剂，病害难以控制。在病害测报、防治及流行规律的分析研究中，都应当抓住指数增长期为关键。若错过这一阶段，预测预报往往失时，防治措施将事倍功半[10]。根据梨黑星病流行时间动态描述模型，2002年和2003年病叶率达到0.05的时间分别是初花后的第60d和第63d，即当年的6月4日和6月18日。因此，梨树初花期后的60d内是防治梨黑星病关键时期。

3 结论与讨论

通过SAS统计软件拟合不同模型（exponent、Logistic、Gompertz、Weibull）的研究结果表明：在梨黑星病的发病流行中，病叶率随时间的变化动态用Logistic模型拟合较好，平均病斑数的发展动态用Gompertz模型拟合较好。梨树初花期后的60d内，是梨黑星病流行的指数增长期，在这一时期，梨黑星可发生2～3代。同时，在此期间梨树的叶片和果实高度感病[11]。因此，这一时期是防治梨黑星的关键时期。对于这一时期梨黑星病的防治，建议在侵染测报的基础上，选用具有内吸治疗效果的杀菌剂，如40%神速福星等，进行防治[12,13]。

植物病害流行的时间动态分析是病害流行测报的基础，是控制病害的重要依据。用模型表示病害流行的发展动态，会有助于全面地了解流行的特征，并可以进行不同项目的比较[14]。

Van der Plank首次把植物病害分为单利型和复利型两类，并把Logistic模型应用于对复利型病害流行过程的描述[15]。Logistic模型是一条关于拐点对称的S形曲线，它的密度分布呈钟状[16]。然而，病害流行的速率分布是不对称的，其峰值较Logistic密度曲线之峰值出现的早[16]。Berger认为：当病情低于0.05和高于0.6时，Logistic模型不能很好地拟合病害增长过程，而Gompertz模型则无此限制，Berger利用9个病害系统共113组流行曲线，对Logistic和Gompertz模型进行拟合，并用线性化参数作为鉴定拟和好坏的判别标准，结果表明后者优于前者[16]。

Pennypacker等人首次对利用Weibull模型描述流行过程进行较详细的研究，并认为该模型的可塑性及准确性可使其成为分析病害发展过程的一个很有用的工具[17]。

不同病害流行的时间动态可用不同的模型进行描述，在实际应用中应进行模型的比较后选取最合适的模型，并可利用选取后的模型指导病害防治，如可利用模型估算在病害流行过程中，病情参数达到某些点的期望天数和病害在这些点时的期望发展速度（病情日增量），为病害的一般测报工作提供数量上的参考依据。

到目前，对梨黑星病病害的分级标准研究较少，尚未有公认的统一科学的分级标准，为了便于相关学者间相互比较和参考，本研究没有采用病情指数这一指标来描述梨黑星病的流行动态，而是采用病叶率和平均病斑数来反映梨黑星病的流行动态。

参考文献

[1] 罗文华．梨黑星病病原及生物学特性的研究［J］．四川农业大学学报，1988，1；59－64

[2] Stanton W R. Field variation *venturia pirina* strains［J］．Brit Mycol Soc，1953，36；90－103

[3] 罗文华，冷怀琼．梨品种对黑星病的抗病性研究［J］．四川农业大学学报，1990，8（2）：141 －146

[4] 汤浩茹，冷怀琼．梨黑星病的遗传育种研究［J］．四川大学学报，1993，11（2）；266－272

[5] 殷继训，俞少嫦．梨黑星病侵染循环的研究［J］．中国果树，1988，1；13－18

[6] 梅本清作．ニホンナシ黑星病の第一次侵染源の种类と初发生における重要性［J］．日本植物病理学会报，1991，56（5）；658－664

[7] Madden，L. V.，Knoke，J. K. and Louie，R. The statistical relationships between aphid trap catches and maize dwarf mosaic virus inoculation pressure. In Plant Virus Epidemiology（Plumb，R. T. and Thresh，J. M. et al.）［M］．Oxford；Blackwell Scientific Publications，1983. 159－168

[8] 王振中，林孔勋．花生锈病流行曲线分析［J］．植物病理学报，1986，16（1）；11－16

[9] 彭昭英．世界统计及分析全才 SAS 系统应用开发指南［M］．北京：北京希望电子出版社

[10] 曾士迈，杨演．植物病害流行学［M］．北京：农业出版社，1986. 93－94

[11] 李保华，赵美琦．梨叶叶龄与梨黑星病菌侵染发病的关系［J］．植物保护学报，2001，28（4）；309－312

[12] 李金堂，李保华，李宝笃，孙秀英．几种杀菌剂防治梨黑星病的持效期的研究［J］．莱阳农学院学报，2004，21（1）；37－39

[13] 李保华，韩红香，赵美琦．梨黑星病内吸治疗剂施药时期研究［J］．植物保护，1998，24（3）；30－31

[14] Butt，D. J. and Royle，D. J. Multiple regression analysis in the epidemiology of plant diseases. In Epidemics of Plant Disease（Kranz，J. et al）［M］．Springer-Verlag，Berlin and New York，1974. 78－114

[15] Van der Plank，J. E. Plant Disease：Epidemics and control［M］．New and London；Academic Press，1963

[16] Berger，R. D. Comparison of Gompertz and Logistic equations to describe plant disease progress［J］．Phytopath，1981，71；716－719

[17] Pennypacker, S. P. , Knoble, H. D. Antle, C. E. , et al. A flexible model for studying plant disease progression [J]. Phytopath, 1980, 70; 232 -235

Analysis of Temporal Dynamics of Pear Scab (Venturia nashicola) Epidemic

LI Jin-tang XIAO Wan-li

(*Weifang University of Science and Technology*, *Shouguang* 262700)

Abstract: Several models were used to fit the temporal data of pear scab monitored in Lai-Yang in 2002 and 2003. Results showd that Logistic model and Gomperts model can reflect respectively the change of the diseased leave percent and average number of lesions per leaf with time better. The optimum prevent time was within 60 days after coming into blossom.

Key words: Pear scab; Epidemic; Logistic model

多杀菌素和荧光桃红 B 对橘小实蝇取食的影响

杜迎刚①
（潍坊科技学院，寿光 262700）

摘　要： 40mg/kg 多杀菌素或 1 000mg/kg、3 000mg/kg 荧光桃红 B 均不影响 3 日龄橘小实蝇雌、雄虫对蔗糖的取食量（$P>0.05$）；与蒸馏水对照和马拉硫磷对照相比，40mg/kg 多杀菌素或 1 000mg/kg 荧光桃红 B 对雌、雄虫吐食率也无显著影响（$P>0.05$），但 3 000mg/kg 荧光桃红 B 对雌、雄虫吐食率有极显著影响（$P<0.01$）。40mg/kg 多杀菌素或 1 000mg/kg 荧光桃红 B 对 6 日龄橘小实蝇雌、雄虫对蔗糖的取食量与蒸馏水对照无差异（$P>0.05$）；3 000mg/kg 荧光桃红 B 对雌虫的取食量与蒸馏水对照有显著差异（$P<0.05$），与马拉硫磷对照无差异（$P>0.05$），对雄虫的取食量与蒸馏水对照无显著差异（$P>0.05$），与马拉硫磷对照有显著差异（$P<0.05$）。与蒸馏水、马拉硫磷相对照，40mg/kg 多杀菌素或 1 000mg/kg 荧光桃红 B 对雌、雄虫的吐食率均无显著影响（$P>0.05$），而 3 000mg/kg 的荧光桃红 B 对雌、雄虫的吐食率均有极显著影响（$P<0.01$）。

关键词： 橘小实蝇；多杀菌素；荧光桃红 B；取食量；吐食率

橘小实蝇（*Bactrocera dorsalis* Hendel），隶属双翅目（Diptera）实蝇科（Tetriphitidae），是外来危险性害虫之一，原产印度和马来半岛，现主要分布于夏威夷群岛、中国台湾等亚洲和太平洋等地区。在大陆，其现已分布到福建、海南、广东、广西、湖南、贵州、云南、四川等省，并在华南、西南地区急剧蔓延、猖獗为害。其寄主范围广，为害柑橘、番石榴、洋桃、芒果等 46 个科 250 多种果树、蔬菜和花卉，是一种毁灭性的害虫，被列为我国二级检疫对象[1~3]。

总结国外 50 多年实蝇防治的成功经验，喷洒蛋白诱剂一直是一项重要的防治措施[4,5]。但蛋白本身不具有杀虫活性，其对实蝇的杀灭作用靠加入其中的杀虫介质来完成。为配合实蝇其他防治措施及保护生态环境，蛋白中所选用的杀虫介质杀虫方式最好以胃毒作用为主。而新近报道的对实蝇具有防治潜力的两种新型农药—多杀菌素和荧光

① 杜迎刚，男，博士，副教授，潍坊科技学院生态与植保研究所所长。研究方向：昆虫生态化学研究。E－mail：jiqinge@ yahoo. com. cn.

桃红 B，主要是胃毒作用[6,7]。农药本身可能导致昆虫发生呕吐反应，实蝇具有吐食习性（正常条件下，实蝇取食后会吐出部分食物，这部分食物可能会被它或其他实蝇再取食）[8]，这些都可能降低农药的杀虫效果。本文通过对比这两种农药与传统蛋白中所用农药—马拉硫磷对橘小实蝇取食习性的影响，进一步评价这两种农药对实蝇的潜在防治可能，同时为蛋白中杀虫物质的选择提供理论依据，为评价农药对昆虫的毒力提出新的视角。

1 材料与方法

1.1 试验虫源

橘小实蝇来自 2002 年福建漳州番石榴园收集的老熟幼虫建立的室内大量饲养种群，约第 60 代。饲养温度 23 ~ 25℃，相对湿度 65% ~ 75%，光周期 12L：12D。

1.2 试验方法

1.2.1 标准曲线制作：配制含荧光素钠 0、0.25、0.5、1.0、2.0、4.0、8.0 μg/ml 的 0.2 mol/L 的蔗糖溶液，491 nm 比色测其光密度值制作标准曲线。

1.2.2 取食量的测定：分别取 3 日龄、6 日龄饥饿 24h 的橘小实蝇雌雄各 20 头，放入 1 000ml 的三角烧瓶中。在光照强度 400 ~ 500lx 下，用 J-管饲喂加含有不同农药（多杀菌素，40mg/kg；荧光桃红 B，1 000 mg/kg、3 000 mg/kg；蒸馏水对照，3 000 mg/kg；马拉硫磷对照，100mg/kg。剂量设计参考 3 种农药对橘小实蝇的 LC50、LT50[10]）和 1.0g/kg 荧光素钠的 0.2mol/L 的蔗糖溶液，1h 后冰冻处死实蝇，用 1.5ml 0.1mol/L 氢氧化钠提取，提取液用 1 μm 的尼龙针筒过滤器过滤，491nm 比色测定光密度值，根据标准曲线计算实蝇取食量[8,9]，重复 3 次。

1.2.3 吐食率的测定：在取出冰冻实蝇的同时，容器也用 0.1mol/L 氢氧化钠溶液少量多次洗涤，洗涤液处理同实蝇提取液，计算实蝇吐食率。

$$\text{吐食率（\%）} = \frac{\text{实蝇吐出量（容器回收量）}}{\text{实蝇取食量}} \times 100$$ [8,10]

1.3 数据分析方法

数据处理用 SPSS11.5 for Windows 统计分析软件，采用单因子方差分析对实验数据进行分析，方差检验用 Tukey's 进行。

2 结果与分析

40mg/kg 多杀菌素或 1 000mg/kg、3 000mg/kg 荧光桃红 B 均不影响 3 日龄橘小实蝇雌、雄虫对蔗糖的取食量（$P > 0.05$）；与蒸馏水、马拉硫磷相对照，40mg/kg 多杀菌素和 1 000mg/kg 荧光桃红 B 对 3 日龄橘小实蝇雌、雄虫吐食率无显著影响（$P > 0.05$），

3 000mg/kg 荧光桃红 B 对其吐食率有极显著影响（P<0.01）。（表 1）

表 1　含不同农药的蔗糖对橘小实蝇取食行为的影响

药剂	浓度（mg/kg）	食量 ♀	食量 ♂	吐食率 ♀	吐食率 ♂
3 日龄					
蒸馏水对照	3 000	3.980 0±0.428 9aA	3.425 6±0.320 9aA	49.913 7±4.420 1bB	47.824 1±4.506 9bB
Phloxine-B	1 000	3.536 6±0.202 0abA	3.558 3±0.298 2abA	52.272 4±4.717 2bB	49.836 3±4.605 1bB
Phloxine-B	3 000	3.736 3±0.251 2abA	3.157 9±0.214 8abA	86.654 0±3.075 7aA	89.450 2±4.748 2aA
多杀菌素	40	3.761 5±0.354 1abA	3.472 7±0.439 1abA	54.469 6±5.356 3bB	51.228 8±4.289 3bB
马拉硫磷对照	100	2.616 0±0.218 7bA	2.275 2±0.245 9bA	57.027 4±3.565 7bB	61.518 8±2.530 5bB
6 日龄					
蒸馏水对照	3 000	5.325 5±0.399 2aAB	4.066 8±0.403 5aA	57.704 7±7.005 9bB	60.965 3±5.885 8bB
Phloxine-B	1 000	5.305 9±0.265 1aAB	4.227 6±0.500 6aA	62.417 5±6.111 9bB	57.867 5±8.082 6bB
Phloxine-B	3 000	3.797 6±0.336 5bBC	4.258 4±0.230 3aA	100.898 7±3.731 6aA	103.648 1±6.025 7aA
多杀菌素	40	5.494 0±0.427 6aA	4.280 1±0.265 4aA	64.847 2±5.207 9bB	60.640 6±4.755 4bB
马拉硫磷对照	100	2.598 9±0.245 3bC	2.616 2±0.259 5bA	55.959 3±6.489 5bB	60.191 4±4.432 4bB

注：表中字母为 Tukey's 多重比较的结果。不同大小写字母分别表示差异达 0.01、0.05 显著水平.

40mg/kg 多杀菌素和 1 000mg/kg 荧光桃红 B 对 6 日龄橘小实蝇雌、雄虫取食量与蒸馏水对照无显著差异（P>0.05），与马拉硫磷对照有极显著差异（P<0.01）。3 000 mg/kg 荧光桃红 B 对雌虫的取食量与蒸馏水对照有显著差异（P<0.05），与马拉硫磷对照无显著差异（P>0.05）；对雄虫的取食量与蒸馏水对照无显著差异（P>0.05），与马拉硫磷对照有显著差异（P<0.05）。与蒸馏水、马拉硫磷相对照，40mg/kg 多杀菌素或 1 000mg/kg 荧光桃红 B 对橘小实蝇雌、雄虫吐食率均无显著影响（P>0.05），但 3 000mg/kg 荧光桃红 B 对橘小实蝇雌、雄虫的吐食率有显著影响（P<0.01）。

与蒸馏水相比，马拉硫磷极显著影响 6 日龄雌性橘小实蝇对蔗糖的取食量（P<0.01），显著影响 6 日龄雄性橘小实蝇和 3 日龄雌、雄性橘小实蝇对蔗糖的取食量（P<0.05），这意味着马拉硫磷在很低的浓度下（100mg/kg，雌、雄性橘小实蝇的 LC50 分别为 253.038 9、272.1 608mg/kg[10]）就对 3 和 6 日龄橘小实蝇的取食行为产生较大影响，表现出一定的驱避性。

3　讨论

诱剂和农药结合从 20 世纪开始就用来防治实蝇[11,12]，马拉硫磷因低毒、低价格和实蝇对其抗性低而被选择[13]作为蛋白诱剂中的常用农药。大量的应用有机磷农药已经导致次要害虫的再猖獗，加上其对环境、人类及天敌的负面影响[14,15]，逼迫人们寻求对哺乳动物和非靶标生物更安全的化合物[16,17]。通过对拟除虫菊酯[18]、苏云金杆菌[19,20]、吡虫啉[21,22]、多杀菌素[23,24]和荧光桃红 B[25,26]等具有新作用位点或新作用方式的农药的研究，最终实蝇诱剂中农药的选择集中在了多杀菌素和荧光桃红 B 上。

从表 1 可以看出，低浓度的马拉硫磷就对橘小实蝇表现出较强的驱避作用，不适合加入诱剂中作为杀虫介质；多杀菌素和荧光桃红 B 是较理想的杀虫物质。3 000mg/kg 荧光桃红 B 除影响 6 日龄雌性橘小实蝇的取食量外，还影响橘小实蝇的吐食率（$P<0.05$），这一现象国内外均未见报道，值得进一步研究。荧光桃红 B 主要是胃毒作用，其毒力大小与光照强度及本身浓度有关，本研究表明，不能单纯靠提高荧光桃红 B 的浓度来缩短 LT50。能否把高浓度胃毒农药影响害虫取食行为的现象也作为评价一种农药毒力的参考指标，有待进一步探讨。

参 考 文 献

[1] 杜迎刚，陈家骅，季清娥等．橘小实蝇对蛋白和糖的反应［J］．福建农林大学学报（自然科学版），2007，36（4）：357－360

[2] 杜迎刚，陈家骅，季清娥．一种新型蛋白诱剂对橘小实蝇引诱作用［J］．福建林学院学报，2007，27（3）：259－262

[3] 吴宇芬．橘小实蝇的地理分布模型［J］．福建农林大学学报（自然科学版），2005，34（2）：168－171

[4] Morton T. C.，Bateman M. A. Chemical studies on proteinaceous attractants for fruit-flies，including the identification of volatile constituents［J］．Aust. J. Agric. Res.，1981，32（6）：905－916

[5] Steiner L. F. Fruit fly control in Hawaii with poison-bait sprays containing protein hydrolysates［J］．J. Econ. Entomol.，1952，45（5）：838－843

[6] Salgado V. L. Studies on the mode of action of spinosad；insect symptoms and physiological correlates［J］．Pestic. Biochem. Physiol.，1998，60（2）；91－102

[7] Jimena B.，Alejandro r.，Luis A. Q. Phloxine B effect on immature stages of the Mediterranean fruit fly，*Ceratitis capitata*（Diptera；Tephritidae）（Wiedemann）［J］．J. Econ. Entomol.，2003，96（3）：662－668

[8] Nigg H. N.，Schumann R. A.，Yang J. J.，et al. Quantifying individual fruit fly consumption with *Anastrepha suspense*（Diptera：Tephritidae）［J］．J. Econ. Entomol.，2004，97（6）：1850－1860

[9] 杜迎刚，陈家骅，季清娥．橘小实蝇个体食量测定［J］．福建农林大学学报（自然科学版），2008，37（2）：122－126

[10] 杜迎刚．橘小实蝇引诱蛋白的研究［J］．福建：福建农林大学植物保护学院，2004 级博士论文

[11] Shaw J. G. Poison-lure sprays for Mexican fruit fly［J］．Calif. Citrogr，1955，40（5）：188－190，192

[12] Toshiyuki N.，Henry A. B.，ASHER O. Comparative effectiveness of malathion and

malathion-yeast hydrolysate bait sprays for control of the melon fly [J]. J. Econ. Entomol., 1957, 50 (5): 680-684

[13] Steiner L. F. The role of attractants in the recent Mediterranean fruit fly eradication program in Florida [J]. J. Econ. Entomol., 1961, 54 (1); 30-35

[14] Daane K. M., Dahlsten D. D., Dreastadt S. H. Effects of Mediterranean fruit fly malathion bait spray on the longevity and oviposition of parasitoids of linden and tuliptree aphids (Homoptera; Aphididae) [J]. Environ. Entomol., 1990. 19 (4); 1130-1134

[15] Hoelmer L. A., Dahlsten D. L. Effects of malathion bait spray on *Aleyrodes spiraeoides* (Homoptera; Aleyrodidae) and its parasitoids in northern California [J]. Environ. Entomol., 1993, 22 (1); 49-56

[16] Stark J. D., Vargas R. I., Thalman R. K. Azadirachtin: effects on metamorphosis, longevity, and reproduction of three tephritid fruit fly species [J]. J. Econ. Entomol., 1990, 83 (6); 2168-2174

[17] Purcell M. F., Stark J. D., Messing R. H. Insecticide effect on three tephritid fruit flies and associated braconid parasitoids in Hawaii [J]. J. Econ. Entomol., 1994, 87 (6); 1455- 1462

[18] Anna M., Isaac I., Amnon F., et al. Toxicological studies of organophosphate and pyrethroid insecticides for controlling the fruit fly *Dacus ciliatus* (Diptera; Tephritidae) [J]. J. Econ. Entomol., 2001, 94 (5): 1059-1066

[19] Jorge T., Pablo L., Trevor W., et al. Toxicity of *Bacillus thuringiensis* β-exotoxin to three species of fruit flies (Diptera; ephritidae) [J]. J. Econ. Entomol., 1999, 92 (5); 1052-1056

[20] David C. R., Jose A. G., Adelaido J. M. Lack of toxicity to adults of the Mexican fruit fly (Diptera; Tephritidae) of β-exotoxin in *Bacillus thuringiensis* endotoxin preparations [J]. J. Econ. Entomol., 2000, 93 (4): 1076-1079

[21] Oscar E. L., Timothy C. H., Amy L. M. Toxicity of imidacloprid-treated spheres to Caribbean fruit fly, *Anastrepha suspensa* (Diptera; Tephritidae) and its parasitoid *Diachasmimorpha longicaudata* (Hymenoptera; Braconidae) in the laboratory [J]. J Econ. Entomol., 2004, 97 (2): 525-529

[22] James D. B., Sridhar P. Feeding and survivorship of blueberry maggot flies (Diptera; Tephritidae) on protein baits incorporated with insecticides [J]. Flo. Entomol., 2005, 88 (3): 268-277

[23] Kirsten S. P., Rufus I., John C. W., et al. Protection of fruit against infestation by apple maggot fly and blueberry maggot (Diptera; Tephritidae) using compounds containing spinosad [J]. J. Econ. Entomol., 2005, 98 (2): 432-437

[24] Vargas R. I., Peck S. L., Mcquate G. T., et al. Potential for areawide integrated management of Mediterranean fruit fly (Diptera; Tephritidae) with a braconid parasitoid

and a novel bait spray [J]. J. Econ. Entomol. , 2001, 94 (4); 817 - 825

[25] Moreno D. S. Photoactive dye insecticide formulations; adjuvants increase toxicity to Mexican fruit fly (Diptera; Tephritidae) [J]. J. Econ. Entomo. l, 2001, 94 (1); 150 - 156

[26] Vargas R. I. , Miller N. W. , Prokopy R. J. Attraction and feeding responses of Mediterranean fruit fly and a natural enemy to protein baits laced with two novel toxins, phloxine B and spinosad [J]. Entomol. Exp. Appl. , 2002. 102 (3): 273 - 282

The Effect of Spinosad and Phloxine-B on the Feeding Behavior of Oriental Fruit Fly Bactrocera dorsalis

DU Ying-gang

(*Weifang University of Science and Technology*, *Shouguang* 262700)

Abstract: 40mg/kg spinosad, 1 000mg/kg and 3 000mg/kg Phloxine-B all brought no statistical differences in ingestion sugar for 3-d-old oriental fruit flies. 40mg/kg spinosad and 1 000mg/kg Phloxine-B did not affect the regurgitation ratio of females and males significantly compared with the distilled water control and malathion control, but the 3 000 mg/kg Phloxine-B affected the regurgitation ratio significantly. 40mg/kg spinosad and 1 000 mg/kg Phloxine-B had no difference in ingestion sugar for 6-d-old oriental fruit flies compared with the distilled water control. The difference between 3 000mg/kg Phloxine-B and distilled water control was significant for females and was not significant for males, but for malathion control the result would be reverse. 40mg/kg spinosad and 1 000mg/kg Phloxine-B did not affect the regurgitation ratio of females and males significantly compared with the distilled water control and malathion control, but 3 000mg/kg Phloxine-B had significant effect on females and males.

Key words: *Bactrocera dorsalis*; Spinosad; Phloxine-B; Ingestion; Regurgitation ratio

葱种质资源数量性状的聚类分析、相关性和主成分分析

苗锦山① 孙 虎 李云玲

（潍坊科技学院，寿光 262700）

摘 要： 为阐明普通大葱和分葱种质资源的亲缘关系以及数量性状间的关联性，在大田栽培条件下以国内外116份葱资源为试验材料进行了数量性状的聚类分析、相关性和主成分分析。结果表明：116份葱种质的12个数量性状遗传变异系数为25.25%～146.38%，基于形态标记划分的5个组群间形态差异明显。单株重与假茎重、叶长、株高、出叶孔间距、叶扁宽和假茎长相关性均达极显著或显著水平。单株重、株高、假茎重3个主成分累积方差贡献率为91.18%，其反映的信息与基于12个数量性状的聚类和相关分析结果基本一致。

关键词： 葱；种质资源；聚类分析；相关性分析；主成分分析

我国是葱的初生起源中心之一。葱栽培历史悠久，遗传变异丰富，是遗传育种研究的宝贵资源。但长期以来，葱的育种工作在我国进展缓慢，生产应用主要以各地方品种为主，尚无杂交种大面积推广应用，因此葱作物的产量和品质潜力尚未被充分挖掘。而我国用于出口创汇的大葱品种也以干物质积累率高、辣味较浓，但生物产量相对较低的日本大葱为主。因此，如何充分利用我国丰富的葱资源，有效协调产量和品质的关系，选育高产优质的本土葱取代进口品种是生产亟待解决的问题。目前，葱种质资源的鉴定及育种材料的选择多根据形态标记进行。因此，从形态学角度研究葱不同种质资源的形态、品质遗传特性，协调其产量和品质之间的关系是葱育种的关键环节之一。

目前，关于葱种质资源数量性状特征和分类研究，主要根据分蘖特征和假茎指数大小划分为普通大葱、分葱和楼葱3个栽培变种，而普通大葱则分为长白葱、短白葱和鸡腿葱3个类型[1~3]。该经验性的方法虽具一定的指导意义，但分蘖数、假茎指数等少数几个性状指标很难全面反映葱茎、叶等收获器官从起源至演化和传播过程中由于自然和人工选择所形成的丰富的遗传变异以及品种间亲缘关系的远近。本文以所搜集的形态差异较大且涵盖了栽培葱的不同类型的116份种质资源，通过确定与产量相关的12个数

---

① 苗锦山，男，博士，副教授，潍坊科技学院作物育种及生物技术研究所所长。研究方向：蔬菜育种及生物技术。E－mail：lnmjs@163.com

量性状指标，进行了葱种质资源主要数量性状的聚类分析、相关性和主成分分析，以期探明葱种质资源所固有的品种遗传特性，为资源的利用、改良和创新以及优良杂交种的组配提供理论依据。

1 材料和方法

1.1 试验材料

本文搜集了国内外包括普通栽培大葱和分葱共116份种质资源作为试验材料（表1）。

表1 研究用试验材料及其来源

序号	试验材料	来源	序号	试验材料	来源
1	鸡腿葱[1]	中国农业大学	23	四川彭县大葱[2]	六盘水师专
2	莱阳大葱[1]	山东农科院	24	贵州四季香葱[2]	六盘水师专
3	寿1105[1]	山东农科院	25	吉藏大葱[1]	安丘农业局
4	八叶齐大葱[1]	寿光农业局	26	天元大葱[1]	安丘农业局
5	大梧桐葱[1]	山东农科院	27	日本5号[1]	山东农科院
6	章丘大葱[1]	山东农科院	28	明彦大葱[1]	安丘农业局
7	天津五叶齐[1]	山东农科院	29	平度老脖子[1]	国家蔬菜资源中心
8	新疆大葱[2]	库尔勒农科院	30	长治葱[1]	国家蔬菜资源中心
9	铁杆寒风王[1]	安丘农业局	31	白葱[2]	国家蔬菜资源中心
10	西华独葱[2]	国家资源中心	32	海阳大葱[1]	国家蔬菜资源中心
11	山东长白葱[1]	库尔勒农科院	33	三叶齐大葱[1]	国家蔬菜资源中心
12	元藏2号[1]	安丘农业局	34	大高板葱[2]	国家蔬菜资源中心
13	中华巨葱[1]	山东农科院	35	义贡大葱[1]	国家蔬菜资源中心
14	夏黑2号[1]	安丘农业局	36	小火葱[2]	国家蔬菜资源中心
15	新疆本地葱[1]	库尔勒农科院	37	高脚白大葱[1]	国家蔬菜资源中心
16	东元一本葱[1]	安丘农业局	38	安阳大葱[2]	国家蔬菜资源中心
17	元宝208[1]	安丘农业局	39	二叉葱[2]	国家蔬菜资源中心
18	日本元藏[1]	安丘农业局	40	雅安大葱[2]	国家蔬菜资源中心
19	天光一本葱[1]	安丘农业局	41	河北大头葱[2]	国家蔬菜资源中心
20	气煞风大葱[1]	山东农科院	42	四叶齐大葱[2]	国家蔬菜资源中心
21	四川渡口葱[2]	六盘水师专	43	杞县大葱[2]	国家蔬菜资源中心
22	长宝大葱[1]	安丘农业局	44	大错叶葱[1]	国家蔬菜资源中心

（续表）

序号	试验材料	来源	序号	试验材料	来源
45	包头孤葱[2]	国家蔬菜资源中心	75	宁夏大头葱[2]	国家资源中心
46	西子大葱[2]	国家蔬菜资源中心	76	Shiddomeokute[2]	WARWICK HRI
47	安阳铁杆王[1]	河南新乡师专	77	white spear[2]	WARWICK HRI
48	新王大葱[1]	国家蔬菜资源中心	78	Yanagawasenebuka[1]	WARWICK HRI
49	河南鸡腿葱[1]	河南新乡师专	79	bunching onion[2]	WARWICK HRI
50	红皮小葱[2]	国家蔬菜资源中心	80	akita hosonegi[2]	WARWICK HRI
51	宝塔大葱[1]	河南新乡师专	81	Aizu[2]	WARWICK HRI
52	新葱 2 号[1]	河南新乡师专	82	Kuronoborinebuka[1]	WARWICK HRI
53	山西太古葱[1]	山西晋城	83	Hakushuu[1]	WARWICK HRI
54	高节白大葱[1]	国家蔬菜资源中心	84	Aiguro[2]	WARWICK HRI
55	独股白大葱[1]	国家蔬菜资源中心	85	Mitsumata[2]	WARWICK HRI
56	四川本地葱[2]	四川遂宁市	86	Yamatohosonegi[2]	WARWICK HRI
57	分葱[2]	国家蔬菜资源中心	87	kujou asagikei[2]	WARWICK HRI
58	新疆章丘大葱[1]	库尔勒农科院	88	Kincho[1]	WARWICK HRI
59	黑油葱[1]	国家资源中心	89	yakko summer bunchin[2]	WARWICK HRI
60	新郑大葱[1]	河南新乡师专	90	Yoshikawabanseifuto[2]	WARWICK HRI
61	菱棒葱[1]	国家蔬菜资源中心	91	Kagoshimabanegi[2]	WARWICK HRI
62	汝阳笨葱[1]	国家蔬菜资源中心	92	Shimonoda[1]	WARWICK HRI
63	陇县大葱[2]	国家蔬菜资源中心	93	Ishikura1[1]	WARWICK HRI
64	三十家鳞棒[1]	国家蔬菜资源中心	94	Ishikura2[1]	WARWICK HRI
65	鞭杆葱[1]	国家蔬菜资源中心	95	Kaga[2]	WARWICK HRI
66	大葱[2]	国家蔬菜资源中心	96	Tokuda[2]	WARWICK HRI
67	千阳旱葱[2]	国家蔬菜资源中心	97	Ishikura3[1]	WARWICK HRI
68	独根葱[1]	国家蔬菜资源中心	98	Cibouble[2]	WARWICK HRI
69	仙鹤腿[1]	国家蔬菜资源中心	99	Chouju[1]	WARWICK HRI
70	毕克齐大葱[2]	国家蔬菜资源中心	100	bunching onion[2]	WARWICK HRI
71	安阳大葱[1]	国家蔬菜资源中心	101	Japanese bunching[2]	WARWICK HRI
72	高杆大葱[1]	国家蔬菜资源中心	102	Ishikuru[1]	WARWICK HRI
73	黑葱[1]	国家蔬菜资源中心	103	Gosenoku[1]	WARWICK HRI
74	嵩县三叶齐[1]	国家蔬菜资源中心	104	Winterover[1]	WARWICK HRI

（续表）

序号	试验材料	来源	序号	试验材料	来源
105	bunching onion[2]	WARWICK HRI	111	kyoto market[2]	WARWICK HRI
106	welsh onion[2]	WARWICK HRI	112	vilr-moscow[2]	WARWICK HRI
107	Vilr[2]	WARWICK HRI	113	koshizu050004[2]	WARWICK HRI
108	Berlin[2]	WARWICK HRI	114	韩国大葱[1]	潍坊农科院
109	Riga[2]	WARWICK HRI	115	山西长白条大葱[2]	山西晋城市
110	Fragrant[2]	WARWICK HRI	116	二生子[1]	山东农科院

注：品种上标“1”表示普通大葱，品种上标“2”表示分葱；WARWICK HRI：英国华威大学园艺中心

1.2 试验方法

试验于2007年3月至2008年12月在中国农业大学寿光蔬菜研究院试验基地进行。试验地为砂浆潮土，0～20cm土层有机质含量0.92%，速效氮53.2mg/kg，速效磷62.3mg/kg，速效钾87.8mg/kg，土壤田间持水量24.0%，容重1.3g/cm^3。2007和2008年，分别于3～5月和3～7月播种育苗，6月下旬露地定植。定植株距10cm，行距90cm，小区面积4m×3.6m，随机区组排列，重复2次。定植前结合整地每667m^{2}施有机肥50kg、高氮复合肥30kg，其他管理同大田。2007年和2008年11月中旬收获，每小区5点取样，每点2株，共选取10株调查葱有关数量性状数据。

1.3 测量项目和方法

测量葱单株数量性状[4]包括单株重（X_1）、株高（X_2）、假茎重（X_3）、假茎长（X_4）、假茎直径（X_5）、叶长（X_6）、叶扁宽（X_7）、宿存叶片数（X_8）、出叶孔间距（X_9）和单株分蘖数（X_{10}）；统计假茎指数（X_{11}：X_4/X_5）、叶形指数（X_{12}：X_6/X_7）。分葱的单株重调查株丛总质量。数据的调查统计方法如下。

单株重：取10株称重计算平均值；株高：葱假茎底部至最长叶片顶端的长度；假茎长：葱假茎底部至倒二叶叶锁口的长度；假茎直径：鸡腿葱直径为底部粗茎和中部细茎和的1/2，其他葱为假茎最粗部分的直径[1~2]；叶长：最长叶片的长度；叶扁宽：将最长叶片压扁，测最宽处长度；宿存叶片数：统计绿色面积超过叶片总面积2/3以上叶片数；出叶孔间距：底部3片叶出叶孔之间的长度除以2。

1.4 数据统计和分析

基本统计和方差分析采用EXCEL统计分析软件，对各性状指标的原始数据分别进行分析；聚类分析时先对调查统计和测定数据进行标准化处理，采用SPSS 13.0软件对116份材料12个形态数量性状的1 392个数据（两年数据的平均值）进行统计分析，类平均法系统分类。性状相关性分析和主成分分析也采用SPSS 13.0统计分析软件进行。

2 结果与分析

2.1 葱种质资源数量性状变异和聚类分析

对116份葱种质资源单株重、株高、单株分蘖数、假茎重、假茎长、假茎直径、假茎指数、叶长、叶扁宽、宿存绿叶数、出叶孔间距和叶形指数12个数量性状的统计分析结果表明，不同种质资源性状间差异较大，遗传变异丰富，不同性状在不同材料之间表现不同程度的多样性（表2）。

根据变异系数大小判断得出葱不同数量性状变异度大小顺序为：单株分蘖数>假茎重>单株重>假茎直径>叶形指数>叶扁宽>出叶孔间距>宿存叶片数>假茎长>假茎指数>株高>叶长。

表2　葱种质资源数量性状变异表

	X_1/g	X_2/cm	X_3/g	X_4/cm	X_5/cm	X_6/cm	X_7/cm	X_8	X_9/cm	X_{10}	X_{11}	X_{12}
平均值	150.24	85.52	103.15	32.34	2.02	53.18	2.65	3.86	2.15	2.35	17.77	23.11
变异范围	9.70~406.84	29.03~137.91	7.25~308.32	9.21~61.33	0.32~3.97	18.31~80.22	0.55~4.82	0.80~8.12	0.52~4.89	0~17	8.27~32.20	7.95~53.64
变异系数(%)	74.26	26.97	75.80	35.68	43.56	25.25	38.49	36.53	38.14	146.38	32.92	39.55

舍去2级统计数据假茎指数和叶形指数，将116份葱种质资源10个数量性状数据标准化处理后，采用类平均法进行聚类分析形成4个组群，其中组群4组内性状差异仍较大，可分为2个亚组。因此，试验葱种质资源的形态分类在D=10.25的结合处可分为5个组群，计算各组群性状值的平均数用于各组特征分析（表3，图1）。

第1组群共有18份种质，其中，国内品种15个，欧洲、日本和韩国葱品种各1个。本组葱主要以国内主栽长白普通大葱为主，基本特征是植株高大，株高基本大于110cm；假茎和叶片均较长，分别在45cm和60cm以上；直径在各分组中最粗，大于2.5cm；假茎指数居中，叶形指数平均值在各组中最大。上述特征决定了本组葱单株生产力最高，假茎质量最大，具有高粗型大葱的基本特征。本组的代表品种有：铁杆寒风王、大梧桐葱、莱阳大葱、安阳铁杆王、日本5号、寿1105、韩国大葱等。但传统短白品种天津五叶齐也划进了本组，可能是因为在长期的生产实践中人为定向选择或繁种技术不规范可能致使其种性发生了一定变化。宝塔大葱形态观察属鸡腿葱，但株高和葱白长分别为119.0cm和45.3cm，具备了长白大葱的某些特征也划为了本组。

第2组群为分葱组，共有21份种质，其中，国内品种9份，欧洲品种12份。本组特征是株高和叶长居中，数值分别大于65.0cm和56.2cm，但假茎和叶片细、窄，假茎直径和叶扁宽分别在1.70cm和2.80cm以下，因而具有高细型葱的特征。多数品种具有7个以上的分蘖数，因其分蘖数较多而单株重和假茎重数值较大，是优良的分葱种质资源。本组葱大多具备南方分葱分蘖较多的特点。代表品种有：白葱、大高板葱、分葱、yakko summer bunchin、bunching onion 和 tokuda 等，但 87 号、91 号和 111 号欧洲分葱蘖数较少，分别为 4、3.4 和 3，具有北方分葱蘖数较少的特点，也划为了本组。

第 3 组群也为分葱组，共有 8 份种质，其中，国内品种 1 份，欧洲品种 7 份。本组葱分蘖数为 3 ~ 9 个，植株矮细，单株生产力低下，如单株重和假茎重均在 40g 和 30g 以下，生产利用价值不大。本组代表品种有：vilr、ciboubLe 和红皮小葱等。

第 4 组中的第 1 亚组属矮粗型普通大葱组群，共 38 份种质，其中，国内品种 15 份，日本品种 10 份，欧洲葱 13 份。本组特征是假茎和叶长居中，数值大多分别小于 100cm 和 50cm，但假茎指数和叶形指数在所有分组中最小，单株生产力低于高粗型大葱和高细型分葱。本组葱一般具有较好的紧实度、干物质率和糖含量，辣味较浓，是优良的熟食、加工品种资源，国内的鸡腿葱和出口短白大葱大多划在本组，主要代表品种有：鸡腿葱、河南鸡腿葱、明彦大葱、天光一本葱、ishikuru 等。

第 2 亚组属矮粗型和矮细型之间的中间类型，接近矮细型，包括普通大葱和少量分蘖较少分葱类型共 31 份种质，其中，国内品种 26 份，欧洲葱 5 份。本组葱的主要特征是株高和叶长数值均小于矮粗型大葱，假茎指数和叶形指数大于矮粗型，单株生产力也显著小于矮粗型。主要代表品种有：安阳大葱、毕克齐大葱、黑葱、Japanese bunching 和 gosenoku 等。

表 3　葱种质资源形态分类的分组资料

组别	1	2	3	4	5
单株重（g）	322.93	315.69	29.63	228.75	133.16
株高（cm）	122.20	82.11	40.61	90.43	75.62
假茎重（g）	229.08	195.10	22.58	154.01	91.96
假茎长（cm）	50.92	25.91	13.90	35.79	27.06
假茎直径（cm）	2.99	1.14	0.60	2.65	1.69
叶长（cm）	71.30	56.22	26.78	54.61	48.52
叶扁宽（cm）	3.59	1.95	0.83	3.38	2.16
宿存叶片数	5.20	29.21	14.38	6.51	7.93
出叶孔间距（cm）	3.55	1.94	0.70	2.22	1.74
单株分蘖数	0.03	7.93	5.83	0.40	1.75
假茎指数	17.21	23.61	24.86	13.84	17.14
叶形指数	20.18	31.12	33.91	16.95	24.15

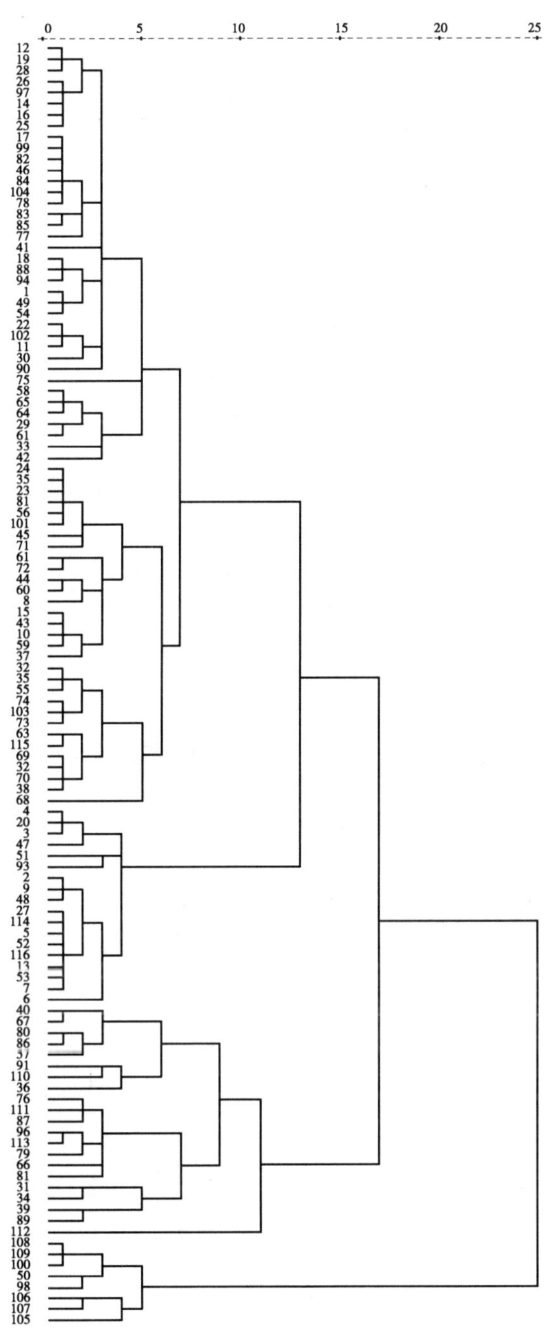

图 1　116 份葱种质数量性状数据统计结果聚类图

2.2　葱种质资源数量性状相关分析和主成分分析

数量性状相关性是作物资源研究和利用的重要内容，也是组配杂交组合过程中所要考虑的重要因素。通过对性状间相关性研究，确定不同性状之间的关系，可以在选择某

一性状的同时预测对其他性状可能产生的影响或选择压。葱种质主要数量性状间均存在显著和极显著相关性，且同一性状受其他多个性状变化的影响。其中，单株重与假茎重、叶长、株高、出叶孔间距、叶扁宽和假茎长均达极显著或显著水平，相关系数分别是0.965**、0.666*、0.616*、0.598*、0.489*和0.459*，假茎重和叶长与株重的相关性最为密切。葱株高与假茎长、出叶孔间距、叶长、假茎重、假茎直径、叶扁宽呈极显著或显著正相关，但与单株分蘖数呈显著负相关，相关系数分别为0.913**、0.965**、0.929**、0.697*、0.666*和−0.417*，其中，叶长和假茎长对株高的影响最大。假茎重与假茎长、假茎直径、叶长、叶扁宽和出叶孔间距呈显著正相关，相关系数分别为0.588*、0.410*、0.691*、0.533*和0.679*。假茎长与假茎直径、叶长、叶扁宽、出叶孔间距呈显著正相关，与宿存叶片数和单株分蘖数呈显著负相关，相关系数分别为0.731*、0.698*、0.644*、0.885*和−0.451*、−0.557*，其中，出叶孔间距和叶长对其影响较大。假茎直径与叶长、叶扁宽和出叶孔间距呈显著正相关，与宿存叶片数、单株分蘖数、假茎指数呈显著负相关，相关系数分别为0.509*、0.829*、0.639*和−0.634*、−0.744*、−0.718*（表4）。株高、假茎长和假茎直径是普通大葱假茎产量的主要构成因素，三者与分蘖数和宿存叶片数呈不同程度负相关表明，随分蘖数的增加分葱的单蘖产量潜力下降。从另一角度也说明分葱产量形成规律与普通大葱明显不同。

表4　葱种质资源数量性状相关矩阵

	X_1	X_2	X_3	X_4	X_5	X_6	X_7	X_8	X_9	X_{10}	X_{11}	X_{12}
X_1	1.000	0.616*	0.965**	0.459*	0.299	0.666*	0.489*	0.266	0.598*	0.105	0.019	−0.556*
X_2		1.000	0.697*	0.913**	0.666*	0.929**	0.613*	−0.286	0.965**	−0.417*	−0.141	−0.532
X_3			1.000	0.588*	0.410*	0.691*	0.533*	0.159	0.679*	0.011	−0.024	−0.532
X_4				1.000	0.731*	0.698*	0.644*	−0.451*	0.885**	−0.557*	−0.144	−0.396
X_5					1.000	0.509*	0.829*	−0.634*	0.639*	−0.744*	−0.718*	−0.612*
X_6						1.000	0.494	−0.095	0.893**	−0.228	−0.118	−0.082
X_7							1.000	−0.506	0.589*	−0.656*	−0.569*	−0.531
X_8								1.000	−0.280	0.899**	0.539	−0.205
X_9									1.000	−0.394	−0.120	−0.205
X_{10}										1.000	0.644*	0.648*
X_{11}											1.000	0.559*
X_{12}												1.000

注：*和**别表示在$\alpha=0.05$和$\alpha=0.01$水平差异显著

舍去2级统计数据假茎指数和叶形指数，根据116份葱种质的形态指标数据应用主成分分析方法（PCA）分析不同数量性状在葱产量构成中的重要性，得到葱形态性状特征值的贡献率和累计贡献率（表5）。在所有产量构成的主分量性状中，前3个主成分

（PC1、PC2 和 PC3）累积方差贡献率为 91.18%，可以综合反映原 12 个形态指标的信息。在实际性状选择中按照累积贡献率大于 85% 的原则，采用单株重、株高、假茎重 3 个主成分作为选择依据进行综合性状选择即可基本达到目的。

表 5　形态主分量性状的特征值、贡献率、累计贡献率

性状	特征值	贡献率（%）	累计贡献率（%）
X_1	6.231	56.648	56.648
X_2	2.831	25.740	82.338
X_3	0.967	8.792	91.180
X_4	0.416	3.778	94.958
X_5	0.208	1.892	96.850
X_6	0.161	1.462	98.312
X_7	0.086	0.785	99.098
X_8	0.052	0.476	99.573
X_9	0.048	0.427	100.00

根据试验种质的主成分值，在 PC1-PC2 和 PC2-PC3 平面上作不同数量性状散点图（图 2）以及种质样点图（图 3）。结果表明：葱 10 个数量性状在 PC1-PC2 和 PC2-PC3 平面图位置分布基本反映了性状间的相关关系。另外，116 份试材散布于 PC1-PC2 和 PC2-PC3 平面图上。其中，PC1-PC2 可以将不同资源有效分开，例如，高粗组 18 份种质主要分布于 PC1 正坐标轴的右边部分；单株质量较小的分葱组 8 份种质主要分布在 PC1 负坐标轴最左边，其余 21 份分葱位于其右边与之相邻。形态分类中第 4 组中的第 1 亚组分布于高粗组的左边，第 2 亚组则位于第一亚组的左边，横跨 PC2 的正负坐标轴。因此，PC1-PC2 和 PC2-PC3 平面可以有效区分葱种质的分布情况，葱形态性状的前 3 个主成分反映的信息与基于 12 个性状的聚类和相关分析结果基本一致，从而在性状选择的过程中达到了简化变量的目的。

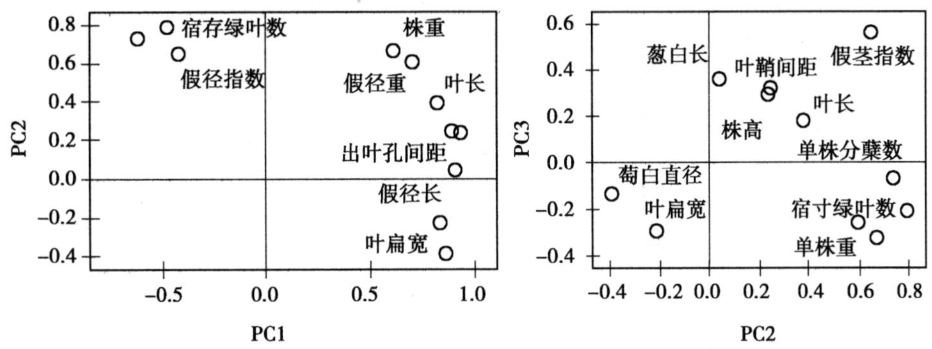

图 2　葱种质不同数量性状的前 3 个主成分值

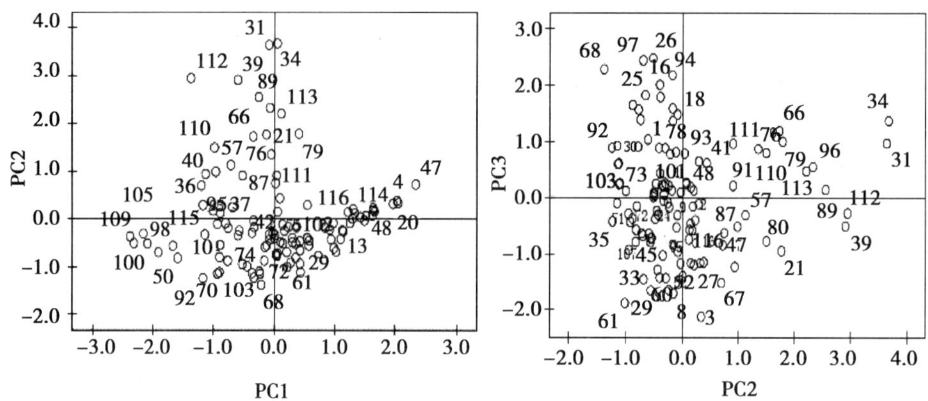

图 3 葱种质数量性状的前 3 个主成分种质样点分布图

3 讨论

3.1 形态标记的主要研究方法及其在育种上的作用

遗传多样性研究是作物遗传育种的重要环节，通过对不同来源种质之间亲缘关系的发现和确认可以为种质保护和有效进行亲本组配提供依据。表型性状是基因型和环境因素互作的结果，数量性状虽易受发育时期和环境条件等因素的影响，但作为多样性研究的最直接方法，形态学标记具有简便、直观、易行、快速的特点，是种质资源评价和优良种质筛选的一个重要手段。其研究法方法主要包括聚类分析、相关性和主成分分析等已成功应用于多种作物资源分类和育种研究，对于作物资源利用和品种选育起到了较好的指导作用[5~11,14~15]，但在葱育种研究上应用较少。

3.2 形态标记研究在葱种质资源分类及亲缘关系研究上的应用

我国是葱的起源中心之一，种质资源丰富是开展育种工作的基础，但长期以来葱种质资源研究和利用相对落后，是育种工作不能取得较快进展的根本原因。陈运起等[5]测定和统计了 23 个棒状大葱品种的 11 个数量性状，采用 Q 型聚类方法将 23 个棒状大葱品种分为高粗型、高细型、矮细型、矮粗型 4 个类型，并建立了 4 个判别分类函数方程式，能较好地将大葱归为不同类型，为葱的分类研究提供了很好借鉴。但该研究试材仅限于普通大葱，且试材资源数量较少，在我国南方、欧洲及日本等地区广泛栽培同样具有丰富的遗传和变异的分葱资源未涉及，未能涵盖葱所有遗传变异类型。

本文搜集了国内外 116 份葱种质，基本包括了除楼葱外的大部分栽培葱类型，具有一定的普遍性。本文未选用不开花或开花不结实和很少结实的分株繁殖分葱资源，主要为保证不同资源生育期等生育条件的一致性。基于葱数量性状的数据资料将供试种质划分为 5 个组群，聚类结果较好地区分了葱主要栽培区种质资源形态相似性和差异，区分了普通大葱之间以及栽培分葱之间的不同类型，从形态学角度初步明确了不同生态区域资源之间的亲缘关系远近，并发现了与葱种质单株产量最为密切的性状是假茎重、叶长和株高，为种质资源在科研生产中的研究利用打下了基础。

从不同类型资源的分组情况看，传统的长白大葱、南方型分葱分类与传统分类方法基本一致。但鸡腿葱和短白葱则基本划为矮粗型大葱亚组，不同于传统分类方法。从解剖学角度观察，鸡腿葱与普通短白葱假茎最大的区别在于其变态叶鞘在基部加厚呈鸡腿状。关于鸡腿葱假茎直径的测量方法多数文献倾向于底部粗茎和中部细茎和的 1/2，也有研究测量基部最粗部分直径，本研究采取了前者，因为 2 级数据假茎指数系为假茎长度与茎粗的比值，而作者认为茎粗测量应尽量接近整个假茎直径的平均值。本研究结果说明两者均属普通大葱范畴，在形态上相似性接近。另外，部分分蘖较少，单株生产力相对较低的北方型分葱和分蘖相对较多的高细型分葱也划为一组，表明单纯根据分蘖数多少作为划分南北分葱类型的方法似乎具有一定的局限性，育种实践中还应综合考虑株重、叶片性状等因素。

此外，根据 5 个分组材料来源分析表明高粗型种质主要以国内品种为主，矮粗型来源较为广泛，分别来自中国、欧洲和日本。高细型种质主要来自中国和欧洲，而矮细型分葱主要为欧洲品种，近矮细型种质则主要以国内品种为主。说明可能由于葱不同生态区域环境因素、食用习惯等差别体现在育种中所造成的选择压不同对种质资源的类型产生了影响。

3.3 形态标记在资源研究利用上应注意的问题

形态分类形成的组群均有明显的形态独特特性或独特基因型，加之数量性状一般呈连续性分布，所以，每一类群内均有某一或多个性状的极端个体，育种过程中实际应用价值较大[13]。根据不同育种目标，利用不同类型优良的基因资源进行基因重组和轮回选择对于种质改良、创新以及杂交种的组配均具有重要的指导意义。

应当指出，表型鉴定和选择受环境及栽培因素影响较大，因此，单从形态学上研究遗传多样性具有一定的局限性。例如，品种平度老脖子属传统长白大葱，但因其在试验区易感软腐病，导致单株生产潜力和相关性状未能充分展现而划为矮粗型大葱组。此外，尽管在相同的生态环境下鉴定作物不同形态的多样性更加能够较好地揭示其遗传本质[5]，但葱属于长日照植物，在本研究中发现南方种质在北方种植初花期有明显提前的现象，表明生育环境的一致性在形态鉴定过程中影响不同生态区域作物形态特性的表现，这是也今后相关研究中需要注意的问题。

4 结论

本研究在同一生态环境下，根据 2 年的数据资料发现葱种质遗传变异丰富，得出在各性状中变异度最大的 3 个性状分别是单株分蘖数、假茎重和单株重。采用类平均法将 116 份种质聚类为 5 个组群，分别为高粗型大葱组、高细型分葱组、矮细型分葱组、矮粗型大葱组和近矮细型葱组，从形态学角度初步明确了组内群体间亲缘关系的远近。对 10 个数量性状的主成分分析发现单株重、株高和假茎重 3 个主成分累积方差贡献率为

91.18%，基本可以综合反映原12个形态指标的信息。另外，不同性状间相关性分析表明单株重与假茎重、叶长、株高、出叶孔间距、叶扁宽和假茎长均达极显著或显著水平。假茎重与假茎长、假茎直径、叶长、叶扁宽和出叶孔间距呈显著正相关。

参 考 文 献

[1] 周长久. 蔬菜种质资源概论 [M]. 北京：北京农业大学出版社，1995：192-210

[2] 王小佳. 蔬菜育种学 [M]. 北京：中国农业出版社，2000：220

[3] 梁艳荣，姜伟，张颖力. 大葱种质资源研究及利用进展 [J]. 中国农学通报，2006，22（9）；302-306

[4] 王海平，李锡香. 葱种质资源描述规范和数据标准 [M]. 北京：中国农业出版社，2008.

[5] 王述民，曹永生，Redden R J 等. 我国小豆种质资源形态多样性的鉴定和分类研究 [J]. 作物学报，2002，28（6）：727-733

[6] 李向华，常汝镇. 中国春大豆品种聚类分析及主成分分析 [J]. 作物学报，1998，24（3）；325-332

[7] 吴舒致，黎裕. 谷子种质资源的主成分分析和图论主成分分类 [J]. 西北农业学报，1997，6（2）；46-50

[8] 陈沁滨，侯喜林，张波等. 洋葱种质资源数量性状的主成分分析和聚类分析 [J]. 江苏农业学报，2007，23（4）：376-378

[9] 易金鑫. 亚洲部分茄子品种资源数量分类 [J]. 园艺学报，2000，27（5）：345-350

[10] 李文嘉，方锋学，李立志等. 结瓜主要农艺性状的相关与通径分析 [J]. 园艺学报，2003，30（6）；734-736

[11] 柯卫东，傅新发，黄新芳等. 莲藕部分种质资源数量性状的聚类分析与育种应用 [J]. 园艺学报，2000，27（5）：374-376

[12] 陈运起，莉敏，刘洪星. 大葱部分种质资源数量性状聚类分析 [J]. 中国蔬菜，2006（8）；25-26

[13] 佟汉文. 乌拉尔甘草种质资源遗传多样性研究 [D]. 北京：中国农业大学，2005

[14] Hotelling H. Analysis of a Complex of Statistical Varieties into Principal Components [J]. Educ. Psychol.，1973，24：498-520

[15] Rao C R. The Use and Interpretation of Principal Component Analysis in Applied Research [J]. Sanhkya，Ser. A，1964，26：329-358

Clustering, Correlation and Principal Component Analysis in Welsh Onion (Allium fistulosum L.) Germplasm Resources

MIAO Jin-shan　SUN Hu　LI Yun-ling

(*Weifang University of Science and Technology*, *Shouguang* 262700)

Abstract: To elucidate the relations between welsh onion (*Allium fistulosum* L.) germplasm resources and correlations between quantity characters, clustering, correlation and principal component analyses were conducted with 116 *A. fistulosum* accessions in the fields. The result showed that coefficients of variation of 12 quantity characters among 116 *A. fistulosum* accessions varied from 25.25% ~ 146.38%. All accessions were clustered into 5 groups, and differences of morphological characters between the five groups were identified. Psudostem weight, leaf length, plant height, distance of the adjacent leaves, leaf width and psudostem length were related to the yields of plants positively. Accumulative variance contribution rate of single plant weight, plant height and psudostem weight was 91.18%, and information of the three principal components corresponded to the tree plot of clustering and correlation analyses based on 12 quantity characters.

Key words: Welsh onion (*Allium fistulosum* L.); Germplasm resource; Clustering analysis; Correlation anlysis; Principal component analysis

北冬虫夏草的研究现状概述

潘好芹① 夏海波

（潍坊科技学院，山东寿光 262700）

摘 要： 北冬虫夏草作为冬虫夏草的最佳替代品，其化学成分、药理学功能及活性物质与天然冬虫夏草相似，已受到广泛关注和重视。本文总结了近年来北冬虫夏草在人工栽培、生物活性物质及药理学功能等方面的研究结果，分析了目前存在的问题和今后研究的重点。

关键词： 北冬虫夏草；蛹虫草；虫草素

冬虫夏草（*Cordyceps sinensis*）是一种珍贵的天然药材，具有提高机体免疫力及抗肿瘤作用，并且对慢性支气管炎、高脂血症、心血管疾病等有很好的疗效。野生冬虫夏草主要产于我国的四川、西藏、青海等省（区）的高寒地带，由于其对地理气候环境的特殊要求、严格的寄生性及近年来的过度采挖，使得野生冬虫夏草产量很低，资源严重缺乏，价格超过黄金，无法满足社会需求。因北冬虫夏草（*Cordyceps militaris*）的有效成分和药理学功能与野生虫草非常相似，并且其主要功能活性物质含量高于天然冬虫夏草，同时具有可人工栽培等特点，已被广泛作为冬虫夏草的最佳替代品，受到国内外学者的广泛关注和重视。本文总结了近年来北冬虫夏草在人工栽培、生物活性成分、药理学等方面的研究结果。

1 北冬虫夏草的人工栽培研究

北冬虫夏草又称蛹虫草、北虫草、东北虫草等，属真菌界，子囊菌门，麦角菌科，虫草属。世界上已发现虫草属真菌约350余种，我国记录61种[1]。北冬虫夏草是虫草属真菌的模式种，与野生冬虫夏草为同一属，寄生于鳞翅目的蚕蛾科、舟蛾科、天蚕蛾科及部分鞘翅目昆虫的蛹体上，为一种蛹草，由子座和菌核（虫体或蛹体部分）两部分组成。北冬虫夏草主要分布在吉林、辽宁、陕西等地[2]，是我国分布广泛的药用价值极高的虫草菌。

北冬虫夏草的自然资源有限，随着人们对其研究的逐渐深入，人工培养技术已获得

---

① 潘好芹，女，博士，副教授，潍坊科技学院微生物研究所所长。研究方向：真菌及真菌资源开发利用。E－mail：never423@163.com

成功，不少地区均有较大规模的生产。目前，北冬虫夏草的栽培生产主要采用3种方法进行：一是子实体固体发酵法。该方法需要采集野生的北冬虫夏草，进行菌种的分离、纯化，然后将菌种接种在大米、小麦等固体培养基上培养。生产过程需在控温、控湿和无菌培养室中进行，整个培养过程分为菌丝体培养和子实体形成与生长两个阶段。菌丝体培养阶段需要在黑暗中，需要约15～20d时间，使菌丝体长满培养瓶表面后可诱导子实体原基的形成。子实体原基的诱导需光照和10℃左右的昼夜温差刺激。子实体的生长需光照和较高的湿度，整个生长周期约需要50～60d。该方法生产子实体的技术和条件要求不高，但因北虫草为子囊菌，菌种退化迅速，因此生产过程中需要不断筛选和复壮菌种；二是菌丝体液体深层发酵法。该方法可以大量获得北冬虫夏草菌丝体，但液体发酵需要发酵罐等设备，发酵成本较高；三是将北冬虫夏草菌种在柞蚕活蛹体或新鲜蚕蛹内，在同第一种方法相同的条件下培养40～50d即可。由于该方法需要合适的寄主和严格的生长条件，较之前两种方法，其技术要求和成本相对较高，但该方法培养出的虫草中有效成分含量较前两种培养方法的高[3]。目前，国内北虫草的人工栽培已逐渐进入到产业化阶段。

2　北冬虫夏草的生物活性成分研究

研究表明，北冬虫夏草的化学成分和营养物质与野生冬虫夏草非常相似，目前，认为重要的生物活性物质包括核苷类物质（如虫草素、腺苷等）、虫草酸（甘露醇）、虫草多糖、蛋白质、超氧化物歧化酶（SOD酶）、氨基酸、维生素及多种微量元素（如硒等）等化学成分[4,5]。研究证明，北冬虫夏草含有粗蛋白28.18%，氨基酸18.28%（共有18种氨基酸，其中7种是人体必需氨基酸），10种以上的脂肪酸，并富含不饱和脂肪酸；20余种矿质元素和多种维生素，如维生素A、B1、B2、B6、B12、C、D2、E、胡萝卜素等。

虫草素（cordycepin）又名虫草菌素、虫草碱等，为3'-脱氧腺苷（3'-deoxyadenosine），分子式为$C_{10}H_{13}N_5O_3$，分子量为251，碱性，溶于水，是虫草中特有的核苷类活性物质。迄今为止，在北冬虫夏草子实体及发酵液中发现10余种核苷类成分，如虫草素、腺苷、肌苷、尿苷、胸苷、腺嘌呤、次黄嘌呤、尿嘧啶等[6]。研究表明，虫草素具有抗菌[7,8]、抗病毒、干扰人体RNA和DNA合成，显著抑制多种肿瘤细胞生长的作用[9]，引起医药界的高度重视。虫草酸（甘露醇）是虫草的一个重要质量指标。虫草中的D-甘露醇的含量为5%～9%，甘露醇具有利尿、提高血浆渗透压、镇喘祛痰、抗自由基等功能，可以显著地降低颅压、促进新陈代谢，使脑溢血和脑血栓病症得到缓解。虫草多糖被认为是当前世界上非常好的免疫促进剂之一，具有增强机体免疫力、抗肿瘤、抗辐射等作用。虫草中还含有蛋白质、氨基酸、高含量的SOD和硒等活性成分，其中SOD具有抗多种疑难病的作用，如抗红斑狼疮、类风湿、皮肌炎、防辐射、抗癌，并有抗衰老和美容肌肤的作用[10,11]，甾醇类物质和硒都具抗癌活性。

国内外一些学者对北冬虫夏草和冬虫夏草化学成分的含量进行了比较研究。结果表明，北冬虫夏草中虫草素、虫草酸、蛋白质等物质的含量明显高于野生冬虫夏草。赵余庆等[12]研究表明北冬虫夏草的虫草素含量高于西藏产冬虫夏草，而两者的氨基酸和微量元素含量基本相近。汤晓云等[13]报道，北冬虫夏草的虫草素和蛋白质含量高于野生冬虫夏草，而虫草多糖含量低于后者。都兴范等[14]对人工培养的北冬虫夏草和野生冬虫夏草化学成分和含量进行研究，结果表明北冬虫夏草中的虫草素、虫草酸、虫草多糖和蛋白质含量都明显高于冬虫夏草，尤其是虫草素、虫草酸和虫草多糖的含量分别为冬虫夏草的2.9倍、2.7倍和3.2倍，而氨基酸含量基本接近。以上研究结果为北冬虫夏草替代冬虫夏草提供了依据。

3 北冬虫夏草的药理学功能研究

近年来，通过药理学的研究，北冬虫夏草对免疫系统、神经系统及心血管系统等疾病有治疗效果，并具有抗肿瘤和抗衰老等作用[15]，认为与冬虫夏草相似[13]。

3.1 提高机体免疫力

北冬虫夏草具有细胞免疫调节作用，同时也有体液免疫调节作用。北冬虫夏草的免疫作用主要与虫草多糖有关。研究表明，虫草多糖能够促进T和B淋巴细胞的增值，提高小鼠腹腔巨噬细胞的吞噬功能；可以提高SOD酶活力，促进红细胞C3b花环形成，对肿瘤患者因化疗引起的白细胞减少具有很高的疗效。来源于北虫草的新型免疫抑制剂FTR720能够直接作用于淋巴细胞，表现免疫抑制效果，可以抑制器官移植等的排斥反应。

3.2 抗氧化、抗衰老作用

北冬虫夏草具有延缓衰老、抗疲劳功能。研究表明，北冬虫夏草虫草提取物能有效防止D-半乳糖致衰老小鼠的多项衰老体征的出现，具有明显的延缓衰老作用，其作用机制可能与其提高抗氧化酶活性、清除自由基、减少过氧化脂质的生成有关[16]。北虫草具有明显抗衰老作用，对治疗老年性痴呆的有效率为37.14%，明显优于维生素E；同时能提高老龄大鼠体内SOD、GSH-Px活性和明显降低LPO含量，从而提示北虫草的抗衰老作用是通过抗氧化作用来实现的。北虫草中的虫草酸能清除人体自由基，明显拮抗组织匀浆产生过氧化脂质，显著增加细胞能荷值，降低血压，扩张心脑血管，调节血液黏稠度，抑制脂质在血液及血管壁上的沉积，对心肌也有保护作用。此外，北虫草对羟自由基的清除作用比同剂量的甘露醇作用强，对四氯化碳所致的肝脏损伤具有明显的保护作用，而对氧自由基的清除作用则不如同剂量的抗坏血酸。

3.3 抗癌作用

北冬虫夏草能抑制癌细胞裂变，阻延癌细胞扩散，显著提高体内T细胞、巨噬细胞的吞噬能力。虫草多糖能选择性地增加脾脏营养性血液量，能使脾脏质量明显增加，脾脏中浆细胞明显增多，具有一定的抗放射作用，此外，还能提高血清的皮质酮含量，促进机体核酸及蛋白质的代谢，具有抑瘤作用。

北虫草中的主要有效成分虫草素对小鼠艾氏腹水癌和人上皮癌细胞均有明显的抑制作用。北虫草不仅本身具有较强的抗肿瘤作用，能增强抗肿瘤药物的疗效，还能通过免疫调节，达到治疗或控制肿瘤的目的。虫草素可以增强抗癌药环磷酰胺的作用，也可以作为临床抗肿瘤药物的辅助药。虫草菌素的抗肿瘤作用与其抑制 DNA 和 RNA 的合成有关。研究表明，虫草素结构与腺苷相似，替代腺苷参与了细胞代谢过程，抑制 mRNA 腺嘌呤加尾，虫草素 5′-三磷酸连至 mRNA3′ 端，因缺少 3′- OH 而导致了 mRNA 无法延伸和成熟，影响蛋白质合成，最终抑制肿瘤细胞的生长。

3.4 抗菌、抗炎作用

北虫草中的虫草素和虫草多糖都具有抗菌抗炎作用。北虫草菌种发酵液中含有耐热的广谱性抗菌物质，能够拮抗革兰氏阴性及阳性菌、芽孢菌和非芽孢菌、链霉菌。其中，虫草素对枯草杆菌等细菌、链球菌、鼻疽杆菌、炭疽杆菌、猪出血性败血症杆菌及葡萄球菌等病原菌的生长有抑制作用；对鸟结核杆菌、枯草杆菌、鼻疽杆菌等结核杆菌也均有抑制作用；对石膏样小芽孢癣菌、絮状表皮癣菌、羊毛状小芽孢癣菌及须疮癣菌等皮肤致病性真菌有抑制作。

3.5 抗惊厥、镇静作用

北虫草含有多种维生素，具有调节神经系统的作用，对植物神经系统具有外周抗胆碱作用，能降低副交感神经兴奋性，使蛹虫草具有镇静作用，并且对心悸、失眠有较好的治疗作用。研究表明，北虫草能明显减少小鼠自主活动，能对抗戊四氮诱发小鼠惊厥，并且能够协同戊巴比妥钠诱发小鼠睡眠，作用强度与冬虫夏草相似，表明北虫草具有镇静催眠作用。

3.6 调节呼吸系统功能

北虫草水提液具有明显的增强肾上腺素分泌、扩张动物支气管、平喘、祛痰等作用，可对肺心病呼吸衰竭发挥辅助治疗作用。胡征等[17]从人工栽培北虫草菌丝的挥发油中发现一种与贝母碱结构类似的物质，证实北虫草是一种对呼吸道疾病有效的药物。北虫草能够通过改变血浆氨基酸，使 BCAA /AAA 比值上升，对肺心病呼吸衰竭发挥辅助治疗作用。

3.7 雄性激素样作用

北虫草能增强睾丸的生精与内分泌功能，促使雄性激素分泌，并能修复腺嘌呤引起的睾丸功能障碍使大鼠血清睾酮含量增加，同时使其体重及皮腺、精囊、前列腺的重量显著增加，有明显的雄性激素样作用[18]。人工栽培的北虫草细粉及复合粉可以不同程度地通过提高睾丸间质细胞酶的活性以促进雄性激素的合成和分泌，从而促进睾丸生精细胞的生长发育及精子的形成，发挥其补肾助阳益精之功效[19]。临床证明，北虫草对肾虚所致阳萎、早泄、肾虚腰痛有良好的治疗及保健作用，对治疗肾虚腰痛、糖尿病、蛋白尿等肾功能障碍者也有较好的效果。

3.8 降血糖作用

人工培养的北冬虫夏草能够显著降低四氧嘧啶糖尿病小鼠的血糖水平和糖基化血清蛋白含量，改善糖尿病小鼠的血糖耐量，提高胰岛素抵抗脂肪细胞的葡萄糖摄取水平，说明人工培养的北虫草对糖尿病小鼠有较好的降血糖作用。北虫草制品可调节体液免疫、细胞免疫、巨噬细胞和 NK 细胞免疫功能，并对正常动物和高血糖模型动物的血糖耐量有一定的增强作用。

3.9 其他作用

北虫草在肺虚咳嗽、急慢性支气管炎、哮喘等病症的治疗上有一定的应用。虫草素具有抗缺氧、增加心肌营养血流量的作用，并可增加犬冠脉血流量，降低冠脉、脑及外围血管阻力。虫草酸能清除人体自由基，显著增加细胞能荷值，降低血压，扩张心脑血管，调节血液黏稠度，抑制脂质在血液及血管壁的沉积。虫草也具有降血脂作用，能使血清中总胆固醇、血清甘油三酯浓度明显降低。此外，北虫草还有减肥、瘦身、美容等功效。

4 展望

北冬虫夏草作为一种蛹草，不仅具有较高的食用价值，而且还具有很高的药用功效。现代药理和毒理实验研究证明，人工北虫草的药效和天然冬虫夏草基本一致，具有提高机体免疫力、抗衰老、抗癌等功效，为人工北虫草替代价格昂贵的天然冬虫夏草提供了科学依据。

伴随着人们生活水平的提高和工作压力的增大，人们对功能保健产品的需求量不断增加。北冬虫夏草作为一种药食两用菌，市场需求也在不断扩大，因此加强其药用和保健价值的开发是今后研究的重点。北虫草作为传统名贵中药冬虫夏草代用品的开发，已经取得不少成果，但对其自身特殊的活性成分及药理作用仍需要继续进行深入研究，如虫草素的代谢途径及主要调控因素还未完全弄清，阻碍了生物合成研究的发展。加强北虫草各种有效成分及药理机制的研究，可为北虫草开发为现代保健品或药品提供科学依据。对于北虫草中有效成分的分离纯化研究工作，我国起步较晚，目前主要停留在制剂的研究上，水平有限，因此加速虫草素等有效成分的分离、纯化及产业化研究亟待进行。同时，进行北虫草优良菌种的选育和高产技术的研究，提高蛹虫草的产量和有效成分含量；北虫草相关产品的研发等，都是今后对北虫草进行研究的重要内容。相信随着对虫草菌的深度开发，将会较大的促进医药产业和保健品产业的发展，具有良好的经济效益和社会效益，开发北虫草具有极其广阔的市场前景。

参考文献

[1] 崔星明. 食（药）用真菌种质资源研究（一）[J]. 上海农业学报，2000，16（3）；94 -96

[2] 李楠，龚长虹，张宏. 北冬虫夏草人工栽培技术研究及保健品研制 [J]. 长春师范学院学报，2001，20（1）；36 -37

[3] 朱宏图. 人工培育蛹虫草的研究 [J]. 中药通报，1987，12（12）；21

[4] 李楠，龚长虹，张宏. 北冬虫夏草人工栽培技术研究及保健品研制 [J]. 长春师范学院学报，2001，20（1）；36 -37

[5] 汤晓云. 蛹草的研究进展 [J]. 基层中药杂志，2002，16（4）；50 -53

[6] Li S P, Yang F Q, K. W. K. Tsim, J. Pharm [J]. Biomed. Anal. 2006, 41；1571 -1584

[7] Suger AM, McCaffrey RP. Antifungal activity of 3'-deoxyadenosine [J]. Antimicrob Agents Chemother, 1998, 42（6）；1424 -1427

[8] Ahn Y J, Park S J, Lee S G, et a1. Cordycepin：selective growth inhibitor derived from liquid culture of Cordyceps militaris against clostridium SPP [J]. Agric Food Chem, 2000, 48：2744 -2748

[9] Nakamura K, Yoshikawa N, Yamaguchi Y, eta1. Antitumor effect of cordycepin（3'-deoxvadenosine）on mouse melanoma and lung carcinoma cells involves adenosine A3 receptor stimulation [J]. Anticancer Res, 2006, 26（1A）：43 -47

[10] 李祝，刘爱英，梁宗琦. 虫草菌素的生物活性及检测方法 [J]. 食用菌学报，2002. 9（1）；57 - 62

[11] 刘东泽，陈伟，高新华等. 虫草菌素（3´-脱氧腺苷）研究进展 [J]. 上海农业学报，2004，20（2）；89 - 93

[12] 赵余庆，于明，陈立君等. 冬虫夏草属真菌化学研究概况 [J]. 中草药. 1999，30（12）；354.

[13] 汤晓云. 蛹草的研究进展 [J]. 基层中药杂志，2002，16（4）；50 -53

[14] 都兴范，李亚杰，王林华等. 北冬虫夏草的发展现状 [J]. 辽宁农业科学，2003，（4）；26 -28.

[15] 马定远. 冬虫夏草及其菌丝的药理学研究进展 [J]. 中药材，2001，24（6）；455

[16] 王玉华，叶加，李长龄等. 冬虫夏草提取物延缓衰老实验研究 [J]. 中国中药杂志，2004，29（8）；773 -776

[17] 胡征，夏服宝，吴小刚等. 冬虫夏草新药效成分分析 [J]. 中国食用菌，2004，23（5）；37 -38.

[18] 刘洁，杨世杰，杨旭等. 蚕蛹虫草的抗肿瘤及激素样作用 [J]. 中国中药杂志，1997，22（2）；111 -113

[19] 贡成良，徐承智，杨昆等．家蚕蛹虫草的毒性研究［J］．中国食用菌，2003，22（6）：54－56

The Research Progress of Cordyceps Militaris

PAN Hao-qin　XIA Hai-bo

(*Weifang University of Science and Technology*, *Shouguang* 262700)

Abstract: As the best substitute for *Cordyceps sinensis*, has the similar chemical components, bioactive substances and medical function with *Cordyceps sinensis*. This article introduces the research in cultivation, bioactive substances and medical function of *Cordyceps militaris*, and also analysis the current problems and important research fields in future.

Key words: *Cordyceps militaris*; Cordyceps; Cordycepin

鲁硕红蔷薇绿枝扦插育苗技术的研究

郎德山① 李美芹 李 祎

（潍坊科技学院，山东寿光 262700）

摘 要： 以鲁硕红蔷薇为试料，按正交设计排列，因素和水平采用 L24（3×4×24），分别研究生根剂类型、培养基质的种类、扦插枝条的木质化程度、插穗所留叶片及其腋芽数量等多个因素对鲁硕红蔷薇插穗生根、植株成活的影响。结果表明：枝条的木质化程度和生根剂种类对生根率的影响最大，基质、插穗所留叶片及其腋芽数量对扦插生根率的影响次之；采用半木质化插穗、用生根剂“根旺”速沾 1 秒钟左右，扦插在沙壤土中，可使其插穗生根率达 89% 左右；上述各因素对移栽大田后的苗木生长无显著影响。

关键词： 扦插育苗；生根率；正交试验；鲁硕红蔷薇

蔷薇属于蔷薇科（*Rosaceae*）蔷薇属（*Rosa*）植物，为落叶或常绿灌木，茎直立或攀援，通常有皮刺。蔷薇属（*Rosa* L.）是世界著名的观赏植物之一，全世界共有约 200 种，广泛分布于北半球亚热带到温带地区[1]。中国是蔷薇属植物重要的分布中心之一，共有 95 种[2]。

蔷薇通常采用播种、嫁接、扦插、组培、水培、压条、分株等方法进行繁殖。采用扦插育苗技术，不仅能保持母株优良性状，避免发生劣变[3,4]，且能加速良种繁育的速度，对迅速发展的无性系育种和林业发展具有重要意义。王维君[5]采用扦插技术繁殖玫瑰蔷薇，分别研究了枝条的木质化程度、生根粉浓度及培养基质对生根的影响，得知半木质化枝条、用 100mg/kg 生根粉浸泡 0.5～1h 扦插在炉渣中生根效果极佳；温爱存[6]对黄蔷薇进行了扦插试验，得知 NAA、IBA 的浓度和水肥管理对其成活率影响极大。

鲁硕红蔷薇为蔷薇科蔷薇属野蔷薇的一个栽培变种，是潍坊科技学院 2007 年从荷兰引进。经试种，该蔷薇在山东寿光的适应性较强，能耐干旱、寒冷、瘠薄，抗病能力极强（尤其是对白粉病，即使高温高湿季节也不易受侵染）。不仅一年内开花数次，而且开花早，花型特大，花期长，颜色非常鲜艳，花量繁多、簇生（一簇多达 87 朵花），香味清雅，株型优美，枝条飘逸，果实红艳光亮，可用来布置花柱、花架、花廊、墙垣

① 郎德山，男，硕士，潍坊科技学院副教授。研究方向：园林园艺植物栽培。E－mail：langdeshan123@126.com

或修剪造型等，开花时远看锦绣一片，红花遍地，近视花团锦簇，鲜红艳丽，叶色墨绿，叶子大而光亮，景观效果极佳；同时，因其皮刺大、硬而浓密，也是机关、学校、厂矿、果园四周等用来做篱笆墙的上等选择；该蔷薇较其他蔷薇具有更高的观赏价值、经济价值及应用前景，但因其繁殖难度较大，数量极少，其园林美化价值仅在个别城市体现，完全没有发挥其应有的作用。因此，有必要开展鲁硕红蔷薇的快繁体系的研究，建立成熟的繁殖体系，为其合理的推广应用奠定基础。

本研究从激素的类型与浓度、培养基质种类、枝条的木质化程度，接穗所留叶片与腋芽数量，扦插后水肥及病虫害管理等各个方面进行研究，探索影响鲁硕红蔷薇扦插生根、成活的主要因素，通过优化组合，最终筛选出适宜的嫩枝扦插方法。

1 材料与方法

1.1 试验地概况

试验地设在潍坊科技学院试验场，位于山东寿光，属暖温带半湿润气候，四季分明，气候温和，年均气温 12.4℃左右，降雨量 608mm，年日照时数约 2 607h，无霜期 195d。扦插苗床设在光照充足、水源条件好、地势平坦的试验田内，采用全光照喷雾技术喷水。

1.2 试验地的准备

提前 15d 左右做成宽 1.2m、高出地面 25cm 的苗床。苗床底层铺河沙、表面 15cm 左右分别以沙壤土、洁净河沙作基质；床上用竹批子搭成 70cm 高的拱，以备下雨时覆盖薄膜。扦插前 1～2d 用 500 倍多菌灵溶液喷洒苗床，以杀死病原菌。

1.3 插条处理与扦插

2009 年 7 月 1 号，供试插穗采集于山东寿光潍坊科技学院试验场，枝条按往年生完全木质化老枝条、当年生半木质化穗枝以及未木质化的顶端嫩枝，分别剪切，长度在 4～10cm，每个插穗保留 1 或 2～3 个腋芽，上端距腋芽 1cm 处剪成平口，下端剪成斜口，使切口斜面与底部腋芽相背；剪去叶片，每个插穗留下单叶的 1/2 或留下 1～3 片单叶，修剪好的穗条立即放于清水中，防止萎蔫。取出穗条，用吲哚乙酸（IAA）、萘乙酸（NAA）、2，4-D、生根剂“根旺”（由四川农科院兰月科技开发公司生产）速蘸 1 秒后扦插，扦插深度为 2～7cm（地面以上只保留一个腋芽），株行距为 5cm × 10cm，插后浇透水。

1.4 试验设计

首先探索不同种类及浓度的生根剂对插穗生根率的影响。取当年生半木质化枝条，剪切成 8cm 左右的插穗，每个插穗保留 2 个腋芽、半片单叶，按上面描述的方法，分别用 125、250、500、1 000、2 000mg/L 的 NAA 和 IAA、50、100、200、400、800mg/

L的2，4-D以及（10、20、40、80、160）$\times 10^3$mg/L的“根旺”蘸根，设置不用任何生根剂处理的插穗作对照（CK），之后扦插于沙壤土基质内，每个处理扦插50株，扦插后分别与10d、20d、40d观察并记录生根与发芽情况，随机取样，每次取10株；取40d后调查的数据统计其生根率。

然后，采用正交试验设计，进一步研究不同生根剂、不同插穗条件（木质化程度、每个插穗所含腋芽数目以及插穗所留的叶片数）及不同基质等多种因素对插穗生根及苗木成活的综合作用，生根剂浓度分别为1 000mg/L的IAA、500mg/L的NAA、200mg/L 2，4-D和80 $\times 10^3$mg/L的根旺（数据来源于第一个实验）。按正交设计排列，采用3水平1因素+4水平1因素+2水平4因素设计，即L24（$3\times4\times2^4$）（见表1），每个处理扦插30株，3次重复，取平均值。40d后调查并统计其生根率。

表1 试验因素与水平

水平	因素				
	A插穗木质化程度	B生根剂	C基质	D插穗叶片数	E插穗芽数
1	未木质化	吲哚乙酸IAA	沙壤土	半片单叶	1个
2	半木质化	萘乙酸NAA	河沙	1~3片单叶	2~3个
3	完全木质化	2，4-D			
4		根旺			

1.5 扦插后管理

扦插后7d内，为防止叶片黄化干枯，每天保持4~8h的喷水时间，并且中午11:30至1:30一直喷水；做到有太阳直射时叶片上多数时间都有小水珠，基质内水分适中、以保持潮湿为标准。之后每天喷水3~5次，每次喷10min左右。等生根后，间隔1~3d喷1次，每次喷透，使苗床基质保持干湿交替。若扦插后2周内下雨，用塑料薄膜覆盖顶部，防止雨水伤害尚未生根的插穗；但底部30cm不覆盖，以保证通风换气。2周后喷洒1次800~1 000倍的多菌灵，防止枝条及落叶腐烂。生根后每隔7d喷1次0.2%的尿素，后期每隔4~5d用0.2%的尿素和0.2%的磷酸二氢钾混合喷洒1次[7,8]。成活后移栽至大田，正常肥水管理，并注意防治病虫害，尤其是地下害虫。

2 结果与讨论

2.1 各种生根剂对插穗生根率的影响

用不同浓度的生根剂处理插穗并扦插，正常管理。10d后，畦面上1/10左右叶片发黄并开始脱落，拔出插穗观察，多数观察不到明显变化，只有约50%用2，4-D和根旺处理的插穗开始出现愈伤。20d后，用NAA、IAA处理的插穗30%左右开始出现白色细根并开始发芽，用2，4-D处理的插穗约60%出现白色嫩根并开始发芽，用根旺处理的插穗约85%出现白色嫩根并发芽；并且用NAA、IAA和根旺处理的插穗发芽时间总体上早于2，4-D处理；NAA、IAA的处理形成根的长度和数目少于2，4-D和根旺的处理，前者只有1～2条根，后者则有3～7条，甚至有的多达11条。用根旺处理的落掉叶子的插穗，其生根率仅达20%左右，并且生根的插穗发芽也慢，可见半片单叶所进行的光合作用对插穗的成活是比较重要的；原因可能是叶片不仅能进行光合作用，提供生根所需的碳水化合物，而且也能合成内源生长素刺激生根，从而为发芽提供条件。没做任何处理的对照几乎没有生根和发芽的。40d后，观察到用2，4-D和根旺处理的插穗长出的幼苗比其余处理的生长旺盛并且粗壮，取出剩余的所有插穗，统计其生根率，结果详见图1。

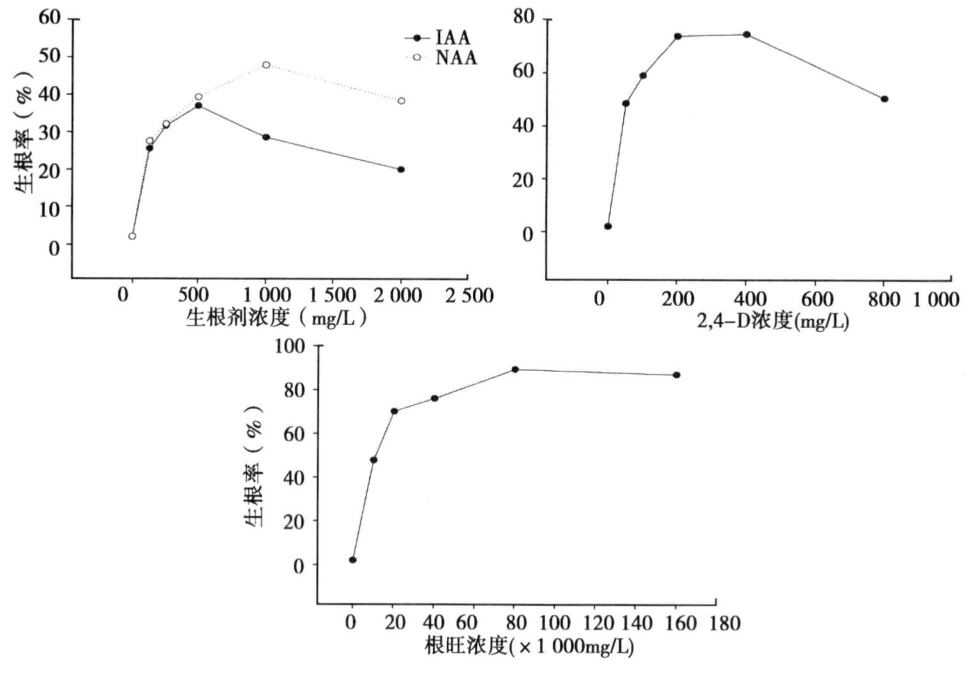

图1 各种生根剂对插穗生根率的影响

2.2 对扦插生根率的影响

将各种条件的插穗采用不同的处理，扦插在不同的基质中，生长40d后，观察结果如下：①枝条的木质化程度对生根率和发芽率影响显著。总体情况是：半木质化程度的插穗生根率和发芽率最高，原因可能是半木质化枝条的组织分生能力强，内源生长促进物质较多，抑制物质较少，细胞分生能力强，愈伤组织形成快，所以扦插成活率高；完全未木质化的插穗，不仅生根率底，而且30%左右生根的插穗在40d内都没发芽，可能是该种插穗的腋芽非常瘪，休眠时间较长的原因；②完全木质化程度的插条在河沙基质中生根率和发芽率均优于在沙壤土基质中，而半木质化和完全未木质化的插条在沙壤土中的生根率和发芽率均优于在河沙基质中，究其原因可能是夏季的高温天气，蒸发量大，河沙保湿性差，插穗在未生根前容易干枯，因此，在河沙基质中选择木质化程度较高的插穗不容易失水干枯，所以其生根效果优于嫩枝或半木质化枝条；反之亦然；③留有1～3片单叶的插穗比半片叶的插穗生根率高，但发芽慢。究其原因可能是在生根期间，叶片多，光合作用强，输送给插穗底部的营养就多，所以生根快；但到后期，叶片制造营养的能力减弱，根吸收的营养过多的分给叶片，发芽就慢；④含2～3个腋芽的插穗生根及发芽情况均略优于1个腋芽的，尤其是下端斜口接近腋芽时，根的数量明显增多。将40d调查统计后的小苗移栽大田后，各种处理再生的幼苗生长状况没有明显区别。可见，不同因素处理对扦插成活率影响较大，而对后期生长的影响不明显。

表2　生根率正交试验结果与分析

试验号	处理						生根率（%）
	A插穗木质化程度	B生根剂	C基质	D插穗叶片数	E插穗芽数		
1	1	1	1	1	1	1	14.9
2	1	2	1	1	2	2	10.8
3	1	3	2	1	2	1	38.6
4	1	4	2	1	1	2	49.2
5	1	1	2	2	2	2	18.7
6	1	2	2	2	1	1	12.4
7	1	3	1	2	1	2	29.3
8	1	4	1	2	2	1	40.7
9	2	1	1	1	1	2	49.7
10	2	2	1	1	2	1	37.6
11	2	3	2	1	2	2	73.6
12	2	4	2	1	1	1	88.5
13	2	1	2	2	2	1	45.2
14	2	2	2	2	1	2	30.8
15	2	3	1	2	1	1	75.4
16	2	4	1	2	1	2	89.9
17	3	1	1	1	2	2	21.3
18	3	2	1	1	2	1	19.8
19	3	3	2	1	2	2	60.5
20	3	4	2	1	1	1	73.1
21	3	1	2	2	2	1	20.8
22	3	2	2	2	1	2	18.1

（续表）

试验号	处理						生根率（%）
	A 插穗木质化程度	B 生根剂	C 基质	D 插穗叶片数	E 插穗芽数		
23	3	3	1	2	1	1	62.3
24	3	4	1	2	2	2	78.4
K_1	214.6	170.6	530.1	537.6	525.0	529.3	
K_2	490.7	129.5	529.5	522.0	534.6	530.3	
K_3	354.3	339.7					
K_4		419.8					
R	34.51	48.38	0.05	1.30	0.80	0.08	
因子主次	A→	B→	C	D	E		
较优因子	A2	B4	C1	D2	E1	2	

正交试验结果见表2。由此可见，A、B 因素对生根率的影响差异极显著，A 因素的3个水平中以当年生半木质化穗条效果最佳，生根率高达89%以上；B 因素4水平中以根旺效果最佳；C、D、E 3种因素中各自的两水平对生根率的影响差异不显著。从表2中K值大小可以看出，本实验中A2 B4 C1 D1 E2为最优水平组合，即取当年生半木质化插穗，留有2~3个腋芽和半片叶，用根旺生根剂处理5s左右，扦插在沙壤土基质中生根效果最佳，发芽效果最好。由极差值R可以看出：5种因素对生根率影响的主次顺序为：B→A→D→E→C。

通过正交方差分析（表3）进一步验证各因素对该蔷薇扦插生根的影响。表3经DPS数据处理系统分析结果与表2结果一致。

扦插生根由多种因素决定，刘海刚[9]推测温度和空气湿度是影响银合欢扦插生根的两个重要因子；王维君[5]、闫恩维[10]都认为绿枝扦插育苗，插条质量和空气湿度是最基本的因素；本实验中，合适的激素处理是该蔷薇生根的前提，插条质量和空气湿度是保证成活的最基本的因素。

表3 正交试验方差分析

因素	平方和	自由度	均方	F值	p-值
插穗木质化程度	4 764.677 5	2	2 382.338 8	46.520 9	0.000 1
生根剂	9 469.116 7	3	3 156.372 2	61.635 8	0.000 1
基质	0.015 0	1	0.015 0	0.000 3	0.986 6
插穗叶片数	10.140 0	1	10.140 0	0.198 0	0.662 7
插穗腋芽数	3.840 0	1	3.840 0	0.075 0	0.788 0
系统误差	0.041 7	1	0.041 7	0.000 8	0.999 9
实验误差	768.109 2	14	54.864 9		
总误差	768.150 8	15	51.210 1		

3 小结

3.1 鲁硕红蔷薇的生根条件

鲁硕红蔷薇的生根条件是必须用生根剂处理，NAA、IAA、2，4-D 和根旺相比较而言，根旺效果最佳。

3.2 综合生根剂、插穗条件

综合生根剂、插穗条件（木质化程度、每个插穗所含腋芽数目以及插穗所留的叶片数）及基质等多种因素对鲁硕红蔷薇的扦插育苗的影响效果，可以得出采用半木质化的插穗、留有半片叶和 2 ~3 个腋芽，用根旺生根剂处理、在沙壤土基质中，插穗生根率和发芽效果较好，加之适当的管理措施，可在每年的 5 月中旬至 9 月进行扦插繁殖该蔷薇，移栽后生长良好。

参 考 文 献

[1] 俞德俊．中国植物志（第 37 卷）[M]．北京；科学出版社，1985，360 -455
[2] Wu Z Y，Hong D Y. Flora of China（9）[M]．Beijing；Science Press，2001，339 -382
[3] 宋仁莲．苗木扦插生根技术 [J]．中国林业，2009，(04)：53
[4] 王艳云．花卉绿枝扦插技术要点 [J]．现代农村科技，2009，(17)：40 -41
[5] 王维君．刺玫蔷薇绿枝扦插繁殖技术 [J]．现代化农业，2008，6，(347)：25
[6] 温存爱．黄蔷薇嫩枝扦插育苗技术试验研究 [J]．科研与技术，2006，8：47 -49
[7] 张水荣．全光照喷雾扦插快速育苗技术（上）[J]．上林业科技通讯，1994，284 (1)：41
[8] 张水荣．全光照喷雾扦插快速育苗技术（下）[J]．上林业科技通讯，1994，285 (2)：40 -41
[9] 刘海刚，李江，段曰汤，李桐森，邱琼．银合欢扦插繁殖研究 [J]．山东林业科技，2009，5；63 -65
[10] 闫恩维，赫家发，刘克武．刺玫蔷薇绿枝扦插繁殖技术的研究 [J]．中国林副特产，2001，4

Seedling Growing Techniques of Greenwood Cutting in LuShuoHong Yardrose

LANG De-Shan　LI Mei-qin　LI Yi

(*Weifang University of Science and Technology*, *Shouguang*　262700)

Abstract: Cutting propagation experiment was carried out with the lushuohong rose from Holland, and the effect of the type of rooting reagents and substrates, the lignified degrees of cuttings, the quantity of leaves and lateral bud containing in every cutting on the rooting rate were studied. L24 (3 ×4 ×24) element orthogonal experiment was designed according to the rooting reagents, lignified degrees of the cuttings, medium etc. The result showed that lignified degrees of the cuttings and the type of rooting reagents were the main influential factor of rooting rate, and the substrates, the quantity of leaves and lateral bud were not distinct. The rooting rate of the yard rose is 89% after the base of the cuttings was dipped in rooting reagent "GenWang" 1 second quickly. The above factors on the growth of seedlings after transplanting to the field had no significant effect.

Key words: Cutting Propagation; Rooting rate; Orthogonal tests; Lushuohong rose

设施菜田土壤 N_2O 季节排放特征及施肥控制技术研究

肖万里[1]① 何飞飞[2] 李俊良[3] 陈 清[4]

（1 潍坊科技学院，寿光 262700；2 湖南农业大学，长沙 410128；
3 青岛农业大学，青岛 266109；4 中国农业大学，北京 10010）

摘 要： 利用静态箱/气相色谱法对寿光市设施菜田进行不同氮素处理下 N_2O 排放通量的季节变化观测，研究结果表明：在农民传统施肥管理措施下，一年中 N_2O 的排放主要集中在全年温度较高、灌溉频繁的2月份移栽后至9月底，在这一时期，影响 N_2O 排放的主要因素是土壤水分状况或养分状况，而不是温度。在温度、土壤养分浓度等适宜的条件下，在一定的土壤水分含量范围内，土壤水分含量是决定 N_2O 排放通量的主要因素。在农民传统施肥管理措施下，各生长季番茄移栽后至第一次追肥之前是 N_2O 的大量排放期，分别占传统处理各生长季累积排放量的54.1%～77.1%，灌溉特别是移栽后第一次灌溉显著地促进了 N_2O 的排放，干湿交替可能是引起此段时期 N_2O 大量排放的主要原因。进入10月后，N_2O 的排放通量长时间维持在较低的水平，温度可能是限制该时期 N_2O 大量排放的主要因素。追肥改变了 N_2O 的排放强度，并没有改变 N_2O 排放通量季节性变化的格局。应用PSNT氮素调控管理技术，来对设施番茄土壤 N_2O 进行减排是可行的。

关键词： 设施菜田；N_2O；季节排放；PSNT 氮素调控

研究表明，农田土壤是全球 N_2O 排放的主要来源[1]；影响农田土壤 N_2O 排放的主要因子是温度、水分、有机质含量、肥料等底物浓度等，其中，肥料、水分的投入是较大的影响因素[2~9]。本研究选取水肥投入量比较大的山东省寿光市设施菜田作为研究对象，首次在该地区运用静态密闭箱法进行了 N_2O 气体季节排放观测，旨在通过 N_2O 气体季节排放观测，探索出 N_2O 气体季节排放规律及设施菜田 N_2O 减排的措施。

① 肖万里，男，硕士，潍坊科技学院讲师。研究方向：设施土壤养分资源综合管理、设施土壤温室气体排放。E－mail：Xiaowanli1818@163.com

1 材料与方法

1.1 试验地点基本状况

试验于2004年2月至2006年1月在山东省寿光市古城街道办事处罗家村（36°55′N，118°45′E）进行，该村为当地典型的设施番茄生产基地。试验选用的日光温室为典型的水泥柱和钢架结构，已连续种植5年，温室内的种植面积为84.0m×7.8m。种植方式为典型的一年两季，2月至6月为春季、8月至来年1月为秋季、7月份休闲。试验地土壤类型为粉质壤土。

本试验供试作物为番茄。2004年春季，番茄在2004年1月10日播种育苗，2月15日移栽定植，6月10日收获完毕（拉秧）；2004年秋季，番茄于2004年7月2日播种育苗，8月8日移栽定植，2005年1月21日收获完毕（拉秧）；2005年春季，番茄在2005年1月8日播种育苗，2月6日移栽定植，6月11日收获完毕（拉秧）；2005年秋季，番茄于2005年7月2日播种育苗，8月6日移栽定植，2006年1月21日收获完毕（拉秧）。栽培方式为传统的畦栽。

1.2 试验处理及观测方法

1.2.1 氮素肥料试验处理

2004—2006年试验期间，连续观测了4个氮素处理土壤 N_2O 的排放情况，4个氮素处理具体设置如下。

（1）NN：对照处理，不施有机肥和氮素化肥；

（2）MN：有机肥处理，不追施化学氮肥。春季基施风干鸡粪8t/hm^2，2004年和2005年有机肥投入的氮素总量分别为260kg/hm^2 和316kg/hm^2；秋季基施风干鸡粪11t/hm^2，2004年和2005年有机肥投入的氮素总量分别为360kg/hm^2 和258kg/hm^2，于定植前均匀撒施后翻耕；

（3）CN：传统氮素处理，春季和秋季基施有机肥情况同MN处理。根据当地习惯操作，2004年春季，在施用同样有机肥基础上补充了270kg/hm^2 的尿素作为基肥；2005年春季由于有机肥投入量较2004年春季高，在施用有机肥基础上只补充了150kg/hm^2（尿素）。根据对当地农户的调查结果，化学氮肥每次追施120kg/hm^2，2004年春季共追施5次；2004年秋季追施6次；2005年春季追施4次；2005年秋季追施6次；

（4）SN：调控处理，春季和秋季基施有机肥情况同MN处理。追肥时，结合PSNT技术原理[10]和番茄各生育阶段追肥后推荐的根层氮素供应值以及各生育阶段作物氮素吸收速率[11]，在综合考虑土壤氮素、灌溉水带入氮素的基础上确定追施氮量，SN处理各次追肥时追肥量计算公式如下。

追施氮量 = 推荐氮素供应值 - 根层 NO_3^- - N 含量 - 灌溉水带入氮素量（公式1）

试验小区选择在温室的中间位置，每个处理设置3次重复，共12个小区，随机区组排列。

1.2.2 静态密闭箱的设置

在1.2.1氮素肥料处理的基础上，在每个重复的4个处理试验小区中间位置分别设置气体采样底座、安放气体采样箱。

采样箱结构如图1所示。由采样箱（地上部分）和底座（地下部分）构成。采样箱底面积为90cm×70cm，高度为60cm，采样箱横截面包括整个施肥灌水沟和2株植株。箱体四周及顶盖均由不锈钢板构成，外包1.5cm厚泡沫塑料，整个箱体外围用不透明的黄色胶带固定。箱体顶部中间加10cm直径的混气扇，其目的是使箱内气体混合均匀；一侧加温度计探头，采样前后用天津产电子温度计测定采样前后箱内气温变化。电扇由12VDC胶体电池供电。采样箱底座由不锈钢板焊接制成，采样箱底座壁高5cm（从水槽底部计），底座地部插入土中部分深10cm，全部埋入土中。测定时，箱体与采样箱底座接触部分用水密封。

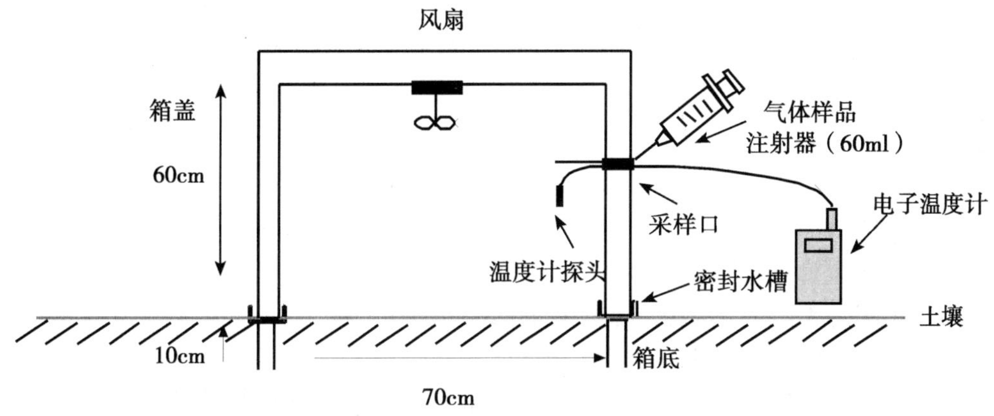

图1　N_2O 采样箱结构示意图

1.2.3 测定指标及测定方法

1.2.3.1　设施内的小气候环境

2004—2006年试验中，观测2cm、10cm深处的土壤温度，所有指标均在上午8：00~11：00随 N_2O 气体采样同步观测。

1.2.3.2　土壤 N_2O 排放通量

每次采样时，在罩箱后0min、7min、14min、21min分别用60ml医用注射器采集箱内气体60ml。采集气体样品的同时，人工测定采样前后箱内气温和地表、地下温度。

（1）N_2O 排放通量季节变化观测。N_2O 气体样品采集时间为施肥前1d、施肥当天，施肥后1周内，1d 1次；1周后，2d 1次；上午8：00~11：00采样。

样品采集结束后及时运回实验室，用GC-14B气相色谱仪（日本岛津公司生产）分析测定 N_2O 浓度。N_2O 标准气体为中国标准物质中心346ppb/L标准气体。N_2O 检测器为ECD（电子捕获检测器），检测器温度310℃，分离柱温度60℃。采用十通进样反吹阀和四通切换阀进样，N_2O 保留时间为4min，载气为99.999%高纯氮气（山东半导体研究所生产），流速为30ml/min，测定 N_2O 气体的变异系数一般小于5%。样品分析完毕后，运用千谱色谱软件判峰，计算各个试验处理的 N_2O 排放通量。

N_2O 排放通量：计算公式见公式 2。

$$F = \rho \times V/A \times \Delta c/\Delta t \times 273/(273 + T) \quad (式 2)$$

式中：F 为气体排放通量（$\mu g\ N_2O\text{-}N \cdot m^{-2} \cdot h^{-1}$），正值为排放，负值为吸收；

ρ 为 标准状态下 N_2O 密度（$ppb \cdot L^{-1}$）；

V 为气体箱体积（m^3）；

A 为气体箱的底面积（m^2）；

$\Delta c/\Delta t$ 为 N_2O 随时间的累积量（$ppb \cdot h^{-1}$）；

T 为气体箱内温度（℃）。

由于技术原因，2004 年春季番茄移栽后 11 天及夏季休闲季所有处理均没有测定 N_2O 的排放，对照处理整个春季均没有测定 N_2O 的排放。

（2）N_2O 排放总量。排放总量由测定期间得到的数据乘以测定的延迟时间累加获得。由于没有观测走道的 N_2O 排放，本研究的排放总量只包括植株生长的施肥灌溉沟，计算公式见公式 3。

$$F_m = \sum_{i=1} (ki \times h \times m) \quad (式 3)$$

式中，F_m 为 N_2O 排放总量（$kg\ N \cdot hm^{-2}$）；

ki 为间隔采样测定中第一个测定时间的排放通量（$\mu g\ N \cdot m^{-2}h^{-1}$）；

h 为到下次采样的延迟时间；

m 为面积系数（观测面积占总面积的比例，0.71）。

1.2.3.3 表层 10cm 土层土壤水分含量

每次 N_2O 气体采样结束后，用小铲在各个试验小区的畦中间位置采集少量 0～10cm 土层土样放入自封袋中，带回实验室混匀后称取 20g 左右（做 3 次重复），于 105℃下烘干 24h，测定土壤水分含量。由于国际上一般用 WFPS%（土壤充水孔隙度，Water-filled pore space）来表示土壤含水量状况，已经测定的土壤重量含水量，需要转换成 WFPS% 的形式。计算公式见公式 4。

WFPS（%）=（土壤重量含水量 × 土壤容重）/土壤总孔隙度

土壤总孔隙度 = 1 − 土壤容重/2.65 （式 4）

1.2.3.4 数据统计与分析

用 Excel、SAS（6.0）系统进行数据方差分析与多重比较。

2 结果与分析

2.1 设施菜田土壤 N_2O 排放通量的季节变化特征

从图 3 可以看出，2004 年和 2005 年传统处理设施番茄土壤 N_2O 排放通量的季节变化特征基本一致，呈现明显的季节变化。2004 年 N_2O 排放通量在 18.5～1 490μg/（$m^2 \cdot h$）之间变化；2005 年 N_2O 排放通量在 −48.4～2 026.5μg/（$m^2 \cdot h$）之间变化。

N_2O排放主要发生在春季番茄移栽至9月底全年温度较高、灌溉频繁的时期，该阶段N_2O排放量分别占2004年、2005年试验观测期间传统处理处理总排放量的90.2%，93.73%。进入10月份后，N_2O排放通量长时间维持在较低的水平，只有2005年11月1日、11月15日追肥灌水之后出现了较为明显的N_2O排放峰。

在2004—2005年设施番茄的4个生长季内，番茄移栽后至第一次追肥之前是菜田土壤N_2O的大量排放期，传统处理累积排放量分别是3.75，1.89，4.48，2.70kg/hm^2，分别占2004年春季、2004年秋季、2005年春季、2005年秋季试验观测期间传统处理累积排放量的54.1%，55.7%，76.2%，77.1%（表1）。灌溉特别是移栽时第一次灌溉显著地促进了N_2O的排放，2004年秋季、2005年春季、2005年秋季移栽第一次灌水后N_2O排放通量分别达到了1 490、1 924、779μg/（m^2·h）。2005年秋季移栽后，N_2O排放最高峰没有出现在第一次灌水后，而是出现在中耕挑沟后的第三次灌溉期间，N_2O排放通量最大值达到了2 026μg/（m^2·h）。

2.2 设施菜田土壤N_2O排放通量的季节变化的影响因素

从2004年及2005年全年的传统处理N_2O排放通量、土壤水分含量、表层土壤温度的观测结果来看（图2a，图2b，图3），N_2O排放通量与土壤水分含量、表层土温的关系较为复杂，N_2O排放通量的季节变化与土壤水分含量（WFPS值），2cm、10cm土温的同步关系均不明显。尽管设施番茄土壤2cm、10cm土温在春季2月份到秋季10月份以前大多高于15℃，具备土壤微生物硝化和反硝化作用形成N_2O的适宜温度条件，但明显的N_2O的排放峰却只出现在此阶段移栽灌水、生育期内追肥灌水以及休闲季施基肥灌水后，这表明在这一阶段影响N_2O排放的主要因素是土壤水分状况或养分状况，而不是温度。

2.2.1 施肥对N_2O排放通量季节变化的影响

在传统设施蔬菜生产中，农民在进行追肥管理时，一般采取将肥料溶入灌溉水中，随水冲施，追肥往往要要结合灌溉来同时进行（表2，图2b）。从传统处理与对照处理N_2O排放通量的季节变化来看（图3），传统处理与对照处理N_2O排放通量的季节变化格局基本一致，追肥只是改变了N_2O的排放强度，并没有改变N_2O排放通量季节性变化的格局。

2.2.2 灌溉对N_2O排放通量季节变化的影响

灌溉是通过影响表层土壤水分含量来对土壤排放N_2O的过程起调节作用的。从图2b和图3可以看出，2月份至秋季10月份以前N_2O排放的变化趋势与表层土壤水分含量（WFPS值）的变化趋势基本一致，该时期N_2O的排放通量与表层土壤水分含量（WFPS值）之间的相关系数r达到了0.44（n=162），呈显著的相关关系，这表明在2月份至秋季10月份以前这段时期内，在温度、土壤养分浓度等适宜的条件下，在一定的土壤水分含量范围内，土壤水分含量是决定N_2O排放通量的主要因素。

随着设施番茄生长季内灌溉等农事操作的交替进行，表层土壤出现了干湿交替的过程，同时N_2O排放通量随土壤水分含量的变化而波动（图2b，图3）。从土壤水分的变化来看，2004 年秋季、2005 年春季、2005 年秋季移栽第一次灌溉后，土壤水分含量（WFPS 值）分别从移栽前的 38.0% ~54.8% WFPS 迅速增加到 101.4% ~105.8% WFPS。

对照处理、有机肥处理、传统处理、调控处理在番茄生长季内 N_2O 排放都集中于移栽后到第一次追肥前这一阶段，分别占各处理各生长季总排放量的 51.0% ~83.9%，51.4% ~83.9%，54.1% ~77.1%，51.4% ~82.9%（表 1），移栽后第一次灌溉时，各处理都出现了 N_2O 的排放高峰，不同处理呈现相同的排放特征（图 3）。本研究认为出现这种现象可能是移栽后灌溉所引起的土壤干湿交替所导致。干湿交替促进 N_2O 大量排放的原因可能与干湿交替促进了微生物硝化和反硝化作用的显著进行有关[12]。

温度对 N_2O 季节排放的影响：

秋季十月份以后设施番茄土壤 2cm、10cm 日平均土温降到 15℃ 附近（图 2a，图 3），个别时间段甚至降低到了 8℃ 左右，N_2O 的排放才明显的受到日平均土温变化的影响，N_2O 的排放通量持续较低，甚至个别时间段还出现了土壤对 N_2O 的吸收现象。在此期间，虽然经历多次追肥灌水（表 2，图 2b），引起的 N_2O 排放的也较为微弱，只有 2005 年 11 月 1 日、11 月 15 日追肥灌水后出现了较为明显的 N_2O 排放峰（图 3），2004 年尽管也经历了多次追肥灌水（表 2，图 2b），但追肥灌水后始终没有出现 N_2O 的排放高峰，这可能与 2004 年此阶段的平均土温相对较低有关（图 2a）。有研究表明，冬季温度低于 15℃ 时，即使追施氮肥，引起的排放也较为微弱[13,14]。结合本研究的观测结果推测，设施番茄进入 10 月份之后，温度可能是控制 N_2O 排放的主控因子。

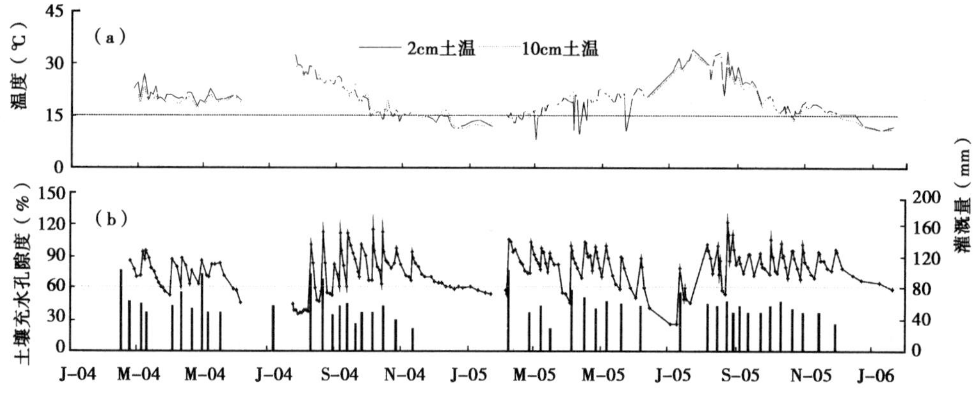

图 2 试验期间（2004 年 2 月至 2006 年 1 月）日光温室内 2cm 土温、10cm 土温（a），灌溉量及土壤含水量（b）

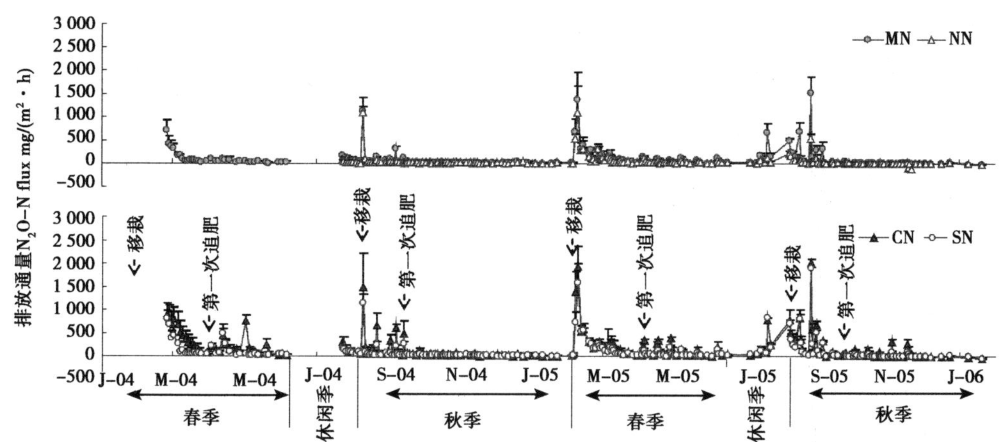

图 3　整个试验观测期间（2004 年 2 月～2006 年 1 月）NN、MN、CN、SN 处理 N_2O-N 的排放通量变化

NN：对照处理；MN：有机肥处理；CN：传统处理；SN：调控处理

表 1　试验期间各试验处理条件下 N_2O 排放量汇总

测定时期	处理[1]	季节排放量（kg/hm^2）	各生长季第一次追肥前排放比例（%）
2004-2-25 至 6-6 2004 年春季	NN	技术原因未测	技术原因未测
	MN	2.48 a	63.8
	CN	6.91 a	54.1
	SN	3.62 a	53.1
2004-7-23 至 2004-8-7 2004 年休闲季[2]	NN	0.12 b	
	MN	0.37 ab	
	CN	0.55 a	
	SN	0.41 ab	
2004-8-8 至 2-2 2004 年秋季	NN	1.67 b	51.0
	MN	2.07 ab	51.4
	CN	3.40 a	55.7
	SN	2.18 ab	51.4
2005-2-3 至 6-11 2005 年春季	NN	2.79 c	78.5
	MN	3.67 bc	81.0
	CN	5.88 a	76.2
	SN	4.27 b	80.6

（续表）

测定时期	处理[1]	季节排放量（kg/hm²）	各生长季第一次追肥前排放比例（%）
2005－6－12 至 2006－8－5 2005 年休闲季	NN	0.57 b	
	MN	1.48 ab	
	CN	2.08 a	
	SN	1.90 ab	
2005－8－6 至 2006－1－21 2005 年秋季	NN	0.83 d	83.9
	MN	1.87 c	83.9
	CN	3.50 a	77.1
	SN	2.46 b	82.9
汇总：			
2004－2－25 至 2006－1－21 2004—2006 年	MN	11.94 b	
	CN	22.32 a	
	SN	14.85 b	
2004－7－23 至 2006－1.21 2004 年休闲季至 2005 年秋季	NN	5.99 c	
	MN	9.46 b	
	CN	15.41 a	
	SN	11.23 b	

1NN，MN，CN，SN 分别表示对照、有机肥、传统和调控处理

2 由于技术原因，休闲季只监测了 2004 年 7 月 23 日至 8 月 7 日的排放

3 同一生长季内同一列中带有相同字母表示不同氮素处理的排放量在

表 2　2004—2005 年试验期间各处理的追肥时间及氮素追施量（kg/hm²）

年份	追肥次数	追施氮肥时间及番茄生育期	各处理追施氮量			
			NN	MN	CN	SN
2004 春季	Ⅰ	48～56 DAT[1] 第一穗果膨大期	0	0	120	178
	Ⅱ	57～66 DAT 第二穗果膨大期	0	0	120	150
	Ⅲ	67～76 DAT 第三穗果膨大期	0	0	120	0
	Ⅳ	77～93 DAT 第四穗果膨大期	0	0	120	0
	Ⅴ	94～117 DAT 第六穗果膨大期至生长季结束	0	0	120	0

（续表）

年份	追肥次数	追施氮肥时间及番茄生育期	各处理追施氮量			
			NN	MN	CN	SN
2004 秋季	Ⅰ	37～49 DAT[1] 第一穗果膨大期	0	0	120	0
	Ⅱ	50～59DAT 第二穗果膨大期	0	0	120	0
	Ⅲ	60～68 DAT 第三穗果膨大期	0	0	120	0
	Ⅳ	69～80DAT 第四穗果膨大期	0	0	120	50
	Ⅴ	81～95DAT 第五穗果膨大期	0	0	120	50
	Ⅵ	96～167DAT 第六穗果膨大期至生长季结束	0	0	120	60
2005 春季	Ⅰ	58～69 DAT[1] 第一穗果膨大期	0	0	120	38
	Ⅱ	70～79DAT 第二穗果膨大期	0	0	120	39
	Ⅲ	80～89DAT 第三穗果膨大期	0	0	120	50
	Ⅳ	90～126 DAT 第四穗果膨大期	0	0	120	0
2005 秋季	Ⅰ	49～57 DAT[1] 第一穗果膨大期	0	0	120	40
	Ⅱ	58～ 67DAT 第二穗果膨大期	0	0	120	0
	Ⅲ	68～77 DAT 第三穗果膨大期	0	0	120	51
	Ⅳ	78 ～87DAT 第四穗果膨大期	0	0	120	0
	Ⅴ	88～ 101DAT 第五穗果膨大期	0	0	120	60
	Ⅵ	102 ～169DAT 第六穗果膨大期	0	0	120	50

[1] DAT：移栽后的天数

2.3 PSNT 氮素调控管理技术 N_2O 减排效应分析

从表 1 可以看出，2004 年 7 月 23 日至 2006 年 1 月 21 日试验观测期间，调控处理 N_2O 排放量与传统处理 N_2O 排放量相比显著降低，这说明本研究采用 PSNT 氮素调控技术来对设施番茄土壤 N_2O 进行减排是可行的。

3 结论

（1）在农民传统施肥管理措施下，一年中 N_2O 的排放主要集中在全年温度较高、灌溉频繁的 2 月份移栽后至 9 月底，在这一时期，影响 N_2O 排放的主要因素是土壤水分状况或养分状况，而不是温度。

（2）在 2 月份移栽后至 9 月底这段时期内，在温度、土壤养分浓度等适宜的条件下，在一定的土壤水分含量范围内，土壤水分含量是决定 N_2O 排放通量的主要因素。干湿交替影响了 N_2O 排放通量的变化。

（3）在农民传统施肥管理措施下，各生长季番茄移栽后至第一次追肥之前是 N_2O 的大量排放期，分别占传统处理各生长季累积排放量的 54.1% ~77.1%，灌溉特别是移栽后第一次灌溉显著地促进了 N_2O 的排放，干湿交替可能是引起此段时期 N_2O 大量排放的主要原因。进入 10 月份后，N_2O 的排放通量长时间维持在较低的水平，温度可能是限制该时期 N_2O 大量排放的主要因素。

（4）传统处理与其他氮素处理 N_2O 排放通量的季节变化格局基本一致，追肥只是改变了 N_2O 的排放强度，并没有改变 N_2O 排放通量季节性变化的格局。

（5）应用 PSNT 氮素调控管理技术，来对设施番茄土壤 N2O 进行减排是可行的。

致谢

对本研究提供技术支持和帮助的有中国农业大学的苏芳老师、黄彬香老师、中国科学院大气物理研究所的王迎红等，谨此致谢！

参 考 文 献

[1] Bouwman AF. Exchange of greenhouse gases betwee terrestrial ecosystems and the atmosphere/Bouwman AF. Soils and the Greenhouse Effect [J]. Chichester; Wiley&Sons Ltd., 1990; 61 -127

[2] 蒋静艳,黄耀. 农业土壤 N_2O 排放的研究进展[J]. 农业环境保护,2001,20(1):51 -54

[3] Ulrike Sehy, Reiner Ruser, Jean Charles Munch. Nitrous oxide fluxes from maize fields; relation-ship to yield, site - specific fertilization, and soil conditions [J]. Agriculture, Ecosystems and Environment, 2003, 99: 97 -111

[4] 张玉铭，胡春胜，董文旭等. 农田土壤 N_2O 生成与排放影响因素及 N_2O 总量估算的研究 [J]. 中国生态农业学报，2004，12（3）：119 -123

[5] 邹建文，黄耀. 农业管理措施对 N_2O 排放的影响 [J]. 农村生态环境，2002，18（1）：46 -49

[6] 焦燕. 土壤理化特性对农田甲烷和氧化亚氮排放的影响 [M]. 南京农业大学博士论文，2003

[7] Simojoki A., Jaakkola A. Effect of nitrogen fertilization, cropping and irrigation on soil air composition and nitrous oxide emissions in a loamy clay [J]. European Journal of Soil Science, 2000, 51 (3): 413 -424

[8] Dobbie, K. E., McTaggart, I. P., Smith, K. A. Nitrous oxide emissions from intensive agricultural systems; variations between crops and seasons, key driving variables, and mean emission factors [J]. Geophys. Res, 1999, 104; 26891 -26899

[9] Mulvaney, R. L., Khan, S. A. and Mulvaney, C. S. Nitrogen fertilizers promote denitrification [J]. Biol, Fertil, Soil, 1997, 24; 211 -220

[10] Hartz, T. K., W. E. Bendixen and L. Wierdsma. The value of presidedress soil nitrate testing as a nitrogen management tool in irrigated vegetable production [J]. HortScience, 2000, 35 (4); 651 -656

[11] 汤丽玲．日光温室番茄的氮素追施调控技术及其效益评估［D］．中国农业大学博士论文．2004

[12] 梁东丽，同延安，OveEmteryd，等．干湿交替对旱地土壤 N_2O 气态损失的影响［J］．干旱地区农业研究．2002，20（2）：28－48

[13] 郑循华，王明星，王跃思等．华东稻麦轮作生态系统的 N_2O 排放研究［J］．应用生态学报．1997，8（5）：495－499

[14] 高志岭．冬小麦/夏玉米轮作体系农田土壤 N_2O 排放和 CH_4 吸收特征［D］．中国农业大学博士论文，2004

Studies on the Seasonal Emission of Nitrous Oxide and Controlling through N Management in Greenhouse Vegetable Field

XIAO Wan-li[1] HE Fei-fei[2] LI Jun-liang[3] CHEN Qing[4]

(1 *Weifang University of Science and Technology*, *Shouguang* 262700;
2 *Hunan Agricultural University*, *Changsha* 410128, *Hunan*;
3 *Qingdao Agricultural University*, *Qingdao* 266109;
4 *China Agriculture University*, *Beijing* 100010)

Abstract: We focused on the seasonal variation of the N_2O emission flux of Various nitrogen treatment of Shouguang greenhouse vegetable soil in the use of the gas chromatograph. The results showed that; With conventional N practice, N_2O emissions mainly concentrated in February to September when the temperature was high, and the irrigation was frequent. During this period, the main influencing factors of N_2O emissions was soil moisture status or nutrient status, rather than temperature. If temperature and soil nutrient was on suitable conditions and the soil moisture content was in a certain range, soil moisture content decided N_2O emission emissions. With conventional N practice, the 54.1% ~ 77.1% of seasonal emission of N_2O was measured from transplanting to the first sidedressing in the four seasons, strongly related to drying-wetting soil process. Low N_2O emission was measured at the later growing stage with relative low soil temperature in the autumn season, and temperature maybe the main limiting factors during this period. Topdressing changed the intensity of N_2O emissions, but it didn' t change the seasonal variation of the N_2O emission flux. Site-specific N treatment with Pre-Sidedress Nitrate Testing (PSNT) reduced the N_2O emissions.

Key words: Green house vegetable soil; N_2O; Seasonal emissions; PSNT

浅谈色彩在园林设计中的应用

张 菲① 郭 洁
（潍坊科技学院，寿光 262700）

摘 要： 色彩在我们生活中无处不在，恰当地运用色彩可以愉悦身心，枯燥和不协调的色彩却让人烦躁不安。随着经济的发展，人们的工作和生活环境发生了日新月异的变化，对环境的要求也越来越高，我国的园林事业也逐渐走向正规。此时，将色彩恰当地运用于园林中显得颇为重要。

关键词： 色彩；艺术美；园林

1 色彩构成与属性

将两个以上的色彩根据不同的目的性，按照一定的原则重新组合、搭配构成新的美的色彩关系就叫色彩构成。物体反射阳光所表现出来的各种颜色，称为色相，如黄、红、绿、蓝等；物体颜色的明暗程度称为明度；物体颜色的浓淡或深浅程度称为彩度或纯度或饱和度，艳丽的色彩其饱和度高，如红色最高，其次是紫、黄、绿等。

将色彩的这些特性恰当的运用到园林设计中，可以增加景观的色彩效果。

2 不同色彩的植物对人的心理作用

人们看不同色彩的植物时，与自己所经历的自然现象和社会现象联系在一起，会产生各种情感，了解色彩的心理联想，有助于创造出符合人们心理的，在情调上有特色的园林景观。

2.1 绿色

绿色是最普通的颜色，也是最容易忽视的颜色。随着季节的变化，绿叶也有一定的季相变化。春天，浓绿色是大多数花色，特别是红色调花卉的完美陪衬；夏天，浓浓绿意是人们休闲、纳凉的最佳色彩；秋天，绿叶显得更为重要，灰绿色、全黄色和具黄斑

---

① 张菲，女，硕士，潍坊科技学院讲师。研究方向：园林植物与观赏园艺。E - mail：feizhang1015@163.com

的均给人们带来美的享受；冬天，一抹绿色可以给人们带来生机。

常见的绿色植物有草坪草、大叶黄杨、松柏类、柳树、睡莲等。

2.2 红色

红色植物非常引人注目，特别在绿色的衬托下，更为醒目和热烈。在中国人的传统观念中，常常把红色与吉祥、喜庆联系在一起，所以在节日花坛布置、婚庆中常用红色。但是，由于红色特有的强视觉刺激性，过多地运用容易使人疲倦。

常用的红色植物有大丽花、月季、紫叶李、一串红、香石竹、合欢等。

2.3 白色

白色是冷色与暖色之间的过渡色，给人干净、纯洁、明快的感觉。开花的园林植物约有1/3的是白色花，若在鲜花丛中点缀白色，会显得清新而富有生气。在中国人的观念中，白色还有肃穆、哀悼之意，会给人以晦气之感因此忌讳用成片的白色。

常用的白色植物有三叶草、百合、玉簪、玉兰、瓜叶菊等。

2.4 黄色

黄色属于暖色调，是明亮、娇美的颜色，给人以明快、纯洁、“万绿丛中耀眼明”的美感。

常用的黄色植物有连翘、万寿菊、黄刺玫、金盏菊、小苍兰等。

2.5 紫色

紫色属于中间色调，有暖色调的紫红色和冷色调的蓝紫色，具有优美高雅、雍容华贵的气度。但在园林配植中紫色面积不宜过大，以免造成沉重感。

常见的紫色植物有三色堇、薰衣草、紫鼠尾草等

3 园林色彩的合理应用

3.1 园林色彩的构图

不同的色彩给人不同的温度感、情调感、距离感、轻重感和疲劳感等，因此，在运用园林因素时，必须考虑不同色彩给人的感觉，注重对这些因素综合考虑，恰当处理色块和大小，营造完美的整体效果。

应注意的构图法则，即变化与统一是构成审美需求的总原则。变化是指不同要素在平面内所具有的不同特征的独立性。例如，方圆、明暗、大小、黑白、粗细等。统一是指调和，即寻找平面要素中的共同性。例如，对称与均衡、对比与调和、节奏与韵律。

3.2 园林色彩的协调、统一

若在较小范围内运用多种色彩的植物，应选用其中一种色彩为主，较大量的应用，

并将其置于重要的位置，其他色彩通过调和和对比处理来衬托主色。色彩相同而深浅浓淡不同的颜色较容易调和，很多花卉均有同色而深浅不同的品种，皆可运用，自然界的色彩丰富多变，可利用色彩学的基本知识作参考，尝试更多更好的色彩搭配，营造更为动人的园林景观。

3.3 以人为本

色彩的选择与搭配要要尊重人性，坚持“以人为本，为人服务”的原则，符合大众的生理、心理和文化特点，与普通公众的审美情趣一致。

3.4 充分利用植物的季相变化

任何事物都要遵循其自然生活规律，园林植物随着其物候的变化，形态、色彩、景象等随之发生改变。因此，充分巧妙地利用其特点，合理布局，可营造出美妙、变化的园林景观。

艺术美与园林美相辅相成，人们对于园林的欣赏水平也日益提高，掌握色彩的特性及运用方式，有利于为我们配置出既符合人性，又遵重园林要素本性的自然化的园林景观。

参 考 文 献

[1] 施淑文．建筑环境色彩设计［M］．北京：建筑工业出版社

[2] 孟兆祯．园林设计之于城市景观［M］．中国园林 2002：13－16

[3] 方明，士景幸平．景观引导制度与城市景观环境形成［M］．城市规划，2000

A Brief Talk on Colour Application in Landscape Design

ZHANG Fei GUO Jie

(*Weifang university of science and technology*, *Shouguang* 262700)

Abstract: Colors in our life everywhere, appropriate use of color can be pleasurable, boring, not harmonious colour but let people be agitated, uneasiness. With the development of economy, China's landscape business gradually formal, people around the working and living environment has been changed the changing. At this time, colour properly by using on garden career appears very important.

Key words: Color; Artisitc Beauty; Landscape

利用地温预测菏泽牡丹花期的研究

张 菲①

（潍坊科技学院，寿光 262700）

摘 要：针对山东菏泽市的国际牡丹花会召开时间与牡丹花期很难吻合，影响当地牡丹产业和牡丹文化发展这一现状，通过分析菏泽地区土壤温度与牡丹盛花期之间的关系，建立了地温（稳定高于4℃的首日到4月10日的平均地温）与盛花期之间的多元非线性回归预测模型，并利用该模型对28年来的盛花期进行了预测。预测结果与实际开花期的误差为±4d，预测效果较好，为确定菏泽国际牡丹花会的召开时间提供了预测方法和模型。

关键词：开花期；多元非线性回归分析；预测模型

牡丹（*Paeonia suffruticosa* Andr.）居中国传统名花之首，品种多、花姿美，历来被视为富贵、平安、吉祥的象征，深受人民喜爱。自1992年以来，菏泽地区为发展经济、招商引资已成功举办了15届国际牡丹花会，年均游客100多万人次。

花会能否与花期吻合直接影响到牡丹花会的顺利召开、牡丹文化的发展和产区的经济效益。菏泽牡丹是自然条件下的大田栽培模式，花期受气候条件的影响很大。根据28年（1963—1987年、2002年、2005年、2006年）调查资料显示，盛花期最早在4月11日，最晚可到4月30日。而且牡丹花期较短，单株花期一般为7d左右[1]，群体花期15d左右。因此，准确预测牡丹盛花期，使国际牡丹花会即时召开，是提高牡丹产区经济效益的必要前提。徐丕商[2]、魏秀兰[3]等都作过气象因子与牡丹花期的研究，但都没有很好地解决国际牡丹花会与牡丹盛花期吻合的问题。所以，能否根据气象因子的变化逐步完善预测模型并用于实践，是牡丹产业发展亟待解决的实际问题之一。

1 资料来源

1963—1987年、2002年、2005年和2006年（1月20日至花期）的气象资料来自山东省菏泽市气象局，气象资料包括地温、日平均气温、逐日最低温度和逐日最高温度等指标；花期资料来自于菏泽市曹州牡丹园、百花园，共计28年的数据。

---

① 张菲，女，硕士，潍坊科技学院讲师。研究方向：园林植物与观赏园艺。E-mail：feizhang1015@163.com

2 主要指标

对植物生长发育起决定作用的环境因子主要有光照、温度、水分等。菏泽春季平均日照时数在7h以上，能够满足牡丹的光照需要[2]；据调查，菏泽地区地下水位较浅，并且牡丹原产我国西北干旱地区，根系深而发达，耐旱力较强，地下水分的供给可以满足牡丹生长发育所需的水分[4]；研究证明，无论正常开花还是反季节催花[5~7]，温度是最为重要的环境因子[8,9]，温度的变化直接影响牡丹花芽休眠的解除及萌发生长。各气象因子中温度是影响牡丹花期的主导因素。

地温是气象观测的一项常规要素，也是影响植物生长的重要气象因子，特别是浅层地温有着更重要的农业气象学意义。例如，在农作物、普通牧草等返青过程中，其贡献率甚至大于其他气象因子[10,11]。一般当地下5cm处土壤温度达到4~5℃时，中原牡丹品种群根部开始生长，生命活动悄然开始[12]。据实际观察发现，自然条件下变幅剧烈、变频较大的气温表现与其对花芽萌发和生长发育的实际效果较难对应，而地温的表现与其对花芽萌发和生长发育的实际效果更趋吻合。

本文采用地温作为预测的主要温度指标，以4℃作为起始温度，以牡丹园中占地面积最大的中花期品种的盛花期作为牡丹群体的盛花期。据气象资料显示，地温稳定通过4℃的首日均在1月20日之后，因此，本研究以1月20日距盛花期的天数作因变量（记为y），地温稳定通过4℃的首日距1月20日的天数作为第一个指标（记为x_1）。考虑到实际发布花会召开时间的预报需要，以稳定通过4℃的首日到4月10日的平均地温作为第二个指标（记为x_2，x_2=首日至4月10日总地温/首日至4月10日的间隔天数）。

3 模型建立

设1月20日作为坐标零点，则根据1963—1987年资料确定了一组x_1、x_2和y的值（表1）。

表1 1963—1987年各个指标及花期资料

年份	首日日期（月．日）	≥4℃首日距1月20日的天数x_1	盛花期（月．日）	盛花期距1月20日的天数y	首日至4月10日的间隔天数	首日至4月10日≥4℃总积温	平均地温x_2
1963	3.12	52	4.25	96	28	269.8	9.635 7
1964	3.4	44	4.28	99	37	321.5	8.689 2
1965	3.8	48	4.23	94	32	337.8	10.556
1966	3.1	50	4.27	98	30	348.8	11.627

（续表）

年份	首日日期（月．日）	≥4℃首日距1月20日的天数 x_1	盛花期（月．日）	盛花期距1月20日的天数 y	首日至4月10日的间隔天数	首日至4月10日≥4℃总积温	平均地温 x_2
1967	3. 8	48	4. 22	93	32	348. 8	10. 9
1968	3. 3	43	4. 21	92	38	422. 1	11. 108
1969	3. 14	54	4. 3	92	26	275. 7	10. 604
1970	3. 4	44	4. 29	100	35	323. 6	9. 245 7
1971	3. 15	55	4. 28	99	25	305. 4	12. 216
1972	3. 4	44	4. 27	98	37	351. 6	9. 502 7
1973	2. 25	36	4. 19	90	44	475. 5	10. 807
1974	3. 13	53	4. 24	95	27	332. 4	12. 311
1975	2. 23	34	4. 2	91	46	457. 1	9. 937
1976	3. 3	43	4. 26	97	38	362. 6	9. 542 1
1977	2. 22	33	4. 16	87	47	574. 1	12. 215
1978	3. 3	43	4. 22	93	36	387. 2	10. 756
1979	3. 2	42	4. 22	93	38	366. 4	9. 642 1
1980	3. 14	54	4. 25	96	27	292. 8	10. 844
1981	2. 17	28	4. 21	92	52	468. 2	9. 003 8
1982	2. 26	37	4. 2	91	42	506. 8	12. 067
1983	3. 1	41	4. 23	94	39	452. 2	11. 595
1984	3. 11	51	4. 26	97	29	296. 6	10. 228
1985	3. 11	51	4. 29	100	29	310	10. 69
1986	3. 3	43	4. 23	94	37	438. 5	11. 851
1987	2. 22	33	4. 25	96	47	401. 2	8. 536 2

用 MATLAB 软件对表（1）中的数据进行了 y 关于 x_1、x_2 非线性回归分析，得到了 y 关于 x_1、x_2三次多项式回归模型：

$$y = 150.6169 - 1.6318x + 0.0315^2 - 0.0004x_1^3 - 6.9716x_2 + 0.3142x_1 \times x_2 \quad (1)$$

其空间结构图形如下：

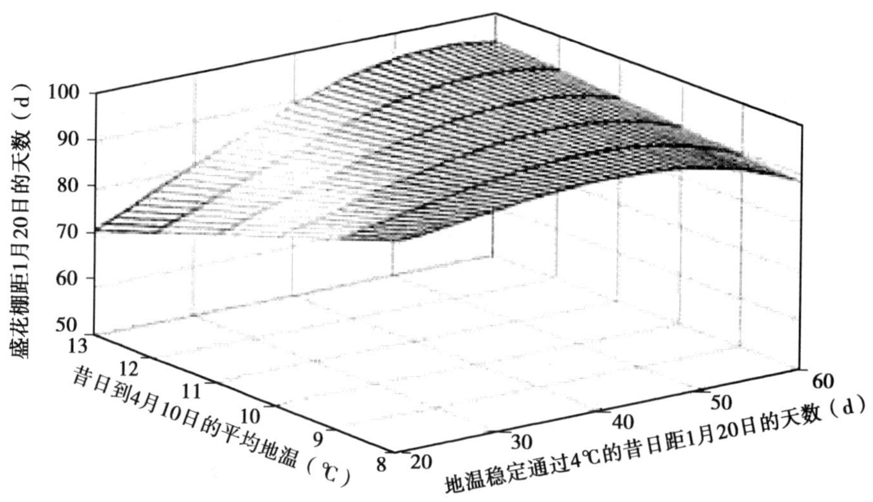

图1　地温与花期关系模型图

4　花期预报与模型的检验

4.1　花期预报

对2002年、2005年、2006年这3年的相关资料和数据进行处理，数据处理结果见表2。

表2　2002年、2005年、2006年各个指标及花期资料

年份	首日日期（月/日）	≥4℃首日距1月20日的天数 x_1	盛花期（月/日）	盛花期距1月20日的天数 y	首日至4月10日的间隔天数	首日至4月10日≥4℃总积温	平均地温 x_2
2002	2.4	15	4.11	81	63	665.2	10.559
2005	2.27	38	4.25	96	42	447.2	10.647 6
2006	2.13	24	4.16	87	54	537.5	9.953 7

利用非线性模型（1）对1963—1987年、2002年、2005年、2006年的花期进行预报，见表3。（“+”代表预报花期比实际花期提前，“-”代表预报花期比实际花期延迟）

表 3　28 年的实际花期和预报盛花期分别距 1 月 20 日的天数的误差情况

年份	实际盛花期距 1 月 20 日的天数	预报盛花期距 1 月 20 日的天数	预报误差(d)	年份	实际盛花期距 1 月 20 日的天数	预报盛花期距 1 月 20 日的天数	预报误差(d)
1963	96	96	0	1977	87	86	+1
1964	99	97	+2	1978	93	95	-2
1965	94	96	-2	1979	93	96	-3
1966	98	96	+2	1980	96	96	0
1967	93	96	-3	1981	92	92	0
1968	92	94	-2	1982	91	89	+2
1969	92	96	-4	1983	94	93	+1
1970	100	97	+3	1984	97	96	+1
1971	99	96	+3	1985	100	96	+4
1972	98	96	+2	1986	94	94	0
1973	90	91	-1	1987	96	95	+1
1974	95	96	-1	2002	81	80	+1
1975	91	92	-1	2005	96	93	+3
1976	97	96	+1	2006	87	87	0

由表 3 可以看到，这 28 年的数据，花期预测的结果最大误差为 4d（散点图如图 2 所示），据调查，牡丹的群体花期一般可持续 15d 左右。因此，该模型实用性较强，为准确地预报菏泽地区牡丹的花期提供了一定的参考依据。

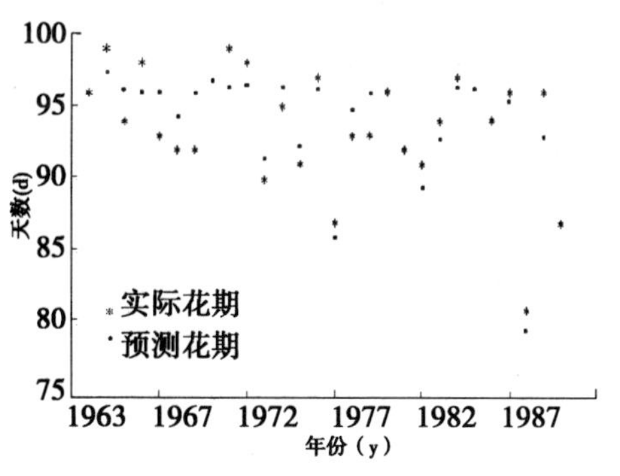

图 2　预测花期与实际花期散点图

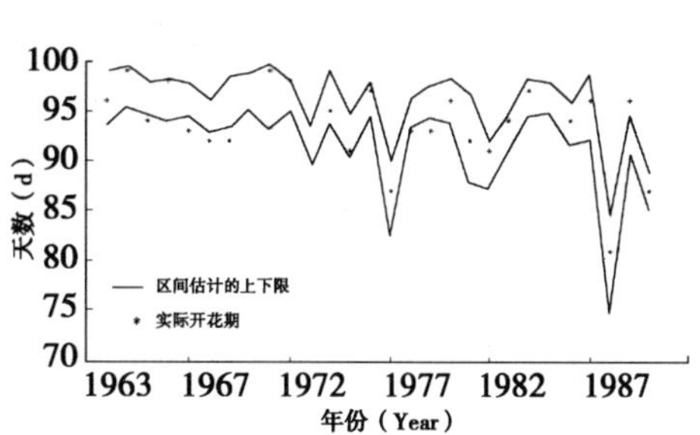

图 3　α = 0.95 的花期预测置信区间估计

4.2 模型的检验

在置信度 2 =0.95 条件下，利用模型（1）给出了 28 年花期预测的区间估计（图3），横坐标表示 1963 年开始的年数、纵坐标表示盛花期距 1 月 20 日的天数。从图中可以看出 28 年中有 20 年的实际开花期均在置信水平 2 =0.95 的置信区间内，且理论预测花期与实际花期最多相差 4d。

5 讨论

（1）本文采用地下 5cm 处土壤的平均温度稳定高于 4℃的首日距 1 月 20 日的天数 x_1 和首日至当年 4 月 10 日的平均地温 x_2 为自变量，并且采用 Matlab 软件对实际数据进行拟合，预测花期与实际开花期的误差为 ±4d，与牡丹的群体花期 15d 相比较小，可用于实践。

（2）本文考虑到实际发布花会召开时间的预报需要，相关地温因子的计算只取到 4 月 10 日，牡丹发育后期出现的异常天气对盛花期造成的影响难以预报，这是本模型的局限性。在模型的检验中，8 年的实际花期没有落在预报置信区间中，也可能与采用的因子不够全面和花农在气候异常年份的应急管理有关。若将其综合考虑、研究，可以提高预测的准确度及精确性。

参 考 文 献

[1] 张圣旺，郑国生，孟丽．钙素对栽培牡丹花衰老的影响［J］．植物营养与肥料学报．2002，8（4）；483 –487

[2] 徐丕商．菏泽牡丹开花期的预报［J］．气象，1988，24（1）；54 –55

[3] 魏秀兰，孔凡中，张宗灏等．菏泽牡丹开花期的长期预报［J］．气象，2001，(06)；55 –57

[4] 郑国生，何秀丽．夏季遮荫改善大田牡丹叶片光合功能的研究［J］．林业科学，2004，42（4）；27 –32

[5] 刘波，郑国生，赵海军．不同低温时数对牡丹花芽解除休眠的影响［J］．山东农业科学，2004，(3)；41 –42

[6] 王宗正．低温处理对牡丹开花及展叶的影响［J］．园艺学报，1996，23（3）；307 –08

[7] 高志民，王莲英．有效积温与牡丹催花研究初报［J］．中国园林，2002（2）；86 –88

[8] 单宏伟，郑爱琴，张长征等．北方温室牡丹促成栽培技术研究［J］．北方园艺，2006（4）；129 –130

[9] T. A. Fulton，A. J. Hall，J. L. Catley. Chilling requirements of Paeonia cultivars［J］. Scientia Horticulturae 89（2001）；237 –248

[10] 周秉荣．土壤热交换、地温的估算［J］．青海气象，2005（3）：53 –44

[11] 李正风，张晓海，刘勇等．不同覆盖方式对植烟土壤温度和水分及烤烟品质的影响 [J]．中国农学通报，2006，11 (11)：224 - 227

[12] 刘波．低温解除牡丹休眠过程中的需冷量及某些生理生化变化的研究 [D]．中国优秀硕士博士学位论文全文数据库

A Study on Florescence of Tree Peony in Heze by Edaphic Temperature

ZHANG Fei

(*Weifang University of Science and Technology*, *Shouguang* 262700)

Abstract: The Tree Peony Exhibition Meeting as the characteristic festival usually did not correspond with the florescence, so affected the tree peony industry, the agricultural economy and culture in Heze badly. According to analyzing the relationship among the days from the first day of edaphic temperature upper 4℃ to January 20, the average edaphic temperature from the first day to April 10 and the florescence, a multivariate nonlinear regression analysis model was set up. And using the model to forecast the 28 years' florescence, the permissible error was 4 days. It could provide the reference for fixing the date of Tree Peony Exhibition Meeting.

Key words: Florescence; Nonlinear Multianalysis Regressing Analysis; Forecasting model

微型月季不定芽诱导及植株再生初探

吕金浮①

（潍坊科技学院，寿光 262700）

摘 要： 探讨了微型月季离体快速繁殖技术中的外植体表面灭菌时间的范围，并运用正交法研究了不同浓度的细胞分裂素6-BA及生长素NAA对离体芽萌发再生的影响。试验结果表明，外植体表面灭菌采用浓度为0.1%的升汞，时间为3min为宜，可使消毒效果达到最佳。微型月季芽分化培养基中，芽分化受细胞分裂素影响较大，而对生长素的反应相对迟钝，对细胞分裂素/生长素的比值反应较敏感，激素浓度为6-BA 2.0mg/L、NAA 0.2mg/L时可获得最大的芽分化率93.3%，且增殖系数大。

关键词： 微型月季；外植体；组织培养；芽分化

微型月季（*Rosa chinensis Minima* 或 *Rosa roelletti*）是蔷薇科蔷薇属多年生木本植物，由原产我国的小月季在18世纪传入欧洲后经过一系列杂交选育而成[1]。株型矮小，花小，开花繁密，花期长，耐寒性较强，可作为地被绿化或盆栽，应用前景广泛[1,2]。但由于微型月季株型矮小，节数少，常规扦插或嫁接繁殖速度慢，繁殖系数低，繁殖速度受到很大限制，成本高，难以大规模应用[3,4]。目前，对微型月季的组织培养报道较少，为了推进微型月季的扩大繁殖，探索规模化组织培养生产技术，为微型月季的快速繁殖和推广提供了一条有效途径，本文针对微型月季的组织培养进行了初步探索。

1 材料与方法

1.1 实验材料

1.1.1 植物材料

微型月季品种来自于寿光红梅园艺。

1.1.2 化学药品

实验所用大量元素、微量元素、有机元素、铁盐、添加剂、植物生长调节剂、升汞均购于潍坊先科。

① 吕金浮，女，硕士，潍坊科技学院讲师。研究方向：园林植物快繁技术。E-mail：jinfu_2008@163.com

1.2 方法

1.2.1 微型月季外植体的获得

选取健壮的当年生的枝条中段（带饱满而未萌发的侧芽），剥去叶柄和叶片及皮刺，用毛刷沾浓洗衣粉水溶液仔细刷洗，再在自来水下冲洗干净，用纱布吸干枝条上的水分，用解剖刀将侧芽外面包裹的鳞片剥去，仅留 2～3 层鳞片包裹。

1.2.2 外植体灭菌时间的筛选

将剥去鳞片的侧芽放到超净工作台上灭菌。先用无菌水冲洗一遍，再用 75% 的酒精灭菌 30s，为了把侧芽外的残留的酒精洗去，再用无菌水冲洗一遍。然后将侧芽放到 0.1% 的升汞溶液中灭菌，分别设置 2min、3min、4min、5min 和 10min 和 5 个时间梯度，最后用无菌水冲洗 6 次，充分洗去侧芽外残留的升汞，以利于外植体的萌发。灭菌后，将侧芽接种于培养基上，培养温度为 25℃、光照强度为 2 500lx、每日光照 14h，记录芽污染及萌发情况。

1.2.3 培养基的筛选

以 MS 为基本培养基，研究了细胞分裂素 6-BA 和生长素 NAA 不同配比浓度对外植体芽萌发及分化的影响。其中，6-BA/NAA 有 18 种浓度配比设计，所用培养基蔗糖的浓度为 30g/L、琼脂为 7g/L、pH5.8。

将外植体下端竖直插入含有不同浓度激素的 MS 培养基上，置于（25 ± 1）℃ 2 500 lx 光照培养，每天光照 14h。每一处理各接外植体 30 个，30d 后，观察不同培养基上芽萌发及再生情况，计算芽分化率芽分化率（%）= 芽分化外植体数/接种外植体数 × 100%。

2 结果与分析

2.1 不同的灭菌时间对外植体芽萌发及分化的影响

实验分别设置 2、3、4、5 和 10min 5 个时间梯度，由此确定外植体灭菌时间对其再生的影响，结果见表 1。

表 1 不同灭菌时间对微型月季芽萌发及分化的影响

灭菌时间（min）	接种外植体数	污染外植体数	污染率（%）
2	30	0	0
3	30	30	100
4	30	15	50
5	30	3	10
10	30	0	0

由表1可见，由自然界采取外植体材料后对其灭菌是必须的。当灭菌时间为2min时，外植体材料全部污染，没有任何外植体萌芽及再生（图1）。当灭菌时间为3min时，外植体材料没有任何污染，在适宜的培养基上，绝大部分外植体都可以再生（图2）。当灭菌时间为4min时，外植体材料没有任何污染，但有50%的外植体死亡，仅有一半的外植体材料保持绿色，随后在适宜的培养基上萌发再生（图3）。当灭菌时间为5min时，外植体材料没有任何污染，但有90%的外植体灭菌后变为褐色，随后死亡，仅有10%的外植体材料保持绿色，随后在适宜的培养基上萌发再生。当灭菌时间延长到10min时，所有的外植体材料全变为褐色而死亡，没有外植体萌发再生的现象（图4）。由此可见，由自然界获得得幼嫩外植体材料要经过灭菌才可以进行组织培养，灭菌时间要依据材料的发育程度确定，一般以嫩芽做外植体时的灭菌时间为3~4min。

图1

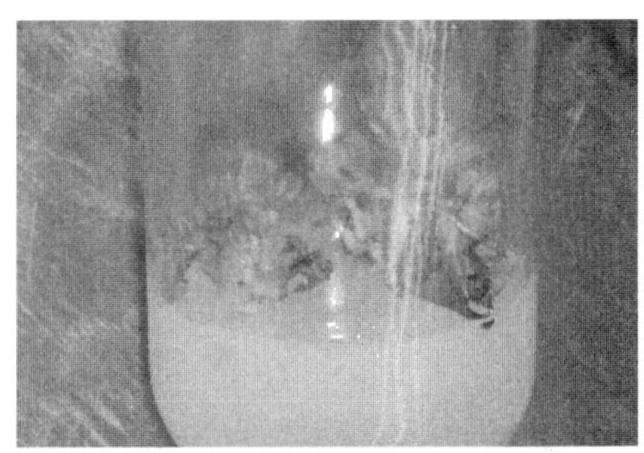

图2

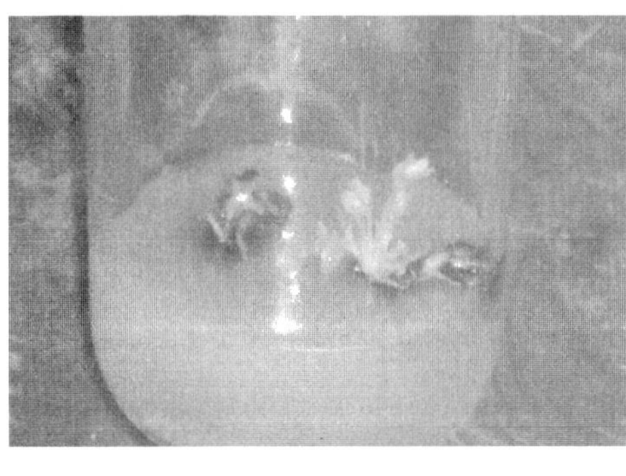

图3

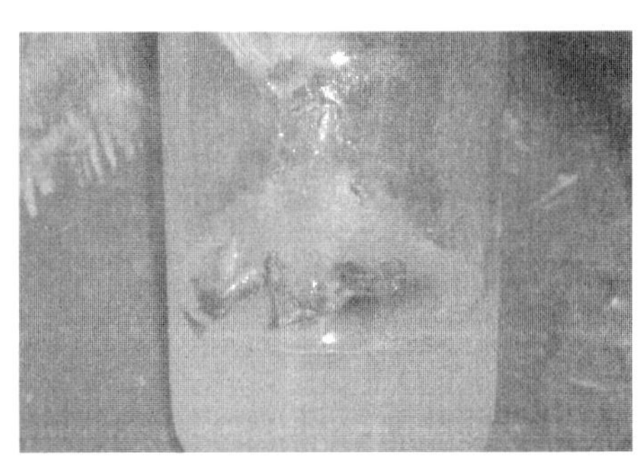

图4

2.2 不同浓度配比的6-BA/NAA对外植体芽萌发及分化的影响

当NAA浓度为0.05、0.1、0.2和0.3mg/L时，把细胞分裂素6-BA设定1.0、2.0、3.0、4.0和5.0 mg/L 5个浓度梯度，研究6-BA对芽萌发及再生的影响（表2、表3、表4、表5）。

表2 6-BA/0.05mg/L NAA 配比对微型月季芽萌发及分化的影响

培养基代号	6-BA 浓度（mg/L）	NAA 浓度（mg/L）	接种外植体数	分化外植体数	分化率（%）
N1	1.0	0.05	30	9	30
N2	2.0	0.05	30	13	43.3
N3	3.0	0.05	30	10	33.3
N4	4.0	0.05	30	5	16.7
N5	5.0	0.05	30	2	6.7

由表2可知，6-BA 浓度在1.0～2.0mg/L 的范围内，随其浓度的增加芽分化率也增加，当6-BA 浓度在2.0mg/L 时，外植体芽分化率达到最高值43.3%，随后在3.0～5.0mg/L 的范围内，外植体芽分化率随6-BA 浓度的增加而降低，当6-BA 浓度为5.0mg/L 时，外植体芽分化率仅为6.7%，比最高值降低了36.6%。可见，细胞分裂素对芽分化在某种程度上起决定作用。

表3 6-BA/0.1mg/L NAA 配比对微型月季芽萌发及分化的影响

培养基代号	6-BA 浓度（mg/L）	NAA 浓度（mg/L）	接种外植体数	分化外植体数	分化率（%）
N6	1.0	0.1	30	13	43.3
N7	2.0	0.1	30	24	80
N8	3.0	0.1	30	16	53.3
N9	4.0	0.1	30	9	30
N10	5.0	0.1	30	6	20

由表3可知，6-BA 浓度在1.0～2.0mg/L 的范围内，随其浓度的增加芽分化率也增加，当6-BA 浓度在2.0mg/L 时，外植体芽分化率达到最高值80%，随后在3.0～5.0mg/L 的范围内，外植体芽分化率随6-BA 浓度的增加而降低，当6-BA 浓度为5.0mg/L 时，外植体芽分化率仅为20%，比最高值降低了60%。

表4 6-BA/0.2mg/L NAA 配比对微型月季芽萌发及分化的影响

培养基代号	6-BA 浓度（mg/L）	NAA 浓度（mg/L）	接种外植体数	分化外植体数	分化率（%）
N11	1.0	0.2	30	17	56.7
N12	2.0	0.2	30	28	93.3
N13	3.0	0.2	30	23	76.7
N14	4.0	0.2	30	14	46.7
N15	5.0	0.2	30	9	30

由表4可知，6-BA浓度在1.0~2.0mg/L的范围内，随其浓度的增加芽分化率也增加，当6-BA浓度在2.0mg/L时，外植体芽分化率达到最高值93.3%，且每个芽增值倍数也最大，随后在3.0~5.0mg/L的范围内，外植体芽分化率随6-BA浓度的增加而降低，当6-BA浓度为5.0mg/L时，外植体芽分化率仅为30%，比最高值降低了63.3%。由此可知，芽分化与否与细胞分裂素和生长素的绝对值有关，还与两者的比例有很大关系。

表5 6-BA/0.3 mg/L NAA配比对微型月季芽萌发及分化的影响

培养基代号	6-BA浓度(mg/L)	NAA浓度(mg/L)	接种外植体数	分化外植体数	分化率(%)
N16	1.0	0.3	30	12	40
N17	2.0	0.3	30	22	73.3
N18	3.0	0.3	30	15	50
N19	4.0	0.3	30	11	26.7
N20	5.0	0.3	30	6	16.7

由表5可知，6-BA浓度在1.0~2.0mg/L的范围内，随其浓度的增加芽分化率也增加，当6-BA浓度在2.0mg/L时，外植体芽分化率达到最高值73.3%，随后在3.0~5.0mg/L的范围内，外植体芽分化率随6-BA浓度的增加而降低，当6-BA浓度为5.0mg/L时，外植体芽分化率仅为16.7%，比最高值降低了56.6%。

表6 6-BA/NAA配比对微型月季芽萌发及分化的影响

培养基代号	6-BA浓度(mg/L)	NAA浓度(mg/L)	接种外植体数	分化外植体数	分化率(%)
N1	1.0	0.05	30	9	30
N6	1.0	0.1	30	13	43.3
N11	1.0	0.2	30	17	56.7
N16	1.0	0.3	30	12	40
N2	2.0	0.05	30	13	43.3
N7	2.0	0.1	30	24	80
N12	2.0	0.2	30	28	93.3
N17	2.0	0.3	30	22	73.3
N3	3.0	0.05	30	10	33.3
N8	3.0	0.1	30	16	53.3
N13	3.0	0.2	30	23	76.7
N18	3.0	0.3	30	15	50
N4	4.0	0.05	30	5	16.7

（续表）

培养基代号	6-BA 浓度（mg/L）	NAA 浓度（mg/L）	接种外植体数	分化外植体数	分化率（%）
N9	4.0	0.1	30	9	30
N14	4.0	0.2	30	14	46.7
N19	4.0	0.3	30	11	26.7
N5	5.0	0.05	30	2	6.7
N10	5.0	0.1	30	6	20
N15	5.0	0.2	30	9	30
N20	5.0	0.3	30	6	16.7

当6-BA浓度一定时，把生长素NAA设定0.05、0.1、0.2和0.3mg/L 4个浓度梯度，研究生长素NAA对芽萌发及再生的影响。由表6可知：当6-BA浓度为1.0mg/L时，NAA浓度在0.05~0.2mg/L的范围内，随其浓度的增加芽分化率也增加，当NAA浓度在0.2mg/L时，外植体芽分化率达到最高值56.7%，随后外植体芽分化率降低，当NAA浓度为0.3mg/L时，外植体芽分化率仅为40%。当6-BA浓度为2.0mg/L时，NAA浓度在0.05~0.2mg/L的范围内，随其浓度的增加芽分化率也增加（图5、图6）。当NAA浓度在0.2mg/L时，外植体芽分化率达到最高值93.3%，这也是所有培养基配方中芽再生分化率最高的一种培养基配比组合，随后外植体芽分化率降低，当NAA浓度为0.3mg/L时，外植体芽分化率为73.3%，比最高值降低了20%，通过研究还发现，6-BA浓度为2.0mg/L的培养基中芽分化率均较高。当6-BA浓度为3.0mg/L时，NAA浓度在0.05~0.2mg/L的范围内，随其浓度的增加芽分化率也增加，当NAA浓度在0.2mg/L时，外植体芽分化率达到最高值76.7%（图7），随后外植体芽分化率降低，当NAA浓度为0.3mg/L时，外植体芽分化率为50%。当6-BA浓度为4.0mg/L时，NAA浓度在0.05~0.2mg/L的范围内，随其浓度的增加芽分化率也增加，当NAA浓度在0.2mg/L时，外植体芽分化率达到最高值46.7%（图8），随后外植体芽分化率降低，当NAA浓度为0.3mg/L时，外植体芽分化率仅为26.7%（图9）。当6－BA浓度为5.0mg/L时，NAA浓度在0.05~0.2mg/L的范围内，随其浓度的增加芽分化率也增加，NAA浓度在0.05mg/L时，外植体芽分化率仅有6.7%（图10），当NAA浓度在0.2mg/L时，外植体芽分化率达到最高值30%，随后外植体芽分化率降低，当NAA浓度为0.3mg/L时，外植体芽分化率仅为16.7%。本研究还发现，当6-BA浓度处于较高水平时，外植体芽分化率均较低，外植体玻璃化现象较严重，受NAA浓度大小影响不明显；而当6-BA浓度处于较低水平时，外植体芽分化率也均较低，且外植体褐变现象严重。可见，微型月季植株再生过程中芽分化受细胞分裂素影响较大，而对生长素的反应相对迟钝，对细胞分裂素/生长素的比值反应较敏感。

图 5

图 6

图 7

图 8

图 9

图 10

3 结论

月季组织培养过程中的影响因素较多，比较重要的有品种、植物生长调节剂、外植体、培养基和培养条件等对月季组织培养的影响[1,5]。本文主要研究植物生长调节剂和外植体灭菌条件等对微型月季芽诱导及愈伤组织诱导的影响。结果表明，由自然界获得的幼嫩外植体材料要经过灭菌才可以进行组织培养，灭菌时间要依据材料的发育程度确定，一般以嫩芽做外植体时的灭菌时间为 3 ~ 4min。植物生长调节剂是诱导外植体分化再生的重要条件，不同的外植体材料使用的植物生长调节剂类型及浓度不一样，在微型月季组织培养过程中，芽分化受细胞分裂素影响较大，而对生长素的反应相对迟钝，对细胞分裂素/生长素的比值反应较敏感。

参考文献

[1] 吴淑平，马汉云，龚凤萍．丰花月季组培快繁技术研究［J］．安徽农业科学，2006，21：15－18

[2] 李海燕，胡国富，胡宝忠．月季组培快繁技术的研究［J］．东北农业大学学报，2004，1：21－26

[3] 张宇斌，游萍，乙引．月季快速繁殖系统的建立［J］．贵州师范大学学报，2003，3：33－36

[4] 李军萍，高云振，王正加．月季组织培养过程中的影响因素［J］．浙江林业科技，2003，4：7－12

[5] 沈国正，钱丽华，赵杭苹．盆栽微型月季离体培养繁殖技术探讨［J］．浙江农业科学，2006，4：16－21

Study on the buds differentiation and the Regenerate in *Rosa chinensis Minima*

LV Jin-fu

(*Weifang University of Science and Technology*, *Shouguang* 262700)

Abstract: Establishment of a Highly Regeneration System in *Rosa chinensis Minima* Involveing the disinfection time and the different levels of 6 - BA and NAA were studied. The results showed that steriled to 3min explant can recover to get best effect with 0. 1% $HgCl_2$. 6 - BA/NAA was the most effective to budinducing in all the plant growth regulatom used in this research. The highest bud differentiation rate 93. 3% in the explant of both hypocotyls and internode Was obtainedwhen the concentration of 6-BA/NAA Was 2. 0/0. 2mg/L.

Key words: Rosa chinensis Minima; Explant; Tissue; Buds differentiation

小麦—中间偃麦草双体异附加系的选育及其染色体构成分析

孙智英①
（潍坊科技学院，寿光 262700）

摘 要：通过形态学和种子醇溶蛋白聚炳烯酰胺凝胶电泳（PAGE）分析表明：本文选育的7个小麦—中间偃麦草双体异附加系（DL1、DL2……DL7）可分为两类：第一类是附加的染色体归属于中间偃麦草的E染色体组，DL1、DL3、DL4、DL6属此类，其中DL4、DL6为同一附加系，DL1、DL3为不同的附加系；第二类附加的染色体归属于中间偃麦草的X染色体组，DL2、DL5、DL7属于此类。

关键词：小麦；中间偃麦草；异附加系；种子醇溶蛋白电泳

中间偃麦草（*Elytrigia intermedium*，2n =42）是与小麦亲缘关系较近的野生植物，具有抗旱、抗寒、抗锈病、耐盐碱和高蛋白等优良性状[1]，且与小麦杂交易成功，国内外许多学者已成功地将其染色体或染色体片断转移进小麦遗传背景中，选育出多种小麦—中间偃麦草异附加系[2~6]，并用不同方法对其进行了研究分类。

选育小麦异附加系的方法有多种，归纳起来主要有常规法、桥梁亲本法、双二倍体回交法、双单体或多重单体附加法和单倍体法。其中，常规法是选育小麦异附加系的经典方法，即在小麦与近缘植物的杂种后代中先选择单体异附加系，再自交选择双体异附加系[7]。本文利用常规法从小麦与中间偃麦草杂交的不同分离世代中选育出7个双体异附加系，并用细胞学方法及种子醇溶蛋白电泳方法对其染色体构成进行了分析。

1 材料与方法

1.1 材料

普通小麦品种烟农15（2n =6X =42）；小麦近缘物种中间偃麦草（2n =6X =42）。烟农15/中间偃麦草不同世代分离材料，八倍体小偃麦中1、中2、中3、中4、中5，

---

① 孙智英，女，硕士，潍坊科技学院副教授。研究方向：作物遗传育种。E－mail：zhiyingsun@163.com

以上材料均由本课题组保存。

1.2 方法

1.2.1 细胞学鉴定方法

1.2.1.1 花粉母细胞减数分裂观察

取花粉母细胞处于减数分裂中期Ⅰ的花药，卡诺氏液（酒精：冰乙酸 =3：1）固定，室温条件下用5N盐酸解离6min，改良卡宝品红染色，然后压片、镜检拍照。

1.2.1.2 根尖细胞有丝分裂观察

种子在室温下浸泡至露白，1～4℃冰箱中冰冻24h，然后在25℃条件下发芽，根长1.5～2.0cm时取根尖，根尖先在冰水中处理24h，再用卡诺氏液于1～4℃条件下固定24h，60℃条件下用1N盐酸解离8min，铁矾—苏木精法染色，用45%乙酸分色，然后压片、镜检并拍照。

1.2.2 种子醇溶蛋白聚炳烯酰胺凝胶电泳（PAGE）分析

参照颜启传（1989）[8]方法，略有改动，具体方法如下。

（1）样品提取：取一粒饱满无病害种子，用样品钳夹碎后置于1ml离心管中，加入200μl提取液［25%（v/v）氯乙醇，1%（v/v）巯基乙醇和1mol/L尿素］，冰箱中过夜提取，5 500转/min离心15min，取上清液备用。

（2）制胶：吸取3ml凝胶溶液，加入1滴0.6% H_2O_2 液，摇匀后迅速倒入凝胶槽封口处，约5～10min聚合；再吸取18ml凝胶溶液，加入2滴0.6% H_2O_2 液，摇匀后倒入电泳槽玻璃板之间，插入样品梳，5～10min聚合。

（3）加样：轻轻拔去样品梳，用滤纸吸去水分，吸取样品离心液8～10μl分别加入样品槽中。

（4）电泳：500V电压下电泳60～80min，甲基绿作指示剂。电极缓冲液用pH值为3.1～3.2的醋酸—甘氨酸混合缓冲液。

（5）固定和染色：用3.5ml 1%考马斯亮兰和100ml 10%三氯乙酸染色过夜，用7%醋酸溶液保存。蛋白质带以任意相对迁移距离（Dm）[9]表示。

2 结果与分析

2.1 小麦—中间偃麦草异附加系的筛选

本研究从普通小麦烟农15与中间偃麦草杂交的不同分离世代中，选择表型性状明显不同于烟农15的植株，对其PMC MⅠ染色体构型进行压片镜检分析，结果表明，镜检133个单株，共获得附加不同数目外源染色体的植株12个，其中，单体异附加株（2n =21Ⅱ +Ⅰ，图版Ⅱ-1）3个，双单体异附加株（2n =21Ⅱ +Ⅰ+Ⅰ，图版Ⅱ-2）2个，其余7个为双体异附加株（2n =22Ⅱ，图版Ⅰ-2-8）。在这3种类型异附加株中，只有2n =22Ⅱ的异附加株遗传性比较稳定，其后代一般不再发生分离。获得的双体异附加株的编号及世代来源列于表1。

表 1 双体异附加株的编号及来源

材料	双体异附加株株号	原始株系（行）	世代
DL1	970086—1	930090—13	B2F3
DL2	970098—3	930091—2	B2F3
DL3	970138—1	930094—9	B3F2
DL4	970123—1	930092—12	B3F2
DL5	970090—2	930090—3	B2F3
DL6	970105—2	930091—9	B2F3
DL7	970109—1	930091—13	B2F3

表 2 双体异附加株花粉母细胞染色体构型及根尖细胞的染色体数目

材料	染色体平均构型	观察细胞数	根尖染色体数目及所占比例			观察种子数
			2n = 42	2n = 43	2n = 44	
DL1	0.25 Ⅰ +21.75 Ⅱ +0.06 Ⅲ	16	1（6.7）	1（6.7）	13（86.6）	15
DL2	0.15 Ⅰ +21.85 Ⅱ +0.05 Ⅲ	20	0	0	13（100.0）	13
DL3	0.12 Ⅰ +21.90 Ⅱ	15	0	1（6.7）	14（93.3）	15
DL4	0.05 Ⅰ +21.90 Ⅱ	20	0	0	14（100.0）	14
DL5	0.19 Ⅰ +21.80 Ⅱ +0.06 Ⅲ	16	0	1（6.7）	14（93.3）	15
DL6	0.20 Ⅰ +21.70 Ⅱ +0.07 Ⅲ +0.07 Ⅳ	15	0	0	15（100.0）	15
DL7	0.28 Ⅰ +21.85 Ⅱ	14	0	0	15（100.0）	15
烟农	15 0.20 Ⅰ +20.90 Ⅱ	10	20(100)	0	0	20

注：括号内数据为其所占观察种子数的百分数

由于异附加系中的外源染色体常出现丢失现象，为了进一步确定所获得 7 个小麦—中间偃麦草双体异附加株的细胞学稳定性，对其花粉母细胞染色体构型进行了分析，并对其当代所收种子的根尖染色体数目进行了观察，结果列于表 2。

染色体构型分析结果表明，在 7 个异附加株所观察的花粉母细胞中，大多数细胞的染色体构型为 2n = 22 Ⅱ，单价体数很少，多价体出现频率极低，表明它们所附加的一对中间偃麦草染色体能很好的联会。

由根尖染色体数目来看，7 个异附加株中，DL2、DL4、DL6、DL7 4 个异附加株自交种子的根尖细胞染色体数均为 2n = 44，外源染色体传递率都是 100%，DL1、DL3 和 DL5 3 个异附加株自交后代个别种子根尖染色体数目为 2n = 43，DL1 自交后代中，有的种子根尖染色体数目为 2n = 42，外源染色体传递率少差一些。但分别达到 86.7%、93.3% 和 93.3%，表明这 7 个双体异附加株具有良好的细胞遗传学稳定性，外源染色体传递率较高。

2.2 小麦—中间偃麦草双体异附加系的鉴定

本研究选育出的 7 个小麦—中间偃麦草双体异附加系，经过细胞学鉴定其染色体构型都为 2n = 22 Ⅱ，为了进一步确定它们所附加染色体的类型，本研究运用形态学、生化两种遗传标记系统，对它们进行了鉴定。

2.2.1 双体异附加系的形态学特点

对选育的 7 个双体异附加系及其亲本的生长发育、植株形态、穗部和籽粒特点进行了观察，结果列于表 3。结果表明，这 7 个异附加，系及其双亲之间在所观察的各项性状上，都存在不同程度的差异，根据各附加系的表型特征，将它们分为 4 类。

第一类：苗叶深绿，株型紧凑，茎秆较细，坚硬，穗形纺锤，无芒，叶片下垂，籽粒大较长，颜色较暗，半透明，DL2、DL5、DL7 属于此类。根据旗叶是否卷曲又可分为两类：DL5、DL7 旗叶卷曲，对白粉病分别表现为免疫和高抗；DL2 旗叶不卷曲，中抗白粉病；

第二类：苗叶绿色，株型紧凑，茎秆粗硬，叶片上举，籽粒中等大小，扁圆形，中抗白粉病，DL4、DL6 属于此类。根据穗形又可将它们分为两种类型，DL4 圆锥形穗，DL6 棒形穗，稍短；

第三类：苗叶绿色，株型紧凑，茎秆粗硬，叶片下垂，旗叶稍卷，纺锤形穗，对白粉病免疫，籽粒较长，色浅，这一类只有 DL1 一个系；

第四类：苗叶深绿，株型紧凑，茎秆粗硬，叶片上举，方形穗，中感白粉病，籽粒皱缩，DL3 属于此类。

2.2.2 小麦—中间偃麦草双体异附加系的种子醇溶蛋白电泳分析

提取所选育的 7 双体异附加系的成熟种子醇溶蛋白，进行聚炳烯酰胺凝胶电泳，结果如图 1。

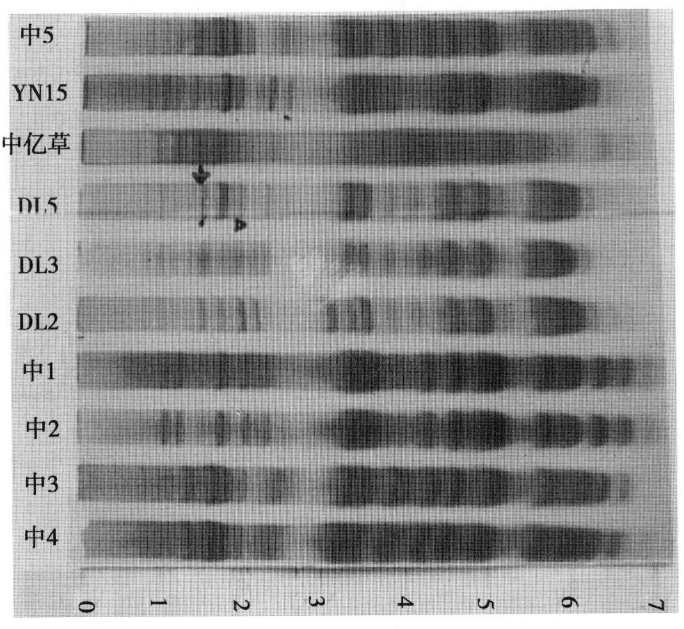

1—A

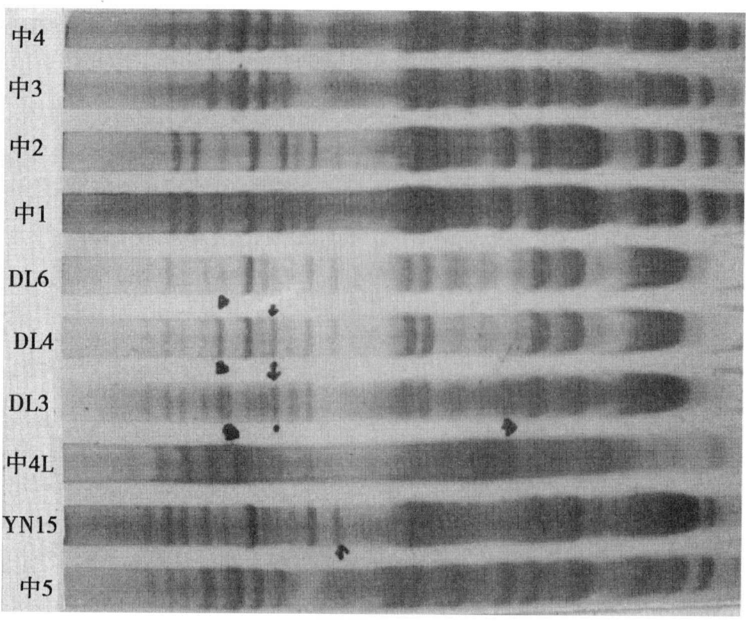

1—B

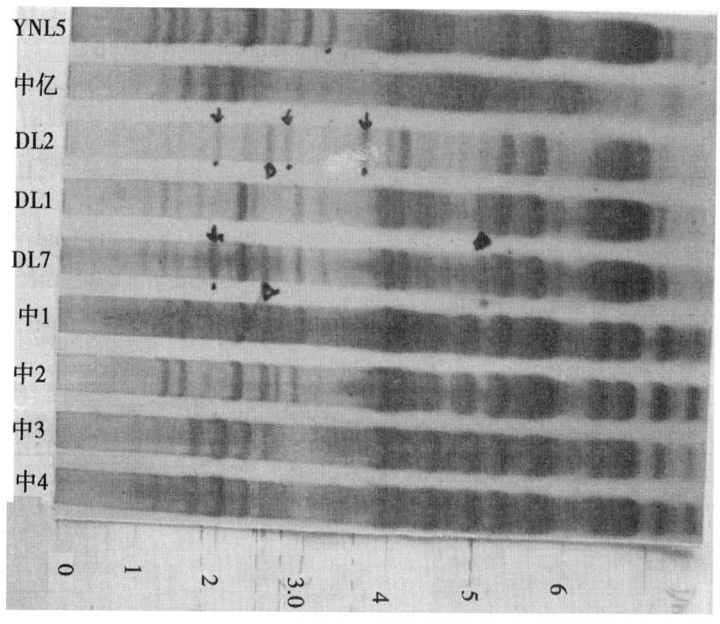

1—C

图1 普通小麦—中间偃麦草双体异附加系的种子醇溶蛋白电泳

▲ E 染色体基组特征带；△X 染色体基组特征带；→新出现

表 3　小麦—中间偃麦草双体异附加系及其亲本的主要性状特点

材料	苗色	幼苗习性	株形	茎秆	白粉病抗性	株高（cm）	抽穗期	穗数/株	穗长（cm）	小穗数/穗	不结实小穗数	粒数/穗	穗形	叶片	旗叶	
															形状	长×宽（cm×cm）
中间偃麦草	深绿	半匍匐	松散	粗硬	1	170.3	2/6	49.5	53.7	29.3	24.1	6.4	细长	下垂	不卷曲	28.7×1.0
烟农 15	深绿	直立	紧凑	粗硬	4	78.9	20/4	7.4	9.4	20	1	54.8	圆锥	上举	不卷曲	21.4×2.0
DL1	绿	直立	紧凑	细硬	1	85.4	21/4	8.4	8.8	19.2	1.8	42.6	纺锤	下垂	稍卷曲	18.6×1.6
DL2	深绿	直立	紧凑	中硬	3	86.2	21/4	12.2	9.2	21.2	1.8	50.2	纺锤	下垂	不卷曲	19.4×2.1
DL3	深绿	半匍匐	紧凑	粗硬	4	74.4	21/4	9.8	8.4	20	1.2	50.2	长方	上举	不卷曲	18.4×1.9
DL4	绿	直立	紧凑	粗硬	3	80.8	22/4	11.4	9.2	21.6	1	50.8	圆锥	上举	不卷曲	17.4×2.1
DL5	深绿	直立	紧凑	中硬	1	87.8	20/4	11	9.4	21.2	1	56.4	纺锤	下垂	卷曲	19.9×1.7
DL6	绿	直立	紧凑	粗硬	3	86.5	23/4	9.8	8.1	21	0.8	52.8	棒状	下垂	稍卷曲	17.9×2.0
DL7	深绿	直立	紧凑	中硬	2	80.8	21/4	10	10.6	20	0.2	56	纺锤	下垂	卷曲	17.3×2.0

注：1. 中间偃麦草和烟农 15 各性状为 10 株平均值，异附加系为 5 株平均值；2. 白粉病反应型分为 5 级：1—免疫，2—高抗，3—中抗，4—中感，5—高感

由图 1—A 知，DL3 在 Dm = 1.85、5.0 处分别出现一条弱带和一条较强的带，这两条带同时出现在中间偃麦草和中 5 的谱带中，而烟农 15 和中 1 却没有，说明 DL3 中的偃麦草染色体属于中 5 所携带的中间偃麦草染色体组，同时，DL3 中缺少了烟农 15 中 Dm = 3.15 的带，说明 DL3 在附加了中间偃麦草一对染色体的同时，可能又代换了烟农 15 的某一染色体，可能是异附加代换系。或者，DL3 中的偃麦草染色体抑制了烟农 15 某一染色体蛋白基因的表达，从而不出现该染色体基因所控制的蛋白质带，若是这样，则 DL3 为异附加系。此外，DL3 中还出现一条 Dm = 2.33 的新带，可能是由于基因互作的结果。

DL4 的图谱与烟农 15 相比，除了含有烟农 15 的所有带外，在 Dm = 1.85 处有一条带同时出现在中间偃麦草和中 5 中，说明 DL4 附加的中间偃麦草染色体属于中 5 中的中间偃麦草染色体组。同时，在 Dm = 2.25 处出现一条新带，可能是由于外源基因与小麦基因互作产生的。

DL6 的图谱与 DL4 的图谱很相似，但在 Dm = 1.85 和 Dm = 2.35 处的带很弱，因此 DL6 附加的染色体也可能属于中 5 所携带的中间偃麦草的染色体组，DL6 与 DL4 可能属于同一异附加系。

由图 1—B 可以看出，DL2 出现了烟农 15 所没有的 4 条新带，其值分别为 1.85、2.45、2.75 和 3.65，同时，也缺少了烟农 15 的 Dm = 3.0 的带纹，其中，Dm = 2.45 也同时出现在中间偃麦草和中 1、中 2 谱带中，而 Dm = 1.85、2.75 和 3.65 的新带为中间偃麦草所没有，说明 DL2 中的中间偃麦草染色体是属于中 1、中 2 所携带的中间偃麦草染色体组，且附加的同时可能代换了烟农 15 中控制 Dm = 3.0 的蛋白质带合成的染色体。因此，DL2 可能为异附加代换系；或者是基因间相互作用的结果。

DL1 在 Dm = 5.0 处出现了一条弱带，烟农 15 不含有该带，但它同时出现在中间偃麦草和中 3、中 4 中，DL1 除了比烟农多了一条 Dm = 5.0 的带外，其余带与烟农 15 相同，所以，DL1 附加的染色体属于中 3、中 4 所携带的中间偃麦草染色体组。

DL7 与烟农 15 的谱带相比，多了 Dm = 1. 85、2. 45 两条带，Dm = 1. 85 是 DL7 特有的，而 Dm = 2. 45 则同时出现在中间偃麦草及中 1、中 2 的谱带中，所以，DL7 附加的染色体应归属于中 1、中 2 中的中间偃麦草染色体组。

由图 1—C 知，DL5 烟农 15 多了 Dm = 1. 40、2. 05 两条谱带，而缺少烟农 15 中的 Dm = 2. 65 的带纹，Dm = 1. 40 为 DL5 特有，而 Dm = 2. 05 则同时出现在中间偃麦草和中 1、中 2 中，说明 DL5 所附加的染色体属于中 1、中 2 中的中间偃麦草染色体组。

由以上分析知，所选育的 7 个异附加系可分为两类：第一类附加的染色体归属于中 1、中 2 所携带的中间偃麦草 X 染色体组，DL2、DL5、DL7 属于此类；第二类附加的染色体归属于中 3、中 4、中 5 中的中间偃麦草 E 染色体基组，DL1、DL3、DL4、DL6 属于此类。

3 结论与讨论

种子醇溶蛋白是一种很好的生化标记，小麦种属间、品种间种子醇溶蛋白组成差别很大，且性质稳定，不同遗传组成的醇溶蛋白电泳图谱都显示出各自独特的谱带组合，这种组合完全取决于遗传因素，不受发育时期生理条件和环境因子影响，因此，小麦醇溶蛋白组份上的差异可以反映出遗传组成的不同[10,11]。近年来，国内外已将种子醇溶蛋白电泳分析应用到遗传育种和种子生产上，如品种鉴定，亲缘关系分析、代换系、附加系鉴定等方面[12,13]。

本文所选育的 7 个双体异附加系的种子醇溶蛋白电泳谱带中都出现了小麦和中间偃麦草均没有的新带型，说明小麦在附加了外源染色体后，其所附加的外源染色体对小麦基因表达的影响是一种多方面的复合作用，但其作用的机理有待于深入研究。

参 考 文 献

[1] Friebe B, et al. C-banding and in situ hybridization analyses of Agropyron intermedium, a partial wheat × Ag. intermedium amphiploid, six derived chromosome addition lines [J]. T. A. G., 1992, 84: 899 - 905

[2] 孙善澄等．小麦与偃麦草远缘杂交的研究 [J]．华北农学报，1987，2：7 - 12

[3] 何孟元等．两套小冰麦异附加系的建立 [J]．中国科学（B 辑），1988，11：1 161 - 1 168

[4] BanksP. M. Xu SJ, Wang RR-C, and Lark in PJ. Varying Chromosome Composition of 56- Chromosome wheat × *Thimmpayrum* intermedium partial amploids [J]. Genome, 1993, 36: 207 - 215

[5] Lima-Brito. J. et al. Molecular cytogenetic analysis of durum wheat × tritordeum hybrids [J]. Genome, 1997, 40 (3): 362 - 369

[6] 李平路．小麦—中间偃麦草异附加系的选育 [D]．硕士论文，1997

[7] 薛秀庄等．染色体工程技术在小麦育种中的应用 [J]．陕西农业科学，1991，(2)：45 - 48

[8] 彦启传. 我国使用的小麦和大麦种子醇溶蛋白 PAGE 电泳鉴定品种的标准程序 [J]. 种子, 1989, (6): 55-57

[9] Jaaska, V. Electrophoretic Survey of seeding Esterases in Wheat in Relation to Their Phylogeny [J]. T. A. G., 1980, 56: 273-284

[10] 滕晓月等. 小麦品种的蛋白鉴定 [J]. 作物学报, 1988, 14 (4): 322-328

[11] Dewey. R, The genome scructure of intermediate wheatgrass [J]. J. Heredity, 1962, 53: 282-290

[12] 张延宾等. SDS-PAGE 在小麦育种中的应用 [J]. 国外农学—麦类作物, 1996, 1: 5-6

[13] 傅宾孝等. 小麦醇溶蛋白电泳的新方法 [J]. 作物学报, 1993, 19 (2): 185-187

Chromosome Configuration of Alien Disomic Additionfor Wheat-Elytrigia Intermedium

SUN Zhi-ying

(*Weifang University of Science and Technology*, *Shouguang* 262700)

Abstract: Get through Morphology and seeds prolamin PAGE analyse indicate, this text breeding 7 wheat-Elytrigia intermedium alien disomic addition plants (DL1, DL2……DL7) divide into two kinds. Frist kind appended chromosome of Elytrigia intermedium E chromosome complement , DL1, DL3, DL4, DL6 of this kind, DL4, DL6 are same addition lion, DL1, DL3 are different addition lion. Second kind appended chromosome of Elytrigia intermedium X chromosome complement, DL2, DL5, DL7 of this kind.

Key words: Wheat; Elytrigia intermedium; Addition lion; Seeds prolamin PAGE

Function and Safety Assessment of *Lactococus lactis* subsp. *lactis* LB12 as Potential Probiotic Strain

ZHANG De-zhen①

(*Weifang University of Science and Technology*, *Shouguang* 262700)

摘　要：The effect of yogurt fermented by *Lactococus lactis* subsp. *lactis* LB12 isolated from traditional Chinese pickled cabbage on serum cholesterol and triacylglycerol levels were investigated in mice. In the same, the characterizations of the strain, such as acid-tolerance, bile-tolerance, antimicrobial activity, antibiotic sensitivity and safety were also examined. The serum total cholesterol, triglyceride and bile acid levels significantly decreased of mice given a high-cholesterol diet supplemented with yogurt fermented by *Lactococus lactis* subsp. *lactis* LB12. Characterization of *L. lactis* subsp. *lactis* LB12 showed that it was bile- and acid-tolerant, resistant to five commercial antibiotics tested, and possessed antimicrobial activity to pathogenic *Escherchia coli* and *Staphylococcus aureus*. None of morphological changes was noted as a result of *L. lactis* subsp. *lactis* LB12 treatment, nor were there significant differences in the visceral weight indices of the lymph nodes, spleen, bacterial translocation, or aberration rate of sperm of mice compared to control. The results indicated that *L. lactis* subsp. *Lactis* LB12 might be effective as a probiotic with cholesterol-lowering activities.

关键词：Yogurt; *Lactococus lactis* subsp. *lactis* LB12; Acid and bile tolerance; Antimicrobial and antibiotic sensitivity; Cholesterol-lowering effect

1 Introduction

Cardiovascular disease is the leading cause of death in many countries and it is strongly associated with hypercholesterolemia (Law et al., 1994). It is therefore important to develop new ways of reducing serum cholesterol. Recently, lactic acid bacteria have attracted attention as potential cholesterol-lowering milk additives (Chandan, 1999; Roos and Matin, 2000). The reduction of cholesterol by lactobacilli and bifidobacteria that can survive in the intestine

① 张德珍，女，硕士，潍坊科技学院讲师。研究方向：食品微生物。E - mail：zhen5198@126.com

has been demonstrated in human, mouse, and pig studies (Kawase et al., 2000; Haberer et al., 2003; Lim et al., 2004; Usman and Hosono, 2000; Nguyen et al., 2007). In contrast, few studies exist on the probiotic activity of lactococci since they are traditionally not considered to be natural inhabitants of the human gastrointestinal tract (Teuber et al., 1995). However, several works showed the possibility of the presence of lactococci in the flora of the human or animal gastrointesrinal tract (Gruzza et al., 1992; Grahn et al., 1994; Klijin et al., 1995). Lactococci are widely used as starter bacteria in manufacturing cheese and other fermented dairy products. Thus, isolation and establishing the effective probiotic properties of lactococci could lead to development of new probiotic foods.

Potherb mustard (*Brassica juncea* Coss.), a member of the *Cruciferae*, often called pickled cabbage, is always brined and stored as pickle in China. Traditionally, the potherb mustard pickle is homemade in the beginning of winter or spring in most of the rural areas and some households in urban areas of China. After harvesting, the mustard leaves are washed and drained, wilted in the sun, then mixed with salt, packed into earthenware pots in layers, and then was pressed tightly by a wooden ladle; spices may be added. The pots are sealed and the leaves allowed fermentation for couple of months.

In the present study, we identified and characterized a lactococci strain screened from traditional Chinese pickled cabbage and evaluated its potential probiotic function.

2 Materils and Methods

2.1 Materials

Strains of *Lactococus lactis* subsp. *lactis* NBRC 12007 (obtained from Biological Resource Center of National Institute of Technology and Evaluation, China, Japan), *Escherchia coli* ATCC 25922 and *Staphylococcus aureus* ATCC 25923 (obtained from the Microbiological Laboratory of Life Science College of Nanjing Normal University, Nanjing, China) were serially transferred at least three times prior to use in present study. Oxgall (Sigma, USA, pH 7.0) and cholesterol were purchased from Shanghai Chemical Co. Ltd. (China); The kits of total cholesterol (TC), high density lipoprotein-cholesterol (HDL-c) and total bile acids (TBA) were purchased from Shanghai Rongsheng Biotech Co. Ltd. (China); Kit of triacylglycerol (TG) from Zhejiang Dongou iotechnology Co. Ltd. (China).

2.2 Isolation of bacterial strains

Serial dilutions of collected Chinese pickled cabbage juice were made in quarter-strength Ringer's solution, and 50 ml of each dilution was spread-plated onto MRS (Sigma) and Rogosa (Sigma) agar. The plates were incubated under microaerobic conditions with 10% CO_2 at 37℃ for 48 h. Colonies were selected from plates of showing highest growth, then subcultured in

MRS broth and restreaked onto MRS agar to ensure purity.

2. 3 Screening of strains with cholesterol-lowing effects

Sterile MRS broth were supplemented with pleuropneumonia-like organism (PPLO) serum fraction obtained from Beijing Sunbio Medical Co. Ltd. (China) and 0. 30% (w/v) oxgall, cholic acid, or taurocholic acid (Sigma) for 24h at 37℃. PPLO served as the source of cholesterol. Oxgall, which is the dehydrated fresh bile, was added to the media in order to mimic conditions that would be encountered in the human gastrointestinal tract. Cholic and taurocholic acid were added as the source of deconjugated and conjugated bile respectively. Aliquots were removed prior to inoculation to determine the initial cholesterol content of the media. Bacterial strains were grown in the absence or presence of 0. 30% (w/v) oxgall in MRS broth containing 2. 0% PPLO under anaerobic conditions at 37℃. Following incubation for 24h, cells were centrifuged at 6 000 rpm for 10 min and the residual cholesterol in the supernatant was determined as described (Rudel and Morris, 1973). The strain with the largest cholesterol-lowing effect was selected for further characterization.

2. 4 Strain identification

The strain used was identified based on Gram staining, morphology, and catalase activity. Scanning electron microscopy was performed as described (Yamauchi and Snel, 2000). The pattern of carbohydrate fermentation was determined by using the API 50 CH system (Biomerieux S. A., La Balme les Grottes, France) according to the manufacturer' s instructions. Sodium dodecyl sulfatepolyacrylamide gel electrophoresis (SDS-PAGE) of whole-cell protein lysates was used to compare the isolated strain with reference *Lactococus lactis* subsp. *lactis* strains as described (Pot et al., 1993). For definite identification, 16S rRNA sequencing was performed using total DNA from the isolate.

2. 5 Preparation of yogurt

For preparation of yogurt, milk (1. 0% fat and 11. 0% solid no fat) was heated at 95℃ for 15 min, then cooled to 43℃, inoculated with a 5% (v/v) liquid culture of *L. lactis* subsp. *lactis* LB12. The inoculated mixes was poured into containers and incubated at 42℃ until pH 4. 6, cooled to 4℃ and stored at that temperature no longer than 2 days before feeding. The numbers of bacteria in freshly fermented yogurt were determined by established procedures to be approximately 109 CFU/ml (International Dairy Federation, 1988).

2. 6 Lowing cholesterol test of *L. lactis* subsp. *lactis* LB12

Four weeks old male Sprague-Dawley mice with an average initial body weight of 220 g (obtained from the Animal Breeding Station of Nanjing Medical University, P. R. China) were used in present experiment. The mice were randomly assigned to four treatments each of twelve. The four dietary treatments were arranged as following: group 1 mice fed commercial diet (purchased from Nanjing Qinglongshan Animal Resources Centre, China), served as model control; group 2 mice fed commercial diet plus 1.0% (w/w) cholesterol, 8.0% (w/w) lard and 0.50% (w/w) oxgall, served as high fat mould; group 3 mice fed commercial diet plus 1.0% (w/w) cholesterol, 8.0% (w/w) lard, 0.50% (w/w) oxgall and 5.0% (v/w) milk (1.0% fat and 11.0% solid no fat, acidifying it to pH 4.6 with 10% lactic acid), and served as experimental control; group 4 mice fed commercial diet plus 1.0% (w/w) cholesterol, 8.0% (w/w) lard, 0.50% (w/w) oxgall and 5.0% (v/w) yogurt fermented by *L. lactis* subsp. *lactis* LB12, and served as experimental. The mice were housed individually in standard cages, maintained at a constant environmental temperature (24 ~ 26℃) and relative humidity (60% ~ 64%) with a 12h light and dark cycle. Diets were given each morning at 120 g/kg body weight and water was freely available. The activity, behavior, and general health of the mice were monitored daily. Food and water intake were measured daily, and body weight was measured weekly.

After feeding for 28 days, the mice were fasted for 12 h and then anesthetized by ether. Blood was obtained from the *arteria cervicalis*, the viscera were excised, weighed and tested for bacterial translocation aseptically. Blood placed in sterile tubes containing EDTA as anticoagulant. Serum samples were isolated from the blood by centrifugation (4 000 rpm for 30 min) and analyzed for total cholesterol (TC), triglycerides (TG), and high density lipoprotein cholesterol (HDL-c) using kits as described by Loh et al. (2002), respectively. Feaces of each group of mice were collected daily on each of the last 5 days of the experimental period and lyophilized. 1.0 g of crushed lyophilized feces were suspended in chloroform-methanol (1: 1 v/v), sonicated for 5 min, then extracted at 60℃ for 60 h. The extract was evaporated and dissolved in methanol for measurement of total bile acids (TBA) with a commercial kit (Loh et al., 2002). The total cholesterol of feaces was determined as described by Rudel and Morris (1973).

2.7 Bacterial translocation

Translocation of bacteria to blood and tissues was assessed as described (Zhou et al., 2000). Briefly, one drop of blood (10 ~ 15μl) was inoculated onto the surface of MRS and brain heart infusion (BHI, Oxoid, Shanghai Qianchen Biological Science Co. Ltd, P. R. China) agar plates prior to being emptied into EDTA tubes. The plates were incubated at 37℃ anaerobically (MRS) or aerobically (BHI) to detect bacteremia. The excised mesenteric lymph nodes (MLN), spleen, and liver were ground with a tissue grinder. Half of each tissue suspension was plated on MRS agar plate and the other half was plated on BHI agar plate. The plates were then incubated anaerobically (MRS) or aerobically (BHI) at 37℃ for 48h.

2.8 Acute toxicity test of *L. lactis* subsp. *lactis* LB12

An acute oral toxicity study was performed in accordance with the Organization of Economic Cooperation and Development guidelines (OECD, 1995). Four weeks-old Kunming mice (purchased from Nanjing Qinglongshan Animal Resources Centre, P. R. China) with a body weight ranging from 18 ~ 22g were randomly divided into two groups, and each group contains ten females and ten males. Yogurt fermented by *L. lactis* subsp. *lactis* LB12 was administered at dose of 100 ml/kg · bw by gastric intubation to single female and male mice once a day throughout the experimental period of 10 days, and served as treated group, control group received sterilized low fat milk (1.0% fat and 11.0% SNF, acidifying it to pH 4.7 with 10% lactic acid) at dose of 100 ml/kg · bw in the similar manner of treated group. Diet and water were freely available, and the housed conditions of mice were similar to lowing cholesterol test.

All the tested mice were observed shortly after dosing, and then each mouse was observed daily for a period of 10 consecutive days, and examined for general behavior signs twice daily. The general behavior signs included changes in the skin and fur, eyes and mucous membranes, excreta and also food and water taking, as well as behavioral pattern. All the tested mice were killed and the vital organs were separated and processed for routine gross and microscopically examination at the end. The epididymus of all male mice were excised and immersed into plates which contained sterilized 0.90% (w/v) NaCl solution for sperm shape abnormality measured, respectively.

2.9 Acid tolerance of *L. lactis* subsp. *lactis* LB12

Acid tolerances were evaluated by growing *L. lactis* subsp. *Lactis* LB12 strain in MRS broth adjusted to acidic pH 1.5, 2.5, 3.5, 4.5 by adding concentrated hydrochloric acid and incubated at 37℃ for 6 h. 1 ml culture was attained aseptically from the media at 2 h intervals during 6 h incubation for determining the viable cell numbers, cells were harvested by centrifugation (5 000 rpm for 10 min at 4℃), diluted by a sterile saline (0.90% NaCl, w/v), evenly spread onto MRS-agar plates (pH 6.8) to confirm the survival of bacteria and incubated at 37℃ for 48 h. Observed colonies in the plates were considered to be the viable cells. The plates were duplicated in all the experiments.

2.10 Bile salt tolerance of *L. lactis* subsp. *lactis* LB12

In order to assess bile salt tolerance of *L. lactis* subsp. *lactis* LB12, the strain was inoculated into MRS broth (pH 7.0) supplemented with 0.10%, 0.20%, 0.30% and 0.40% (w/v) oxgall (Sigma, pH 7.0) respectively, and incubated at 37℃ for 6 h. 1 ml culture was attained aseptically from the media at 2h intervals during 6 h incubation for determining the viable cell numbers, cells were harvested by centrifugation (5 000 rpm for 10 min at 4℃), diluted by a sterile saline (0.85% NaCl, w/v), evenly spread onto MRS-agar plates (pH 6.8) to confirm the survival of bacteria and incubated at 37℃ for 48 h. Observed colonies in the plates were considered to be the viable cells. The plates were duplicated in all the experiments.

2.11 Antimicrobial test of *L. lactis* subsp. *lactis* LB12

The antimicrobial tests of the culture, clear supernatant of culture (5 000rpm for 10 min at 4℃) and sterilized culture (85℃ for 15 min) of *L. lactis* subsp. *lactis* LB12 were tested on the pathogenic *E. coli* ATCC 25922 and *S. aureus* ATCC 25923 using the agar-gel diffusion inhibition test. In the agar-gel diffusion inhibition test as described by Opara and Ansa (1993), 0.2 ml of a 24 h broth culture of each of the test microorganisms was aseptically introduced and evenly spread using bent sterile glass rod on the surface of gelled sterile Mueller-Hinton agar plates. Four wells of about 3.0 mm diameter were aseptically punched on each agar plate using a sterile cork borer, allowing at least 30 mm between adjacent wells and between peripheral wells and the edge of the petri dish. 0.05ml of the culture, clear supernatant of culture and sterilized culture of *L. lactis* subsp. *lactis* LB12 were then introduced into the wells in the plates, respectively. 0.05 ml of sterilized MRS broth, the culture medium of *L. lactis* subsp. *lactis* LB12, was introduced into the remainder well as the control. pH value of all above culture was adjusted to 7.0 before filling into the well. The plates incubated at 37℃ for 24h for the test bacteria, and were duplicated in all the experiments.

2.12 Antibiotic resistance testing of *L. lactis* subsp. *lactis* LB12

Antibiotic resistance of *L. lactis subsp. lactis* LB12 was assessed by disc diffusion assay using antibiotic disks (Hangzhou Microbiology Reagent Factory, Hangzhou, China) (Bauer et al., 1966). The antibiotics tested were ampicillin (10μg), tetracycline (30μg), gentamicin (10μg), roxithromycin (15μg), and cefoxitin (30μg). The commercial antibiotic discs were placed on nutrient agar plates previously seeded with 18 h broth culture of the strain in duplicate. The plates were incubated at 37℃ for 48 h, after which zones of inhibition were examined. Earlier, the potencies of all the antibiotics used in the study were confirmed using susceptible strain of *S. aureus* ATCC 25923.

2.13 Statistical analysis

Results were presented as mean ± standard error of mean for all groups. Student t-test was used for test of significance between two groups.

3 Result

3.1 Strain isolation and identification

Ten strains isolated on MRS and Rogosa agar from pickled vegetable juice were preliminarily indentified as lactic acid bacteria. The strain with the largest cholesterol-lowing effect was a sphere-shaped, Grampositive, and able to grow at temperatures between 10 and 45℃. The patterns of carbohydrate fermentation and SDS-PAGE analysis of the isolate were similar to those of the *L. lactis* group. Partial sequencing of 16S rRNA indicated 98% identity with *L. lactis* subsp. *lactis* NBRC 12007. Therefore the isolate was confirmed as a strain of *L. lactis subsp. lactis*, and was designated *L. lactis* subsp. *lactis* LB12.

3.2 *Lactococus lactis* subsp. *lactis* LB12 on serum lipids and bile acid levels of mice

The results of assigned diets on serum lipids and bile acid levels of mice are presented in Table 1. Levels of serum total cholesterol (TC) and triacylglycerols (TG) in group 2 mice were significant increased compared to the model control mice (group 1) when the high-cholesterol diets were fed to the mice. It meant that the high fat mould mice had set up. Mice fed yogurt (group 4) fermented by *L. lactis* subsp. *lactis* LB12 had significantly lower total cholesterol, triacylglycerols and total bile acid compared to the experimental control mice (group 3). It suggested that yogurt fermented by *L. lactis* subsp. *lactis* LB12 had cholesterol-lowering effect.

Table 1 Different diets fed for 28 days on serum lipids and bile acid levels of the mice

Treatment	Serum TC (mmol/L)	Serum TG (mmol/L)	Serum HDL-c (mmol/L)	Serum TBA (μmol/L)
Group 1	1.35 ±0.24	1.08 ±0.21	0.92 ±0.13	8.11 ±3.15
Group 2	4.34 ±1.32*	1.46 ±0.35*	0.87 ±0.12	12.27 ±3.59*
Group 3	4.43 ±0.99	1.37 ±0.28	0.86 ±0.12	12.41 ±4.51
Group 4	3.25 ±0.56*	1.15 ±0.20*	0.88 ±0.12	8.64 ±2.30*

Treatments: Group 1 (model control) mice were fed commercial diet (purchased from Nanjing Qinglongshan Animal Resources Centre China); group 2 (high fat mould) mice were fed commercial diet plus 1.0% (w/w) cholesterol, 8.0% (w/w) lard and 0.50% (w/w) oxgall; group 3 (experimental control) mice were fed commercial diet plus 1.0% (w/w) cholesterol, 8.0% (w/w) lard, 0.50% (w/w) oxgall and 5.0% (v/w) low fat milk; group 4 (experimental) mice were fed commercial diet plus 1.0% (w/w) cholesterol, 8.0% (w/w) lard, 0.50% (w/w) oxgall and 5.0% (v/w) yogurt fermented by *L. lactis subsp. lactis* LB12.

* Significant ($P < 0.05$) compared to experimental control (group 3); * greatest differences ($P < 0.01$) compared to mould control (group 1)

3.3 Bile acid and cholesterol concentration in feaces

The effects of assigned diets on feaces bile acid and cholesterol content of mice are illustrated in Figure 1 (a, b). The bile acid and cholesterol content of feaces in mice given high-cholesterol diets (group 2, 3 and 4) were significantly higher than those in model control mice (group 1). The bile acid and cholesterol level in feaces of the mice fed with yoghurt (group

4) were significant higher than those of experimental control (group 4) and high fat mould mice (group 2). It suggested that *L. lactis* subsp. *lactis* LB12 could promote the excretion of bile acid and cholesterol.

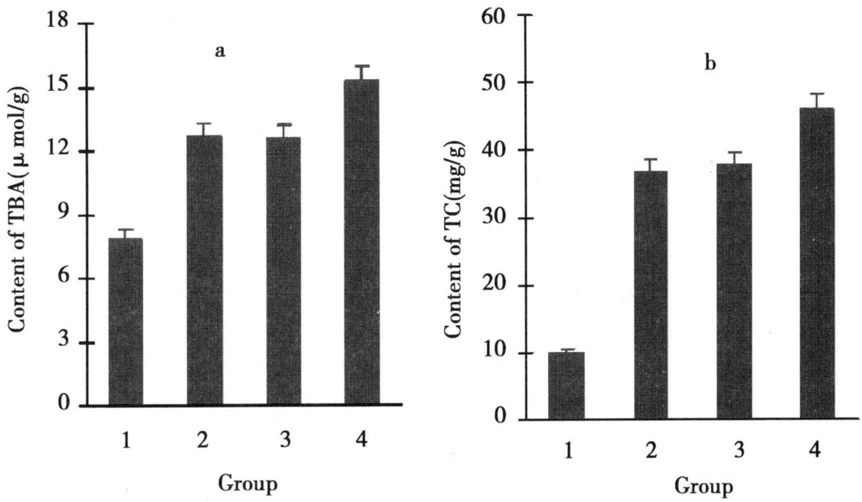

Figure 1 Effect of feeding of commercial diet (group 1), mixture of commercial diet plus cholesterol plus lard plus oxgall (group 2), commercial diet plus cholesterol plus lard plus oxgall plus low fat milk (group 3), commercial diet plus cholesterol plus lard plus oxgall plus yogurt fermented by *L. lactis* subsp. *lactis* LB12 (group 4) on the total bile acids (TBA) concentration (A) and cholesterol (TC) concentration (B) of feces of mice. Values are means ± SD of measurements from 12 mice

3.4 Effects of *L. lactis* subsp. *lactis* LB12 on body and viscera weight of the mice

The body weight and viscera weight index is showed in Table 2. There are no significant difference in body weight, weight percentage of nates and spleens to body weight among all groups. The weight percentage of liver to body was significant ($P < 0.01$) increased in high fat mould mice (group 2), experimental control mice (group 3) and yogurt treated mice (group 4) compared to that of model control mice (group 1), suggesting that there are more fat stored in liver of high fat mould, experimental control and yogurt treated mice than that of mould control mice. However, the weight percentage of liver to body was significantly ($P < 0.05$) decreased in yogurt treated mice than those in high fat mould and experimental control mice. This suggests that there was fewer fat stored in liver of group 4 than those of groups 3 and 4.

3.5 Safety assessment of *L. lactis* subsp. *lactis* LB12

In lowing cholesterol test, there are no significant difference in body weight, weight percentage of nates and spleens to body weight among all groups (Table 2). No deaths or differences in behavior among groups were noted.

Table 2 Different diets fed for 28 days on body and viscera weight indexs of the mice

Treatment	28day body weight (g)	liver/body (w/w,%)	nate/body (w/w,%)	spleen/body (w/w,%)
Group 1	359 ±34	3.53 ±0.34	0.68 ±0.05	0.43 ±0.10
Group 2	385 ±42	5.12 ±0.43	0.60 ±0.06	0.46 ±0.12
Group 3	363 ±34	5.10 ±0.56	0.59 ±0.05	0.48 ±0.07
Group 4	354 ±32	4.60 ±0.45	0.59 ±0.06	0.43 ±0.08

Treatments: Group 1 (model control) mice were fed commercial diet (purchased from Nanjing Qinglongshan Animal Resources Centre China); group 2 (high fat mould) mice were fed commercial diet plus 1.0% (w/w) cholesterol, 8.0% (w/w) lard and 0.50% (w/w) oxgall; group 3 (experimental control) mice were fed commercial diet plus 1.0% (w/w) cholesterol, 8.0% (w/w) lard, 0.50% (w/w) oxgall and 5.0% (v/w) low fat milk; group 4 (experimental) mice were fed commercial diet plus 1.0% (w/w) cholesterol, 8.0% (w/w) lard, 0.50% (w/w) oxgall and 5.0% (v/w) yogurt fermented by *L. lactis subsp. lactis* LB12.

Data are mean ± SD of measurements from 12 mice.

Significant and greatest differences: $P<0.05$ and $P<0.01$. * $P<0.05$ compared to high fat mould and experimental control (group 2 and 3); $P<0.01$ compared to mould control (group 1)

During acute toxicity test, no deaths were also observed, no significant difference in body weight or differences in behavior between experimental and control group mice were noted. All tested mice did not show any significant abnormality in the skin, fur, eyes and mucous membranes, as well as behavioral pattern, and also had no obvious signs of toxicity or change in other physiological activities. The body weight, body weight gain (Table 3) and excreta of the mice treated with yogurt had no significant change, as well as no significant difference in food and water tacking compared with those of the control group. At necropsy, the pathological examination of the internal organs related showed that no gross histopathological alterations were found in all the tested animals and the control group, and the aberration rate of sperm had no significant difference between yoghurt treated mice and control mice.

Table 3 Different diets fed on body weight gain of the mice

Treatment	0day body weight (g)	10day body weight (g)	Body weight gain (g)
Control	18.90 ±0.70	25.80 ±1.95	6.90
Experimental	19.30 ±1.10	26.60 ±2.50	7.30

Treatments: Control and experimental group mice were administered sterilized low fat milk (1.0% fat and 11.0%。SNF, acidifying it to pH4.7 with 10% lactic acid) and yogurt fermented by *L. lactis* subsp. *lactis* LB12 at dose of 100 ml/kg · bw by gastric intubation once a day throughout the experimental period of 10 days, respectively. Commercial diet (purchased from Nanjing Qinglongshan Animal Resources Gentre, China) and water were freely available to all mice.

Data are mean ± SD of measurements from 20 mice.

A translocation-positive animal is defined as an animal that had at least one tissue sample (including blood) containing one or more viable bacterial cells. Positive translocation tissue is defined as the tissue from which at least one viable bacterial cell was recovered (one colony). Statistical analysis of results did not reveal any significant differences in the percentage of animals and tissues between the different groups ($P > 0.05$). No bacteria isolated from the tissue samples matched with the test strain fed to the mice.

3.6 Low pH tolerance of *L. lactis* subsp. *lactis* LB12

Low pH tolerance of *L. lactis* subsp. *lactis* LB12 was assessed in pH 1.5, 2.5, 3.5 and 4.5, respectively. As shown in Figure 2a, the strain grew obviously for 6h incubation in pH 3.5 and 4.5, and slightly for 6 h incubation in pH 2.5, suggesting that this strain had the ability to survive at pH 2.5 ~ 4.5, and the viable cells could still reach 106 CFU/mt after incubated in pH 1.5 for 6 h. It indicated that *L. lactis* subsp. *lactis* LB12 was low pH tolerant.

3.7 Bile salt tolerance of *L. lactis* subsp. *lactis* LB12

Results of bile salt tolerance were shown in Figure 2b. It showed that the viable cells increased obviously in the condition of 0.10% bile salt, and decreased obviously in the condition of 0.20%, 0.30% or 0.40% bile salt. However, the viable cells were determined above 107 CFU/ml when incubated in 0.20% bile salt for 6 h, and 106 CFU/ml in 0.30% and 0.40% bile salt for 4 h.

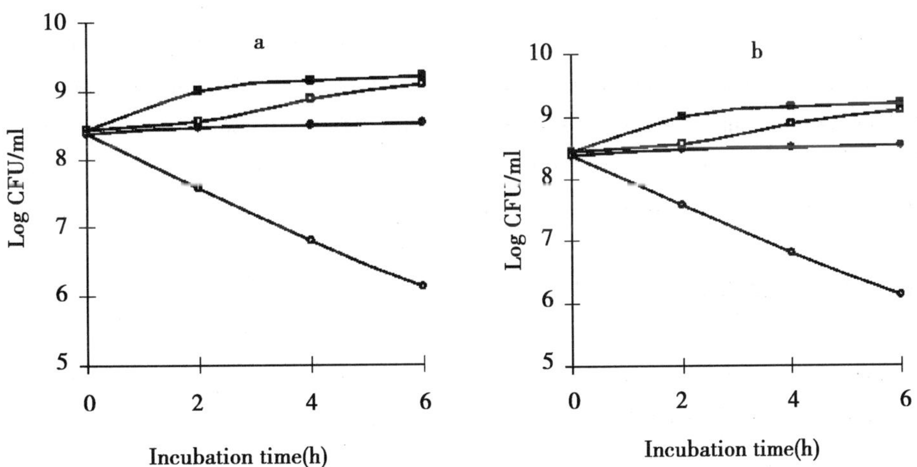

Figure 2 Effect of pH (A) (-■-, -□-, -●-, and -○-, the culture pH of 4.5, 3.5, 2.5 and 1.5) and bile salt (B) (-■-0.10%, -□-0.20%, -●-0.30%, -○-0.40% bile salt) on viability of *L. lactis* subsp. *lactis* LB12. Values are means ± SD of measurements from 3 experiments

3.8 Antimicrobial activity of *L. lactis* subsp. *lactis* LB12

The antimicrobial activities results of *L. lactis* subsp. *Lactis* LB12 to the pathogenic *E. coli and S. aureus* are showed in Table 4. The diameter of inhibition zones caused by the culture (A), clear supernatant of culture (B) and the sterilized culture (C) of *L. lactis subsp. lactis* LB12 were all more than 17 mm and significant larger than that of control (D). However there are no significant difference among A, B and C, indicating that there could exist some inhibitory substance in the culture produced by the strain during fermentation.

Table 4 Antimicrobial activities of *L. lactis* subsp. *lactis* LB12 on the test organisms using agar-gel diffusion test

Treatment	Diameter of inhibition zones (mm)			
	A	B	C	D
E. coli	18.02 ±2.15*	17.53 ±1.98*	17.51 ±1.47*	7.83 ±1.06
S. aureus	17.62 ±2.11*	17.42 ±2.32*	17.42 ±1.96*	7.81 ±1.24

A, B, C and D expressed the groups of culture, clear supernatant of culture, sterilized culture of *L. lactis* subsp. *lactis* LB12 and MRS broth samples, respectively.

Data are mean ± SD of measurements from 3 experiments.

Significant difference: $P < 0.01$ compared to control group (D)

3.9 Antibiotic resistance of *L. lactis* subsp. *lactis* LB12

The diameters of inhibition zones caused by ampicillin, tetracycline, gentamicin, roxithromycin and cefoxitin to *L. lactis* subsp. *lactis* LB12 were 13mm, 14.5mm, 7.2mm, 16.1mm and 7.0mm, significant lower than the 15mm, 17mm, 12mm, 18mm and 10mm were caused by these antibiotics to the contrast strain of *S. aureus* ATCC 25923, respectively. This indicates that the strain was resistance to the antibiotics tested.

4 Discussion

Lactic acid bacteria are normal components of the intestinal microflora in both humans and animals and have been associated with various health-promoting properties. One beneficial effect is a reduction in serum cholesterol levels. The results from the present study strongly suggest that *L. lactis* subsp. *lactis* LB12 screened from traditional Chinese pickled cabbage juice significantly reduced serum cholesterol of mice.

Different hypotheses have been advanced to explain how the hypocholesterolemic effect of lactic acid bacteria is possible. In this study, the cholesterol and bile acid levels in the serum of mice fed with yogurt fermented by *L. lactis* subsp. *lactis* LB12 decreased significantly, while the cholesterol and bile acid content increased in mice feces. These effects may be due in part to the deconjugation of bile salts by strains of bacteria that produce the enzyme bile salt hydrolase (BSH) (Taranto et al., 1997; Brashears et al., 1998; Pereira et al., 2003). As deconjugated bile salts are more readily excreted in the feaces than conjugated bile salts (Gilliland and Walker, 1990; De Smet et al., 1994; De Rodas et al., 1996), bacteria with BSH activity may effectively reduce serum cholesterol byenhancing the excretion of bile salts, with a consequent increase in the synthesis of bile salts from serum cholesterol; or by decreasing the solubility of cholesterol, since bile acid is essential for gastrointestional absorption of cholesterol (Sugao and Imaizumi, 1986), and thus reducing its uptake from the gut.

The gastric tract contains gastric juice of low pH due to the high hydrochloric acid concentration of the secreted gastric acid, and the intestinal tract contains bile juice containing bile salts (Holzapfel et al., 1998). As such, probiotic bacteria should have the ability to survive the passage through the gastrointestinal tract, resisting the acidic conditions in the stomach and the bile acids at the beginning of the small intestine (Taranto et al., 1998; Hyronimus et al., 2000; Park et al., 2002). The present results indicated that the strain of *L. lactis* subsp. *Lactis* LB12 screened from traditional Chinese pickled cabbage juice had a high level of bible tolerance and acid resistance.

Assessment of pathogenicity is one important component of probiotic safety studies (Zhou et al., 2000; Marteau et al., 1997), the indicators for which include splenomegaly and hepatomegaly. None of these morphological changes was noted as a result of *L. lactis* subsp. *lactis* LB12 treatment, nor were there significant differences in the visceral weight indices of the lymph nodes, spleen, or liver. In addition, bacterial translocation, the process by which intestinal bacteria pass through the mucosal epithelium and invade other organs, is another important safety consideration, as it may cause bacteremia, septicemia, and even multiple organ failure (Borriello et al., 2003). The bacterial translocation in the present study was not significantly different between experimental and control groups. Moreover, *L. lactis* subsp. *lactis* LB12 is resistant to the tested common commercial antibiotics, and possesses antimicrobial activity to pathogenic *E. coli* and *S. aureus*, suggesting that the organism would not be affected by therapies using these antibiotics and might help maintain the natural balance of intestinal microflora during antibiotic treatments.

Serum triglycerides and relative weight of the liver were also lowered as a result of the *L. lactis* subsp. *lactis* LB12 treatment. This suggests that the hypolipemic effect of the bacteria may not be due to a redistribution of lipids from the plasma to the liver, but rather to decreased intestinal absorption of lipids or increased lipid catabolism (Taranto et al., 1998).

The results of this study indicate that *L. lactis* subsp. *lactis* LB12 is a safe probiotic with the potential to reduce serum cholesterol and triglyceride levels. Further studies will be required to determine the mechanism underlying the cholesterol-lowering effect. It will also be necessary to test more animals, using varying doses of this strain over longer times, to assess the long-term probiotic potential of *L. lactis* subsp. *lactis* LB12.

References

[1] Bauer AW, Kirby WMM, Sherris JC, Turck M Antibiotic susceptibility testing by a standardized single disk diffusion method [J]. Am J Clin Pathol. 1966, 45: 493 -496

[2] Borriello SP, Hammes WP, Holzapfel WH, Marteau P, Schrezenmeir J, Vaara M, Valtonen V. Safety of probiotics that contain Lactobacillus or Bifidobacteria [J]. Clin. Infect. Dis. 36: 2003, 775 -780

[3] Brashears MM, Gilliland SE, Buck LM. Bile salt deconjugation and cholesterol removal from media by *Lactobacillus casei* [J]. Dairy Sci. 1998, 81: 2 103 -2 110

[4] Chandan RC. Enhancing market value of milk by adding cultures [J]. Dairy Sci. 1999, 82: 2 245 -2 256

[5] De Rodas BZ, Gilliland SE, Maxwell CV. Hypocholesterolemic action of *Lactobacillus acidophilus* ATCC 43121 and calcium in swine with hypercholesterolemia induced by diet [J]. Dairy Sci. 1996, 79: 2 121 -2 128

[6] De Smet I, Hoorde LV, Saeyer ND, Woestyne MV, Verstraete W. In vitro study of bile salt. 1994, 34: 33 -35

[7] hydrolase activity of BSH isogenic *Lactobacillus plantarum* 80 strains and estimation of cholesterol lowering through enhanced BSH activity. Microb. Ecol. Health Dis. 7: 315 -329

[8] Gilliland SE, Walker DK. Factors to consider when selecting a culture of Lactobacillus acidophilus as a dietary adjunct to produce a hypocholesterolemic effect in humans. J. Dairy Sci. 1990, 73: 905 -911

[9] Grahn E, Holm SE, Lilja H, Sellgren K. Interference of a *Lactococcus lactis* strain on the human gut flora and its capacity to pass the stomach and intestine. Scand. J. Nutr. 1994, 38: 2 -4

[10] Gruzza M, Duval-Iflah Y, Ducluzeau R. Colonization of the digestive tract of germ-free mice by genetically engineered strains of *Lactococcus lactis*: study of recombinant DNA stability. Microbiol. Releases. 1992, 1: 165 -171

[11] Haberer P, Du Toit M, Dicks LMT, Ahrens F, Holzapfel WH. Effect of potentially probiotic lactobacilli on faecal enzyme activity in minipigs on a high-fat, high-cholesterol diet-a preliminary *in vivo* trial. Int. J. Food Microbiol. 2003, 87: 287 -291

[12] Holzapfel WH, Haberer P, Snel J, Schillinger U, Huis in' t Veld JHJ. Overview of gut flora and probiotics. Int. J. Food Microbiol. 1998, 41: 85 -101

[13] Hyronimus B, Le Marrec C, Hadj Sassi A, Deschamps A. Acid and bile tolerance of spore-forming lactic acid bacteria. Int. J. Food Microbiol. 2000, 61: 193 -197

[14] International Dairy Federation. Yogurt: enumeration of characteristic microorganisms. Colony count technique at 37℃. IDF Stand. 117A. Int. Dairy Fed. , Brussels, Belgium. Kawase M, Hashimoto H, Hosoda M, Morita H, Hosono A (2000) . Effect of

administration of fermented milk containing whey protein concentrate to mice and healthy men on serum lipids and blood pressure. J. Dairy Sci. 1988, 83: 255 -263

[15] Klijin N, Weerkamp AH, De Vos WM. Genetic marking of *Lactococcus lactis* shows its survival in the human gastrointestinal tract. Appl. Environ. Microbiol, 1995, 61: 2 771 -2 774

[16] Law MR, Wald NJ, Wu T, Hackshaw A, Bailey A. Systematic underestimation of association between serum cholesterol concentration and ischaemic heart disease in observational studies: data from BUPA study. Br. Med. J. 1994, 308: 363 -366

[17] Lim HJ, Kim SY, Lee WK. Isolation of cholesterol-lowering lactic acid bacteria from human intestine for probiotic use. J. Vet. Sci. 2004, 4: 391 -395

[18] Loh TC, Foo HL, Tan BK, Jelan ZA. Effects of palm kernel cake on growth performance and blood lipids in mice. Asian-Austr. J. Anim. Sci. 2002, 15: 1 165 -1 169

[19] Marteau P, Minekus M, Havenar R, Huis JHJ. Survival of lactic acid bacteria in a dynamic model of the stomach and small intestine: validation and the effects of bile. J. Dairy Sci. 1997, 80: 1 031 -1 037

[20] Nguyen TDT, Kang JH, Lee MS. Characterization of *Lactobacillus plantarum* PH 04, a potential probiotic bacterium with cholesterol-lowering effects. Int. J. Food Microbiol. 2007, 113: 358 -361

[21] OECD. Guideline No. 420. Acute Oral Toxicity-Fixed Dose Method. Opara NV, Ansa MA (1993) . The antibacterial activity of Tea and Coffee on selected organisms. J. Med. Lab. Sci. 1995, 3: 45 -48

[22] Park YS, Lee JY, Kim YS, Shin DH. Isolation and characterization of lactic acid bacteria from feces of newborn baby and from dongchimi. J. Agric. Food Chem. 2002, 50: 2 531 -2 536

[23] Pereira DI, McCartney AL, Gibson GR. An in vitro study of the probiotic potential of a bile salt hydrolyzing Lactobacillus fermentum strain, and determination of its cholesterol-lowering properties. Appl. Environ. Microbiol, 2003, 69: 4 743 -4 752

[24] Pot B, Vandamme P, Kersters K. Analysis of electrophoresis of whole cell protein fingerprints. Chemical Methods in Prokaryotic Systematics. John Wiley & Sons, New York, NY, USA; 1993: 493 -521

[25] Roos MN, Martin KB. Effects of probiotic bacteria on diarrhea, lipid metabolism, and carcinogenesis: a review or papers published between 1988 and 1998. Am. J. Clin. Nutr, 2000, 71: 405 -411

[26] Rudel LL, Morris MD. Determination of cholesterol using 0-phthalaldehyde. J. Lipid Res. 1973, 14: 364 -366

[27] Sugao H, Imaizumi K. Choleaterol, Sankyo Syuppan, Tokyo, 1986: p. 122 -145

[28] Taranto MP, Medici M, Perdigon G, Holdago APR, Valdez GF. Evidence for cholesterolemic effect of *Lactobacillus reuteri* in hypercholesterolemic mice. J. Dairy Sci. 1998,

81: 2 336 – 2 340

[29] Taranto MP, Sesma F, Holdago APR, Valdez GF. Bile salts hydrolase plays a key role on cholesterol removal by *Lactobacillus casei.* Biotechnol. Lett, 1997, 19: 845 – 847

[30] Teuber M, Geis A, Neve H. The genus *Lactococcus.* In The Prokaryotes. Balows A, Truber HG, Dworkin, Harder MW, Schleifer KH, editors. Vol II. 2nd. Springer Verlag, New York, NY, 1995: 1 482 – 1 501

[31] Usman A, Hosono A. Effect of administration of *Lactobacillus gasseri* on serum lipids and fecal steroids in hypercholesterolemic mice. J. Dairy Sci. 2000, 83: 1 705 – 1 711

[32] Yamauchi KE, Snel J. Transmission electron microscopic demonstration of phagocytosis and intracellular processing of segmented filamentous bacteria by intestinal epithelial cells of the chick ileum. Infect. Immun, 2000, 68: 6 496 – 6 504

[33] Zhou JS, Shou Q, Rutherfurd KJ, Prasad J, Gopal PK, Gill HS. Acute oral toxicology studies on potentially probiotic strains of lactic acid bacteria. Food Chemical Toxicol, 2000, 38: 153 – 161

钾素对棉花生长发育和叶片生理特性的影响

郭　英[①]　范世杰　亓延凤
（潍坊科技学院，寿光　262700）

摘　要： 本文在大田试验条件下，研究了钾素营养对棉花生长发育及叶片生理特性的影响。试验设2个品种，4个施钾量。结果表明，施钾增加了棉花的株高和果枝数，降低了第一果枝着生节位，且随施钾量的增加幅度呈增加趋势；与不施钾相比，施钾提高了中后期棉花功能叶片的光合速率和气孔导度，同时施钾还增加了棉花功能叶片叶绿素荧光动力学参数Fv/Fo、Fv/Fm、φPSⅡ、ETR和qP，降低了qN值。可见，适量的施用钾肥能提高棉花功能叶片的光合特性，延缓了叶片的衰老。

关键词： 钾素；棉花；生长发育；生理特性

一直以来，早衰成为棉花生产上制约其产量和纤维品质的重要因素之一，棉花的早衰不仅影响棉花产量，而且导致棉花纤维强度降低、长度变短、整齐度下降，从而降低棉纤维的成纱质量，有关早衰的研究成为学者关注的焦点。有研究指出可以通过环境因子的调节措施来预防棉花叶片早衰以及对出现叶片早衰后的稳产措施，如采用植物生长调节剂，肥料，以及水分、光照、温度、气体等，其中，施用钾肥就是重要措施之一，钾素有“品质元素”之称，是棉花生长发育所必需的大量元素之一，研究发现，钾素可以促进棉花不同叶位主茎叶的干物质积累，促进棉花叶片叶绿素的合成，硝态氮含量的增加和硝酸还原酶活性的增强，促进棉花叶片中SOD活性的增强，改变叶片中各种内源激素含量，对防止棉花叶片早衰有重要作用[1-6]。而棉花的早衰多表现在棉花生长的中后期阶段，因而，加强棉花中后期生长发育及叶片生理特性研究，对于揭示棉花早衰现象，指导棉花生产具有重要的意义。本文为了进一步探讨钾素对棉花早衰生理的影响机理，在大田条件下，进行钾素对棉花中后期生长发育和叶片生理特性的研究，旨在为通过施钾防止棉花早衰，提高棉花产量及改善纤维品质提供理论依据。

① 郭英，女，硕士，潍坊科技学院讲师。研究方向：作物栽培与耕作。E－mail：luer168_ 2000 @163. com

1 材料与方法

1.1 实验设计

本试验土壤养分状况：土层含有机质 1.24%，全氮 0.88 g/kg，速效磷 34.00 mg/kg,速效钾 89.00mg/kg。

试验选用棉花品种为鲁棉研 18 号（L18，前期长势中等，中后期长势强）和中棉所 41 号（ZH41，前期长势强，后期长势一般）。在施 N 180kg/hm^2 和 $P_2O_5$120kg/hm^2 的基础上，设 3 个不同施钾量为 K_2O 60、180、300 kg/hm^2，分别用 Treat. Ⅰ、Treat. Ⅱ、Treat. Ⅲ表示，以不施钾处理作对照，记为 CK。氮、磷、钾肥分别为尿素（含纯 N 46%）、过磷酸钙（含 P_2O_5 16%）和氯化钾（含 K_2O 60%）其中，过磷酸钙和氯化钾均做基肥一次性施入，尿素 1/2 作为基肥，1/2 作为追肥在花铃期施用。小区面积 5.6m×10m，随机区组排列，重复 3 次。4 月 18 日播种，行距 80cm，株距 33cm，其他管理同一般大田。

1.2 中后期棉花生育状况调查及取样方法

在叶片展开当天挂牌标记第 9~11 果枝上的主茎叶和对应果枝上的第一果枝叶。自挂牌后 15d 开始，每隔 15d 进行光合和荧光参数的测定，并分别取 15~20 片叶，部分用液氮速冻保存测定内源激素含量，部分冷冻保存，进行其他生理生化指标的测定。于 7 月 15 日调查第一果枝着生节位、9 月 10 日测量株高和调查果枝数。

1.3 测定项目及方法

1.3.1 光合特性测定

利用 CIRAS-2 便携式光合仪测定，自叶片展开后 15d 开始，每隔 15d 测定一次。测定时，选择晴天 10：00~14：00 在自然光下测定标记叶片，每处理重复 5 次。

1.3.2 荧光动力学参数测定

利用 FMS-2 便携调制式叶绿素荧光仪，自叶片展开后 15d 开始，每隔 15d 测一次。测定时，选择晴天 10：00~14：00 在自然光下测定标记叶片，每处理重复 5 次。

2 结果与讨论

2.1 钾素对棉花生长发育的影响

株高是常常被用来表征地上部营养生长的重要指标之一，土壤养分状况的变化亦会引起株高的相应变化。由表 1 可看出，各施钾处理的最终株高均高于对照，且随施钾量的增加，增幅呈增大趋势。两品种比较存在一定差异，L18 表现为各施钾处理的株高与 CK 间以及 Treat. Ⅲ与 Treat. Ⅰ间差异均达极显著，Treat. Ⅱ与 Treat. Ⅰ间差异显著。

ZH41 Treat. Ⅲ、Ⅱ与 CK 间差异显著，其余各处理间差异不显著。说明施钾对棉花株高的影响存在品种间差异，两个品种相比，对 L18 的最终株高影响作用较大。

表 1 钾素对棉花生长发育的影响

品种	处理	株高 (cm)	第一果枝着生节位 (NO.)	果枝数 (NO.)
L18	CK	68. 44 Cd	8. 36 Aa	13. 18 Ab
	Ⅰ	78. 06 Bc	8. 18 Aa	13. 43 Ab
	Ⅱ	85. 85 ABb	7. 46 Aab	14. 18 Aab
	Ⅲ	92. 77 Ab	7. 18 Ab	15. 10 Aa
ZH41	CK	83. 52 Ab	8. 80 Aa	13. 58 Aa
	Ⅰ	90. 70 Aab	8. 36 Aa	13. 60 Aa
	Ⅱ	96. 18 Aa	8. 11 Aa	14. 00 Aa
	Ⅲ	96. 72 Aa	8. 27 Aa	14. 27 Aa

施钾也对棉花第一果枝着生节位和果枝数有重要影响。各施钾处理的第一果枝着生节位均低于对照，两品种对不同施钾量反应不同，L18 的 Treat. Ⅲ与 CK 间差异达显著水平，其余处理间差异不显著；ZH41 各处理间均无显著差异。施钾增加了单株果枝数，且随施钾量增加，增加幅度加大，两品种果枝数对钾肥发应也存在一定差异，L18 Treat. Ⅲ的果枝数与 CK 间差异达显著水平，其余各处理间差异不显著；ZH41 的各施钾处理与 CK 间均无显著差异。说明施钾对棉花第一果枝着生节位和果枝数的影响存在品种间差异，两品种相比，对 L18 的影响作用较大。

2.2 钾素对棉花功能叶片光合特性的影响

2.2.1 光合速率的动态变化

由图 1 可以看出，随着叶龄的增长，两个品种叶片的光合速率变化规律一致，均呈先增大后减小的趋势，到叶片展开后 30d 达最大值，然后逐渐减小。施钾对两品种叶片光合速率动态变化的影响趋势一致，施钾明显提高了叶片的光合速率，且随着施钾量的增大，光合速率提高幅度加大。经方差分析，两品种的 Treat. Ⅰ、Ⅱ和 Treat. Ⅲ在叶片生长各个时期光合速率均与 CK 差异达极显著水平，但 Treat. Ⅱ和 Treat. Ⅲ间差异水平在不同时期表现不同，在叶龄达 15d 和 30d 时，两处理间差异达极显著，在 45d 和 60d 时差异不显著。

2.2.2 蒸腾速率的动态变化

随着叶龄的增长，两个品种叶片蒸腾速率的变化规律与光合速率相似，也呈先增加后降低的趋势。施钾提高了叶片的蒸腾速率，且随施钾量增加，增幅呈增大趋势。两品种对钾的敏感性表现不同，L18 3 个施钾处理与 CK 间差异不明显；ZH41 的 3 个施钾处理与对照相比均能明显提高叶片的蒸腾速率，但 3 个施钾处理间变化不明显（图 2）。由此说明，施钾可提高叶片的蒸腾速率，且对 ZH41 的影响大于 L18。

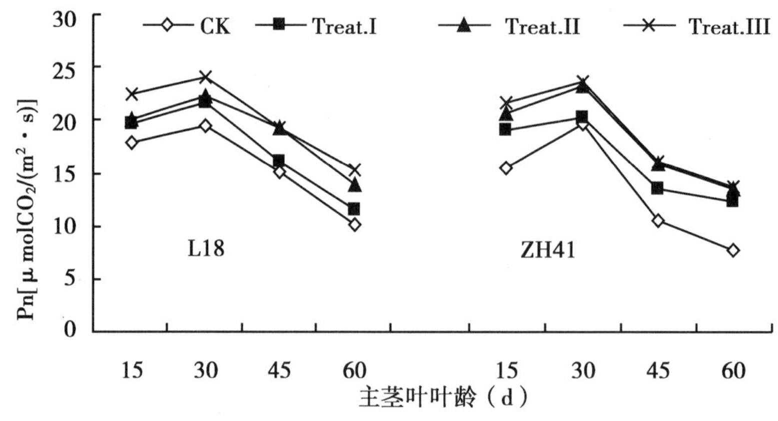

图1 钾素对棉花叶片光合速率的影响

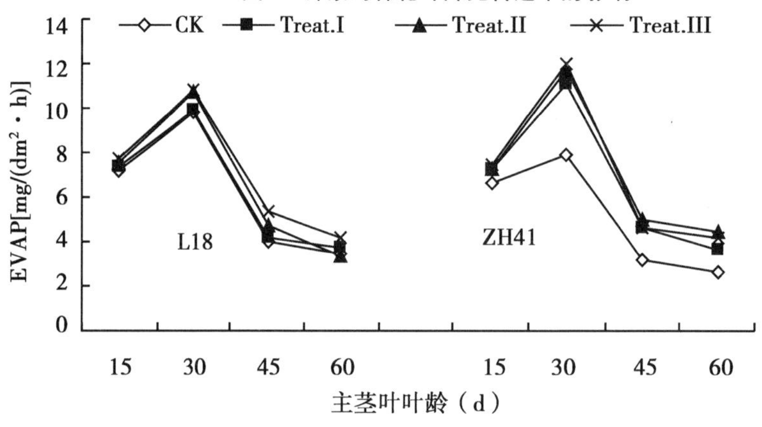

图2 钾素对棉花叶片蒸腾速率的影响

2.3 钾素对棉花功能叶片叶绿素荧光动力学参数的影响

2.3.1 Fv/Fm 和 Fv/Fo 的动态变化

由图3可以看出，随着叶片展开时间的延长，两个品种叶片的 Fv/Fm 和 Fv/Fo 的变化趋势相同。施钾对 Fv/Fm 和 Fv/Fo 的影响趋势两品种表现一致。在叶片生长的各个时期，各施钾量处理中 Fv/Fm 和 Fv/Fo 均比 CK 高，且随着供钾水平的提高，呈逐渐增大的趋势。但两品种相比也存在一定差异，各施钾处理对 L18 的 Fv/Fo 影响明显大于对 ZH41 的影响，尤其是在叶龄达 30d 以后，差异更明显。说明施钾利于棉花叶片维持较高的 PSⅡ潜在活性，提高棉花叶片中 PSⅡ光化学最大效率，两个品种相比，L18 表现更为敏感。

2.3.2 qN 和 qP 的动态变化

由图4可以看出，在叶片生长过程中，施钾对 qN 值的影响，均随供钾水平的提高而降低，到叶片生长后期降低趋势更明显，两个品种表现趋势一致。当叶龄达 60d 时，两个品种 Treat. Ⅰ、Treat. Ⅱ和 Treat. Ⅲ与对照 CK 相比，降幅分别为 9.24% 和 33.86%、34.46% 和 4.38%、12.8% 和 35.04%，说明施钾在叶片生长后期可明显降低 qN 值，而且施钾越多，降幅越大。两个品种相比，施钾对 L18 的影响大于 ZH41。

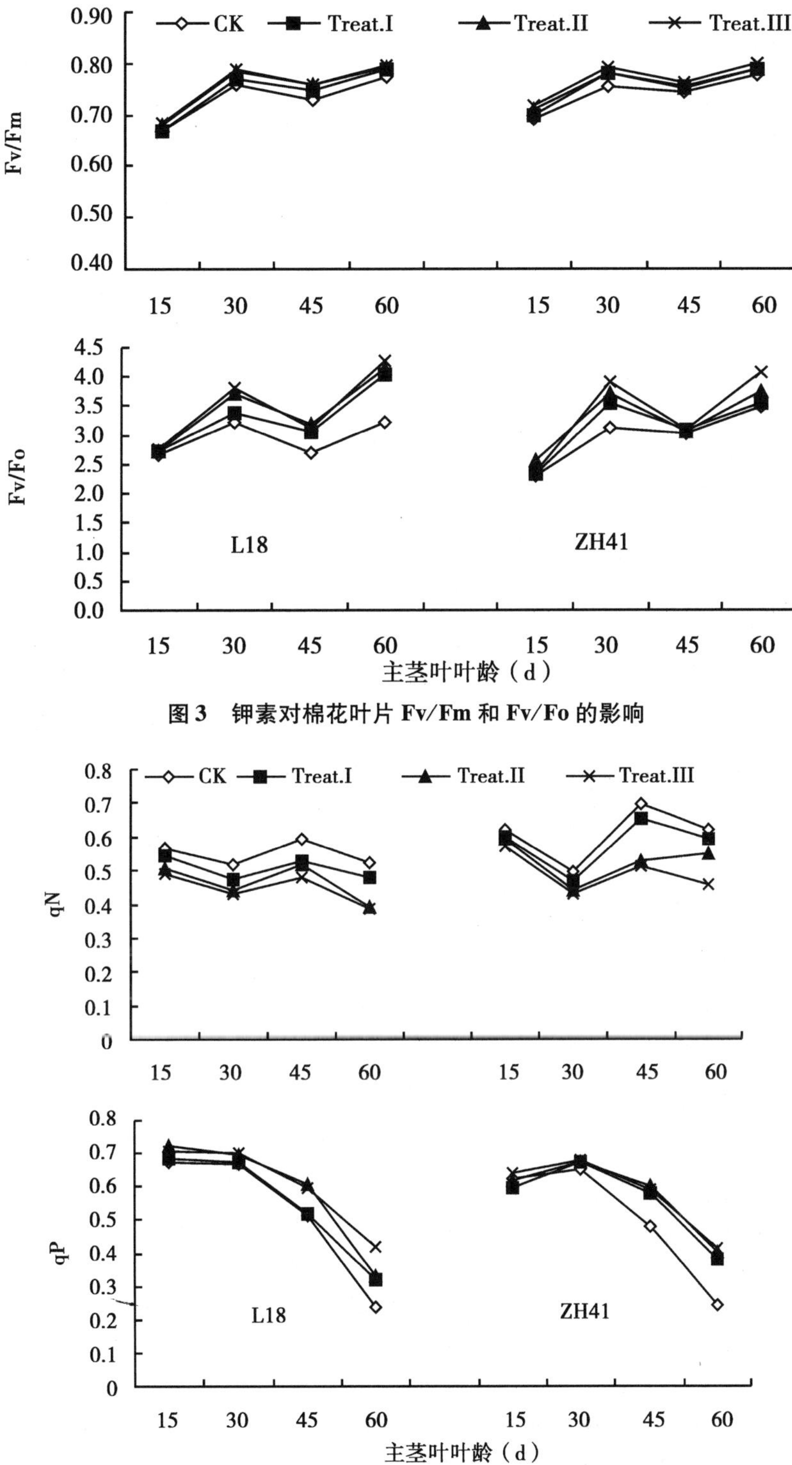

图 3　钾素对棉花叶片 Fv/Fm 和 Fv/Fo 的影响

图 4　钾素对棉花叶片 qN 和 qP 值的影响

与此相反，随供钾水平的提高，qP 值呈增大趋势，到叶龄达 30d 以后增加幅度更明显。由此说明，施钾提高了后期棉花叶片的荧光光化学猝灭系数，利于 PSⅡ反应中心维持较高比例的开放部分，降低了荧光非光化学猝灭系数，使叶片减少非辐射能量的耗散，从而利于叶片把所捕获的光能较充分地用于光合作用，施钾越多效果越明显。

2.3.3 φPSⅡ和 ETR 的动态变化

由图 5 可以看出，在叶片的生长发育过程中，φPSⅡ和 ETR 均呈先增后降的趋势，当叶龄到 30d 时达最大值。施钾对 φPSⅡ和 ETR 的影响，两个品种表现出相同的趋势。各施钾处理对 φPSⅡ的影响，在不同时期表现不同，在叶龄达 30d 前影响不明显，30d 后则明显提高 φPSⅡ值。对 ETR 的影响，3 个施钾量间差异不同，Treat. Ⅰ与 Treat. Ⅱ和 Treat. Ⅲ间差异明显，而 Treat. Ⅱ和 Treat. Ⅲ间无明显差异。

3 结论与讨论

前人关于钾素营养对棉花生长发育性状影响研究已有较多报道，研究指出，随着施钾量的增加，棉花株高能够明显增加；但也有人指出，施钾对棉花株高无明显影响[6]。本研究结果表明，施钾增加了棉花株高，且随施钾量的增加，增幅加大，当施钾 300kg/hm^2 时，L18 和 ZH41 的株高与不施钾处理间差异均达极显著和显著，同时，施钾还增加了果枝数，降低了第一果枝着生节位，增幅和降幅均随施钾量的增加呈逐渐加大趋势。

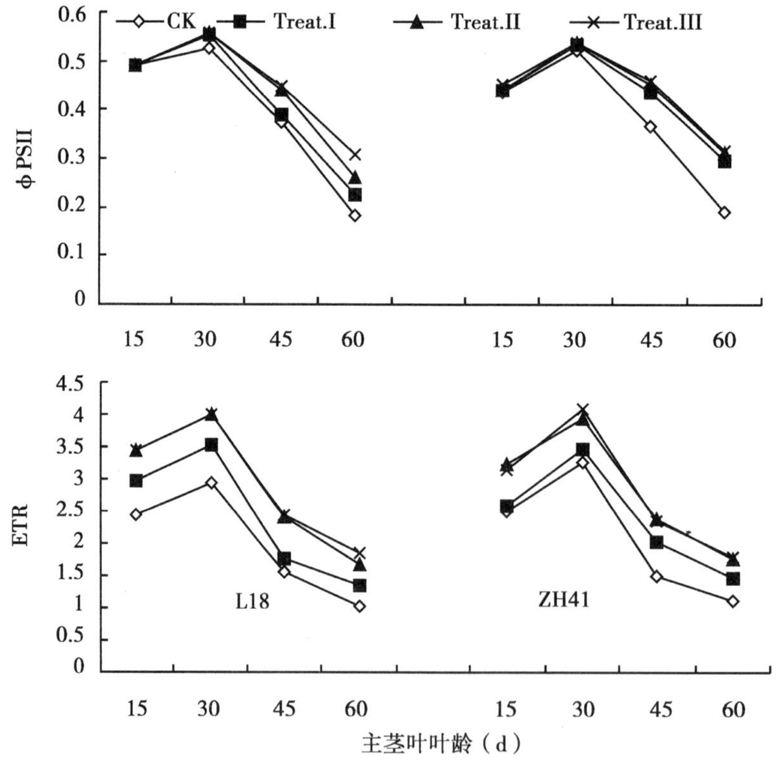

图 5 钾素对棉花叶片 φPSⅡ和 ETR 的影响

净光合速率（Pn）能够直观表示棉花叶片的光合特性，而叶绿素荧光动力学技术是近期发展起来的新技术，它在测定叶片光合作用过程中，光系统对光能的吸收、传递、耗散、分配等方面具有独特的作用，与“表观性”的气体交换指标相比，叶绿素荧光参数更具有反映“内在性”特点，被称为测定叶片光合功能快速、无损伤的探针[5-8]。且有研究表明，施钾对苗期叶绿素荧光动力学参数有重要影响作用。在此基础上，本文研究了施钾对中后期棉花叶片光和特性的影响，结果表明，施钾提高了中后期棉花叶片的净光合速率和气孔导度，施钾增加了棉花功能叶叶绿素荧光动力学参数Fv/Fo、Fv/Fm、φPSⅡ、ETR 和 qP，降低了 qN 值。说明施钾增强了中后期棉花叶片 PSⅡ的潜在活性和 PSⅡ光化学最大效率，提高了 PSⅡ反应中心开放部分的比例[9-12]，提高了 PSⅡ的实际量子效率（φPSⅡ）和光合电子传递速率（ETR），减少了叶片非辐射能量的耗散，使叶片把所捕获的光能较充分地用于光合作用，延缓中后期棉花叶片衰老。

参考文献

[1] Pettigrew W T. Potassium deficiency increases specific leaf weights and leaf glucose levels in fieldgrown cotton [J]. Journal article Agronomy Journal. 1999, 91 (6): 962 -968

[2] 宋美珍，毛树春，邢金松. 钾素对棉花光合产物的积累及产量形成的影响 [J]. 棉花学报，1994，6（增刊）：52 -57

[3] 梁德印，徐美德，王晓琪等. 钾营养对棉花养分吸收和干物质积累的影响 [J]. 1992，25（2）：69 -74

[4] 郭英，孙学振，宋宪亮等. 钾素营养对棉花苗期生长及其叶片生理特性的影响 [J]. 植物营养与肥料学报，2006，12（3）：363 -368

[5] 刘连涛，李存东，孙红春等. 棉花叶片衰老生理研究进展 [J]. 中国农学通报，2006，22（7）：316 -321

[6] 方贵来，王昊，祁家凤. 棉花施钾效应初探 [J]. 乡镇经济研究，1998，（4）：47 -48

[7] 张旺锋，勾玲，王振林等. 氮肥对新疆高产棉花叶片叶绿素荧光动力学参数的影响 [J]. 中国农业科学，2003，36（8）：893 -898

[8] 宋美珍，杨惠元，蒋国柱. 黄淮海棉区钾肥效应研究 [J]. 棉花学报，1993，5（1）：73 -78

[9] 梁金香，王玉朵，韩梅等. 棉花施钾的增产效果及其技术研究 [J]. 土壤肥料. 2003（3）：17 -19

[10] Pettigrew W T. Relationships between insufficient potassium and crop maturity in cotton [J]. Agronomy Journal，2003，95（5）：1 323 -1 331

[11] Cassman K G，Kerby T A，Roberts B A，et al. Potassium nutrition effects on lint yield and fiber quality of Acala cotton [J]. Crop Science. 1990（30）：672 -676

[12] Bennett O L，Rouse R D，Ashley D A，et al. Yield，fiber quality and potassiumcontent of irrigated cotton plants as affected by rates of potassium [J]. Agronomy Jurnal. 1965，57：296 -299

Effects of Potassium Nutrition the Cotton Growth and Development and Leaf Physiological Characteristics

GUO Ying　FAN Shi-jie　QI Yan-feng

(*Weifang University of Science and Technology*, *Shouguang*　262700)

Abstract: Effects of Potassium (K) nutrition on the cotton growth and development and on the cotton leaf physiological traits were studied in the field experiment condition. Two different cultivars and four different Potassium application rates were adopted in the study. The results showed that, cotton plant height and the number of fruit-branches were increased with the use of Potassium, while the first fruit-branch' s location site was lowered and further more, the lowered degree were increased with the increasing Potassium application rates. Meanwhile, Potassium application improved the functional leaves' photosynthesis and stomatal conductance , and the parameters of Chlorophyll (chl) fluorescence such like Fv/Fo、Fv/Fm、φPS Ⅱ、ETR and qP were also increased, in contrast, the value of qN was decreased. In conclusion, proper Potassium application could enhanced the photosynthetic characteristics of functional leaf and could postpone senescence in cotton.

Key words: Potassium; Cotton; Growth and development; Physiological characteristic

昆虫病毒增效蛋白研究进展

郭 洁[①]
（潍坊科技学院，寿光 262700）

摘 要： 概述了昆虫病毒增效剂方面的研究进展，重点述及生物增效剂病毒增效蛋白的增效活性特点和增效机理，以及病毒增效蛋白分子生物学方面研究进展。已明确病毒增效蛋白增效作用与昆虫围食膜的破坏有关，其他增效机理有待进一步研究。还就增效剂的应用前景进行了展望。

关键词： 昆虫病毒；病毒增效蛋白

昆虫病原病毒具有杀虫效果专一、持久、无抗药性，对人、畜及高等植物无害等特点，并且能在害虫种群中形成流行病而长期控制虫口，从保持生态平衡和减小化学农药对环境污染战略考虑，作为生物杀虫剂的开发和应用颇具潜力。然而，病毒杀虫剂的应用尚存在以下 3 个问题：一是杀虫范围窄；二是作用速度较慢；三是杀虫效率比化学杀虫剂低，大大限制了病毒杀虫剂的大面积生产应用，目前仅占整个农药市场的 0.2%[1]。为此，如何提高天然昆虫病毒的利用效率就成了病毒研究的热点。其中，利用病毒增效蛋白，提高病毒的杀虫效果是其中研究内容之一。

1 病毒增效蛋白

来源于昆虫病毒，曾被称之为病毒促进因子、病毒增强因子（viral enhancing factor）、增强因子（enhancin）或病毒增强素（synergistic factor），现统称增效蛋白（enhancing protein）。杆状病毒增效蛋白是由某些杆状病毒基因编码的具有促进核型多角体病毒感染的一类金属蛋白酶，这种蛋白酶能增强 NPV 对体外培养细胞的感染力，还能提高苏云金杆菌（*Bacillus thuringiensis*，Bt）等其他生物杀虫剂的功效[2]。它具有酯酶活性，在颗粒体病毒、痘病毒及核型多角体病毒中均有发现[3]。Tanada（1959）首次发现美洲黏虫（*Pseudaletia unipuncta*，Pu）颗粒体病毒（granulosis virus，GV）对其核型多角体病毒（nuclear polyhedrosis virus，NPV）存在增效作用[4]，PuGV 增效蛋白的活性并不限于美洲黏虫，它也增强 PuNPV 对不同宿主的感染性。在离体条件下 PuGV 增效蛋白能增强苜蓿银纹夜蛾（*Autographa californica*，Ac）NPV、粉纹夜蛾

① 郭洁，女，硕士，讲师。潍坊科技学院研究方向：农业昆虫与害虫生物防治。E－mail：guojie0125@126.com.

(*Trichoplusia ni*, Tn) NPV、PuNPV 等病毒对草地贪夜蛾(*Spodoptera frugiperda*)Sf21 细胞的感染[5]。PuGV 增效蛋白对马尾松毛虫(*Dendrolimus punctatus*)质型多角体病毒(CPV)分别感染棉铃虫(*Helicoverpa armigera*, Ha)、马尾松毛虫也有很高的增效活性[6]。在东方黏虫(*Pseudaletia separata*, Ps)中增殖的 PuGV 对东方黏虫、棉铃虫、黄地老虎(*Agrotis segetum*)3 种夜蛾科害虫的 NPV 有显著的增效作用[7]。

自从 PuGV 中分离出增效蛋白,随后在粉纹夜蛾、棉铃虫、小菜粉蝶(*Pierisrapae*)、旋幽夜蛾(*Scotogrammatrifolli*)[8]、云杉卷夜蛾等 9 种昆虫 GV[9] 和蓓带夜蛾(*Mamestra configurata*)NPV[10]以及东方黏虫痘病毒(entomopoxvirus, EPV)中发现了增效蛋白的存在[11]。在用五月鳃金龟痘病毒(*Anomala cuprea* entomopoxvirus)进行增效试验时,发现该痘病毒的球状体和纺锤体对 BmNPV 口服毒性均有增效作用[12]。而最近在测定黏虫(Pu)痘病毒对 AcNPV 的增效作用时发现,AcNPV 能明显的增强 PuEPV 的侵染[13]。在用芹菜夜蛾核型多角体病毒(AfMNPV)和菜粉蝶颗粒体病毒(*Pieris rapae*, PrGV)混合感染 3 ~4 龄菜粉蝶幼虫时发现,AcNPV 能明显提高杀虫效果并缩短了幼虫的存活时间,表明 AfMNPV 可能对 PrGV 存在增效作用[14]。

1.1 病毒增效蛋白的增效活性

病毒间增效作用具有如下特点。

(1)增效活性包括提高杀虫活性、杀虫速度及扩大杀虫谱。例如,黏虫的痘病毒能提高黏虫核型多角体病毒的感染能力[15];AfMNPV 和 PrGV 混合侵染菜粉蝶幼虫时,缩短了幼虫的存活时间[14]。

(2)病毒增效蛋白的增效作用具有一定程度的广谱性,例如,美洲黏虫颗粒体病毒(PuGV)增效蛋白可同时提高 PuNPV 对美洲黏虫、东方黏虫 NPV 对东方黏虫,斜纹夜峨 *Spodoptera litura* NPV(S1NPV)对斜纹夜峨的感染力,但降低了家蚕 *Bombyx mori* NPV(BmNPV)对家蚕的感染力[16]。

(3)病毒增效蛋白的增效活性受其用量及存在状态(是经纯化还是存在于病毒包涵体中)、寄主昆虫龄期、被增效病毒种类等影响,例如,PuGV 对 PuNPV 的增效活性最高,PsNPV 次之,S1NPV 最低,而对 BmNPV 则无增效作用;八字地老虎 *Xestia cnigrum* GV(XcGV)在以八字地老虎 5 龄幼虫为靶标对象时对 XcNPV 有显著增效作用,在以 4 龄幼虫为对象时则无增效活性[17];PuGV 活体对 PuNPV 的增效倍数为 14 000 ~17 000倍,而纯化增效因子的增效倍数为 1 100 ~5 300倍[16]。

1.2 病毒增效蛋白的分子生物学研究

增效蛋白是由病毒基因编码的一种磷脂蛋白。在 GV 中,增效蛋白存在于包涵体包膜蛋白中,约占 GV 蛋白质的 5%。由多肽和磷脂构成,磷脂部分为卵磷脂[18],是起增效作用所必须的。进一步的研究表明,颗粒体病毒增效因子是一种金属蛋白酶[19]。增效蛋白具有金属蛋白酶活性,能降解昆虫中肠围食膜,PuGV 的增效蛋白还具有酯酶活性[2]。有报道称,用脂蛋白染色法并未检测到脂类的存在,但生物测定结果证实所提取的 PuGV 的增效蛋白对 PsNPV 北京毒株仍有很高的增效活性,并由此认为,对于增效因子的增效活性不应片面强调磷脂的作用，其活性至少是蛋白分子与磷脂协同作用的结果[20]。

在昆虫痘病毒中研究较多的是 PuEPV 增效蛋白，早期研究表明 PuEPV 增效蛋白存在于球状体，该蛋白质分子量为 38kD，是一种均一的糖蛋白，可稳定地冻存于碱液里，与颗粒体病毒增效蛋白氨基酸组成上相似，酸性氨基酸比例较高，但血清学特性与颗粒体病毒增效蛋白不同[21]。此后，通过免疫反应发现，昆虫痘病毒增效蛋白存在于昆虫痘病毒球状体和纺锤体，而不存在于来源于球状体的病毒粒子[22]。近来，李永丹等又在亚洲小车蝗（*Oedaleus asiaticus*，Oa）痘病毒发现了增效蛋白，该蛋白的分子量约为 40kD，存在于包涵体蛋白上[23]。

虽然已发现具有增效活性的核型多角体病毒，但还未提纯核型多角体病毒增效蛋白，只是发现了与颗粒体病毒增效基因有一定同源性的基因 。其中，在蓓带夜蛾（Mc-NPV）中发现的增效基因与其他增效基因在编码的氨基酸上有 20% 的同源性，表达的蛋白质分子量为 98kD，也为一种金属蛋白酶。将 McNPV 增效基因插入 AcNPV 中，获得的重组病毒对蓓带夜蛾的毒力提高了 4.4 倍。而黄地老虎 NPV （AsNPV）多角体蛋白和病毒粒子均可提高 HaNPV 的感染力和杀虫速度，免疫研究表明 AsNPV 多角体、病毒粒子和 PuGV 增强素之间无同源性，但与 HaNPv 多角体间有较高的同源性[24]。

现已测定了 8 种病毒增效基因的序列，它们分别为：PuGV，TnGV，HaGV，XcGV，云杉卷叶蛾 *Choristoneura fumiferana* NPV （CfNPV），LdMNPV，McNPV 和 PsEPV，其中，在 XcGV 和 McNPV 中分别发现了 4 个和 2 个不同的增效基因[10,25~31]。这 12 种增效基因除 XcGV E4 基因外所编码的蛋白质均具有典型的锌结合域，表明增效蛋白为一种金属蛋白酶。

不同增效蛋白的氨基酸序列在不同区域其同源性存在着较大差异，TnGV、PuGV、HaGV 3 种 GV 的增效蛋白氨基酸序列 1 ~ 550 的同源性为 89%，551 ~ 901 的同源性为 69%，表明增效蛋白 N 端的氨基酸对其生物学活性比 C 端的重要，其功能域很可能在高同源性的 N 端[32]；也曾有试验构建了分别表达 3 种 N 端部分缺失的 TnGV 增强蛋白的重组杆状病毒，这 3 种蛋白在 N 端分别缺失了 150、186 和 250 个氨基酸。用重组病毒感染 Tn5B14 细胞，成功地表达了这 3 种蛋白，并得到了纯化的蛋白质。通过体外降解围食膜的方法检测这些部分缺失的增强蛋白的活性，结果证实，这 3 种蛋白均失去了增强蛋白的降解围食膜黏蛋白的活性。这一结果表明，增强蛋白的 N 端对其降解围食膜黏蛋白的功能是必需的[33]。

1.3 病毒增效蛋白的作用机理

目前研究认为，增效蛋白主要通过两种方式达到增效作用：一是发挥金属蛋白酶的活性，降解昆虫中肠围食膜上的肠粘蛋白和糖蛋白，从而破坏围食膜的物理屏障，使病毒粒子更易进入中肠细胞，增加病毒的相对感染量；二是改变中肠围食膜的通透性和孔径大小，使毒力蛋白和病毒粒子更易通过围食膜，感染宿主昆虫[34~36]。

自然界的病毒传染主要经口进入昆虫肠道，释放出病毒粒子。由于昆虫前肠、后肠内壁有角质层护膜，病毒只能从中肠入侵[37]。中肠上皮细胞与肠腔之间有一层围食膜

（Peritrophic membrane，PM），是由中肠细胞分泌的非细胞结构，主要由蛋白质、糖和几丁质构成，无孔和缝[38~40]，是防止微生物入侵及物质对中肠细胞磨损的一道屏障。它是由几丁质排列的规则或不规则的网络结构，其间有多种蛋白与其相连。

对增效因子的作用方式研究主要集中在蛋白分子对宿主昆虫 PM 的影响[41~42]，认为增效因子作为破坏围食膜的蛋白水解酶，增大围食膜的孔径从而增加对病毒的通透性。王平等鉴定了 TnGV 增效蛋白的作用底物——粉纹夜蛾幼虫中肠围食膜一种蛋白：粘蛋白（Mucin），并克隆了粘蛋白的 cDNA 和分析了其序列[43]。在离体条件下对围食膜渗透性的影响和作用试验表明，TnGV 增效蛋白能够改变和提高围食膜对包括 AcMNPV 病毒粒子等标记分子的渗透性。离体状态下，增效蛋白并不增加 AcMNPV 病毒粒子与粉纹夜蛾幼虫中肠细胞连接与融合[36]。

袁哲明等用大肠杆菌表达的粉纹夜蛾颗粒体病毒重组增效蛋白 P96[44]，可显著或极显著提高棉铃虫核型多角体病毒、苏云金杆菌和阿维菌素对棉铃虫幼虫的致死率，对苜蓿丫纹夜蛾核型多角体病毒感染甜菜夜蛾幼虫也有明显增效作用[45]。相关报道还有 TnGV 增效因子 C 末端片段[46]、HaGV 增效蛋白基因 5′端截短的 21kb[11]、17 和 22kb 片段[32]、全长的 HaGV 基因[47,48]、Ps 痘病毒增效蛋白基因[49]。以上报道均显示了明显的增效活性，其作用机理主要是通过降解宿主中肠围食膜上的肠粘蛋白，使病毒等病原微生物更易进入幼虫中肠细胞[36]。

2 病毒增效剂的应用展望

增效蛋白能够增加病毒对昆虫的感染力，且可通过双重方式起作用，在实践应用中具有极广阔的前景，因而倍受关注。增效蛋白可通过以下 4 种途径进行应用。

首先，将增效蛋白纯化后与病毒制剂混合施用，或直接将具有增效作用的两种病毒组合混用，在田间可达到提高病毒杀虫效果的目的。

其次，将增效蛋白基因重组到杆状病毒基因组中，获得高效的重组病毒。目前已有的研究结果表明，带有增效蛋白基因的重组病毒，其杀虫效果较野生型病毒的杀虫效果有明显提高。

再次，将增效蛋白基因转入目的植物中。其在植物体内的表达既可解决转基因植物的抗性问题，也可提高田间病毒制剂的杀虫效果。

最后，将增效蛋白基因导入 Bt 等细菌或其他真菌中构建工程菌，利用增效蛋白对 Bt 有增效作用的特点及 Bt 等可大规模发酵生产、成本低、生产技术成熟等特点，解决病毒制剂不能大规模生产和易失效的问题。

参考文献

[1] 郭慧芳，方继朝，韩召军．昆虫学报［J］．2003，46（6）：766－772

[2] 马永平，欧洋，孟小林等．中国病毒学［J］．1999，14（3）：185－189

[3] 刘平，孟小林，徐进平等．中国生物防治［J］．1999，15（4）：188－189

[4] Tanada Y，Descriptions and characteristics of a nuclearpolyhedrosis virus and a granulosis

virus of the armyworm, Pseudaletia unipuncta (Haworth) (Lepidoptera, Noctuidae) [J]. Insect Pathol, 1959, 1: 197 -214

[5] 彭建新，杨红，洪华珠. 中国生物防治 [J]. 2000, 16 (2): 87 -91

[6] 刘强，丁翠. 应用与环境生物学报 [J]. 1999, 5 (3): 300 -304

[7] 刘强. 粘虫颗粒体病毒增效因子的研究 [D]. 北京: 中国科学院北京动物研究所, 1998

[8] Roelvink P W, Corsaro B G, Grandos R R. Journal of General Virology [J]. 1995, 76: 269 -270

[9] 洪靖君，段家龙，彭辉银. 中国病毒学 [J]. 2002, 17 (3): 270 -275

[10] Li Q, Li L, Moore K, Donly C, Theilmann D A, Erlandson M. Characterization of Mamestra configurata nueleopolyhedrovirus enhanein and its functional analysis via expression in an Autographa californica M nucleopo lyhedmvirus recombinant [J]. Gen. Virol, 2003, 84: 123 -132

[11] 欧洋，孟小林，徐进平. 生物工程学报 [J]. 2000, 16 (5): 595 -598

[12] Furta Y, Mitsuhashi W, Kobayashi J, Hayasaka S, Imanishi Y, Chinzei Y, Sato M. Peroral infectivity of non-occluded viruses of Bombyx mori nucleopolyhedrovirus and polyhedron-negative recombinant baculoviruses to silkworm larvae is drastically enhanced when administered with Anomata cuprea entomopoxvirus spindles [J]. General Virology, 2001, 82: 307 -312

[13] 李国勋，郭巍，李长友等. 苜蓿丫纹夜蛾核型多角体病毒增效作用的研究 [J]. 走向21世纪的中国昆虫学, 1072 -1076

[14] 王晓容，匡石滋. 2种昆虫病毒混合悬液对菜粉蝶的增效作用 [J]. 华中农业大学学报, 2005, 24 (1): 21 -24

[15] Xu J, Hukuhara T. Biochemical properties of an enhancing factor of an entomopoxvirus. Inverteb Pathol [J]. 1994, 63 (1): 14 -18

[16] Hukuhara T, Tamura K, Zhu Y F. Synergistic factor shows specificity in enhancing nuclear polyhedrosis virus infections [J]. Appl. Ent. Zool, 1987, 22 (2): 235 -236

[17] Goto C. Enhancement of a nuclear polyhedrosis virus (NPV) infection by a granulosis virus (GV) isoloated from the spotted cutworm, Xestia c-nigrum L. (Lepidoptera: Noctuidae) [J]. Appl. Ent. Zool., 1990, 25 (1): 135 -137

[18] Kozuma K, Hukuhara T. Invertebr Pathol [D]. 1992, 59: 328

[19] Lepore L, Roelvink P R, Granados R R. Enhancin. the granulosis virus protein that facilitates nucleopolyhedrovirus (NPV) infections. is a metalloprotease [J]. Invertebr. Pathol, 1996, 68: 131 -140

[20] 刘强，丁翠，蔡秀玉. 病毒学报 [J]. 1998, 14 (4): 352 -358

[21] Xu J H, Hukuhara T. Biological prope rties of an enh an cing factor of an entomopoxvirus [J]. Invenebr Pathol, 1994, 68 (1): 14 -18

[22] Wijonarko A, Hukuhara T. Detection of a virus enhancing factor in the spheroid. Spin-

dle. and virion of an entomopoxvirus [J]. Invenebr Pathol, 1998, 72 (1): 82 -86

[23] 李永丹，赵朝阳，王丽英．亚洲小车蝗痘病毒增效因子的初步研究 [J]．中国病毒学，2003，18 (5)：478 -481

[24] 白小东，丁翠．黄地老虎 NPV 增效作用的研究 [J]．应用环境与生物学报，2000，6 (1)：52 -55

[25] Bischoff D S, Slavicek J M. Molecular analysis of an enhancin gene in the Lymantra diapar nuclear polyhedrosis virus [J]. virol. , 1997, 71: 8 133 -8 140

[26] Holly J R, David S B, James M S. Both Lymantria dispar nucleopolyhedrovirus enhancin genes contribute to viral potency [J]. Virol, 2001, 75 (18): 8 639 -8 648

[27] Hashimoto Y, Corsaro B G. Location and nucleotide sequence of the gene encoding the viral enhancing factor of the Trichoplusia ni granulosisvirus [J]. Gen. Virol. , 1991, 72: 2 645 -2 651

[28] Hayakawa T, Xu J H, Hukuhara T. Cloning and sequencing of the gene for an enhancing factor from Pseudaletia separata entomopoxvirus [J]. Gene, 1996, 177: 269 -270

[29] Hayakawa T, Ko R, Okano K, Seong S L, Goto C, Maeda S. Sequence analysis of the Xestia c-nigrum granulosis virus genome [J]. Virology, 1999, 262: 277 -297

[30] 刘强，叶寅，白小东等．粘虫颗粒体病毒增效因子的基因定位 [J]．昆虫学报，2001，44 (2)：148 -154

[31] Roelvink PW, Corsaro BG, Granados R R. Characterization of the Hclicoverpa armigera and Pseudaletia unipuncta granulovirus enhancin Genes [J]. Gen. 1irol, 1995, 2 693 -2 705

[32] 刘相国，杨恭，邱并生等．微生物学报 [J]．2001，41 (2)：167 -172

[33] 李志广，尹隽，钟江．中国病毒学 [D]．2002，17 (4)：326 -330

[34] WangP, Hammer DA, Granados RR. Interaction of Trichoplusia ni granulosis virus- encoded enhancing with the midgut epithelium and peritrophic membrane of four lepidoteran insects [J]. Gen Virol, 1994, 75: 1 961 -1 967

[35] Peng J, Zhong J, Granados RR. A baculovirus enhancing alters the permeability of a mucosal midgut peritrophic matrix from Lepidopteran larvae [J]. Insectc physiol, 1999, 45: 159 -166

[36] Wang P, Granados RR. An intestinal mucin is the target substrate for a baculovirus enhancin [J]. Proc Natl. Acad Sci (USA), 1997, 94: 6 977 -6 982

[37] Hukuhara T, Wijonarko A. Enhanced fusion of a nucleopolyhedrovirus with cultured cell by a virus enhancing factor from an entomopoxvirus [J]. Invertebr Pathol. 2007, 77 (1): 62 -67

[38] Richarads A G, Richards P A. The peritrophic membrane of insect [J]. Ann. Rev. Entomol, 1977, 22: 219 -240

[39] Santos C D, Terra W R. Distribution and characteristic of oligomeric digestive enzyme

from Erinnyis ello larvae and inference concern secretary and the peritrophic membrane [J]. Insect Biochem, 2006, 16 (4): 691 - 700

[40] Spence K D, Kawata M Y. Permeability characteristics of the peritrophic membrane of Manduca Sexta larvae [J]. Insect physiol, 1993, 39 (9): 785 - 790

[41] Hara S, Tanada Y, Omi EM. Isolation and characterization of a synergistic enzyme from the capsule of a granulosis virus of the army worm, Pseudaletia unipuncta [J]. Inverteb Pathol, 2006, 27: 115 - 124

[42] LeporeL S, Roelvink P R, Granados RR. Inhancin, the granulosis virus protein that facilitate nucleopolyhedrovirus (NPV) infection is a metalloprotease [J]. Inverteb Pathol, 1996, 68: 131 - 140

[43] Wang P, Hammer DA, Granados RR. Binding and fusion of Autographa californica nucleopolyhedrovirus to cultured insect cells [J]. Gen Virol, 1997, 78: 3 081 - 3 089

[44] 袁哲明，孟小林，刘树生．粉纹夜蛾颗粒体病毒增效基因 3′端 2. kb 片段在大肠杆菌中的表达 [J]．昆虫学报，2001，44 (2)：155 - 160

[45] 袁哲明，孟小林，昆虫病毒重组增效蛋白的广谱增效活性 [J]．中国生物防治，2004，20 (1)：31 - 33

[46] 刘平，孟小林，徐进平等．中国生物防治 [J]．1999，15 (4)：188 - 189

[47] 刘相国，杨恭，邱并生等．微生物学报 [J]．2000，40 (4)：379 - 383

[48] 胡蓉，孟小林，徐进平等．中国病毒学 [J]．2001，16 (4)：364 - 368

[49] 袁哲明，孟小林，刘树生．中国病毒学（杀虫微生物专刊）[J]．2000，15：55 - 60

Research Progress of Insect Viral Enhancing Protein

GUO Jie

(*Weifang University of Science and Technology*, *Shouguang* 262700)

Abstract: This paper summarized the recent advances in insect viral enhancing factor, including the enhancing characteristics and mechanism of viral enhancing, a biological characteristics from insect viruses, It has been confirmed that the destruction of peritrophic membrane contributed to the enhancement of viral infectivity by viral enhancing protein. Other mechanism related to the nhancement needs fur—ther study. Finally the use of insect virus synergists was discussed.

Key words: Insect virus; Viral enhancing protein

中国农作物秸秆资源及其在设施栽培中的应用

亓延凤[①] 郭 英

（潍坊科技学院，寿光 262700）

摘 要： 秸秆是农作物生产系统中一项重要的生物资源。中国是世界上秸秆资源最为丰富的国家之一。论文介绍了中国农作物秸秆的资源及其应用现状，阐述了作物秸秆在设施栽培中的利用途径和效果，并简要分析了未来的应用前景和当前存在的主要问题。

关键词： 作物秸秆；中国；设施栽培

作物秸秆是农作物生产系统中的一项重要的生物资源，秸秆还田（包括直接还田和腐解还田）、栽培基质（包括种植食用菌）、饲料、燃料、制造燃气或作为其他工业原料等都是秸秆利用的有效途径。秸秆利用涉及到农作物废弃资源再利用、水土保持以及环境安全等可持续发展问题，因此已引起世界各国的普遍关注，对其进行合理开发和利用成为发展可持续农业的重要方面[1,2]。

1 中国农作物秸秆资源及其利用概况

中国是一个农业大国，也是秸秆资源最为丰富的国家之一。秸秆是农作物的主要副产品，也是十分宝贵的生物资源，其中，碳、氧、氢 3 种化学成分总和占 95 %以上，其余为钾、氮、磷、硅、钙、镁、硫等矿质元素；有机成分以纤维素、半纤维素为主，其次为木质素、蛋白质、脂肪、灰分等。资料表明，2000 年，中国的秸秆资源总量达到 5.541×10^8t[3]。近年来，随着农作物单产的提高，秸秆产量还在不断增加，平均每年以 1251.2×10^4t 的速度增长[28]。中国的秸秆资源以水稻、玉米和小麦秸秆为主，约占秸秆资源总量的 76.1%，其中，水稻秸秆最多，占秸秆总量的 31.6%，其次是玉米和小麦，分别占秸秆总量的 23.9% 和 21.6%，杂粮、油菜和豆类作物秸秆所占比例只有 4.1%、3.8% 和 2.7%[3]。随着种植业结构调整，经济作物秸秆的比重有所增加。从地理分布上讲，稻秸主要分布于中南、华东地区及西南的部分省份；玉米秸主要分布于东北、华北地区及华东和中南的部分省份；小麦秸秆主要分布在华东、中南和华北等

---

① 亓延凤，女，硕士，潍坊科技学院讲师。研究方向：蔬菜栽培。E－mail：saduyanfeng@163.com

地区[2]。

中国自古就有利用秸秆的优良传统。在传统农业阶段，秸秆主要是被直接用作肥料、燃料或饲料。随着传统农业向现代化农业转变、经济社会发展和科技进步，秸秆利用途径也发生了很大转变。现阶段中国秸秆资源的利用途径主要包括肥料、饲料、燃料、原料等，另有相当部分的秸秆被焚烧和弃置。从表 1 中可以看出，目前的秸秆资源以作为肥料利用（包括直接还田）的数量最多，占秸秆总量的 36.6%，其次是燃料和饲料，分别占秸秆资源的 23.7% 和 22.6%，焚烧和弃置乱堆占 17%[3]。小麦、水稻、玉米等作物秸秆主要是用作肥料。

表 1　各种秸秆利用方式占秸秆资源总量的百分数[3]（%）

作物	肥料	饲料	燃料	原料	焚烧	弃置乱堆	合计
小麦	40.2	14.3	20.3	8.3	9.0	7.9	100.0
玉米	32.2	27.1	24.7	1.8	5.4	8.9	100.0
水稻	41.7	16.2	25.5	5.6	7.8	3.1	100.0
杂粮	11.5	67.8	10.5	2.8	1.0	6.4	100.0
油菜	34.1	20.4	26.6	1.0	12.5	5.4	100.0
棉花	16.0	15.5	56.6	4.4	2.3	5.3	100.0
花生	26.0	41.5	23.0	1.0	0.7	7.7	100.0
豆类	16.8	34.4	41.6	1.2	1.9	4.1	100.0
其他	47.6	27.5	14.6	1.1	3.7	5.5	100.0
合计	36.6	22.6	23.7	4.4	6.6	6.1	100.0

现阶段，中国秸秆资源的利用仍存在利用率与利用效率低的问题。一方面相当数量的秸秆被焚烧或弃置，浪费了资源，污染了环境；另一方面，大部分秸秆未经任何技术处理直接利用，处理后加以利用的比例尚少，仅占 2.6%[28]。合理利用秸秆资源，对于保护生态环境，促进农业生产可持续发展具有重要意义。中国政府对此高度重视，近年来，无论是对基础研究，还是应用开发，都从资金、政策等方面给予大力扶持，极大地促进了秸秆资源的综合利用。近年来发展起来的秸秆优质化能源利用技术，以及其他工业化利用技术，都具有很好的发展潜力[2]。

2　作物秸秆在中国设施栽培中的应用

2.1　中国设施农业发展概况

中国设施栽培历史悠久，但是直到 20 世纪 80 年代后期才开始快速发展起来，目前已初步形成了具有中国特色的设施生产体系，成为世界上设施栽培面积最大的国家。设施结构和装备由简单到复杂，功能由单一到综合，管理由粗放到集约。随着经济发展、科技进步和社会需求多元化，设施利用已由单纯的蔬菜栽培拓展到花卉、林果、药用植物、大田作物栽培以及水产养殖、畜禽饲养等诸多领域。

2004 年，中国的设施蔬菜面积已经发展到 253.7 万 hm^2，但设施花卉面积只有 2.87 万 hm^2，设施果树面积只有 7.87 万 hm^2。在各类设施中，温室和大拱棚面积约占设施总面积的65%。中国的温室以日光温室为主体，其中，80%以上为节能型日光温室。现代化大型连栋温室由于建造投资和运行成本较高，在中国发展缓慢，至 2003 年底只有 1 000hm^2左右。

无土栽培是一项重要的设施栽培技术，中国自 20 世纪 70 年代后期开始在生产中推广应用。由于无土栽培具有高产优质高效、节约肥水和劳动力、克服温室连作障碍、不受地域限制、易于实现工厂化和自动化等优点，近年来在中国得到了较为快速的发展。截至2005 年，中国的无土栽培面积已超过1 250hm^2，并呈现加速度发展的趋势，其中，绝大多数为基质培，以有机生态型为主，玉米等作物的秸秆得到了初步应用。

2.2 作物秸秆在设施栽培中的应用及其效果

2.2.1 作为肥料

秸秆含有丰富的有机质和矿质营养，为土壤微生物繁殖与活动提供了重要的环境保障，有助于以细菌为主导的各类土壤微生物的相对均衡生长，对加速土壤有机体分解，提高有机质含量，促进养分转化具有重要作用[4,5]。作为肥料进行秸秆还田主要有两种方式[28]，一种是直接还田，包括粉碎还田、整秆还田及覆盖栽培还田；另一种是间接还田，包括堆沤还田、烧灰还田、过腹还田、菇渣和沼渣还田等。秸秆堆沤还田也称高温堆肥，是解决有机肥源短缺的主要途径。目前，已由传统的高温堆沤发展到添加微生物菌种或加快秸秆腐熟的化学制剂进行堆沤，缩短了沤制时间，提高了堆沤效果[26]。近年来，相继出现了一些专门的有机肥制造厂家，利用高新技术进行菌种的培养和繁殖，通过专用设备控制温度、湿度和时间，经机械翻抛、高温堆腐、生物发酵等过程，将秸秆转化成优质的有机肥，具有自动化程度高、腐熟周期短、产量和肥效高等特点。

施用作物秸秆可以增加土壤腐殖质组分中新鲜的有机质，提高全氮、全磷、全钾和速效 N、P、K 含量，增强土壤的供肥能力[5,6,26]，尤其对于瘠薄、缺钾土壤是一条培肥地力的有效途径。单纯施用氮、磷化肥容易造成土壤硫素缺乏和亏损，而施用秸秆却可以在某种程度上延缓土壤硫素下降，甚至提高速效硫和有机硫含量，并且未腐熟玉米秸秆直接还田优于腐熟玉米秸秆还田[7]。秸秆还田还能提高土壤微量元素的含量，如施用玉米秸秆能提高土壤中有效锌、锰、铁、铜含量[8]。

2.2.2 作为栽培基质

岩棉、草炭在无土栽培基质中占有重要地位，但从 20 世纪后期，世界各国从环境保护和资源可持续利用出发，都在寻找其可替代的资源，其中，有机废弃物利用成为研究的热点。农业废弃物是可资源化利用的有机废弃物中最理想的材料，不但富含作物生长所必需的各类营养元素，而且基本没有城市垃圾中的重金属污染等。可供利用的农业废弃物主要有作物秸秆、树皮、稻壳、椰壳等。Jespersen[10]研究发现，将腐熟有机废弃物（水貂粪、牛粪、麦秸和鲜木片）按20%～40%的体积比与泥炭混合，其栽培效果优于或近于泥炭。在中国南方一些地区，应用炭化稻壳、椰壳纤维等废弃资源作为栽培基质已经相当成熟和普遍[11,12]。北方地区将玉米秸、稻秸用于无土栽培和育苗过程也有报道[13,26]。由于秸秆基质容重偏小，大小孔隙比偏大，因此，多数是作为复合基质的组分加以利用，与重型基质材料复配可显著改善其物理性状，主要研究方向包括秸秆处理、秸秆与其他材料的配比、秸秆基质理化性状及其在栽培过程中变化。

2.2.3 改良设施土壤

农作物秸秆还田是补充和平衡土壤养分、改良土壤的有效方法。秸秆富含纤维素、半纤维素等物质，施入土壤后，改善了土壤中的C/N，为微生物的活动提供了丰富的碳源和氮源，使微生物区系、数量发生很大变化[19,21]。土壤微生物的活动直接影响到土壤的物理、化学和生物学性状，在养分供给、肥料有效利用、有害生物防治及土壤保持等方面起着重要作用。研究发现，施用作物秸秆可增加土壤中的放线菌和真菌数，但亚硝酸细菌、硝酸细菌、反硝化细菌数随秸秆用量增加而减少，从而可有效地抑制硝化作用和反硝化作用，降低土壤有效氮损失，减轻由硝化、反硝化作用产生的NO_2^-、N_2O所带来的环境污染[16]。

土壤中所进行的一切生物和化学过程都需要由酶的催化作用才能完成。水解酶类，包括脲酶、磷酸酶、纤维素酶和转化酶等，对土壤肥力具有更重要的作用[17]。施用作物秸秆可提高脲酶、磷酸酶、纤维素酶和转化酶活性，但不同作物秸秆的效应存在一定差异，玉米根茬优于大豆根茬[18]。

设施生产具有高度集约化、复种指数高和作物种类单一等特点，随着种植年限的增加，容易引起连作障碍，土壤理化和生物学性状恶化，土传病虫害加重，作物产量和品质下降。对设施连作土壤的改良和连作障碍的综合治理近年来为中国的研究人员所关注[19,20]。研究表明，施用未腐熟作物秸秆能明显增加连作土壤的有机质和孔隙度，降低土壤容重和电导度，改善其理化性质，减缓次生盐渍化，促进蔬菜生长发育[15]。同时，施用秸秆还可改善微生物群体结构，抑制病原微生物的活动，减轻连作障碍[21]。

在一些设施栽培主产区，为减轻连作障碍的危害，通过秸秆利用达到了土壤消毒和施肥的双重效果。方法是在夏季高温休闲季节，将石灰氮（氰铵化钙）和碎麦草混合施入温室土壤中，然后深翻、起垄、浇水、覆膜、密闭，高温处理15d以上，可杀灭多种土传病虫害。

2.2.4 改善生态环境

冬季设施环境的突出特点是低温、弱光、高湿，以及CO_2亏缺。郭卫华等[22]研究表明，将稻草和膨化鸡粪按适当比例配合撒施可以提高番茄叶绿素含量，增强光合作用，并显著提高产量。而且，稻草的持续分解可使温室内CO_2在生育后期仍能保持较高浓度，满足长季节栽培条件下番茄生长发育对CO_2的需求。然而，不同稻草施入方法对温室CO_2的影响不同，土壤深埋优于均匀散施和地表覆盖[24]。近年来，一种秸秆的高效利用技术——“秸秆反应堆”技术，在设施生产中得到较大面积的开发。该法利用作物秸秆等材料，接上适宜菌种后进行发酵，酵解过程中产生的CO_2、热量和微生物孢子等可提高设施内CO_2的浓度，增加气温和地温，减轻病虫为害，改善生长环境，促进作物生长发育[26]。

秸秆地表覆盖还能提高土壤总孔隙度和毛管孔隙度，提高土壤的导水率和蓄水能力，减少土表水分蒸发，增加土壤湿度，降低空气湿度，协调水、气、热矛盾，促进作物生育。秸秆是热的不良导体，在覆盖情况下能够调节土壤温度，形成低温时的“高温效应”和高温时的“低温效应”，缓解气温骤变对作物的伤害，并有利于设施作物栽植后的缓苗和前期生长[27]。

3　作物秸秆在设施栽培中的应用前景和问题

中国农作物秸秆资源丰富，具有利用秸秆的优良传统，尤其是近些年来，越来越多的研究人员开始致力于作物秸秆资源利用方面的研究和开发，取得了显著成效。未来中国农业的发展，必须走资源节约型、可持续发展的道路，设施农业也不例外。中国现已成为世界上设施栽培面积最大的国家，为秸秆资源利用提供了广阔的空间，这将有利于实现高产优质高效和可持续发展。到目前为止，秸秆在设施栽培中的应用，无论数量和比例都较低，发展速度相对较慢。分析原因主要有以下几方面。(1) 秸秆处理、加工的技术和设备尚不成熟和完善，作物秸秆利用的基础研究、工程设备和技术水平与一些发达国家相比尚存一定差距。秸秆利用多数仍沿用传统的方法，缺乏具有自主知识产权、适应性能好、推广价值高的先进技术，长期困扰其发展的根本问题没有得到解决。(2) 中国秸秆资源虽然丰富，但分布不均匀，种类和来源多样，自身特性和应用效果不同，受到多种因素的影响，制约了秸秆资源化利用的步伐。(3) 秸秆的收集和工厂化处理是秸秆综合利用的一条新途径，但收集相对困难，操作不便，成本较高。秸秆还田劳动强度大，费时费工。秸秆再利用总体效益较低，农民缺乏积极性和主动性。(4) 秸秆中富含纤维素、半纤维素和木质素，在土壤中分解转化时间较长，给操作管理带来不便。腐解过程中易造成土壤微生物与作物争氮，影响作物生长发育。设施土壤复种指数高，倒茬时间短，给秸秆还田带来了困难。(5) 近年来，无土栽培虽然得到快速发展，但社会化进程较慢，设备、技术水平尚低，基质生产作为一个产业只是刚刚出现。未来无土栽培，尤其是有机基质培在中国将会有更大的发展潜力，为秸秆的设施应用拓展了空间。

加快秸秆的综合利用，一方面要加大宣传，把保护自然资源、防止环境污染确立为综合利用的主导思想，提高对秸秆利用价值的认识；另一方面，必须加强秸秆利用的基础和应用研究，注重引进、消化吸收国外先进的技术和设备，提高作物秸秆利用的技术水平。同时，注重研究和探索以科技为依托、市场为导向、产业化的秸秆综合利用路子。

参考文献

[1] 全国农业技术推广服务中心. 中国有机肥料资源 [J]. 北京: 中国农业出版社, 1999: 121-139

[2] 韩鲁佳, 闫巧娟, 刘向阳等. 中国农作物秸秆资源及其利用现状 [J]. 农业工程学报, 2002, 18 (3): 87-91

[3] 高祥照, 马文奇, 马常宝等. 中国作物秸秆资源利用现状分析 [J]. 华中农业大学学报, 2002, 21 (3): 242-247

[4] 蔡晓布, 钱成, 张元等. 西藏中部地区退化土壤秸秆还田的微生物变化特征及其影响 [J]. 应用生态学报, 2004, 15 (3): 463-168

[5] 吴志杰, 张海军, 许广山等. 玉米秸秆还田培肥土壤的效果 [J]. 应用生态学报, 2002, 13 (5): 539-542

[6] 朱林, 彭宇, 袁飞. 施用稻草等有机物料对黄瓜连作土壤速效养分的影响 [J]. 中国农学通报, 2001, 17 (2): 30-36

[7] 颜丽, 关连珠, 祝凤春. 玉米秸秆配施化肥对土壤钾、硫养分的调节作用 [J]. 土壤通报, 1994, 25 (7): 61-63

[8] 陈丽荣, 姜岩. 玉米秸秆及其根茬不同分解时间对土壤有效微量元素的影响 [J]. 吉林农业科学, 2000, 25 (6): 23-25

[9] Jespersen L M. Production of compost in a heat compoating plant and test of compost mixtures as growing media for greenhouse culture [J]. Acta Hort. 1993, 342: 127-142

[10] 张德威等. 几种无土栽培基质的理化性质 [J]. 浙江农业学报, 1993, 5 (3): 166-171

[11] 邹志荣. 玉米芯预腐熟温度和时间对黄瓜幼苗生长的影响 [J]. 陕西农业科学, 1993, 8 (1): 10-11

[12] 齐维强, 贺超兴, 张志斌等. 施用秸秆有机肥对温室番茄生长发育的影响初探 [J]. 陕西农业科学, 2003, 5 (2), (6): 3-5

[13] 宋述尧. 玉米秸秆还田对塑料大棚蔬菜连作土壤改良效果研究 [J]. 农业工程学报, 1997, 13 (1): 135-139

[14] 殷永娴, 张春兰, 姚惠琳. 增施秸秆对蔬菜保护地土壤微生物的影响 [J]. 土壤通报, 1996, 27 (5): 239

[15] 宋日, 吴春胜, 牟金明等. 玉米根茬留田对土壤微生物量碳和酶活性动态变化特征的影响 [J]. 应用生态学报, 2002, 13 (3): 303-306

[16] 牟金明, 宋日, 姜亦梅等. 不同作物根茬还田对土壤酶活性的影响 [J]. 吉林农业大学学报, 1997, 19 (4): 65-69

[17] 朱林, 张春兰, 沈其荣. 施用稻草等有机物料对黄瓜连作土壤 pH、EC 值和微生物的影响 [J]. 安徽农业大学学报, 2001, 28 (4): 350-353

[18] 于占东, 宋述尧. 稻草配施生物菌剂对大棚连作土壤的改良作用 [J]. 农业工程学报, 2003, 19 (1): 177~179

[19] 袁飞，彭宇，张春兰等．有机物料减轻设施连作黄瓜苗期病害的微生物效应［J］．应用生态学报，2004，15（5）：867－870

[20] 郭卫华，李天来．有机质配施对日光温室 CO_2 浓度及番茄生理的影响［J］．园艺学报，2003，30（5）：592－594

[21] 武春成，曹霞，齐明芳等．稻草不同施入方法对温室土壤主要环境因子的影响［J］．沈阳农业大学学报，2006，37（3）：528－530

[22] 朱德文，陈永生，程三六．我国设施农业发展存在的问题与对策研究［J］．农业装备技术，2007，2（3）：34－35

[23] 金伊洙，郝翠翠，齐心等．稻草秸秆穴盘育苗基质对辣椒秧苗质量的影响［J］．吉林农业科学，2005，30（2）：23－24

[24] 曹启光，陈怀谷．稻秸秆覆盖田小麦根际和非根际土壤中细菌多态性及其拮抗物质的分析［D］．华东植物病理学术研讨会论文集，2005，12（7）：21－22

[25] 卜玉山，苗果园，周乃健等．地膜和秸秆覆盖土壤肥力效应分析与比较［J］．中国农业科学，2006，39（5）：1 069－1 075

[26] 陈泮江，车献水，刘志刚等．秸秆生物发酵综合利用日光温室蔬菜效益显著［J］．中国蔬菜，2005，22（1）：22－23

[27] 高新昊．农作物秸秆资源化利用及日光温室番茄长季节栽培肥水管理技术［J］．南京农业大学，2006，12（2）：17－18

[28] 刘丽香，吴承祯，洪伟等．农作物秸秆综合利用的进展［J］．亚热带农业研究，2006，2（5）：13－14

Application of Crop Residues in Protected Cultivation in China

QI Yan-feng　GUO Ying

(*Weifang University of Science and Technology*, *Shouguang*　262700)

Abstract: China is a country with abundant crop residue resources and the largest area of protected cultivation in the world. The resources of crop residues in China and their application status are briefly introduced in this paper. Aimed at the reuse of agricultural waste resources and the sustainable development of protected cultivation, the utilization and effects of crop residues under protected cultivation are presented. The future prospects and current problems of crop residue application have also been analyzed.

Key words: Crop straw; Soil amendment; Organic fertilizer; Growing media; Agricultural waste

植物无籽果实发生机理研究综述

祝海燕[①] 肖万里
（潍坊科技学院，寿光 262700）

摘 要： 无籽果实以其含糖量高，口感好，食用方便等优点一直深受人们的喜爱。但无籽果实发生的机理并不都是一样的，本文从两大方面阐述了无籽果实产生的原因，望对植物无籽果实新品种的研究培育提供理论依据。
关键词： 无籽果实；单性结实；胚乳培养；三倍体果实；无核基因

植物的祖先大都是靠种子繁殖的，但是由于种种原因，个别植株或枝条发生变异，使子房没有经过授粉受精而发育成果实或授粉受精后胚发育中途停止，从而结出无籽果实，人类在实践活动中发现了这些无籽果实，就采用营养繁殖的方式栽培保存下来，形成了无籽品种。

无籽果实以其含糖量高，口感好，食用方便等优点一直深受人们的喜爱。例如，世界上所消费的葡萄80%以上是无籽的。为了满足市场经济和人民的需求，除了大自然的恩赐之外，我们要加大对无籽果实的研究，应用现代的科学知识和技术，培育出品种更多的无籽瓜果。

1 用传统方法生产无籽果实

1.1 单性结实

从植物本身的遗传特性来说，植物的开花结果，大多要经过传粉，受精等一系列过程。但一些植物由于长期的自然演化变异，不用传粉受精，或者只需花粉或激素的刺激，不需进行受精，就能结出正常的果实，这种现象在植物学上称为单性结实[1]。由于单性结实未经受精，所以，产生的果实就没有种子，即为无籽果实。

1.1.1 天然单性结实

在自然条件下，子房不经过授粉受精而发育成果实称为天然单性结实或自发性单性结实。如柑橘，葡萄，柠檬，柿子，黄瓜，茄子等。我们知道，植物果实的膨大需要种

① 祝海燕，女，硕士，潍坊科技学院讲师。研究方向：蔬菜遗传育种。E－mail：zhuhaiyan1978@126.com

子形成过程中合成的大量生长素的刺激，只有在这些生长素的作用下，子房才能发育成果实[2~3]。那么，这些无籽果实的子房又是如何发育成果实的呢？祁业凤认为，种子并非果实生长所需的激素的全部来源，果肉生长激素的来源除自身合成外，发育着的茎、嫩叶和根也可为其提供一定量的激素[4]。并且大量的研究也表明，天然单性结实的果实子房内含有较高的生长素，并在开花前就已开始积累，开花后期子房中也合成了较多的生长素，因此，不经过授粉受精子房就可以直接发育成果实[5]。王玖瑞在研究枣可育品种与败育品种中胚珠及果肉激素含量的变化时发现，在枣硬核期前后胚的败育与否直接关系到了胚与果肉所含激素的浓度 。胚发生败育的枣，果肉内所含的 IAA、GA_3、ZT 等明显高于核内的胚。且无种子果实果肉中激素的含量高于有种子果实果肉中的激素含量，从而使得果肉生长和竞争营养的能力强于幼胚造成胚败育[6]，形成了无籽果实。据测定无核柑橘品种子房内生长素含量比有核品种的也高很多。

1.1.2 刺激性单性结实

子房在花粉，外界环境条件或外援激素的刺激下，不经过受精而发育成果实的现象称为刺激性单性结实或人工单性结实。例如，霜害可引起无籽梨的形成，较低温度和较高光照可诱导番茄产生无籽果实，而瓜类在短日照和较低的夜温下易产生无籽果实。这可能是因为低温或霜害抑制了胚珠的正常受精所致。

利用某些生长物质处理，可人工诱发单性结实。早在 1935 年，美国植物生理学家贾斯塔弗逊，用人工合成的萘乙酸等植物激素，第一次魔术般地使番茄，茄子，辣椒，西葫芦获得了单性结实的无籽果实，使植物激素成为了诱导无籽瓜果的“点金术”。现在，农业生产上这一技术已十分普遍。例如，用生长素处理茄子、甜椒、黄瓜、番茄都能形成无籽果实，而苹果、桃、梨、葡萄的无籽果实需用赤霉素进行处理才能形成[7~8]。这种方法得到的无籽特性是不能遗传的，所以，每次都要进行处理才能得到无籽果实。

1.1.3 假单性结实

有些植物传粉受精后，由于各种原因，胚只稍稍发育就转向败育，但其子房或花托等部分可继续发育，从而形成无籽果实，KOBEL（1931）将此现象称为假单性结实（或伪单性结实）。王近卫等对无核白葡萄的无核果形成过程的研究发现部分受精的胚珠，由于胚乳核和幼胚的早期退化导致败育产生无核果[9~12]。在柑橘上对“塔 1”芦柑的无核性研究表明，其雌配子体基本正常，胚及胚乳早期亦发育正常，但盛花后 21 ~24d 发生胚乳退化现象，几乎是同时胚也发生中途败育而消失[13]。而无核纪州蜜柑，花粉育性高，胚囊能正常形成，但受精后合子不进行分裂，从而退化消失造成无籽。

1.2 三倍体果实

三倍体植物由于减数分裂的异常不能形成正常的种子，因而，所结果实也为无籽果实。在这方面，无籽西瓜和香蕉是最好的例子。

普通西瓜为二倍体（2n＝2X＝22），细胞内有两个染色体组，共 22 条染色体。用 0.2% ~0.4% 的秋水仙素溶液处理普通二倍体西瓜，可使染色体数加倍，成为具有 4 个染色体组，44 条染色体的四倍体（2n＝4X＝44）。将四倍体的西瓜与二倍体的西瓜杂交，就得到了有33条染色体的三倍体（2n=3x=33）。三倍体西瓜在减数分裂时三组染色体不能平均分配，这样最终导致配子中的染色体数有多有少，致使不能形成正常配子，所以，三倍体西瓜雄花的花粉大多空瘪，不能给雌花正常授粉。

为了使西瓜果实能正常发育，开花时，在三倍体植株的雌蕊柱头上授以二倍体西瓜的花粉刺激诱导其形成无籽西瓜。其原因是二倍体西瓜的花粉中含有生长素，同时，还含有使色氨酸转变为吲哚乙酸的酶系，当二倍体花粉萌发时，形成的花粉管伸入三倍体西瓜子房的同时，将色氨酸转化为吲哚乙酸的酶系也分泌到子房中，从而引起子房合成大量生长素促进子房膨大形成无籽果实。

香蕉的情况也很类似，不过它是由野生香蕉自然演变而形成的三倍体。野生香蕉为二倍体，细胞内有22条染色体。在野生香蕉进行有性繁殖时，形成了没有减数的二倍体卵细胞，当这种卵细胞和正常的精子结合后，就形成了三倍体种子，由三倍体种子长出的植株所结出的果实既为无籽果实。

胚乳是由精细胞和两个极核融合发育而成的，因此胚乳本身即为三倍性，在适宜的培养条件下诱发即可产生三倍体植株。从20世纪30年代开始，Lampe和Mills即着手进行玉米胚乳培养。近年来，我国科学工作者利用细胞工程技术，开展了柑橘、苹果[14]、猕猴桃[15]、枸杞[16]等的胚乳培养工作，目前已获得了猕猴桃、枸杞的三倍体植株，得到了种子数目明显减少的果实。尤其是三倍体的枸杞，果实无籽，少籽，多糖，氨基酸等含量高于二倍体，口感好，易加工，是理想的制干与加工鲜汁的食用枸杞。

2 利用基因工程生产无籽果实

无籽果实的产生与子房中的生长素含量相关，单性结实的植物子房中含有大量的生长素和赤霉素，可刺激果实膨大生长。通过对番茄单性结实突变体——pat突变体的研究发现，pat突变体的一些基因产物可能影响番茄体内赤霉素的代谢水平，并进一步研究了番茄子房中与天然单性结实有关的基因的表达。将番茄的正常结果株系和近等基因单性结实系的子房分离，并从子房中提取RNA。对其进行双向聚丙烯凝胶电泳和体外翻译，结果发现，至少有6个体外翻译产物在这对近等基因系材料间存在差异，其中，一个30kD的蛋白质在其他的单性结实突变体的子房中也存在[17~21]。因此，通过相应得基因克隆有望得到番茄的单性结实基因。1996年，当时尚在堪萨斯州立大学生物系工作的李义教授带领他的实验室用生长素合成基因构建了广谱性的无籽瓜果基因，并获得了专利。并且研究者在枣中也找到枣无核的目的基因片段[22]。

一般来说，单性结实的果实子房中生长素浓度较高，可见，单性结实与子房中的生长素含量有关。因此，从理论上讲，运用转基因技术，在植物子房中表达生长素和细胞分裂素生物合成的基因可诱导单性结实。例如，根瘤农杆菌Ti质粒T-DNA区存在有laaM基因编码的色氨酸单加氧酶，它在IAA生物合成途径中催化色氨酸转变为吲哚乙酸胺。Rotino等已将DefH9启动子与laaM基因融合，并将其导入茄子和烟草中[23]。在10株转基因烟草中有5株可单性结实。在转基因茄子的研究中获得了更令人满意的效果，6 个株系均可单性结实。并且这种转基因茄子在冬季也能座果，而在相同的条件下，正常结果植株则不能结果，从而更加显示出了单性结实的转基因植物的商业潜力。

3 问题和展望

无籽果实以其品质高、口味好、食用方便等优点赢得了诸多消费者的亲睐，但传统生产无籽果实的方法存在着很多问题，例如，天然单性结实的品种少；使用激素诱导时激素浓度难以掌握；而利用三倍体获得无籽果实，则面临着四倍体品种不易获得，种子产量低，制种周期长等缺点。因此，限制了无籽果实的大量生产。但随着科学技术的发展，无核基因的发现和克隆，转基因技术及植物组织培养技术已越来越多的应用到无籽果实新品种的培育中，尽管这些技术在实际的运用和推广中还存在着一些问题和阻力，但我们有理由相信通过转基因技术和组织培养技术生产无籽果实将弥补传统技术的不足，和传统技术一起并驾齐驱为人类培育出更多的无籽果实新品种。

参考文献

[1] 王忠．植物生理学 [M]．北京：中国农业出版社，2003

[2] 吕忠恕，王保民，张承烈．开花前后子房生长调节物质的变化及其与结果及单性结果的关系 [J]．植物生理学报，1979，5（3）：253－261

[3] 吕忠恕，王保民．开花前后子房中生长调节物质的变化及其与结果的关系 [J]．植物生理学报，1991，17（5）：1－5

[4] 祁业凤．枣胚败育机理与胚培养研究 [D]．保定：河北农业大学，2002，22（4）：2－4

[5] 张上隆，陈昆松，叶庆富．柑桔授粉处理和单性结实子房（幼果）内源激素 IAA、ABA 和 ZA 含量的变化 [J]．园艺学报，1994，21（2）：117－123

[6] 王玖瑞．枣树雄性不育和胚败育研究 [D]．保定：河北农业大学，2004

[7] 邱似德，单性结实与激素 [J]．植物生理学通讯，1984，（2）：15

[8] 龚束芳，杨国慧，王军虹．赤霉素诱导葡萄无核原因研究 [J]．北方园艺，2000（5）：51.

[9] 陶建敏，陈长春，徐喜楼．无核葡萄育种技术研究进展 [J]．果树科学，1998，15（1）：78－83

[10] 马之胜，贾云云．果实无核的成因及生产无核果的途径 [J]．生物学杂志，1991，40（2）：5－7，4

[11] 王近卫，堀内昭作，林伯年等．无核白葡萄的无核果形成组织形态学研究 [J]．园艺学报，1992，19（1）：1－6

[12] 张宏明等．无核葡萄胚珠发育及早期离体培养的研究 [J]．激素对胚珠离体培养的研究 [J]．北京农业大学学报，1990，16（2）：227－282

[13] 陈大成，李志勇，胡桂兵等．“塔 1”芦柑无核机理探讨 [J]．华南农业大学学报，1998，19（2）：36－40

[14] 杜学梅，李登科．植物生长调节剂在苹果组培上的应用［J］．中国农学通论，2002，18（4）

[15] 秦永华，张上隆．猕猴桃的组织培养和遗传转化研究进展［J］．细胞生物学杂志，2004，26（1）

[16] 王立英，李健．枸杞胚乳不同发育时期的离体培养研究初报［J］．宁夏农林科技，1999（4）：12－15

[17] Mazzucato A. The parthenocarpic fruit (pat) mutant of tomato (Lycopersicum esculentum Mill.) sets seedless fruits and has aberrant anther and ovule development [D]. Development, 1998, (125): 107－114

[18] Fos M, Nuez F. Expression of genes associated with natural parthenocarpy in tomato ovaries [J]. Journal of Plant Physiology, 1997, (151): 235－238

[19] 肖祥希，李明，邱栋梁．果实无核机理研究进展［J］．经济林研究，2009，(3)：6

[20] 肖金平，陈力耕，叶伟其等．“丽椪 2 号”无核椪柑花粉育性及超微结构观察［J］．浙江林业科技；2006，1

[21] 白晓庆．“温敏”无核荔枝不同类型果实中的生理变化研究［J］．甘肃农业大学，2009

[22] 彭建营，束怀瑞，彭士琪等．与枣核性状相关联 RAPD 标记的筛选［J］．果树科学，2001，18（5）：288－290

[23] Rotino G L, Perri E, Zottini M. Genetic engineering of parthenocarpic plants [J]. Nature Biotechnology, 1997 (15): 1 398－1 401

Studies on the Cytological Mechanism of Plant Seedless Fruit

ZHU Hai-yan XIAO Wan-li

(*Weifang University of Science and Technology*, *Shouguang* 262700)

Abstract: Seedless fruit have many advantages and are very popular among customers. More than one reason can explain the cytological mechanism of plant seedless fruit. In this paper, the author studies the cytological mechanism of plant seedless fruit on two facets and provides the theoretics how to foster the new breed of plant seedless fruit.

Key words: Seedless fruit; Parthenocarpy; Endosperm culture; Triploid fruit; Seedless gene

萝卜异倍体间的特征特性比较

祝海燕① 肖万里

(潍坊科技学院，寿光 262700)

摘　要： 本研究以萝卜品种北京白为试材，对已获得的同源四倍体，同源三倍体的特征、特性、细胞学特点进行了观察比较。结果表明，二、三、四倍体萝卜特征特性比较，三倍体的综合表现最好；三倍体萝卜减数分裂的突出特点是染色体的姊妹染色单体在后期Ⅰ提前解离。

关键词： 萝卜；四倍体；三倍体

植物多倍体一般具有器官变大、抗性增强、品质提高等突出优点，因此多年来，多倍体育种一直受到国内外广大育种工作者的重视，选育出了四倍体的大白菜、小白菜、菜心、芥蓝，三倍体的葡萄、西瓜、柑橘、甜菜等许多在生产上应用价值较高的多倍体新品种或新材料[1~8]。它可以克服远缘杂交的不孕性，通过进一步杂交选育获得单体和三体等重要的遗传材料[9~10]。

萝卜作为我国主要蔬菜之一，食用器官是肉质根，不以种子为主要经济产品，因此特别适合多倍体育种。但关于萝卜多倍体育种的研究很少。本研究以夏秋栽培的萝卜品种北京白为试材，对已获得的同源四倍体、同源三倍体的特征特性、细胞学行为进行了观察比较，旨在为萝卜多倍体新品种选育种及遗传研究奠定基础。

1　材料与方法

1.1　材料

供试材料为白萝卜品种——北京白，及其同源三倍体、同源四倍体。

1.2 方法

1.2.1　植株外部形态特征特性

在同一栽培管理条件下，观测不同倍性植株的生长发育特点和外部形态特征。主要包括植株生长势，叶形，叶色，肉质根大小，形态，株高，分枝数，花色等。

① 祝海燕，女，硕士，潍坊科技学院讲师。研究方向：蔬菜遗传育种。E - mail：zhuhaiyan1978@126. com

1.2.2 肉质根品质

用手持测糖仪测定肉质根中部的区域的固形物质含量。

2，6-二氯酚靛酚滴定法，测定肉质根中部区域的维生素 C 含量。

品尝法，测定肉质根中部区域的脆度和辣味等。

1.2.3 气孔大小、密度及叶绿体数目的测定

取展平的叶片，撕取下表皮，置载玻片上，滴 1 滴 1% 的 I-KI 染液，盖上盖玻片，在 40 倍镜下用显微测微尺测量气孔的大小，统计单位面积的气孔密度和保卫细胞内的叶绿体数。

1.2.4 花粉大小和活性的测定

取新鲜花粉散在载玻片上，用显微镜测微尺在 40 倍镜下测量花粉的大小；取新鲜花粉散在载玻片上，滴 1 ~ 2 滴用 10% 蔗糖配制的 0.5% 的 TTC 染色液，盖上盖玻片，置铺有湿滤纸的培养皿中，在 35℃ 下染色 40min，然后在显微镜下观察统计红色花粉粒的数目和无色花粉粒的数目，计算花粉的活性。

1.2.5 减数分裂行为观察

于上午 9：00 ~ 10：00 取开花初期的小花序，用 Carnoy 固定液（95% 乙醇三份，冰醋酸 1 份）固定，4℃ 冰箱内保存。选取大小适宜的花蕾，剥取花药，置载玻片上，加少许铁矾-苏不精染色液，用小镊子挤出花粉母细胞，去除药壁，盖上盖片，染 3min 后，用吸水纸吸去染色液，轻压，在 OlympnsBH-2 光学显微镜下观察照相。

1.3 结果分析

1.3.1 生长发育及外部形态特征比较

二倍体、三倍体和四倍体相比较，二倍体生长发育最快，肉质根形成最早，春季开花也最早；三倍体肉质根形成最晚，但后期生长快，春季开花晚；四倍体肉质根形成期和春季开花期介于二倍体和三倍体之间，但肉质根始终生长较慢。二倍体的肉质根最长，外表光滑，长柱形；叶色浅绿，叶裂宽且浅，叶片较柔软。四倍体的肉质根短小，外表不光滑，尾部多分叉；叶色浓绿，叶裂窄且深，叶片厚挺直。三倍体的肉质根较二倍体的短小，但较二倍体的粗，圆柱形，外表光滑，尾部无分叉；叶色和叶形介于四倍体和二倍体之间。二倍体花枝细，分枝多，花小，淡紫色；四倍体花枝粗，分枝少，花大，色浓；三倍体介于四倍体和二倍体之间。二倍体的荚细长，四倍体和三倍体的荚粗短。对秋季种植 85d 后的肉质根进行调查，结果见表 1。三倍体的肉质根虽然较二倍体的短，但平均重最高，较二倍体的增重 16.7%，较四倍体的增重 84.42%。

表 1 二、三、四倍体萝卜的特征、特性比较

倍性	肉质根的长（cm）	肉质根的粗（cm）	肉质根重量（g）	肉质根的形状
二倍体	38.5	6.73	2 100	长柱、无分叉、匀称、光滑
三倍体	29.05	8.13	2 450	长柱、无分叉、匀称、光滑
四倍体	23.03	4.57	1 300	长柱、无分叉、不匀称、不光滑

1.3.2 二、三、四倍体的品质比较

表2 二、三、四倍体萝卜的品质比较

倍性	可溶性固形物含量（%）	维生素 C 含量（mg/100FW）	口感
二倍体	7.15	6.58	脆、味淡、有辣味
三倍体	8.15	8.33	脆、味较浓、略有辣味
四倍体	8.35	9.13	较脆、味浓、有辣味

由表2可见，二倍体加倍成四倍体后，固形物含量和维生素C含量都有明显的提高，但脆度降低，辣味增强，商品价下降。而三倍体固形物含量和维生素C含量略低于四倍体，但明显高于二倍体，且脆甜，味浓，品质好，具良好的商品价值。

1.3.3 二、三、四倍体萝卜的气孔大小、密度及保卫细胞叶绿体数目比较

气孔大小、密度及保卫细胞内的叶绿体数目在同一植物类型的不同倍性间一般存在着差异，因此，可作为鉴别植物倍性的一个指标。由表3可见，萝卜二倍体的保卫细胞最小，为（25.2×18.7）μm，气孔密度最高，为17.9个/mm²，保卫细胞内的叶绿体数目最少，为6.3个/保卫细胞（图1）；四倍体的保卫细胞最大，为（32.2×21.5）μm，气孔密度最低，为8.80个/mm²，叶绿体数目最多，为11.3个/保卫细胞（图3）；三倍体的介于两者之间，分别为（28.7×19.1）μm，11.7个/mm²和9.7个/保卫细胞（图2）。

表3 萝卜二、三、四倍体气孔大小，密度和叶绿体数比较

倍性	气孔大小长×宽（μm×μm）	气孔密度（个/mm²）	叶绿体数（个/保卫细胞）
二倍体	25.2×18.7	17.9	6.3
三倍体	28.7×19.1	11.7	9.7
四倍体	32.2×21	8.80	11.3

1.3.4 二、三、四倍体萝卜的花粉大小和生活力比较

对二倍体、三倍体和四倍体的花粉大小和生活力进行了测定，结果见表4。从表4可以看出，花粉粒大小随倍性增加而增大，纵横轴径的比值随倍性增加而变小，如二倍

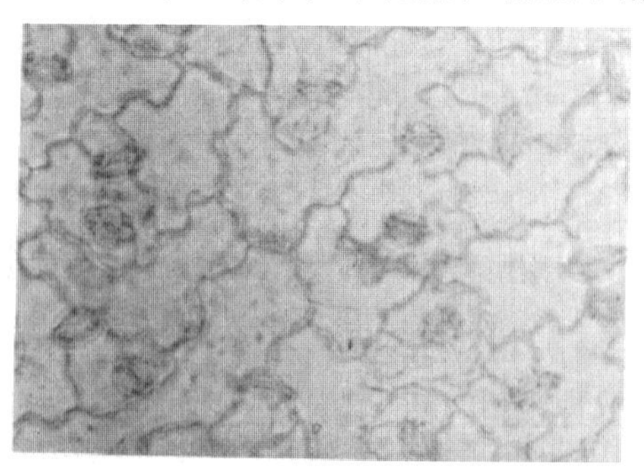

图1 二倍体植株的叶绿体细胞

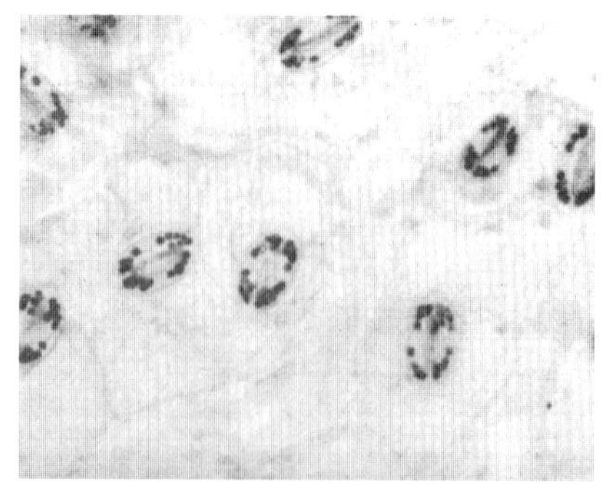

图2 三倍体植株的叶绿体细胞

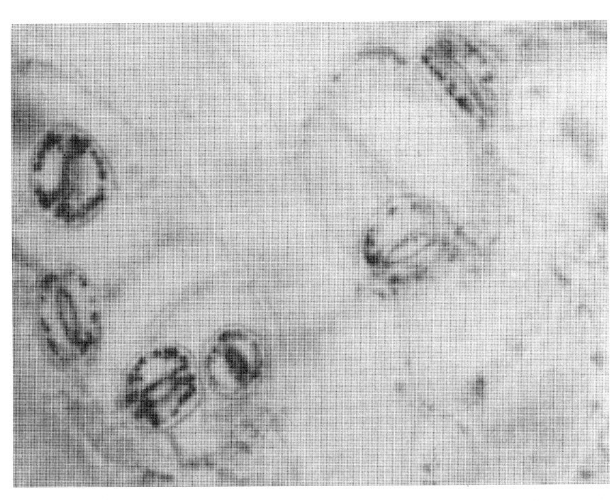

图3 四倍体植株的叶绿体细胞

体的平均大小（26.5 × 14.3）μm，纵轴横轴经的比值为1.85，四倍体的平均大小（34.7 ×25.3）μm。纵轴横轴经的比值为1.37，三倍体平均大小为（30. 3 ×18.7）μm，纵轴横轴经比值为1.62。可见，花粉粒大小和纵横轴的比值亦可作为鉴别倍性的一个参考指标。由表4还可以看到，萝卜三倍体、四倍体的花粉数有较高的生活力，其中三倍体的为59.43%，四倍体的为79.95%。这与大白菜、菜心、芥蓝和甘蓝等十字花科蔬菜多倍体的花粉生活力基本相似。

表4 二、三、四倍体萝卜的花粉大小和生活力比较

倍性	花粉大小（长×宽）（μm×μm）	红色花粉粒数	无色花粉粒数	花粉活力（%）
二倍体	26.5×14.3	503	22	95.81
三倍体	30.3×18.7	312	213	59.43
四倍体	34.72×5.3	383	143	72.95

1.3.5 二、三、四倍体的萝卜减数分裂行为

减数分裂观察表明，二倍体减数分裂正常，终变期可见有9对染色体，中期Ⅰ9对染色体排列在赤道板两侧，后期Ⅰ，同源染色体分开，在纺锤丝的牵引下分向两极，每极各有9条染色体。萝卜的减数分裂属同时型，即末期Ⅰ后细胞质并不分裂，而直接进行第二次分裂，到末期Ⅱ后，细胞质同时进行分裂，形成四面体的四分孢子。萝卜四倍体减数分裂比较紊乱，终变期同源的4个染色体大多联会成一个四价体（Ⅳ），个别联会成一个三价体和一个单价体（Ⅲ + Ⅰ）。中期Ⅰ四价体和三价体排在赤道面上，单价体游离在赤道面两侧，后期Ⅰ个别染色体的两个姊妹染色单体提前解离，使分向两极的染色体数大都多于18条染色体（表5，图4）。三倍体的每个同源染色体组有3个染色体，终变期各同源组大多联会成三价体（图5），三价体的形态不同，有Y字状、链状等形式，萝卜三倍体减数分裂的突出特点是姊妹染色单体在后期Ⅰ的提前解离，大量观察表明：后期Ⅰ很少见有姊妹染色单体未发生提前解离的细胞，因此，分到两极的染色

体的总数几乎都多于27条染色体（表5）。

表5 二、三、四倍体萝卜的后期Ⅰ分离及频率

倍性	联会方式	后期Ⅰ分离方式及频率（%）				
		9/9	18/18	13/14	18～23/18～23	14～17/14～17
二倍体	Ⅱ	100	0	0	0	0
三倍体	Ⅲ，Ⅱ+Ⅰ	0	0	0	76.7	23.3
四倍体	Ⅳ，Ⅲ+Ⅰ，Ⅱ+Ⅱ	0	4	0	100	0

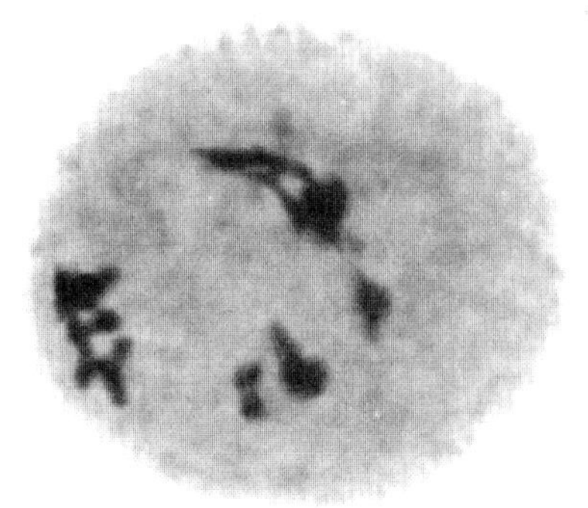

图4 三倍体植株花粉母细胞减数分裂后期Ⅰ

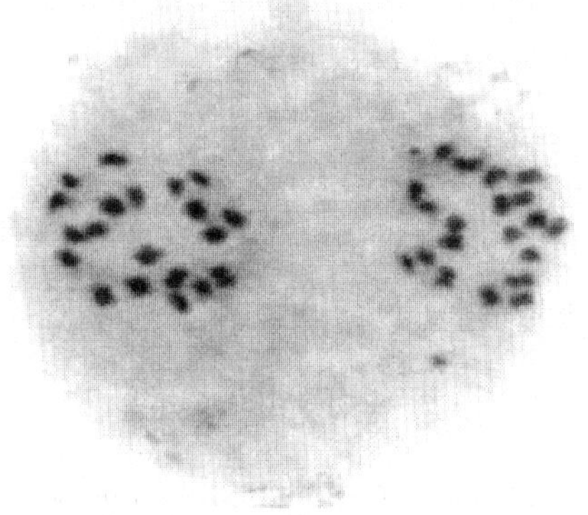

5 四倍体植株花粉母细胞减数分裂后期Ⅰ

2 讨论

人工诱导获得的同源四倍体萝卜可溶性固形物含量和维生素C含量较二倍体有明显提高，但肉质根变小分叉，商品形状变差，因此，没有更好的提高栽培价值。但用四倍体与二倍体杂交获得的三倍体，则无论是外观形状和品质均优于其二倍体。可见，三倍体对萝卜的生长发育是一个比较适宜的倍性，这与糖用甜菜的三倍体优于其二倍体和四倍体的表现是一致的。

三倍体的减数分裂不规则是正常现象，但后期Ⅰ姊妹染色单体一般并不常发生提前解离。而本研究的萝卜三倍体（2n＝3x＝27）则不同，后期Ⅰ分到两极的染色体数总和均多于总数27，一般为32～40，这表明，染色体的姊妹染色单体在减数分裂后期Ⅰ已提早发生了解离。萝卜三倍体在减数分裂中发生姊妹染色单体提前解离的现象国内外尚未见研究报道，其原因尚有待进一步研究探讨。

参考文献

[1] 张志毅，李凤兰．白杨染色体加倍技术研究及三倍体育种［J］．北京林业大学学报，1992．14（增刊）：52－58

[2] VeilleuxR. Diploid and polyploidgametes in crop plants ： mechanisms of fomation and uti-

lization in plant BreadingReviews [J]. 1985. 3: 252 -288
[3] 朱之悌，林惠斌，康向阳. 毛白杨异源三倍体 B301 等无性系的选育的研究 [J]. 林业科学，1995. 31 (6): 499 -505
[4] 谭素英等. 三倍体无籽西瓜的优越性及无籽西瓜新品种 [J]. 中国西瓜甜瓜，1994，4: 22 -23
[5] 罗耀武，朱子英. 人工诱导获得四倍体玫瑰香葡萄的研究 [J]. 园艺学报，1977，24 (2): 125 -128
[6] 张成合，刘世雄，申书兴. 大白菜同源四倍体的诱导剂细胞学研究 [J]. 园艺学进展，1994，(11): 143 -146
[7] 王子欣，刘学岷. 四倍体大白菜的选育 [J]. 华北农学报，1992，7 (3): 32 -35
[8] 尚爱芹，张成合，刘世雄. 菜心四倍体的获得及细胞学研究 [J]. 园艺学进展，2000，(14): 256 -260
[9] 秦瑞珍，宋文昌. 同源四倍体水稻培养在育种中的应用 [J]. 中国农业科学，1992，25 (1): 6 -11
[10] 张成合，祝海燕，申书兴. 结球甘蓝一套初级三体的获得与鉴定 [J]. 中国农业科学，2006，6 (2): 25 -31

Comparison of the Characters of Radish Heteroploid

ZHU Hai-yan XIAO Wan-li

(*Weifang University of Science and Technology*, *Shouguang* 262700)

Abstract: BeijinWhite radish which grow in summer or autumn was used as material to study the means of tetraploid inducement , also, the morphological characteristics and cytological specialty were observed in this paper. The results showed as follows: (1) Comparison of diploid, triploid and tetraploid, the triploid radish shows the best in integrated characteristics. (2) extruding character of the meiosis of the triploid radish was that the sister chromatids at anaphase divided ahead.

Key words: *Radish*; *Triploid*; *Tetraploid*

长江流域日本沼虾遗传多样性分析

李法君① 高俊平 梁 弘
（潍坊科技学院，寿光 262700）

摘 要： 利用9对微卫星分子标记对长江上中下游4个日本沼虾群体进行了遗传多样性分析。结果表明，在9个基因座中，共检测到40个等位基因，每个座位检测到的等位基因数为1～8个，4个群体的平均等位基因数Na为3.777 8～4.111 1个，平均有效等位基因数Ne为2.326 3～3.192 4，平均观察杂合度Ho为0.552 1～0.656 2，平均期望杂合度He为0.494 4～0.625 1，平均多态信息含量PIC为0.433 8～0.542 3。4个群体间的遗传相似系数为0.819 7～0.980 9，遗传距离为0.019 3～0.198 8。遗传距离分析显示，JJ与WH群体的遗传距离最近，而JY与JLJ群体的遗传距离最远；群体间遗传分化微弱（Fst＝0.065），群体内变异占总变异的93.45%。上述结果表明，4个日本沼虾群体仍保持着较高的遗传多样性，群体间未产生明显的遗传分化。

关键词： 日本沼虾；微卫星；遗传多样性

日本沼虾（*Macrobrachium nipponensis*）俗称青虾，属于甲壳纲，十足目，长臂虾科，沼虾属。具有适应性强，分布广，食性杂，生长快，养殖经济效益高等特点，是我国淡水虾类的一个重要养殖品种。当前对日本沼虾的研究工作多数集中于生长特性[1]、核型分析[2]和育苗[3]等方面。由于日本沼虾的遗传背景资料相当有限，仅见RAPD[4]分析。为得到高信息量的遗传信息以便更加准确地了解日本沼虾的资源状况，开展更加广泛的DNA分子水平的研究极为必要。

微卫星（*Microsatellite*）DNA又称简单重复序列（simple sequence repeat，SSR），是一种由1～6个核苷酸为重复单位串联组成的长达几十个核苷酸的序列，微卫星具有十分丰富的多态性。其中以双核苷酸重复最为常见[5]。由于微卫星在真核生物基因组中是随机分布的，作为分子标记又有着非常高的多态性和共显性，在物种遗传多样性检测[6]，遗传图谱的构建[7]，亲缘关系鉴定[8]等方面倍受青睐．由于磁珠富集法具有高效富集微卫星DNA的作用，因而被广泛应用于微卫星位点的筛选[9,10]。至今未见将微卫星分子标记应用于日本沼虾的报道，本文拟首次用微卫星分子标记对长江上中下流的

① 李法君，男，硕士，潍坊科技学院讲师。研究方向：水生生物遗传育种。E－mail：lifajun1976@163.com

日本沼虾野生群体进行遗传多样性分析。

1 材料与方法

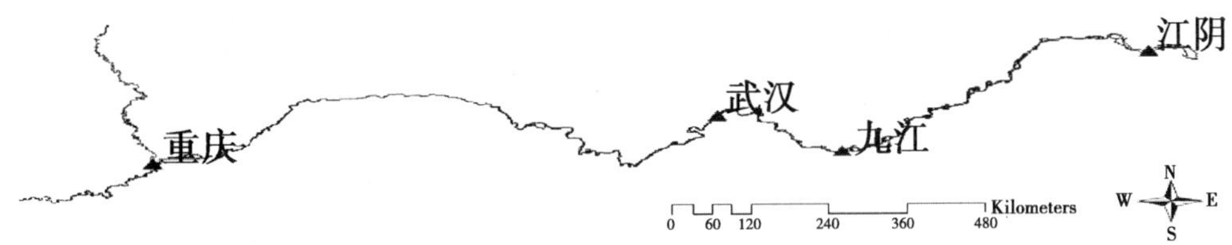

图1 4个采样点的地理分布

1.1 材料

日本沼虾分别取自长江重庆嘉陵江段（简称JLJ，下同）、湖北武汉段（WH）、江西九江段（JJ）、江苏江阴段（JY），每个地理种群各取32尾，无水已醇保存。微卫星引物来自本实验室筛选的微卫生序列（待发表）。序列见表1。

表1 9对微卫星引物的特征

位点	引物序列（5′—3′）	退火温度（℃）	产物设计长度 bp
WX01	F：GGG TAG TGT CTT CAT TCT CA R：GTG TTC ACA GTT CAC TTT CAT	54	151
WX02	F：AGA GGC AAT TGT AGC CGA GA R：TGG CAC GAT AGG AAG GAG TT	54	236
WX03	F：CAAGAAGAAAGAAGCAGGTAA G R：ATT CGT GAT TGG CGA TGA T	50	222
WX04	F：GAG CGT GGG AAA TGT TAG AGA R：GGA GAA GGC TGC GAT TAG AA	56	118
WX05	F：TTG GCA AGT CTC GTC TGA TG R：CGA GGA AAC GCC TGC TAC	54	146
WX06	F：CGT GAC GGA CGT TTA CTG R：ATC GTT TAC GAA TGA CTA AT	54	212
WX07	F：GTC ACT GAC TATGAACAATAA CA R：GGT TTG ATC TGG AAG TTT AG	52	119
WX08	F：GCC ATT TTC TCA TAA GGG T R：ACG GTG GTA TTC AGG GAT	52	176
WX09	F：ATC CTG CGA AGA TCA TAC GG R：TGC ATT TGC AAT CCA CTC AT	54	165

1.2 方法

1.2.1 基因组 DNA 提取

基因组 DNA 的提取参照 Strauss[11]的方法（略作修改）进行。

1.2.2 PCR 反应

采用25μl 反应体系，其中，10mmol/LdNTP 1μl，10xbuffer 2.5μl，25mmol/L $MgCl_2$ 2μl，8pmol/μl 两侧引物各 2μl，5U TaqDNA 聚合酶 0.2μl，50ng/μL 的 DNA 模板 2μl，用超纯水补足 25μl。

PCR 反应程序为：94℃预变性 5min；反应程序为 94℃预变性 3min；94℃变性 30s，复性 30s，72℃延伸 30s，35 个循环；最后 72℃延伸 5min。4℃保存。反应结束后，PCR 产物用 8%的非变性聚丙烯酰胺凝胶电泳分离。

1.2.3 数据处理

用 PopGene（Version 3.2）软件统计各微卫星基因座的等位基因频率（Allele Frequency，P）、等位基因数（Observed number of alleles，Ae）、有效等位基因数（Effective number of alleles，Ne）、观测杂合度（Observed heterozygosity，Ho）、期望杂合度（Expected heterozygosity，He）、群体内固定系数（fixation index，Fis）、群体间分化系数（differentiation index，Fst）、遗传距离（Genetic distance，D）。多态信息含量（Polymorphism Information Content，PIC）由公式（1）计算。

$$PIC = 1 - \left(\sum_{i=1}^{n} P_i^2\right) - \left(\sum_{i=1}^{n-1}\sum_{j=i+1}^{n} 2P_i^2 P_j^2\right) \tag{1}$$

其中，n 为某一位点上等位基因数，Pi、Pj 分别为第 i 和第 j 个等位基因在群体中的频率，j = i + 1。

根据遗传距离用 Mega3.1 构建 4 个群体的 UPMGA 聚类图。

2 结果与分析

2.1 4 个地理种群的微卫星扩增结果

本实验选用的 9 对微卫星引物在检测群体中均能扩增出稳定的条带，用 8% 的非变性聚丙烯酰胺凝胶电泳分离。位点 WX08 在 4 个种群的扩增图谱如下。

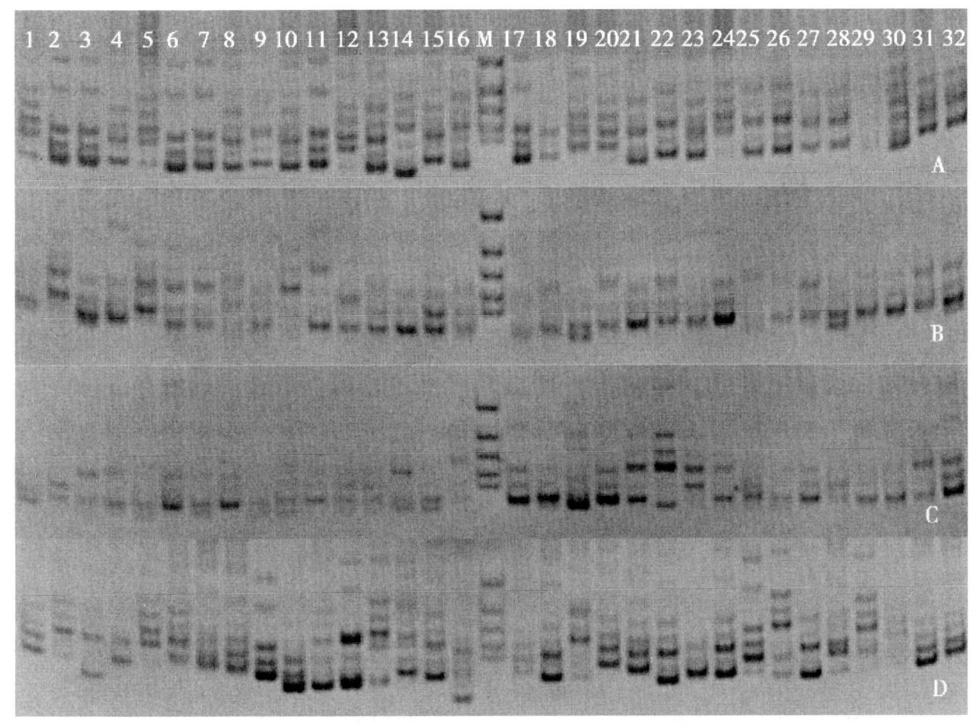

图 2 微卫星位点 WX08 在四个种群的电泳图谱

A：嘉陵江段；B：九江段；C：武汉段；D：江阴段 1～32 为不同的个体。M 为 PBR322/*BsuR* I Marker

2.2 群体遗传多样性分析

表 2 日本沼虾 4 个群体在 9 个微卫星位点的遗传多态性分析

群参	体数	WX01	WX02	WX03	WX04	WX05	WX06	WX07	WX08	WX09	平均
武汉段	Na	2	4	2	4	4	3	2	8	5	3.7778
	Ne	1.908 7	2.615 6	1.031 7	1.432 2	3.676 8	2.245 6	1.753 4	2.400 9	3.871 5	2.326 3
	PIC	0.362 7	0.539 9	0.030 2	0.284 6	0.680 3	0.455 5	0.337 3	0.562 7	0.695 1	0.438 7
	Ho	0.781 2	0.875 0	0.031 2	0.065 2	0.718 8	0.750 0	0.625 0	0.562 5	0.695 1	0.593 8
	He	0.483 6	0.627 5	0.031 2	0.306 5	0.739 6	0.563 5	0.436 5	0.592 8	0.753 5	0.503 9
	Fis	-0.641 0	-0.416 6	-0.051 9	0.792 9	0.012 7	-0.352 1	-0.454 5	0.036 0	-0.264 0	-0.148 7
	PHW	**	**	NS	**	**	*	**	NS	*	

（续表）

群体	参数	位点									平均
		WX01	WX02	WX03	WX04	WX05	WX06	WX07	WX08	WX09	
九江段	Na	2	4	3	3	4	2	3	7	5	3.666 7
	Ne	1.398 0	2.395 3	1.099 3	1.823 7	3.871 5	1.932 1	1.919 4	3.020 6	4.531 0	2.443 4
	PIC	0.244 1	0.493 1	0.088 1	0.397 7	0.694 1	0.366 0	0.400 8	0.639 7	0.743 7	0.451 9
	Ho	0.343 8	0.750 0	0.093 8	0.031 2	0.843 8	0.687 5	0.625 0	0.718 8	0.875 0	0.552 1
	He	0.289 2	0.591 8	0.091 8	0.458 8	0.753 5	0.490 1	0.486 6	0.679 6	0.791 7	0.514 8
	Fis	−0.207 5	−0.287 5	−0.037 8	0.930 8	−0.137 6	−0.425 1	−0.304 8	−0.074 5	−0.122 8	−0.074 1
	PHW	NS	*	NS	**	**	*	*	NS	NS	
江阴段	Na	2	4	3	1	4	3	3	8	6	3.777 8
	Ne	1.519 3	2.149 0	1.099 3	1.000 0	3.145 9	2.892 7	2.037 8	6.440 3	3.605 6	2.655 4
	PIC	0.283 4	0.434 8	0.088 1	—	0.621 7	0.579 9	0.394 5	0.825 6	0.676 7	0.433 8
	Ho	0.375 0	0.812 5	0.093 8	—	0.656 2	0.781 2	0.875 0	0.937 5	1.000 0	0.614 6
	He	0.347 2	0.154 3	0.091 8	—	0.693 0	0.664 7	0.517 4	0.858 1	0.734 1	0.494 4
	Fis	−0.097 1	−0.519 6	−0.037 8	—	0.037 9	−0.194 0	−0.718 1	−0.109 8	−0.383 8	−0.252 7
	PHW	NS	*	NS	-	*	**	**	*	*	
嘉陵江段	Na	2	4	3	2	4	3	3	8	8	4.111 1
	Ne	1.788 6	2.913 2	2.050 1	1.969 2	2.589 1	2.476 4	2.185 7	6.989 8	5.769 0	3.192 4
	PIC	0.343 7	0.605 3	0.409 3	0.371 0	0.552 2	0.518 1	0.437 8	0.840 1	0.803 4	0.542 3
	Ho	0.406 2	0.781 2	0.500 0	0.312 5	0.531 2	0.781 2	0.906 2	0.718 8	0.968 8	0.656 2
	He	0.447 9	0.667 2	0.520 3	0.500 0	0.623 5	0.605 7	0.551 1	0.870 5	0.839 8	0.625 1
	Fis	0.078 6	−0.189 6	0.023 8	0.365 1	0.134 4	−0.310 4	−0.670 6	0.161 3	−0.171 9	−0.064 4
	PHW	NS	**	NS	*	*	**	**	**	NS	

注：NS：此位点处于 HW 平衡；*：$P<0.05$；**：$P<0.001$

表 3　9 个微卫星位点的遗传变异参数

位点	等位基因数	有效等位基因数	多态信息含量	平均杂合度	遗传分化指数
WX01	2	1.669 0	0.308 4	0.385 9	0.037 4
WX02	4	2.712 6	0.516 8	0.597 9	0.053 0
WX03	4	1.311 9	0.153 8	0.180 9	0.239 1
WX04	4	1.580 2	0.351 1	0.311 4	0.151 9
WX05	4	3.739 8	0.629 6	0.691 4	0.056 2

（续表）

位点	等位基因数	有效等位基因数	多态信息含量	平均杂合度	遗传分化指数
WX06	3	2. 557 0	0. 479 8	0. 571 9	0. 060 8
WX07	3	2. 005 8	0. 392 6	0. 490 1	0. 022 6
WX08	8	5. 037 4	0. 717 0	0. 738 5	0. 078 6
WX09	8	4. 666 5	0. 729 7	0. 767 6	0. 023 1
平均数	4. 444 4	2. 808 9	0. 466 6	0. 526 2	0. 065 5

日本沼虾 4 个群体的遗传变异参数如表 2，表 3。通过对日本沼虾 9 个多态性位点的扩增，共得到 40 个等位基因，每个座位检测到的等位基因数为 1 ~8 个，平均每个位点扩出 4. 444 4个基因。其中，最多的是 WX08 、 WX09 两个位点都扩出 8 个等位基因，而 WX01 最少扩出两个等位基因，WX04 位点在江阴段则只扩出一个基因。有效等位基因从 1. 311 9（WX03 位点）到 5. 037 4（WX08 位点）不等。各个位点的 PIC 值从 0. 153 8到 0. 729 7，在 4 个位点（WX02、WX05、WX08、WX09）表现为高度多态（PIC >0. 5）。通过计算基因型的 P 值检验，位点 WX02 、 WX05 、 WX06 、 WX07 在四个种群中都表现为偏离 Hardy-Weinberg 平衡，在有些位点的偏离极其显著，如 WX02 在武汉段和嘉陵江段，WX07 在武汉段、江阴段和嘉陵江段。而位点 WX03 则在 4 个种群中都符合 Hardy-Weinberg 平衡；从群体来看，4 个群体中符合 Hardy-Weinberg 平衡最多的为九江段，共有 4 个位点符合 Hardy-Weinberg 平衡。群体内固定系数 Fis 值显示，9 个位点在 4 个群体中大部分表现为杂合子过度，例如，在九江段中，除 WX04 位点表现为杂合子缺失外，其余 8 个位点全部表现为杂合子过度，其次为江阴段为 7 个，武汉段为 6 个，而表现为杂合子过度的最少的为嘉陵江段为 4 个。在所有位点杂合子过度的比例为 71. 4% 。

2. 3 群体间的遗传关系

各个位点上的遗传分化指数（Fst）为 0. 022 6 ~0. 239 1，4 个群体 9 个位点的平均 Fst 为 0. 0655，表明只有 6. 55% 的变异是群体分化形成的，而 93. 45% 的变异来源于群体内。由表 4 可知，武汉段与九江段的遗传距离最近为 0. 019 3，而嘉陵江段与江阴段遗传距离最远为 0. 198 8。根据群体间的遗传距离用 Mega3. 1 软件的 UPGMA（Unweighted Pair Group Method with Arthmetic Mean）法对 4 个地理群体进行聚类分析（图 3）。从图中可以看出，4 个地理群体分为 3 类。遗传距离最近的武汉段与九江段先聚在一起，两者再与江阴段聚为一类，最后与嘉陵江段聚在一起。

表 4 日本沼虾 4 个地理种群的遗传相似系数（上三角）和遗传距离（下三角）

群体	JY	JJ	WH	JLJ
JY	*****	0. 946 6	0. 938 5	0. 819 7
JJ	0. 054 8	*****	0. 980 9	0. 858 8
WH	0. 063 4	0. 019 3	*****	0. 884 3
JLJ	0. 198 8	0. 152 3	0. 123 0	*****

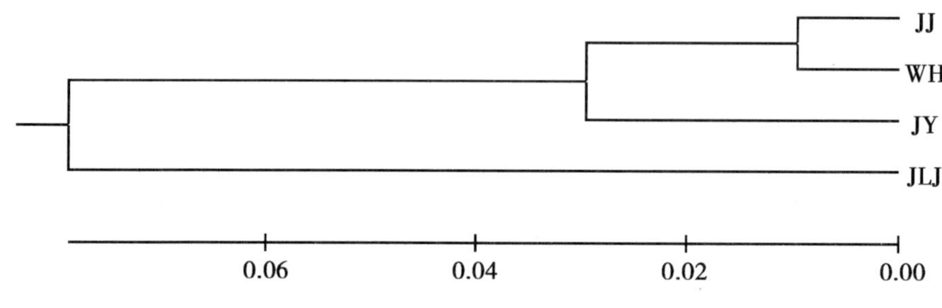

图 3 4 个日本沼虾群体的 UPGMA 聚类图

3 讨论

微卫星标记因其特异的引物序列及高度的多态性，与其他的标记系统相比能更多的揭示群体的遗传变异水平而广泛应用于群体遗传研究[12]。本研究首次运用微卫星标记对 4 个地理群体进行 PCR 扩增，经检测确定，扩增条带清晰，稳定性好。平均每个位点 4. 4444 个基因，可以较好的用于日本沼虾的遗传多样性分析。

遗传杂合度（H）又称基因多样度，可反应各个群体间在多个位点的遗传变异，即可反应群体的一致性的程度。群体 H 越低，表明该群体的一致性越高，群体的遗传变异越少，遗传多样性越低。用微卫星标记计算出的群体杂合度值一般在 0. 3 ~0. 8[13]。4 个群体的观测杂合度（Ho）和期望杂合度（He），除江阴段差距略大（Ho 为 0. 614 6，He 为 0. 494 4）外。其他三个群体的观测杂合度（Ho）和期望杂合度（He）都在 0. 5 ~0. 6 之间，差距微乎其微。嘉陵江段的观测杂合度（Ho）和期望杂合度（He）分别为 0. 656 2和 0. 625 1，在 4 个群体中表现为遗传多样性最高，这也与聚类图中表现的相一致，嘉陵江段处在长江上游，由于地理位置而产物的隔离使其产生更多的遗传变异。在 H 上呈现为更多的遗传多样性。4 个群体的遗传杂合度（H）值，表明日本沼虾在天然水域中所受自然选择的压力较小，群体的遗传变异较大，遗传多样性丰富，种质资源良好。蕴藏着较大的进化潜力以及丰富的育种和遗传改良潜力。

多态信息含量（PIC）是指一个后代所获得的某个等位基因标记来自于它亲代的同一个等位标记的可能性大小，平均 PIC 是衡量等位基因片段多态性的理想指标。当PIC >0. 5时，为高度多态性位点，表明该遗传标记能够丰富的提供遗传信息；当 0. 25 < PIC <0. 5 时为中度

多态位点，表明该遗传标记能够较为合理的提供遗传信息；PIC 小于 0.25 时为低度多态位点，表明该遗传标记提供的遗传信息较差[14]。本实验所采用的 9 个微卫星位点，PIC >0.5 的为 5 个，0.25 ~0.5 之间的为 3 个，PIC <0.25 的为 1 个。平均 PIC 值为 0.47。能够较好的反应日本沼虾遗传多样性。在遗传连锁分析中，PIC > 0.7 的微卫星 DNA 标记为最理想的选择标记，位点 WX08、WX09 的平均 PIC 值均大于 0.7，这两个标记对日本沼虾遗传多样性的进一步分析以及未来遗传图谱的构建有着重要意义。

群体内固定系数（Fis），是用来测量群体遗传动态的重要指标，也是度量近交衰退和远交衰退的重要参数。Fis 反应了 Ho 和 He 之间的平衡关系，Fis 越接近 0，基因型的分布越接近于平衡状态；Fis 为正时，反应杂合子过度（Heterozygosity excess）；Fis 为负时，反应杂合子缺失（Heterozygosity deficit）。本研究中，9 个位点在 4 个群体中大部分表现为杂合子过度，所有位点杂合子过度的比例为 71.4%。其他的水产动物中也有类现象，孙昭宁[15]在研究中国对虾家系时，发现 5 个家系在所有位点都表现出杂合过度，她认为出现这种现象的原因有 4 个：①具有无效等位基因的个体，事实上是纯合的；②杂合过度的位点具有很高的突变率；③这些家系不是随机交配的；④取样误差。董秋芬[13,16]在研究石斑鱼也发现有杂合过度现象。他认为杂合子过度现象一般出现在研究对象为相对较小的群体或者封闭的群体中。联系日本沼虾的生活习性，个人认为后一种说法能更好的解释本研究中出现的杂合子过度现象。因为日本沼虾运动能力较差，喜欢生活在湖泊或水流较缓的河湾中，群体之间的生殖交流较少。正是因为生活在处在相对封闭群体中，导致了 4 个群体的微卫星位点出现大面积杂合子过多度的现象。

群体间分化系数（Fst）是依据等位基因频率入群体大小来计算的。Fst 值在 0 ~ 0.05 之间，群体分化较弱；0.05 ~0.15 之间群体分化中等；0.15 ~0.25 之间，表示群体遗传分化较大；当 Fst >0.25 时，表示分化极大。本研究中检测到的 9 个位点平均 Fst 为 0.065 表明 4 个群体遗传分化中等偏下。仅有 6.55% 的变异是由群体间分化导致的，而总变异的 93.45% 发生于群体内。相互间的遗传距离表明，武汉段与九江段的遗传距离最小为 0.019 3，而嘉陵江段与江阴段的遗传距离最大为 0.198 8。蒋速飞[4]在用 RAPD 对六安、龙感湖、淮南、高淳 4 个群体的遗传多样性进行分析发现遗传距离最大的为龙感湖群体与高淳群体间为 0.171 2，与本研究差距不大。但最小遗传距离为六安群体与淮南群体的 0.144 6，这与本研究差距较大。表明封闭的环境更有助于加大遗传距离。

综合本研究结果可见，位于长江上、中、下游的 4 个群体间的遗传分化较弱，长江流域的日本沼虾的保持较高的遗传多样性，具有较大的选育潜力。这与长期生活在开放式环境密切相关，长期的自然选择使之适应环境的能力增强。从资源开发和利用的角度出发，利用微卫星分子标记分析群体的遗传结构，为制定科学的保护措施提供理论依据。使日本沼虾的种质资源得到合理的保护和开发利用，具有重要的实际意义。

参 考 文 献

[1] 刘军，龚世园．湖北武湖日本沼虾的生长特性［J］．湖泊科学，2003，15（2）：177 －183

[2] 杨万喜，周宏. 日本沼虾生精细胞核的形态变化及其在真虾部 Caridea 生殖进化中的地位 [J]. 应用生态学报，2000，11 (5)：763 -766

[3] 何绪刚，龚世园. 日本沼虾规模化育苗试验 [J]. 内陆水产，2003，28 (11)：36 -38

[4] 蒋速飞，傅洪拓，龚永生等. 日本沼虾 4 个地理群体遗传变异的 RAPD 分析 [J]. 长江大学学报 (自科版)，2006，3 (2)：179 -182

[5] Powell W, Morgante M, Andre C, et a1. The Comparison of RFIP, RAPD, AFLP and SSR (microsatellite) Markers for Germplasm Analysis [J]. Mol Breed, 1996, 12: 225 -223

[6] Nielsen E, Heino M B. Looking for a Needle in a Haystack: Discovery of Indigenous Atlantic Salmon (Salmosalar L.) in Stocked Population [J]. Conservation Genetics, 2001, 2: 219 -232

[7] Nichols K M, Young W P, Danzmann R G, et a1. A Consolidated Linkage Map for Rainbow Trout (Oncorhynchusmykiss) [J]. AnitaGenet, 2003, 34 (2): 102 -115

[8] 张于光，李迪强，饶力群等. 东北虎微卫星 DNA 遗传标记的筛选及在亲子鉴定中的应用 [J]. 动物学报，2003，49 (1)：118 -123

[9] Edwards K J, Barker J H, Daly A, et a1. Microsatellite libraries enriched for several microsatellite sequences in plants [J]. Biotechniques, 1996, 20: 758 -760

[10] Carleton K L, Streelman J T, Lee B Y, et a1. Rapid isolation of CA microsatellites from the tilapia genome [J]. Animal Genetics, 2002, 33: 140 -144

[11] Skinner D D, and Denoya C D, 1993, Simple DNA polymerase chain reaction method to locate and define orientation of specific sequences in cloned bacterial genomic fragments [J], Microbios, 5: 125 -129

[12] 鲁双庆，匡刚桥，刘臻等. 高识别力的微卫星标记系统在鳜属 (Siniperca) 物种鉴定的应用 [J]. 海洋与湖沼，2007，38 (4)：379 -384

[13] 董秋芬，刘楚吾，郭昱嵩等. 9 种石斑鱼遗传多样性发生关系的微卫星分析 [J]. 遗传，2007，29 (7)：837 -843

[14] Botstein D, White RL, Skolnick M, Davis RW, Construction of a genetic linkage map in man using restriction fragment length polymorphisms [J]. American Journal of Human Genetics, 1980, 32 (3): 314 -331

[15] 孙昭宁，刘萍，李健等. 微卫星 DNA 技术用于中国对虾家系构建中的系谱认证 [J]. 中国水产科学，2005，12 (6)：694 -700

[16] 董秋芬，刘楚吾，郭昱嵩等. 青石斑鱼微卫星标记的筛选及群体多态性分析 [J]. 水产学报，2007，31 (6)：841 -847

Analysis of Genetic Diversity among Macrobrachium nipponensis Populations in the yangtze river using microsatellite markers

LI Fa-jun GAO Jun-ping LIANG Hong

(*Weifang University of Science &Technology*, *Shouguang* 262700)

Abstract: Nine microsatellite markers were used to analyze the genetic diversity of four Macrobrachium nipponensis populations in the up、middle and lower reaches of the Yangtze River. A total of 40 different alleles were found and the number of alleles in each locus ranged from 1 to 8. In the four populations, the average number of alleles was 3. 777 8 to 4. 111 1, the number of mean valid alleles was 2. 326 3 to 3. 192 4, the value of average observed and expected heterozygosity ranged from 0. 552 1 to 0. 656 2 and 0. 494 4 to 0. 625 1, and the mean PIC was 0. 433 8 to 0. 542 3. Fst value indicated that the populations were minimum differentiated. The genetic similarity coefficient of the five populations was 0. 819 7 to 0. 980 9, and the genetic distance of the populations was 0. 019 3 to 0. 198 8. The analyses of genetic distance indicated the closest relationship was between JJ and WH, and the largest distance was observed between JLJ and JY. Only little genetic differentiation was detected among the 4 populations (Fst =0. 065), and the internal variation was 93. 45% of the total variation. Therefore, it is concluded that Macrobrachium nipponensis populations in different regions of the Yangtze River. still kept high genetic diversity, and the genetic differentiation among populations was not significant.

Key words: *Macrobrachium nipponensis*; Microsatellite; Genetic diversity

日本沼虾 AFLP 反应体系的建立

李法君① 于丽艳 王志和
（潍坊科技学院，寿光 262700）

摘 要： 目前运用扩增片段长度多态性（AFLP）对日本沼虾进行分析尚未见报道。本文对基因组酶切、选择性扩增中 Mg^{2+}、dNTP 浓度、预扩产物稀释倍数及选扩引物（M+3）/（E+3）配比等进行了比较分析，构建了日本沼虾 AFLP 分析体系。研究结果表明，酶切 5h，选扩 25μl PCR 反应体系中 Mg^{2+} 2mmol/L，dNTP 1.2mmol/L，预扩产物稀释 40 倍，选扩引物（M+3）/（E+3）配比为 8∶1，所得产物在毛细管电泳中可得到稳定的结果。该体系的构建为 AFLP 技术在日本沼虾相关研究中的应用奠定了基础。

关键词： 日本沼虾；AFLP；反应体系

日本沼虾（*Macrobrachium nipponensis*）俗称青虾，属于甲壳纲，十足目，长臂虾科，沼虾属。具有适应性强，分布广，食性杂，生长快，养殖经济效益高等特点，是我国淡水虾类的一个重要养殖品种。当前，对日本沼虾的研究工作多数集中于生长特性[1]、核型分析[2]、育苗[3]等方面。由于日本沼虾的遗传背景资料相当有限，仅见 RAPD[4]分析。为得到高信息量的遗传信息以便更加准确地了解日本沼虾的资源状况，开展更加广泛的 DNA 分子水平的研究极为必要。

AFLP（扩增片断长度多态性）是荷兰科学家 Zabeau 和 Vos[5]于 1993 年建立的一种 DNA 多态性的分子标记技术。结合了 RFLP 和 RAPD 的优点，具有高效、快速、稳定、可靠等特点[6]。已应用在水产动物中，例如，大黄鱼（*Pseudosciaena Crocea*）[7]，大菱鲆（*Scophthalmus maximus*）[8]和中国对虾（*Penaeus chinensis*）[9]。而目前运用 AFLP 对日本沼虾进行分析尚未见报道。本文拟将 AFLP 运用于日本沼虾，对反应体系的多个因子作了优化，建立适用于日本沼虾的 AFLP 反应体系。

① 李法君，男，硕士，潍坊科技学院讲师。研究方向：水生生物遗传育种。E - mail：lifajun1976@163.com

1 材料与方法

1.1 材料

日本沼虾分别取自江苏太湖、山东微山湖、湖北洪湖、安徽龙感湖。

实验所用主要试剂：用荧光标记的选扩引物 M +3/E +3，购自 TaKaRa 公司。

实验所用主要仪器设备：冷冻离心机，遗传分析仪（CEQ8000）购自 BECKMAN 公司。

1.2 基因组 DNA 提取

基因组 DNA 的提取参照 Strauss[10] 的方法（略作修改）进行。取约 200 mg 日本沼虾背部肌肉组织剪碎，放入 1.5 ml 离心管内，加入 600μl STE 缓冲液（30 mmol/LTris-Cl，pH 8.0；200mmol/L EDTA，pH 8.0；50mmol/LNaCl），混匀后加入 SDS 至终浓度为 1%，RNaseA 至终浓度 20μg/ml，37℃ 温浴 1h。加入蛋白酶 K 至终浓度为 200μg/ml，55℃ 消化。加入蛋白酶 K 后不断上下颠倒，至溶液澄清。冷却后加入等体积的饱和酚（pH 8.0）1 次；酚：氯仿：异戊醇（25：24：1）1 次；氯仿：异戊醇（24：1）1 次，氯仿 1 次。离心后取上清，加入两倍体积的无水乙醇沉淀 DNA. 收集絮状沉淀，70% 乙醇洗涤两次，干燥后加入适量 TE 溶解。将样品 DNA 稀释至 200ng/μl，-20℃ 保存备用。

1.3 AFLP 反应体系的建立

AFLP 反应体系的建立参照 Vos[11] 等的方法。

1.3.1 酶切与连接

采用 EcoR I 和 MseI 双酶切模板 DNA，酶切连接分两步进行。酶切时间设 2h、3h、4h、5h、6h、12h 共 6 个处理。在水溶缸上 37℃ 酶切后，72℃ 灭活酶 10min 以终止反应。然后用加入接头连接液，16℃ 连接过夜。酶切产物用 1.2% 琼脂糖凝胶电泳检测。酶切、连接体系见表 1。

1.3.2 预扩增

预扩增体系见表 1，将酶切连接产物稀释 10 倍作为预扩增模板，用引物 E + A，M + C 进行扩增。PCR 扩增程序为：94℃ 4min；94℃ 20s，56℃，30s，72℃ 2min，20 个循环；72℃ 10min，4℃ 保存。预扩增产物用 1.2% 琼脂糖凝胶电泳检测。对预扩增后的产物分别稀释 10 倍、20 倍、40 倍、60 倍、80 倍、100 倍进行选择性扩增。

1.3.3 选择性扩增

选择性扩增体系见表 1。体系优化参考黄文坤[12] 的方法。用江苏太湖日本沼虾预扩增产物并稀释 40 倍的产物，对选择性扩增体系中影响实验结果的关键因素进行了优化。在保持其他因子不变的情况下，先对 Mg^{2+} 浓度设计 6 种梯度实验，筛选其最佳浓度；然后再利用最佳 Mg^{2+} 浓度，在保持其他因子不变的情况下，依次筛选 dNTP、引物之间的配比、预扩增产物的最佳浓度（表2）。PCR扩增程序：预变性94℃ 4min；第一轮扩增参数：94℃ 30S、65℃ 30S、72℃ 80S，以后每轮循环温度递减0.7℃，扩增12轮；接着按94℃ 30S，55℃ 30S，72℃80S扩增20轮；终延伸72℃ 5min。4℃保存。

表1 日本沼虾AFLP反应体系

酶切体系	连接体系
5μl 10×Buffer	1μl 10×T4 Ligase Buffer
0.5μl 100×BSA	1μl EcoR I adapter mix（20pmol/μl）
10 U EcoR I（final）	1μl Mse I adapter mix（20pmol/μl）
10 U Mse I（final）	1μl T4 Ligase
3μl DNA（200ng/μl）	
ddH_2O to 50μl	ddH_2O to 10μl
总体积（50μl）	总体积（10μl）

预扩体系	选扩体系
2.5μl 10×Taq buffer	2.5μl 10×Taq buffer
2μl Mg^{2+}（25mmol/L）	2μl Mg^{2+}（25mmol/L）
1.2μl dNTP（2.5mmol/L）	1.2μl dNTP（2.5mmol/L）
1U Taq polymerase	1U Taq polymerase
0.5μl EcoR I primer（25pmol/μl）	0.5μl EcoR I primer（25pmol/μl）
0.5μl Mse I primer（25pmol/μl）	0.5μl Mse I primer（25pmol/μl）
1μl 酶切连接模板	1μl 预扩增稀释模板
ddH_2O to 25μl	ddH_2O to 25μl
总体积（25μl）	总体积（25μl）

表2 日本沼虾AFLP选择性扩增反应体系各因子梯度设计

因子	单位	浓度梯度
Mg^{2+}	mmol/L	1、1.5、2、2.5、3
dNTP	mmol/L	0.6 0.8 1 1.2 1.4 1.6
预扩产物稀释倍数		10 20 40 60 80 100
选扩引物（M+3）/（E+3）配比		1:1 2:1 4:1 6:1 8:1

1.3.4 扩增产物的毛细管电泳分析

将选扩产物在用1.2%琼脂糖凝胶电泳检测合格后，取1μl在遗传分析仪（CEQ8000）上进行毛细管电泳。

2 结果

2.1 基因组 DNA

从电泳结果看，所提基因组 DNA 主带清晰，几乎没有降解（图 1）。DNA 浓度测定仪测定结果 OD_{260}/OD_{280} 比值在 1.7～1.9 范围内，说明 DNA 纯度高，蛋白质含量极少，完全能满足 AFLP 分析对 DNA 的要求。

2.2 AFLP 体系的建立与优化结果

2.2.1 基因组双酶切结果

基因组 DNA 经 EcoRI/MseI 双酶切后，产物经琼脂糖凝胶电泳，结果显示原基因组 DNA 主带消失，电泳条带呈“Smear”状。表明基因组 DNA 酶切完全，可用于连接反应。双酶切后基因组 DNA（图 2）。对设置的 6 个酶切时间进行对比分析，确定 5h 最好。酶切时间过短，酶切不完全；酶切时间过长，易产生“star”活性，降低特异性[12]。

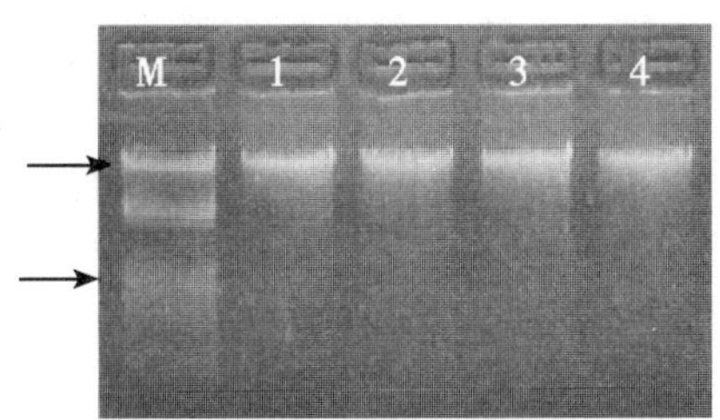

图 1　基因组 DNA 电泳结果

泳道 M：Marker；1：太湖；2：微山湖；3：洪湖；4：龙感湖

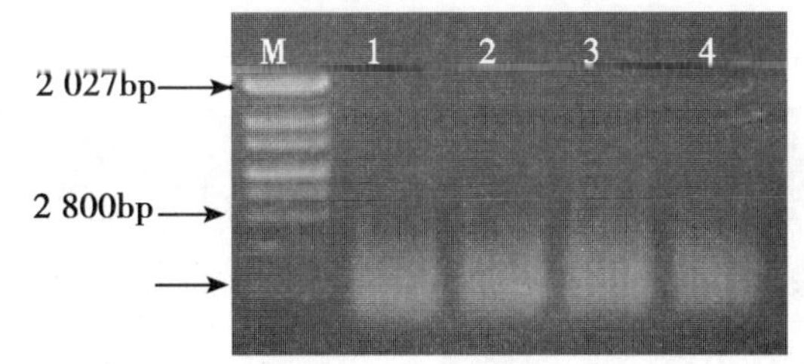

图 2　基因组 DNA 双酶切后电泳结果

泳道 M：Marker；1：太湖；2：微山湖；3：洪湖；4：龙感湖

2.2.2 预扩增

预扩增反应起着承上启下的作用，既反映酶切和连接效果的好坏，又直接影响着选择性扩增的电泳结果。预扩增检测（图 3），可看出其弥散带分散均匀且连续成一片，片段大小在 100～800bp 之间，稀释后可以作为选择性扩增的模板。同时表明，前面基因组 DNA 的提取和双酶切及连接也是符合要求的。

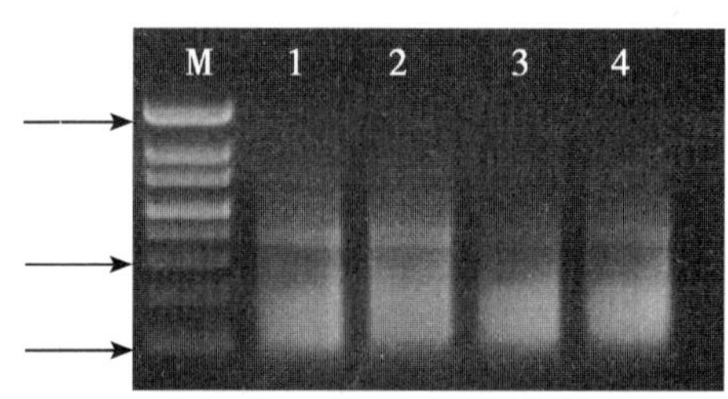

图 3 日本沼虾基因组 DNA 预扩增产物电泳图谱

泳道 M：Marker；1：太湖；2：微山湖；3：洪湖；4：龙感湖

2.2.3 选择性扩增体系的建立

2.2.3.1 Mg^{2+} 对选择性扩增体系的影响

对 5 种不同的 Mg^{2+} 扩增产物在琼脂糖凝胶电泳初检测发现：1 mmol/L，1.5 mmol/L 条带较弱，2 mmol/L 条带晴晰且稳定，2.5 mmol/L，3 mmol/L 条带呈明显分散状。毛细管电泳显示 2 mmol/L 体系较其他体系更稳定。因此，选用 2 mmol/L 体系。

2.2.3.2 dNTP 对选择性扩增体系的影响

对 6 种不同浓度的 dNTP 扩增产物在琼脂糖凝胶电泳初检测发现：均能扩增出条带，毛细管电泳结果表明，以 1.2mmol/L 为最好。

2.2.3.3 预扩产物稀释倍数对选择性扩增体系的影响

通过对 6 种不同的稀释倍数的扩增产物在琼脂糖凝胶电泳初检测和毛细管电泳发现：均能扩增出条带，没有太多差异。本实验选用稀释 40 倍。

2.2.3.4 选扩引物（M+3）/（E+3）配比对选择性扩增体系的影响

选扩引物（M+3）/（E+3）不同的配比对选择性扩增体系的影响较大：本实验发现，（M+3）/（E+3）在 1：1、2：1、4：1、6：1 之间在琼脂糖凝胶电泳初检测条带呈明显弥散状，8：1 条带清晰。毛细管电泳显示此配比信号更稳定。因此，选用（M+3）/（E+3）配比为8：1（图 4）。

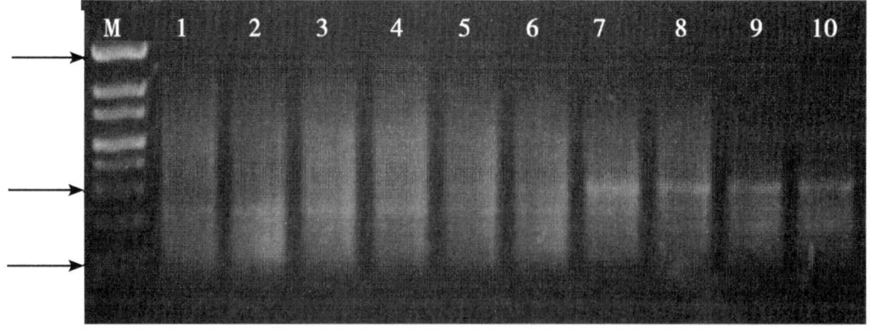

图 4 选扩引物 M+3/E+3 配比不同配比的电泳图

泳道 M：Marker；1~2：1：1；3~4：2：1；5~6：4：1；7~8：6：1；9~10：8：1

2.2.4 毛细管电泳结果

在建立 AFLP 分析技术体系的基础上，以太湖虾和洪湖虾两个点的基因组 DNA 进行引物筛选。筛选出 5 对多态性较高、带型质量较好的引物。5 对引物共扩增出 557 条带，其中多态性条带为 407 条，多态性比率达 65.6% ~78.7%（表 3），为后续的不同地理种群紫茎泽兰 AFLP 分析奠定了基础（图 5）。

表 3 不同引物对日本沼虾荧光标记 AFLP 选择性扩增的结果

引物对	扩增位点	多态性位点	多态性位点比例（%）
E-ACG/M-CAA	115	89	77.4
E-ACG/M-CTG	107	72	67.2
E-ACG/M-CTC	93	61	65.6
E-CAA/M-AAC	125	93	74.4
E-CAA/M-AAG	117	92	78.7
总数	557	407	—

3 讨论

日本沼虾是我国一种重要的淡水经济养殖品种。但其已知基因组 DNA 序列信息较少，至今 GENBANK 上还没有登录微卫星序列，这也限制了微卫星等需要利用 DNA 序列信息的分子标记技术的大规模应用；RAPD 技术存在重复性差的问题；RFLP 而则费时耗力。AFLP 技术无需预先知道被研究物种的 DNA 序列信息，是目前可以应用于日本沼虾的一种较好的分子标记技术。

基因组 DNA 通过限制性内切酶产生连接反应和扩增反应的亚片段。所以，基因组的充分酶切是 AFLP 成功的一大关键。在使用限制性内切酶切基因组时，一定要彻底。同一 DNA 样本完全酶切与不完全酶切形成的 AFLP 指纹分布方式不同，而这却并不代表真实的 DNA 多态性。不完全酶切的产物扩增后在电泳凝胶上会出现额外的条带，主要是一些高分子量的带型[13,14]. 理论上双酶切反应体系中的 EcoRI 为低频切点的内切酶，需要较长时间才能完全酶切基因组 DNA，因此有必要延长反应时间。实验中将酶切时间延长至 5h，同时将 EcoRI 用量加大到 10U，保证了酶切的完全。

Mg^{2+} 浓度不仅影响 Taq 酶的活性，还能与反应液中的 dNTP、模板 DNA 及引物结合，影响引物与模板的结合效率、模板与产物的解链温度以及产物的特异性和引物二聚体的形成[15]. 而 dNTP 是 AFLP 反应的原料，dNTP 浓度过高，会导致 PCR 错配，从而使扩增出现非特异性扩增，浓度过低又会影响合成效率。本实验中来看，预扩产物稀释在一定范围内对选择性扩增影响不大。这也从另一方面验实了 AFLP 反应对模板浓度的变化不敏感，DNA 浓度在 1 000倍的范围内变化时，对反应的影响都不太大。由于 EcoRI 为低频切点的内切酶，而 MseI 为高频切点的内切酶。两种酶产生的酶切片断数各不相同，所以选扩引物 M +3/E +3 不同的配比对选择性扩增体系的影响较大，本实验所

Bin	Dye	Samples	Fragments	XMin	XMax	XMean	XVar	YMean	1	2	3	4
197	D4	4	4	196.84	196.91	196.88	0.00	18223	1	1	1	1
198	D4	4	4	197.92	198.01	197.97	0.00	32964	1	1	1	1
199	D4	2	2	198.84	199.06	198.95	0.01	7322	0	0	1	1
200	D4	1	1	199.88	199.88	199.88	0.00	8738	0	0	1	0
202	D4	3	3	201.45	201.58	201.51	0.00	7503	1	0	1	1
204	D4	3	3	204.15	204.46	204.25	0.02	8489	1	0	1	1
208	D4	4	4	207.54	207.72	207.64	0.00	18913	1	1	1	1
209	D4	3	3	208.96	209.19	209.07	0.01	6741	1	0	1	1
211	D4	2	2	210.44	210.68	210.56	0.01	9021	0	1	1	0
211	D4	3	3	211.21	211.49	211.31	0.02	6689	1	0	1	1
214	D4	4	5	213.35	214.15	213.54	0.09	6435	1	1	1	2
216	D4	2	2	215.53	215.77	215.65	0.01	6954	1	0	1	0
217	D4	4	4	216.78	217.00	216.88	0.01	7325	1	1	1	1
222	D4	2	2	221.65	221.89	221.77	0.01	7058	1	0	1	0
223	D4	2	2	223.21	223.24	223.22	0.00	7339	1	1	0	0
224	D4	2	2	224.07	224.10	224.08	0.00	16795	0	0	1	1
225	D4	1	1	225.24	225.24	225.24	0.00	8336	1	0	0	0
227	D4	2	2	227.25	227.59	227.42	0.03	6150	0	0	1	1
229	D4	4	4	228.95	229.02	228.99	0.00	10980	1	1	1	1
230	D4	4	4	230.01	230.16	230.10	0.00	20436	1	1	1	1
233	D4	1	1	232.92	232.92	232.92	0.00	6316	0	0	0	1
235	D4	1	1	234.54	234.54	234.54	0.00	5254	0	0	1	0
236	D4	1	1	235.97	235.97	235.97	0.00	4916	0	0	0	1
237	D4	4	4	237.32	237.53	237.43	0.01	27696	1	1	1	1
239	D4	1	1	238.89	238.89	238.89	0.00	11743	1	0	0	0
243	D4	4	4	242.49	242.60	242.54	0.00	11312	1	1	1	1
243	D4	3	3	243.25	243.37	243.30	0.00	8821	1	0	1	1
245	D4	1	1	244.91	244.91	244.91	0.00	8594	1	0	0	0
249	D4	1	1	249.42	249.42	249.42	0.00	6942	0	0	1	0
255	D4	3	3	254.84	254.92	254.89	0.00	7028	1	0	1	1
257	D4	4	4	257.34	257.49	257.43	0.00	11968	1	1	1	1
260	D4	3	3	259.95	260.10	260.04	0.00	6701	1	0	1	1

图5　选扩引物 E-CAA/M-AAC 毛细管电泳图

1：太湖；2：微山湖；3：洪湖；4：龙感湖

得的最佳配比为8∶1，与季士治[8]在大菱鲆中得到的6∶1稍有不同。这与不同物种间双酶切间产生的片断不尽相同有关。但总体而言，两者差距不大。

毛细管电泳分析与聚丙烯酰胺凝胶电泳相比具有分离效率高、速度快和灵敏度高、而且所需样品少、自动化操作简便等特点，更能够反应选扩产物的丰富度。特别是100bp之下的条带能很好的呈现出来。而且各个信号从峰图上来看，信号稳定。不像聚丙烯酰胺凝胶电泳那样条带有强有弱，难以区别。

近年来，AFLP技术在水生生物中得到了广泛的应用。匡友谊[16]对黑龙江水系呼玛河塔河河段呼玛河哲罗鱼的遗传多样性进行分析。结果显示呼玛河水系哲罗鱼群体内有严重的近亲交配现象。赵金良[17]运用8对选择性引物对我国引进的萨罗罗非鱼群体进行了AFLP指纹的研究，结果表明群体间遗传变异较小。喻达辉[18]运用AFLP技术构建了合浦珠母贝的遗传连锁图谱。刘云国用AFLP筛选出牙鲆抗鳗弧菌病的两条高显性高显性基因频率的标记，为实现牙鲆分子标记辅助育种和抗病基因克隆奠定了一定基础。而日本沼虾的遗传背景知之甚少，本文建立了一套稳定的 AFLP 反应体系，为今后利用该技术开展日本沼虾的相关研究奠定了基础。

参 考 文 献

[1] 刘军，龚世园．湖北武湖日本沼虾的生长特性［J］．湖泊科学，2003，15（2）：177－183

[2] 杨万喜，周宏．日本沼虾生精细胞核的形态变化及其在真虾部 Caridea 生殖进化中的地位［J］．应用生态学报，2000，11（5）：763－766

[3] 何绪刚，龚世园．日本沼虾（*Macrobrachium nipponensis*）规模化育苗试验［J］．内陆水产，2003，28（11）：36－38

[4] 蒋速飞，傅洪拓，龚永生等．日本沼虾 4 个地理群体遗传变异的 RAPD 分析［J］．长江大学学报（自科版），2006，3（2）：179－182

[5] Zabeau M，Vos P. Selective restriction fragment amplification：ageneral method for DNA fingerprinting［P］．European Patent Application 94102629.7（Publication No：05348A1）Paris：European Patent Omee，1993

[6] Smith J J，Scottemig J S，Leadbetter J R. Charaterization of random amplified polimophie DNA（RAPD）products from Xanthomonas campesris and some comments on the use of BAPD products in phylogenetie analysis［J］．Mol Phylogenet Evol，1994，3：135－145

[7] 王晓清，王志勇．人工雌核发育大黄鱼（*Pseudosciaenacrocea*）的 AFLP 分析［J］．海洋与湖沼，2007，38（1）：22－28

[8] 季士治，王伟继．大菱鲆 AFLP 分析体系的建立［J］．海洋水产研究，2007，28（1）：7－12.

[9] 李朝霞，李健．中国对虾人工选育快速生长群体不同世代间的 AFLP 分析［J］．高技术通讯，2006，16（4）：435－440

[10] Strauss W M. Preparation of genomic DNA from mammalian issues. Current Protocol in Molecular Biology［J］．New York：John Wiley and softs，1989，221－222

[11] Vos P，Hogem R，Bleeker M，et al. AFLP：A new technique for DNA fingerprinting［J］．Nucl Acid Res，1995，23（21）：4407－4414

[12] 黄文坤，郭建英．紫茎泽兰 DNA 的提取及 AFLP 反应体系的建立［J］．武汉植物学研究，2007，24（6）：498－504

[13] MAHESWARAN M. SUBUDHI P K. NANDI S. et a1. Polymorphism. distribution and segregation of AFLP markers in a double haploid rice population［J］．Theor. App1. Genet. 1997，94：39－45

[14] MEKSEM K I. PEPEMAN D. et a1. A high resolution map on potato chromosome V based on RFLP and AFLP markers［J］．Mal. Gen. Genet. 1995，249：74－81

[15] Sambrok J，David W Russel1. 分子克隆实验指南［M］．北京：科学出版社，

1993, 611 -618
[16] 匡友谊，佟广香，尹家胜等．呼玛河哲罗鱼遗传多样性的 AFLP 分析 [J]．中国水产科学，2007，14 (4)：615 -621
[17] 赵金良，王伟伟，李思发等．我国引进萨罗罗非鱼群体的 AFLP 遗传指纹 [J]．上海水产大学学报，2007，16 (3)：293 -296
[18] 喻达辉，王小玉，黄桂菊等．合浦珠母贝遗传连锁图谱的构建 [J]．中国水产科学，2007，14 (3)：361 -368

Establishment of AFLP analysis system for Oriental River Prawn (*Macrobrachium nipponensis*)

LI Fa-jun YU Li-yan WANG Zhi-he
(*Weifang University of Science and Technology*, *Shouguang* 262700)

Abstract: Up to know, AFLP (Amplified Fragment Length Polymorphism) was not applied to Macrobrachium nipponensis. AFLP analysis system for Macrobrachium nipponensis was established in this study, with the relative processes being presented, including DNA double enzymes digestion reaction, the dilute multiple for the preamplification production and the concentration of Mg^{2+}、dNTP in the selective amplification reactions system, different proportion in selective primers (M +3) / (E +3). It was proved that quite steady results could be achieved in capillarity electrophoresis by using 5h for double enzymes digestion, Mg^{2+} 2mmol/L、dNTP 1.2mmol/L, 40 dilute multiple for the preamplification production, 8 : 1 for (M +3) / (E +3) selective primer in 25μl PCR reaction volume. The establishment of the system might lay a foundation for the application of AFLP techniques to the relative research of Macrobrachium nipponensis.
Key words: *Macrobrachium nipponensis*; AFLP; Reaction system

浅谈植物源农药发展前景与对策

于丽艳①

（潍坊科技学院，寿光 262700）

摘 要： 植物源农药具有环保、有机、长效、易光解、无残留等优点，应用中可分为杀虫剂、除草剂和杀菌剂3种。但植物源农药在推广应用中仍存在局限性，针对我国现状，本文从多方面探讨了植物源农药的发展前景与对策。

关键词： 植物源农药；有机农业；可持续发展；前景

随着人们健康意识的提高，大多数国家都非常重视农产品的安全性，对农药残留的限制十分严格，无公害农产品、有机食品的需求量大大增加。但2000—2008年中，国内引起震动的食品安全案件达30多件[1]。对外出口中，中国近几年农产品出口面临着非常严峻的"绿色壁垒"，因此造成的经济损失和社会负面影响极大，其中农药残留超标是经常遇到的问题。同时，在生态农业发展和生态园林城市的建设中，对有害生物的可持续控制，保护农田生态环境和城市生态环境的重要手段是利用生物防治，并能全面而有效的开展生物防治。植物源农药作为生物防治和实现药物无残留的重要组成部分，加速其产业化是保证农业可持续发展重要手段，是今后农药工业发展的一大方向。

1 植物源农药发展概况

我国植物资源十分丰富，在《中国有毒植物》一书列入有毒植物1 300多种，其中，许多具有杀虫（菌）作用，或已被作为植物农药利用。在近30 000种高等植物中，约有近千种植物含有杀虫（菌）性物质，主要集中于30多科，据曹长青等报道目前仅长白山地区可作植物源农药开发的植物有28种，分属17科[2]。多数研究者认为楝科、豆科、卫矛科最有开发植物源农药的利用价值。

所谓植物源农药，就是利用植物的某些部位或提取其有效成分制成具有防治、杀虫或杀菌作用的有机农药。近20年来，国内企业可谓投入了大量的人力物力进行植物源农药的开发和研究，并取得了明显成效。据统计资料显示，全国有13个省2个直辖市的31个厂家生产39种植物源农药产品。"十五"和"十一五"期间，国家科技攻关重大项目、科技成果转化基金等项目都有植物源农药项目资助或规划[3]。

---

① 于丽艳，女，硕士，潍坊科技学院讲师。研究方向：果树生物技术。E－mail：xiaoyu602602@163. com

1.1 植物源杀虫剂的研究概况

Crainge 和 Ahmed 报道，约有 2 400种植物具有控制害虫的生物活性[4]。对植物源杀虫剂的许多基础研究已取得重要成果，大多数植物源活性物质都对害虫正常行为有干扰作用，使其拒食、忌避、生长发育受阻、抗产卵甚至不育。目前，已明确了许多植物性杀虫剂的活性物质、有效剂量及对害虫的作用方式，并已开发出许多植物活性物质系列制剂和复配剂。

1.2 植物源杀菌剂的研究概况

在植物源农药中，杀菌剂的研究相对于杀虫剂要少得多，但近几年也发展迅速。Wilkings 和 Board 于 1989 年撰文报道有 1 389 种植物有可能作为杀菌剂，其中包含了许多不同类型的化合物。冯俊涛等对 56 种植物的抽提物进行抑菌活性测定，结果表明，许多植物的抽提物能抑制某些病菌孢子的萌发或阻止病菌的侵入。

1.3 植物源除草剂的研究概况

目前，已在 30 多个科的植物中发现了上百种植物含有除草活性的物质，如醌酚类、生物碱类、苯嗪酮类、酮类、肉桂酸类、香豆素类、噻吩类、腈类、类黄酮类、噻嗯聚乙炔类及萜烯类等 10 余种天然杀草化合物。其中，一些已被开发成天然除草剂。直接从植物中提取有除草活性的物质作为除草剂比较困难，但可利用特定功能的分子簇，即一系列结构简单且具有不同作用机制的次生物质合理组合而产生新一代除草剂。

2 植物源农药的活性成分及作用机理

2.1 植物源杀虫剂的活性成分

可作用的植物源杀虫剂的活性成分非常多[5]，介绍如下。

2.1.1 生物碱类

目前，人们发现的生物碱已有 6 000多种[6]，已证明有杀死害虫作用的主要有烟碱、喜树碱、百部碱、藜芦碱[9]、苦参碱、雷公藤碱、小薛碱、木防己碱、苦豆子碱等。该类化合物对昆虫的作用方式多种多样，如毒杀、拒食和忌避及抑制生长发育等。

2.1.2 萜烯类

萜烯类化合物是植物源农药中含量较多、研究比较广泛的一类化合物，其中，精油的大部分组成为萜烯类化合物。目前，从植物源农药中发现的萜烯类主要有单萜类、倍半萜类、二萜类和三萜类化合物。主要作用方式为熏杀作用、拒食、胃毒、内吸作用和影响试虫的产卵、孵化等生殖行为消灭害虫。

2.1.3 酮类

黄酮类化合物多以甙或甙元、双糖甙或三糖甙状态存在，具有防治害虫作用的主要有鱼藤酮、毛鱼藤酮、类鱼藤酮、胡桃醌、苦参素等。作用方式为拒食和毒杀作用。

2.1.4 番荔枝内酯

番荔枝内酯是番荔枝科植物特征性生物活性成分之一，它与以往发现的各类天然产物的结构类型相比有较大区别[7]，由35~39个碳原子构成化合物骨架，分子中的四氢呋喃环和末端Y-内酯环通过碳链相连接，碳链上常带有羟基、酮基和乙酰氧基等。番荔枝内酯通过强烈的胃毒和拒食作用来体现其杀虫活性，研究表明，它比世界公认的高效植物源农药鱼藤酮及有机磷农药乙酰甲胺磷的效果还要好。

2.1.5 精油类

精油是一类分子量较小的植物次生代谢物质，此类不仅具有毒杀、熏杀、忌避或引诱、拒食、抑制生长发育等作用，还具有昆虫性外激素和引诱作用，多用于防仓库害虫，如桉树油、薄荷油、百里香油、松节油、菊蒿油、茼篙油、芸香精油、肉桂精油、猪毛蒿油、芜香精油等。

2.1.6 光活化毒素类

这类物质在光照下对害虫杀伤力成几倍甚至上千倍的提高，它们在植物中广泛存在。如噻酚类的a-三连噻酚；聚乙炔类的茵陈二炔；醚类的金丝桃素；香豆素类的花椒毒素；呋喃喹啉碱类的小蘗碱等。

2.1.7 甾体类

此类具有拒食、毒杀和抗生作用，主要有Nic-1、Nic-2及植物质蜕皮酮、羊角扭总甙、牛藤甾酮等。

2.2 植物源杀虫剂的作用原理

植物源杀虫剂主要通过各种毒杀作用、拒食和忌避作用、干扰正常的生长发育作用来实现控制虫害的目的。

2.2.1 各种毒杀作用

植物对昆虫最直接、最有效的作用方式就是毒杀作用，毒杀机理也不尽相同。

胃毒毒杀作用的物质都可以破坏昆虫的中肠组织，使中肠亚细胞结构发生变化，也可阻断昆虫的神经传导，抑制多种解毒酶，发挥神经毒剂的作用。胃毒毒杀作用的症状为虫体脱水缩短，拉稀粪便，甚至拉出直肠或囊泡状物，直至死亡。

内吸作用是一种特殊的胃毒方式，与喷雾相比，这种方式对环境污染小，不易杀伤天敌。许多植物源杀虫物质具有典型的内吸毒杀活性。

害虫接触到具有触杀作用的物质，表现出兴奋状，其神经中枢即被麻醉，并且使害虫的蛋白质凝固堵死虫体的气孔，从而使害虫窒息死亡。

大部分精油都具有熏杀作用，精油可使害虫表皮蜡质层颗粒排列发生变化，破坏中肠组织，抑制中枢神经电位自发放。鉴于熏杀的特殊方式，可将精油用于防治仓储害虫和大棚温室害虫。

光活化毒杀作用是植物源农药的活性物质借助于光敏化剂发挥作用，光敏化剂是光活化毒杀作用的关键。

2.2.2 拒食和忌避作用

具有拒食作用和忌避作用的物质并不直接杀死害虫，而是允许其存在，但是迫使害虫转移选择目标。具有拒食和忌避作用的物质可改变害虫的体内外信息，然后影响神经，迫使害虫做出柜食和忌避的行为。

2.2.3 干扰正常的生长发育作用

许多植物源农药能够干扰害虫的生长发育，使卵不能正常孵化，幼虫不能正常蜕皮化蛹，蛹不能正常羽化或出现畸形，在害虫的整个生长过程中起到主导调节作用。目前，认为该类活性成分是干扰了昆虫正常的内分泌系统，导致生长发育出现异常。这种方式，对当代或当年的害虫影响不太明显，但可以控制下一代害虫的发生。

2.3 植物源杀菌剂的活性成分及作用机理

植物源杀菌剂主要通过从植物中提取的活性物质对植物病菌起直接的抑制作用；同时，含有一些活性物质和营养成分，既可刺激植物自身产生抗病菌活性物质和机能。又可以提高和改进植物营养生长条件而提高抗病能力。其体内含多种类型的抗菌化合物。如生物碱类、类黄酮类、蛋白质类、脂肪酸类和酚类化合物等。对于植物源杀菌剂作用机理方面的研究，多采用植物提取液对病原菌的直接作用，如抑制菌丝生长、抑制游动孢子的产生、附着胞形成及侵入丝形成、对线虫的致死、对病毒的病株抑制及体外钝化效果等；对寄主的作用，如诱导寄主产生抗性、增强寄主的生长及繁殖能力、保鲜及贮藏能力等。植物源杀菌剂对植物病害作用机理仅限于初步了解，其真正的作用机理还需进行深入细致的研究。

2.4 植物源除草剂的活性成分及作用机理

植物源除草剂主要是利用植物的次生代谢产物对其他植物具有的异株克生作用，来影响其他植物的生长发育和代谢过程。在植物相互的化学关系中，杂草和作物竞争，在绝大多数情况下并不是致命的，作物对杂草的化学防御没有作物对害虫和病菌化学防御剧烈，植物产生释放的能够致死其他植物的次生物质很少。而且植物所释放的次生物质往往是多样而微量的，同一次生物质又具有多重生态功能，直接从植物中提取有除草活性的物质作为除草剂比较困难，但可利用特定功能的分子簇，即一系列结构简单且具有不同作用机制的次生物质合理组合而产生新一代除草剂。

3 植物源农药的优缺点及推广应用现状

3.1 植物源农药的优缺点

植物源农药作为一种新型农药，来源于自然具有环保、有机、长效、易光解、无残留、高效、能与环境相容、作用机理独特、开发费用低廉、来源广泛等特点，具有明显的生态效益、经济效益和社会效益，是发展有机农业，促进农业可持续发展的理想农药，并越来越为农民所欢迎。作为未来农药的发展方向，无疑具有广阔的发展前景。

概括起来，植物源农药具有以下优点。

植物源农药一般为水剂，由于它们所含的有效成分为天然物质，不是人工合成的化学物质，受阳光或微生物的作用后容易分解，半衰期短，残留降解快，具有低毒、低残留的特点，能够保持农产品的高品质，同时，具有良好的环境相容性。

由于植物源杀虫剂杀虫成分较多、作用方式独特，使害虫较难产生抗药性。同时，植物源杀虫剂选择性强，对人、畜及天敌毒性低，对害虫天敌伤害小，对作物具有营养作用，可提高农产品的营养价值，开发和使用成本相对较低。

从作用原理上看，植物可以为药，用它制作的药物，不仅可以用来防治作物的病虫害，而且中医学认为还可以作为人用药、兽用药[8]。我国植物种类繁多，习性也各有差别，有的奇臭无比，有的又苦又毒，完全可以造药。有人说，植物源农药药力不强，其实不然，有的植物毒性大。连人都害怕，何况作物上的几个小虫。至于说药力不够，只是因为还没有找到对号入座的植保农药罢了。

目前，植物源农药研究的主流在于为创制新农药探索具有生物活性的先导化合物，这是一项要求刻意创新、追求原始性创新的工作。创新的目标在于两个层面：其一是获得具有农药活性化学结构新颖的化合物；其二是化合物是已知的，但活性是新颖的或者未曾报道过的。植物源农药研究是一项生物与化学密切结合的课题，生物学研究单位具有生测方面的优势，而化学研究单位具有提取分离和结构鉴定等基础研究的优势，如果两方面能够加强合作研究，将达到优势互补的目的，这对推动植物源农药的研究十分有利。

3.2 植物源农药在中国推广应用上的不足及对策

虽然植物源农药优点较多，但其源于植物本身，还是有其自身的缺陷，包括化学结构复杂不易合成或合成成本太高，活性成分易分解，制剂成分复杂，不易标准化；发挥药效慢，喷药次数多，残效期短；由于植物的分布存在地域性，在加工厂地的选择上受到的限制因素多；植物的采集具有季节性等。近年来，国内从事植物源农药生产的单位多为一些地方性小厂，产品多为水剂或乳油，至今没有形成规模。而且目前开发的植物源农药产品中有效成分含量低，植物源农药的药效发挥受环境因素（温度、湿度、pH值、土壤肥力等）的影响较大，存在速效性不够，制剂的贮藏稳定性差，质量上不易控制等缺陷，直接导致了植物源农药产业化发展较为缓慢。我国和国际上同类研究相比，就整体水平而言还有一定差距，究其原因有以下几个方面。

（1）与政府的鼓励政策和市场宣传机制有关。

韩国和日本等国家均出台了对使用植物源农药进行补贴的政策。而在中国，对植物源农药的基础研究投入太少，环保宣传也少。只有上海市政府提倡使用绿色环保农药[9]，并予以政府补贴，一定程度上限制了植物源农药推广。

（2）作用速度缓慢，推广受限，机理研究尚待加深。

植物源农药由于其见效慢的特性，在市场推广中受到了限制。同时，机理方面的研究仅是探索阶段，没有明确的方式和方法，因此源农药应用范围较窄，只是对少数的病虫害起作用，缺乏广谱性，需要进一步深入研究，并明确作用机理。

（3）有效成分提取和检测困难，影响开发利用。

有效成分复杂，一般不容易确定和检测。不能明确植物中何种物质是主要的活性成分，只能以总的提取物表示和体现其产品的药效，不利于商品注册和形成产品；直接利用的有效成分含量较低，市场上销售的制剂有效成分含量只有千分之几，有的甚至只有万分之几。而且，植物源农药的活性成分为植物的一类或几类次生代谢物质，其种类、含量受自身遗传因子、外界环境条件（如土壤、温度、光照、土壤 pH 值）的影响，会有地域性和季节性等变化；并且活性成分在植物不同部分含量亦不同，特别是有些活性成分对光和热不稳定；可投产的植物源农药，为解决降解问题，绝大多数是乳油剂型，原药无毒，加上乳化剂、有机溶剂，反而变成有毒制剂[10]。这些都给植物源农药开发利用带来一定的影响。

（4）开发不良可能会导致生态破坏。

直接利用植物资源为原料生产农药，由于植物体内活性成分含量一般很低，直接加工需大量植物材料，会带来过度采挖而造成资源枯竭和生态环境的破坏。

4 植物源农药的发展前景与对策

在植物源农药发展中尽管存在以上问题，但我国植物资源丰富，研究开发药用植物历史悠久，积累了丰富经验，同时，随着色谱技术、核磁共振、质谱、单晶、X-射线衍射技术的进步，使植物天然化学研究有了显著的发展，为植物源农药带来了良好的开发应用前景。同时，随着人们环保意识的逐渐增强以及对生活质量的要求愈来愈高，特别是我国加入 WTO 后，农产品在出口创汇中面临的绿色壁垒问题，使新型的、无污染的、低残留的植物源农药越来越受到广大科技工作者的重视。国内外许多农药公司和厂家纷纷转向对植物源农药的投资为加速开发植物源农药提供了广阔的前景。但由于植物源农药的研究太少，有的尚属空白，为此，针对以上存在的问题，应加强以下几方面的工作。

4.1 加大政策支持和管理、宣传机制

1996 年，我国成立南、北两个国家级农药创制开发（工程）中心，已取得了一批国内外技术专利，创制了一批很有发展前景的新型活性化合物和生物农药。但由于经费投入有限，无法形成一个自主创制新农药的体系。要想大力发展生物农药．还需政府给予一定的政策优惠和资金上的支持。要切实建立起品质检测和质量价格运行机制，用质量和价格的双重杠杆来调节和激发农民放弃使用高毒农药。各涉农部门应加大对生物农药的宣传与推广力度，使广大农民提高环保意识，掌握使用技能。

4.2 开发同时做好生态保护工作

植物农药在植物体内的含量十分有限，一般小于 1%。植物源农药资源的开发应注重环境与生态的保护，尤其是对国家级、省级保护的珍稀树种，如银杏、樟树、厚朴、喜树等。因此，植物源农药的研究，应在弄清活性物质的化学结构与活性的基础上进行结构优化，有针对性地开发实用化合物。应积极引种繁育，扩大栽培，营造农药用林或林药两用林。探索速生、丰产栽培技术，走可持续发展道路，否则将造成新的人为生态

灾难。对于这种现状，国内植物源农药需要加强基础研究，改进产品质量，顺应国际潮流。

4.3 作用机理研究深化，应用方法灵活多样

利用色谱法、同位素示踪法等深入研究植物源农药对靶标的作用点及作用机理，为更好地开发利用植物源农药提供科学依据。针对植物源农药作用方式特殊，作用速度缓慢的特点，其田间使用除与常规农药相同外，还应根据其特点灵活运用，以保证防治效果正常发挥。从中草药药理分析，许多中草药对真菌和细菌性疾病抑制作用十分明显，从中可以找出一些对植物病害有较好防治效果的新型杀菌剂加以开发利用。

4.4 提高技术水平，实现环保药效

药用植物的提取液作用于寄主时，其渗透能力、延展能力都是有限的。应设法采用植物源助剂和化学药剂中的助剂来增加渗透能力和延展能力，充分发挥药效。充分吸收多学科的研究成果，避免有毒的有机溶剂，采用无毒有机溶剂的微乳剂来代替乳油，对易光解的活性成分用 b-CD 分子胶囊，提高稳定性，防止光分解，提高生物防治效果。

21 世纪，生物防治将成为控制农业生物灾害、保护农田生态环境健康和城市生态环境等的重要手段。植物源农药以其绝大的优势，顺应了人类生活质量提高和社会进步，加速其产业化和规范化发展是生物防治的必然需求，前景无限。

参 考 文 献

[1] 徐汉虹．食品安全法推动下的植物源农药［J］．农药科学与管理，2010，8：7 - 11

[2] 曹长清，刘秀珍，傅锋．长白山区常用植物源农药［J］．中国林业，2010，11：50

[3] 论坛．植物源农药前景看好［J］．山东农药信息，2006，11：18 - 19

[4] 史秀娟，王学海．植物源农药现状与展望［J］．现代农业科技，2006，2：20 - 21

[5] 唐英，谭世语，孙大贵等．我国植物源农药的研究进展［J］．西南民族大学学报（自然科学版），2003，3：15 - 18

[6] 张鑫，叶非．植物源农药中生物碱提取与纯化技术进展［J］．山东农药信息，2007，4：21 - 22

[7] 吴文君，高希武．生物农药及其应用［M］．化学工业出版社，2004，9：65 - 67

[8] 黄文九．广西生物农药发展现状及对策研究［J］．企业科技与发展，2010，21：1 - 4

[9] 陈秋芳．植物源农药的应用［M］．湖南农业，2010，10：20

[10] 刘爱民．微生物资源与应用［M］．东南大学出版社，2008，7：231 - 235

Prospects and Countermeasures for the development of botanical pesticides

YU Li-yan

(*Weifang University of Science and Technology*, *Shouguang* 262700)

Abstract: Botanical pesticides are eco-friendly, organic, long-lasting, easy to photolysis, no residue, etc. , applications can be divided into pesticides, herbicides and fungicides. However, application of plant pesticides still exist in the promotion of the limitations of view of the status quo, this paper discusses several aspects of its development prospects and countermeasures.

Key words: Botanical Pesticide; Organic Agriculture; Sustainable Development; Prospect

飞碟南瓜的栽培技术要领

王志和[①] 李培之 肖万里
（潍坊科技学院，寿光 262700）

摘　要： 本文简单介绍了飞碟南瓜的栽培技术，包括，播种、培育壮苗和定植技术，重点介绍了栽培管理中的注意要领。
关键词： 飞碟南瓜；栽培技术

飞碟南瓜属于南瓜的变种，其色彩鲜艳，果形奇特、可爱，如扇贝，皮嫩黄色或白色，重 80g 左右，茎短蔓生，既可用于公园绿地的造景，又可充当家庭盆景美化居室，在观赏园艺的发展中，越来越受到人们的青睐。现结合笔者的栽培经验，介绍一下飞碟南瓜的栽培技术要领。

1　适期播种

飞碟南瓜原产美洲热带地区，性喜高温，但对温度有较强的适应性，种子发芽适宜温度在 27℃左右。温室、大棚等保护地设施内全年均可种植，也可于春秋两季进行露地栽培。春植一般在 3 月中下旬播种，秋植以 8 月下旬为宜。

2　培育壮苗

目前，多采用营养钵育苗，育苗的营养土配制，可选用蛭石 2 份、珍珠岩 3 份、草炭土 5 份，并在每立方米营养土中加入 1kg 氮、磷、钾复合肥，经混合均匀，消毒后配制成营养土即可用来育苗。在育苗过程中，要注意控水控温，防止发生徒长现象，一般以保持 25℃为宜。若出现幼苗长势弱或叶色泛黄的现象，可喷洒 2 次 0.5% 的复合肥液，每次间隔 7d 左右。当苗出现 4 ~5 片真叶时就可定植[1]。

3　定植

定植前整平地面，清除枯枝病叶。因为南瓜对粪肥反应良好，因此整地前一般每

① 王志和，男，硕士，潍坊科技学院讲师。研究方向：设施园艺。E - mail：feilongwu918@163.com

667m² 施腐熟鸡粪1 000～1 500kg以保证基肥充足。畦宽设置为1.2m，株距40cm，每667m² 可种1 100株左右。定植时，宜选择晴天的傍晚或阴天进行，防止水分过度蒸发降低成活率。于定植前1d浇透水，定植后浇一遍定根水，夏季要注意遮阳降温利于缓苗。若用花盆栽培，可选取直径40cm、高50cm左右的塑料盆，在盆底预先放入鸡粪作基肥，草炭土、煤灰、珍珠岩按照5∶4∶1的比例混合配制成培养土。

4 栽培管理

4.1 温度管理

飞碟南瓜生长、开花和结果期均需要较高温度，植株生长温度不能低于12℃，开花结果要求的温度也在15℃以上，果实发育最适温度为23～25℃。生产中应注意温度的调控。

4.2 水分管理

飞碟南瓜因叶片大而多，蒸腾作用旺盛，缓苗后要注意保持土壤湿润，生长盛期及开花结果后需水量加大，此时，要保证充足的水分供应。

4.3 肥料管理

飞碟南瓜的追肥应掌握薄肥勤施、多肥配合的施肥原则。苗期以氮肥为主，缓苗后可喷1次1%的尿素作追肥，以促生新根，使幼苗发棵，抽蔓至开花前，每7d浇1次2%的复合肥液，使植株生长健壮。植株坐果后，配合施用磷钾肥料，以促果实肥大，提高坐瓜率。一般在第2个果坐稳后至盛果期每7d结合浇水施1次1%的复合肥。可在茎基部采用穴施或条施，注意不能靠茎基部过近施肥，以防烧根。施肥后应及时浇水[2]。

4.4 引蔓整枝

当植株高40cm左右时采用金属支架（盆栽时）、竹竿或吊线引蔓。飞碟南瓜生长过程中分生侧蔓较多，应注意及时摘除侧芽，以免消耗营养，影响主蔓结瓜。在主蔓上棚架后，可根据造型需要适当保留2～3条侧蔓增加结瓜。

4.5 人工授粉

为提高坐瓜率，开花后最好采用人工授粉。可于上午9时选择当天盛开的雄花，剥除花冠后用毛笔将花粉蘸下，涂到雌花柱头上[3]。

4.6 常见病虫害防治

飞碟南瓜易发生白粉病、病毒病、蚜虫等病虫害。病毒病可拔除病株，并喷洒20%病毒A可湿性粉剂进行防治；白粉病可用25%粉锈宁可湿性粉剂600倍液喷施防治；用30%乐果乳油喷雾防治蚜虫，喷药时应均匀喷洒病株，提高防治效果。

参 考 文 献

[1] 顾业芹．飞碟瓜露地栽培高产高效技术［J］．辽宁农业科学，2003.2
[2] 严泽生．南瓜·苦瓜·黄瓜栽培技术一点通［M］．成都：四川科学技术出版社
[3] 张建．日光温室飞碟瓜有机栽培技术［J］．长江蔬菜，2009，12

Main Points of Culture Technique about UFO pumpkin

WANG Zhi-he　LI Pei-zhi　XIAO Wan-li
(*Weifang University of Science and Technology*, *Shouguang* 262700)

Abstract: In this paper , the author conducts cultivation techniques of the UFO pumpkin, including planting, nurturing seedlings and planting techniques, focusing on the essentials of cultivation and management.

Key words: UFO pumpkin; Cultivation techniques

一种提取茶树基因组 DNA 的方法——改良的 CTAB 法

范世杰[①] 唐玉海
（潍坊科技学院，寿光 262700）

摘 要：采用改良的 CTAB 法与常规的 CTAB 法提取茶叶基因组 DNA 进行比较，结果证明改良的方法得到 DNA 浓度和纯度高，无蛋白质和 RNA 等杂质影响，并且可以很好的应用于 ISSR 分子标记分析。

关键词：茶树；基因组 DNA 提取

随着分子生物学研究的深入，基因组学也越来越广泛的应用在茶树（*Camellia sinensis*）方面的研究上，而质量比较高的 DNA 的提取纯化是整个工作的基础。为了提高茶树基因组 DNA 的质量，茶叶工作者进行过一系列的探讨：朱旗[1]等采用改进的 SDS 法，就不溶性聚乙烯吡咯烷酮（PVP）对茶树基因组 DNA 纯度的影响进行了系统研究，认为不溶性 PVP 能明显地提高所提茶树基因组 DNA 的纯度；在纯化过程中，加入不溶性 PVP 效果更佳。陈亮[2]等采用在细胞核被解裂之前去除细胞质中的茶多酚和蛋白质，而后用 SDS 裂解细胞核，异丙醇和乙醇沉淀基因组 DNA，获得的基因组 DNA 能有效扩增。高峻[3]等采用 CTAB 改良法提取云南茶树基因组 DNA，获得 RAPD 扩增成功。梁月荣[4]等采用植物 DNA 提取试剂盒法提取茶树基因组 DNA，进行了茶树品种资源遗传多态性 RAPD 分析。袁长春[5]等用改良的 CTAB 法成功的富含多酚类物质的植物中提取了 DNA。郭玉琼[6]等采用 4mol/L 的 LiCl 沉淀 RNA 的方法也得到了较为纯净的 DNA。本研究在综述前人的研究结果基础上，采用了改良的 CTAB 法，发展了一种操作简单并且能够得到高质量的 DNA 的方法。我们用此方法提取得到了高质量的 DNA，并且成功用于 ISSR 分子标记。

1 方法与材料

1.1 材料

供试材料为采自福建省农业科学院茶叶研究所的福鼎大白茶，福鼎大毫茶，优 3，

① 范世杰，男，硕士，潍坊科技学院讲师。研究方向：作物栽培与耕作。E - mail：fans201@163. com

优 10 和优 108 5 个品种以及玉龙，肉桂，瑞香，黄旦，铁观音，毛蟹，福云 10 号，福鼎大毫茶，福鼎大白茶，白样观音，铁罗汉，福云 8 号，福云 6 号，云南大叶 207，优 3 和优 10 16 个品种，取样时取一芽二叶。

1.2 基因组 DNA 的提取

1.2.1 方法1

（1）取茶树的一芽二叶，用液氮迅速研磨至细末，然后装入 2.0ml 的 eppendorf 离心管，加入提取预处理液 1ml（0.4mol/L 的葡萄糖，3% 的聚乙烯吡咯烷酮），混匀后 5 000rpm 离心，然后倒掉上清液，留下沉淀备用。

（2）加入 630μl 预热（65℃）1.5 × CTAB 提取缓冲液（1.5% CTAB，1.5mol/L NaCl，15mmol/L EDTA，100mmol/I Tris-HCl pH 8.0，0.2% β-巯基乙醇），加入 70μl 的无水乙醇，然后 65℃温浴 45min（隔 5min 左右翻动一下以便使之混合受热均匀）。

（3）取出 2mleppendorf，冷却后，加入 600μl 氯仿：异戊醇（24：1）混合均匀，然后 10 000rpm 离心 10min，取出后吸取上清液到新的 2ml eppendorf 管中。

（4）加入 2/3 体积的预冷的异丙醇混合均匀，置于 -20℃ 冰箱中约 30min，此时，出现白色絮状沉淀，用干净的枪头挑出沉淀物。若沉淀不明显则 5 000rpm 离心 3min，去上清

（5）加入 800μlTE buffer（10mmol/L Tris-HCl pH 8.0，1mmol/L EDTA pH 8.0），溶解 DNA。

（6）加入等体积的酚：氯仿：异戊醇（25：24：1）混合均匀，然后 10 000rpm 离心 10min，取出后吸取上清液到新的 eppendorf 管中。

（7）加入 2 倍体积的无水乙醇，混合均匀，沉淀 DNA，4 000rpm 离心 3min，去上清液。

（8）加入 500μl 75% 乙醇洗涤 2 次，置于超净工作台吹干。

（9）加入 50μl TE 缓冲液溶解 DNA，备用。

1.2.2 方法2

步骤 1 时，研磨的细末装入 2.0ml 的 eppendorf 离心管，不加入提取预处理液，直接加入预热的 1.5 × CTAB 提取缓冲液，其余步骤同步骤 1。

1.3 基因组 DNA 电泳检测

取溶解后的样品 5μl，加 1μl 上样缓冲液，采用 1% 琼脂糖凝胶，150V 电压下电泳 40min 后，于凝胶成像系统下观察，保存图象。

2 结果分析与讨论

2.1 琼脂糖凝胶电泳法测定基因组 DNA

DNA 电泳检测，取 5μl 加 1μl 上样缓冲液，采用 1% 琼脂糖凝胶，150V 电压下电

泳 40min 后，于凝胶成像系统下观察，保存图象。

由图可见，改良的 CTAB 法提取的茶叶基因组 DNA 电泳后呈现出一条迁移率很小的整齐条带，无弥散的荧光区出现，表明提取的 DNA 样品比较纯，无 RNA 污染。也没有多糖等其他杂质污染。DNA 片断大小在 21kb 左右。从浓度和纯度上基本满足 ISSR 分析的要求。

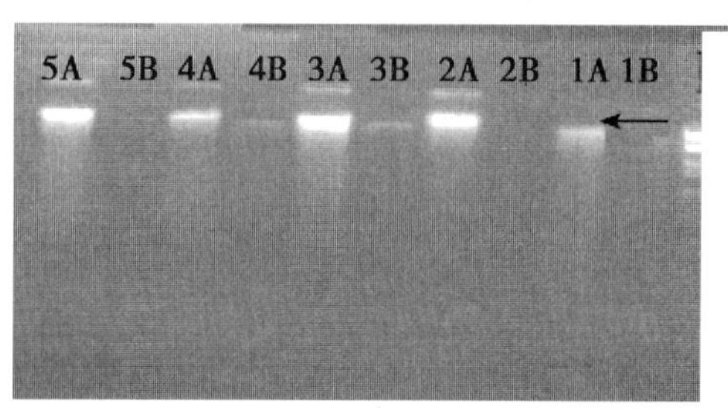

图 1　5 个样品两种方法提取的基因组 DNA 的琼脂糖凝胶电泳图

注：Marker 为 λDNA/EcoR Ⅰ + Hind Ⅲ Marker

A 表示方案 1，B 表示方案 2，样品 1～5 分别为品种福鼎大白茶、福鼎大毫茶、优 3、优 10、优 108

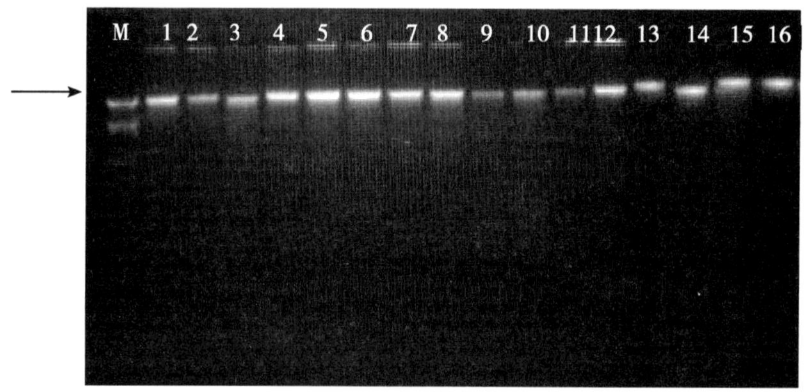

图 2　16 个样品采用改良方法提取基因组 DNA 的琼脂糖凝胶电泳图

注：Marker 为 λDNA/EcoR Ⅰ + Hind Ⅲ Marker

样品 1～16 依次为玉龙，肉桂，瑞香，黄旦，铁观音，毛蟹，福云 10 号，福鼎大毫茶，福鼎大白茶，白样观音，铁罗汉，福云 8 号，福云 6 号，云南大叶，优 3，优 10

2.2　分光光度法测定基因组 DNA

用 Ultrospec 2100 pro UV/Spectrophotometer 型核酸蛋白仪对本实验选用的 16 个茶树品种样本的基因组 DNA 分别进行了总 DNA 纯度和浓度的测定，得出 OD_{260}/OD_{280} 比值集中 1.62～1.99 之间，大多数样品的比值在 1.8 左右，完全符合 PCR 扩增的要求。

2.3　DNA 样品质量的 ISSR-PCR 检测

为了检验我们提取的 DNA 能否用于 PCR 扩增，我们选用一个 ISSR 引物，参照姚明哲[7,8]等建立的 ISSR-PCR 体系，该引物序列为 ACACACACACACACAC（CT）T，反应体系为 20μl 反应体系，PCR 组分如下：2μl10 × PCR buffer，200μmol/L dNTP，1.0U TaqDNA 聚合酶，0.4μmol/L 引物，50ng 的模板 DNA。

PCR 循环程序如下：94℃ 预变性 7min；94℃ 变性 30s，56℃ 退火 1min，72℃ 延伸 2min，共 40 个循环；最后延伸 7min。PCR 结束后，PCR 产物用 1.5% 的琼脂糖凝胶电泳检测，150V 电压下电泳 60min，于凝胶成像系统下观察保存图片。

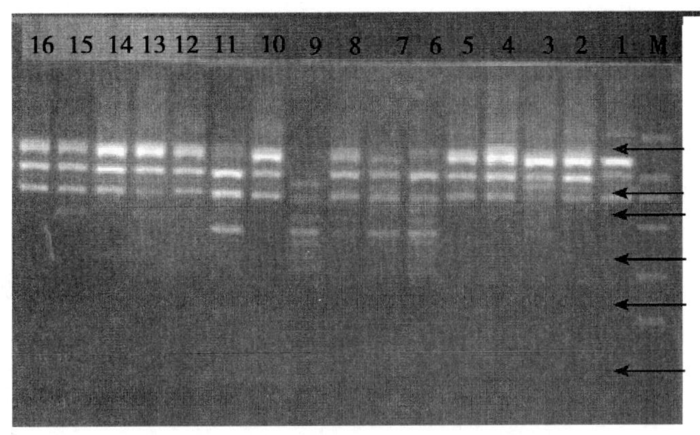

图 3　引物 46 对茶树基因组 DNA 的 ISSR－PCR 扩增结果

注：M 为 Takara 公司的 DL2000 样品 1～16 依次为玉龙，肉桂，瑞香，黄旦，铁观音，毛蟹，福云 10 号，福鼎大毫茶，福鼎大白茶，白样观音，铁罗汉，福云 8 号，福云 6 号，云南大叶，优 3，优 10

从结果可以看出，用改良的方法提出的 DNA 用于 ISSR-PCR 能够扩增出完整清晰的条带，说明用此方法提取的 DNA 质量较高，完全可以应用于 ISSR-PCR 的检测。

3　讨论

由于茶树叶片中富含茶多酚和生物碱等次生物质，DNA 的提取相对比较困难，本研究采用的两种方案提取 DNA 的效果差异比较大，未加预处理液的样品在提取过程中褐变现象明显，而且得到的沉淀为凝胶状，经纯化得到很少或者得不到 DNA；而在提取前加入提取预处理液的样品，整个提取过程中提取液均保持原来的绿色，无褐变现象发生，并且得到的 DNA 经电泳检测显示条带整齐，无 RNA 或者多糖等杂质污染，无论从纯度还是浓度均符合试验要求。

改良的 CTAB 法提取 DNA 具有步骤简单，耗时间少的特点，所用试剂也均为普通试剂。SDS 异丙醇法步骤繁琐，而且用到试剂较多。普通的 CTAB 法虽然步骤简单，但其主要用于草本植物和不含酚类或含酚类较少的植物的 DNA 的提取，并不适合富含多酚类物质的茶叶基因组 DNA 的提取，而且不能有效去除蛋白质和多糖等其他杂质，对此，本研究采用酚：氯仿：异戊醇（25：24：1）的试剂加以纯化，未纯化前呈现乳白色的沉淀物，沉淀呈透明状的黏稠物，得到了纯度高的 DNA 沉淀物。

参 考 文 献

[1] 朱旗，任春梅，洪亚辉等．茶树叶片 DNA 提取纯化与检测［J］．湖南农业大学学报，1994，20（2）：114－117

[2] 陈亮，陈大明，高其康等．茶树基因组 DNA 的提取与鉴定［J］．茶叶科学，1997，17（2）：177－181

[3] 高峻，蔡新，许明辉．云南茶树 DNA 提取和 RAPD 分子标记和探讨［J］．云南农业大学学报，2000，15（2）：126－128

[4] 梁月荣，田中淳一，武田善行．茶树品种资源遗传多态性 RAPD 分析［J］．浙江林学院学报，2000，17（2）：215－218

[5] 袁长春，施苏华，叶创兴．从富含酚类的茶类植物叶中提取纯净的总 DNA［J］．中山大学学报论丛，2001，21（3）：1－4

[6] 郭玉琼，孙云，赖钟雄等．一种新的茶树 DNA 提取方法——LiCl 沉淀法［J］．福建茶叶，2005，8（4）：15－16

[7] 姚明哲，黄海涛，余继忠等．ISSR 在茶树品种分子鉴别和亲缘关系研究中的适用性分析［J］．茶叶科学，2005，25（2）：153－157

[8] 姚明哲，王新超，陈亮等．茶树 ISSR-PCR 反应体系的建立［J］．茶叶科学，2004，24（3）：172－17

A Modified Method for Extracting Genome DNA of Tea-Modified CTAB Method

FAN Shi-jie　TANG Yu-hai

(*Weifang Uiniversity of Science and Technology*, *Shouguang*　262700)

Abstract: Modified CTAB method and ordinary CTAB method for extracting DNA from tea were compared in this study, DNA by the modified CTAB method was good in quantity, it has high concentration and high purity. It has no protein or RNA pollution and can be well used in ISSR molecular markers

Key words: Tea (*Camellia sinensis*); DNA extraction

香石竹的杂交育种技术

王爱丽[①]
（潍坊科技学院，寿光　262700）

摘　要： 香石竹，又名康乃馨，石竹科石竹属。花色娇艳，单朵花的花期较长，是当今重要的切花植物。各国广泛种植，广受欢迎，目前出现了很多专门进行育种、繁育的公司。本文主要介绍了香石竹的品种分类，产地分布，形态特征，以及培养香石竹的方法，育种技术，栽培管理技术。

关键词： 繁育；种植；栽培；防治

1　简介

香石竹（*Dianthus caryophyllus*），又名康乃馨，石竹科石竹属。花色娇艳，单朵花的花期较长，是当今重要的切花植物。香石竹原产于南欧、地中海北岸、法国和希腊一带，现在世界各地广泛栽培，主要产区在意大利、荷兰、波兰、以色列、哥伦比亚、美国等。随着香石竹商品化生产，出现了许多专门进行育种、繁育的公司。这些公司在品种类型上各有优势，每年都能推出一定数量的新品种，以增强市场竞争力，同时也给香石竹鲜花的持续发展注入了更强的活力。我国的香石竹育种工作起步较晚，国内市场流行的品种大都为引进的国外品种，目前上海市花卉育种中心经过多年的育种研发，已培育出几个获得自主知识产权的香石竹品种。

1.1　形态特征

香石竹多年生根宿草本。株高30~60cm，茎簇生、光滑，微具白粉，茎上有膨大的节。对生叶，线状披针形，全缘，基部抱茎，具白粉而呈灰绿色，有较明显的叶脉3~5条。花多为单生茎顶，少有数朵簇生者，花色有白、粉、红、紫、黄及杂色，具香味，有单瓣重瓣之分。蒴果，种子黑色。

1.2　生长习性

香石竹喜温暖、较干燥、空气流通及阳光充足的环境，喜肥，要求排水良好、腐殖

① 王爱丽，女，硕士，潍坊科技学院讲师。研究方向：园林植物遗传育种。E－mail：13668668226@163.com

质丰富的微酸性、稍黏质土壤。忌连作，不耐炎热。类型及品种较多，依栽培方式有露地栽培的一季开花类，如花坛香石竹；四季开花类，如巨花型香石竹；还有温室栽培的，如四季开花型香石竹，用作切花栽培的多为此类，可连续开花数年。

1.3 园林应用

应用以切花为主，是世界上产量最大，产值最高，应用最普遍的四大切花之一。园林布置中偶然用于花坛。香石竹为伟大母爱的象征，按照欧美的习惯，母亲节这天，要把红色的香石竹献给健在的母亲，把白色的香石竹献给已故的母亲。

2 繁殖培育

播种、扦插、压条繁殖均可，也可组织培养，但一般均采用扦插繁殖。除盛夏外，其他时间均可进行，尤其1月下旬至2月上旬成活率最高。插穗应取中部侧芽2~3个，当侧芽长至4~5cm长时，用于掰取，基部带踵易于成活，县需带叶扦插，插入土中1cm为宜，插后庇荫，喷水，保持13~15℃，20~30d可生根[2]。

育种者在育种之前必须对香石竹的习性、分类、育种目标、发展情况有所了解。品种分类有各种分类标准，按用途可分为盆花（花坛）香石竹和切花香石竹两大类。按着花方式（花序）可将香石竹分为常花香石竹或独头香石竹（Standard carnation）和聚花（多花、小花）香石竹（Spray carnation）。前者保留一枝一花；后者一茎多分枝、多花。按花茎大小可分为大花（8~9cm）、中花（5~8cm）、小花（4~6cm）和微型花（2.5~3cm）4类。按花色分，可分为纯色香石竹和异色香石竹和双色香石竹等。

2.1 育种目标

香石竹育种目标除观赏性状之外，还有园艺性状。观赏性状要求花色鲜明，外花瓣不下垂，不见雌蕊，有香气，花瓣全开并能同时开花；花萼不易脱落，花朵持久性好；花梗挺直、秆硬、柔韧、不易折断；叶片较大，附着蜡层，不卷曲，不干枯；花枝匀称，腋芽发芽节位低，二次花早；根系强壮。从生态育种来说，欧洲的香石竹育种以冬季弱光照下能生长开花为目标。从抗病育种来看，欧洲以镰刀菌属引起的立枯病危害严重，日本则以假单胞菌属引起的细菌性斑点问题较大，我国目前以链格胞属引起的叶斑病比较普遍且严重。抗病育种已成为香石竹育种的重要目标。另外，耐热性、早熟性、丰产性也是香石竹育种研究中的重要目标。

2.2 杂交育种技术

花粉是选择父本的重要条件，香石竹为重瓣花，由雄蕊变瓣而成，花粉不易采集；多数品种的雌蕊正常。利用现有品种，可与具抗病性的石竹属原种进行种间杂交。杂交育种需要常年累月，坚持不懈，各方分工协作很有必要。

2.2.1 杂交育种主要操作流程

（1）亲本选配→交配→采种→实生→开花选择→营养繁殖（扦插）。基本杂交技术。通常母本要在花瓣露色时小心去掉花瓣和雄蕊，然后套上纸袋，以杜绝外来花粉污染。

在空气干燥，气温18～25℃的9～11月和3～4月的10：00～14：00适宜授粉。雌蕊授粉适期是开花的中后期，在柱头分叉、发亮、有粘液时授粉；雄蕊开4～5成较好。授粉量多效果好，可采用重复授粉的方法。

每朵花授粉完毕后，授粉工具（镊子或毛笔）必须用75%的酒精消毒，及时套袋并挂上写明父母本杂交组合名称、杂交日期等的标牌。

一般杂交后10d左右可将套袋取下利于子房发育成长，对杂交后的植株要加强肥水管理和病虫害控制，特别是增施钾、硼肥，有利于种子的成熟。通常40～50d后，膨大的子房顶部由绿变褐时，说明种子已成熟，应及时采收。采收下来的种子随标牌一起分别按组合保存，防止混杂，放干燥皿中保存种子。

处理过的种子在温室内播种，可播于花盆或育苗盘上，保持室温20～25℃。待苗长出2～3对真叶时，移苗一次，移苗后每周叶面喷营养液一次，待苗长至8～10cm时，可定植到栽培床上。

（2）植株处理：定植后的小苗精细管理，不摘心，基部留4～5个侧芽，让顶芽先开花，对有用杂交继续自交或回交，以稳定性状，并用无性繁殖方式，扩大生产种苗。对实生苗中生长不良、长势不旺的个体宜及早拔除。由于香石竹遗传组成上的杂合性，会得到与双亲不同的子代个体。开花时进行第一次选择，对花色、花形优良的中选个体进行扦插繁殖，然后再进行选择（此为无性系选种），最后获得综合指标优良的新品种，组培生产推广。

2.2.2 栽培设施要求

避雨栽培。香石竹在高温高湿条件下易被镰刀菌等感染致病。上海夏季有一段黄梅雨季节，利用大棚顶膜，进行避雨栽培，可以免去夏季雨水，创造一个干燥环境，减少发病因子。

通风。大棚必须设置两头山墙开门通风及两侧窗通风。两侧的通风窗离地至少55cm，以免冬季通风时引起“穿堂风”。

遮荫材料。由于夏季炎热高温，对香石竹正常生长形成威胁，晴天在10：00～15：00采用遮荫网遮荫，是必要的。

支撑防倒。香石竹植株较高，为防倒伏，须支撑3层网，以维持植株直立，一般最低离地10cm，第二、第三层间距15～20cm，网眼以10cm×10cm为宜。

3 种植方法

3.1 准备

香石竹属须根系植物，疏松透气、蓄水保肥性能好的土壤，最适于香石竹的生长。因此最好选用沙质土壤，再加10%容量或更多的泥草炭，也可用没有完全腐烂的有机质如厩肥、树叶、碎稻草或木屑替代一部分或全部泥草炭作为栽培土。因为金山地区多数土壤都较黏重，所以种植前首先要进行土壤改良。具体方法是施入大量猪粪、牛粪或鸡粪等有机肥及砻糠灰等，每亩可施入 8 ~ 9t 有机肥。基于上海地下水位高的原故，一般每棚作 1 ~ 1.2m 高畦头 3 畦，深沟。在移栽前如土壤一直处于避雨状态，植前须浇灌大量水“盐”。临种植前，土壤保持湿润。为避免影响植株生长，降低产量，不提倡使用化学除草剂除草。

3.2　种植方法

香石竹定植突出“浅”字，以促使小苗快速发根，同时也可减少因丝核菌引起的茎腐病发生。浅植的标准是植株生根基质上部略露土表为好，在第一次浇水时，相当一部分苗倒伏到需要扶直的程度。第一次浇水为“沾根水”，一定要浇足，使根系与土壤充分接触。

3.3　种植密度

种植密度取决于定植时间和摘心次数，一般 3 月前定植摘心一次的为每平方米 30 株，摘心二次的为每平方米 24 株；如果是 4 ~ 5 月前定植的摘心一次半的为每平方米 30 ~ 36 株，摘心二次的为每平方米 25 ~ 30 株；如是 6 月后定植的摘心二次的为每平方米 36 株。总之要求有利植株通风透光，多争有效分枝数，形成一个理想的丰产群体结构[3]。

3.4　花期的控制

香石竹的花期是通过不同定植时间和摘心次数来调节控制的。

1、2 月初定植进行一次摘心，可在 6 月底始花，7 月为第一批采花高峰；第二批在元旦、春节上市；第三批花在翌年的 5、6 月上市，也可延至 7 月初。

2、3 月初定植不摘心，6 月底开花，一般一个月采花结束；第二批花国庆上市；第三批花在翌年的 3 ~ 4 月。

3、4、5 月定植摘心一次，8 月上旬始花，为一级枝开的花，10 ~ 11 月为二级枝形成的花。如进行二次摘心，则第一批花在 10 ~ 11 月上市，并延续到元旦，到翌年的 4 ~ 5 月又有一个高峰，此时花的质量好，而且可延续到“母亲节”前后。

4、6 月上旬定植进行二次摘心，主要满足春节供应，元旦期可有大量鲜花上市，延续到春节，第二批可在“母亲节”形成高峰。

5、9 月上旬定植进行一次摘心，4 ~ 5 月为采花高峰，7 ~ 8 月仍有优质花供应。

3.5　肥水温度管理

香石竹适宜生长在疏松肥沃、含丰富腐殖质的土壤中。基肥占总肥量的 1/3，追肥则根据生长状况要求薄肥勤施。

香石竹的生育适宜湿度为 1.5 ~ 2.0 微微法拉（PF）。一般夏季 1 ~ 2d 浇一次水，在清晨或晚间进行，春、秋、冬季 4 ~ 5d 浇一次水，要求在上午 10：00 以后进行。

香石竹的生育适温为 15 ~ 20℃。在冬季要做好保温工作，一般在 11 月中下旬上二道膜，有霜冻时上三道膜，确保夜温在0℃以上。而在夏季时要做好降温工作，具体可采用遮荫、喷雾降温等措施。

4 病虫害防治

香石竹很易患病，而且虫害较多，其主要病虫害为叶斑病、立枯病、蓟马等。因此在防治中强调综合防治，要求减少病虫菌发源地、控制病菌传播途径和使用化学药剂综合进行。

使用无病、优质、健壮的种苗，定植前土壤进行严格消毒，及时将病株拔除及枯黄叶摘除烧毁，同时搞好环境卫生。

如果采用基部滴水装置，能够有效地减少病菌顺水流蔓延扩散途径。在春秋季节要及时通风，以降低大棚内的温湿度，阻止病源菌的萌发。

在药剂防治时应注意做到，各种农药要交替使用，以防止产生抗性；药剂防治时，应在傍晚或清晨对叶片的正反面进行均匀喷施，提高防率。

叶斑病是由镰刀菌引起的对香石竹危害最大的病害，除了综合防治外，还要用扑海因、75%百菌清、代森锰锌、50%克菌丹等杀菌剂500～800倍液和1%波尔多液，每周定期喷药防治，特别注意的是切花后一定要及时用药保护伤口。

防治蓟马用强内吸杀虫剂—呋喃丹，在定植前每667m^2 3kg，以后根据测报情况再用药。

5 栽培管理

5.1 露地栽培

通常在秋季植苗，越冬后翌年夏季收花。栽植时要施足有机肥料。夏季为防止暴雨，可搭塑料棚遮顶，但四周不加遮挡，便于通风透气。作为二年生栽培时，可于10月底将植株在近地面第一个明显伸长的节间处剪掉，露地越冬。气温在0℃以上时可以不加覆盖，但华东地区一般要覆盖保温。翌春萌发出新枝条继续开花。为减少疾病，保持土壤肥力，应与其他花卉轮作。土壤每隔3～4年消毒1次。

5.2 大棚及温室栽培

定植的时间，取决于市场。一般9～10月份定植，采花时间为4～5月，5～6月定植，采花时间为冬季及春节。定植前土壤要潮湿，因香石竹是浅根性花卉，切忌栽植过深，只要盖住根，不倒即可。栽后第一遍水要浇透，栽培密度视栽培条件和品种而异。一年生栽培行株距为17cm×20cm或15cm×17cm，二年生栽培为20cm×25cm或17cm×20cm。

植株长高后，要架设网格固定，使其直立生长，一般第一层网格离地约10cm左右，以后随着植株长高增加两到三层网格，层间距离20～25cm，各层网的密度也不尽相同。

香石竹定植后2~4周，即要开始摘心[4]。以后陆续进行，利用它来控制花期，例如要使12月至翌年1月开花，可在7月底停止摘心。摘心后逐渐升高温度，以刺激新芽萌发。小苗摘心后每隔10d施一次稀释液肥，肥的浓度不可太高，否则盐类物质聚结土壤表层，引起香石竹生理干旱而出现生长停止、叶卷曲、新根不发、下部叶严重枯黄等症状。

光照时间长短可控制香石竹的花期，在长江以北9月份种植的香石竹，到冬季植株长到5~6对叶片时给予人工光照1个月，同时提高温度，翌年5月便可开花，若不给予人工光照，则要到6月份。温室及大棚用人工光照，一般每13m^2用100W灯泡1只，在植株上面1m处照射3h左右即可。

在温度管理上，7~9月温室或大棚内温度过高，要注意通风降温。10月中旬以后，当夜温在10℃以下，则要注意保温，11月上旬起，夜间密闭，白天仅在中午通风换气，有条件的可开始加温，使夜温保持在13~15℃，这样可使第一次盛花在12月中下旬至翌年1月上旬，第二次盛花期在3月中旬至4月上旬，此时正是切花淡季，效益最好。

香石竹由于栽培时间长，生长量大，需要不断追肥，平均每月1~2次，固体肥和液肥间用。特别是9~10月和3~4月，此时生长旺盛，需要大量养分，如发现土壤表面板结，可结合施肥浅锄，促进根系生长。

在生长过程中，开花枝条上再发生的侧芽要及早去除，质量好的可作扦插用。待茎端生有几个花蕾时，留中间一个大的花蕾，其余的应及早摘除，使养分集中于中间的一个花蕾。

香石竹常会出现裂萼现象，这与品种的遗传性及温差变化有关。昼夜温差超过10℃，或室内温度忽高忽低，变化太大，都会引起裂萼。

6 采收与贮藏

采花宜在下午进行，当第一片花瓣刚露出一点时即可采收。收后整理，剔除不合格的，将好的分级，包装，翌晨即可上市。暂不出售的，先让其吸足水，然后可放在3℃左右的冷库中贮藏。但要注意，不能和蔬菜、水果、月季、郁金香、紫罗兰放在一起[5]。

切花贮藏保鲜是调节市场、进行周年供应的重要措施。香石竹有集中开花的特性，在气温适宜的季节大量开花，而在冬季和盛夏产花很少，国外也普遍采用冷藏法来贮藏鲜花。常用的有湿藏法和干藏法，前者即将花枝成束插入水中或保鲜液中，温度控制在1~4℃，相对湿度为90%~95%，此法可贮藏5~30d；后者即是将花蕾尚未开放时采收，包装在聚乙烯薄膜袋或箱中，在冷室内经过预冷后转入贮藏冷库（0~1℃），此法可贮藏4~6个月。

参考文献

[1] 荆延德，亓建中，张志国．花卉栽培基质研究进展［J］．浙江林业科技，2001
[2] 康黎芳，曹冬梅，王云山等．香石竹栽培基质的研究［J］．山西农业科学，2000
[3] 向桂福，刘丽辉等．香石竹基质栽培技术试验［J］．湖南农业科技，1997
[4] 董华强，汪跃华等．不同处理对香石竹切花的保鲜作用［J］．现代园艺，2006
[5] 邱璐，罗春梅等．香石竹扦插技术［J］．云南农业，2007

Breeding Technology of Carnation

WANG Ai-li
(*Weifang University of Science and Technology*, *Shouguang* 262700)

Abstract: Carnation, named alias carnation. Design and color is delicate and charming, single flower bloom is longer, it is important cut plants in nowadays. It's planted widely and popular, there are a lot of breeding companies. This paper mainly introduces the variety classification, producing area distribution of carnation, morphological characteristics, and cultivating carnation method, breeding technology, cultivation and management technology.

Key words: Breed; Plant; Cultivation; Prevention

苜蓿属6种牧草种子萌发时期耐盐性鉴定

李春燕①

（潍坊科技学院，寿光 262700）

摘 要： 苜蓿属牧草是优良的豆科饲料作物，对其进行萌发期耐盐鉴定，可提高其引种筛选利用效率，为抗盐育种提供基础资料。在实验室条件下用浓度为0、20、40、60、100、140、200 mmol/L 7个浓度的氯化钠溶液对苜蓿属6份种子进行鉴定。通过相对发芽势、发芽率、相对发芽率、发芽指数和胚根、胚芽长对植物种子的耐盐性进行了比较，结果表明：低浓度盐溶液对6种苜蓿属植物的种子萌发均有促进作用，随着盐浓度的增加，与发芽相关的各项指标均下降，抑制了种子萌发。不同苜蓿材料对氯化钠盐分的适应情况有差异，就相对发芽势和相对发芽率而言，黄花苜蓿和中苜一号较其他品种的耐盐性要高，中苜二号种子的的耐盐性最差。胚根对盐胁迫的敏感程度要大于胚芽。

关键词： 苜蓿；萌发；耐盐性；指标

盐害是21世纪世界农业的重要问题[1]，我国的盐碱地面积非常大，各类盐碱土总面积0.991亿 km^2，占国土面积的1/10。因此，要改变我国农业生产现状，提高土地资源利用率，除了要改良盐碱地之外，耐盐性植物材料的选育，培养植物耐盐性品种也是一个重要方面。

作为盐碱地利用先锋植物的牧草，因其自身遗传和栽培条件不同物种间耐盐性存在着明显差异[2]，其中，利用较多的苜蓿属牧草具有叶片排盐机制[3]，能在轻度盐碱地种植，是畜牧业生产中的重要饲草[4]。耐盐性鉴定是选育苜蓿属耐盐品种的基础，目前这方面的研究较多。韩清芳等[5]对国内外19个苜蓿品种进行了种子萌发期耐盐力比较试验，得出结论是不同浓度氯化钠溶液对苜蓿种子发芽率影响很大。周丽霞等[6]在土壤含盐量0%～0.8%范围内对10种苜蓿的出苗、成活率、株高、根长、鲜重等进行了比较研究，当盐浓度超过0.4%时，各项指标均大幅度下降，苜蓿生长受到明显抑制。耿华珠等[7]对32种苜蓿品种进行了抗盐性研究，结果得出切罗克、秘鲁、公农一号等表现较好，它们在1% NaCl浓度中的发芽率均能达到60%以上。对牧草的耐盐性

---

① 李春燕，女，硕士，潍坊科技学院助教。研究方向：植物种质资源。E－mail：309606054@qq.com

的研究多集中于萌发期和幼苗期两个阶段。王榕楷等[8]的研究认为，植物的耐盐性随个体的发育阶段而变化。龚明等[9]也指出，植物在萌发及幼苗期耐盐性最差，其次是生殖期，而其他的发育阶段对盐胁迫相对不敏感。王占升等[10]对5种禾本科牧草不同生育阶段的耐盐力进行比较实验得出，牧草苗期耐盐力较低，中期较高。种子是植物重要的繁殖材料，它在发芽阶段的耐盐状况一定程度上反映了该物种的耐盐程度[11]。种子耐盐程度是耐盐碱植物筛选与早期鉴定的主要依据之一[12]。

进行苜蓿属牧草耐盐性研究，对其在盐碱地萌发并成功建植，改善苜蓿的栽培管理方法有一定作用。本研究利用不同浓度的氯化钠单盐溶液对6种苜蓿属植物种子的萌发期的耐盐性进行比较，以评价其萌发时期耐盐性差异，为苜蓿属耐盐性品种选育及在盐碱胁迫条件下改善种子的萌发特性提供帮助。

1 材料与方法

1.1 实验材料

黄花苜蓿（*Medicago falcate* L.），内蒙古农业大学提供种子；中苜一号紫花苜蓿（*Medicago sativa* L. *cv. zhongmu No.* 1），中苜二号紫花苜蓿（*Medicago sativa* L. *cv. zhongmu No.* 2）；阿尔冈金（*Medicago sativa* L. *cv. algonquin*），甘农三号（*Medicago sativa L. cv. Gannong No.* 3），大叶苜蓿（*Medicago sativa L. cv. Daye*），中国农业大学种子检验中心提供。单盐溶液由分析纯氯化钠（北京化学试剂公司生产）配制，纯度≥99.5%。

1.2 试验方法

试验选用氯化钠溶液作为种子发芽的培养液，设定0（CK）、20mmol/L（M1）、40mmol/L（M2）、60mmol/L（M3）、100mmol/L（M4）、140mmol/L（M5）、200 mmol/L（M6）7个浓度。

种子用10%的次氯酸钠溶液消毒5min，依照国际牧草种子检验规程[13]，发芽床采用滤纸法。在恒温20℃的培养箱内用培养皿做发芽试验，设置每天8h光照，16h黑暗，每皿放50粒种子，加等体积的盐溶液10ml，每一种处理重复4次，并用称重法每两天补充其所损失的水分[14]。从第4d开始统计记录发芽数目，10d后发芽数量不再变化，结束发芽试验。在发芽结束时，测定其根长和芽长。

1.3 测定指标

发芽势从第4d统计，6、8、10d各统计一次。计算各处理下的相对发芽势，发芽率，相对发芽率，发芽指数，根长，苗长。各指标计算方法如下。

种子发芽势 = 发芽初期（规定日期内）正常发芽粒数/供检种子粒数 ×100%

相对发芽势为一定氯化钠溶液处理下的发芽势与对照溶液下发芽势的百分比

种子发芽率 = 发芽终期（规定日期内）全部正常发芽粒数/供检种子数 ×100%

相对发芽率为一定氯化钠溶液处理下的发芽率与对照溶液下发芽率的百分比。

发芽指数（GI）＝∑（Gt/Dt），式中，Gt 为不同时间的发芽数，Dt 为相应的发芽日数，∑为总和。

根长和芽长测定：每个培养皿选取 5 株用直尺进行测量，取平均值。

1.4 数据处理

数据通过 Excel 和 SPSS11.5 软件进行单因素方差分析（ANOVA）处理分析。

2 结果与分析

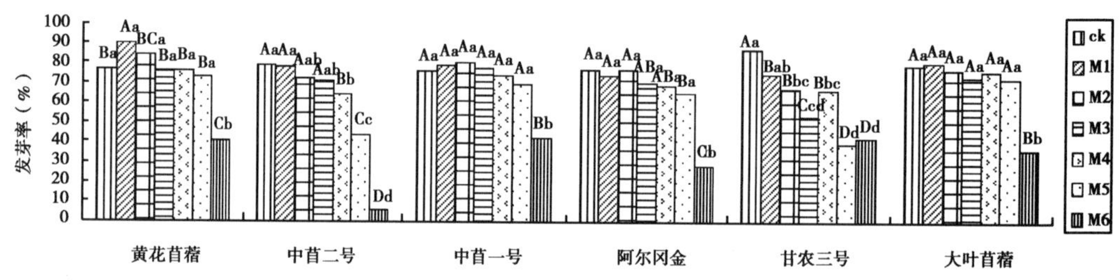

图 1 不同浓度氯化钠溶液处理下不同苜蓿品种的发芽率

注：不同大、小写字母分别表示同品种间差异显著（P<0.05）同品种间差异极显著（P<0.01）

2.1 不同浓度氯化钠溶液对种子发芽率和相对发芽率的影响

由图 1 可以看出，在低浓度盐处理（20，40mmol/L）下，各品种苜蓿的发芽率都略高于或是接近于对照，说明低浓度盐分对种子萌发有促进作用，这种现象可能与低盐促进细胞膜渗透调节有关，也可能与微量的无机离子（Na^+）对呼吸酶激活作用有关[15]。这与大多数耐盐植物的研究相符合[16]。随胁迫浓度的增加，各个品种的发芽率呈下降趋势，说明盐胁迫对苜蓿种子萌发有一定的抑制作用。但因品种的不同抑制的程度有所不同，其中黄花苜蓿、中苜一号苜蓿、阿尔冈金苜蓿和大叶苜蓿在低浓度（20，40mmol/L）和中浓度（60，100 mmol/L）下发芽率均能达到 60% 以上，并且在各个浓度之间差异不显著（P>0.05），说明这 4 个品种的耐盐力相当。而在高浓度氯化钠单盐胁迫下（200 mmol/L），各个品种的发芽率受到极显著抑制（P<0.01）。中苜二号品种在 20～60 mmol/L 盐胁迫下，发芽率差异不显著（P>0.05），但是在 100～200mmol/L 盐浓度下，发芽率均受到极显著抑制作用（P<0.01）。甘农三号品种发芽率随浓度的变化较为反常，规律不明显，在个别盐浓度下的发芽率有略高于前一浓度的现象，这可能与实验存在误差有关。

由表 1 可知，6 种苜蓿的相对发芽率随氯化钠盐浓度的增加而逐渐受到抑制。在 100 mmol/L 盐胁迫下，各个苜蓿品种的相对发芽率都达到 80% 以上，说明此浓度下的 4 个苜蓿品种还有较强的耐盐力，并且黄花苜蓿、中苜一号和大叶苜蓿的相对发芽率均达到 90% 以上，与中苜二号和甘农三号在此浓度下的相对发芽率相比达到显著水平

(P<0.05)。在140 mmol/L盐浓度下，中苜二号品种和甘农三号的相对发芽率迅速下降，与其他4个品种的差异达到极显著水平（P<0.01），说明此浓度下的中苜二号和甘农三号耐盐力较差，而其他4个品种仍有一定的耐盐力。当盐浓度达到200 mmol/L时，各个品种的相对发芽率均大幅度下降，在此盐浓度基础上以相对发芽率的显著水平评定这六种苜蓿的耐盐力的顺序为：中苜一号>黄花苜蓿>大叶苜蓿>阿尔冈金>甘农三号>中苜二号。

表1 不同苜蓿品种在不同盐浓度胁迫下的相对发芽率

植物材料	NaCl浓度（mmol/L）					
	M1	M2	M3	M4	M5	M6
黄花苜蓿	116.88Aa	109.09Aa	98.70Aa	98.70Aa	94.37Aa	53.25Aa
中苜二号	98.73BCb	91.77Bb	89.37Aa	81.01Bb	55.06Bb	7.60Cb
中苜一号	103.95Bb	105.92Aab	101.75Aa	97.71Aab	90.79Aa	55.92ABa
阿尔冈金	96.52Cb	99.78ABab	91.30Aa	89.56ABab	84.78Aa	37.17Ba
甘农三号	86.13Dc	78.03Cc	61.27Bb	76.87Bc	45.66Bb	36.55Ba
大叶苜蓿	101.89Bb	96.83Bb	92.4Aa	96.2Aab	91.77Aa	46.2Ba

注：不同大、小写字母分别表示同列内差异显著（P<0.05）表示同列内差异极显著（P<0.01）。

2.2 不同浓度氯化钠溶液对种子发芽势（相对发芽势）的影响

由图2可看出，6个苜蓿品种在不同浓度单盐处理下相对发芽势随浓度的增加而降低，其中，中苜二号和甘农三号较为明显。在低浓度盐（20、40mmol/L）处理下，黄花苜蓿、中苜一号和大叶苜蓿的相对发芽势略高于对照，其他品种也较为接近，差异不明显。在第4d时，除中苜二号和甘农三号外，其他品种在低于200mmol/L下，相对发芽势均大于0.6，并且在其后的时间变化不大，说明苜蓿种子的发芽力在200mmol/L盐浓度以下其变化较不明显，盐浓度的变化对其不是很敏感，其发芽力在一定盐浓度范围内随盐胁迫时间的延长而减弱。0~200mmol/L的盐溶液对中苜二号和甘农三号的相对发芽势影响较为均匀，浓度达到140mmol/L，相对发芽势低于50%，严重抑制其萌发能力。各个品种在高浓度盐处理下（140、200mmol/L）随着时间的推移，相对发芽势呈增长趋势，说明高浓度下种子后期的发芽力较强。

2.3 不同浓度氯化钠溶液对苜蓿种子发芽指数的影响

发芽率这一指标可以反映盐分对种子萌发的影响，但不能反映出苗的整齐度。发芽指数这个指标则表示种子萌发速度和田间出苗的一致性[17]。从发芽指数上看，由图3可知在低浓度20mmol/L盐胁迫下，除黄花苜蓿略高于对照外，其余5种苜蓿的出苗率较为一致。黄花苜蓿在20~140 mmol/L盐浓度胁迫下，其发芽指数差异不显著（P>0.05），200mmol盐浓度胁迫下差异极显著（P<0.01）。中苜一号、阿尔冈金和大叶苜

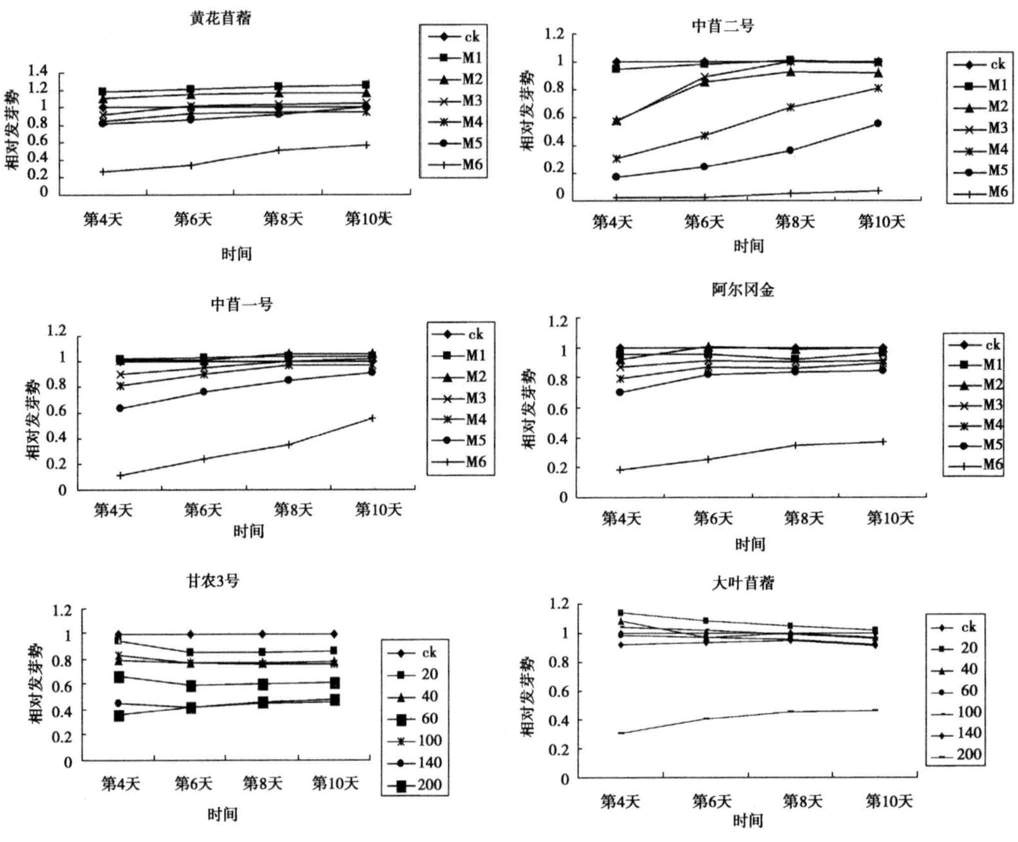

图 2 不同浓度氯化钠处理下不同苜蓿品种的相对发芽势

蓿在 20～60mmol/L 盐浓度胁迫下发芽指数差异不显著，在 100～200mmol/L 盐浓度下差异显著（$P<0.05$）。而随着盐浓度的增加，中苜二号和甘农三号发芽指数则呈现明显下降趋势，差异达到极显著水平（$P<0.01$），说明中苜二号种子在中高浓度盐溶液胁迫下萌发出苗整齐度不是很高。

2.4 不同浓度氯化钠溶液对苜蓿种子萌发胚根胚芽的影响

根是植物的重要生长器官，根系的生长直接关系着植物对土壤水分和养分的吸收，营养物质的储存与转化，影响着植物地上部分的生长和发育[18]。研究胁迫环境对种子萌发的影响时，多以根的生长为指标之一[19]。由表 2 可知，当盐浓度大于 40 mmol/L 时，随着盐浓度的增加，各个苜蓿品种的胚根生长均受到抑制。这是由于在盐胁迫环境下苜蓿幼苗的根细胞失水，影响了根的正常生长[20]。在 20mmol/L 盐浓度下，黄花苜蓿、大叶苜蓿和中苜一号的胚根长和胚芽长，中苜二号和阿尔冈金的胚芽长均高于对照，说明低盐对苜蓿品种的胚根和胚芽均有促进作用。在 20～100 mmol/L 盐浓度胁迫下，各苜蓿品种的胚芽长在此浓度间差异不显著（$P>0.05$），而其胚根长却差异显著（$P<0.05$），有的还达到极显著水平（$P<0.01$）。说明盐分对胚根的影响大于胚芽，胚根对盐分胁迫来说是一个较为敏感的部位。这与石东里等[19]研究较为一致。

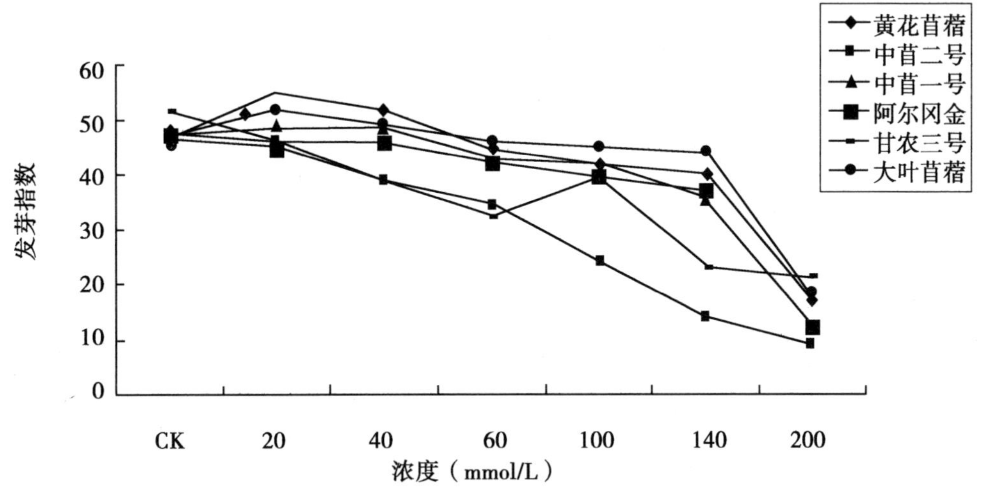

图 3　不同浓度氯化钠溶液处理下不同苜蓿的发芽指数

表 2　不同浓度氯化钠溶液处理下不同苜蓿品种胚芽胚根长

浓度	黄花苜蓿		中苜二号		中苜一号		阿尔冈金		甘农 3 号		大叶苜蓿	
(mmol/l)	胚芽长	胚根	胚芽长	胚根	胚芽长	胚根	胚芽长	胚根	胚芽长	胚根	胚芽长	胚根
ck	1.48Aab	3.38Bb	1.30Aab	6.96Aa	1.75Aab	5.89Aa	1.72Aa	5.62Aa	1.39ABab	6.58Aa	1.89Aa	5.47ABa
20	1.47Aab	4.24Aa	1.33Aa	5.06Bab	1.85Aa	6.16Aa	1.73Aa	5.46ABa	1.32BCab	5.30Bab	1.88Aa	6.41Aa
40	1.55Aa	4.46Aa	1.28Aab	3.78BCbc	1.61ABab	5.20Ba	1.65Aab	5.03ABCa	1.26BCb	4.88BCb	1.84Aa	5.26Ba
60	1.43Aab	3.30Bb	1.30Aab	4.48Bbc	1.64ABab	3.98Cb	1.36ABab	4.488CDab	1.6Aa	3.85CDbc	1.88Aa	3.25Cb
100	1.37Aab	3.34Bb	1.20 Aab	3.64BCbc	1.61ABab	3.92Cb	1.31ABab	4.592BCab	1.2BCbc	3.63DEbc	1.45Bb	3.33Cb
140	1.12Bbc	2.25Cc	0.96Bb	2.48Ccd	1.35Bb	2.66Dc	1.16Bab	3.642Db	1.1CDbc	2.59Ecd	1.18Cbc	2.84Cb
200	0.95Bc	0.72d	0.50Cc	0.75Dd	0.89Cc	1.25Ed	1.01Bb	1.13Ec	0.94Dc	1.13Fd	1.04Cc	1.17Dc

注：不同大写字母表示同列内差异显著（$P < 0.05$）；不同小写字母表示同列内差异极显著（$P < 0.01$）

3　小结与讨论

低浓度的氯化钠胁迫能促进种子的萌发，随着盐胁迫浓度的增加，不同苜蓿种子萌发的各项指标均呈下降趋势。在中低浓度盐胁迫下，各苜蓿品种的抗盐性差异并不很明显，但在高浓度盐胁迫下，各苜蓿品种间的抗盐性差异显著。就相对发芽率、相对发芽势而言，中苜一号、黄花苜蓿和大叶苜蓿的耐盐性较为接近，大于阿尔冈金、甘农三号和中苜二号。中苜二号和甘农三号就萌发率和出苗整齐度而言都显著低于其他 4 种牧草。就这 6 种苜蓿而言，140 ~ 200mmol/L 盐浓度适宜作为其耐盐性萌发鉴定地胁迫浓度。

胚根胚芽作为植物萌发期耐盐性的重要指标，其胚根的敏感度要大于胚芽。

实验采用不同浓度的氯化钠单盐对不同苜蓿种子进行萌发试验，可能并不能完全代表大田天然盐的胁迫效果，需要采集不同盐碱地地区的盐结皮对其进行进一步验证。另外，苜蓿的耐盐性与其生理生化作用是分不开的，因此，应进一步研究其发芽时期的生理指标来更好的鉴定其耐盐性。

参 考 文 献

[1] Flowerst Salinisation and Ortiz cultural production [J]. Scientia Horticulture, 1999, 78: 1241

[2] 谢振宇，杨光穗．牧草耐盐性进展 [J]. 草业科学，2003，20 (8)：11 -17

[3] 翟凤林，曹庆鸣等．植物的耐盐性及改良 [M]. 北京：农业出版社，1989：341 -335

[4] 王玉民，刘艳芝，王中伟等．我国苜蓿耐盐性研究现状及评述 [J]. 吉林农业科学，2005，30 (6)：47 -49

[5] 韩清芳等．不同苜蓿品种种子萌发期耐盐性研究 [J]. 西北植物学报，2003，23 (4)：597 -602

[6] 周丽霞等．盐分含量不同对不同休眠性苜蓿出苗与生长的影响 [J]. 草业科学，1998，15 (2)：55 -59，61

[7] 耿华珠等．苜蓿耐盐性鉴定初报 [J]. 中国草地，1990，(2)：69

[8] 王榕楷等．三种草坪草的耐寒性及其与超氧化物歧化酶作用关系初步研究 [J]. 中国草地，2001，23 (1)：46 -49

[9] 龚明，刘友良，丁念成等．不同生长阶段小麦耐盐性差异 [J]. 西北植物学报，1994，14 (1)：1 -7

[10] 王占升，朱汉等．牧草耐盐力及盐碱地引种试验 [J]. 中国草地，1995，(2)：38 -42 ，19

[11] Gupta G N. Salt tolerance in dome tree species at seedling stage [J]. Indian Forest, 1987，12：101 -112

[12] 阎顺国，沈禹颖．生态因子对碱茅种子萌发期耐盐性影响的数量分析 [J]. 植物生态学报，1996，20 (5)：414 -422

[13] 牧草种子检验规程 [S]. GB/ T 2 930，1 - 2 930. 11 -2 001

[14] 薛勇．不同品种紫花苜蓿种子萌发期耐盐性比较试验 [J]. 当代苜蓿，2007，3：39 -40

[15] 赵可夫．NaCl 抑制棉花幼苗生长的机理——盐离子效应 [J]. 植物生理学报，1998，24 (4)：173 -176

[16] 沈禹颖，阎顺国，余玲．盐分浓度对碱茅种子萌发的影响 [J]. 草业科学，1991，3：68 -71

[17] 李昀，沈禹颖，阎顺国．氯化钠胁迫下 5 种牧草种子萌发的比较研究 [J]. 草业科学，1997，14 (2)：50 -53

[18] 石东里，赵丽萍，姚志刚．大穗结缕草萌发期耐盐能力试验 [J]. 湖北农业科学，2007，46 (5)：782 -784

[19] Muller D A. Germination and root growth of 4 osmosis conditioned cool-season grasses [J]. Range Manage, 1996, 49: 117 - 120
[20] 崔辉梅，陈曾．盐胁迫对白菜种子萌发和幼苗生长的影响 [J]．安徽农业科学，2006，34（18）：4 680 - 4 682

Research of Salt Tolerance During Germinating Period of Six Alfalfa Varieties

LI Chun - yan
(*Weifang University of Science and Technology*, *Shouguang* 262700)

Abstract: Alfalfa is good leguminous grass. By identifying the salt tolerance during sprouting period, it can improve the efficiency of introduction and provide basic data for breeding for salt resistance. Under laboratory conditions, 6 alfalfa varieties were identified by 7 different concentrations of NaCl solutions: 0、20、40、60、100、140、200 mmol/L. Salt tolerance of 6 kinds of seeds was compared according to relative germination energy, germination percentage, relative germination percentage, germination index and radical length, germ length. The results showed that: low NaCl concentration can promote the germination of 4 kinds of alfalfa seeds . But as the concentration increasing, all indexes were decreasing and the germination was inhibited. Different varieties adapt to different NaCl concentration. As relative germination energy and relative germination percentage, seeds of Medicago falcate L. and Medicago sativa L cv. zhongmu No. 1 are more tolerated than other varieties under NaCl stress, but seeds of Medicago sativa L cv. zhongmu No. 2 is the lest tolerated. It also showed that radicle is more sensitive than germ under NaCl stress.

Key words: Alfalfa; Germination; Salt tolerance; Index

苎麻细胞质雄性不育“三系”ISSR特异片段克隆和序列分析

李建永① 周荣廷 高俊平 李法君
（潍坊科技学院，寿光 262700）

摘 要：利用ISSR分子标记技术对苎麻细胞质雄性不育“三系”mtDNA进行多态性分析；在选用的38个ISSR引物中，有6个引物的扩增产物在不育系、保持系和恢复系之间存在差异。对这些特异性片段进行克隆和序列测定，结果表明，片段21-MS（GenBank登陆号：EU122345）全长956bp，包含一个525bp的完整编码区，共编码174个氨基酸。片段31-M/R（GenBank登陆号：EU122344）全长778bp，包含一个404bp的不完整编码区，共编码134个氨基酸；其核苷酸和氨基酸序列与已报道的多种植物中的番茄红素β-环化酶基因分别存在71%~76%和73%~77%的同源性。

关键词：苎麻；线粒体DNA；简单重复序列间区（ISSR）；番茄红素β-环化酶；细胞质雄性不育

高等植物的细胞质雄性不育（Cytoplasmic male sterility，CMS）是普遍存在的，到目前为止已在300多种植物中发现[1]。雄性不育在杂种优势利用中占极为重要的地位，长期以来，人们一直都在对其不育机理进行探讨。大量研究结果表明，CMS属于母性遗传，与线粒体基因组密切相关，但雄性不育的生理学和遗传学机制还远未阐明。苎麻雄性不育特性早在20世纪60~70年代就被发现存在于若干地方品种之中[2]。苎麻以收获营养体为目的，其杂种优势利用比其他收获种子的作物更为便利，因此备受育种工作者重视[3]。从苎麻雄性不育特性被发现以来，人们对其机理的研究主要集中在生理生化方面[4]，在分子生物学方面的研究国内外还未见报道。

ISSR（inter-simple sequence repeats）标记技术对简单重复序列（simple sequence repeats SSR）之间的DNA序列进行扩增。由于微卫星在基因组中广泛分布，而且等位变异特别丰富，ISSR因此可以检测到基因组多个位点的差异，而且无需预知研究对象的基因组序列[5]。

苎麻是我国的传统特产，是最优良的纤维作物之一，其种植面积和产量占世界总量

① 李建永，男，硕士，潍坊科技学院助教。研究方向：植物基因工程与遗传育种。E-mail：ljy_19810520@163.com

的90%以上。苎麻雄性不育杂种优势组合已应用于生产，但雄性不育的分子基础研究还罕见报道。本实验采用ISSR分子标记技术对苎麻胞质雄性不育系（SS370）、保持系（GS13-X_1）和恢复系（细叶青）mtDNA进行多态性比较，对相关特异性片段进行克隆和序列分析，探讨这些特异片段与苎麻CMS的关系，期望为揭示苎麻雄性不育的分子遗传学机制积累资料。

1 材料与方法

1.1 实验材料

实验材料为苎麻（*Boehmeria nivea*（L.）Gaud.）胞质雄性不育系SS370（A），相应的保持系GS13-X_1（B）和恢复系细叶青（R）。其中不育系和保持系为项目组成员在前期工作中从同一品种的孤雌生殖诱导后代中培育获得，恢复系则通过测交获得；不育系经遗传分析推测为核-质互作型不育[6]。

1.2 实验试剂

ISSR引物（加拿大哥伦比亚大学提供序列）由上海生工（Sangon）合成；dNTP、*Taq*酶为MBI公司产品；pGEM-T载体及T4连接酶购自Promega公司；DNA分子量标准和胶回收试剂盒购自北京天根生化科技有限公司；大肠杆菌DH5α为本实验室保存；其他试剂均为国产分析纯。

1.3 苎麻mtDNA提取

苎麻mtDNA提取主要参考Scotti等[7]的蔗糖衬垫法，略有改动。

1.4 ISSR-PCR扩增

根据ISSR反应体系优化结果设定20μl PCR反应体系：1×Taq酶配套缓冲液，2.5mmol/L $MgCl_2$，1.5U *Taq*酶（MBI），25ng模板DNA，0.75μmol/L引物，dATP、dCTP、dGTP、dTTP各0.15mmol/L。扩增程序为：94℃预变性5min；94℃变性30s，52℃退火45s，72℃延伸80s，共40个循环；72℃完全延伸10min。

1.5 多态性比较分析

选用38个ISSR随机引物（加拿大哥伦比亚大学提供序列，序列见表3-1），先排除其中无条带和无多态性的引物，再对有多态性的引物作2~4次重复，最后选取重复性和稳定性较好的引物进行多态性比较分析。

表1 使用的 ISSR 引物

引物	序列	引物	序列
ISSR-1	5′-(GCT)(AGT)(GCT)$(CA)_6$-3′	ISSR-22	5′-$(CT)_8$T-3′
ISSR-2	5′-(AGC)(ACT)(AGC)$(GT)_7$-3′	ISSR-23	5′-$(CT)_8$(AG)G-3′
ISSR-3	5′-(AGT)(GCT)(AGT)$(GA)_7$-3′	ISSR-24	5′-CGCC$(GA)_6$-3′
ISSR-4	5′-G$(CA)_4$C-3′	ISSR-25	5′-$(GGGGT)_3$-3′
ISSR-5	5′-$(CT)_8$(AG)G-3′	ISSR-26	5′-$(GA)_8$(CT)G-3′
ISSR-6	5′-$(CT)_8$(AG)C-3′	ISSR-27	5′-$(AT)_8$C-3′
ISSR-7	5′-CCC$(GT)_6$-3′	ISSR-28	5′-$(GT)_8$(CT)C-3′
ISSR-8	5′-G(GC)G$(GT)_6$-3′	ISSR-29	5′-$(CT)_8$(AG)C-3′
ISSR-10	5′-GC(AT)$(GA)_6$G-3′	ISSR-30	5′-$(GAA)_5$-3′
ISSR-11	5′-CCA$(GAG)_4$-3′	ISSR-31	5′-$(AG)_8$CG-3′
ISSR-12	5′-GCG$(AC)_6$A-3′	ISSR-32	5′-CCA$(GAG)_4$-3′
ISSR-13	5′-$(TAT)_5$-3′	ISSR-33	5′-GGA$(GTG)_4$-3′
ISSR-14	5′-$(GGC)_5$-3′	ISSR-34	5′-CCA$(GTG)_4$-3′
ISSR-15	5′-$(AGC)_5$-3′	ISSR-35	5′-$(TG)_8$(AG)G-3′
ISSR-16	5′-$(ACTG)_4$-3′	ISSR-36	5′-GCGCATATG$(GACA)_3$GC-3′
ISSR-18	5′-$(TGCA)_4$-3′	ISSR-37	5′-$(GGAT)_5$-3′
ISSR-19	5′-$(GGGGT)_3$-3′	ISSR-38	5′-$(GATA)_4$-3′
ISSR-20	5′-$(AT)_8$T-3′	ISSR-39	5′-$(CAG)_5$-3′
ISSR-21	5′-$(CA)_8$(AG)T-3′	ISSR-40	5′-$(GGAGA)_3$-3′

1.6 特异条带的回收、克隆和测序

将差异片段用无菌消毒刀片在长波紫外灯下从琼脂糖凝胶上切下，用胶回收试剂盒进行纯化、回收。用 pGEM-T 克隆载体连接并转化到感受态大肠杆菌 DH5α 中；涂布于加有氨苄青霉素、IPTG 及 X-gal 的抗性 LB 平板上进行蓝白斑筛选。挑取白色菌落，在液体 LB 培养基中扩大繁殖。用碱裂解法[8]从菌液中提取质粒，以通用测序引物 T7 和 SP6 进行常规 PCR 检测。对阳性克隆进行序列测定（由上海生工代为完成）。

1.7 序列分析

将测序得到的核苷酸序列用开放阅读框（Open Reading Frame，ORF）分析软件 ORF Finder（http://www.ncbi.nlm.nih.gov/projects/gorf）查找其编码区（即 ORF）；登陆 GenBank，用 BLAST 程序（http://www.ncbi.nlm.nih.gov/BLAST）对其核苷酸序列及编码的氨基酸序列进行同源性检索分析。

2 结果与分析

2.1 苎麻 mtDNA 纯度和完整性

经琼脂糖凝胶电泳、EB 染色后可在紫外灯下观察到 23kb 左右的 mtDNA 带，所含杂质少，没有出现大量降解的现象，说明通过上述提纯方法，能得到相对完整的线粒体 DNA（图 1）。

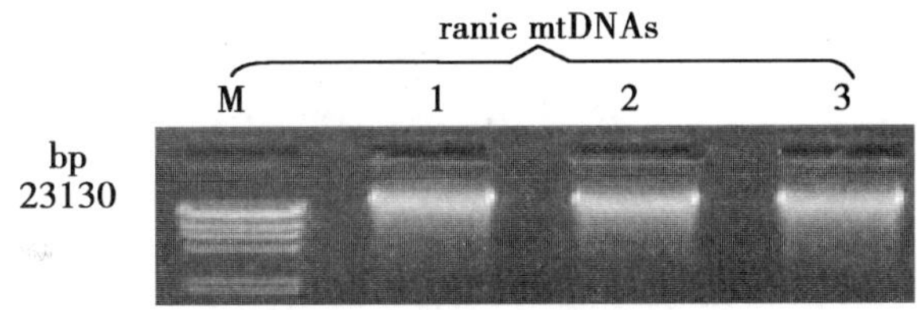

图 1 苎麻 mtDNA 琼脂糖凝胶电泳检测

M. DL250$^+$ DNA 标准分子量；1. SS370；2. GS13-X_1；3. 细叶青；白色箭头指示多态性条带

根据经验数据，OD_{260}/OD_{280}比值在 1.7～1.9 之间时，DNA 的纯度较高。测定所提取的 mtDNA 的 OD_{260}/OD_{280}，SS370 为 1.84，GS13-X_1 为 1.78，细叶青为 1.68，说明所提取的 mtDNA 的纯度较高，可满足后续实验的需要。

2.2 苎麻“三系”mtDNA 的多态性分析结果

在选用的 38 个引物中，有 5 个无扩增产物或扩增产物带谱不清晰，其他引物均能扩增出 1～6 条清晰可辨的条带。初选出 15 个具多态性的引物，再经多次重复，只有 6 个引物能够扩增出具有较高稳定性和重复性的多态性条带（图 2）。

回收并克隆引物 ISSR-21 的扩增产物中不育系特异多出约 1 000bp 的条带（命名为：21-MS，下同）；引物 ISSR-23 的扩增产物中不育系特异多出约 900bp 的条带（23-MS）；保持系和恢复系均多出约 750bp 的条带（23-M/R01）和 500bp 的条带（23-M/R02）；引物 ISSR-31 的扩增产物中保持系和恢复系均多出约 750bp 的条带（31-M/R）；引物 ISSR-35 的扩增产物中不育系特异多出约1 400bp 的条带（35-MS），保持系和恢复系均多出约 1 000bp 的条带（35-M/R）。克隆结果经重组检测后，选取其中的阳性克隆进行序列测定（3～5 个重复）。

2.3 ISSR 特异片段序列分析结果

测序结果经分析后，除片段 21-MS 序列和 31-M/R 序列外，其他的 5 个特异片段均为无研究意义的非编码序列。

片段 21-MS 序列（GenBank 登陆号：EU 122345）全长 956bp，A + T 含量为 57.85%。序列包含一个 525bp 的完整编码区（即 ORF，位于 233～757bp 区域），共编码 174 个氨基酸（图 3）。用 Omiga2.0 进行启动子序列结构分析发现，在其 ORF 上游

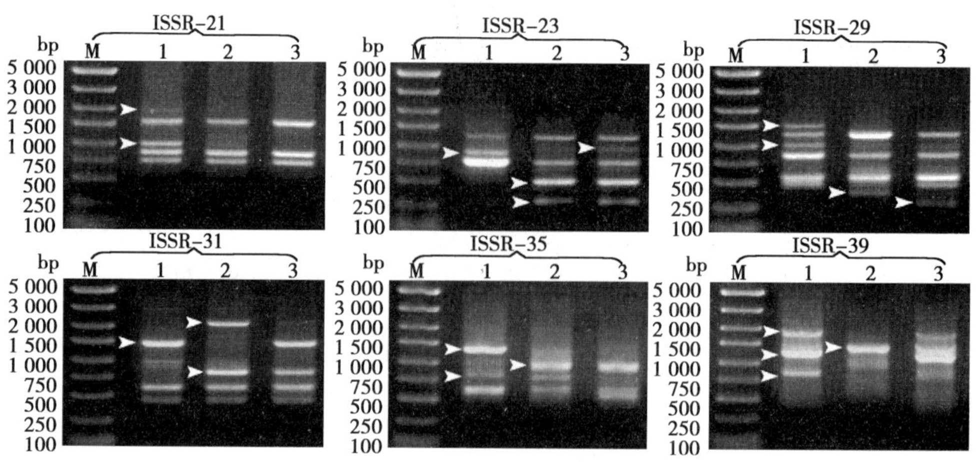

图 2 苎麻“三系”mtDNA 的 ISSR-PCR 扩增结果

M. DL250⁺ DNA 标准分子量；1. SS370；2. GS13-X_1；3. 细叶青；白色箭头指示多态性条带

区域存在 4 个 TATA 盒（分别位于 28 ~ 34bp、163 ~ 170bp、184 ~ 189bp、199 ~ 202bp 区域）和 1 个 CAAT 盒（126 ~ 131bp 区域）（图 3）。

21-MS sequence

```
CACACACACACACACAATAATATCACCTATATTAGTACTCATTCTCTCTTTGCCACACCCAAAAGCTCTAAAATGTGCCT   80
                           TATA box
CTCTCAACCCTTCTCTGTCTCTTTTGCCTTTAGTACTATTAACCACCCAATACACAGTAAGCCCACATAGCGGTTTCACT   160
                                            CAAT box
ATTATAAATACTCTCATTATTATTATAAAGTTCTCACATATAGGCACACATTTTTTTTTTCCTTTCAAAGTTATGGATTT   240
  TATA box                TATA box                                     ORF—■ D F
TGGAGTGGTGGGTTTGGATCACCATCATCACCATCATCATGGATTGGGAATTTCTTCTTCTTCCTCTTCTTCTTCGGCCG   320
 G  V  V  G  L  D  H  H  H  H  H  H  H  G  L  G  I  S  S  S  S  S  S  S  S  A  G
GTTTTGGTCCCAACACTGTGATATCTTCTTCTTCTTGCTCAGATCCTGAGACCAAGCAGAGAACATTATACGGATCTGGG   400
  F  G  P  N  T  V  I  S  S  S  S  C  S  D  P  E  T  K  Q  R  T  L  Y  G  S  G
CTGTGCTGTAACAACAACAACAACAATAATAATAACAATAACAACAATAGCGACGTTATAAAGCAAGAGAGATCTGCAGG   480
L  C  C  N  N  N  N  N  N  N  N  N  N  N  N  N  S  D  V  I  K  Q  E  R  S  A  G
CTCGGGTCTCGAGGAGTATTGGAGGAGCTCCAAGGTCGCCAAGGCCAGTGGTTGTGGCGTCGTTGTTGTTGATGACGATG   560
 S  G  L  E  E  Y  W  R  S  S  K  V  A  K  A  S  G  C  G  V  V  V  V  D  D  D  D
ATTTCTCATCGGCCTGCAAAGGAATGATGTTTCAGCAGAGGAACAGTCACAACACTTTGCTGAGATCTAATTCCAACACT   640
  F  S  S  A  C  K  G  M  M  F  Q  Q  R  N  S  H  N  T  L  L  R  S  N  S  N  T
GCTAGTACCACTGCTTCCACTACCACTCTCAGCTTCTTGGACAATGAGCAACACTATAACCAACAGAGCCACCAAATGCT   720
A  S  T  T  A  S  T  T  T  L  S  F  L  D  N  E  Q  H  Y  N  Q  Q  S  H  Q  M  L
CAGCTTCTCTACTTCTGCTTCTTCTCCTTCTGCCTAATCAGAGGCTCATAACATCGCTACATTGCCTTACTTTCCCAGTG   800
 S  F  S  T  S  A  S  S  P  S  A  *
CTTACGCCGGTAGAAATACAGGGTAATATATGTTGTCATACAAAGTTGAAGTTTTTAGCTTTTCATTTTTGGGTTGGTTG   880
TTTGCATGGAGAGAATGGCTGGGTGCTTTAGTGGGTTTTGCTTTTTAGTTAGTGTGAGACTGTGTGTGTGTGTGTG   956
```

图 3 苎麻不育系特有片段 21-MS 核苷酸序列及其 ORF 编码的氨基酸序列

片段 31-M/R 序列（GenBank 登陆号：EU 122344）全长 778bp，A + T 含量为 55.14%。序列包含一个 404bp 的不完整编码区（位于 375 ~ 777bp 区域），共编码 134 个氨基酸（图 4）。

BLAST 分析表明，21-MS 的核苷酸序列及其 ORF 编码的氨基酸序列与以知基

31–M/R sequence

```
ACACACACACACACACCGTTCACATCATAAAAATCTCTCCTTTGAGAGTCCTCAAAAGGGCTTGTTTCTTTGTTTCTTTC 80
CATTAGCCTCTCCGATGTTTGGGTATCTAAAATGCTATATTCTCTGGTAAGTCCTCAACTTAATTACTCTTCCTAGCAGT 160
ATTAGTTTTTGCCGTGAAGAATTTTTTTTGTTTGTTTTGATTTCTGCTAAATTTTGCCTCTTCTAGGTGAAAAGTAAGTT 240
CCTTTACATGACCATGAGCCCAAAGACCCGTCCATGGAATTGATTTTCTGAGAATCAGAATCGGAATCATTGGAAATTTG 320
AGGTTACCCAGATAGGATTTTGCAGAGATATCGCCGACCCAGATTAGGATTTCCATGGATACTTTACTCAAAACACACAA 400
                                                     ORF—■ D T L L K T H N
CAAGCTTGAATTTTTGCACCCACTTCATGGGTTCTCGGAGAAATTGAGCAATTCAAACCCATCGAGGTTTCAAGAGCTTA 480
 K L E F L H P L H G F S E K L S N S N P S R F Q E L R
GGTTTGGACTGAAAAAGTCTCACATGAACTTGGGCAGGACTTCTTGTGTCAGGGCTAGTAGTACTAGTAGTAGTGCTCTT 560
  F G L K K S H M N L G R T S C V R A S S T S S S A L
CTTGAGCTTGTGCCTGAGACCAAAAAGGAGAATCTTGATTTTGAGCTTCCCTTGTATGACCCGTCGAAGGGCCTCGTCG 640
L E L V P E T K K E N L D F E L P L Y D P S K G L V V
TGACCTTGCGGTCGTTGGTGGCGGTCCTGCGGGGCTCGCTGTTGCTCAGCAAGTCTCGGAGGCGGGGCTATCGGTGTGCT 720
 D L A V V G G G P A G L A V A Q Q V S E A G L S V C S
CGGTTGACCCGTCCCCCAAGCTGATTTGGCCCAACAATTACGGTGTGTGTGTGTGTGT 778
  V D P S P K L I W P N N Y G V C V C
```

图 4 苎麻保持系与恢复系特有片段 31-M/R 核苷酸序列及其 ORF 编码的氨基酸序列

因同源性均低于 50%，表明该片段为不育系（SS 370）特有的新序列。31-M/R 中的一段核苷酸序列（位于 365～773bp 区域，长 409bp）与甜橙（*Citrus sinensis*，AY 679168）、葡萄（*Vitis vinifera*，AM 432668）、温州蜜橘（*Citrus unshiu*，AY 166796）、番木瓜（*Carica papaya*，DQ 415894）、烟草（*Nicotiana tabacum*，X 81787）等多种植物中番茄红素 β-环化酶（lycopene beta-cyclase allozyme，Lyc-b）基因部分序列存在 71%～76% 的同源性（表 2）；其 ORF 编码的氨基酸序列与甜橙（AAU05146）、温州蜜橘（AAN 86060）、葡萄（CAN 69313）、番木瓜（ABD 91578）、烟草（CAA 57386）等多种植物中 Lyc-b 的部分氨基酸序列存在 73%～77% 的同源性（表 2，图 5）。

表 2 苎麻保持系和恢复系特有片段 31-M/R 核苷酸及其编码氨基酸序列与其他植物 Lyc-b 基因同源性比较

Taxon	Homology in nucleotide sequence (%)	Homology in amino acid sequence (%)
Citrus sinensis	76	75
Citrus unshiu	75	75
Vitis vinifera	75	77
Carica papaya	74	73
Nicotiana tabacum	71	74

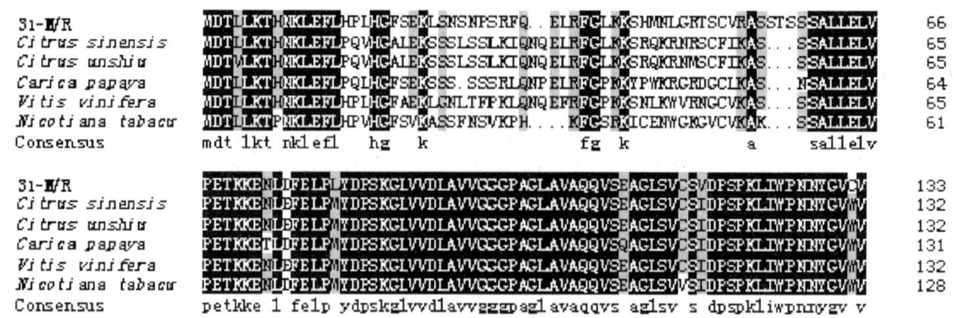

图5 苎麻保持系和恢复系特有片段31-M/R中ORF编码的氨基酸序列与其他植物Lyc-b氨基酸序列同源性比较

3 讨论

导致植物细胞质雄性不育的因素可能不止一种。从前人研究结果来看，CMS与线粒体基因组的结构变化和新的嵌合基因的产生有关，而其中已经鉴定的与CMS相关的嵌合基因大多与ATP合成酶或细胞色素c氧化酶有关，如碧冬茄中*Cox*基因以及其他植物*atpA*、*atp*6、*atp*9基因等[9,10]。前人对CMS的研究多用RAPD[11~13]和RFLP[14]等技术，利用ISSR技术对CMS的研究少见报道。

本研究利用ISSR分子标记技术对苎麻CMS“三系”mtDNA进行了多态性比较分析，在6个ISSR引物中找到了不育系、保持系和恢复系之间的差异片段，这些片段中有不育系特异缺失的，也有不育系特异多出的。序列分析结果表明特异片段21-MS的ORF上游区域存在RNA聚合酶和特异转录因子的结合位点TATA盒及CAAT盒。而仅由TATA盒及转录起始点即可构成最简单的启动子，因此，该序列内的ORF极有可能表达，但其表达产物是否引起雄性不育还需要下一步的实验证据。

特异片段31-M/R的编码区与一些植物的Lyc-b基因存在较高的同源性，而Lyc-b是将线性番茄红素转化为具环类胡萝卜素的关键酶[15]。植物中类胡萝卜素作为光捕获辅助色素和光氧化作用保护剂，在光合作用中发挥重要作用；同时，它也是构成花、果色泽的主要色素；有些类胡萝卜素还是ABA合成的前体[16]。若类胡萝卜素的合成受到抑制，将会直接影响植物的正常生长发育，而不育系中Lyc-b基因序列发生了变异。笔者猜测可能不育系恰好因为这一原因影响了细胞能量代谢，使得小孢子不能正常发育，最终导致CMS；而可育系因为Lyc-b基因正常，其育性并未受到影响。

参 考 文 献

[1] Kaul M L H. Male sterility in higher plants [M]. Berlin: Springer Verlag Press, 1988

[2] 李宗道. 苎麻生理生化与遗传育种 [M]. 北京: 中国农业出版社, 1989: 158－167

[3] Zhang Z-H (张中华), Wei G (魏刚), Yang Y (杨燕), *et al.* Breeding and utilization of ramie male sterility line “C26” [J]. *China's Fiber and Products* (中国麻业),

2005, 27 (3): 109 - 112

[4] Shong J (宋军), Zhang Z H (张中华), Pan G T (潘光堂), 2007. Physiological and biochemical characteristics in ramie male sterile lines [J]. *Journal of Tropical and Subtropical Botany* (热带亚热带植物学报), 2007, 15 (5): 423 - 428

[5] He Y Q (何予卿), Zhang Y (张宇), Sun H (孙海), *et al.* Studies on the relation ship between cultivated and wild Rice using ISSR markers [J]. *Journal of Agricultural Biotechnology* (农业生物技术学报), 2001, 9 (2): 123 - 127

[6] Liu F H (刘飞虎), Liang X N (梁雪妮), Zhang S W (张寿文), *et al.* Identification and heredity analysis of sterility for ramie male sterile lines [J]. *China' s Fiber Crops* (中国麻业), 2000, 22 (1): 6 - 9

[7] Scotti N, Card T, Marechal-Drouard L. Mitochondrial DNA and RNA isolation from small amounts of potato tissue [J]. *Plant Mol Biol Rep*, 2001, 19: 67a-67h

[8] 王关林, 方宏筠. 植物基因工程（第二版） [M]. 北京: 科学出版社, 2002: 734 - 735

[9] Hanson M R, Bentolia S. Interactions of mitochondrial and nuclear genes that affect male gametophyte development [J]. *Plant Cell*, 2004, 16: S154 - S169

[10] Kim D H, Kim B D. The organization of mitochondrial *atp*6 gene region in male fertile and CMS lines of pepper (*Capsicum annuum* L.) [J]. *Curr Genet*, 2006, 49: 59 - 67

[11] Yang J B (杨剑波), Wang X F (汪秀峰), Zhao C S (赵成松), *et al.* Cloning and Sequencing Analysis of the Specific DNA Fragment of Mitochondria From Maintainer of WA Type Rice [J]. *Journal of Plant Physiology and Molecular Biolog* (植物生理与分子生物学学报), 2003, 29 (3): 199 - 205

[12] Wang X L (王小利), Zhang G S (张改生), Liu H W (刘宏伟), *et al.* RAPD Analysis of Cytoplasmic Male Sterile Lines of Nian-Type Wheat [J]. *Acta Bot Boreal-Occident Sin* (西北植物学报), 2005, 25 (4): 681 - 68

[13] Zhang D S (张德双), Zhang F L (张凤兰), Wang Y J (王永健), *et al.* Cloning and Sequencing for RAPD Specific Fragments in Chinese Cabbage Cytoplasmic Male Sterile [J]. *Chinese Agricultural Science Bulletin* (农业生物技术科学), 2006, 22 (2): 44 - 50

[14] Huan W (黄威), Wang L (汪莉), Yi P (易平), *et al.* RFLP Analysis for Mitochondrial Genome of CMS-Rice [J]. *Acta Genetica Sinica* (遗传学报), 2003, 33 (4): 330 - 338

[15] Liang Y (梁燕), Wang M (王鸣), Chen H (陈杭), *et al.* The characteristics functions and relation ships of *LYCs* in plant [J]. *Acta Bot Boreal-Occident Sin* (西北植物学报), 2002, 22 (4): 993 - 998

[16] Rock C D, Zeevaart J A D. The ABA mutant of Ara-bidopsis thaliana is impaired in epoxy- carotenoid biosynthesis [J]. *Proc Natl Acad Sci USA*, 1991, 88: 7 496 - 7 499

Cloning and Sequencing for ISSR Specific Fragments in Cytoplasmic Male Sterile, Maintainer and Restorer Lines of Ramie (*Boehmeria nivea* L. *Gaud.*)

LI Jian-yong ZHOU Rong-ting GAO Jun-ping LI Fa-jun

(*Weifang University of Science and Technology*, *Shouguang* 262700)

Abstract: The polymorphic analysis of mtDNA from ramie cytoplasmic male sterile (MS), maintainer (M) and restorer (R) lines (three lines) were performed by using ISSR technique. Thirty-eight ISSR primers were used for testing mtDNA polymorphism and different amplified bands were observed in six primers in ramie "three lines", these specific bands were cloned and sequenced. Among those bands, the fragment 21-MS (GenBank accession number: EU122345) had 956bp in total length and a 525bp intact coding region that encoded a polypeptide consisting of 174 amino acids. Fragment 31-M/R (GenBank accession number: EU122344) had 778bp in total length and a 404bp incompletely coding region that encoded a polypeptide consisting of 134 amino acids; this fragment had 71% ~76% and 73% ~77% of homology in nucleotide and amino acid sequences with lycopene beta-cyclase allozyme gene in many other plants.

Key words: Ramie (*Boehmeria nivea* (L.) Gaud.); Mitochondrial DNA; Inter-simple sequence repeats (ISSR); lycopene beta-cyclase allozyme (Lyc-b); Cytoplasmic male sterile line

区域土地利用时空变化图谱分析——以海河流域为例

徐友信[①] 李宗珍

（潍坊科技学院，潍坊 262700）

摘 要： 运用地学信息图谱理论和方法，在 RS 和 GIS 的支持下，以海河流域 40a（1970—2008 年）土地利用 5 期空间数据（1970 年，1980 年，1990 年，2000 年，2008 年）为基础，合成了一系列土地利用图谱，包括 4 个时序单元的土地利用变化图谱，40a 变化过程图谱，并通过图谱重构，提取了海河流域 40a 土地利用变化的“涨势”系列图谱、40a“涨势”变化过程图谱和 40a 土地利用时空演变模式图谱。通过图谱分析，逐一分析了不同时序单元、不同空间尺度土地利用格局的变化规律，并总结了 40a 土地利用的分异规律。

关键词： 土地利用图谱；图谱分析；海河流域

自 20 世纪 90 年代以来，土地利用/覆被变化（LUCC）已成为全球环境变化研究的热点和核心领域[1~3]。地学信息图谱自 1988 年由陈述彭提出以来，以其图谱简单化、时空一体化和图谱直观化等特点，为土地利用/覆被变化研究提供了崭新的方法论和理论体系。国内外许多学者从不同角度和侧面对地学信息图谱进行了初步探讨和实践[4~9]。

本文以海河流域 5 期（1970—2008 年）土地覆盖动态监测数据为基础，利用地学信息图谱理论和方法，合成了一系列土地利用图谱。通过图谱分析，总结了海河流域 40a 土地利用的发展分异规律，以期为海河流域土地利用合理发展提供借鉴。

1 地学信息图谱基本原理

地学信息图谱是按照一定指标递变规律或分类规律排列的一组能够反映地球科学时空信息规律的数字形式的地图、图表、曲线或图像[10]。其基本组成单元为图谱单元。地学信息图谱单元是记录时空复合信息的基本单元，由“相对均质”的地理单元和

① 徐友信，男，硕士，潍坊科技学院助教。研究方向：生态修复，资源利用。E－mail：kelexu_ 0526@163. com

“相对均质”的时序单元复合而成。对于那些记录“最均一过程”和“最均质空间”的地学信息图谱单元，则称为“最小地学信息图谱单元”[11]。每个图谱单元上都对应着某一时刻、某位置上该单元的某些属性。地学信息图谱正是以图谱单元为依托来揭示土地利用发展变化规律的。图谱单元最大限度的保证了空间上的“同质性”和时间上的“唯一性”，可以采用能够同时反映空间差异和时序变化过程的状态变量 P（P1，P2，P3，P4，…，Pn）进行描述。在时间轴上，从起始采样时刻 T0 开始，其后续的采样点 T1，T2，T3，…上记录着相应时刻的空间位置与属性特征数据。采用 GIS 空间叠加的方法将各时刻的数据两两合成，得到的信息单元记录着 T0 ~ T1，T1 ~ T2，…两个或者连续时间段内的空间—属性一体化状态[12]。这样我们就可以提取所研究区域的时间转移过程及空间位置变化。土地利用地学信息图谱就是各时间段内土地利用变化的时空复合体数据。借助地学信息图谱单元，提取研究地理过程的时空复合体数据，以达到总结土地利用的发展分异规律、为区域决策服务的目的。

2 研究区概况

研究区位于东经 1 120° ~1 190°、北纬 350° ~420°之间，西与山西高原与黄河流域接界，北与蒙古高原与内陆河流域接界，南界黄河，东临渤海。包括河北、河南、山西、内蒙古、北京和天津 4 省 2 市（图 1），流域面积 23.2 万 km^2，占全国总面积的 2.4%。据 1993 年统计，海河流域内人口 1.176 亿人，约占全国总人口的 10%；耕地 1.63 亿亩，占全国耕地的 11%。海河流域处于中国干旱和湿润气候的过渡地带，多年年平均降水量为 548mm。流域多年平均水资源总量为 419 亿 m^3，产水系数（水资源总量与降水量之比）为 24%。人均水资源占有量仅有 $338m^3$，不足全国的 1/6。流域西北高，东南低，主要地貌类型为平原、山地、丘陵和台地。海拔最高处 3 059m，最低地方仅为 0m。

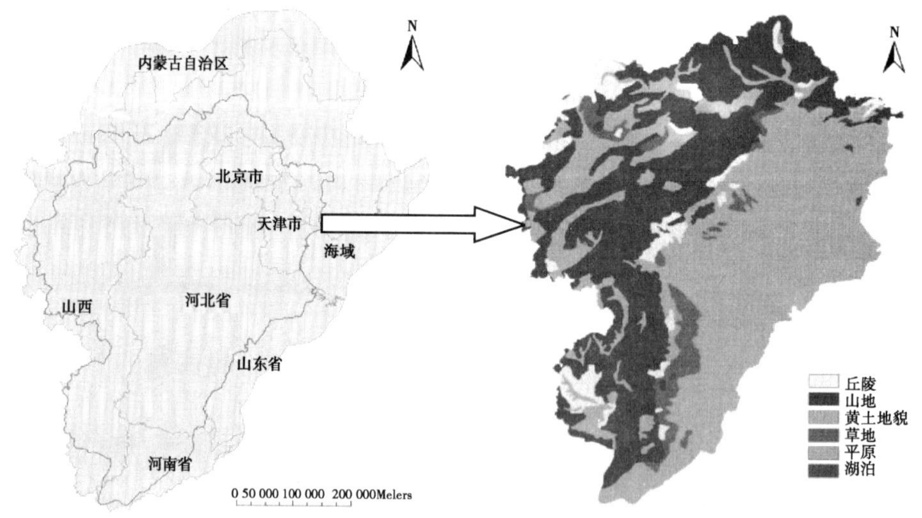

图 1 研究区位置示意图（右图为地貌图）

3 数据来源及处理

地学信息图谱单元的提取需要有具有一定时间间隔的土地利用状况数据作为基础。本文以海河流域生态环境治理工程项目，海河流域 5 期（1970 年，1980 年，1990 年，2000 年，2008 年）土地利用数据为基础，参照 2000 年矢量化底图，利用 GIS 和 RS 软件进行地图矢量化。对不同期影像进行配准，保证误差不超过 3 个像元，参照不同期遥感影像，对照统计数据，采用人机交互的方法对遥感影像进行分类，最终得到 5 期土地利用数据。利用野外调研数据进行检验，并采用误差矩阵进行评价，精度都达到 90%以上。

在已有各期土地利用数据的基础上，对土地利用类型进行重编码，以获取能最大反映土地利用变化的基本地物类别。为了便于进行空间数据之间的地图代数运算和编码的提取、综合以及图谱重构，以期能更好的在空间上反映各土地利用类型的时序变化状况，本文将土地利用类型编码设定为 6 类，分类方案见表 1。

表 1 土地利用分类编码

编码	1	2	3	4	5	6
土地类型	耕地	林地	草地	水域	建设用地	未利用地

对已有矢量数据进行归一化、标准化处理，选取 5 期数据的共有边界作为流域边界进行数据裁切，以确保不同期数据的统一性。各期数据统一采用 Custom Albers Equal-Area Conic 投影，其投影椭球体为 Krasovsky_ 1940，投影带中央经线为 105°E′第一标准纬线 25°N′第二标准纬线 47°N′所有数据均采用 grid 数据格式，取 30m × 30m 格网单元进行重采样。

4 土地利用系列图谱合成

土地利用变化图谱单元是进行土地利用图谱分析的基本单元，图谱单元是由相对均质的空间单元和相对均一的时间单元集合而成的[11]。图谱单元的确定和提取是进行系列图谱分析的关键。本文在图谱单元提取与确定的基础上，采用地图代数方法进行系列图谱合成，构造步骤如下：

（1）图谱单元的确定。①空间单元的确定。由于地理环境条件的连续性、渐变性和波动性等特征，最小地理单元的确定显得尤为重要。地理空间单元选取过大，则不能较好的反映空间的异质性；相反，则不能很好反映空间的同一性。通常地理单元的确定要以单元内部相对均质、单元之间具有较大的异质性为宜。在实际工作中，经常采用规则网格法，即采用具有一定分辨率的规则网格作为基本地理单元。因其图形规则简单，易于进行网格运算和操作。本文选取 30m 的规则格网作为基本地理单元。②时间单元的确定。利用数据反映了不同时期的土地利用状况。不同时序单元的土地利用数据也代表了区域土地利用发展变化过程的不同状态。应该说，研究土地利用变化过程的最小时序单元应该为 1 年[12]。但限于历史数据的可获取性以及现有数据提取时间的限制，本文提取了上述 5 期土地利用数据，其时序单元分别为 10a（1970—1980 年）、10a（1980—1990 年）、10a（1990—2000 年）和 8a（2000—2008 年）。

（2）以提取的图谱单元为基础，利用 Arcgis 空间分析功能，将不同期土地利用数据进行空间叠加，得到一系列空间—属性—过程一体化图谱单元。具体实现方法是以时间序列为轴，对每一个空间的 1 位编码的 value 值进行操作，将时间上相邻的各期数据两两合成，生成 2 位数编码的复合数据[12]。此时，生成的系列时空复合体数据，就是土地利用图谱（图 2 - 5）。分别为 1970—1980 年、1980—1990 年、1990—2000 年和 2000—2008 年 4 个时序单元土地利用图谱。同样，将 5 期土地利用数据合成 value 值为 5 的时空复合体数据，即海河流域 40a 土地利用变化过程图谱（图 6）。

（3）土地利用的变化包括两个方面：一是转入，即由其他土地利用类型转移到本土地利用类型；二是转出，即本土地利用类型转移到其他土地利用类型[13]。为进一步揭示土地利用的内在转化规律，也就是分析土地利用转移的来源及去向，本文通过确定分类原则，建立重映射表，运用图谱重构合成了“涨势”系列图谱（图 7）和海河流域 40a“涨势”变化过程图谱（图 8）。最后，本文够造了土地利用变化模式图谱（图 9），以研究海河流域 40a 来土地利用时空演化的基本规律。

5 土地利用系列图谱分析

土地利用图谱分析包括 3 个部分：土地利用时空复合体数据、主要图谱单元排序表和转移矩阵[12]。其中，时空复合体数据是核心，它由记载着时间—属性—过程一体化的图谱单元构成，并可通过图谱查询检索获取土地利用变化类型的转移去向及数量变化情况。主要图谱单元排序表记录了主要的土地利用类型变化及数量。转移矩阵则可以反映变化时段内各个土地利用类型的转化状况。通过图谱分析，我们就可以清晰的把握海河流域研究时段内土地利用时空格局演化的基本规律。

5.1 1970—1980 年土地利用变化图谱分析

1970—1980 年土地利用变化图谱（图 2），由 1970 年和 1980 年两期土地利用数据叠合而成。图谱合成后，共生成了 36 类图谱单元。通过图谱排序运算，其中，12 个变化图谱单元占到了变化图谱总面积的 90.7%。从主要变化类型列表（表 2）中可以看出，在各种变化图谱单元中，草地转化为林地最为明显，占变化总面积的 20.2%，面积为 $990.34\times10^3hm^2$，主要分布在坝上高原以及山区向平原的过度地带；其次就是林地转化为草地，占变化总面积的 15.7%，面积为 $768.45\times10^3hm^2$，主要分布在林草交界生境脆弱且易受人为干扰的地区；第三就是耕地向建设用地的转移，占变化总面积的 10.7%，面积为 $523.01\times10^3hm^2$，主要分布在大型城市及村镇的周边地区。

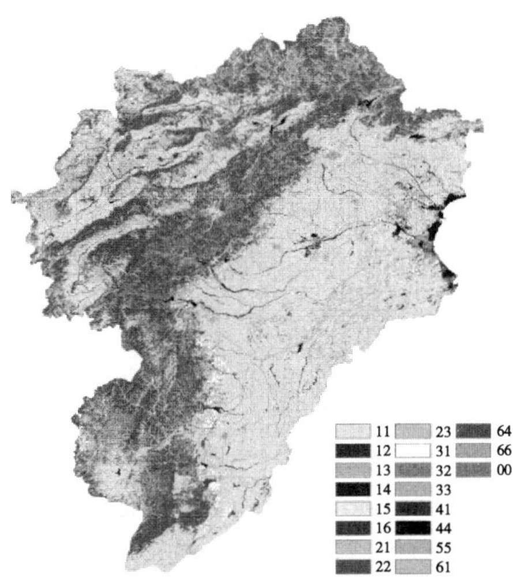

图 2　1970—1980 年土地利用变化图谱

注：11. 不变耕地；12. 耕地→林地；13. 耕地→草地；14 耕地→水域；15. 耕地→建设用地；16. 耕地→未利用地；21. 林地→耕地；22. 不变林地；23. 林地→草地；31. 草地→耕地；32. 草地→林地；33. 不变林地；41. 水域→耕地；44. 不变水域；55. 不变建设用地；61. 未利用地→耕地；64. 未利用地→水域；66. 不变未利用地；00. 其他

表 2　海河流域 1970—1980 年主要土地利用变化类型排序表

编码	变化格网数	变化比率（%）	累计百分率（%）	面积（$10\times10^3 hm^2$）	图谱单元类型
32	11003744	20.19	20.19	990.34	草地～林地
23	8538322	15.67	35.85	768.45	林地～草地
15	5811220	10.66	46.52	523.01	耕地～建设用地
31	5293363	9.71	56.23	476.40	草地～耕地
13	4986034	9.15	65.38	448.74	耕地～草地
12	4175653	7.66	73.04	375.81	耕地～林地
41	2613162	4.79	77.83	235.18	水域～耕地
21	2408425	4.42	82.25	216.76	林地～耕地
14	2316780	4.25	86.50	208.51	耕地～水域
61	1215001	2.23	88.73	109.35	未利用地～耕地
16	623826	1.14	89.87	56.14	耕地～未利用地
64	435747	0.80	90.67	39.22	未利用地

5.2　1980—1990 年土地利用变化图谱分析

1980—1990 年土地利用变化图谱（图 3），由 1980 年和 1990 年两期土地利用数据叠合而成。图谱合成后，共生成了 36 类图谱单元。通过图谱排序运算（表 3），可知期间最大的土地利用变化类型是耕地的转出，占变化总面积的 35.6%。其中，有 $219.03\times10^3 hm^2$ 转化为建设用地，$212.06\times10^3 hm^2$ 转化为草地，$164.24\times10^3 hm^2$ 转化为林地，$116.56\times10^3 hm^2$ 转化为水域。第二大土地利用变化类型是草地的转出，占变化总面积的 27.7%。转化为林地 381.5 ×10³hm²，另有 198.55 ×10³hm² 开垦为耕地，主要分布在林草交界及山区向平原过度等生境脆弱地带。第三大变化类型是林地转化为草地，占变化总面积的 19.5%，变化面积 407.8 ×10³hm²。应该说，林地的次生草地化，人为干扰居主要地位。

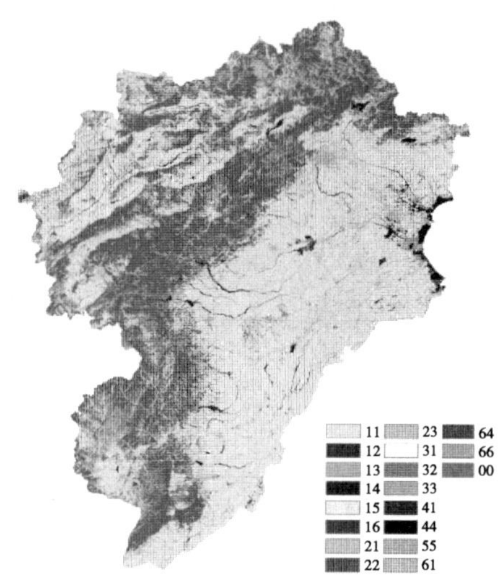

图 3　1980—1990 年土地利用变化图谱

11. 不变耕地；12. 耕地→林地；13. 耕地→草地；14 耕地→水域；15. 耕地→建设用地；16. 耕地→未利用地；21. 林地→耕地；22. 不变林地；23. 林地→草地；31. 草地→耕地；32. 草地→林地；33. 不变林地；41. 水域→耕地；44. 不变水域；55. 不变建设用地；61. 未利用地→耕地；64. 未利用地→水域；66. 不变未利用地；00. 其他

表 3　海河流域 1980—1990 年主要图谱单元排序表

编码	变化格网数	变化比率（%）	累计百分率（%）	面积（10 ×10³hm²）	图谱单元类型
23	4531159	19.50	19.50	407.80	林地 ~ 草地
32	4238834	18.24	37.74	381.50	草地 ~ 林地
15	2433672	10.47	48.21	219.03	耕地 ~ 建设用地
13	2356192	10.14	58.35	212.06	耕地 ~ 草地
31	2206068	9.49	67.85	198.55	草地 ~ 耕地
12	1824915	7.85	75.70	164.24	耕地 ~ 林地

5.3　1990—2000 年土地利用变化图谱分析

1990—2000 年土地利用变化图谱（图 4），由 1990 年和 2000 年两期土地利用数据叠合而成。图谱合成后，共生成了 36 类图谱单元，其中，12 类变化图谱单元覆盖了整个变化图谱单元的 91.4%。通过图谱排序运算（表 4），可知此期间变化最大的图谱单元仍然是耕地的转出，占变化总面积的 33.52%，向建设用地、草地、林地和水域的转出面积分别为 377.49 ×10³hm²、353.13 ×10³hm²、235.09 ×10³hm² 和 184.04 ×10³hm²。其中，耕地向林草的转化主要分布在北部山区坝上高原等地。其次是林地向草地的转化，占变化总面积的24.6%，变化面积865.29×10^3hm^2。经分析可知，林地退化次生多为人为采伐破坏所致。第三大变化类型是草地正向演替为林地，占变化总面积的15.9%，变化面积558.63×10^3hm^2，是自然演替与人工造林共同作用的结果。

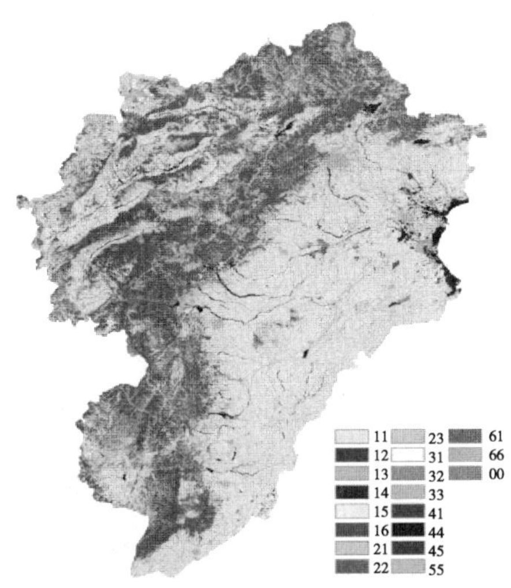

图4 1990—2000年土地利用变化图谱

11. 不变耕地；12. 耕地→林地；13. 耕地→草地；14 耕地→水域；15. 耕地→建设用地；16. 耕地→未利用地；21. 林地→耕地；22. 不变林地；23. 林地→草地；31. 草地→耕地；32. 草地→林地；33. 不变林地；41. 水域→耕地；44. 不变水域；45 水域. →建设用地；55. 不变建设用地；61. 未利用地→耕地；66. 不变未利用地；00. 其他

表4 海河流域1990—2000年主要图谱单元排序表

编码	变化格网数	变化比率（%）	累计百分率（%）	面积（10×10^3hm^2）	图谱单元类型
23	9614342	24.57	24.57	865.29	林地~草地
32	6206954	15.86	40.43	558.63	草地~林地
15	4194288	10.72	51.15	377.49	耕地~建设用地
13	3923701	10.03	61.18	353.13	耕地~草地
12	2612135	6.68	67.85	235.09	耕地~林地
31	2487109	6.36	74.21	223.84	草地~耕地

5.4 2000—2008年土地利用变化图谱分析

2000—2008年土地利用变化图谱（图5），由2000年和2008年两期土地利用数据叠合而成。图谱合成后，共生成了36类图谱单元，其中12类变化图谱单元覆盖了整个变化图谱单元的91.7%。通过图谱排序运算（表5）以及土地利用转移矩阵（表6），可知这一期间仍以耕地的转出最为剧烈，占变化总面积的40.7%，其中，向草地转化403.7×10^3hm^2，向建设用地转化339.53×10^3hm^2，向林地转化290.61×10^3hm^2。经分析可知，这一时期的退耕还林还草力度较大，尤以北部山区较为明显。同时，建设用地的扩张进一步加剧，侵占了大量耕地。整体而言，这一时期的耕地降幅加剧。第二大土地利用变化类型是草地的转出，占变化总面积的27.5%，分别向林地和耕地转出562.5×10^3hm^2和

234. 13 ×10^3hm^2。可知这一时期，草地的正向演替较为明显，大部分草地转化为林地，另外，草地也有一部分被开垦为耕地。第三大变化类型是林地转化为草地，占变化总面积的14%，变化面积406. 38 ×10^3hm^2，主要分布在太行山脉沿线的敏感脆弱地带。

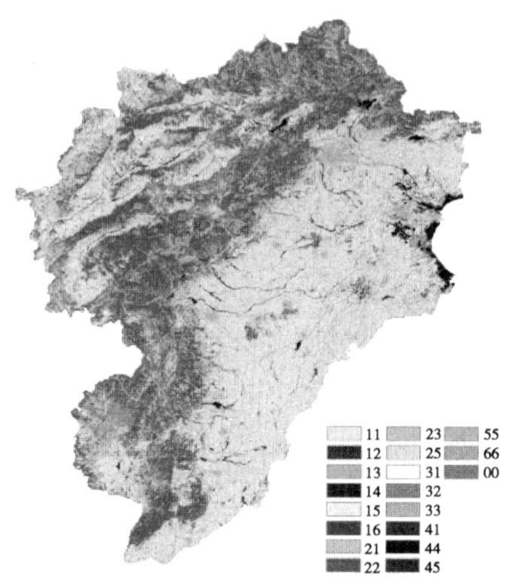

图5 2000 ~ 2008 年土地利用变化图谱

11. 不变耕地；12. 耕地→林地；13. 耕地→草地；14 耕地→水域；15. 耕地→建设用地；16. 耕地→未利用地；21. 林地→耕地；22. 不变林地；23. 林地→草地；25. 林地→建设用地；31. 草地→耕地；32. 草地→林地；33. 不变林地；41. 水域→耕地；44. 不变水域；45 水域. →建设用地；55. 不变建设用地；66. 不变未利用地；00. 其他

表5 海河流域2000—2008年主要图谱单元排序表

编码	变化格网数	变化比率（%）	累计百分率（%）	面积（×10^3hm^2）	土地利用变化类型
32	6250005	19. 43	19. 43	562. 5	草地 ~ 林地
23	4515371	14. 04	33. 47	406. 38	林地 ~ 草地
13	4485525	13. 94	47. 41	403. 7	耕地 ~ 草地
15	3772605	11. 73	59. 14	339. 53	耕地 ~ 建设用地
12	3229026	10. 00	69. 2	290. 61	耕地 ~ 林地

表6 2000—2008 年土地利用变化面积转移矩阵 单位：×10^3hm^2

类型	2000—2008					
	耕地	林地	草地	水域	建设用地	未利用地
耕地	9 203. 43	290. 61	403. 7	95. 73	339. 53	47. 98
林地	161. 02	6 543. 65	406. 38	10. 83	22. 23	1. 98
草地	234. 13	562. 5	1 991. 93	14. 78	18. 31	3. 03
水域	70. 58	9. 83	12. 2	723. 72	21. 07	11. 4
建设用地	81. 92	8. 31	5. 05	11. 08	1 734. 23	1. 73
未利用地	17. 83	5. 29	6. 72	17. 44	1. 89	99. 69

5.5 1970—2008 年土地利用变化过程图谱分析

40a 土地利用变化过程图谱（图 6）是由 40a 的 5 个采样时刻的土地利用类型数据共同合成，图谱共产生了 4 301类具有 5 位编码的图谱单元。其中，461 类图谱单元覆盖了变化面积的 96%。从图谱中可以看出，40 年来，利用方式没有发生变化的耕地主要分布在研究区域地势平坦的东部平原和地势较高的西部和南部平原。发生变化的耕地主要集中在西北地势较高的平原、沿海以及大型城市的周边地区。特别是沿海地区耕地的次生盐碱化，耕地和水体湿地的频繁转换，以及城市及高新开发区的建设，致使沿海地区的土地利用类型转化剧烈。

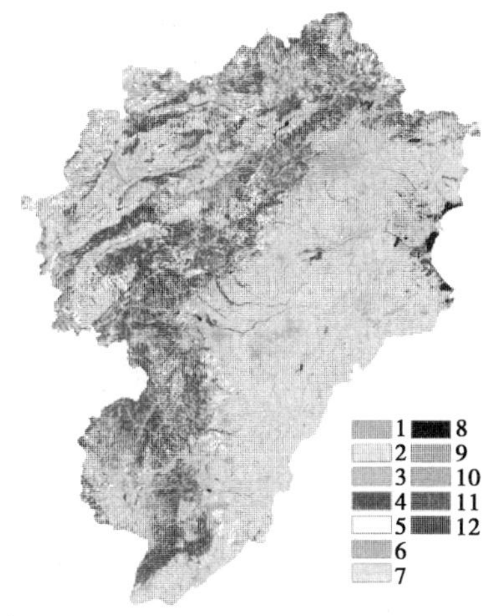

图 6 1970 ~ 2008 年土地利用变化过程图谱

1. 耕地变化区；2. 不变耕地区；3. 林地变化区；4 不变林地区；5. 草地变化区；6. 不变草地区；7. 水域变化区；8. 不变水域区；9. 建设用地变化区；10. 不变建设用地区；11. 未利用地变化区；12. 不变未利用地区

40a 来整个海河流域呈现从西部、北部的耕牧交错区到中西部的山区，经过草地过渡带到东部、南部的耕地、盐碱地、水域直到海域的土地利用格局。在这种变化格局中，耕地始终占据着优势，在北部山区的耕牧交错区，耕牧之间的转化较为频繁。特别是在近年来，随着退耕还林还草力度的加强，耕地—草地—林地之间的转换进一步加剧。同时，草地向林地和耕地的转换也较为明显，原因是草地的正向演替以及草地的开垦。应该说，农牧交错区、林草交错区及沿海地区的土地利用变化较为频繁，生态较为脆弱。

5.6 1970—2008 年土地利用变化“涨势”系列图谱分析

根据土地利用的转入状况，本文通过建立重映射表，设定分类原则，进行图谱重构，生成了“涨势”系列图谱（图 7）。分析 40a 涨势系列图谱可知，1970—1980 年间，变化面积最大的图谱单元类型为新增林地、园地（表 7），为 $14.12\times10^5\text{hm}^2$，主要分布在流域的中部的太行山山脉一线，在流域的北部和南部山区也有零星分布。第二大变化图谱单元类型为新增草地，面积 12.66 × 10^5hm²，主要分布在流域西北部到西南部的山脉沿线。草地的增加大部分来源于林地的逆向演替，也有一部分来源于耕地的转化。此外，新增耕地 12.31 × 10^5hm²，成为面积位居第三的土地利用变化类型，集中分布在流域中南部平原向山区的过度地带，在北部山区及沿海也有增加，分布零散。1980—1990年间，土地利用变化面积最大的是新增草地，为 6.31 × 10^5hm²，草地的增加主要集中在流域北部的张家口、赤诚和怀来一带，另外，沿太行山山脉一线也有零星分布。与草地的增长方式不同，林地的增长多为成片的增加，面积 5.56 × 10^5hm²，成为第二大变化图谱单元类型。主要分布在流域的北部山区，平原上也有零星增加。1990—2000 年，草地的增加趋势明显，面积 12.59 × 10^5hm²，集中分布在流域西北部的山区，多呈块状分布。另外，林地也有明显增加，面积 8.3 × 10^5hm²，山区增加的林地多成片状，平原上多为零星散布。2000—2008 年，林地的增加占据主要地位，面积 8.77 × 10^5hm²，主要来源于北部山区的退耕还林以及平原区果园的增加。第二大变化图谱单元类型为新增草地，面积 8.34 × 10^5hm²，主要分布在流域的西北部山区，多为退耕还草的结果，另外其他新增草地多为块状分散分布，多为林地采伐逆向演替为草地所致。这 4 期土地利用涨势图谱结构的变化，见图 8。

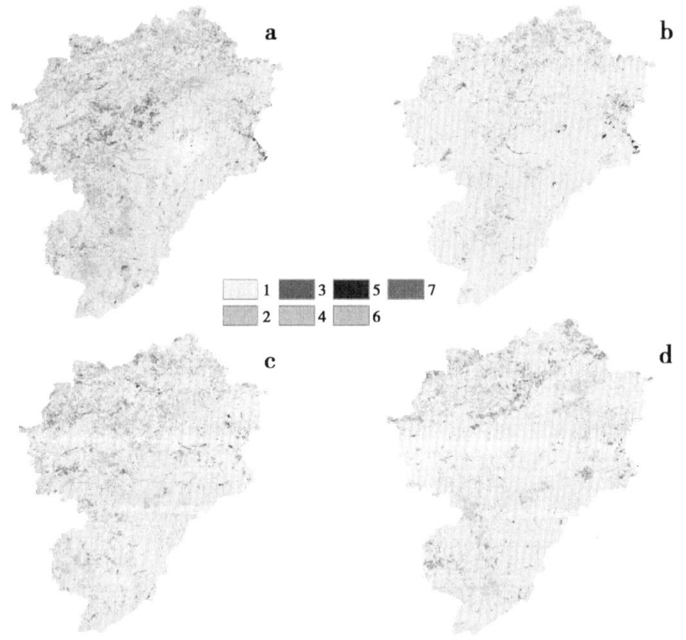

图 7　1970—2008 年土地利用“涨势”系列图谱

(a) 1970 ~ 1980 年土地利用“涨势”图谱；(b) 1980 ~ 1990 年土地利用“涨势”图谱；(c) 1990 ~ 2000 年土地利用“涨势”图谱；(d) 2000 ~ 2008 年土地利用“涨势”图谱；1. 稳定区域；2. 新增耕地；3. 新增林地；4. 新增草地；5. 新增水域；6. 新增建设用地；7. 新增未利用地

表 7 "涨势"系列 4 个时序单元图谱结构列表 （单位：$\times 10^3$ hm^2）

编码	图谱单元类型	1970—1980 年	1980—1990 年	1990—2000 年	2000—2008 年
1	不变区域	18 286	21 100	19 670	20 297
2	新增耕地	1 231	415	684	565
3	新增林地	1 412	556	830	877
4	新增草地	1 266	631	1 259	834
5	新增水域	310	192	259	150
6	新增建设用地	583	244	434	403
7	新增未利用地	103	53	57	66

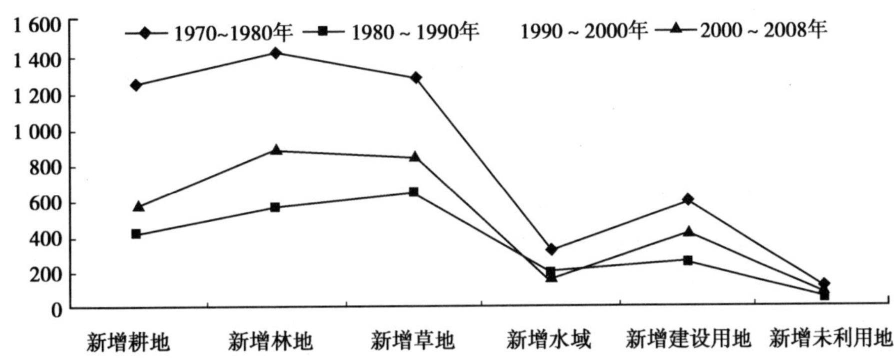

图 8 "涨势"系列 4 个时序单元变化图谱结构折线图

6 海河流域 40a 土地利用模式图谱特征分析

为了从宏观上了解海河流域土地利用转变方式的时空特征，本文将叠加而成的具有 5 位编码的土地利用变化过程图谱的图谱单元根据其稳定性重新进行分类构造出海河流域 40a 土地利用时空演变模式图谱。根据图谱单元的变化特点及其稳定性，归纳出了 18 类土地利用时空演变模式特征，见表 8。这样，同一图谱单元记录了相同空间位置上 4 个时序时段内土地利用的不同转化状态。

海河流域 40a 土地利用变化具有显著的时空分异特征（图 9），具体变现在以下几方面：

（1）40a 中，稳定型土地利用模式图谱面积共计 1 511.17 $\times 10^4$ hm^2，在排序表中位居第一，占研究区面积的 65%。其中，面积最大的稳定性图谱单元是耕地，计 814.82 $\times 10^4$ hm^2，主要分布在流域东部的农业耕地区，在西北部山区高原也有少许分布，东部平原区由于地势平坦，农业集约化水平较高，为流域较为稳定的农业耕地区。

（2）第二大土地利用模式图谱类型为反复摆荡型，面积 29.68 $\times 10^4$ hm^2，占研究区面积的 13%。主要分布在山区到平原的过度带以及易于受人为干扰的地区。其中最大的反复摆荡型图谱单元面积 29.68 $\times 10^4$ hm^2，为林草的反复转化区域。

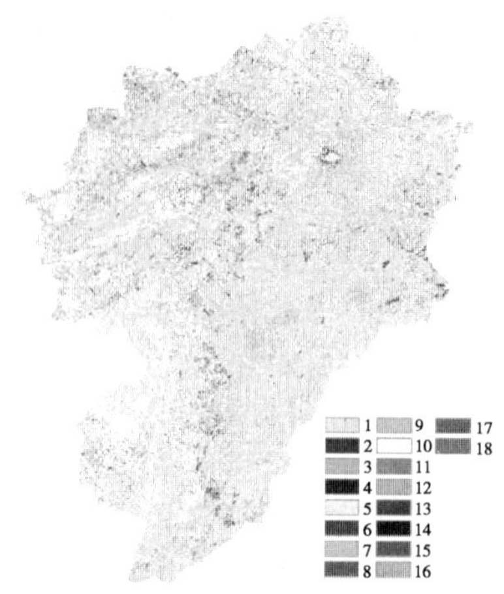

图9 1970~2008 年土地利用变化模式图谱

1. 稳定型；2. 平稳转换型；3. 最近转换型；4. 反复摆荡型；5. 新稳态转换型；6. 趋频转换型；7. 降频转换型；8. 反复后降频型；9. 间歇转换型；10. 中间转换型；11. 波变；12. 反复后趋频型；13. 趋频后间歇型；14. 反复后间歇型；15. 趋频后反复型；16. 前翁后趋频型；17. 趋频后稳定型；18. 连续转换型

（3）平稳转换型主要集中在城镇与耕地的交错区域，为快速的城镇化进程侵占大量耕地所致，面积 $179.13\times10^4\ hm^2$，占流域面积的 7.72%，位居排序表第 3 位。其中变化最大的图谱类型面积 $41.91\times10^4\ hm^2$，为早期耕地向城镇的稳定转移区域。

（4）第四大土地利用模式图谱类型为最近转换型，面积 $116.57\times10^4\ hm^2$，占流域面积的 5%。其中最大图谱单元面积为 $27.76\times10^4\ hm^2$，为耕地向建设用地的转化区，是 2000 年以后快速的城市化的结果。

（5）新稳态转化型面积 $94.63\times10^4\ hm^2$，占流域面积 4%，成为第五大土地利用模式图谱类型。具有代表性的最大图谱单元面积为 $20.88\times10^4\ hm^2$，仍为耕地新增为城镇的区域，是第 3 时段内城镇的扩张所致。

综上所述，通过分析海河流域 40a 土地利用模式图谱发现，40a 海河流域的土地利用主要以“耕地—草地—林地”和“耕地—建设用地”之间的转化较为明显，其他的土地利用转化类型也占据了相当的地位。各种土地利用类型都有始终稳定不变的区域，尤以耕地最为明显，主要分布在流域东部的农业耕地区。除了稳定区域外，耕地向建设用地的转化以及“耕地—草地—林地”三者之间的转化平衡成为流域土地利用变化的主要模式。

7 结论和讨论

40a 海河流域土地利用变化具有明显的时空特征，在时段上表现为：1970—1980 年间，土地利用方式的改变以林草的转化以及垦殖和开发为主；到了 1980—1990 年间，耕地的转出以及林草之间的转化成为主要的土地利用转移方式；在 1990—2000 年间，退耕还林还草力度加强，林草之间的转化以及耕地的转出，使得草地大幅度增加；2000—2008 年间，进一步加快的城镇化进程使得耕地大幅度转出，退耕还林还草也使得耕地有进一步减少趋势，耕地的快速下降成为此期土地利用变化方式的主旋律。在空间格局上表现为：在滨海，耕地—水域—未利用地之间的转换趋于频繁，空间位置不固定；在平原，耕地和建设用地表现出“此消彼长”的趋势，平原区果园的增多使得耕地进一步转出，在平原到山区的过度地带，耕地向草地的转出使得耕地进一步减少，但同时也有大量草地被开垦为耕地；在山区，林草之间的转化较为频繁，特别是林草交界区以及山区的采矿和林地采伐区，使得林草的空间位置出现较大的波动状态；在北部高原，耕地和草地的转化频繁，随着退耕还林还草力度的加大，使得耕地和林草地的空间位置处于频繁变换当中。应该说，海河流域的这种时空动态变化，是由自然因素和人为因素双重作用的结果。

参 考 文 献

[1] 李秀彬. 全球环境变化研究的核心领域——土地利用/土地覆被变化的国际研究动向 [J]. 地理学报，1996，51 (6)：553 - 558

[2] Turaer Ⅱ BL，SkoIe D，Sanderson S et a1. Land-use and land-cover science/research plan. IGBP Report No. 35 and HDP Report No. 7 [J]. Stochkholm：IGBP，1995

[3] Alcamo J，Kreileman E，Leemans R. Integrated scenarios of global change [J]. In：Global Environmental Change. London：Pergamon Press，1996

[4] 唐中实，李小乙. 澳门城市遥感信息图谱 [J]. 地理学报，2001，(B09)：38 - 42

[5] 田永中，岳天祥. 地学信息图谱的研究及其模型应用探讨 [J]. 地球信息科学，2003，(3)：103 - 106

[6] 陈毓芬，廖克. 中国自然景观综合信息图谱研究 [J]. 地球信息科学，2003，(3)：97 - 102

[7] 张百平，周成虎等. 中国山地垂直带信息图谱的探讨 [J]. 地理学报，2003，(2)：163 - 171

[8] 吕红峰，王静爱等. 土地利用结构优化图谱研制——以科尔沁沙地典型样区为例 [J]. 地球信息科学，2005，(4)：131 - 134

[9] 武国胜，林惠花等. 福建省生态环境空间格局图谱分析 [J]. 地球信息科学，2005，(1)：116 - 121

[10] 齐清文，池天河. 地学信息图谱的理论和方法 [J]. 地理学报，2001，(B09)：8 - 18

[11] 叶庆华等. 基于 GIS 的时空复合体—土地利用变化图谱模型研究方法 [J]. 地理科学，2002，21 (4)：350 - 357

[12] 叶庆华，刘高焕等. 黄河三角洲土地利用时空复合变化图谱分析 [J]. 中国科学 D 辑，地球科学，2004，34 (5)：461 - 474

[13] 刘胜和，何书金. 土地利用动态变化的空间分析测算模型 [J]. 自然资源学报，2002，17 (5)：533 - 539

TuPu Analysis of Regional Land Use Change —A Case Study on Haihe River Basin

XU You-xin LI Zong-zhen

(*Weifang University of Science and Technology*, *Shouguang* 262700)

Abstract: According to theories and methods of Geo-information TuPu, based on RS and GIS, with five pieces of land use data (1970, 1980, 1990, 2000 and 2008) from 1970 to 2008 of Haihe River Basin, a series of land use TuPu are defined. Including four periods of land use change TuPu and 40 years land use change progress TuPu. With TuPu reconstruction, a series of land use change "zhangshi" TuPu, land use change progress of "zhangshi" TuPu and land use spatio- temporal evolve pattern TuPu in 40 yearsf Haihe River basin are extracted. By TuPu analysis, summed up land use change rule in different spatial units with diverse time-scale, and summa-ries the rule of land use differentiation.

Key words: Land use TuPu; TuPu analysis; Haihe River Basin

HACCP 体系在豆类杂粮质量控制中的应用探讨

李宗珍 [①]徐友信
（潍坊科技学院，寿光 262700）

摘 要： 农产品质量安全是人类生存的基础，是国家繁荣的保障，是国家食品安全管理的重要组成部分。为确保豆类小杂粮质量安全，本文应用 HACCP 原理对豆类小杂粮生产过程进行危害分析，确定了关键控制点，并制定了具体的控制措施，以期通过 HACCP 计划的实施，能够有效保障豆类小杂粮的质量安全，为粮食质量控制提供可供借鉴的新途径。

关键词： HACCP；蔬菜；关键控制点；危害分析

豆类小杂粮蛋白质含量高，富含各种维生素、矿物质，兼备医、食双重功效，能够满足家庭餐桌饮食环保、营养、健康的要求，在人们的膳食结构中占有重要位置。山东省是华北大平原的一部分，属于暖温带半湿润季风型气候区，气候温和，四季分明，春秋短暂，冬夏较长，光照充足，温度适宜，雨热同季，降雨适中，主要集中在 6～8 月，较适合大豆生长发育对光、温、水的需求和大豆优质高产栽培的基本原理[1]。近年来，我国大豆产业整体形势日趋严峻，消费不断增长，国内生产滑坡，国际依存度过高。山东是夏大豆主产区之一，栽培历史悠久，但由于种植方式不合理、病虫害严重、产量低、规模效益不高等原因，种植面积呈现逐年下降的趋势，由于“工业三废”和单一追求农业高产量，导致农业环境质量出现不同程度的污染[2-3]，给豆类小杂粮的质量安全带来隐患。食品安全不仅关系到消费者的身体健康和生命安全，而且还直接或间接影响到食品、农产品行业的健康发展。农产品种植过程作为食品链的初端，直接影响农产品 及其加工食品的安全水平。HACCP 体系涵盖了食品从农场到餐桌的全过程，可以加强农产品和食品质量安全工作，从生产源头上控制农产品的质量安全。本文将 HACCP 的基本原理应用豆类小杂粮整个生产过程中，通过对工艺流程进行危害分析，确定了种植地块选择（CCP1）、农资采购（CCP2）、病虫草害控制（CCP3）、肥料使用（CCP4）、灌溉（CCP5）、收获（CCP6）、包装（CCP7）7 个关键控制点，提出了关键控制点的关键限值以及监控方法和纠正措施等。

① 李宗珍，女，硕士，潍坊科技学院助教。研究方向：微生物，农业经济管理。E－mail：kelexu_ 0526@ 163. com

1 HACCP 体系介绍

HACCP 的全称是“Hazard Analysis Critical Control Point”，即危害分析与关键控制点系统，是以科学为基础，通过系统研究，确定具体的危害及其控制措施，以保证食品的安全性。HACCP 是一个评估危害并建立控制系统的工具，其控制系统着眼于预防而不是依靠最终产品的检验来保证食品的安全，它是迄今人们总结出的最有效的保障食品安全的管理方法。有别于传统的质量控制方法，HACCP 区别于传统的最终检验，它更注重在危害分析、风险评价的基础上，对食品制造过程中微生物学、化学和物理性的潜在危害因素进行系统的预防和控制，以有限的资源，有重点地将食品的安全卫生方面的风险降低到可以接受的水平。

2 确定工艺流程

2.1 种植阶段工艺流程

种植地块选择→农资采购→栽培管理（病虫草害控制、肥料使用、灌溉、植株调整）→采摘→包装→储运。

2.2 生产加工阶段工艺流程

原料接收→筛选→烘干→分级→包装→储运。

3 确定关键控制点

关键控制点是在特定的生产体系的某一或某几个点（或程序）失控，可能导致对公共卫生产生危害的那些生产环节上加以控制。确定关键控制点可将危害消除或降低到最小限度，关键控制点的确定除了应用危害发生的可能性及严重性分析之外，更重要的是充分利用国际组织公认的“CCP 判断树”以问答形式来判定各危害因素的关键性。运用确认关键控制点的判断树，对每一个生产程序造成的各种危害，确定关键控制点（表 1、表 2）。

表 1 种植阶段关键控制点的确定

工艺流程	本工序存在的潜在危害	是否显著	判断依据	应采取的防范措施	是否关键点
种植地块选择	B：致病菌	是	前作种植造成土壤中可能存在未杀灭致病菌	选择没有污染源的地区，产地环境符合《绿色食品产地环境技术条件》的地区建立种植基地	是，CCP1
	C：重金属、有毒化合物污染	是	农药残留、重金属等或土壤、空气、水受到污染		
	P：石块、碎玻璃等	否	地块中可能存有大量的物理性杂质		
农资采购	B：致病菌	是	肥料中可能含有致病菌	制定统一的采购标准，统一采购经检测合格的农资，定期评估农资供应商	是，CCP2
	C：重金属、有毒化合物污染	是	肥料、农药中可能导致产品中重金属超标，农药可能带来农药残留量超标		
	P：石块、碎玻璃等	否	肥料中可能含有碎玻璃等		
栽培管理 病虫草害控制	B：无 C：重金属、有毒化合物污染 P：无		农药使用不当造成农药残留	严格《绿色食品农药使用准则》	是，CCP3
栽培管理 肥料使用	B：致病菌	否	肥料中可能存在未杀灭致病菌	严格执行《绿色食品肥料使用准则》	是，CCP4
	C：重金属、硝酸盐等	是	肥料使用不当可能带来重金属、硝酸盐超标		
	P：无				
栽培管理 灌溉	B：致病菌	否	水中含有致病菌	严格按《绿色食品产地环境技术条件》农田灌溉水质标准要求	是，CCP5
	C：重金属、农药残留等	是	灌溉水受污染造成农药残留、重金属超标		
	P：无				
栽培管理 植株调整	B、C、P：无				
收获	B：微生物	否	人员、工具的微生物污染	禁止在农药安全间隔期内收获豆类杂粮，执行《无公害食品 粮用豆》	是，CCP6
	C：农药残留	是	农药安全间隔期不够		
	P：外来污染物	否	采收时外来物污染		
包装	B：微生物		人员、工具的微生物污染	严格包装	否
	C：有毒化学物质		不合格的包装材料含有对人体有害的化学物质		
	P：外来污染物		泥沙等杂物混入包装袋内		
储运	B：微生物 C：变质 P：无		运输、仓储的温湿度不理想，变质等都有可能产生相应的化学危害和生物危害	控制运输和销售过程的温湿度，明确贮存条件	否

注：B-生物性危害，C-化学性危害，P-物理性危害

表2 生产加工阶段关键控制点的确定

工艺流程	本工序存在的潜在危害	是否显著	判断依据	应采取的防范措施	是否关键点
原料接收	B：致病菌	是	库存过程中可能受致病菌污染	MP、SSOP	否
	C：药物等化合物污染	是	贮存、运输中受到环境污染		
	P：石块、碎玻璃等	否	运输过程中可能混有大量杂物		
筛选	B：致病菌污染		滋生霉菌	MP、SSOP	否
	C：无				
	P：不完善粒、杂物		存在干瘪、不成熟粒、小石块等杂物		
分级	B：微生物	否	人员、工具的微生物污染	GMP、SSOP	否
	C：无				
	P：外来污染物	否	工作人员带入杂物		
包装	B：微生物		人员、工具的微生物污染	严格控制	是，CCP7
	C：有毒化学物质		不合格的包装材料含有对人体有害的化学物质	GMP、SSOP	
	P：外来污染物		泥沙等杂物混入包装袋内		
环境卫生	B：微生物	是	消毒效果差	GMP、SSOP	否
	C：药物残留	是	消毒不当引起的药物残留		
	P：无				
储运	B：微生物、霉菌	是	饲料成品在贮存过程中可能受霉菌污染	GMP、SSOP	否
	C：无				
	P：无				

综上所述，绿色食品豆类小杂粮生产加工过程中的关键控制点有：种植地块选择（CCP1）、农资采购（CCP2）、病虫草害控制（CCP3）、肥料使用（CCP4）、灌溉（CCP5）、收获（CCP6）、包装（CCP7）。

3.1 关键控制点的关键限值、监控程序、纠正措施

关键限值（CL）是与一个CCP相联系的每个预防措施所必须满足的标准。一个关键限值（CL）用来保证一个操作生产出安全产品的界限，每个CCP必须有一个或多个关键限值（CL）来控制显著危害。当加工偏离了关键限值（CL）时，则可能导致产品的不安全，因此必须采取纠偏措施以保证安全。合适的CL可以从科技刊物、法规性指标、专家及实验研究等渠道获得，也可以通过实验和经验的结合来确定。建立CL应做

到合理、适宜、适用和可操作性强。如果过严，会造成即使没有发生影响到食品安全危害，也要去采取纠正措施。如果过松，又会产生不安全的产品，应为每一个有关 CCP 的预防建立关键限值。

好的 CL 应该是：直观、易于监测、仅基于饲料安全、能使只出现少量被销毁或处理的产品就可采取纠正措施、不能违背法规、不能打破常规方式的措施。

针对以上确定的 7 个关键控制点，HACCP 小组制定了 HACCP 系统的详细工作计划表 3，其中规定了 7 个关键控制点的关键限值。

表 3　HACCP 计划表

关键控制点	显著危害	关键限值	监控				纠偏措施	记录	验证
			对象	方法	频率	人员			
种植地块选择 CCP1	致病菌重金属、有毒化合物污染	土壤各项污染物的含量限值 mg/kg 耕作 条件旱田 pH 值 <6.5　6.5~7.5　>7.5 镉　0.30　0.30　0.40 汞 0.25　0.30　0.35 砷　25　20　20 铅　50　50　50 铬　120　120　120 铜　50　60　60	土壤	实验检验	申请生产基地前	土肥检测站	拒绝检验不合格的地块	检测记录	各级绿色食品管理部门监督检查
		空气各项污染物含量浓度值（mg/m^3） 项目　日平均　1h 平均 总悬浮颗粒物 0.30　—— 二氧化硫　0.15　0.50 氮氧化物　0.10　0.15 氟化物 7（$\mu g/m^3$）　20（$\mu g/m^3$） 1.8［μg/（dm2.d）］	空气	实验检验	申请基地前	土肥检测站	拒绝检验不合格的地块	检测记录	各级绿色食品管理部门的监督检查
农资采购 CCP2	致病菌	高温堆肥卫生标准 沼气发酵肥卫生标准	有机肥	实验检验	每年	化验员	重新堆肥发酵	检测记录	组长审核记录，随机进行抽样，进行检测
	重金属、有毒化合物污染	煅烧磷酸盐、硫酸钾、腐殖酸叶面肥料质量指标	化肥	实验检验	每批	化验员	重新购置	检测记录	
病虫草害控制 CCP3	重金属、硝酸盐等	绿色食品禁止使用的农药	农药	检查合格证明	每批	采购员	严格控制农药品种和用量	检测记录	组长审核记录
肥料使用 CCP4	致病菌、重金属、硝酸盐等	见 CCP2							

（续表）

关键控制点	显著危害	关键限值	监控				纠偏措施	记录	验证
			对象	方法	频率	人员			
灌溉 CCP5	重金属、农药残留等	灌溉水各项污染物浓度限值（mg/L） pH 值 5.5~8.5 总汞 0.001 总镉 0.005 总砷 0.05 总铅 0.1 六价铬 0.1 氟化物 2.0	农田灌溉用水	实验检验	申请基地前	省土肥检测站	拒绝检验不合格的地块	检测记录	各级绿色食品管理部门的监督检查
收获 CCP6	农药残留	药物残留检测符合各项安全指标	小杂粮	实验检验	每批	化验员	严格控制农药使用品种次数间隔	检测记录	审核记录，随机抽样检测
包装 CCP7	致病菌污染	没有患腹泻、手外伤、呕吐、咳嗽、发热及其他皮肤病人上岗，包装前先洗手消毒，带一次性手套，每半小时更换一次手套	工作人员	主动报告被动询问巡检	工作时间	管理人员	患病人员下岗休息，洗手消毒	健康检查记录	组长审核记录，每月抽查

3.2 监督控制

根据豆类杂粮的生产过程，对确定的关键控制点进行日常监控，保证各个关键点在所监控的范围内，当发现关键限值发生偏离时，要及时分析原因，提出有计划的纠正措施，并付诸于行动，对受影响的产品进行处理和防止同样问题的再次发生。日常管理主要有受过技术培训的农户和农业企业的技术人员协作来完成，并做翔实的生产纪录，管理人员要定期检查，以确保监督控制的有效性。

3.3 建立档案

对生产过程的每个环节做出完整、真实、可靠的记录，有条件的可以建立数字化电子档案，档案保存期与豆类杂粮的销售期相同，或者至少 18 个月，以便查询。

3.4 计划验证

根据豆类杂粮生产过程中的情况变化，对 HACCP 要进行修订，以保证因地制宜、因时制宜的执行。根据标准变化、技术进步和市场反馈的意见等，对 HACCP 体系进行检测，检测控制措施是否得当，及时发现新的关键控制点，改进 HACCP 体系，并加以记录。

HACCP 体系的正常运行，能够保障豆类杂粮的品质，在出口贸易中，避免一些国家的贸易技术壁垒，增加出口创汇额。豆类杂粮的标准化生产不仅能够满足消费者的健康需要，也必将为我国农业的现代化建设、提高人民生活水平做出更大的贡献。

参 考 文 献

[1] 张同法．山东省夏大豆配套优质高产栽培技术［J］．现代农业科技，2008，15：12－14

[2] 刘光德，王莉玮，李其林等．重庆市农业环境及农产品污染评价研究［J］．农业环境科学学报，2005，24（5）：952－956

[3] 赵中金，黄昀，周优良．重庆市农业环境质量安全现状与防治对策［J］．四川环境，2006，25（4）：123－126

[4] 李杰霞，杨志敏，陈庆华等．重庆市农业面源污染负荷的空间分布特征研究［J］．西南大学学报（自然科学版）2008，30（7）：145－151

Analysis in the Application of the HACCP System for the Supervision Over the Quality of the Grains

LI Zong-zhen　XU You-xin

(*Weifang University of Science and Technology*, *Shouguang*　262700)

Abstract: The Quality and Safety of the agricultural products is the basis for human survival and the safeguard of the protection of national prosperity and an essential part of the national food safety management. To ensure the quality and safety of grains, this article analysised side effect of the production process by using the application of the HACCP theary . Then i-dentified the key points of this process and worked out several steps inorder to ensure the quality and safety of the grains and provide new approaches to identify these stuffs.

Key words: HACCP; Vegetable; Key points of this process; Analysis of the sideeffect

棉花 T-DNA 标签雄性不育突变体的遗传分析

高俊平①[1] 李法君[1] 张 军[2]
(1 潍坊科技学院，寿光 262700；2 山东棉花研究中心，济南 250100)

摘 要：利用农杆菌介导 T-DNA 插入得到棉花雄性不育突变体，与野生型陆地棉(*Gossypium hirsutum* L.) Coker312 杂交得到 F_1 代。F_1 代植株出现了不育与可育两种性状的分离，分离比是 1:1。对 F_1 代进行形态学观察，卡那霉素和除草剂抗性鉴定，PCR 扩增检测以及遗传学分析，证实雄性不育突变性状的表现与 T-DNA 插入共分离。我们认为，突变是由 T-DNA 插入引起的显性杂合突变。为我们利用 T-DNA 标签法进行雄性不育有关基因的克隆奠定了基础。

关键词：棉花；T-DNA；雄性不育突变体；遗传分析

在植物的基因克隆和功能分析研究中有许多种策略，利用突变体就是其中之一[1]。产生突变体的方法主要有理化诱变、T-DNA 插入、转座子插入等[2]。其中，利用农杆菌介导的 T-DNA 标签法[3]是目前研究植物功能基因组最有效、使用最广泛的手段，据统计有 40% 的拟南芥突变基因是用 T-DNA 标签法克隆的[4]。对这些基因功能的研究和利用将为提高作物的产量、品质、抗逆提供更有效的途径。

棉花是世界上重要的经济作物，提高皮棉的产量和纤维的品质具有重要的经济效益。目前利用不同品种间的杂交优势是提高皮棉产量和纤维品质的主要手段。但是大面积推广的组合，仍然以人工去雄授粉为主，制种成本过高已经成为棉花杂种优势利用的主要限制因素[5]，因此，利用基因工程手段克隆育性相关的基因并加以利用创造理想的雄性不育系就成为了提高棉花产量和品质的新途径。

本研究利用野生型 Coker312 花粉与根癌农杆菌介导的 T-DNA 插入得到的 T_0 代转基因棉花雄性不育突变体杂交，获得突变体的 F_1 代植株。在对 F_1 代植株进行育性观察、卡那霉素和除草剂抗性鉴定、PCR 扩增检测的基础上，对突变体进行遗传分析，为下一步利用 T-DNA 标签法[6]克隆与棉花雄性不育相关的基因奠定基础。

---

① 高俊平，男，硕士，潍坊科技学院助教。研究方向：功能基因。E－mail：gjp0921@126.com

1 材料与方法

1.1 植物材料

野生型陆地棉（*Gossypium hirsutum* L.）品系 Coker312，T-DNA 插入突变体 T0 代植株。

1.2 育性鉴定

雄性不育突变体与野生型 Coker312 杂交得到的 F_1 代，以及 F_1 代中不育株与 Coker312 杂交得到的 F_2 代，种植于温室和临清试验田，以野生型 Coker312 为对照，进行表型观察和数据统计分析。

1.3 卡那霉素和除草剂抗性鉴定

将脱脂棉撕成小条蘸取 500mg/L 的卡那霉素溶液涂抹棉花叶片，5d 后统计抗性植株和非抗性植株比例[7]。同样用脱脂棉条蘸取 1% 的草甘膦溶液涂抹棉花叶片，统计抗性植株和非抗性植株比例。

1.4 转基因棉花的分子鉴定

DNA 抽提按照王芙蓉等改进的的 CTAB 法从棉花叶片中提取总 DNA，具体方法参照文献[8]。参照 T-DNA 上含有的抗草甘膦基因和 NPTII 基因设计引物，进行抗草甘膦基因和 NPTII 基因 PCR 扩增。

表 1 用于扩增 T-DNA 上特异片段的 PCR 引物序列

引物名称	引物序列（5’-3’）
GR-f	TTTACAAGTGGCCACCTAGCT
GR-r	TGGTTCGTGTCTCATGCACTT
NPTII-f	CCTGTCCGGTGCCCTGAATGAAC
NPTII-r	CCACACCCAGCCGGCCACAGTCG

2 结果与分析

2.1 雄性不育突变体性状表现

我们从 T-DNA 插入株系中获得了一个突变体，该突变体叶片和株高发育正常，但是花丝短，柱头较长，花药不开裂，不能正常散粉，进行自交后不结铃。利用 Coker312 花粉进行人工授粉后结铃并获得种子，说明该突变体柱头发育正常，雄蕊发育异常，属于雄性不育突变体。对该突变体进行全生育期的观察，雄性不育突变表型在生长发育过程中表现稳定（图1）。

图1 T-DNA 插入突变体雄性不育表型

A 为突变体雄性不育花；B 为野生型正常花

2.2 遗传分析

突变体与野生型 Coker312 杂交得到的 F_1 代，种植于温室和临清试验田，以野生型 Coker312 为对照，进行表型分析。F_1 代共 41 株，19 株表现为雄性不育，22 株可育，符合 1∶1 的分离假设（χ2C = 0.220 < χ20.05 = 3.84），据此我们认为，该突变类似于显性突变。为验证突变性状的稳定性，将 F_1 代分离出的不育株再授以 Coker312 的花粉，得到 F_2 代植株共 185 株，有 90 株表现雄性不育，95 株可育，分离比仍然是 1∶1（χ2C = 0.135 < χ20.05 = 3.84），结果与 F_1 代完全一致。进一步证明该突变是显性杂合突变。

2.3 卡那霉素和除草剂抗性鉴定

由于 T-DNA 区含有抗草甘膦基因和 NPTII 基因（图 2），对卡那霉素和除草剂有抗性，因此，可对 F_1 代进行抗性鉴定。用 500mg/L 的卡那霉素溶液涂抹 F_1 代棉花叶片，在处理后 5 天就可以明显地识别对卡那霉素具有抗性与否。F_1 代中 19 株雄性不育棉花的叶片没有任何斑点，正常生长，显示出明显的抗性；22 株可育棉花的叶片处理部位出现黄斑、萎缩。除草剂抗性的表现与卡那霉素鉴定的结果一致。结果证实，突变体植株显示出明显的野生型植株所不具备的抗性，卡那霉素和除草剂抗性表现与育性表型一致，表明雄性不育突变性状与卡那霉素和除草剂抗性基因共分离。

2.4 转基因棉花的分子鉴定

鉴于 T-DNA 区含有抗草苷膦基因和 NPTII 基因，为了从分子水平上验证突变是否

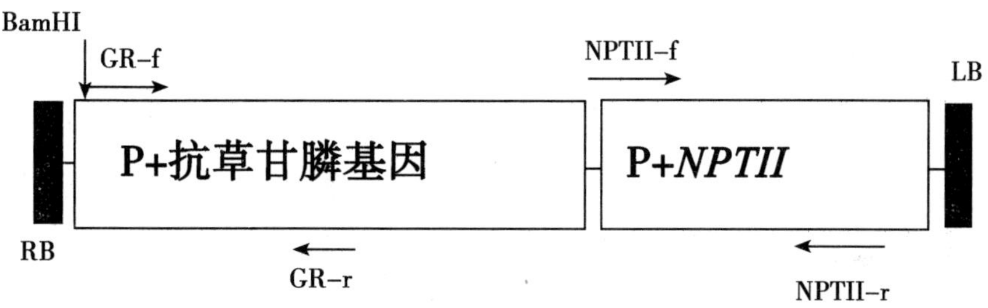

图 2 插入到棉花基因组中的 T-DNA 结构，带有抗草苷磷基因和新霉素磷酸转移酶（*NPT*II）两个抗性筛选基因及实验中引物的位置。水平箭头示引物的位置

与 T-DNA 插入有关，对 F_1 代中的 41 株进行抗草苷膦基因和 NPTII 基因的 PCR 扩增。利用引物 GR-f、GR-r 扩增 F_1 代棉花基因组中 T-DNA 上的抗草苷膦基因（图 3）；利用引物 NPTII-f 和 NPTII-r 扩增 F_1 代棉花基因组中 T-DNA 上的 NPTII 基因（图 3）。结果表明 F_1 代中，19 株不育植株能扩增出一条抗草苷膦的 1 199bp 片段和一条 NPTII 的 488bp 片段（图 3 的第 1、4 泳道）；而育性正常的 22 株植株（如泳道 2、4、5）中均无特异性的扩增条带出现。即基因组 DNA 的 PCR 扩增结果、卡那霉素和除草剂鉴定结果与和棉花育性表型具有一致性。表现为：转基因 F_1 代棉花中有 19 株雄性不育棉花同时具有卡那霉素和除草剂抗性，并可扩增出抗草苷膦基因和 NPTII 基因的特异性片段；22 株育性正常棉花不具有卡那霉素和除草剂抗性，也无特异性条带扩增。这也表明雄性不育突变性状与抗草苷膦基因和 NPTII 基因共分离，即雄性不育突变性状与 T-DNA 的插入相关，提示该突变体可能含有单个 T-DNA 插入位点且与 T-DNA 共分离，因此，可以通过 T-DNA 标签法分离突变基因。为了进一步验证，我们利用研究得到的 T-DNA 插入位点的基因组序列设计引物组合，扩增突变体基因组和野生型基因组。如果突变体是纯合体，由于 T-DNA 的间隔，PCR 就不会有扩增产物。结果突变体和野生型得到了相同的扩增结果（结果未显示），并且巢式引物也说明了反应产物是特异性产物，充分说明 F_1 代突变体为杂合体，突变为显性突变。因而，从分子水平证实该突变是显性杂合突变。

3 讨论

突变体是遗传学研究的基本材料，在植物的基因克隆和功能分析研究中有重要作用。T-DNA 标签法是研究植物功能基因组最有效、使用最广泛的人工诱导产生突变体的手段，其优点是一旦确定突变性状由 T-DNA 插入引起，就可以通过测定 T-DNA 的旁侧序列而快速分离到相应的突变基因[6]。棉花作为世界上重要的经济作物，提高皮棉产量和纤维品质具有重要经济效益，目前，利用不同品种间的杂交优势是实现这一目标的主要手段。但是人工去雄授粉为主的杂交组合，制种成本过高已成为限制杂种优势利用的主要因素。虽然棉花已经鉴定了一些不同类型的雄性不育系，但一直难以在杂交制种中应用[5]。因此，可以利用 T-DNA 标签法克隆育性相关的基因，研究雄性不育的分子机理，并加以利用创造理想的棉花雄性不育系类型。

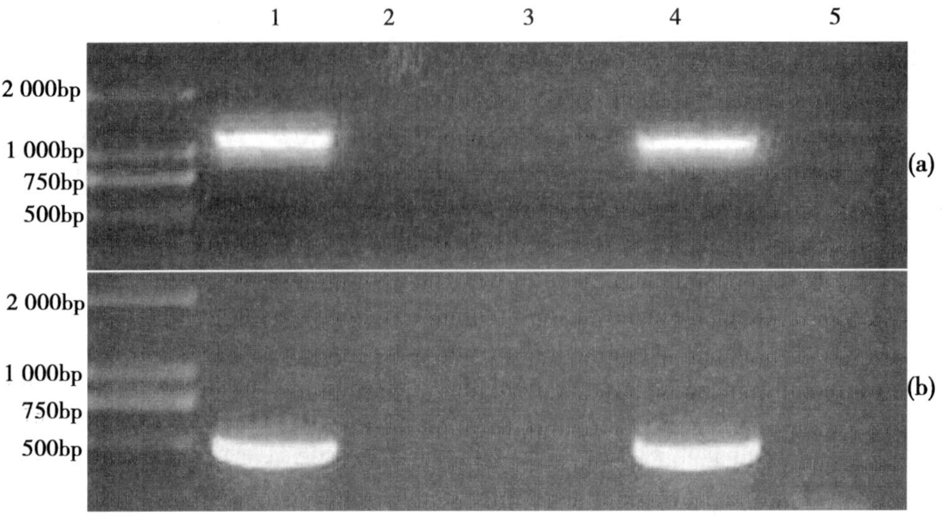

图3　引物 GR-f、GR-r 扩增 F_1 代5棵棉花基因组中 T-DNA 上的抗草苷膦基因（a）；引物 NPTII-f 和 NPTII-r 扩增 F_1 代5棵棉花基因组中 T-DNA 上的 NPTII 基因（b）

结果：1、4有 PCR 产物；2、3、5没有 PCR 产物。说明1、4为转基因植株，2、3、5则为分离出来的正常植株

本研究中，我们利用 T-DNA 插入得到雄性不育的 T_0 代突变体，用野生型 Coker312 花粉与之杂交获得 F_1 代植株。F_1 代以及 F_2 代植株均出现1：1的育性分离，与卡那霉素和除草剂抗性鉴定以及 PCR 检测结果一致，进一步的分子鉴定结果证实突变是由 T-DNA 插入引起的显性杂合突变，因此可以通过测定 T-DNA 的旁侧序列而快速分离到相应的突变基因。大多数情况下，雄性不育表型是纯合的隐性基因（ms/ms）造成的，杂合（+/ms）具有正常的花粉。该基因座位可能蕴含了一种新的雄性不育的遗传机制。对该位点及其附近基因的克隆，并研究其在棉花生殖发育中的功能，将有助于更好的了解棉花甚至植物的生殖发育，为棉花雄性不育机理研究奠定基础，进而可能成为促进杂种优势利用，提高棉花产量和品质的新途径。

参考文献

[1] Richards, S. J. , A. Hill, P. Hillmen. Recent advances in the diagnosis, monitoring, and management of patients with paroxysmal nocturnal hemoglobinuria [J]. Cytometry B Clin Cytom, 2007, 72 (5): 291-298

[2] 王歆，于恒秀，唐丁等．一个显性矮秆水稻突变体的获得及其遗传分析［J］．中国农业科学，2008，41（12）：3 959-3 966

[3] 方卫国，张永军．根癌农杆菌介导真菌遗传转化的研究进展［J］．中国生物工程杂志．2002：40-44

[4] Meinke D W, Meinke L K, Showalter T C, et al. A sequence-based map of Arabidopsis genes with mutant phenotypes [J]. Plant Physiol, 2003, 131: 409-418

[5] 高俊平，韩广津，宫永超，王芙蓉．棉花雄性不育的分子生物学研究进展［J］．

现代农业科技，2008，2：116－117
[6] 汪得凯，张红心，胡国成，付亚萍，斯华敏，孙宗修．一个水稻大叶角度突变体 lla 的遗传分析及基因克隆［J］．科学通报，2005，50（4）：399－401
[7] 郭敬，唐灿明等．利用卡那霉素间接鉴定法进行大规模的棉花转基因育种技术［J］．棉花学报，2000，12（5）：270－276
[8] 王芙蓉，张军，刘任重，刘勤红，张传云，刘国栋．海岛棉 DNA 导入陆地棉栽培品种获得变异种质的初步遗传分析［J］．中国农业科学，2005，38（8）：1 528－1 533

Genetic Analysis on T-DNA Tagging Male Sterile Mutant in Upland Cotton (*Gossypium hirsutum L.*)

GAO Jun-ping[1] LI Fa-jun[1] ZHANG Jun[2]

(1 *Weifang University of Science and Technology*, *Shouguang* 262700;
2 *Shandong Cotton Research Center*, *Jinan* 250100)

Abstract: An upland cotton (*Gossypium hirsutum L.*) male sterile mutant by T-DNA insertion was crossed with a wildtype upland cotton (cv. Coker312). The segregation ratio of male sterile to male fertile was 1 : 1 in generation of F1. The results of morphological observation, Kanamycin and herbicide resistance assay, PCR identification and corresponding genetic analysis showed that the male sterile was co-segregated with the T-DNA insertion. This male sterile mutant was considered as Dominant heterozygous mutation caused by the T-DNA insertion and the genetic analysis on which was the basis of cloning the male sterile related genes of upland cotton by T-DNA tagging.

Key words: Upland cotton; T-DNA; Male sterile mutant; Genetic analysis

纳豆菌培养条件的初探

李婷婷[①]
（潍坊科技学院，寿光 262700）

摘 要： 本试验以 OD_{600} 为指标，研究了培养条件对纳豆菌生长的影响。试验结果表明，该菌株最适培养条件为温度37℃，pH值7.0，接种量3%，培养时间24 h，装液量60ml/250ml，摇床转数150 r/min，最适碳源为葡萄糖，最适氮源为蛋白胨。

关键词： 纳豆菌；培养条件；发酵

纳豆具有溶血栓、抗肿瘤、降血压、抗氧化性、防止骨质疏松、抗凝血等作用。目前，我国纳豆食品工业的自主研发能力有限，大多数产品是引进日本生产线生产的传统纳豆食品，纳豆作为新时期的健康食品，其生产工艺和设备装备的要求精度较高，科技含量有待于进一步提高。本文研究测定了纳豆菌液体发酵过程中的碳源、氮源、初始pH值、装液量、发酵温度、摇瓶转速、发酵时间、接种量等因素的影响，确定纳豆菌的最适培养条件，以便为生产纳豆产品提供理论依据，并为纳豆激酶产酶条件优化奠定良好的基础。

1 材料与方法

1.1 材料

黑豆（市售）；纳豆杆菌B0604（本研究室保藏菌种）；其他药品及试剂均为分析纯。

1.2 仪器与设备

斜面培养基：蛋白胨1%，牛肉膏0.5%，NaCl 0.5%，pH值7.0～7.2；种子培养基：蛋白胨1%，葡萄糖1%，酵母膏0.5%，牛肉膏0.5%，NaCl 0.3%。

---

① 李婷婷，女，学士，潍坊科技学院助教。研究方向：食品微生物。E－mail：rmlt@163.com

1.3 纳豆菌发酵条件的研究

1.3.1 纳豆菌的培养方法

液体种子培养：500ml 锥形瓶分装 60ml 基础种子培养基，接种后，在温度 37℃，转速 150r/min 的条件下振荡培养 24h，作为培养条件优化的种子液。

发酵培养：无菌条件下，将接种种子培养液装至蒸煮杀菌后的大豆中，在温度 37℃的培养箱中培养 18h。

1.3.2 OD 值测定方法

发酵完成后，取 1ml 发酵液，以接种前培养基为空白，用分光光度计测定波长 600nm 处的 OD 值。

2 纳豆菌发酵条件的探讨

2.1 培养时间对菌株生长的影响

在 250ml 的三角瓶中装入 60ml 的培养基，调整 pH 值为 7.0，高温 121℃，20min 灭菌冷却后，在超净工作台中接入 3% 的菌种，在 37℃，150r/min 摇床上振荡培养，每隔 2h 测定 OD 值。

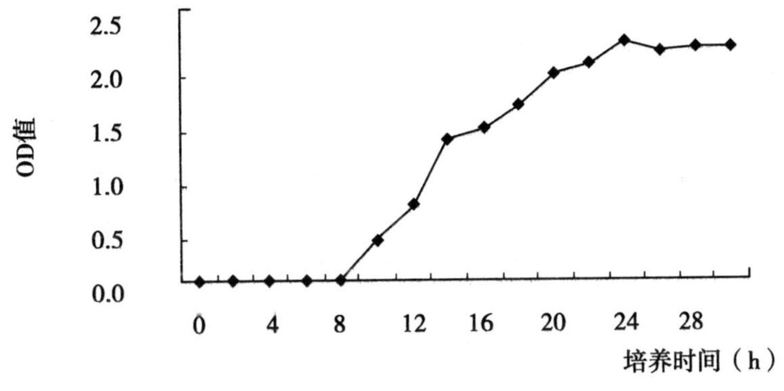

图 1 培养时间对菌株生长的影响

从图 1 可以看出：纳豆菌发酵，在 0 ~ 6h 内纳豆菌几乎不生长，OD 值趋向 0；在 6h 后纳豆菌开始进入对数期，趋于直线生长，到 24h 达到最大值，OD 值为 2.200，24h 后菌种生长进入平衡期，由此可见，纳豆菌的最佳培养时间是 24h。

2.2 温度对菌株生长的影响

在 250ml 的三角瓶中装入 60ml 的培养基，调整 pH 值为 7.0，高温 121℃，20min 灭菌冷却后，在超净工作台中接入 3% 的菌种，分别在温度 30℃，37℃，40℃，45℃下培养，24h 后测定 OD 值。

由图 2 可以看出：当温度为 30℃ 时，菌株生长比较缓慢，24h 后，OD 值仅为

1.320。而当温度为45℃，24h后OD值为1.541。温度为37℃时，菌株培养24h后，OD值达到2.203，明显高于其他温度的OD值，因此，37℃为菌株最适生长温度。

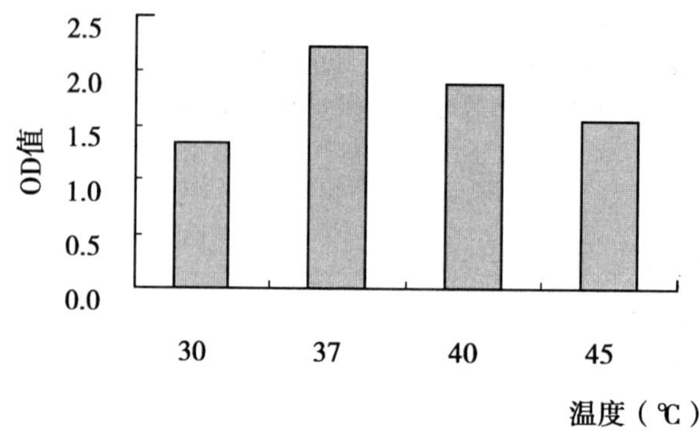

图2 温度对菌株生长的影响

2.3 pH值对菌株生长的影响

在250ml的三角瓶中装入60ml的培养基，配制初始pH值分别为5.0，6.0，7.0，8.0，9.0，10.0的培养基，高温121℃，20min灭菌冷却后，在超净工作台中接入3%的菌种，在37℃，150r/min摇床上振荡培养，24h后测定OD值。

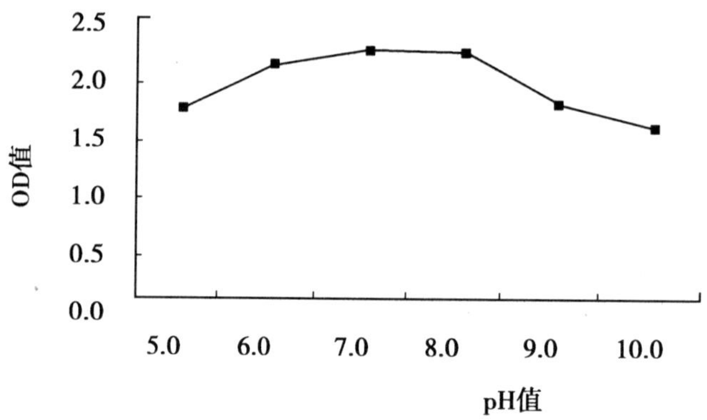

图3 pH值对菌株生长的影响

每个菌株都有最适范围，pH值对菌株的生长有很大的影响。由图3可以看出：pH值为6~8时培养24h后，OD值均高于2.100，菌株生长旺盛。所以，此纳豆菌生长的最适pH值在6.0~8.0之间。

2.4 摇床转速对菌株生长的影响

在250ml的三角瓶中装入60ml的培养基，调整pH值为7.0，高温121℃，20min灭菌冷却后，在超净工作台中接入3%的菌种，在37℃，转速120，150，180，210，240r/min下培养，24h后测定OD值。

由图4可以看出：摇床转速为120r/min培养，24h后OD值为1.340，菌株生长受

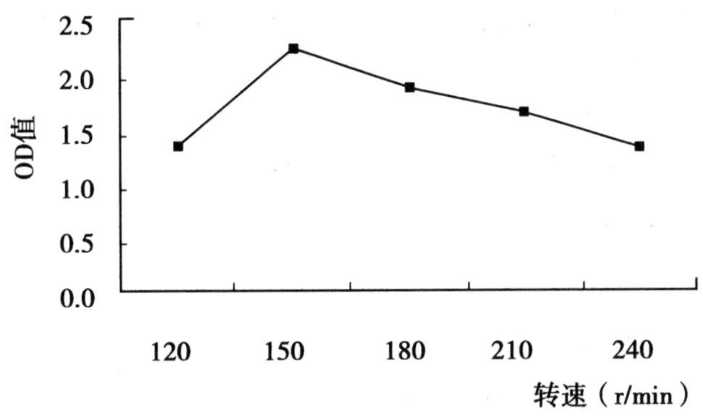

图4　不同转速对菌株生长的影响

到抑制；摇床转速为150r/min时有利于菌株的生长，培养24h后OD值为2.230；摇床转速为180，210，240r/min培养，OD值小于150r/min时。所以摇床转速为150r/min时最适合菌株的生长。

2.5　装液量对菌株生长的影响

在250ml的三角瓶中分别装入20、40、60、80、100ml的培养基，调整pH值为7.0，高温121℃，20min灭菌冷却后，在超净工作台中接入3%的菌种，在37℃，150r/min摇床上振荡培养，24h后测定OD值。

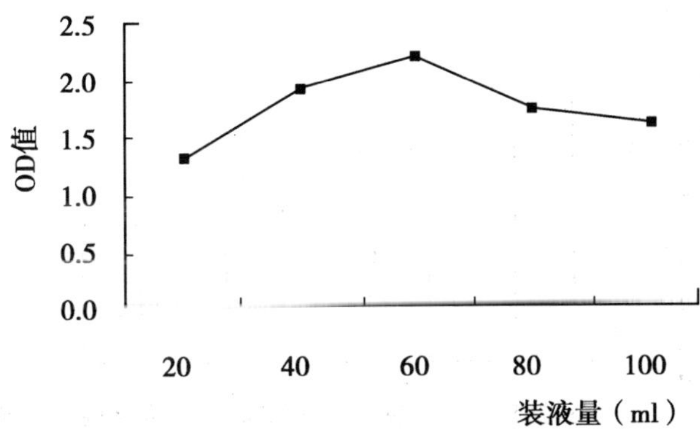

图5　装液量对菌株生长的影响

由图5可以看出：20、40ml的装液量，培养24h后OD值均小于60ml，因为20、40ml的装液量虽然有利于纳豆菌生长，但培养过程中，培养基水分挥发，如果装液量过少，会使细菌较早进入衰亡期，这样，20、40ml的装液量反而不利于菌体生长，当装液量为80ml、100ml时，氧的溶解度低，不利于菌株的生长。综合考虑，选择60ml装液量较为合适。

2.6　接种量对菌株生长的影响

在250ml的三角瓶中装入60ml的培养基，调整pH为值7.0，高温121℃，20min

灭菌冷却后，在超级工作台中分别以1%，2%，3%，4%，5%的接种量接种于培养基中，摇床培养，24h后测定OD值。

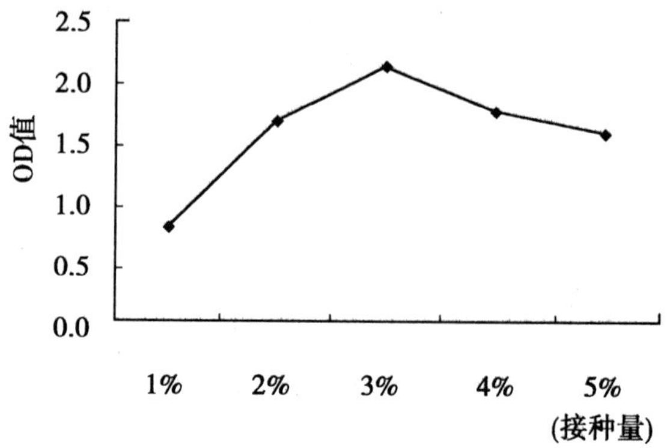

图6 不同接种量对纳豆菌生长的影响

由图6可以看出：3%接种量有利于菌株生长，菌株培养24h后，OD值为2.210，而接种量为4%，5%时，培养基被纳豆菌大量消耗，不利于菌株生长，接种量为1%、2%时，纳豆菌生长缓慢，均小于3%的OD值。因此，3%为最适接种量。

2.7 碳源种类对菌株生长的影响

把培养基中的碳源换成同浓度的葡萄糖、果糖、蔗糖、乳糖，其他成分不变，接种培养，24h后测定OD值。

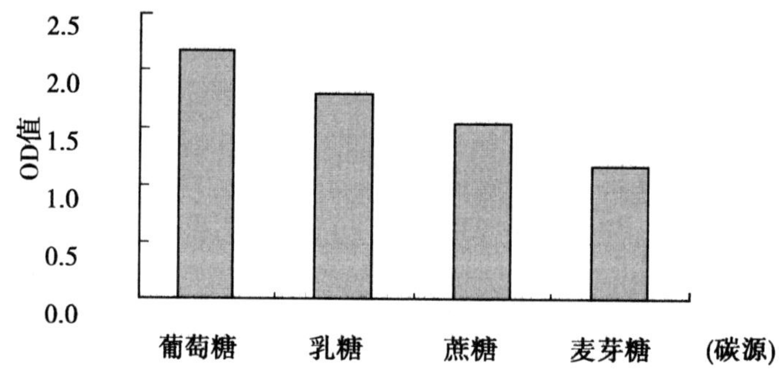

图7 不同碳源对纳豆菌生长的影响

由图7可以看出：以葡萄糖作为培养基的碳源优于其他碳源，培养24h后，OD值达到2.170，纳豆菌生长旺盛，乳糖、蔗糖做碳源时，其OD值低于葡萄糖，麦芽糖，不能被纳豆菌充分利用，培养24h后，OD值仅为1.170。所以，葡萄糖为菌种生长最适宜的碳源。

2.8 氮源种类对菌株生长的影响

把基础种子培养基中的氮源去掉其中一种，其他成分不变，接种培养，24h后测定OD值。

蛋白胨、牛肉浸膏、酵母浸膏都是纳豆菌生长所需要的氮源，由图8可以看出：除去蛋白胨后，纳豆菌的生长生长受到严重抑制，24h 培养后，OD 值为 1.29；除去酵母浸膏后，培养 24h，OD 值接近三种氮源都有的培养基，OD 值为 2.109，由此可知在纳豆菌的培养过程中，蛋白胨是非常重要的氮源。

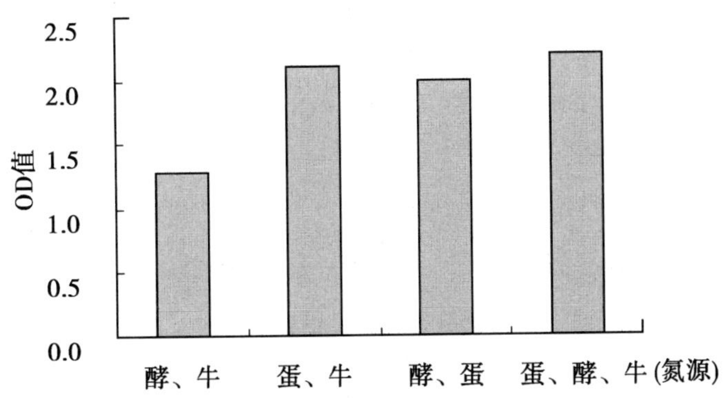

图8 氮源种类对菌株生长的影响

3 结论

通过对纳豆菌培养条件的探索，确定纳豆菌 T-3 液体发酵的最适条件为：温度 37℃，pH 值 7.0，装液量 60ml/250ml，摇床转速 150r/min，接种量 3%，培养时间 24h，最适碳源为葡萄糖，最适氮源为蛋白胨。

纳豆菌发酵条件的优化为纳豆激酶的发酵提供参考，同时，为生产其他纳豆菌产品提供了试验依据和指导。

参考文献

[1] 谢秋铃，郭勇．纳豆——一种多功能食品［J］．食品工业科技，1999，20（1）：71-72

[2] 田艳．纳豆菌液体发酵产生纤溶酶的研究［J］．华南热带农业大学，2001（5）：32

[3] 李麒．纳豆的营养与保健价值［J］．中国食品与营养，2002，(1)：48-49

[4] 齐凤兰，奚锐华，陈有容．纳豆工艺的优化［J］．食品工业，2004，(3)：50-52

[5] 徐速，梁金钟．益康纳豆的研制［J］．大豆通报，2004，(3)：18-20

[6] 满丽莉，向殿军．纳豆菌培养条件的初步研究［J］．农产品加工，2008，(8)：51-54

[7] 宋俊梅，鞠洪荣．新编大豆食品加工技术［M］．山东大学出版社，2002.12

[8] 王正刚，丁责平，蔡正森．纳豆激酶的发酵工艺研究［J］．氨基酸和生物资源，2001，23（2）：17-23

[9] 钟青萍，余世望，王开祥等．纳豆加工工艺的探究［J］．食品工业科技，2001，22（5）：20－22

[10] SumiHamada H. TsushimaH. Minara H. Muraki. A ovel-Fibrinolytic-Enzyme (Nattokinase) in the Vegetable Cheese Natto: A Typical and Popular Soybean-Food in the Japanese Diet [J]. Experientia, 1987, 43: 1 110

[11] Takahashi C, Kikuchi N, etal. Possible anti - tumor - pronoting activity of components in Japanese soybean fermented food, natto: effect on gap junction intercellular communication [J]. Carcingenesis, 1995, 16 (3): 471 -476

The Best Cultural Conditions Of Bacillus Batto

LI Ting-ting

(*Weifang University of Science and Technology*, *Shouguang* 262700)

Abstract: In the experiment, I make OD_{600} as index, and the cultural conditions which are effect on the growth of bacillus natto were studied. The results of experiment demonstrated that the best cultural conditions for growth are 37℃, pH 7.0, 3% of inoeulation amount, 24h of the cultural time, 60ml/250ml of medium amount, rotary speed 150r/min, the optimum carbon source is glucose and the best nitrogen source is Peptone.

Key words: Natto; Cultural conditions; Ferment

热激蛋白与植物抗热性关系的研究

裴华丽① 李美芹 薛其勤 乔 宁 刘永光 杨天慧
（潍坊科技学院，寿光 262700）

摘 要： 概述了有关热激蛋白的发现、种类以及表达调控情况，介绍了热激蛋白在植物抗热性方面的作用，并进一步提出和讨论了该领域尚待解决的问题。
关键词： 热激蛋白；抗热性；耐热性

在农业生产中温度逆境是限制其地域分布的主要因子，近年来，全球性温室效应不断加剧，据预测我国各地的增温幅度将明显高于全球，整个农业将面临严重挑战[1]。以我国重庆、四川为最主要干旱中心的西南部地区因为长时间的高温缺水使农业生产遭受了巨大的经济损失，蔬菜生产遭受损失尤为严重。此外随着生产的发展及消费水平的提高，特别是对各种蔬菜作物周年生产和供应的现实需求，但其生育期往往受到高温逆境的影响，同时蔬菜作物对于高温胁迫的响应也并非是完全被动的，其体内会发生相应的适应反应来降低胁迫造成的危害，以维持基本的代谢过程，甚至通过开启某些基因的表达来缓解高温的伤害[2]。近年来，对蔬菜作物的高温伤害及其耐热性进行了一些研究，某些方面已深入到细胞与分子水平。本文就有关热激蛋白与植物的抗热性的关系作一简要综述。

1 热激蛋白的发现

热激蛋白 Heat Shock Proteins（HSPs）又称热休克蛋白或应激蛋白（Heat Stress Proteins），是细胞应激原（如高温）刺激下所生成的一组蛋白质。HSP 首先是在果蝇体内发现的，1962 年 Ritossa 发现，若将果蝇的培养温度从 25℃ 升高到 30℃（热刺激温度升高），30min 后就可在多丝染色体上看到蓬松现象（或称彭突 puff）。表明这些地区基因的转录加强并可能有某些蛋白质合成的增加[3]，并将此类蛋白命名为热激蛋白（Heat Shock Proteins HSPs）。1974 年，Tisseres 从热激果蝇幼虫的唾液腺等部位分离到了 6 种新的蛋白质，即 HSP[4]。它是生物体在受环境胁迫时产生并藉此防止细胞免受胁迫和修复正在遭受的胁迫伤害。

---

① 裴华丽，女，硕士，潍坊科技学院讲师。研究方向：蔬菜生物技术及分子遗传育种。E－mail：peihuali2@163.com

大多数热激蛋白的研究是以微生物动物材料为主，有关植物热激反应的研究起步较晚，20 世纪 80 年代初期才开始研究高等植物中的热激蛋白。目前，热激蛋白的研究已取得重大进展，已成为植物生物工程中较为活跃而且发展较快的领域之一[5]。

2 HSP 的产生与种类

热激蛋白（Heat Shock Proteins，简称 HSPs）是生物体受到高温、干旱、低温、缺氧、饥饿、重金属离子等不良环境因素影响时诱导合成的一类应激蛋白。在逆境条件下，从细菌到人类都能诱导合成热激蛋白，以保护细胞免受进一步的损伤。温度的改变是形成热激蛋白的主要因素。温度控制热激基因的表达，蛋白质与植物的抗性具有密切的联系。通常认为，诱导合成 HSP 的理想条件是比正常生长温度高出 10℃ 的热激处理[6]。植物在热激 3 ~ 5min 内 HSP mRNA 的量增加，在 20min 内可以检测到新合成的 HSP[7]。如果植物一直处于热激状态，HSP 的合成可以持续几个小时[8]。HSP 广泛存在于植物细胞膜、细胞质、叶绿体、线粒体等组织中。

HSPs 的种类很多，通常根据分子量（kD）的大小，将其分为高分子量热激蛋白（High Molelcular Weight HSPs，简称：HMW HSPs）（M. W > 50kD）和低分子量热激蛋白（Low Weight HSPs，简称：LMW HSPs）（M. W < 50kD）两大类，如热激蛋白的 HSP110、HSP90、HSP70、HSP60 家族均为高分子量热激蛋白。植物 HSPs 的特点是低分子量 HSPs 相当丰富，高等植物中存在约 20 多种 LMW HSPs，这些 LMW HSPs 大小差距很大(从 12 000 ~ 30 000)，分布在细胞质、内质网、叶绿体和线粒体等有监护蛋白（chaperone，Cpn）的部位。已研究过的豌豆、向日葵、小麦、水稻、玉米、绿豆和黍等植物中 LMW HSPs 种类都很丰富。除植物外，其他生物的 LMW HSPs 种类都很多，常为 1 ~ 5 种不等，HMW HSPs 在动物中较多，而在植物中较少，种类也不那么复杂[6]。

3 热激蛋白的表达调控

热激时 HSP 基因转录被激活，多数正常蛋白质基因的转录被抑制，同时正常温度下存在的大多数 mRNA 的翻译降低或停止。生物优先翻译 HSPmRNA，合成 HSPs 迅速对热激作出反应。关于 HSP 基因表达的信号传递途径目前还不清楚，由于诱导 HSP 合成的逆境可直接损伤蛋白质或合成异常蛋白质，因此，认为异常蛋白质的积累激活了 HSP 基因的表达。

热激蛋白的表达既参与细胞的正常生理过程，又是细胞对外环境变化或刺激所作出的应答或防御反应。虽然不同种类的热激蛋白功能各异，但在执行某些功能时又相互协作，如作为“分子伴侣”，数种热激蛋白均参与细胞内新合成蛋白质的折叠、加工、转运及蛋白质变性后的复性、降解，维持胞内环境的稳定。因此，热激蛋白在植物抗高温中的作用不言而喻。

4 HSPs 与植物的抗热性的关系

细胞膜系统是热损伤和抗热的中心，细胞膜的热稳定性反映了植物耐热能力。许多研究表明：HSPs 的生成量与植物抗热性呈正相关。因此认为，HSPs 可提高细胞的应激能力。当细胞受热或受其他应力刺激时，能获得抗性或耐热性，以保护细胞免受损伤。1961 年，虽然还没有发现 HSPs，但 Yarwood[9] 已发现，蚕豆、黄瓜、无花果、烟草叶片，经 50℃热激 5 ~ 30min 后，在 12 ~ 48h 内能忍受 55℃高温的时间是未经热激预处理的三倍。但近几年来的研究已证明了某些 HSPs 的出现的确与植物细胞抗热潜力的发挥有关，它的出现为植物提供了一种暂时的保护机制。例如，在热激时，HSP70 迅速移向核内，并在核仁和核质中积累；在热激恢复时，又回迁到细胞质，具有保护细胞或机体免受损伤的作用。大豆叶绿体 HSP26 ~ HSP28 可保护光合系统Ⅱ的反应中心在热激时免受损伤，其中细胞耐热与生物膜热稳定性有关。热激过程中有大量的 HSPs 表达，它们聚集在膜组分中，有可能担当了阻止膜蛋白的热变性，防止生物膜破碎的功能。细胞受热后 HSP70 和 smHSPs（小分子量热激蛋白）以膜外周蛋白的形式连接在质膜和液胞膜上，与膜蛋白发生分子互作，可阻止膜蛋白的变性，稳定细胞膜系统，对膜微囊有热保护功能。与 70 kD HSP 相比较，14kD HSP 可能是细胞质热保护的重要因子[10]。

热锻炼过程中有大量热激蛋白的表达，大量的热激蛋白富集在膜组分上，具有阻止膜蛋白的变性、防止生物膜热破碎的功能。Jakob[11] 在体外热变性实验中证明，LMW HSPs 可阻止葡萄糖氧化酶和柠檬酸合成酶的热变性，而且还可加速这些变性的蛋白质复性。进入叶绿体的大豆 HsP 26 ~ 28 kD 可以保护光合系统Ⅱ（PSⅡ）的反应中心热激时免受损伤。刘箭研究证实线粒体小分子热激蛋白可以减缓柠檬酸的热变性，并促进热变性的柠檬酸合成酶活性，说明高温下线粒体小分子量热激蛋白对柠檬酸合成酶有保护功效[12]。如用不能合成 HSP 的实变体，HSP70 合成受阻遏的细胞以及不能合成 HSP70 的细胞为材料，发现热激时这些细胞对热敏感性增加甚至死亡[13,14]。

乙烯的产生可以提高植物对热胁迫的抵抗能力。Aloniu et al[15] 发现高温胁迫可使辣椒中乙烯含量发生变化，花对乙烯的敏感性以及花内的乙烯含量与抗热性有关，但前者可能对异常落花的影响更大；脱落酸（ABA）在提高植物的抗性方面作用显著，但 Ofrim et al[16] 的研究中指出蔓生菜豆中高温胁迫与 ABA 并无相关性，同时，他发现吲哚乙酸（IAA）从花芽内的输出量与植物耐热性有关，但 ABA 在高温条件下可使叶温升到抑制蒸腾作用的程度，从而加重高温伤害。

对于 HSP 研究的深入可能会促进对植物抗热性的了解，从而进一步通过生物基因工程方法提高植物抗热性，另外对于热激蛋白的诱导机理需要更加深入地的研究使之更好的有目的的为植物抗热性的研究服务。实现培育新的抗性品种的突破。

参 考 文 献

[1] 高亮之，金之庆．全球气候变化和中国的农业［J］．江苏农业学报，1994，19（1）：1 -10

[2] 张志忠，黄碧琦，吕柳新．蔬菜作物的高温伤害及耐热性研究进展 [J]．福建农林大学学报（自然科学版）Advances in high-temperature in jury and heat resistant of vegetables）2002. 6

[3] Ritossa, F. A new puffing pattern induced by temperature shock and DNP in Drosphila [J]. Experientia. 1962, 18: 571 –573

[4] Tisseres, A. A. K. Mitchell. Some new proteins induced by temperature shock in Drosophila [J]. Mol. Biol., 1974, 84: 389 –398

[5] 邓家术，段彬江，刘中来．植物热激蛋白的研究进展及其应用 [J]．生命的化学，2003，23：226 –228

[6] 吴厚雄，肖辉海，李必湖．植物热激蛋白的研究进展 [J]．生物技术通报，2003，4：6 –11

[7] Ken J L, Gurley W B, Nagao R T, et al. Multigene families of soybean heat shock proteins. In Vloten-Dotung LV, Groot Gsp, Hall TC (eds). Molecular Form and Function of the Plant Genonce [M]. New York: Plenum Press, 1985, 81

[8] Song S Q, Kenneth M, Fredlund et al. Changes in lowmoleculai weight heat shock protein 22 of mitochondria during high-temperature accelerated ageing of beta vulgaris [J]. Seed, 2002, 1 577 (1): 17

[9] Yarwood, C. E. Acquired tolerance of leaves to heat [J]. Science 134: 941 –942

[10] 黄祥富，黄上志，傅家瑞．植物热激蛋白的功能及其基因表达的调控 [J]．植物学通报，1999，16（5）：530

[11] Jakob U. Gaestal M Engel K et a1. Sma ll heat shock protein are molecular chaperons [J]. Biol Chem, 1993, 268: 1 517 –1 520

[12] 刘箭，庄野真理子．高温下线粒体小分子热激蛋白对柠檬酸合成酶、线粒体和花粉粒的保护作用 [J]．植物生理学报，2001，27（5）：375 –380

[13] 陈忠，苏维埃．豌豆中可与 GroEL 抗体发生免疫学反应的热激诱导蛋白 [J]．植物学报，1998，40（10）：933 –938

[14] Galili G, Shimoni Y, Giorini-Silfen S et a1. wheat storage proteins: Assembly, transport and depo sition in protein bodies [J]. Plant Physiol Biochem, 1996, 34: 245 ~ 252

[15] ALONIU B, KARNI L, ZAIDMAN Z, et a1. The susceptibility Of pepper (*Capsicum annuum*) to heat induced flower abscission: possible involvement of ethylene [J]. Journal of Horticultural Science, 1994, 69 (5): 923 –928

[16] OFRIM, GROSSY, BANGERTHF. High temperature effects on pod and seed production as related to hormone levels and abscision of reproduction structures in common bean (*Phasealus vulgaris L.*) [J]. Scientic Horticulture, 1993, 55 (3): 201 –211

Studies on the Relationshop of Heat Shock Protein and Heat Resistant of Plant

PEI Hua-li LI Mei-qin XUE Qi-qin QIAO Ning LIU Yong-guang YANG Tian-hui
(*Weifang University of Science and Technology*, *Shouguang* 262700)

Abstract: Studies on the discoverment, varieties and expression of heat shock protein. The relationshop of heat shock proteins and heat resistant of plant were introduced. Some problems in this field which would be invesistant futher, were also pointec out and discussed.
Key words: Heat shock proteins; Heat resistant; Themwtolerance

寿光蔬菜产业可持续发展面临的问题与对策探讨

薛其勤[①] 李美芹 裴华丽 乔 宁 苗锦山

（潍坊科技学院，寿光 262700）

摘 要： 通过深入蔬菜产业发展的各环节进行调查研究，综合分析了寿光蔬菜产业中所面临的突出问题，调查发现：优质高端蔬菜数量相对不足；农业生态环境随蔬菜种植年限的增长日益恶化；蔬菜商品化处理及深加工发展滞后；蔬菜种植过程中机械化程度较低；乏具有自主知识产权的蔬菜优良品种；农民素质相对偏低等成为制约寿光蔬菜产业可持续发展的主要问题。研究并对实现寿光蔬菜产业的可持续发展提出了相应对策，主要包括建立和执行新的科学的土壤整治体系；扩大有机蔬菜生产规模，提高蔬菜的深加工水平；借鉴国外先进经验，提高寿光蔬菜产业的机械化水平；加强与国内科研院所的合作，提高蔬菜种子的国产化水平；加大培训力度，提高菜农整体素质等几个方面。

关键词： 蔬菜产业；可持续发展；问题与对策

山东省寿光市是全国闻名的“中国蔬菜之乡”，是中国最大的设施蔬菜生产基地，也是全国蔬菜种子重要集散地和日光温室推广应用较早的地区之一[1]。蔬菜产业是寿光市县域经济的重要支柱产业，短短十几年蔬菜产业的发展打造了一个经济强县，创造了产业发展史上的一个奇迹[2]。寿光蔬菜作为一个产业发展到今天，产生过许多可以借鉴的成功经验，但随着产业的发展，制约产业健康和可持续发展的矛盾问题日益凸显。如何在新形势下继续保持寿光蔬菜的领先优势及其对全国的辐射带动作用，实现产业发展升级及可持续发展值得研究。

1 寿光蔬菜产业中所面临的突出问题

寿光拥有一流的蔬菜栽培技术和先进的蔬菜经营管理经验，蔬菜种植一直走在全国的前列。但是随着时代的进步和社会的发展，寿光的蔬菜产业也出现了许多值得我们深

① 薛其勤，男，硕士，潍坊科技学院讲师。研究方向：植物生物技术和宏观农业研究。E-mail：xueqiqin@163.com

思的问题。

1.1 蔬菜的产量高，但绿色蔬菜、有机蔬菜等优质蔬菜相对不足

寿光市蔬菜常年种植面积逾 4 万 hm^2，其中设施栽培蔬菜，包括日光温室和部分塑料拱棚共 3 万多 hm^2，温室栽培品种超过 400 个，蔬菜年产量达 40 亿 kg。寿光的蔬菜种植规模和产量均位居全国前列，但寿光绿色蔬菜，特别是有机蔬菜等高端优质蔬菜的种植规模较小。而安全、优质的放心菜已逐渐成为民众的消费趋势，因此提高寿光高端蔬菜的种植规模和水平对寿光蔬菜的可持续发展至关重要。

1.2 农业生态环境问题日益突出

寿光蔬菜产业的可持续发展应以良好的生态环境为基础，生态环境的良好发展必然为蔬菜产业的可持续发展提供契机。然而近年来，随着蔬菜种植年限的增长，寿光的农业生态环境，特别是土壤质量的退化问题日趋严重。

1.2.1 土壤肥力状况的下降是制约蔬菜产业发展的重要因素

寿光蔬菜早年为了片面追求蔬菜产量，以施用化学肥料为主，对土壤肥力造成了一定影响。虽然近年来开始注重施用有机肥改良土壤、提高地力，但有机肥施用过量或不当都会引起比较严重的后果，如施用过量会使土壤中硝酸离子成份聚积，硝酸盐含量超标[3]；另外，畜禽粪便主要来自规模化的养殖场，这种畜禽粪便中的重金属、抗生素含量较高，长期施用容易造成土壤肥力状况下降和地下水污染。

1.2.2 土壤中的农药残留直接限制了有机蔬菜的发展

保护地特殊的环境条件使病虫害更易发生，因此农药施用量相应增加。但同时特殊的环境改变了农药在土壤中的消解行为，农药在保护地的消解速率显著下降，导致农药在土壤中积累[4]。寿光的设施蔬菜起步早，发展时间长，土壤中积累的难降解农药数量较多，严重影响了土壤质量，也成为发展有机蔬菜的制约因素。

1.2.3 土传病害危害日益严重

寿光有很多蔬菜大棚的使用年限较长，土传病害发生频繁，已成为主要病害。调查发现寿光的蔬菜大棚中土传病害发生严重的占 73.2%，其中根结线虫发生严重和较严重的大棚占 42.5%。温室中发生最为普遍、危害最为严重的瓜类、茄果、豆类、叶菜类立枯病、枯萎病、猝倒病、菌核病、炭疽病、根腐病等众多病害都是典型的土传病害。土传病害已成为寿光蔬菜产业必须面对的严肃问题。

1.3 蔬菜商品化处理及深加工发展滞后，蔬菜出口形势严峻

寿光的蔬菜绝大部分都是内销，而且都是未经加工的初级“新鲜菜”，主要通过各地农贸市场销往全国各地，而经过本地企业深加工后出口的只有很小的一部分，出口一直是制约寿光蔬菜产业发展的瓶颈。这使寿光蔬菜产品的附加值很低，利润也不高。寿光的蔬菜产业升级必须很好的解决这一问题。

1.4 蔬菜种植过程中机械化程度较低，菜农劳动强度大

寿光的蔬菜种植设施和种植技术先进，但是在蔬菜生产过程中的机械化水平较低。

从事蔬菜种植的农民劳动时间长、强度大，加之设施蔬菜特殊的生产环境，菜农长时间处于超体力劳动状态中，各种职业病例如风湿、腰腿疼痛、颈椎病等经常困扰着菜农，致使菜农的健康质量和生活质量下降。同时，这种种植管理方式也增加了蔬菜的生产成本，降低了寿光蔬菜的竞争力。

1.5 育种工作滞后，缺乏具有自主知识产权的蔬菜优良品种

寿光的蔬菜生产和流通一直走在全国的前列，但蔬菜生产的核心技术——制种业一直是寿光蔬菜产业的软肋。该市种子年交易量达 8 000多 t，其中 2/3 以上来自国外种子公司，菜农每年购买蔬菜种子的花费达 3 亿元。缺乏具有自主知识产权的蔬菜优良品种，使寿光蔬菜产业发展的核心长期受制于人，国际竞争力差。

1.6 农民素质有待于进一步提高

寿光从事蔬菜种植的农民一般都具有丰富的栽培管理经验，但由于技术缺乏规范，个人凭自己的经验行事，对不同土壤特性、不同作物和不同茬次的蔬菜不能区分管理，往往会出现施肥用药过频、过量的问题。这既造成了环境污染，加大了生产成本，又影响了蔬菜的品质和质量安全。另外，农民对生产高质量、安全的放心菜意识不强，生产过程中存在一定的侥幸心理。因此，有必要提高农民的整体素质，这也是生产高品质蔬菜必须解决的问题。

2 实现寿光蔬菜产业可持续发展的策略探讨

寿光在蔬菜产业的发展过程中遇到的一些问题是由多方面因素造成的，其中，最主要的原因是科技创新能力缺乏及科技储备不足，要实现蔬菜产业的可持续发展必须加大科技创新力度，加快新技术的应用。

2.1 建立和执行新的科学的土壤整治体系，全面提高土壤质量

2.1.1 充分利用微生物降解土壤中农药残留

解决土壤农药残留的本质是在土体中将其进行充分降解、转化，使分子结构中 C-C 键和 C-H 键发生断裂，药效消失，减少危害。农药残留降解最主要的方式是微生物降解，土壤中的微生物能够通过各种生物化学作用参与分解土壤中的有机农药[5]。例如，一种黄杆菌可降解对硫磷、杀螟松、水胺硫磷、甲基对硫磷；芽胞菌属、无色杆菌属和假单胞菌属的有些菌株能降解“666”；产碱杆菌属和无色杆菌属的某些菌株可以降解 DDT[6]。因此我们可以针对寿光的土壤农药残留状况分离出相应的农药降解菌株，借助基因工程技术放大其表达，并通过多种菌株混合的协同作用，对农药具有强烈的分解能力。

2.1.2 采用新型绿色环保肥料，科学施肥，提高土壤肥力

新型肥料要求既要环保，又能显著提高地力，同时还能提高作物的品质。生物腐殖酸肥料的推广为我们提供了一个很好的选择，这种肥料是以特殊微生物发酵工艺，将蔗

渣、锯末、秸秆粉、花生壳等工农业有机废弃物变成富含活性腐殖酸和有益微生物种群的混合物，其具有改良土壤、提高肥效、增加产量、提高作物免疫机能、改善农产品品质等功能[7]。实践证明，生物腐殖酸与传统的矿物腐殖酸相比，生物活性更高，具有更优良的应用效果。如果寿光能够利用当地的工农业有机废弃物生产这种绿色环保肥料，必将为寿光农业的可持续发展提供重要保障。

实施科学施肥策略，切实做到测土配方施肥。政府部门不仅要成立测土配方施肥检验站，更要安排农技人员包片定期到农户大棚取土检测，给予农民及时的指导和建议，真正做到按需定量施肥，提高肥料利用率，同时改善土壤质量。

2.1.3 多措并举，加强土传病害的防治

克服土传病害，我们可以采取以下措施，第一，因地制宜，选用抗病品种，科学管理，提高蔬菜自身的抗病能力；第二，制定合理的栽培制度，通过合理的安排茬口和科学轮作改变土壤中病原菌的生活环境，抑制其生存和发展，从而减少土壤中病原菌的数量，降低发病率，实践证明，实行科学合理的间作与轮作是控制土传病害行之有效的措施；第三，进行土壤消毒。土壤消毒后能够明显降低蔬菜生产过程中用药次数和用药量。土壤消毒一般采取药剂消毒、高温灭菌和熏蒸消毒。

另外，在现有防治土传病害的基础上，可采用施肥防病的新方法。其思路是通过施肥调控土壤微生物生态，提高土壤微生物多样性，从根本上提高土壤健康质量，在微生物生态水平上抑制土传病害[8]。这是一项新颖的绿色防病技术途径，也使肥料拓展了防病功能，对于寿光发展绿色有机蔬菜、实行农业清洁生产和保障食品安全具有重大战略意义。

2.2 扩大有机蔬菜生产规模，提高蔬菜的深加工水平

有机蔬菜对种植基地的条件要求非常严格，因此，首先必须采用上述土壤质量改良方法进行土壤改良：降解土壤残留农药，改善肥力状况，优化土壤的微生物种群，克服土传病害。在种植过程中要制定严格的管理措施，不能添加农药、化肥、除草剂和激素等人工合成物质。采用物理防治和生物防治相结合的病虫害防治策略，并施用有机菌肥。此外，在有机蔬菜发展前期，政府应该积极引导，提供技术指导，并给予政策扶持。尽管有机蔬菜的生产要求高，管理复杂，推广难度大，但从长远看，寿光市发展有机蔬菜，最大限度提高单位面积产出，实现蔬菜产业的飞跃是必由之路。

寿光要想在短时间内提高蔬菜深加工水平，必须转变观念，改变过去政府对农投资大多集中在原材料生产上，也就是种植业，要加大对食品加工和产品销售环节的投资力度。对具有出口优势的蔬菜深加工种类政府应积极在政策扶持、资金投放、信息引导、技术辅导等方面给予支持。加工企业要开阔思路，放眼全球，引进国内外先进的蔬菜加工设备和加工技术，在传统的保鲜出口和冷冻出口的基础上，积极增加调味调理食品、真空冷冻干燥食品、浓缩果菜汁、蔬菜泥、蔬菜卷等高科技含量的深加工产品，实现与国际市场的高点对接。同时，要搞好蔬菜原料供应基地建设，发挥寿光蔬菜种植方面的优势和辐射带动作用，建立高品质的蔬菜深加工原料基地。

2.3 借鉴国外先进经验，提高寿光蔬菜产业的机械化水平

寿光的设施蔬菜与国外园艺发展水平发达的国家相比，起步晚，设施农业机械发展缓慢。因此寿光在提高蔬菜生产的机械化水平上，可借鉴国外的先进经验，例如，美国等国家对温室中作业机具进行了系统的开发，研究，推广和应用，从整地播种到收获以及采后处理，都实现了全盘机械化，部分作业还实现了自动化。我们可以结合寿光的实际情况，采用先进的蔬菜农机器具，逐步提高蔬菜生产的机械化水平，提高劳动生产率，把菜农从繁重的体力劳动中解脱出来。另外，政府可以借鉴我国在小麦、玉米等农机购置上的补贴政策，对菜农购买设施蔬菜农机器具也给予一定补贴，提高菜农民购置农业机械的积极性。

2.4 加强与国内科研院所的合作，提高蔬菜种子的国产化水平

蔬菜育种是一个周期长的系统工程，同时需要广泛的种质资源。寿光可根据当地的蔬菜种植情况，选取几个重点蔬菜种类作为育种目标，加强与国内科研院所的深入合作，借鉴他们先进的育种方法和技术；广泛征集种质资源，建立蔬菜种质库；政府应加大在政策和资金上的扶持力度，鼓励有实力的企业开展育种工作。

2.5 加大培训力度，提高菜农整体素质

菜农是蔬菜生产过程中的主体，菜农的素质水平直接决定了蔬菜产业的发展水平。提高菜农的素质，必须加强对菜农的培训，定期委派农技人员到田间地头进行宣传指导；同时培养一批骨干村民，利用骨干村民的辐射带头作用加快对新技术、新观念的传输，在提高菜农种植管理水平的同时，提高菜农种植优质、安全蔬菜的自觉性。

总之，寿光的蔬菜产业取得了举世瞩目的成就，也带动了地方经济的发展，但是在产业发展的过程中会不可避免的出现新问题，因此要未雨绸缪，及时调整发展思路，实现产业的升级转变。要从注重数量为主向提高质量转变，从劳动密集、粗放经营为主向劳动、技术密集集约经营转变，从立足国内市场为主向国际国内两个市场一起抓转变，使寿光蔬菜产业继续为农业增效、农民增收和发展现代农业做出更大贡献。

参 考 文 献

[1] 潘子龙，刘立功，柴玉梅等．寿光蔬菜产业发展20年［J］．中国蔬菜，2001（2）：53－55

[2] 苗锦山，刘文波，沈火林．寿光蔬菜产业发展的经验、启示和对策［J］．中国蔬菜，2008（10）：8－10

[3] 雷宝坤，陈清，范明生等．寿光设施菜田碳、氮演变及其对土壤性质的影响［J］．植物营养与肥料学报，2008，14（5）：914－922

[4] 尹可锁，吴文伟，郭志祥等．保护地蔬菜病虫害发生及土壤农药残留污染状况［J］．云南大学学报（自然科学版），2008，30（S1）：174－177

[5] Donna Chaw，Ulrica Stoklas，Cocomposting of cattle manure and hydrocarbon contamina-

ted flare pit soils [J]. Compost Science & Utilization, 2001, 9 (4): 322 -335
[6] 李玉梅，王根林，于洪久等．土壤农药残留微生物降解研究进展［J］．北方园艺，2007 (4): 72 -74
[7] 贾爱萍，赵冰，廖宗文．生化腐植酸的肥效及作用机理研究［J］．腐植酸，2005 (2): 15 -19
[8] 蔡燕飞，廖宗文，章家恩等．生态有机肥对番茄青枯病及土壤微生物多样性的影响［J］．应用生态学报，2003. 14 (3): 349 -353

Issues and Countermeasure on the Substainable Developmen of Vegetable Industry in Shouguang

XUE Qi-qin　LI Mei-qin　PEI Hua-li　QIAO Ning　MIAO Jin-shan
(*Weifang University of Science and Technology*, *Shouguang* 262700)

Abstract: By making a deep investigationg and research through various links in the production chain, the result showed that there are five restrictive factors for vegetable industry's developmen: High-quality and high-end vegetable products are relatively insufficien; The agroecological environment worsens day by day along with the growth of vegetables planting agelimit; The vegetables commercial and intensive processing have lagged behind; The level of mechanization for vegetables planting is low; The excellent varieties of intellectual property rights are insufficient; The peasantry quality is relatively low. Based on these restrictive factors, some strategies on how to carry out the sustainable development are offered. Suggestions contain carrying out the new soil management system; Expanding the organic vegetables production and enhancing the intensive processing; Using the experience of other countries for reference and enhancing mechanization and automation for vegetables industry. Strengthening cooperation with research institutions and raising widely the level of domestic vegetables seed; Reinforcing training to improve the peasantry quality.

Key words: Vegetable industry; Substainable developmen; Issues and countermeasure

空气污染对梨枣开花坐果的影响

马兴云① 肖万里[1] 张 菲[1] 朱元玖[2]

（1 潍坊科技学院，寿光 262700；2 潍坊市临朐县第三职业中专，临朐 262600）

摘 要： 近几年来，因空气粉尘污染，致使处在花期的梨枣，遭遇危害而严重影响坐果。尽管花期采取多种综合技术措施，总因不敌粉尘污染强度而近乎绝产。经对树体淋洗液化验分析，查清了空气粉尘污染严重影响坐果的事实。

关键词： 粉尘；梨枣；坐果

近几年入夏以来，山东省寿光市因修公路使用机械车辆运送石灰、水泥、沙料等，调制混凝土处理路基。由于数日影响，致使因公路西侧处在花期阶段的成龄枣树，遭受空气粉尘污染不能正常坐果，尽管花期采取了多项提高坐果率的综合技术措施，终因不敌粉尘污染强度而近乎绝产。

1 受害叶片及花器官症状表现

田间观察发现，受害叶片向上翻卷，叶色浓淡不匀，重者叶片质地变脆、边缘及叶尖焦枯；有的枣吊上的枣花未开即黄化脱落；有些枣花开放后干缩失水或花簇开放不久，花瓣边缘干枯，整个花簇变黄，一触即落。显微镜下观察则见，有的枣花开放后，表面干燥、无粘液或出现褐变，有的吸附着尘状物。

为确定空气粉尘污染影响梨枣坐果，采用自来水淋洗树冠，并提取淋洗液，采用原子吸收分光光度计、紫外分光光度计，进行检测分析，查清了空气污染是导致枣树花期不能正常坐果的主要原因。

① 马兴云，学士，潍坊科技学院副教授。研究方向：果树栽培技术。E－mail：maxingyun321@126. com

2 试验过程

2.1 花期阶段气候特点及技术措施

表1 气候特点及措施

时间（日/月）	气候特点	相对湿度（%）	物候期	技术措施
9/6	雨转晴	79	初花	喷2 500倍爱多收液肥
11/6	小雨	85	初花	全园放蜂
12/6	晴	73		主干环剥
14/6	晴	73	盛花	喷40mg/L赤霉素
23/6	雨	100	盛花	
24/6	阵雨	85		
25/6	小雨	85		
30/6	雨转晴	81		

表1表明，整个花期晴雨相间，空气湿润，相对湿度都在70%以上，有利于枣树开花坐果，且采取了多种提高坐果率的技术措施，但最终坐果率近乎为零。

2.2 污染物及污染源

表2 测检项目及结果　　单位：mg/L

pH	碳酸钙	氟化钙	铁	锰	铜	锌	镉	铅	砷
7.61	261	0.8	0.03	0.007	0.013	<0.1	<0.01	<0.025	<0.025

上述测检结果可知，除铁、铜、锰、锌外，其他重金属元素和氟化物不仅不是梨枣树生长发育的必需元素，反而会对其开花结果产生极为严重的毒害作用。

3 结果分析

在正常情况下，氟化物（氟化氢）要比二氧化硫的毒性高出上千倍，且有长期积累在受害部位很少转移的特性，即使在较低浓度的条件下，也会因持久性污染造成植物酶和叶绿素的破坏作用。其危害主要是氟与酶蛋白中的金属元素，例如，与钙、镁离子结合成络合物，使酶失去活性，阻碍代谢活动正常进行，致使叶肉细胞发生质壁分离和萎缩。氟也可使叶绿素合成受阻，影响梨枣的光和作用。镉的主要来源是工业所排放的三废和大气中镉飘浮的沉降物，镉被树体吸收后，能长期积累于根部，阻碍根系生长，导致根系生理机能衰竭，吸收能力下降，从而使地上部生长发育受到抑制。

铅与镉对植物产生的危害有许多相似之处，它不仅能在植物根部积累，还能有极少部分转移到地上部，随着地上部旺长中心的转移而转移，是新的生长点遭受危害。其主要来源是使用了含铅的农药或长期使用过磷酸钙肥料，而公路西侧的梨枣受害，则来自汽车、机械设备中长期排放的尾气。

砷有多种化合物，广泛存在于自然界。在微量的情况下，能刺激某些作物生长，在超出界定浓度下则对作物产生危害作用。它对花期梨枣树的危害主要是阻碍体内水分的运输，影响体内磷的代谢，继而使梨枣树整体生长发育受到抑制，砷的来源比较广泛，但工业“三废”和酸雨是造成农业污染的主要途径。

由于叶面和花器长期吸附着以石灰粉为主的多种空气微尘，造成了梨枣的光合作用、呼吸作用和授粉受精等生理机制的直接损害；在石灰粉遇到水（雨）生成氢氧化钙、碳酸钙的过程中，pH 值及瞬间产生热量的影响，导致了幼嫩的花器官组织的严重伤害；加之当月雨量多，空气潮湿，碳酸钙长期作用于叶片和花器，造成了梨枣树的光合作用、呼吸作用、代谢等生理功能失调，造成整体及间接损害，影响了梨枣的坐果。

4 结论

梨枣原产我国，适应性广泛，对环境条件无特殊要求，梨枣坐果率低的原因主要是由于空气之中的粉尘及重金属污染物造成的；由于近年我国工业及交通运输业的迅速发展，无疑对原有的生态环境产生了负面效应。我国加入 WTO 后，人们追求绿色果品的欲望与日俱增。因此兴建果园，建立绿色果品基地，要远离工业区，避开交通要道，否则，即造成梨枣落花、落果严重产量低，又不能做到生产真正的绿色果品。

参 考 文 献

[1] 刘家尧，陈继贞．环境生物学［M］．1994：207－208
[2] 马骏，蒋锦标．果树生产技术［M］．2008：302－315
[3] 雍文等．枣树栽培实用技术［M］．2007：87－90

Air Pollution on the Influence of Lizao Flowering Fructifications

MA Xing-yun[1] XIAO Wan-li[1] ZHANG Fei[1] ZHU Yuan-jiu[2]
(*Weifang University of Science and Technology*, *Shouguang* 262700;
LinQu Third Professional Technical Secondary School, *Linqu* 262600)

Abstract: In recent years, by air dust pollution, causes the LiZao, encounter in flowering and fruiting harm seriously affected. Although flowering adopt various out of integrated technical measures, not the total because dust pollution intensity and to produce certainly. Through the analysis of tree body eluent test and analysis, found out the air dust pollution seriously affect fruit-bearing facts.

Key words: Dust; LiZao; Fruit-bearing

去除蔬菜和水果上农药残留的研究进展

刘振龙① 王延梅 高洪燕
（潍坊科技学院，寿光 262700）

摘 要： 去除蔬菜和水果上农药残留的方法很多，从性质上说，有物理法、化学法、微生物降解法，其中，包括一些比较简单的方法，如储藏，用自来水冲洗、沸水煮等；还有一些其他的方法，如洗涤剂、化学氧化剂或在水中加入盐、醋等方法，这些都可以一定程度地去除蔬菜和水果上的残留农药。

关键词： 蔬菜；水果；农药残留；去除

随着生活水平的日益提高，人们越来越关注蔬菜和水果中的农药残留问题，如何能最大程度地减少蔬菜和水果中的农药残留，降低对人体的危害成为近年来的研究热点。当然，解决农药残留问题最根本的方法在于科学合理使用农药以减少农药源头污染，但由于农药使用问题在当前农业生产中时有发生，因此研究蔬菜和水果中农药残留去除技术，从而指导消费者在餐桌前降低农药残留危害也是其中重要的解决办法之一。本文对近几年来有关蔬菜和水果中农药残留去除的研究进行了综述。

1 普通方法

1.1 储藏法

新鲜蔬菜采收后，仍能继续进行呼吸和新陈代谢活动。在蔬菜储藏期间，空气中的氧气和蔬菜中的酶及色素等活性物质对残留农药可进一步氧化分解。A. A. K. Abou-Arab[1]将处理过的番茄放于 -10℃下分别存放 1、3、6、12d 后，每种农药的残留量随着时间的推移都有所减少，如六氯苯、林丹、pp′-滴滴涕属于有机氯类，性质较稳定，存放 6d 后，残留量分别下降 5.28%、7.02%、5.74%；12d 后，残留量分别下降 10.6%、16.3%、13.0%。有机磷类效果明显，存放 6d 后，乐果、丙溴磷、甲基嘧啶磷分别减少 28.5%、26.6%、26.2%；12d 后，残留量分别下降 32.6%、28.2%、31.4%。青菜中的高效氯氰菊酯残留量逐渐较少，存放 72h 的消解率为 28.01%，而储藏在常温下的马铃薯中的噻菌灵 56d 后下降小于 10%。氨基甲酸酯类杀虫剂硫双威的

① 刘振龙，男，潍坊科技学院硕士，讲师。研究方向：农用化学品配方工艺及分析。E - mail：lzl121@126.com

残留在 -10℃是稳定的，但在4.5℃消解较快[2]。

1.2 清理和去皮法

A. A. K. Abou-Arab[1]1999年分析，用药处理过的番茄表皮、汁液、果肉和种子等不同部位的残留量，除极少量的有机氯农药六氯苯、林丹、pp′-滴滴涕、pp′-滴滴涕渗入果肉和有机磷类农药乐果、丙溴磷渗入果肉、种子、汁液外，大部分残留于番茄果皮上。因此，去皮可以除掉番茄中80.6%的六氯苯、82.4%的林丹、81.2%的pp′-滴滴涕、85.0%的乐果、83.3%的丙溴磷和89.2%的甲基嘧啶磷。运用类似的方法，Soliman[5]等用六氯苯、林丹、pp′-滴滴涕、乐果、马拉硫磷、甲基嘧啶磷处理马铃薯后，去皮可以使残留量减少75.3%、72.7%、71.2%、70.8%、70.7%、71.4%。但对于少数内吸性农药，其亲酯性较强，残留会随时间渗透到蔬菜的内部，而使得去皮后去除率有限，例如，马铃薯中的甲拌磷和乙拌磷，去皮后残留量只分别降低了50%和35%[2]。

1.3 日光照射和紫外光照射法

日光的多光谱效应会使蔬菜中部分残留农药分解，破坏。例如，1945年，Gunther首先观察到杀虫剂pp′-滴滴涕在夏天喷到田间由于自然光照降解而很快失去毒效。另外，蔬菜在阳光下照射5mn，有机氯、有机汞农药的残留量会显著减少[5]。

紫外照射消解农药的作用机理是通过施加高能量，加速农药分子的化学键断裂。如菊酯类农药含有双键和环丙烷环等光敏感点，在溶液中易发生光氧化反应。张存政等[3]研究了不同紫外光照射时间对青菜上高效氯氰菊酯的消解研究，紫外照射处理10min时的消解率比对照高10%，且随照射时间延长，消解率增加，这表明紫外照射对残留高效氯氰菊酯消解有一定的加速作用。

1.4 清水洗

洗涤是人们日常生活中最常用的一种方法，它去除残留的效果不仅取决于农药在水中的溶解度，而且与残留的位置、残留时间以及洗涤的温度和作物类型有关。极性较大的农药种类，其水溶性强，亲酯性差，渗透能力差，比较容易被除去，而对于亲酯性强的农药，会随时间延长，向表皮渗透。对于部分残存在蔬菜表面的农药，用水洗法比较容易除去。但是个别农药清洗较难，如谭燕琼等[7]系统研究了自来水流水冲洗，多次水浸洗和长时间水浸洗对喷雾1d后蔬菜上甲胺磷的去除率。室温下，将蔬菜放在4L水中浸泡，15、30、60、120min取样，结果表明甲胺磷从蔬菜渗出到水中的过程缓慢，在60min时，甲胺磷的浓度减少65%，但随着浸泡时间的增长，甲胺磷的浓度没有再进一步降低。多次水浸洗即用4L水浸洗15min分别1、2、3、4次，总共1h，甲胺磷减少至62%，再多浸洗效果也不会改善。

1.5 洗涤剂洗

果蔬洗涤剂主要成分是表面活性剂（如：直链烷基苯磺酸钠等）、助剂（柠檬酸钠等）和一些辅助成分[8,9,10]。洗涤剂洗的效果不仅与洗涤剂类型有关，还有洗涤剂浓度、水温及农药类型有关。宗荣芬等[11]研制了以椰子油衍生物为主要成分的蔬果洗涤剂，并比较了该种洗涤剂与3种市售洗涤剂、清水和1% 食用碱、1% 食用盐对甲胺磷和氧乐果在青菜上的去除效果，该洗涤剂去除率达87.7%，另外3种洗涤剂平均去除率分别为66.8%、64.4%、68.1%。张俊亭等[12]同样用其自制的蔬菜水果专用洗涤剂研究了对硫磷、氯氰菊酯、硫双灭多威、乐果、甲胺磷在黄瓜、油菜、苹果和梨上的洗涤去除率，其平均值超过70%。陈淑芹等[13]则对比了白猫牌清洁精、安利蝶新清洁剂、臭氧水及清水对敌敌畏、氧乐果、抗蚜威在夏白菜上的去除效果，结果表明，安利蝶新清洁剂对敌敌畏效果最佳，白猫牌清洁精对氧乐果的去除率最高。张存政[3]等研究了两种浓度的洗涤剂对青菜上高效氯氰菊酯的去除效果，2%浓度洗涤剂的洗涤效果是0.05%浓度的近2倍，与清水相比，差异达到显著程度。

1.6 热水或沸水洗

利用水煮过程对作物中农药残留去除方式有3种：（1）为加热分解农药残留；（2）为将残留于作物组织内农药带入水溶液中；（3）随水蒸汽而蒸发。利用加热可以去除部分农药，常用于芹菜、菠菜小白菜、圆白菜、青椒、菜花、豆角等。谭燕琼[7]等用沸水处理了被甲胺磷处理过的蔬菜，分别浸泡1、3、5、10min，其去除率都为92%，比室温下自来水冲洗、张春贵[6]等用沸水处理被3种杀虫剂和2种杀菌剂污染的苋菜、空心菜和卷心菜，10min后各农药去除效果良好。

2 特殊方法

2.1 碱液、盐水、酸液

Zohair[14]研究了各种酸性溶液（胡萝卜酸、柠檬酸、维生素C、乙酸、过氧化氢）、中性溶液（氯化钠）和碱性溶液（碳酸钠）对马铃薯上狄氏剂、异狄氏剂、艾氏剂、滴滴伊、滴滴滴、滴滴涕等有机氯和丙溴磷、马拉硫磷等有机磷农药的去除效果。结果表明，5% 和10%胡萝卜酸可以去除pp′-滴滴涕滴滴伊外的所有残留；柠檬酸、维生素C可以洗去残留在马铃薯上的所有丙溴磷、林丹、pp′-滴滴涕 滴滴涕等残留。碱性溶液可以去除所有残留的有机磷和滴滴涕。A. A. K. Abou-Arab[1]和Soliman[4]分别于1999年和2001年将2%、4%、6%、8%、10% 的氯化钠和乙酸溶液洗涤用下述6种农药处理过的番茄和马铃薯；随着浓度的增大，对马铃薯和番茄中残留农药的去除作用也相应增大，其中4%、6%、8%的3种浓度氯化钠和醋酸溶液与清水洗涤的效果相比，所有杀虫剂均有明显差异。

刘义等[15]总结5%醋、5%盐和5% 碳酸钠溶液对豆角、菠菜、白菜、韭菜上甲基对硫磷、马拉硫磷、甲胺磷、氧乐果残留的洗涤效果。结果显示，对于上述4种农药，5%盐溶液的去除效果略好，而5% 醋和5% 碳酸钠溶液与清水的洗涤去除效果相当。

2.2 烹调

烹调过程中温度、时间、吸水量以及系统是否开放都会影响到最终的农药残留量。大多文献中处理蔬菜的方法都是煮沸、油炸或微波。谭燕琼[7]则使用了国内炒煮的方式，在平底锅中加入粟米油，将样本炒煮30s，加水10ml，继续3min，其对青菜中甲胺磷的去除率达69%。

2.3 化学氧化剂

人们能够经常使用的化学氧化剂有次氯酸钙、二氧化氯、过氧化物等。

次氯酸钙是漂白粉和漂白精的有效成分，一种有较高稳定性的强氧化剂，有消毒、杀菌和漂白功能。Eun－Sun Hwang等2001年研究了500、500mg/kg两种浓度次氯酸钙溶液对苹果上1、3mg/kg浓度代森锰锌的去除效果，30min后的去除效果均在90%以上，与对照蒸馏水相比，均有极显著的差异，且浓度越大，对代森锰锌的去除效果越好。

与氯相比，二氧化氯在水中反应具有不形成三卤甲烷等致癌物质，不与酚反应，且比氯氧化性更强等优势，世界卫生组织将其列为安全消毒物质中A_1级产品。Eun－Sun Hwang等[16]2001年研究了5、10mg/kg两种浓度二氧化氯对苹果上1、3mg/kg浓度代森锰锌的去除效果稍逊于次氯酸钙，但与对照蒸馏水相比，均有极显著的差异。

2.4 臭氧

臭氧是一种强氧化剂，其氧化还原电位仅次于氟，为2.07V（氟为2.78V），正是它的强氧化性，在水中污染物的分解、脱色、除臭、杀菌、灭藻与病毒失活；除铁、锰、除硫化物、除酚、除氰、除农药、除石油及合成洗涤剂、除水中致癌物质，降解BOD、COD等，都具有特殊的效果。

得益于臭氧的强氧化性，人们将臭氧气体通入浸泡有残留农药蔬菜的水中与残留农药发生反应，生成相应的酸、醇、胺或其氧化物，这些小分子化合物易溶于水，可被洗涤除去，是一种安全、无残留污染的消毒剂。杨学昌[17]等用臭氧处理番茄、白菜、黄瓜、扁豆等果蔬上的百菌清、氧乐果、敌百虫、杀灭菊酯和敌敌畏，处理后的农药残留量均达到国际允许标准。

在臭氧消解水果上农药残留的研究方面，Eun－Sun Hwang等[16]2001年研究了两种浓度臭氧对苹果上两种代森锰锌及其代谢产物的消解效果，与对照相比，差异极显著，3mg/L的臭氧水作用30min时，苹果上仅有不到10%的残留，代森锰锌的降解产物乙撑硫脲没有被检测到。

2.5 微生物降解法

国内对农药微生物降解研究较晚，且主要集中于农药在环境中的行为及降解机理，而利用微生物进行作物中残留农药降解研究尚少。程国锋等[18]筛选出了分别以甲胺磷为唯一碳源的生长的菌株NM-J_5和以乐果为唯一碳源生长的菌株NM-L_3，两种菌株的菌液分别处理喷有甲胺磷和乐果的小白菜，对两种残留农药有明显的去除作用。

参 考 文 献

[1] Abou-Arab A. A. A. K. Behavior of pesticides in tomatoes during commercial and home preparation [J]. Food Chem, 1999, 65: 509 – 514

[2] Holland P T, Hamiltom D, Ohlin B, et al. Effects of storage and processing on pesticide residues on plant products [J]. Pure Appl Chem, 1994, 66 (2): 335 – 356

[3] 张存政，骆爱兰，王冬兰等．消解去除食用菜叶中高效氯氰菊酯残留方法的研究 [J]. 农业环境科学学报，2000，24 (1): 196 – 200

[4] Soliman K M. Changes in concentration of pesticide residues in potatoes during washing and home prepration [J]. Food Chem Toxicol, 2001, 39 (8): 887 – 891

[5] 你知道怎样去除蔬菜上的农药残留吗?[J]. 中国自然医学杂志，2001，3 (2): 107

[6] 张春贵、谢建元、许秀夫．在叶菜类上农药残留减量方法的评估 [J]. 台湾农业化学与食品科学．2005，43 (1): 46 – 55

[7] 谭燕琼，李伟安．清除蔬菜甲胺磷污染的方法研究 [J]. 卫生研究，1998，27 (1): 62 – 65

[8] 宗荣芬，刘文卫，梅建新．蔬果洗涤剂对农药残留去除率的研究 [J]. 中国卫生检验杂志，2003，13 (4): 441 – 442

[9] 龙万凯，温木盛．蔗糖酯洗涤剂去除农药残留的试验 [J]. 化工技术与开发，2002，31 (4): – 18

[10] 孔凡春，陆胜民，王群．臭氧在果蔬保鲜农药残留上的应用 [J]，食品与机械，2003，5: 24 – 26

[11] 宗荣芬，梅建新，刘文卫．去除蔬果中农药残留的方法研究 [J]. 职业与健康，2004，20 (10): 8 – 9

[12] 张俊亭．蔬菜水果清洗剂对农药残留洗除率的测定及效果 [J]. 农业环境保护，1998，17 (6): 258 – 259

[13] 陈淑芹，孙治强，王兰菊等．清洗液对夏白菜中农药残留洗除效果的对比试验 [J]. 安徽农业科学，2004，32 (2): 307 – 308

[14] Zohair A. Behaviour of some organophosphorus and organochlorine pesticides in potatoes during soaking in different solutions [J]. Food Chem Toxicol, 2001, 39 (7): 751 – 755

[15] 刘义，王刚，张秀慧．蔬菜农药残留去除方法 [J]. 中国卫生工程学，2002，1 (2): 101 – 103.

[16] Eun-Sun Hwang. Cash Jeny N . Postharvest treatments for the reduction of Mancozeb in fresh apples [J]. Journal of agricultural and food chemistry 2001, vol. 49, pp. 3 127 – 3 132

[17] 杨学昌，王真，高宣德等．蔬菜水果农药残留处理的新方法 [J]. 清华大学学报，

1997, 37 (9): 13 - 15.
[18] 程国锋等. 微生物降解蔬菜残留农药研究 [J]. 应用与环境生物学报, 1998, 4 (1): 81 - 84

Removal of Pesticide Residue on Vegetable and Fruit after Harvest

LIU Zhen-long　WANG Yan-mei　GAO Hong-yan
(*Weifang University of Science and Technology*, *Shouguang*　262700)

Abstract: How to reduce pesticide residue on vegetable and fruit after harvest effectively is our research hotspot . There are a lot of methods about removal of pesticide residue, for example, physical, chemical or microbe-degradation methods, including some simple methods, such as storage, tap water-wash, boiling water-wash, and so on; Other methods, such as detergent, chemical oxidant, salt or vinegar in water. All can remove residue pesticide on vegetable and fruit in some degree.

Key words: Vegetable; Fruit; Pesticide residue; Removal

城市有机混合垃圾的蚯蚓堆制处理

杨文霞① 梁 弘

（潍坊科技学院，寿光 262700）

摘 要： 为了探讨加速城市生活垃圾的堆制处理及其资源化利用的有效措施，以采自南京市水阁有机废弃物填埋场的垃圾为代表，加入秸秆或牛粪，调节m（C）/m（N）和水分含量，预堆制15d后，接种赤子爱胜蚓（Eisenia foetida）进行室内堆制处理。结果表明：30%牛粪+70%新鲜有机混合垃圾处理（NH处理）和20%秸秆+80%新鲜有机混合垃圾堆制处理（JH处理）的赤子爱胜蚓总体生长良好。蚯蚓堆制处理显著降低了有机混合垃圾堆制残留物干重，其中NH处理减少的最多。蚯蚓的接种显著降低了新鲜有机混合垃圾（HL）、堆制腐熟有机混合垃圾（DL）和JH处理的有机碳和全氮质量比，提高了NH处理的有机碳和全氮质量比。研究表明：城市有机混合垃圾在加入牛粪的基础上接种蚯蚓，其堆制效果较好，是处理有机混合垃圾的有效措施。

关键词： 环境工程学；蚯蚓堆制处理；赤子爱胜蚓；城市有机混合垃圾

城市生活垃圾产生量不断增加。2008年，世界已有超过50%的人口生活在城市，全球年产垃圾超过100亿t[1]。截至2005年底，我国城市生活垃圾的年产生量达1.5亿t，还以每年8%～10%的速度递增，少数城市（如北京）达15%～20%，至2010年，我国城市生活垃圾年产生量将达1.8亿t[2,3]。而人均垃圾清运量从1980年的0.94kg/d增长到2004年的1.79kg/d，24年增长了90.3%，平均每年增长2.7%[4]。城市垃圾产生量的逐年增长对人们的生存环境和健康都构成了严重威胁。另外，全国城市生活垃圾历年堆存量已达60多亿t，侵占土地面积超过5亿m^2，垃圾无害化处理率较低。全国已有许多城市不同程度出现了“垃圾围城”的局面[5]。

大部分城市生活垃圾沿用简易填埋的落后处理方式，占用大量土地，污染环境，危害人体健康，而且这种状况日益突出[6]。如何有效处理日益增多的废弃物已经成为各国普遍关注的问题。城市生活垃圾中含有很多对人类有用的成分，这些成分加以合理回收利用，就可以变废为宝。赤子爱胜蚓多以半腐烂的有机物为食，可用于有机废弃物的无害化处理。因此，有机废弃物的蚯蚓堆制处理（Vermicomposting）[7,8]应运而生，这是根据蚯蚓在自然生态系统中具有促进有机物质分解转化的功能而在垃圾发酵处理

① 杨文霞，女，硕士，潍坊科技学院讲师。研究方向：环境生态。E-mail：ywxty@163.com

(Composting) 的基础上发展起来的一项主要针对城市有机生活垃圾和农业有机垃圾的生物处理技术。另外，蚯蚓本身在医药、保健、畜禽养殖、水产养殖中有广泛的应用，蚯蚓排泄物蚓粪还含有丰富的养分，可以作为优质有机肥，进行有机果蔬的生产。

因此，本文旨在探讨蚯蚓在城市有机混合垃圾堆制处理中的作用，为城市有机垃圾的无害化、减量化、资源化处理提供一个可行的途径，其副产物蚯蚓也可以为畜禽养殖、水产养殖提供经济可行的饲料，为城市有机混合垃圾更充分更有效地处理和资源化利用提供理论依据。

1 材料与方法

1.1 供试材料

1.1.1 供试蚯蚓

赤子爱胜蚓（Eisenia foetida）由南京市大厂区长芦镇蚯蚓养殖场提供。

1.1.2 供试有机物料

蚓粪：为南京农业大学奶牛场的新鲜牛粪经蚯蚓堆制处理后的产物，挑出蚯蚓与蚓茧，自然风干，过 2 mm 筛，装入聚四氯乙烯袋中，放置干燥通风处，备用。

新鲜有机混合垃圾：取自南京市水阁有机废弃物填埋场的新鲜混合垃圾，经过手工分拣，剔除玻璃、砖瓦块、塑料制品、金属制品等物质，剩余的有机混合垃圾破碎、混匀后备用。

堆制腐熟有机混合垃圾：新鲜有机混合垃圾混匀后，堆成长、宽、高各 0.9 m 的条垛进行静态堆肥。采用翻堆方式通风供氧，以堆体中心温度达到 55 ℃为翻堆标志。前期含水量控制在 50%，后期保持自然，堆制 4 个月，为鲜样。

秸秆：采自江西鹰潭红壤生态站晚稻秸秆，风干，剪碎过 5 mm 筛孔。

牛粪：取自南京农业大学奶牛场的新鲜牛粪自然风干，同上。

供试有机物料的基本理化性质见表 1。

表 1 供试有机物料的基本理化性质

试验材料	含水量 (g/kg)	pH 值 (H_2O)	有机碳 (g/kg)	全氮 (g/kg)	m (C) / m (N)
新鲜有机混合垃圾	853.4	6.31	356.58	13.88	25.7
堆制腐熟有机混合垃圾	450.7	7.97	183.09	11.99	15.3
秸秆	129.2	6.5	352.71	6.85	51.5
牛粪	81.1	7.82	415.45	17.12	24.4
蚓粪	68.6	7.31	147	11.79	12.5

1.2 试验设计

试验采用上口直径为 28cm，下底直径为 20cm，高 26cm，底部有透水孔的塑料钵

24 个，底部放有细纱网防止蚯蚓逃逸。每钵内细纱网上放风干蚓粪 200g（干重），蚓粪上面放有粗纱网（孔径 5 mm），以便于分离垃圾，蚯蚓可以自由穿过。并按不同处理分别加相当于500g 干重的新鲜有机混合垃圾、相当于 500g 干重的堆制腐熟有机混合垃圾、相当于500g 干重的秸秆与新鲜有机混合垃圾的混合物（按2∶8 比例）和相当于500g 干重的牛粪与新鲜有机混合垃圾的混合物（按 3∶7 比例）于粗纱网上。先在盆钵中自然堆制 15d[9]，为了防止产生的热量使蚯蚓逃逸，每隔 24h 翻 1 次堆排除有害气体。然后接种大小相当且处于生殖期的蚯蚓 50 条[10,11]，每条约重 0.3g，总生物量约 15.0g。在钵口蒙上细纱布，防止蚯蚓逃逸。试验设 8 个处理，每个处理设置 3 个重复。于室内阴暗处培养，堆制过程中水分含量通过称重法，用外加入的蒸馏水来控制水分质量比在 600 ~ 800g/kg。通过空调将温度控制在 22 ~ 28 ℃[12,13]。具体各处理初始物料的含量见表 2。

表 2　各处理初始物料的含量

处理	蚓粪（g）	新鲜有机混合垃圾（g）	堆制腐熟有机混合垃圾（g）	秸秆（g）	牛粪（g）	m（C）/ m（N）
HL	200	500	0	0	0	25.7
DL	200	0	500	0	0	15.3
JH	200	400	0	100	0	24.2
NH	200	350	0	0	150	22.1

注：(1) HL 表示新鲜有机混合垃圾，DL 表示堆制腐熟有机混合垃圾，JH 表示 20% 秸秆 + 80% 新鲜有机混合垃圾，NH 表示 30% 牛粪 + 70% 新鲜有机混合垃圾，每个处理分接种蚯蚓（ + E）和不接种蚯蚓（-E）两种情况，共 8 种处理；(2) 秸秆、牛粪以烘干重计，物料比为干重比

分别在接种蚯蚓堆制 15d、30d、45d、60d 时进行蚯蚓计数和称重。计数时先将上层堆制垃圾缓慢倒出，仔细挑出上层垃圾和粗网下蚓粪中的成蚓、幼蚓和蚓茧，对成蚓和幼蚓进行计数和称重，对蚓茧进行计数。堆制 60d 后，收集粗网上混合垃圾堆制残留物并风干称重。经蚯蚓处理完全的垃圾会通过蚯蚓的取食、排泄和携带等作用进入粗网下，将粗网下的垃圾处理物与蚓粪充分混匀作为堆制产物，测定其有机碳和全氮质量比。而未接种蚯蚓的处理，粗网上的有机物料除分解完全的极少部分会落入网下外，其余部分不会落入网下。

1.3　测定分析方法

1.3.1　蚯蚓生长、繁殖特性的测定方法

蚯蚓日增重倍数[14] = （堆制一定天数后蚯蚓总重量 - 初始蚓重）/（初始蚓重 × 堆制天数）　　(1)

蚯蚓日增殖倍数[14] = （堆制一定天数后蚯蚓总条数 - 初始蚯蚓条数）/（初始蚯蚓条数 × 堆制天数）　　(2)

式中蚯蚓总条数包括成蚓数、幼蚓数和蚓茧数，每个蚓茧按 1 条蚯蚓计算，处理时

间以 d 计，蚓重以 g 计。

由于接种蚯蚓而加速降解的有机物料干重占总干重的百分数 =（未接种蚯蚓处理堆制 60d 后有机垃圾堆制残留物干重 - 接种蚯蚓处理堆制 60d 后有机垃圾堆制残留物干重）/初始物料干重 ×100% (3)

1.3.2 样品测试项目及方法

水分含量及干物质重，pH 值和全氮采用常规法；有机碳测定先采用固体稀释法，再采用 $K_2Cr_2O_7$ - H_2SO_4 外加热氧化法测定有机碳质量比。

2 结果与讨论

2.1 蚯蚓在城市有机混合垃圾堆制过程中的生长和繁殖特性分析

2.1.1 蚯蚓在城市有机混合垃圾堆制过程中的生长特性分析

在 0～15d，蚯蚓的日增重倍数以 NH 处理最高，达到 0.030，极显著高于其他各处理（$P<0.01$，下同），见图 1。DL 处理为最低，呈现负增长。说明在有机物料堆制的最初 15d 内，NH 处理中有机物料最适合蚯蚓的生长。而 JH 处理中的有机物料不适合蚯蚓的生长，这可能与该处理中稻草秸秆的存在有关。稻草秸秆含有纤维素、半纤维素以及结构复杂的木质素和难降解的蜡质，稻草秸秆的灰分（矿物质）含量较高，为其他秸秆含量的 3 倍[15]，对蚯蚓的适口性较差，同时稻草秸秆腐烂降解的初期会产生各种有机酸，抑制了蚯蚓的生长。在 15～30d，蚯蚓的日增重倍数在各处理间有显著差异（$P<0.05$，下同），以 JH 处理为最高（0.024），其次是 NH 处理（0.019），DL 处理最低，仍为负值。这说明堆制 30d 时蚯蚓已经适应了秸秆和牛粪的堆制环境，同时由于秸秆和牛粪的腐解为蚯蚓的生长提供了充足的碳源和营养物质，使蚯蚓在 15～30d 的堆制期间生长迅速。30～45d 堆制期间，各处理的蚯蚓日增重倍数均显著降低，除 HL 处理外，其他处理均降低为负值。其原因可能是堆制期间蚯蚓的生长消耗了大量养分，堆制残余物中可利用养分的量相对蚯蚓的生长越来越缺乏。45～60d 堆制期间，蚯蚓的日增重倍数趋于稳定，均降低为负值，以 HL 处理为最低。

随着堆制时间的延长，各处理蚯蚓日增重倍数变化各不相同。HL 处理在堆制的 0～30d 内有一个缓慢增加的过程，从 30d 开始降低，最终出现负增长。DL 处理在堆制的各个时期蚯蚓日增重倍数均为负值，表明堆制时间内蚯蚓的重量一直在减小。其原因是堆制垃圾中 m（C）/m（N）值较低，缺乏足够蚯蚓生长的碳源，使该处理蚯蚓日增重倍数为负值。JH 处理的蚯蚓日增重倍数是先迅速增大，堆制 30d 时达到最大，然后又迅速减小，在 45d 时降到最小，并逐渐变为负增长，最后趋于稳定。NH 处理的蚯蚓日增重倍数则是从堆制 15d 后就一直减小，堆制 45d 时降到最小，之后趋于稳定。一定比例稻草秸秆和牛粪的加入，为蚯蚓提供了充足的碳源，使蚯蚓生长良好。

2.1.2 蚯蚓在城市有机混合垃圾堆制过程中的繁殖特性分析

从图 2 可以看出，0～15d 堆制期间，各处理蚯蚓日增殖倍数几乎没有变化，说明这段时间内蚯蚓还没有开始繁殖。15～30d 堆制期间，DL 和 NH 处理的蚯蚓已开始繁

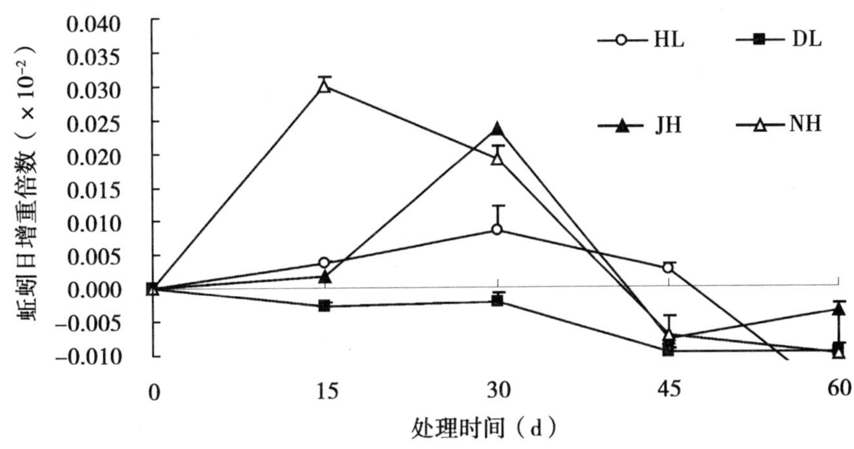

图1 接种蚯蚓各处理赤子爱胜蚓日增重倍数

殖，且DL处理蚯蚓繁殖迅速，日增殖倍数显著高于其他各处理，而NH处理与处理蚯蚓的日增殖倍数变化不大。30～45d堆制期间，各处理蚯蚓的日增殖倍数仍然是以堆制腐熟有机混合垃圾DL处理最大（0.055），且显著高于其他各处理，其他处理的蚯蚓日增殖倍数从大到小依次为HL、NH、JH，其中JH处理蚯蚓的日增殖倍数为0，仍未开始繁殖。堆制60d时，NH处理蚯蚓的日增殖倍数显著高于其他各处理，HL处理和JH处理差异不显著，而DL处理在45～60d堆制期间迅速减小为负值。

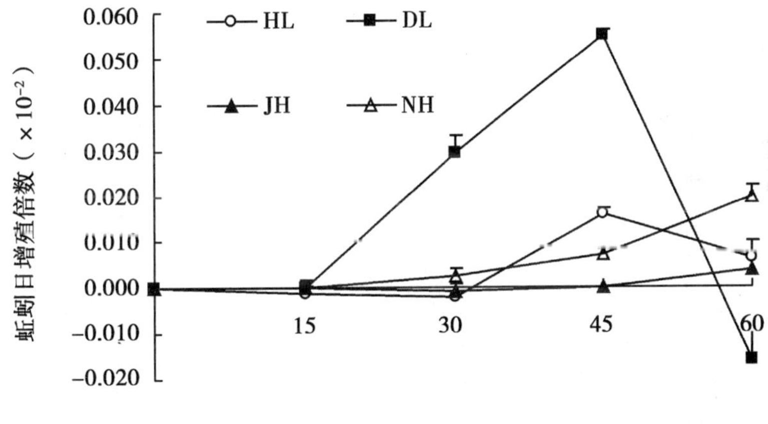

图2 接种蚯蚓各处理赤子爱胜蚓日增殖倍数

0～30d，HL处理的蚯蚓日增殖倍数为负值，蚯蚓的繁殖受到了抑制，在30～60d堆制期间，HL处理的蚯蚓的日增殖倍数先逐渐增大，最后又逐渐减小。有机混合垃圾在堆制初期腐烂降解，产生大量渗滤液，含有有机酸等物质，抑制了蚯蚓的繁殖。DL处理的蚯蚓日增殖倍数先快速增大，在堆制45d时达到最大（0.051），其后又迅速减小。这可能是堆制后期堆制产物剩余量较小，再加上其保水性较差使得水分含量变化较大，抑制了蚯蚓的繁殖[11]。JH 处理各个堆制时期蚯蚓的日增殖倍数均最小，且无显著变化，这与稻草秸秆抑制蚯蚓日增重倍数的原因相似。NH 处理的蚯蚓日增殖倍数在堆制期间一直在缓慢增大。

上述结果表明，堆制时间内，DL 处理蚯蚓繁殖最好。一定比例稻草秸秆和牛粪的加入，增加了有机混合垃圾的通气性，调节了由于有机混合垃圾的腐烂产生的过量水分，但稻草秸秆和牛粪对蚯蚓的影响却不同。稻草秸秆的加入一定程度上抑制了蚯蚓的繁殖，这可能是因为稻草秸秆腐烂降解时产生的各种有机酸以及放出的热量抑制了蚯蚓的产茧和繁殖。而牛粪的加入则促进了蚯蚓的繁殖，并且随着时间的延长，蚯蚓的数量逐渐增加，这与 Bintoro 等[16]对蚯蚓繁殖率的研究结果相似。尽管有报道称农业有机废弃物对蚯蚓的生长和繁殖有不利影响[12]，但从本文蚯蚓的生长和繁殖情况看，在有机混合垃圾中加入牛粪有利于蚯蚓的生长。

2.2 蚯蚓对城市有机混合垃圾堆制残留物干重的影响

利用蚯蚓处理有机垃圾的一个主要依据就是通过蚯蚓与微生物的协同作用可以加速有机物质的分解转化。由赤子爱胜蚓对城市有机混合垃圾堆制残留物干重的影响可以看出（图 3），经过 60d 的堆制，接种蚯蚓处理的粗网上有机混合垃圾堆制残留物干重显著小于未接种蚯蚓的对应处理。表明接种蚯蚓可以明显加速有机物料的降解，加快了堆制速度。因此，通过式（3）计算 HL、DL、JH 和 NH 处理由于接种蚯蚓而加速降解的有机物料干重所占总干重的百分数分别为 27.97%、27.49%、26.75% 和 34.88%。从这一结果可看出，接种蚯蚓后 NH 处理的堆制产物干重减少程度最大。一方面是由于蚯蚓对饵料的需求较大［0］，而该处理初始有机物料 m（C）/m（N）为 22.1，碳氮营养均衡，较适合蚯蚓生长；另一方面由于蚯蚓的接种提高了堆制产物中微生物生物量，微生物与蚯蚓的这种协同作用加速了有机物料的降解，其具体机理还需进一步研究。

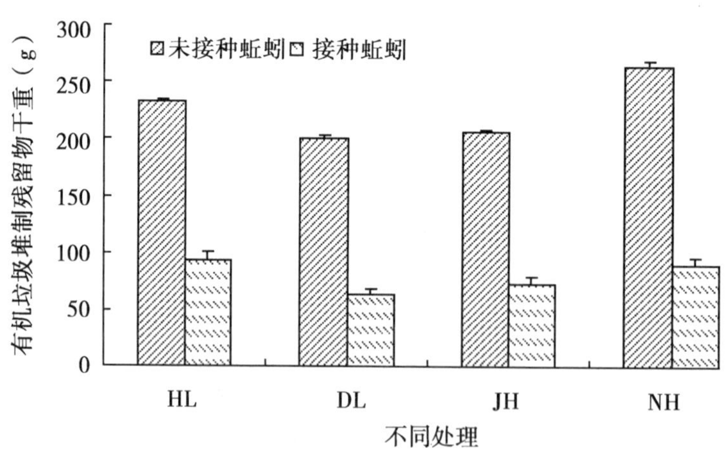

图 3 赤子爱胜蚓对城市有机混合垃圾堆制残留物干重的影响

2.3 蚯蚓对有机混合垃圾堆制产物有机碳、全氮质量比和 m（C）/m（N）的影响

无论是接种蚯蚓还是未接种蚯蚓处理，经过 60d 的堆制，堆制产物有机碳的质量比均相应的低于初始物料（表 1，表 3）。接种蚯蚓后 HL、DL、JH 处理的有机碳质量比显著低于未接种蚯蚓的相应处理，表明蚯蚓的接种促进了有机质的矿化。这主要因为有机物料接种蚯蚓后，蚯蚓消耗碳源，使大量的有机碳以 CO_2 的形式损失[17]。JH 处理除上述原因外，秸秆含有更多易被微生物分解的糖类、淀粉等物质，被微生物利用的物质越多说明其碳素有效率越高[18]，从而加速了有机物料中碳的矿化。NH 处理接种蚯蚓后有机碳质量比有所增加，但是并未达到显著差异。其原因可能为 NH 处理有机物料在降解的过程中通气性逐渐变差，部分抑制了堆制物料中 CO_2 的挥发损失，使部分有机碳在矿化后并未能以 CO_2 的形式损失，而留在了堆制物料中。

表 3 试验各处理堆制产物有机碳、全氮质量比及 m（C）/m（N）

处理	有机碳（g/kg）		全氮（g/kg）		*m*（C）/*m*（N）	
	-E	+E	-E	+E	-E	+E
HL	166.14 ±4.41cA	144.98 ±3.93cB	13.25 ±0.05abA	12.08 ±0.31bB	12.54 ±0.29bA	12.00 ±0.08dB
DL	159.48 ±2.1cA	135.33 ±3.48dB	13.10 ±0.09bA	10.94 ±0.26cB	12.18 ±0.08bA	12.37 ±0.05cA
JH	173.89 ±1.15bA	160.94 ±1.43bB	13.74 ±0.16aA	12.36 ±0.08bB	12.66 ±0.07bB	13.02 ±0.04bA
NH	181.69 ±5.25aA	187.20 ±4.6aA	13.43 ±0.57abA	13.99 ±0.28aA	13.55 ±0.90aA	13.38 ±0.18aA

注：（1）多重均值比较采用 Duncan's 方法；（2）同一列中小写字母相同表示无显著差异（$P<0.05$），同一行中大写字母相同表示无显著差异（$P<0.05$）；（3）-E 表示不接种蚯蚓，+E 表示接种蚯蚓

伴随着有机碳的矿化，各处理全氮质量比也显著增加，这已为很多研究[9,12]所证实。可能是由于堆制过程中有机物的矿化分解，CO_2 的损失以及水分的蒸发引起干物质减少所致；另外，堆制后期固氮菌的固氮作用也有助于堆制产物全氮量的增加。接种蚯蚓后 HL、DL 和 JH 处理的全氮质量比均显著降低，其原因各个处理并不相同。HL 和 JH 处理由于 m（C）/m（N）分别为 25.7 和 24.2，比较适合有机物料的堆制和蚯蚓及微生物的取食，大量氮素被消耗。DL 处理主要是随着堆制时间的进行，堆制产物剩余量越来越小，又由于蚯蚓较高的生物量，使有机物料中大量可利用的碳源和氮源被蚯蚓和微生物所消耗，同时由于堆制后期堆制产物的 m（C）/m（N）过低，氮易被微生物转化为氨而损失掉[19-20]。而 NH 处理的全氮质量比在接种蚯蚓后有所增加，其原因可能是蚯蚓活动所形成的孔道和孔隙环境有利于固氮菌的生长，进而有助于堆制产物全氮量的增加。当然，堆制产物中全氮质量比的高低最终还取决于原始物料中氮的含量和试验结束时物料的堆制程度。

经过 60d 的堆制，各处理堆制产物的 m（C）/m（N）与初始物料相比均有显著降低，由堆制前的 15.3～25.7 降低到 12.0～13.6，可参考表 2 和表 3。但各处理的 m

（C）/m（N）在接种蚯蚓后的变化情况并不相同，HL和NH处理的m（C）/m（N）在接种蚯蚓后有所降低，此结果与国外研究者的结论一致[12~13]。原因可能是：蚯蚓及其肠道内微生物和酶以及有机物料中微生物的存在促进了堆制物料的降解[21]。而DL和JH的m（C）/m（N）在接种蚯蚓后却有所升高。由以上分析可以看出，经过60d堆制，有机物料有机碳质量比和m（C）/m（N）均显著降低，全氮质量比显著增加，有机废弃物在堆制60d后已明显矿化分解。有机物料中接种蚯蚓，增加了NH处理中有机碳和全氮质量比，m（C）/m（N）的减小反应了有机物料的降解，表明蚯蚓的存在可以加速牛粪和有机垃圾混合物料的矿化分解。

3 结论

从蚯蚓在城市有机混合垃圾堆制过程中的生长和繁殖特性分析可看出，NH和JH堆制处理赤子爱胜蚓总体生长良好。接种蚯蚓处理的有机混合垃圾堆制残留物干重显著小于未接种蚯蚓的相应处理，其中，NH处理减少的最多。经过堆制后，有机物料有机碳质量比和m（C）/m（N）均显著降低，全氮质量比有所增加。接种蚯蚓的HL、DL和JH处理的有机碳和全氮质量比均显著低于未接种蚯蚓的相应处理，而NH呈相反趋势，有机碳和全氮质量比均有所增加，m（C）/m（N）有所降低。

参考文献

［1］刘伟，秦霞，王芳芳．城市生活垃圾收运系统优化综述［J］．安全与环境学报，2009，9（5）：91－94

［2］薛强，陈朱蕾．生活垃圾管理与处理技术［M］．北京：科学出版社，2007

［3］刘长玮．城市生活垃圾收运系统优化模型及其应用研究［D］．重庆：重庆大学，2007

［4］王建明．我国城市生活垃圾现状的实证分析［J］．当代经济，2006，10：22－24

［5］胡建杭，王华，吴枕芬等．城市生活垃圾焚烧灰渣熔融特性的分析［J］．安全与环境学报，2007，7（1）：83－87

［6］国家环保总局污染控制司．城市固体废物管理与处理处置技术［M］．北京：中国石化出版社，2000

［7］LEE KE. *Earthworms：their ecology and relationships with soil and land use*［M］．Australia：Acdemic Press，1985：15－16

［8］邱江平．蚯蚓及其在环境保护上等应用：Ⅲ．蚯蚓在处理有机废弃物和生活污水上的应用［J］．上海农学院学报，2000，18（1）：53－58

［9］BANSAL S，KAPOOR K K. Vermicomposting of crop residues and cattle dung with *Eisenia foetida*［J］．*Bioresource Technology*，2000，73：95－98

［10］仓龙，李辉信，胡锋等．赤子爱胜蚓处理畜禽粪的最适湿度和接种密度研究［J］．农村生态环境，2002，18（3）：38－42

［11］李辉信，胡锋，仓龙．蚯蚓堆制处理对牛粪性状的影响［J］．农业环境科学学报，

2004，23（3）：588－593

[12] KAUSHIK P，GARG V K. Dynamics of biological and chemical parameters during vermicomposting of solid textile mill sludge mixed with cow dung and agricultural residues [J]. *Bioresource Technology*，2004，94（2）：203－209

[13] MABOETA M S，RENSBYRG L V. Vermicomposting of industrially produced woodchips and sewage sludge utilizing *Eisenia foetida* [J]. *Ecotoxicology and Environmental Safety*，2003，56（2）：265－270

[14] 胡秀仁，方田，李国鼎．蚯蚓处理垃圾的试验研究［J］．农村生态环境，1991，7（4）：44－49

[15] 党佩珍，张凤祥，王绛辉等．秸秆养牛新技术［M］．南昌：江西科技出版社，1998

[16] BINTORO G，EDWARDSd C A. The influence of different moisture levels on the growth，fecundity and survival of *Eisenia fetida*（Savigny）in cattle and pig manure solids [J]. *European Journal of Soil Biology*，2003，39（1）：19－25

[17] 中国土壤学会农业化学专业委员会．土壤农业化学常规分析方法［M］．北京：科学技术出版社，1983：67－73

[18] 邵月红，潘剑君，孙波．长期施肥对红壤不同形态碳的影响．中国生态农业学报，2006，14（1）：125－127

[19] 刘庄泉，周毅，杨健．蚯蚓在城市生活垃圾中的综合应用［J］．重庆环境科学，2003，25（11）：196－198

[20] 杨云，黄耀，姜纪峰．土壤理化特性对冬季菜地 N_2O 排放的影响［J］．农村生态环境，2005，21（2）：7－12

[21] WHISTON R A，SEAL K J. The occurrence of cellulases in the earthworm *Eisenia foetida* [J]. *Biological Wastes*，1988，25（3）：239－242

Vermicomposting of Mixed Waste of Municipal Solid Organic Waste Using Eisenia Foetida

YANG Wen-xia LIANG Hong
(*Weifang University of Science and Technology*, *Shouguang* 262700)

Abstract: The article is to introduce our study results of treating a vermicomposting of mixed waste of municipal solid organic waste by means of Eisenia foetida. Firt of all, the wastes we sampled from Shuige organic wastes bury field of Nanjing, and then hand-sorted to remove glass, tiles, plastic, metal and other wastes of such sorts. Next, the sampled wastes were added with straw and cow dung as well as some other organic waste remnants. After pre-composting for 15 days, Eisenia foetida was inoculated in a proper density into the mixture, and then placed with optimal moisture and proper temperature in the lab conditions. Daily growth and reproduction of Eisenia foetida were monitored in the process of vermicomposting. And then 60 days of vermicomposting later, it is advisable to test the dry weight and the chemical characteristics of vermicomposts. Results of our experiments show that the Eisenia foetida grew well in the straw and cow dung treatments in the period of the 60 days of incubation. With the mineralization of the organic waste significantly accelerated and dry weight of remnant of the cow dung and Eisenia foetida reduced, the organic C content and the total N of the mixed organic waste would also significantly decreased, the reduced C/N ratio of fresh and cow dung mixed with the vermicomposts. The results of the treatments during the 60 days proved the best treatment indicate that the addition of 30% cow dung and inoculation of earthworms are highly effective and beneficial for the urban solid organic waste reduction, and recycled use. Therefore, vermicomposting of the urban organic wastes treated by earthworms helps not only to transform the wastes into high quality organic fertilizer, but also effectively reduce the environmental pollution so as to reach the goal of eliminating soil second pollution and protecting the soil environment, as well as enhancing virtuous recycle of waste material in agricultural production.

Key words: Environmental engineering; Vermicomposting; Eisenia foetida; Municipal solid organic waste

重金属污染对水稻土土壤微生物量和群落结构的影响

杨文霞[①]
（潍坊科技学院，寿光 262700）

摘 要： 重金属污染可能影响土壤中微生物生物量与活性及群落结构。文章以太湖地区典型的水稻土为研究对象，采集了金属冶炼产业区周边重金属污染的稻田和未明显污染稻田的表土样品，利用 PCR-DGGE 技术分析重金属复合污染下土壤微生物数量和细菌群落结构的变化。结果表明，重金属污染增加了土壤中细菌的数量，而显著降低了放线菌和真菌的数量，并强烈的降低了土壤真菌与细菌的比例，结合 DGGE 图谱，可以看出重金属污染降低了土壤细菌的多样性和群落结构，影响了土壤微生物对有机碳的矿化分解，为今后水稻土有机碳的研究提出了新的课题。

关键词： 重金属污染；土壤微生物量；群落结构

近年来，随着采矿、冶金业的迅速发展，污水灌溉以及农药、化肥的大量使用，我国稻田土壤重金属污染已日趋严重[1~2]。土壤重金属污染可能影响土壤中微生物生物量、群落结构及微生物活性，同时，使土壤酶的活性等生态功能受损，从而使水稻土有机质的矿化受到影响。关于土壤重金属污染对微生物生态影响的研究已有许多报道[3~4]，但是，许多研究都是通过添加外源重金属来模拟污染土壤，难以反映田间土壤的实际污染情况。对于田间水稻土重金属污染下微生物群落结构变化的研究报道还很少。许多土壤微生物是不可培养的，所以用传统的平板计数法，分离鉴定到的微生物只占土壤微生物总数的 1% ~10%[5]。随着分子生物学的发展，有几种新方法被引用到土壤微生物分析中，如 PCR-DGGE、PLFA 法等。DGGE 技术自从 1993 年被引入微生物生态学以来[6]，该技术被广泛地用作分子工具比较微生物群落的多样性和监视种群动态。该技术具有可靠、可重复、快速和容易操作等特点。本文用 DGGE 以重金属污染的水稻土为研究对象，探讨重金属污染对稻田土壤中微生物量和微生物群落结构组成等微生物生态特性的影响，以期为研究重金属污染下土壤生物学质量和功能以及有机质的矿化提供科学依据。

---

① 杨文霞，女，硕士，潍坊科技学院讲师。研究方向：土壤生态和环境。E－mail：ywxty@163.com

1 材料和方法

1.1 试验地概况

本试验点位于宜兴市宜丰镇徐舍村。土壤类型为太湖地区典型的乌泥土。当地气候属亚热带季风气候，全年温暖湿润。热量条件好，年平均气温 15.7℃。降水丰沛，全年有雨，年平均雨日 136.6d，年平均降水量 1 177mm，春夏雨水集中。地面水、地下水丰富。农作物一年两熟。土壤种植水稻已经有 1 000年的历史。本试验田块的重金属主要污染源来自于一个金属冶炼厂，在距离其 1 000m 远地方选择了一块无污染田块作为对照。两田块都为稻麦轮作，而且它们的灌溉、施肥等农业管理措施相同。土壤基本性质和重金属含量见表 1 和表 2。

表 1　两田块表层土壤（0～15cm）的基本性质

土　样	容重（g/cm^3）	黏粒含量(g/kg)	总氮(g/kg)	CEC(cmol/kg)	pH 值(H_2O)
无污染	1.38	317.5	2.80	16.34	6.94
污染	1.40	319.6	2.99	18.05	6.81

表 2　表层土壤的重金属含量（mg/kg）

	Hg	As	Cu	Zn	Pb	Cd	Cr	Ni
无污染	0.36	4.46	34.48	33.81	45.84	0.66	23.44	13.22
污染	0.45	48.80	56.51	127.31	279.95	5.67	69.58	33.87

注：采样时间为 2008 年水稻种植前期

1.2 样品采集与处理

样品的采集时期为 2008 年 10 月，水稻收获后。采样深度为耕层土壤（0～15cm）。每块田设 3 个采样点，每个点采集 3 份样品，野外混匀获得混合样。拣出植物根系后，其中一部分过 10 目筛后放入 4℃冰箱保存，进行土壤微生物的平板计数，另一份样品在 －20℃保存用于提取土壤基因组 DNA，进行微生物细菌群落结构分析。

1.3 土壤细菌、真菌、放线菌总数的测定

土壤微生物计数采用稀释平板法[7]。细菌培养基为牛肉膏蛋白胨培养基；真菌培养基为链霉素—马丁氏孟加拉红培养基；放线菌培养基为高氏一号培养基。每个样品 3 次重复。

实验步骤：称取 1g 土壤放入盛有 99ml 无菌水及玻璃珠的 250ml 三角瓶中，手摇 20min，静置 5min，用 5ml 移液管吸取悬浊液 5ml（注意：保持移液管插入液面的深度一致）移入干燥灭菌的试管中，即为 10^{-2}稀释液。用 1ml 移液管从 10^{-2}稀释液中吸取

0.5ml 转入装有 4.5ml 无菌水的试管中，制成 10^{-3}稀释液，依次系列稀释至 10^{-6}。吸取 0.1ml 菌液涂布平板：细菌用 10^{-5}稀释度，放线菌用 10^{-3}稀释度，真菌用 10^{-2}稀释度。28℃恒温倒置培养：细菌培养 4d，放线菌 3d，真菌 2.5d。

菌落形成单位计算（cfu）：选取菌落数在 30~300 的平板进行计数，则细菌用 10^{-5}稀释度，放线菌用 10^{-3}稀释度，真菌用 10^{-2}稀释度的平板进行计算。

$$cfu/g = n \times 稀释倍数 \times 10/烘干土重$$

式中，n 为平板上的菌落数，乘 10 的原因：涂布平板时所涂菌液为 0.1ml，则 1/0.1 = 10

1.4 微生物群落结构分析（16SrDNA-DGGE）

1.4.1 土壤基因组 DNA 提取

采用 Q. BIOgene 公司的土壤 DNA 快速提取试剂盒（FastDNA ® Kit for Soil）从土壤样品中提取基因组 DNA。

1.4.2 基因组 DNA 的 PCR 扩增

16S rRNA 基因 V3 区的扩增 将提取的基因组 DNA 作为聚合酶链式反应（PCR）的模板，使用 Eppendorf 的 Mastercycler ep gradient S 型快速梯度 PCR 仪，采用对大多数细菌和古细菌的 16S rRNA 基因的特异性 V3 区都通用的引物对 F338-GC 和 R518[8]。它们的序列分别为：F338-GC，（5'-CgCCCgCCgCgCgCggCgggCggggCgggggCACggggggCCTACgggAggCAgCAg-3'）；R518，（5'-ATTACCgCggCTgCTgg-3'），扩增产物片段长约 250bp。

PCR 反应体系：25μl 的 PCR 反应体系组成如下：2.5μl 的 10 × Taq buffer，1.5μl $MgCl_2$（25mM），2.5μl dNTP 2.5（mM），1μl DNA 模板（genomic DNA，10ng/μl），0.5μl 的 Taq DNA 聚合酶（1.5U/ml）；双蒸水补足 25μl。

PCR 反应条件如下：92℃ 3min；30 个循环：92℃ 1min，55℃ 30sec，72℃ 1min；最后在 72℃下延伸 6min。扩增后的 PCR 产物用 2% 琼脂糖凝胶电泳检测质量。

1.5 PCR 反应产物的变性梯度凝胶电泳（DGGE）

梯度变性凝胶的制备使用 Bio-Rad 公司 475 型梯度灌胶系统（Model 475 Gradient Delivery System），变性梯度从上到下是 30% 到 60%，聚丙烯酰胺凝胶浓度是 10%；60℃电泳，先在 200V 的电压下电泳 10min，后 75V 电压下约 10h。

电泳完毕后，将凝胶采用银染法[9]染色。将染色后的凝胶用 Bio-RAD 的 Gel Doc-2000 凝胶影像分析系统分析，观察每个样品的电泳条带并拍照。

1.6 数据处理

用 Quantity One 分析软件分析得到相似性指数；以香农（Shannon-Wiener）指数反映细菌物种多样性，香农指数计算方法采用 Hedrick[10]的方法；数据处理用 Microsoft Excel 2003 进行，统计与显著性检测是利用 SPSS11.0 软件进行的。

2 结果分析

2.1 重金属污染对水稻土微生物数量的影响

土壤微生物量是指土壤中体积小于 $5\times10^3\mu m^3$ 的生物的总量，包括细菌、真菌、放线菌和小型动物，但不包括植物体。细菌、放线菌和真菌是土壤微生物主要组成类群，是生态系统的分解者，它们共同参与生态系统中物质循环与能量流动，在维持生态系统的结构与功能方面起着十分重要的作用[11]。

表 3 显示，重金属污染土壤中细菌的数量为 10.60×10^7CFU/g，显著高于无污染土壤的细菌数量 6.67×10^7CFU/g，增加幅度为 58.9%。而重金属污染却极显著的降低了真菌和放线菌的数量，降低幅度分别为 88.8% 和 63.6%。这说明重金属污染抑制了真菌和放线菌的生长而刺激了土壤中细菌数量的增长，但是重金属污染对真菌和放线菌的抑制程度远大于对细菌的增加幅度。一般认为，微生物会对土壤污染表现出灵敏的响应，细菌比真菌对重金属污染更敏感[12]。这里的结果印证了这一观点。本实验室用相同的土壤样品利用 PLFA 分析方法，同样也显示了真菌/细菌 PLFA 的量的变化程度更大[13]。

表 3 显示，重金属污染土壤样品的真菌/细菌显著的低于无污染土壤，降低了 65.8%。因此，我们认为，重金属污染虽然同样降低了稻田的微生物生物量，但是真菌/细菌比值的变化显示出这种影响更大地表现为相对组成的变化，真菌/细菌比值的大幅度改变无疑会影响到 C、N 等营养元素的循环过程，并由此深刻影响到土壤质量和生态功能的变化，当然这些还需要进一步的野外和实验室的研究。

表 3 两块田的土壤微生物数量的比较

	细菌 ($\times10^7$CFU/g)	真菌 ($\times10^4$CFU/g)	放线菌 ($\times10^6$CFU/g)	真菌/细菌 ($\times10^3$)
无污染	6.67 ±1.68a	7.25 ±1.16A	2.89 ±0.27A	1.11 ±0.18A
污染	10.60 ±2.74b	3.84 ±1.19B	1.34 ±0.12B	0.38 ±0.14B

2.2 重金属污染对水稻土微生物群落结构的影响

提取后的土壤基因组大小约为 23Kb，用 1% 琼脂糖凝胶电泳，得到图谱如图 1；PCR 扩增后 16S rDNA 中 V3 区片段大小接近 250bp，用 2% 琼脂糖凝胶电泳，图谱如图 2。重金属污染与非污染条件下的样品 DGGE 结果如图 3，从图谱中可以初步看出，重金属污染条件下的条带与无污染条件有所不同。两种土壤都有很大一部分相同的亮带，这说明它们拥有一些共同的优势细菌，图 3 也可以看出，两田块的土壤样品都有自己独有的亮带，这说明它们有自己独特的优势种群。

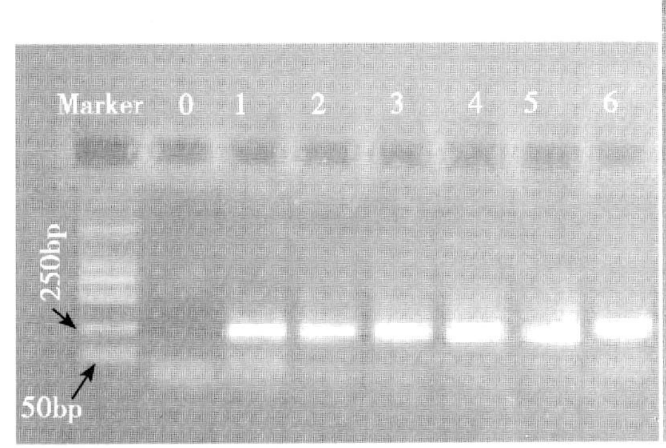

图1 重金属污染与无污染条件下水稻土壤微生物总 DNA 图谱

1,2,3:污染土壤样品;4,5,6:非污染土壤样品

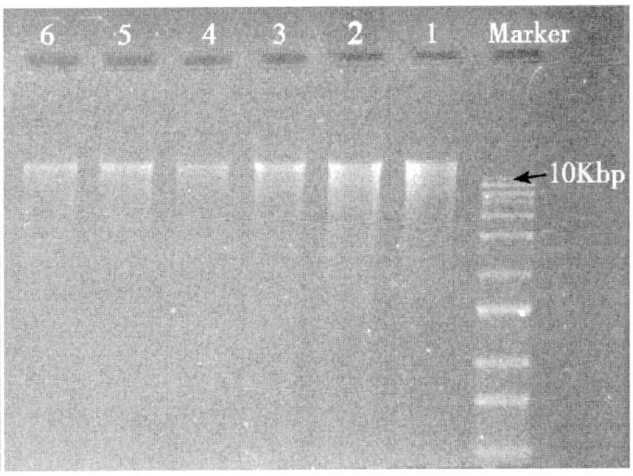

图2 PCR 扩增 16SrDNA 中的 V3 区产物图谱

Marker：阴性对照；1，2，3：污染土壤样品；4，5，6：非污染土壤样品

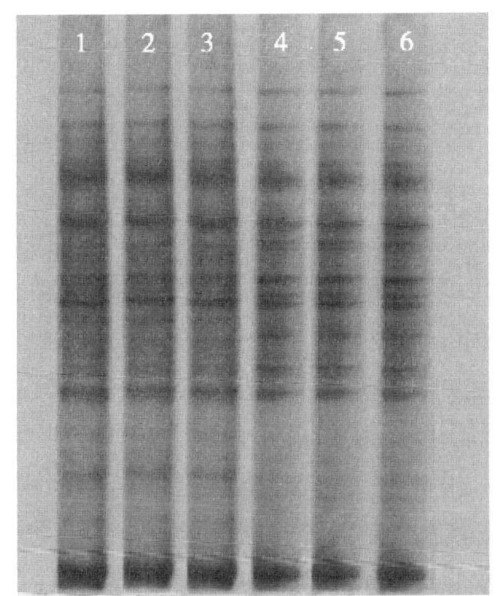

图3 PCR 产物的 DGGE 图谱

1，2，3：污染土壤样品；4，5，6：非污染土壤样品

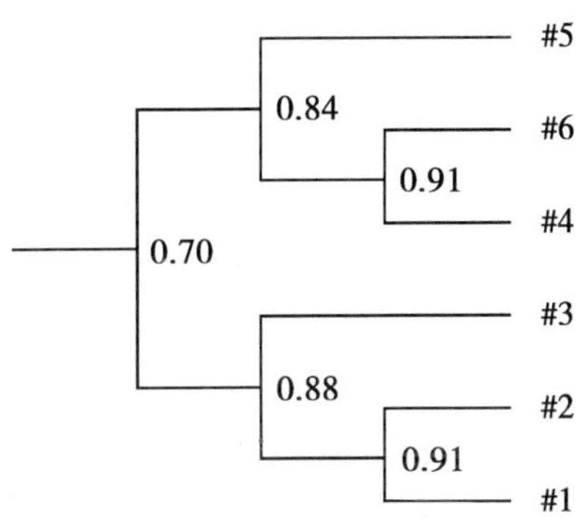

图4 细菌群落结构的相似性系统发育树图谱

1，2，3：污染土壤样品；4，5，6：非污染土壤样品

对图谱进一步分析，得出重金属污染和非污染条件下水稻土壤微生物群落结构相似性约为 0.70，如图 4；而在其水稻土土壤细菌多样性指数方面，重金属污染过的土壤显著低于非污染的土壤，如表 4。

土壤微生物多样性的影响因素包括气候条件，土壤肥力特性和农业管理措施等。本试验中，仅土壤的重金属污染状况不同。所以重金属的污染使土壤微生物群落结构发生了明显的改变，而且其细菌多样性指数比没有污染的显著降低（表 4）。

表4 土菌群落多样性指数

样 品		香农指数	CV（%）
水稻土	污染	3.324 ±0.001a	0.029
	非污染	3.483 ±0.004b	0.120

3 讨论

关于重金属对土壤微生物群落结构的影响已有较多报道。许多研究表明重金属污染能明显影响土壤微生物群落结构，即土壤微生物多样性[12]，然而，杨元根等[14]的研究结果是轻度的重金属污染并不会导致微生物群落结构的变化。腾应等[3]研究结果表明，随着尾矿污染区土壤中几种重金属含量的增加，尾矿区土壤微生物区系组成和各生理类群发生了明显变化，土壤细菌、真菌、放线菌以及各生理类群数量均显著降低。Kuperman[15]等对一个多种重金属复合污染的草原土壤的研究表明，细菌和真菌生物量较未污染的对照分别下降了29%和45%。阎姝，潘根兴等[13]利用PLFA分析重金属污染下的水稻土，显示重金属污染下土壤微生物群落结构发生了明显的变化，细菌和真菌PLFA的变化幅度达到30%以上，革兰氏阳性菌与革兰氏阴性菌的脂肪酸比值升高，而真菌/细菌的比例降低了约70%。这与本文用平板计数法测定的真菌与细菌比值降低了65.8%的结果非常接近。重金属污染可能影响土壤中微生物生物量与活性及群落结构，但这种影响随土地利用和土壤类型、污染物类型而异[16]。

本文利用DGGE图谱及根据图谱计算的细菌群落结构多样性指数表明重金属污染改变了水稻土的细菌群落结构，降低了细菌群落结构的多样性。王秀丽[12]等发现重金属污染导致了微生物群落的变异性增大，降低了群落的稳定性，微生物群落结构产生了系统性的改变。一般认为重金属污染会减少微生物对单一碳底物的利用能力，减少群落的多样性。有研究表明[17]，在土壤微生物发生明显变化以前，整个微生物区系已经发生质的变化，不适应的微生物数量下降，适应生长的微生物数量增大并积累。因此，重金属胁迫对微生物种群结构产生一定影响。土壤微生物生物量比较的结果，表明了重金属污染下土壤中微生物结构发生了变化，影响到了微生物的功能，这对我国稻田土壤的碳固定提出了一个新的问题。

4 小结

重金属污染显著提高了土壤中细菌的数量，而降低了放线菌和真菌的数量，但是后者得到抑制的程度更高。同时，重金属显著降低了土壤中真菌与细菌的比例，这似乎说明了重金属改变了土壤微生物的结构。

通过PCR-DGGE的图谱，可以得出重金属污染降低了土壤中细菌群落的多样性，这说明重金属污染改变了土壤微生物的群落结构和多样性，影响到了水稻土对有机碳的固定。

参考文献

[1] 安中华，董元华，安琼等．苏南某市农田土壤环境质量评价及其分级［J］．土壤，2004，36（6）：631－635

[2] 刘洪莲，李艳慧，李恋卿等．太湖地区某地农田土壤及农产品中重金属污染及风险评价［J］．安全与环境学报，2006，6（5）：60－63

[3] 腾应，黄昌勇，骆永明等．重金属复合污染下红壤微生物活性及其群落结构的变化［J］．土壤学报，2005，42（5）：819－828

[4] 廖敏，陈雪花，陈承利等．土壤-青菜系统中铅污染对土壤微生物活性及多样性的影响［J］．环境科学学报，2007，27（2）：220－227

[5] McCarthy C M，Murray L. Viability and metabolic features of bacteria indigenous to a contaminated deep aquifer［J］．Microbial Ecology. 1996，32：305－321

[6] Muyzer G，De Waal E C，Uitterlinden A G. Profiling of complex microbial population by denaturing gradient gel electrophoresis analysis of polymerase chain reaction-amplified genes encoding for 16SrRNA［J］．Appl. Environ. Microbiol. 1993，59（3）：695－700

[7] 李振高，骆永明，滕应．土壤微生物研究法［J］．中国科学院南京土壤研究所微生物室．北京科学出版社，1985

[8] Nakatsu C. H.，Torsvik V.，and Øverås L. Soil Community Analysis Using of 16S rDNA Polymerase Chain Reaction Products［J］．Soil Sci. Soc. AM. J，2000，64：13 82－1 388

[9] Bassam B J，Caetano-Anollés G，Gresshoff PM. Fast and sensitive silver staining of DNA in polyacrylamide gels［J］．Analytical Biocheistry，1991，196：80－83

[10] Hedrick，D. B，Peacock，A.，Stephen，J. R.，Macnaughton，S. J.，Brüggemann，J.，White，D. C. Measuring soil microbial community diversity using polar lipid fatty acid and denaturing gradient gel electrophoresis data［J］．Journal of Microbiological Methods，2000，41：235－248

[11] 李延茂，胡江春，汪恩龙等．森林生态系统中土壤微生物的作用与应用［J］．应用生态学报，2004，15（10）：1 943－1 946

[12] 王秀丽，徐建民，姚槐应等．重金属铜、锌、镉、铅复合污染对土壤环境微生物群落的影响［J］．环境科学学报，2003，（1）：22－27

[13] 阎姝，潘根兴，李恋卿．重金属污染降低水稻土微生物商并改变 PLFA 群落结构—苏南某地污染稻田的案例研究［J］．生态环境，2008，17（5）：1 828－1 832

[14] 杨元根．重金属铜的土壤微生物毒性研究［J］．土壤通报，2002，33（2）：55－60

[15] Kuperman R G，Carreiro M M. Soil heavy metal concentrations，microbial biomass and enzyme activities in a contaminated grassland ecosystem［J］．Soil Biology and Biochemistry，1997，29（2）：179－190

[16] Schutter M E, Sandeno J M, Dick R P. Seasonal, soil type, and alternative management influences on microbial communities of vegetable cropping systems [J]. Biol. Fertil. Soils, 2001, 34: 397 -410

[17] 刘霞，刘树庆，王胜爱等．重金属复合污染对土壤微生物生态特征的影响研究[J]．农业环境科学学报，2007，26：17 -21

Effects of Heavy Metal Pollution on Soil Microbial Biomass and Microbial Community Structure

YANG Wen-xia

(*Weifang University of Science and Technology*, *Shouguang* 262700)

Abstract: Heavy metal pollution may lead to changes in soil microbial biomass, community structure and functioning activity in soil. The topsoil samples are sampled from a unpolluted rice paddy and a polluted paddy near a metal smelter, both collected from a county in the southern Jiangsu, China. Soil microbial biomass carbon was measured by the conventional procedure and microbial community structure analyzed by PCR-DGGE. The result indicated that heavy metal pollution has increased the number of bacteria in soil, and significantly reduced the number of actinomycetes and fungi, and strongly reduced the ratio of fungi / bacteria in paddy soil. Soil bacterial diversity and structure of community were found to be reduced by DGGE, thus affected the microbial mineralization of organic carbon. Heavy metal pollution can be seen to change the structure of soil microbial community and effect the function of microbial community.

Key words: Heavy metal pollution; Soil microbial biomass; Community structure

四角蛤蜊的育肥养殖技术及食用方法

李群峰① 代惠洁
（潍坊科技学院，寿光 262700）

摘 要： 四角蛤蜊的分布很广，具有生长快、生产周期短的特点，适于在滩涂养殖上作为人工管养的良好品种。研究其育肥养殖技术及食用方法，对于提高其食用价值及经济价值有着重要的现实意义。

关键词： 四角蛤蛎；育肥；经济价值

四角蛤蜊俗称“白砚子”，广泛分布于我国南北沿海，尤其在有淡水注入的河口半咸水区，其资源蕴藏量较大。在所有天然海洋贝类中，其整体数量占绝对优势，沿海及内地居民有一年四季食用四角蛤蜊的习惯，其味道及肉质鲜美，绝不逊于文蛤、青蛤，具有很大的发展空间。

1 育肥养殖的技术原理

根据四角蛤蜊的生物学及生态学原理，创造适宜的生物学及生态学环境，在尽量短的时间内，吐尽残存在体内的泥沙；再投喂小球藻，增加肥满度，提高出肉率；通过育肥养殖，加速体内新陈代谢，除去在浅海生活环境中形成的异味。最终达到不含泥沙、出肉率高、没有异味的绿色环保食品。

2 生态学特征

四角蛤蜊生活于潮地带中、低潮区及浅海泥沙滩中，埋栖深度为 5 ~ 10cm，因受其生活习性的影响，腮腔中存有较多泥沙。其适应的水温是 0 ~ 35℃，适宜生长的温度是 8 ~ 30℃，最适宜的生长水温是 18 ~ 30℃；适应盐度是 5‰ ~ 35‰，适宜生长的盐度是 17‰ ~ 29‰，最适宜盐度是 20‰ ~ 25‰左右；营被动虑食性生活，饵料为单细胞藻类及原生动物等；喜弱光；繁殖季节因地区不同而有差异，每年繁殖 2 ~ 3 次，第一次繁殖的时间为：辽宁 5 ~ 9 月，山东 4 ~ 6 月，江苏 3 ~ 6 月，广东 2 ~ 3 月。处于繁殖期的

---

① 李群峰，男，副教授，潍坊科技学院水产研究所所长。研究方向：水产养殖。E - mail：595780861@ qq. com

四角蛤蜊肥满度、出肉率最高，煮熟出肉率达35%～40%，此时食用价值最大。

3 小球藻的培育方法

育肥养殖四角蛤蜊离不开单细胞藻类，而小球藻无论是从育肥效果还是其培育性能都是最好的。其培育方法一是鱼藻混养模式，通过在鱼池接种小球藻，利用鱼的代谢产物及残饵作为小球藻的营养盐，使小球藻旺盛繁殖，通过小球藻的繁殖净化养鱼用水，降低氨氮、硫化氢含量、降低化学耗氧量、平衡水的酸碱度，改善水质环境，建立一种生态化养鱼模式，使鱼、小球藻互为共生，同池培育，相得益彰，当小球藻密度达到每毫升40万个细胞后结合换水，泵入四角蛤蜊育肥养殖池；二是小球藻的工厂化专门培育模式，建立专门的椭圆、环形养殖池，池深60～80cm，面积以养殖规模而定，接种小球藻后，以电机带动水车旋转，让培育中的小球藻液处于流动状态，不至于下沉，按照小球藻的常规养殖方法，适时加入氮、磷等营养盐，通入气体二氧化碳作为碳源；养殖水源为地下卤水及地下淡水的混合水，盐度与四角蛤蜊育肥养殖用水的盐度一致。小球藻在培育过程中，藻液要每隔5～7d定期用$0.3 \sim 0.5 \times 10^{-6}$二氧化氯、三氯异氰尿酸粉消毒，杀死藻液中的细菌，使藻液处于无菌状态。藻液在育肥养殖使用前2～3d，停止施肥及消毒剂消毒，此种模式培育的小球藻也可以作为其他水产动物的饵料用。

4 育肥养殖的技术

4.1 水源

地下卤水及地下淡水的混合水。与近海海水相比较，地下水具有不受外界污染的特点，即不受海洋原生动物及细菌等有害生物的影响，也不受大陆径流污染的影响，无色无味，水质指标恒定，符合水产养殖用水标准，且在滨海地区容易获得，使用极其方便。卤水盐度可在四角蛤蜊适宜范围内调节，一般在20‰～25‰。

4.2 初捕四角蛤蜊的处理

在四角蛤蜊的捕捞过程中，由于采捕工具的原因，往往将死壳及其他杂质一同捞起，同时，也会使部分活四角蛤蜊的壳受伤，所以，首先要剔除空壳、杂质、破壳蛤蜊。空壳的特征是颜色很暗，有的双壳紧闭，包含有泥沙。破壳四角蛤蜊容易死亡，死亡后流出体液并繁衍大量弧菌，污染水质，且能引起正常个体的大量死亡。所以，不管是在吐沙还是育肥养殖过程中，要经常剔除破壳及死亡的四角蛤蜊。闭壳肌松弛，双壳张开，意味着死亡或即将死亡。

4.3 吐沙

体内沙含量是影响四角蛤蜊商品质量的一个重要指标。若不经过吐沙处理，不谙吃法的人买回来即下锅煮熟，结果满锅是沙。吐沙池类似于专门的小球藻培育池，环道型，环道的体积依据养殖规模而建造，在水车的带动下使水流能在环道中慢慢流动，如同潮汐运动，既能带来丰富的溶解氧，又能使饵料分布均匀。环道底部部分凹陷，较池底凹 20cm，其横断面约占总面积的 1/20，吐出的沙及污物随水流的流动沉积于凹陷处，凹陷处设有排污孔。吐沙池上方设玻璃钢棚顶或遮阳网，便于调节光线及温度，还可以防止雨淋。吐沙时每平米放 15～20kg 四角蛤蜊，约经 8～10h 的吐沙时间，即能吐出体内 90%～95% 的沙，依据沙量及污物的多少，在吐沙的过程中适时、适量的换水及排污，始终保持水质的清新，影响吐沙效果的因素有：温度、盐度、光线、酸碱度、溶解氧、水质的清新度。

4.4 育肥养殖

经 8～10h 的吐沙处理后，泵入洁净的小球藻液，使水色呈淡绿色，小球藻的密度达每毫升 20 万～30 万个，水的透明度在 30～40cm 左右，最好能见底部，便于观察四角蛤蜊的活动状态。四角蛤蜊喜欢清水，虑食小球藻的速度极快，一般 2～3h 即能虑食尽，食尽后水变得无色，绿色粪便在池底清晰可见，应及时补充新鲜藻液，在育肥养殖的过程中根据水中污物及水质情况，适时、适量换水。

4.5 育肥养殖的结果

在水质条件较好，小球藻供应充足的前提下，影响育肥养殖时间的因素是，四角蛤蜊的肥满度、是否因受海区的污染而带有异味。若在繁殖期间，肥满度较高并且无异味，经 1d 左右时间的养殖吐尽体内的泥沙即可，时间不宜过长，否则会产卵。非繁殖季节，肥满度较低（最瘦时煮熟出肉率在 5%～10%），且带有异味，这种四角蛤蜊在条件适宜时，经 3～5d 的育肥养殖，煮熟出肉率能达到 30%～40%，出肉率提高 2～3 倍，且异味消失，极大的提高了其食用价值。育肥养殖结束，作为商品出售前 6～8h，应停止投喂小球藻，使其排空体内粪便，并且在低温弱光下保存，便于之后的运输及食用。

5 食用方法

四角蛤蜊体内易附着寄生虫，严禁生食，需煮熟食用。煮熟的标志是闭壳肌与贝壳容易分离，整个软体部游离于贝壳中。煮熟剥离后的蛤肉可做汤、烧菜、油炸、凉拌，也可以直接食用。煮熟的方法有以下 3 种。

5.1 加水并放盐煮熟

这是较传统的吃法，这样煮熟的四角蛤蜊肉松软，口感不好，且四角蛤蜊本身体液中含盐量较高，重复加盐使得蛤肉变咸，蛤汤咸而不浓，降低蛤肉及汤的鲜度，这种煮熟法是不科学的。

5.2 不加水煮熟

四角蛤蜊软体部分本身含水量较高，放锅中先慢火加热，因受热体液开始渗出，等大量渗出后，急火加热，这样煮熟的蛤蜊肉结实且口感好，盐度适中，体液浓缩，颜色洁白，味美，可直接饮用或做汤菜。

5.3 蒸汽穿透

将四角蛤蜊放蒸笼中，通入蒸汽至熟，将流出的体液收集浓缩，类似于蚝油加工，可制成调味品。

后两种煮熟法较科学，值得提倡。

参考文献

[1] 崔广法，于业绍，于志华等．四角蛤蜊人工育苗的初步研究［J］．海洋科学，1985，3

[2] 李宝华，孙广明，张福瑞．调味四角蛤蜊软罐头的研制［J］．中国水产，1995，7

[3] 国俭文，李永明，王希芬等．提高四角蛤蜊加工产品质量的探讨［J］．中国水产，1999，6

Fattening Technology and Edible Method of Mactra veneriformis

LI Qun-feng　DAI Hui-jie

(*Weifang University of Science and Technology*, *Shouguang*　262700)

Abstract: Mactra veneriformis has a very distribution with fast growth, short production cycle, which is suitable to breed in infertidal mudflat. The research mainly studys fattening technology and edible method of Mactra veneriformis, which has important practical significance for improving edible value and economic value.

Key words: Mactra veneriformis; Fatten; Economic value

矮小型粉壳蛋鸡羽色自别系的研究

代惠洁[①] 李群峰

（潍坊科技学院，寿光 262700）

摘 要： 现代规模化饲养的粉壳蛋鸡都是通过白来航鸡与褐壳蛋鸡杂交实现的，商品代雏鸡大都通过羽速自别雌雄。运用现代育种技术选育隐性白羽的来航鸡可以实现粉壳蛋鸡的羽色自别。本研究对矮小型粉壳蛋鸡配套白来航母系进行隐性白羽的选择，经过两个世代的测交和个体选育，证明矮小型粉壳蛋鸡配套系的商品代雏鸡可以实现羽色自别。商品代中红羽雏鸡都是母雏，公雏则全部为白羽，而红羽雏鸡占全部母雏的比例达到 27.7%。

关键词： 蛋鸡；矮小型；羽色自别；隐性白；白来航

蛋鸡生产专门化和集约化的过程中，应尽早鉴别雏鸡的雌雄，以便公母分群饲养，降低育雏成本。国内外主要褐壳蛋鸡基本都实现了雏鸡的羽色自别，而白壳蛋鸡和粉壳蛋鸡大都是通过快慢羽自别雌雄。和快慢羽自别相比，羽色自别的效率更高、准确性也相对更高。此外金色羽蛋鸡淘汰时其市场价格会高于白羽母鸡，具有更大的市场潜力。目前粉壳蛋鸡没有实现羽色自别的主要原因是白来航带有显性白羽基因 II，后代雏鸡遗传显性白基因，羽毛颜色呈现白色或近似白色。农大 3 号小型粉壳蛋鸡是中国农业大学育种专家选育成功的高效粉壳蛋鸡新种，比普通型蛋鸡的饲料利用率提高 15%。由于配套系的母鸡是白来航型，因此商品代雏鸡只能靠翻肛和羽速自别的方法区分初生雏的性别，在生产中使用不够方便。本研究的目标是选育隐性白羽来航鸡，使商品代雏鸡能够实现羽色的自别雌雄。

1 材料与方法

1.1 选育素材

选用北京北农大种禽有限责任公司的农大 3 号小型粉壳蛋鸡配套系的白来航母系，对其进行隐性白羽的选择。配套父系是矮小型的褐壳蛋鸡，羽色为金色羽。

---

① 代惠洁，女，硕士，潍坊科技学院讲师。研究方向：动物遗传育种。E - mail：aidai - climsion@ 163. com

1.2 测交和选择方法

（1）用金色羽公鸡（快羽）和白来航母鸡（慢羽）交配，采用个体输精，每只公鸡配 10 只母鸡，按母鸡个体收集种蛋，收集 14d 种蛋入孵，种蛋不足 7 枚的母鸡个体淘汰，孵出的雏鸡按快慢羽鉴别公母，将残、弱、死雏和毛蛋收集起来，逐一解剖检验其雌雄，并按羽色分类，统计公雏和母雏中金色羽和银色羽两种颜色的数量（包括头部或颈部有红斑点，背部有红条纹以及全身淡红色）。并选出后代是金色羽母雏的母鸡个体进行第二个世代的测交。

（2）在继代选育时对测交后代有金色羽母雏的母鸡重点留种，并扩大留种比例，所有的公鸡都来自这些留种母鸡。第二年继续对留种母鸡进行选育，每只公鸡配 10 只母鸡，按母鸡个体收集种蛋孵化，观察后代羽毛颜色。

1.3 羽色观察

出雏时从后代中选出纯白羽、白羽头部有红斑和白羽背部有红斑的母鸡 100 只，带翅号并在同一条件下混群饲养至 70 日龄，每周记录羽毛颜色一次，观察羽色的变化规律。

1.4 数据处理

用 Excel 分析软件和 SAS 软件中的 TTEST 过程对数据进行分析处理。

2 结果与分析

2.1 第一次测交结果

此次测交共孵出雏鸡 12 791 只，其中，公雏全为白羽鸡，母雏则出现了不同程度的红羽。将母雏按羽色分类，见表 1。纯白羽母鸡共 5 936 只，占全部母雏的 93.4%；头部有红斑的母雏是 335 只，占全部母雏的 5.3%；而背部有红斑的母雏则占了 1.3%，其中也有少部分是背部有 2 条或 3 条条纹，其他部位呈银羽。

表 1 第一次测交母雏的羽色分布情况

羽色	数量（只）	比例（%）
纯白羽	5 936	93.4
白羽头有红斑	335	5.3
白羽背有红斑	85	1.3

2.2 第二次测交结果

二次育种中，公雏仍然呈白色羽，母雏出现红羽的比例比上个世代提高了 10%，而后代全是红羽母雏的比例提高了 0.5%，部分后代是红羽母雏的比例提高了 9.5%。将母雏按羽色分类，见表 2。纯白羽母雏有 2 568 只，占全部母雏的 72.3%；头部有红斑的母雏有785只，占母雏总数的22.1%；背部有红斑（或红条纹）的雏鸡共199只，占全部母雏的5.6%。

表2　第二次测交母雏的羽色分布情况

羽色	数量（只）	比例（%）
纯白羽	2 568	72.3
白羽头有红斑	785	22.1
白羽背有红斑	99	5.6

2.3　羽色观察结果

雏鸡混群饲养到70日龄，八周龄时羽毛颜色基本稳定。饲养的母雏中有9只是纯白羽雏鸡，86只是红斑雏鸡，饲养结束时羽色类型发生了一定的变化，其中，有3只纯白羽雏鸡变成了红羽，同时有4只红羽雏鸡变成了纯白羽。

将羽毛颜色的变化按照不同的部位列表，见表3。由表3看出，雏鸡出生时红斑主要表现在脸部、头部和背部，其他部位基本没有表现出来。一日龄雏鸡脸部出现红斑的比例是51%，在以后的几周内比例有所下降，而当雏鸡的羽毛颜色基本稳定（八周龄）时，比例恢复到51%；初生母雏的头部出现红斑的母鸡比例是72%，羽色稳定后比例达到83%；背部有红斑或者红条纹的雏鸡在羽色稳定后比例达到58%；雏鸡翅部在一周后相继出现了红羽，羽色稳定后出现红羽的比例达到76%；尾部在两周龄时出现红羽，羽色稳定后比例达到26%；颈部在三周龄时也出现了红羽，饲养结束时出现红羽的比例达到81%；鸡的腹部和腿部在八周龄时出现了不同程度的红羽。

表3　羽色变化（%）

	一日龄	一周龄	二周龄	三周龄	四周龄	五周龄	六周龄	七周龄	八周龄
脸部	51	51	43	36	32	25	30	31	51
头部	72	73	73	65	54	68	75	83	83
背部	17	35	23	30	33	35	36	56	58
翅部	0	20	33	56	62	62	63	76	76
尾部	0	0	4	12	19	17	20	26	26
颈部	0	0	0	56	73	74	73	80	81
腹腿部	0	0	0	0	0	0	0	0	15

3　讨论与结论

（1）从两个世代的选种结果可以看出后代出现红羽的母鸡群在整个群体中的比例有了很大的提高，这说明红羽的出现是可以遗传的，不是因为环境等偶然因素引起的。而且后代中的红羽雏鸡均为母雏，公雏全为白羽，这说明雏鸡羽色自别雌雄是可以实现的。

（2）白来航属于显性白品种，携带纯合的显性白 II，它抑制色素形成。若 I 基因存在，不论其他羽色类型为何种基因型，均因其抑制色素形成而表现为无色羽。但 I 的等位基因 i 基因不抑制色素的形成，它允许有色基因的表达，粉壳蛋鸡商品代出现红羽可能是由于母本群体中出现了野生型 i 基因，允许了金色羽 s 基因在后代中的表达，使得商品代中出现了红羽。本研究的结果正在应用定量 PCR 等方法进行进一步验证，筛选隐性白羽母鸡，完全实现粉壳蛋鸡商品代的羽色自别雌雄。

（3）从羽色观察中可以得出，虽然雏鸡在 3 周龄左右开始换毛，使得羽毛颜色的观察有些误差，但主要部位能够保持金色羽。不同部位羽毛颜色的变化是由金银羽（s/S）基因控制的，符合金银羽的变化规律。

参 考 文 献

[1] 康相涛，赖银生，王俊士等．豫州蛋鸡不同羽色类型对雏鸡自别雌雄准确率的影响 [J]．华北农学报，1995，10（2）：116－119

[2] 廖纪朝，康海琴等．粉壳蛋鸡羽色自别雌雄品系的成功选育 [I]．广西畜牧兽医，1999，15（4）：3－7

[3] 刘敬顺．家鸡羽色色遗传及应用 [I]．养禽与禽病防治，1995，4)：5－7

[4] 卢克伦，许明，姜庆林等．鸡羽色性状的研究现状及应用探讨 [I] 动物科学与动物医学，2004，21（3）：20－21

Studies on Strains of Feather Color Auto-sexing in Dwarf Pink Egg Chicken

DAI Hui-jie　LI Qun-feng

(*Weifang University of Science and Technology*, *Shouguang*　262700)

Abstract: Pink egg chicken are produced by hybridizing between White Leghorn and brown layer, and most of the commercial squabs are auto-sexing throng feather growing. Applying modern breeding theories, cultivating recessive white Leghorn may realize auto-sexing by feather color in dwarf pink egg chicken. The research was conducted to breed recessive white strains from the maternal line of dwarf pink layer. The result shows that the commercial squabs of the dwarf pink layer can be auto-sexing by feather color after two generations test-cross and individual selection. Chicken with feather color of purely red are all pullets, the ratio of which reaches 27.7%, and all cockerels are purely white feather.

Key words: Egg chicken; Dwarf; Feather color auto-sexing; Recessive white; White Leghorn

Gemini 表面活性剂的研究进展

郑兴荣① 韩金宏
（潍坊科技学院，寿光 262700）

摘 要：Gemini 表面活性剂具有独特的性质和应用。本文从其合成进展、发展前景提出了一些看法。

关键词：Gemini 表面活性剂；合成；结构设计

Gemini 表面活性剂的出现，为表面活性剂科学开拓了广阔的前景。它的自缔合浓度比传统的表面活性剂低几百倍，而界面活性比传统的高几千倍[1]。为此，它已成为当今界面和胶体化学的研究热点。

1 Gemini 表面活性剂的分子结构

Gemini 表面活性剂从结构类型上可以分为阳离子型、阴离子型和非离子型表面活性剂[2]。

传统的表面活性剂由一个亲水头基和一个疏水链组成，而 Gemini 表面活性剂是通过联结基团将两个两亲体在头基处或紧靠头基处连接起来的化合物。从各类型的 Gemini 表面活性剂分子结构来看，它们具有一定的模式。联结基团种类较多，主要有两类：一类是柔性链，如亚甲基（$-CH_2-$）n、聚氧乙烯；另一类是刚性链，如对苯基等。由于联结基类型不同，它们构成的表面活性剂具有各自的特点，如柔性联结基团弯曲趋势强，更容易适应环境，降低表面张力能力强。长碳链的种类也有两类，一类为纯碳链，另一类碳链接有其他基团如酯基、酰胺基、氟等[3]。

极性头的种类与普通表面活性剂相关不大，阳离子型主要是季铵盐，阴离子型主要有碳酸盐、磷酸盐、磺酸盐及硫酸酯盐。非离子型主要有多羟基和环氧乙烷的缩合基团[4,5]。

---

① 郑兴荣，女，潍坊科技学院讲师。主要研究方向：基础化学。E-mail：zxr7332@163.com

2 Gemini 表面活性剂的合成与设计

2.1 合成概况

第一个 Gemini 表面活性剂早在 20 世纪 70 年代初就已问世。1971 年，Bunton 等合成了 Gemini 表面活性剂 2，4—二硝基氯（或氟）苯亲核取代反应的催化剂[6]。1985 年，Devinsky 先后合成了一些不同联结基团和不同疏水链的新季铵盐 Gemini 表面活性剂。

20 世纪 90 年代以后，Zana 小组[7]、Menger 小组、Rosen 小组和其他许多化学家发表了大量相关论文，申请了多项专利。

1990 年，Cambon 及其同事就已报道了全氟烃的 Gemini 表面活性剂；1993 年，Zhu 和 Okahara 报道了阴离子表面活性剂；1997 年 Cireln 报道了第一个非离子型表面活性剂；Holmberg 等先后合成了具不同头基的杂 Gemini 表面活性剂。考虑对环境保护和社会经济可持续发展的需要，又开发了无毒或低毒、利用再生资源以及功能性的 Gemini 表面活性剂，同时，也报道了环 Gemini 表面活性剂以及不对称 Gemini 表面活性剂等。

由此可见，Gemini 表面活性剂的合成，随着研究者的期望升高而复杂。因此寻找新的化合物是合成化学的重要任务之一。

目前，我国已生产一些双季铵盐类表面活性剂，即 Gemini 表面活性剂，然而没有认识它们与传统表面活性剂的根本区别。近年来已有从双子角度探索的研究文章，但不多且主要是综述。

2.2 合成路线

根据 Gemini 表面活性剂分子结构，其合成路线归纳起来有以下 3 种：（1）用联结基团将两个或多个两亲体在头基外键合起来；（2）用联结基团先将两个尾链联结起来，再接上头基；（3）用联结基团将头基联结起来，再接上尾链。

2.3 从分子结构水平上设计 Gemini 表面活性剂

表面活性剂的最基本性质是界面（表面）定向吸附和溶液中形成缔合结构，其他具体应用性质均由这两个基本性质派生而成。决定表面活性剂性质的主要因素是其结构（内因）及其所处环境（外因），并且结构是最主要因素。例如，普通表面活性剂在水溶液中的缔合结构类型受到两种作用力控制：一种是烷烃链之间的疏水作用，它是形成缔合结构的驱动力；另一种是头基间的静电斥力或水化层形成的空间阻碍造成的排斥力。这两种作用力的平衡结果，加上表面活性剂分子几何形状产生的空间体积效应，最终决定了表面活性剂分子形成缔合结构的类型。Israelachvili 提出了表面活性剂分子形成聚集体开头的判据：几何结构参数 $p = V/a_0Le$，其中 V 为表面活性剂单元分子烷烃链体积；Le 为烷烃链最大伸展长度；a_0 为头基面积。

当 $p < 1/3$ 时形成球形或椭球形胶团；$1/3 < p < 1/2$ 时形成柱状或棒状胶团；$1/2 < p < 1$ 时形成囊泡；$p = 1$ 时形成层状胶团；$p > 1$ 时形成反相胶团。

该判据虽然离实际情况有一定偏差，但对设计表面活性剂分子结构有一定指导意义。如纳米粒子制造、生物酶催化反应，微乳 CO_2 超临界萃取等，都要求形成反相微乳液，大多数反相微乳增溶都选用 AOT，因为它有两条碳链，通过计算 $p>1$，易形成反相胶团。而 Gemini 表面活性剂至少有两条碳链，因此，可通过设计联结基长度及碳链长度、种类及构型来达到 $p>1$，满足应用要求。这样可开发出比 AOT 性能更优良的专用表面活性剂来满足上述行业及科研工作的需要，促进相关高新技术的发展。分散剂、缓蚀剂、柔软剂，要求界面吸附紧密牢固，Gemini 表面活性剂也符合这种需求，它至少有两个头基，因此吸附牢固。另外由于联结基使两条碳链相距更近，因此吸附得更紧密。这样我们可以根据需求开发多头基、多碳链的 Gemini 表面活性剂。

当今，计算机模拟已成为除理论计算、实验验证以外的第三种研究手段，并且已取得较大成功。这些成功的经验同样可用来指导表面活性剂的分子设计。

3 展望

传统表面活性剂已广泛用于化工各领域，人们称为工业味精，Gemini 表面活性剂则将是工业味精的新一代精品。由于 Gemini 表面活性剂的特殊结构，它不仅具有高表面活性，而且可产生新形态聚集体和奇异性质，为多学科交叉创造条件，将在化学生物学、纳米科技、超分子化学的发展中受到重视。预期在抗 HIV、抗肿瘤、基因转染方面，在环境保护、三次采煤和新型功能材料制备等工业中有较好的应用前景。

Gemini 表面活性剂作为新一代表面活性剂，虽然具有许多优良性能，并已有少数几种产品实现了工业化生产，但是离大规模工业化生产并取代普通表面活性剂还有一段时间。从其结构类型和合成路线来看，大多数合成步骤多、所用原料昂贵、工业化生产难。因此，要实现此类产品的大规模工业化生产，促进我国表面活性剂工业的发展，还有很长的路要走。

参 考 文 献

[1] 钟声，王伟，朱建民．表面活性剂的研究进展［J］．鞍山科技大学学报，2006（2）

[2] 张青山，郭炳南，张辉森．［J］化学进展，2003，16（4）：345－348

[3] 赵剑曦．日用化学工业［J］，2002，32（3）：39－42

[4] 罗明道，颜肖慈，张高勇．日用化学工业［M］，2002，32（3）：5－7

[5] 赵剑曦．低聚表面活性剂——两亲分子表面活性的突破［J］．鞍山科技大学学报，2000（2）

[6] MENGER F M. LITTAU C A. Adsorption of zwitterionic gemini surfactantsat the air-water and solid-water interfaces. 2002（203）

[7] Zana Levy Alkanediyl-α，ω-bis（dimetyl alkyl ammoniumbromide surfactants6 CMC of theethandiy 1-1，2-bi（dimethyl alkyl ammonium bromide）series 1997（127）

Research and development of Gemini surfactants

ZHENG Xing-rong HAN Jin-hong

(*Weifang University of Science and Technology*, *Shouguang* 262700)

Abstract: Gemini surfactants have unique properties and applications. In this paper, we put forward some views about the progress of synthesis and the prospects of development.

Key words: Gemini surfactants; Synthesis; Structure design

浅谈米糠的研究现状与进展

韩金宏[①] 李云玲 董美华 唐玉海
（潍坊科技学院，寿光 262700）

摘 要： 米糠是稻米加工中碾米工序得到的主要副产物。米糠中主要含有大量的蛋白、油脂、膳食纤维、多糖和一些微量成分。长期以来，国内多数地区仅将米糠作为喂养畜禽的饲料，造成极大的浪费。目前，米糠大多数用来提取米糠油，米糠油是一种营养价值很高的食用油脂，富含γ-谷维醇、植物甾醇、矿物质营养素、B族维生素、维生素E等。米糠资源的综合利用，越来越受到人们的关注。

关键词： 米糠；理化性质；生理功能；技术工艺

水稻是世界上最重要的两大粮食作物之一。我国是世界上最大的稻米生产国，稻谷年产量约2亿t，占世界稻谷总产量的37%左右。而作为稻谷加工副产物米糠的年产量为1 000万t以上，约占世界总产量的1/3[1]。因此，米糠资源十分丰富，是我国大宗农副产品之一。长期以来，我国把米糠主要作为畜禽饲料，而对其营养成分没有进行充分提取和利用，造成极大的资源浪费。

2002年3月15日，由国家计委、国家经贸委和农业部联合颁布的全国食品工业“十五”发展规划中明确指出了合理利用米糠资源，提高综合利用水平，积极开发米糖蛋白、米糠营养油、米糠多糖、膳食纤维以及γ-谷维醇等功能食品[2]。

米糠中含有大量的营养物质和功能成分，如米糠蛋白的低过敏性、抗癌活性和保健功能；米糠油的降低人体血清胆固醇功能；米糠多糖抗肿瘤、增强免疫力和降血糖的功能；米糠植酸钙促进人体新陈代谢、骨骼组织生长发育等的功能等。目前，米糠大多数用来提取米糠油。米糠油是一种营养价值很高的食用油脂，含有88.1%～89.2%的中性脂、6.3%～7.0%的糖脂和4.5%～4.9%的磷脂。米糠中含粗脂肪14%～24%，含蛋白质12%～18%，无氮浸出物为33%～53%，水分为7%～14%，灰分为8%～12%，其中米糠蛋白质含量几乎高出普通精米的一倍[3]。此外，米糠中还富含矿物质营养素、B族维生素和维生素E等。脱脂米糠中含有15%～20%的蛋白质，其氨基酸总量及其组成均与大豆相差不大，以此可以制得优质的米糠蛋白。脱脂米糠还可以用作配合饲料，它是蛋白质、纤维素、矿物质和维生素的良好来源[4]。近年来还发现，米

① 韩金宏，女，硕士，潍坊科技学院讲师。研究方向：食品质量与安全。E-mail：hanjinhong2004@163.com

糖中存在一种具有抗癌作用的多糖物质，这种多糖类可望成为一种提高人体免疫力、防止癌细胞增长的药物[5,6]。

1 米糠的主要成分和理化性质

1.1 米糠蛋白

米糠中含有12%～20%左右的蛋白质。研究表明，米糠中的蛋白质是一种低过敏性蛋白；其氨基酸组成完全，接近FAO/WHO的推荐模式，赖氨酸含量比大米胚乳、小麦面粉以及其他谷物中的蛋白质都要高；生物效价（PER值2.0～2.5）与酪蛋白相近（PER值2.5），消化率达90%以上，是一种极具开发潜力的新型植物蛋白[7,8]。传统提取米糠蛋白的方法是碱法提取，但在高碱条件下不但改变了蛋白的营养学特性，而且，蛋白质的半胱氨酸和丝氨酸的ε-氨基酸结合形成赖-丙氨酸，这种物质不但有毒，而且还会引起营养物质的损失[9]。据报道目前用纤维素酶和复合蛋白酶水解米糠制蛋白效果较好，蛋白收率分别达54.75%和58.93%[10]。随水解度的提高，蛋白质的溶解度显著提高，但乳化活性在水解度为3%时最高，过度水解对蛋白质的乳化活性明显降低。经过适当水解能提高蛋白质的功能性质[11]。蛋白水解产物经高效凝胶过滤色谱分析分子量从200～50 000不等[12]。

近年来，以米糠蛋白为原料进行多功能活性肽的开发研究较为活跃。日本东京大学副教授吉川正明从米蛋白的酶解物中，获得了具有降血压和增强免疫功能的活性肽，使米糠蛋白得到更有效的利用。但是另一方面，米糠中天然存在的蛋白如脂酶和氧化酶，又很容易造成米糠的酸败变质。

1.2 米糠膳食纤维

米糠是一种较好的营养物质和膳食纤维的来源，其膳食纤维的含量较高。米糠营养纤维的成分包括47.41%不溶性膳食纤维和0.64%可溶性膳食纤维[13]。主要有整肠、抑制血清胆固醇上升和大肠癌三大作用，对高血脂及高胆固醇等与饮食有关的现代文明病有重要疗效[14]。

米糠中的纤维较粗，人们在口感上难以接受，并且不利于营养物质的消化和吸收。若能将米糠纤维部分降解成可溶性片段，同时保留其他营养成分，可将米糠制成消费者喜爱的保健食品。米糠纤维用纤维素酶处理米糠，将米糠中的部分不溶性纤维降解为可溶性片断，其他营养物质均不被破坏，这样就可得到制得膳食纤维食品的中间产品，再经过加工可制得多种膳食纤维食品[15]。

1.3 米糠多糖

20世纪80年代初，日本学者伊藤悦男发现米糠中含有抗肿瘤成分，其化学本质是一种具有生物活性多糖，自此米糠多糖引起人们的兴趣。米糠多糖存在于稻谷的颖果皮层，据周瑞芳等研究报道，主要是由α-1，6葡萄糖苷键连接的葡萄糖构成。目前，对于米糠多糖的提取主要采用热水抽提法。水溶性米糠多糖与一般均聚糖不同，是一种结构复杂的杂聚糖，由木糖、甘露糖、鼠李糖、半乳糖、阿拉伯糖和葡萄糖等组成。米糠多糖采用不同的提取工艺可以得到多种米糠多糖，它们都有着显著的生物活性和保健功能。

1.4 米糠油

米糠含油量为14% ~24%，作为中低含油量的一种特殊油料，很适于通过一次浸出提取毛糠油[16]。毛糠油经过精炼得到具有营养保健功能的食用米糠油[17]。米糠油是一种很好的油脂，它含有80%左右的油酸和亚油酸，经医学研究证明，具有降血清胆固醇沉积、软化心脑血等重要的医疗作用。近20年来，国际上对米糠制油、糠油精炼等技术，作了不懈的努力，取得了显著效果，如米糠稳定作用（钝化酶）使酸价不再升高、采用先进脱蜡技术提高了精油得率，开拓米糠色拉油、调和油的生产[18]。

不过，米糠中由于含有脂肪分解酶（脂肪氧化酶）造成新鲜米糠不能较长储存，毛糠油的酸价会因储存时间长、温湿度高而迅速增大，致使精炼损失太大；另一方面，米糠油中含有糠蜡等物质不易除尽，增加了精炼的困难，从而影响米糠油的生产发展与提高。

我国对谷维素的研究开始于20世纪70年代，成功地开发出产品，并作为医药，命名为谷维素，用于治疗植物神经功能失调、经前期紧张症及更年期综合症。1975年，被收入国家药典标准，并一直被使用至今。到目前为止，我国对谷维素的生理功能还未开展深入、系统的研究。米糠作为一种再生资源，来源丰富、价格低廉，对于其中的功能活性因子——谷维素进行系统全面的研究，将有利于米糠的综合开发和利用[19]。

表1 米糠中谷维素的组成

种类	含量（%）
24-亚甲基环木菠萝烯醇阿魏酸酯	35 ~ 40
环木菠萝烯醇阿魏酸酯	25 ~ 30
菜籽甾醇阿魏酸酯	10 ~ 12
环木菠萝醇阿魏酸酯	8 ~ 10
β-谷甾醇阿魏酸酯	6 ~ 8
环米糠醇阿魏酸酯	2 ~ 3
豆甾醇阿魏酸酯	1 ~ 2
24-甲基环木菠萝烯醇阿魏酸酯	0.5 ~ 1.0
24-甲基环木菠萝醇阿魏酸酯	0.2 ~ 0.5
24-乙基环木菠萝醇阿魏酸酯	微量
25-羟基环木菠萝醇阿魏酸酯	微量

米糠油中植物甾醇是不皂化物中营养成分的主要成分之一，它本身属于天然物质，没有毒性，但具有抗炎等特性。绝大部分甾醇在米糠油精炼过程中以下脚物的形式提取

出来。植物甾醇也是一类有生理价值的物质，可用于合成调节水、蛋白质、糖和盐代谢的甾类激素，植物甾醇作为治疗心血管疾病、皮肤鳞癌和顽固性溃疡药物已被应用[20]。

1.5 米糠蜡

米糠蜡又称糠蜡，是米糠油精炼时分离出来的一种副产物。精制糠蜡是白色或淡黄色固体，熔程为79～82℃。糠蜡不溶于水、乙醇，溶于乙酸乙脂、石油醚等有机溶剂，与动物蜡相比，具有安全无毒的特点。糠蜡主要组成为偶碳长链脂肪酸和偶碳长链脂肪醇构成的蜡。据报道，蜡酯的碳链总长度为，C_{44}～C_{62}其中C_{50}以上的蜡酯占大多数。其中的二十八烷醇、三十烷醇含量较高[21]。

二十八烷醇具有生物活性的功能性物质，它具有抗疲劳、提高人体机能等作用，在国外它已经在功能性食品、医药、化妆品、饲料等行业有广泛应用，国内这方面研究较少。

目前，我国米糠蜡的年产量约1 200t左右，除了湖南、江西、浙江等省小规模提取，年产粗制糠蜡约200t，大部分被当作皂料卖掉，资源利用率极低。

近年来，国外已经开始采用超临界流体萃取技术从米糠中提取糠蜡，该法仍处于实验室阶段。我国提取糠蜡的研究起步比较晚，主要采用袋滤法、压滤皂化法和溶剂萃取法等。但是这些方法都存在糠蜡分离效果差、污染环境等缺点，需开发高效、实用的糠蜡精制工艺。

1.6 米糠微量成分

米糠中含有一定量的植酸、肌醇、维生素E[22]。植酸不仅可以作为饮料的解渴剂、高档水果的保鲜剂，还能够促进人体对强化大米中矿质元素铁的吸收。肌醇属于维生素药物及降血脂药物。维生素E具有延缓衰老和抗不孕症的作用。

2 展望

米糠含有丰富的功能性成分，是多种天然功能性物质的来源。米糠不仅能够提取功能性物质，而且能开发出高营养的米糠食品（如米糠面条、米糠面包、米糠饼干）。再者，米糠还能作为其他食品的原料，用来制作饮料、糖液等。提取米糠油后的米糠渣还能用来酿造酒。长期以来，国内多数地区仅将米糠作为饲料喂养畜禽，使其具有的营养价值和资源效益没有得到充分的发挥，造成极大的浪费。综合利用米糠资源，不局限于提取米糠油的单一途经，增加米糠的附加值，具有广阔的前景。

参考文献

[1] International Grains Council, US. Department of Agriculture. World Grain, 2000 (11): 1

[2] 李长河. 米糠多糖的研究性状和发展前景 [J]. 现代化农业区, 2005 (1): 39-41

[3] 吴建平．一种开发米糠蛋白的新方法［J］．粮食与饲料工业，1997（10）：33－34
[4] Wayne E. Marshall. Rice Science and Technology. New York：Marcel Dekker-Inc. 1993. 381－404
[5] 戚奋．米糠的医药用途［J］．粮食与饲料工业，1994（8）：16－18
[6] 周秀琴．日本开发米糠抗癌新品 EGMP［J］．药学杂志，2003（2）：46
[7] Slauders R M. The Properties of Rice Bran as a Food Stuff［J］. Cereal Foods World，1990，35（7）：632－636.
[8] Jamuna Prakash. Rice Bran Proteins：Properties and Food Uses［J］. Criti Reviews in Food Sci and Nutri，1996，36（6）：537－552.
[9] M. Wang. Preparation and Functional Properties of Rice Protein isolate［J］Agric. Food Chem，1999，47，411－416
[10] 王雪飞，于国萍，徐红华．不同酶类提取米糠蛋白的研究［J］．中国粮油学报，2004，19（1）：8
[11] 金世合，陈正行，周素梅．酶解米糠蛋白的功能性解米糠蛋白的功能性质研究［J］．中国粮油学报，2004，25（3）：56－57
[12] 陈季旺，姚惠源，陈尚卫．米糠可溶性蛋白酶解物的分子量分布的研究［J］．中国油脂，2004，29（1）：36－39
[13] 朱文华，姚惠源，谈新刚．米糠的不稳定机理与稳定化的研究［J］．粮食与饲料工业，2001，（10）：174.
[14] 孙兰萍，许晖．挤压法制备米糠膳食纤维的研究［J］．农机化研究，2005（4）：98－100
[15] 王领军．米糠营养纤维的生产和应用［J］．粮油加工与食品机械，2003（9）：61－62
[16] 胡国华，余迎利，黄绍华．米糠半纤维素的研究及应用［J］．粮食与饲料工业，1998（2）：42－43
[17] 宋莲军．酶法水解米糠纤维的工艺研究［J］．粮油食品，2003，11（4）：18－20
[18] 李长河．米糠多糖的研究性状和发展前景［J］．现代化农业区，2005（1）：39－41
[19] 钟科贤．米糠一次浸出及米糠油物理精炼［J］．中国油脂，2004，29（4）：56
[20] 韩秀丽，张如意等．米糠的综合利用及其前景［J］．农产品加工，2007（7）：62－64
[21] Leandro Danielski，Carsten Zetzl，Haiko Hense. A process line for the production of raffinated rice oil from rice bran［J］. J. of Supercritical Fluids，2005，34：133－141
[22] 龚院生．米糠谷维醇的生理功能及其应用研究［M］．无锡轻工业大学博士论文，2000，12

Review on Rice bran

HAN Jin-hong LI Yun-ling DONG Mei-hua TANG Yu-hai

(*Weifang University of Science and Technology*, *Shouguang* 262700)

Abstract: Rice bran is a by-product of rice processing, obtained through the polishing of the rice grain. The rice bran mainly contains the massive proteins, the fat, the meals textile fiber, the polysaccharide and some ingredients. For many years, the people in most areas of our country only feed rice brain to poultry, which causes a large waste. At present, rice bran oil can be extracted from rice bran, which is considered as an excellent source of nutritionally beneficial compounds, containing γ-oryzanol, the phytosterin, the mineral substance nutrinet, the B race Vitamin, Vitamin E etc. The comprehensive utilization of rice bran absorbs more and more people's attention.

Key words: Rice bran; Physical and chemical property; Physiological function; Technical crafts

不同植物激素对生姜组织培养快繁的影响

刘艳梅①
（潍坊科技学院，寿光 262700）

摘 要： 采用D206回归设计方法，进行了生姜快繁激素优化试验，建立了繁殖系数、株高与KT、NAA以及6-BA、NAA用量之间的二元二次数学模型。通过模型分析得出，KT对繁殖系数的影响最大，其变化对繁殖系数的影响也最敏感。而NAA对株高的影响最显著，其变化对株高的影响最敏感，并且激素之间存在交互效应，并得出当KT 2.65mg/l与NAA 0.43mg/l搭配时繁殖系数最大为6.4。

关键词： 生姜；植物激素；繁殖系数；株高

生姜（*Zingiber officinal* Rosc.）系姜科姜属植物，原产我国和东南亚热带地区。它以老熟地下根状茎繁殖，其繁殖系数低，因而栽培成本高[1]，且青枯病单胞杆菌极易通过种姜积累和传播，诱发姜瘟，田间发病率高达70%～80%，有时甚至绝收，对生姜生产构成严重威胁[2]。此外，由于生姜体内病菌的存在，在贮存过程中易腐烂，从而降低了生姜的商品性。通过生姜茎尖培养脱菌和离体快繁技术研究，不仅这几年可有效的克服生姜的上述缺点，而且达到提高产量的目的[3～4]。

近年来，由于数学方法的渗透和计算机的应用，使得回归设计理论和系统分析技术有了较大的发展，二元饱和最优设计以其处理数较少而中心点附近信息丰富等特点，在农业试验上得到了广泛的应用，用该法进行的农业试验设计，可求出农业生态环境与产量，品质等目标函数间的多项式回归方程，为此，笔者把该设计方法应用于生姜组织培养快繁激素优化试验研究。

1 材料与方法

1.1 材料来源与处理方法

供试材料为培养继代30d的莱芜大姜脱毒试管苗。快繁培养基采用附加卡拉胶4g/L的MS培养基，pH值为5.8，其中，KT、NAA和6-BA、NAA各2个变量因子，采用

① 刘艳梅，女，硕士，潍坊科技学院讲师。研究方向：番茄育种及生姜组织培养。E－mail：65291273@qq.com

D206 饱和最优设计。将继代培养 30d 的莱芜大姜脱毒试管苗从培养瓶内取出，用无菌水洗净培养基，在无菌条件下将试管从生苗分割成单株，并去根、剪茎（仅保留基部 0. 5 ~ 1cm 长的茎），转入不同处理培养基进行培养。试验设计编码及因子处理水平详见表 1。

表 1 试验设计编码及因子处理水平

处理	KT（mg/L）	NAA（mg/L）	繁殖系数	株高（cm）	处理	6-BA（mg/L）	NAA（mg/L）	繁殖系数	株高（cm）
1	0	0	1. 7	1. 8	7	0	0	1. 7	1. 3
2	4	0	4. 7	1. 5	8	6	0	3. 3	2. 3
3	0	1	1. 3	3. 8	9	0	1	2. 1	3. 7
4	1. 7	0. 4	6. 0	4. 4	10	2. 6	0. 4	4. 3	4. 9
5	4	0. 7	5. 0	3. 2	11	6	0. 7	4. 2	3. 5
6	2. 8	1	4. 3	3. 2	12	4. 2	1	3. 8	3. 6

1. 2 培养条件

培养室温度保持在（25 ±2）℃，相对湿度保持在 60% ~80%，光强为 4 000 lx，光照时间为 12h/d。

2 结果与分析

2. 1 模型建立与统计检验

将结果输入计算机，通过运算，得到以繁殖系数为目标函数的回归模型为：

$$y_A = 6.17 + 1.25x_1 - 1.92x_1^2 - 0.42x_2 - 0.25x_1x_2 - 1.51x_2^2$$

$$y_B = 4.48 + 0.77x_1 - 0.89x_1^2 + 0.13x_2 - 0.06x_1x_2 - 0.96x_2^2$$

对方程进行 F 检验，得 F_A 值为 19. 38 > $F_{0.01}$（5，12）=9. 89，F_B 值为 18. 50 > $F_{0.01}$（5，12）=9. 89 说明回归模型成立，y_A 可以反映 KT 和 NAA 与繁殖系数之间的关系，y_B 可以反映 6-BA 和 NAA 与繁殖系数之间的关系。

同理，可求得以株高为目标函数的回归模型：

$$y_C = 4.42 - 0.48x_1 - 0.64x_1^2 + 0.66x_2 - 0.31x_1x_2 - 1.45x_2^2$$

$$y_D = 5.06 - 0.13x_1 - 1.19x_1^2 + 0.57x_2 - 0.65x_1x_2 - 1.53x_2^2$$

经检验，y_C 可反映可以反映 KT 和 NAA 与株高之间的关系，y_D 可以反映 6-BA 和 NAA 与株高之间的关系。

2. 2 模型解析

2.2.1 主因素效应

因回归方程为无量纲线性编码算得，各偏回归系数已经标准化，因此，直接比较其绝对值的大小，可判明诸因子的重要程度。

从线性项看，繁殖系数回归模型 y_A 的偏回归系数 $x_1 > x_2$，y_B 的偏回归系数 $x_1 > x_2$，这说明激素对繁殖系数的影响 KT > NAA，6-BA > NAA。

株高回归模型 y_C 的偏回归系数 $x_1 < x_2$，y_D 的偏回归系数 $x_1 < x_2$，这说明激素对株高的影响，KT < NAA，6-BA < NAA。

2.2.2 单因子效应

单因子效应反映的是单一激素用量对目标结果的影响。分别将试验求得模型中的两个变量固定在 0 水平，即可得到剩余因素的单因子的效应方程。据此，可得繁殖系数的单因子效应方程：

$$y_{A1} = 6.17 - 1.25x_1 - 1.92x_1^2 \quad y_{A2} = 6.17 - 0.42x_2 - 1.51x_2^2$$

$$y_{B1} = 4.48 - 0.77x_1 - 0.89x_1^2 \quad y_{B2} = 4.48 - 0.13x_2 - 0.96x_2^2$$

同理，可求得株高的单因子效应方程：

$$y_{C1} = 4.42 - 0.48x_1 - 0.64x_1^2 \quad y_{C2} = 4.42 - 0.66x_2 - 1.45x_2^2$$

$$y_{D1} = 5.07 - 0.13x_1 - 1.19x_1^2 \quad y_{D2} = 5.07 - 0.57x_2 - 1.53x_2^2$$

将各单因子效应方程绘成图 1，可直观反映出各目标结果随激素用量而变化的趋势。

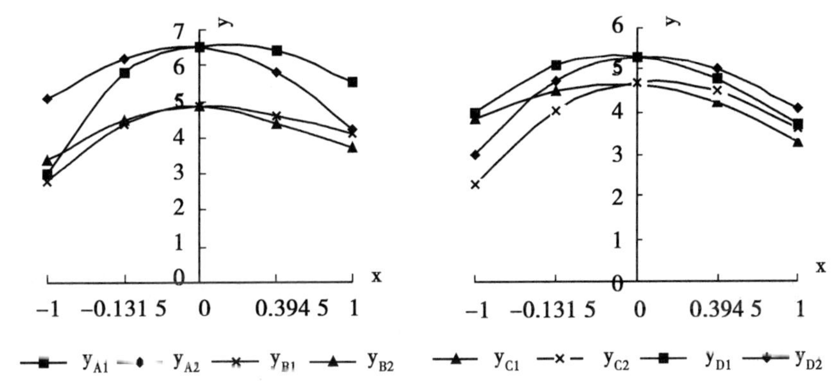

图 1 单因子效应分析

表 2 KT 和 NAA 对繁殖系数的交互作用分析

		x_2 编码				统计参数		
		-1	-0.13	0.395	1	平均值	标准差	CV
X_1 编码	-1	1.667	3.006	2.71	1.333	2.179	0.805	0.369
	-0.132	4.852	6	5.587	4.077	5.129	0.847	0.165
	0.395	5.376	6.408	5.924	4.333	5.51	0.891	0.162
	1	4.667	5.564	5	3.316	4.637	0.955	0.206
统计参数	平均值	4.14	5.245	4.805	3.265			
	标准值	1.676	1.531	1.448	1.358			
		0.405	0.292	0.301	0.416			

表3 6-BA和NAA对株高的交互作用分析

	x_2 遍码				统计参数			
	-1	-0.132	0.395	1	平均值	标准差	CV	
X_1 编码	1	2.133	4.319	4.519	3.7	3.668	1.081	0.295
	-0.13	3.373	5.067	4.969	3.807	4.304	0.844	0.196
	0.395	3.252	4.648	4.37	3	3.818	0.813	0.213
	1	2.3	3.353	2.867	1.258	2.444	0.9	0.368
统计参数	平均值	2.765	4.347	4.181	2.941			
	标准值	0.638	0.73	0.913	1.178			
		0.231	0.168	0.218	0.401			

2.2.3 因子交互效应分析

本试验确定的回归模型存在互作项，说明在综合激素条件下，繁殖系数的提高不单纯是各因子单独效应的线性累加，还存在着配合效应，即因子交互效应。因子交互效应对不同目标结果的影响不同，既是对同一目标结果，因子交互效应的大小也不同。

将各因子固定在0水平，即可得到KT与NAA的互作效应方程：$y_{12}=6.17-1.25x_1-0.42\ x_2-0.25x_1x_2-1.92x_1^2-1.51x_2^2$，分别令 x_1，$x_2=-1$、-0.1315、0.3945、1代入上述方程可得KT、NAA交互效应表（表2）。从表2可以看出，KT与NAA的交互效应有一最优区域，即当 x_1 取 -0.1315～0.3945（即KT1.7～2.8mg/L），x_2 取 -0.1315～0.3945（NAA 0.4～0.7mg/L）时，繁殖系数在5～6.5之间，超出这一区域，无论是增加还是减少，繁殖系数均表现下降。同理，可以推出6-BA与NAA的效应也有一个最优区域，即 x_1 取 -0.1315～0.3945（6-BA 2.6～4.2mg/L），x_2 取 -0.1315～0.3945（NAA 0.4～0.7mg/L）时，繁殖系数在4～4.5之间。

同理，将各因子固定在0水平，即可得到6-BA、NAA与株高的互作效应方程，从表3可以看出，6-BA与NAA的交互效应也有一个最优区域，即当 x_1 取 -0.1315～0.3945（6-BA 2.6～4.2mg/L），x_2 取 -0.1315～0.3945（NAA 0.4～0.7mg/L）时，株高在4.5～5.0之间。同理KT、NAA与株高的互作效应亦存在一最优区域，即当 x_1 取 -0.1315～0.3945（即KT 1.7～2.8mg/L），x_2 取 -0.1315～0.3945（NAA 0.4～0.7mg/L）时，株高在4.0～4.5之间，超出此范围株高均会下降。

2.2.4 因子边际效应

边际效应是单位激素用量变化所引起的目标结果的变化大小，可分析目标结果随激素用量变化而变化的速率[5]。各单因子效应方程对自变量的导数即是边际效应方程，因此本试验条件下，繁殖系数的单因子边际效应方程如下：

$$dy_{A1}/dx_1=1.25-3.83x_1 \qquad dy_{A2}/dx_2=0.42-3.02x_2$$

$$dy_{B1}/dx_1=0.77-1.79x_1 \qquad dy_{B2}/dx_2=0.13-1.01x_2$$

株高的单因子边际效应方程如下：

$$dy_{C1}/dx_1=0.48-1.28x_1 \qquad dy_{C2}/dx_2=-0.66-2.90x_2$$

$$dy_{D1}/dx_1=-0.13-2.38x_1 \qquad dy_{D2}/dx_2=-0.57-3.06x_2$$

将各目标结果的因子边际效应方程绘成图2，可看出各单因子边际效应方程中所决定的直线陡度的大小。图2－1中，y_{A1}的直线陡度大于y_{A2}大于y_{B2}大于y_{B1}，说明KT变化对繁殖系数的影响最大，其次为6-BA，NAA影响最小。从图2－2中得出，NAA对株高影响最大，其次为6-BA，KT影响最小。

上述各方程决定的直线与x轴有交点，说明当激素使用过多时，繁殖系数或株高不仅不增加，反而会下降。所以，在进行组织培养时，一定要注意激素用量，切不可盲目多用。

2.3 优化方案分析

利用计算机进行模拟试验，得出本试验条件下利于组织培养的激素方案（表4）。从表4可以看出，各种激素均有一定的最适施用范围，超出这一范围要得到良好效果是不可能的。本试验条件下，KT、NAA搭配时，只有当KT取2.1～3.4mg/L，NAA取0.24～0.74mg/L时，或者在6-BA、NAA搭配时只有当6-BA取2.7～5.9mg/L，NAA取0.41～0.72mg/L时繁殖系数才能达到4.0以上。而从表4可以看出，在KT、NAA搭配时只有KT取0.55～2.7mg/L，NAA取0.47～0.83mg/L时或者在6-BA取1.76～4.3mg/L，NAA取0.38～0.78mg/L时，株高才能达到3.0cm以上。

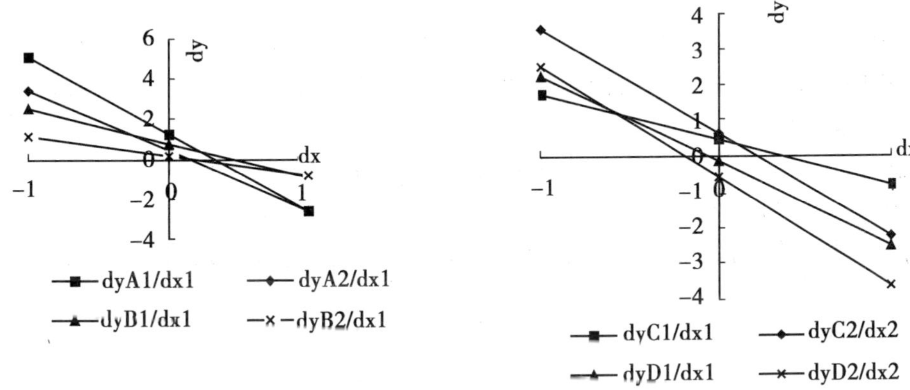

图2 单因子边际效应

表4 株高（大于3.0cm）影响因素取值的频率分布

变量因子		频率			
		x_1（KT）	x_2（NAA）	x_1（6-BA）	x_2（NAA）
因子水平	-1	0.333 3	0	0.230 8	0.153 8
	-0.131 5	0.333 3	0.444 4	0.307 7	0.307 7
	0.394 5	0.222 2	0.333 3	0.307 7	0.307 7
	1	0.111 1	0.222 2	0.153 8	0.230 8
平均值		-0.178	0.295	0.004	0.158
标准差		0.714	0.468	0.689	0.669
95%置信区间		-0.727～0.37	-0.064～0.655	-0.412～0.42	-0.246～0.562
农艺方案		0.55～2.7	0.47～0.83	1.76～4.3	0.38～0.78

3 结论与讨论

生姜组织培养中繁殖系数和株高与激素使用量之间有密切关系，本试验所建模型可充分反映他们之间的数量关系。本实验条件下，以 KT 对繁殖系数的影响最大，其变化对繁殖系数的影响也最敏感，其次为 6 - BA。而 NAA 对株高的影响最显著，其变化对株高的影响最敏感。而且无论是繁殖系数还是株高只有在激素的最适施用范围内，才能得到良好的效果。

本试验条件下 KT、NAA 搭配时，只有当 KT 取 2. 1 ~ 3. 4mg/L，NAA 取 0. 24 ~ 0. 74mg/L 时，或者在 6-BA、NAA 搭配时只有当 6-BA 取 2. 7 ~ 5. 9mg/L，NAA 取 0. 41 ~ 0. 72mg/L 时繁殖系数才能达到 4. 0 以上。对株高的影响，在 KT、NAA 搭配时只有 KT 取 0. 55 ~ 2. 7mg/L，NAA 取 0. 47 ~ 0. 83mg/L 时或者在 6-BA 取 1. 76 ~ 4. 3mg/L，NAA 取 0. 38 ~ 0. 78mg/L 时，株高才能达到 3. 0cm 以上。并且当 KT 取 2. 65mg/l 与 NAA 取 0. 43mg/L 搭配时繁殖系数最大为 6. 4；当 6-BA 取 4. 32mg/l 与 NAA 取 0. 53mg/l 搭配时繁殖系数为 4. 7，可见 KT 与 NAA 搭配时繁殖效率明显高于 6-BA 与 NAA 搭配。

参 考 文 献

[1] 赵得婉，徐坤，艾希珍．生姜高产栽培 [M]. 北京：金盾出版社，2000

[2] 王金陵，李勤．姜青枯病发生规律及药剂防治试验 [J]. 福建农业科技，1995 (2)：18 - 19

[3] 高山，卞云云，陈柏君．生姜组织培养脱毒、快繁和高产栽培 [J]. 中国蔬菜，1999 (3)：40 - 41

[4] 徐坤，杨俊华．脱毒生姜及高产栽培技术 [J]. 长江蔬菜，2000 (8)：8 - 9

Different Hormone on The Rapid Propagation in Ginger Tissue Culture

LIU Yan-mei

(*Weifang University of Science and Technology*, *Shouguang* 262700)

Abstract: The experiment designed in D206 trial design with two factors of KT and NAA or 6-BA and NAA. The result shows, a mathematic model describing the relation between the yields and content of KT, 6-BA, NAA was established through calculation with an electronic computer. When analyzed, the model showed that the rapid propa -gation coefficient was influenced largely by KT, its change is most sensitive to propagation coefficient. The height of plant was influenced largely by NAA, its change is most sensitive to the height of plant, and there are mutual effects between the hormone. And the most suitable rapad-propagation medium is KT 2. 65mg/l and NAA 0. 43mg/l, the breed -ing coefficient reach 6. 4.

Key words: Ginger; Plant hormone; Tissue culture; Rapid propagation coefficient

大豆卵磷脂的制备工艺及其在食品工业中的应用

董美华[①] 唐玉海 韩金宏
（潍坊科技学院，寿光 262700）

摘 要： 本文对大豆卵磷脂的理化性质和功能特性进行了介绍说明，综述了目前比较常用的大豆卵磷脂的制备工艺，并阐述了大豆卵磷脂在食品工业中的应用，对大豆卵磷脂功能的开发利用作了展望。

关键词： 大豆卵磷脂；制备工艺；食品工业；应用

卵磷脂是一种具有重要的生理功能和乳化性能的天然物质，在动植物中分布很广，特别是在蛋黄和大豆中。大豆卵磷脂是和脑磷脂、肌磷脂、磷脂酸等构成磷脂类混合物大豆磷脂的一种甘油醇磷脂，又称磷脂酰胆碱。据报道，高纯度的卵磷脂有利于生成水包油型（O/W）的乳状液而被用作高档乳化剂[1]，同时卵磷脂因具有降低胆固醇，提高血清中胆碱水平，抑制乙醇引起的肝纤维化和肝硬化，促进胶原的瓦解并增强大脑记忆力的作用而引起医药、食品等领域的广泛重视。随着大豆磷脂生产加工技术的进步以及对大豆磷脂生物活性成分研究的深入，研制高纯度单一成分磷脂产品并拓展其应用空间已成为大豆磷脂开发的新趋势。本文对目前制备高纯度大豆卵磷脂的常用方法进行了概述，并对其在食品加工领域的应用作了描述，对大豆卵磷脂的开发前景作了展望。

1 大豆卵磷脂的制备工艺研究现状

大豆加工豆油的油脚中含有 40% ~50% 的磷脂，其中，大豆卵磷脂含量约为 16% ~20%。通过分离提纯可将大豆加工豆油的油脚中的油脂等杂质萃出，从而得到含丙酮不溶物含量达 95% 以上的纯净的粉末状磷脂，这是多种磷脂的混合物。目前从中提取出大豆卵磷脂即磷脂酰胆碱的制备方法有有机溶剂法、柱层析法、制备薄层色谱法、高效液相法、膜分离法、无机盐复合沉淀技术、超临界萃取技术、乙醇分馏法等。

1.1 有机溶剂法

传统的卵磷脂生产多采用有机溶剂进行提取，它具有生产能力大、周期短、便于连

---

① 董美华，女，学士，潍坊科技学院讲师。研究方向：食品科学与工程。E - mail：dongmeihua588@126.com

续操作、容易实现自动化、溶剂价格相对比较便宜、便于回收利用等优点。其原理是利用各磷脂组分在某些溶剂中溶解度的不同，将卵磷脂与它组分进行分离，所用溶剂一般为 C1～C4 的低碳醇、正己烷、石油醚、乙醚、乙酸乙酯等。卵磷脂在低碳醇中的溶解度较大，脑磷脂和鞘磷脂在低碳醇中溶解度较小。但卵磷脂不溶于丙酮。一般的工艺流程为先用丙酮溶解油的性质把大豆油脚中的油先除去，得到粗磷脂，再用低级醇，最常用的是乙醇把卵磷脂从几种磷脂的混合物提取出来。溶剂提取法的关键在于找到一个好的溶剂或溶剂系统，它对于被提取的目标产物应具有良好的溶解性和选择性。在提取时必须控制好温度、溶剂用量、溶剂浓度等。肇立春[2]总结出在卵磷脂的生产工艺中，浓缩前进行毛油过滤与油脚离心分离的操作，浓缩后浸洗前进行一次烘干除水，萃取时用浓度为 85% 的乙醇，控制丙酮液的 pH 值在 8.5 左右，吸附剂选择粉状活性碳，可得到较高产率的卵磷脂。关润伶等[3]用丙酮和乙醇对油脚进行提取，确定最佳提取条件为：用丙酮对油脚脱油的温度在 45℃为宜，脱油时间 60min，得到粗磷脂后，再用乙醇对其进行纯化提取，温度为 70℃，提取时间在 60min 以内，吸附剂选择粉状活性碳，得到了纯度为 82% 的卵磷脂。

1.2 柱层析法

柱层析是以吸附剂为固定相，移动相中的溶质在通过固定相时，由于它们的吸附和解吸能力的不同从而达到分离的目的。常用的吸附剂为硅胶、氧化铝、硅藻土等。洗脱液常选用氯仿、低碳醇等几种溶剂的混合物。曹栋等[4]用 Al_2O_3 装柱，用单一的无毒溶剂 95% 乙醇作洗脱剂，制得的卵磷脂纯度和得率均大于 90% 产品。为高纯度卵磷脂产品的制取提供了一定的实验基础。这一方法最大的特点是避免使用 CH_3OH 及 $CHCl_4$ 这类有一定毒性的溶剂。李卫等[5]以硅胶为吸附剂，用梯度差为（1∶2）～（2∶1）的甲醇和氯仿的混合液对卵磷脂进行梯度洗脱，洗脱剂用量仅为柱体积的 5～6 倍，洗脱时间仅为 6h。柱层析虽然可以得到含量 90% 左右的高纯度卵磷脂，但是处理量十分有限，而且要用到许多有一定毒性的有机溶剂。溶剂的蒸发消耗大量能源，以及产品中的溶剂残留都是这种方法的缺点。

1.3 制备薄层色谱法

经典的 TLC 法用于分离磷脂中各组分，彭一鸣等[6]用制备薄层色谱（PTLC）法对市售级大豆卵磷脂进行纯化，可得到纯度较高的卵磷脂，能作为薄层扫描实验中的标准样品，该提纯方法简单、快速、效果好，在科研过程中较为实用。

1.4 膜分离法

此法是根据磷脂中不同组分分子量的大小，它们通过半透膜的难易程度不同，可将卵磷脂从混合物中分离出来。例如，用己烷—异丙酮混合溶剂溶解的粗卵磷脂溶液通过聚丙烯半透膜，收集流过膜的溶液并蒸发，可大大提高纯度。有人提出将膜技术跟其他工艺合作，能有效分离磷脂，如李卫等[7]提出了用吸附剂、微滤膜去色、除杂，用金属盐沉淀剂除去脑磷脂的新工艺。膜技术由于没有使用化学试剂、节能，吸引了很多化学工程师的研究。膜抗污染的能力已经得到了很好的改善，但渗透量和膜的寿命仍制约着膜工艺的工业化。

1.5 无机盐复合沉淀技术[7]

该法是利用卵磷脂可和某些无机盐生成沉淀的性质，把卵磷脂从磷脂中提取出来，从而达到与其他磷脂分离、除去蛋白质和脂肪的目的。这样可大大提高卵磷脂纯度，为工业生产提供了一种方法。例如徐晨[8]对几种无机盐，$CdCl_2$、$MgCl_2$、$CaCl_2$、$ZnCl_2$ 提取大豆磷脂进行比较实验后认为 $MgCl_2$、$CaCl_2$ 的提纯卵磷脂纯度不高、卵磷脂的回收率很低。$CdCl_2$、$ZnCl_2$的提纯效果好，但 $CdCl_2$ 的毒性较大，不宜使用，$ZnCl_2$ 是较为理想的沉淀剂。李卫[9]通过对 5 种离子 Zn^{2+}、Mg^{2+}、Ba^{2+}、Fe^{2+}、金属离子 Ca 进行沉淀实验，从实验数据看出 Mg^{2+}、Ba^{2+}、Zn^{2+}对卵磷脂和脑磷脂的沉淀率相当，达不到分离的目的。Zn^{2+}对卵磷脂的沉淀效果较好，但同时对脑辚脂也产生较多的沉淀。Fe^{2+}对脑磷脂的沉淀率较高，但同时对卵磷脂也产生较大的沉淀，造成了卵磷脂的浪费。5 种离子中 Ca 是最佳的脑磷脂沉淀剂，几乎可以将乙醇浸提液中的脑磷脂全部沉淀下来，而对卵磷脂的沉淀很小，金属离子 Ca 是最佳的沉淀剂。有机溶剂无机盐复合沉淀法，实质上也属于有机溶剂法，只是在提取的过程中选择一种无机离子与卵磷脂或是脑磷脂形成沉淀而与另一种磷脂能混溶从而达到两种磷脂相分离的目的。该法可制得高纯度的卵磷脂，同时也得到了其他磷脂组分，实现物尽其用，减少“三废”污染。

1.6 超临界萃取技术

超临界流体萃取技术是 20 世纪 70 年代兴起的一门新的分离技术，尤其是超临界 CO_2 的应用开辟了一个全新的研究领域，成为多学科交叉的热点。由于超临界 CO_2 萃取操作参数易于控制，极为适合处理热敏性的物质，可制得高品质的粉末磷脂。超临界流体萃取技术是利用压力、温度高于临界点的超临界流体为溶剂进行物质提取。超临界流体既具有液体对溶质有较大的溶解度的特点，又具有气体易于扩散和运动的特性，在临界点附近，压力和温度的微小变化都可以引起流体密度很大的变化，并相应的表现为溶解度的变化。因此，人们可以利用压力、温度的变化来实现萃取和分离的过程。Dunford 等[10]用超临界二氧化碳—乙醇混合溶剂萃取 Canola 脱油磷脂，研究表明，在 55.2MPa、45℃，乙醇含量 13.0%（W%）的超临界条件下，得到萃取物中磷脂的卵磷脂含量高达 89%，但是得率很低。原因是脱油磷脂不像油粕那样疏松多孔，它很容易在萃取过程中成膏状，使得溶剂不易渗透进人内部萃取，所以萃取率较低。Teberiklcr 等[11]在 17.2MPa、60℃、10% 的乙醇为携带剂萃取脱油磷脂时，发现萃取物磷脂中 91% 是卵磷脂。提高压力到 20.7MPa，可以提高萃取率和卵磷脂的含量，卵磷脂在磷脂中的含量可以提高到 95%；但提高温度到 80℃时，萃取率和卵磷脂含量都下降，原因是温度升高，混合溶剂密度下降，对卵磷脂的溶解能力和选择性都下降。穆筱梅等[12]以溶剂法-超临界 CO_2 萃取法从大豆油脚中制取高纯度的大豆卵磷脂，工艺条件为：萃取压力 25MPa，温度 36℃，萃取 20min。用高效液相色谱测定，其纯度大于 95%。曾虹燕[13]等应用超临界 CO_2萃取技术从大豆中直接提取大豆油和纯度为 95.98% 的大豆磷脂。其确定的最佳萃取条件为：萃取压力 25MPa，温度 50℃，CO_2 流量 30 kg/ h，萃取时间 150 min，大豆磷脂夹带剂乙醇的流量为 3kg/h，得率分别为 15. 72% 和 19. 54% 。与传统提取工艺相比较，超临界 CO_2 流体萃取工艺具有节约溶剂、工艺流程简单等优点，适用于工业化生产。

1.7 其他方法

其他制备卵磷脂的方法还有高效液相法，乙醇分蒸馏法，乙酰化法等。

2 大豆卵磷脂在食品工业中的应用[14,15]

卵磷脂理化特性及其在食品加工上的应用实验研究证实，卵磷脂具有多种功能特性如乳化、防溅、速溶、润湿、分散、脱膜、改善黏度、发泡、晶化控制、结合蛋白质及营养源等，在食品加工领域有着广泛的用途。同时，因卵磷脂具有降低胆固醇，防止动脉硬化，保肝健脑的作用，可应用于新型保健食品的研制。

2.1 人造奶油和起酥油

卵磷脂是人造奶油和起酥油生产最常用的防溅剂和乳化剂，其用量一般为脂肪的 0. 1% ~0. 5%，通常与单甘酯或二甘酯混合使用，它能防止渗水与防溅，促进烘干过程的褐变，增强起酥效果，强化奶油中维生素 A 的抗氧化性。

2.2 巧克力、焦糖、涂覆层中

卵磷脂具有再乳化性、防黏结、释放性和黏度调节能力，对糖果产品性能产生重要影响，可以控制黏度、降低发粘及控制结晶。卵磷脂用于巧克力中可以提高巧克力的柔脆性，降低粘性并阻止表面起霜。

2.3 速溶食品

卵磷脂是良好的乳化剂、润湿剂和促溶剂。卵磷脂可以增加固液界面间的亲和性，使粉末食品颗粒迅速水合。在可可粉、早餐饮品、咖啡、代乳品、布丁等生产制作过程中加入适量的卵磷脂可有效的提高产品的速溶性。

2.4 烘焙食品

在面包、卷饼、炸面包圈、蛋糕、小甜饼、面制糕点等食品中，卵磷脂是必不可少的乳化剂、润湿剂和脱膜剂。它可促进面团中起酥油均匀分布，有利于发酵与水分吸收，改善面团加工过程，增加产品的营养性能，使产品质地更加柔顺细腻。此外磷脂的三维空间结构容易被包进直链淀粉的螺旋结构中，从而阻止直链淀粉发生重结晶，有助于延缓淀粉老化，保持淀粉新鲜、松软。卵磷脂亦能与面筋形成脂蛋白复合物，增加面筋的弹性和柔韧性，改善面团持气性，使焙烤产品获得更大的体积。

2.5 面点食品

由于卵磷脂是一种可提高水和油脂亲合性的物质，因此，在使用油脂加工食品中适用度很高。就面品而言，使用油脂的代表性面制品就是快餐面，加工快餐面时，为改善原料对油脂的亲合度可使用卵磷脂。吴正达[16]研究发现在不需使用油脂的切面和熟面添加卵磷脂后，能改变面的食感。具体来说，使面润滑、柔软且弹性增加，对面加工过程中的“作业性”产生良好的影响。此外，在炒面及中国汤面（汤中有油）中加入卵磷脂可使面味更加鲜美。

2.6 乳制品

在婴儿奶粉、代乳品、代蛋品、冰淇淋及调味品等乳制品中，卵磷脂可用作乳化剂、润湿剂、防溅剂和脱膜剂，在天然乳酪和人造乳酪中，还可用作有效的乳化剂和切片分离剂。

2.7 肉和家禽冻胶层、宠物食品中

卵磷脂是肉和家禽冻胶层、玩赏动物食品的棕色剂、乳化剂、磷酸盐分散剂及膳食补充剂，可防止脂肪分离。当配方设计合理时，磷脂可以大大降低甚至完全消除辣椒罐头、流质咖啡、肉汁及其他高含量动物脂肪产品的“脂肪覆盖现象”。

2.8 食品涂层和色拉

卵磷脂在食品涂层和色拉中用作乳化剂和控制结晶。

2.9 包装辅料中

卵磷脂添加于包装辅料中用作密封剂和脱膜剂，可提高食品包装材料的密封性，并可防止食品与外包装相粘。

2.10 用于操作装置

如用于煎炸成型机、挤压机、输送设备、烘焙用具、干燥器、混合机等，卵磷脂可作为有效的润滑剂、内外脱膜剂。可防止食品粘在烘烤工具上，从而减少用油量，降低产品损失，提高挤出食品的挤出流畅性，并协助食品成型，从而减少清理时间，提高生产效益。

2.11 营养保健食品

将卵磷脂与维生素 E、植物油脂、维生素等混合封入明胶软胶囊内制成滋补品，其营养价值很高；在婴儿食品中添加卵磷脂，有助于婴儿大脑的发育；同时，也可将卵磷脂制成糖尿病患者的营养品。刘丽影等[17]以卵磷脂、刺五加为原料，佐以其他成分，研制开发出一种营养丰富、口感较好的营养保健治疗口服液，长期服用对冠心病、脑动脉硬化、哮喘、失眠等病症能起到综合治疗加保健的双重作用。

3 展望

我国是一个大豆生产国，拥有丰富的大豆磷脂资源。但目前，我国市场上的卵磷脂产品80%以上为浓缩磷脂，而浓缩磷脂由于其乳化性能不好、异味大，应用受到很大限制。同时，医药、保健品、化妆品等行业需要大量的高纯度卵磷脂。因而高纯度卵磷脂的生产已是当前国家重点支持的技术开发领域之一。目前，最具发展前景的还属超临界 CO_2 提取法，但其工艺复杂，成本较高，对规模化生产有难度，还需进一步研究优化工艺，实现工业化，降低成本，以满足不断增长的需求。随着更先进技术的研发，相信大豆卵磷脂在今后会有更广阔的发展前景。

参考文献

[1] 王墨林，安红，陈志强等．大豆磷脂的系统研究与开发．精细化工，2001，18（1）：7－13

[2] 肇立春．大豆卵磷脂生产工艺探讨．粮油加工与食品机械，2003，（3）：40－41

[3] 关润伶，朱红．大豆磷脂的纯化研究．中国食品添加剂，2006，（4）：45－47

[4] 曹栋，裘爱泳等．三氧化二铝柱层析法分离大豆磷脂中磷脂酰胆碱的研究．中国油脂，2001，26（6）：51－53

[5] 李卫．柱层析法分离卵磷脂和脑磷脂．湖北工学院学报，2001，16（2）：63－65

[6] 彭一鸣，蒋笃孝．PTLC 法纯化大豆卵磷脂及鉴定．中国油脂，2002，27（6）：62－64

[7] 李卫，邵友元．高纯度大豆卵磷脂制备研究．中国油脂，2001，26（2）：6－8

[8] 关润伶，邹静，朱红．大豆磷脂的分离纯化研究进展．中国食品添加剂，2005，（5）：44－47

[9] 徐晨．大豆卵磷脂的提纯研究，天然产物研究与开发，1998，10（2）：75－78

[10] Nurhan Turgut Dundord，Feral Temelli. Exbaction of Phospho-lipids form Canola with Supercritical Carbon Dioxide and Ethanol. JAOCS，1995，72（9）：1 009－1 015

[11] Leyla Teberikler. Selective Extraction of Phosphatidylch0line from lecithin by Supercritical Carbon Dioxide/Ethanol Mixture. JAOCS，2001，78（2）：115－118

[12] 穆筱梅，方芳等．大豆卵磷脂脂质体制备的研究．中国油脂，2003，28（3）：45－46

[13] 曾虹燕，方芳，蒋丽娟．超临界 CO_2 萃取大豆油与大豆磷脂工艺条件研究．生物技术，2003，13（2）：37－39

[14] 庞坤，韩立强，李维琳．卵磷脂的性质及其应用．安徽农业科学，2006，34（9）：1 772－1 773

[15] 朱杰，张百刚．卵磷脂在食品加工与营养保健研究中的应用．食品研究与开发，2005，26（3）：131－133

[16] 吴正达．卵磷脂在面条中的应用．粮油加工，2003，（1）：19－20

[17] 刘丽影，刘国华等．大豆卵磷脂口服液的研制．食品加工，2002，6（23）：91－92

The Preparation Process of the Soybean Lecithin and its Application in Food Industry

DONG Mei-hua　TANG Yu-hai　HAN Jin-hong
(*Weifang University of Science and Tecnology*, *Shouguang* 262700)

Abstract: This paper mainly introduced the physical and chemical properties and functional characteristics of the soybean lecithin, reviewed its preparation processes used commonly and elaborated its application in the food industry. At the same time, the functional development and availability of the soybean lecithin was introduced prospectively.
Key words: Soybean lecithin; Preparation process; Food industry; Application

ISSR 标记在 17 个茶树品种遗传多样性中的应用研究*

唐玉海① 崔香菊 董美华 韩金宏

(潍坊科技学院，寿光 262700)

摘 要：用筛选到的 12 个 ISSR 引物对 17 个茶树品种的基因组 DNA 进行扩增，结果共扩增出 61 条带，其中多态性条带 53 条，多态性为 87.08%，平均每个引物组合扩增出 5.08 条带。根据 Nei-Li 系数将 17 个茶树品种聚为两类。结果显示，ISSR 是一种重复性好、高效率的分子标记，可以用于茶树品种的遗传多态性分析。

关键词：ISSR；茶树；聚类分析；分子标记

茶树优良品种的选育对茶叶产量和品质有着重要的作用。茶树由于通常采用杂交育种，所以亲本的选配尤为重要，福建省茶树品种资源丰富，掌握其遗传关系是茶树育种工作的关键。随着分子生物学的发展，分子标记技术已越来越广泛地应用于茶树品种鉴定和亲缘关系上，分子标记是基因组 DNA 水平差异的直接反映，多态性好，且不受环境的影响。目前，已经有一些 DNA 分子标记如 RAPD[1~6]、RFLP[7,8,9]、AFLP[10~13] 等相继应用于茶树品种鉴定和亲缘关系分析上。但这些方法都有一定的局限性：RAPD 虽然操作简单，但由于引物序列较短，退火温度低，所以重复性难以保证，而 AFLP、RFLP 由于步骤繁琐，技术要求高，成本高，所以也难以广泛应用。

1994 年，Zietkiewicz[14] 等发展了 ISSR（inter-simple sequence repeat）标记，它是根据基因组内广泛存在的微卫星序列设计单一引物，对两侧具有反向排列 SSR 的一段 DNA 序列进行扩增，ISSR 引物通常为 16~18 个碱基，由于微卫星在基因组中广泛分布且等位变异特别丰富，因而 ISSR 可以检测到很高的多态性，其产物多态性比 RFLP、SSR、RAPD 更加丰富；同时，由于其引物序列较长，所以 ISSR 具有更好的重复性。ISSR 在茶树种质资源鉴定和亲缘关系的分析上已经有所应用[15~20]，本研究利用 ISSR 标记方法来分析供试材料的遗传多样性，试图为茶树种质资源的鉴定和遗传多样性的分析提供技术支持。

---

* 基金项目：福建省自然科学基金项目（B0510025）；福建省教育厅科技计划项目（JA05333）

① 唐玉海，男，硕士，潍坊科技学院讲师。研究方向：蛋白质化学和分子标记。E－mail：tangyh209@163.com

1 材料和方法

1.1 材料

本实验所用17个茶树品种及来源详见表1。取样地点为福建省农业科学院茶叶研究所种质资源圃，取一芽二叶，置于-20℃冰箱备用。实验用ISSR引物由上海闪晶生物工程公司合成，所用Taq聚合酶、dNTP等购自大连宝生物Takara公司。

表1 供试材料名称和编号

编号	品种名	原产地
1	凤凰黄枝香单枞	广东潮安
2	白毛2号	广东英德
3	白样观音	福建安溪
4	鸿雁1号	广东英德
5	优4	福建福安
6	鸿雁7号	广东英德
7	福鼎大白茶	福建福鼎
8	鸿雁9号	广东英德
9	玉龙	福建福安
10	太姥山野茶	福建福鼎
11	尧山秀绿	广西桂林
12	武义早	浙江武义
13	丹桂	福建福安
14	浙农117	浙江杭州
15	茂绿	浙江杭州
16	浙农139	浙江杭州
17	春兰	福建福安

1.2 方法

1.2.1 DNA的提取

所有茶树样品基因组DNA的提取参照罗军武[21]文献中的CTAB法，并作适当改进，具体方法为：用液氮迅速研磨叶片至细末，然后装入2.0ml的eppendorf离心管，加入提取预处理液1ml（0.4mol/L的葡萄糖，3%的聚乙烯吡咯烷酮），混匀后5 000 rpm离心，然后倒掉上清液，留下沉淀，其余步骤按照常规的CTAB法进行操作。1%的琼脂糖凝胶电泳检测质量，并用Ultrospec2100pro UV/Spectrophotometer型核酸蛋白仪测定浓度。

1.2.2 ISSR－PCR 扩增和产物检测

参照姚明哲等[20,21]建立的茶树 ISSR-PCR 体系，反应体系总体积为 20μl，PCR 组分如下：2μl10 × PCR buffer，200μmol/L dNTP，1. 0U Taq 酶，引物 0. 4μmol/L，50ng 的模板 DNA。扩增程序为：94℃预变性 7min；94℃变性 1min，退火 45s（各引物退火温度见表 2），72℃延伸 90s，35 个循环；循环结束后 72℃延伸 7min。扩增反应在 Eppendorf Mastercycle PCR 扩增仪上进行。PCR 产物用含 0. 5μg/ml EB 的 1. 5% 的琼脂糖凝胶 140V 电泳 1h，用 VILBER LOURMAT 公司凝胶成像系统照相并保存。

1.2.3 数据处理与分析

将保存的图片采用人工计数，同一位置条带有记为 1，无则记为 0，建立 Excel 表格的数据库，根据 Nei[22]的方法计算相似系数 F，$F = 2N_{xy} / (N_x + N_y)$，式中 Nxy 为 X 和 Y 扩增的共有条带数；Nx 和 Ny 分别为 X 和 Y 的扩增总条带数. 遗传距离指数 D（Genetic Distance index）：$D = 1 - F$。根据遗传距离用类平均聚类法（UPGMA）对供试品种进行聚类分析，绘制遗传关系树状图。

2 结果与分析

2.1 茶树基因组 DNA 检验

改良的 CTAB 法提取的茶叶基因组 DNA 电泳后，呈现出一条迁移率很小的整齐条带，提取的 DNA 样品比较纯，无 RNA 污染，也没有多糖等其他杂质污染。DNA 片断大小在 21kb 左右。用 Ultrospec2100 pro UV/Spectrophotometer 型核酸蛋白仪对本实验选用的 17 个茶树品种样本的基因组 DNA 分别进行了总 DNA 纯度和浓度的测定，得出 OD_{260}/OD_{280} 比值集中 1. 62 ~ 1. 99 之间，符合 ISSR-PCR 扩增的要求。

2.2 ISSR 扩增产物多态性

从 100 个 ISSR 引物组合中，选用了 12 个多态性较好引物对 17 个茶树品种进行扩增，共产生了 61 条带，其中多态性条带 53 条，占总条带的 87. 08%，条带大小大约在 250 ~ 1 500bp，不同引物扩增的条带数 3 ~ 8 条不等，平均每个引物扩增 5. 08 条，多态性最高为 100%，最低为 67%（表 2）。引物 20 号、823 号扩增出的条带数最多（8 条），而引物 848 号只扩增出 3 条。按不同茶树品种计算扩增条带数，则扩增条带数最多的品种（凤凰黄枝香单枞、优 4）能产生 45 条，最少的 27 条（玉龙）。引物 46 号和 818 号的扩增结果见图 1、图 2。

表 2　ISSR-PCR 产物多态性

引物编号	引物序列（5’ ~3’）	退火温度（℃）	条带总数	多态性条带数	多态性比例（%）
77	TCTCTCTCTCTCTCTCG	56	4	4	100
814	CTCTCTCTCTCTCTCTA	52	5	4	80
815	CTCTCTCTCTCTCTCTG	52	4	4	100
818	CACACACACACACACAG	56	6	5	83
823	TCTCTCTCTCTCTCTCC	52	8	7	87. 5

（续表）

引物编号	引物序列（5'～3'）	退火温度（℃）	条带总数	多态性条带数	多态性比例（%）
858	TGTGTGTGTGTGTGTGRT	56	5	4	80
848	CACACACACACACACARG	52	3	2	67
20	GGGTGGGGTGGGGTG	56	8	7	87.5
21	GGAGAGGAGAGGAGA	56	5	4	80
46	ACACACACACACACAC（CT）T	56	5	4	80
825	ACACACACACACACACT	52	4	4	100
826	ACACACACACACACACC	52	4	4	100
	总计			61	53
	平均		5.08	4.42	87.08

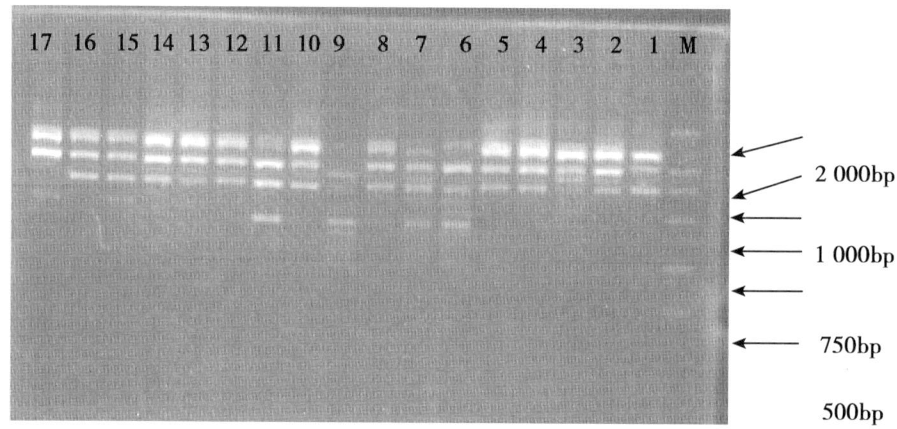

图 1 引物 46 对茶树基因组 DNA 的 ISSR－PCR 扩增结果电泳图谱

注：M 为 Takara 公司的 DL2000；1～17 代表的品种名与表 1 一致

2.3 茶树品种间的遗传距离和聚类分析

根据 ISSR 扩增产物的电泳结果，根据 Nei 的方法计算出 17 个茶树品种间的遗传距离。根据统计分析结果，用 UPGMA 法构建了 17 个茶树品种的分子系统树（图 3）。由图 3 可以看出，供试品种的遗传距离在 0.12 到 0.692 31之间，茂绿和浙农 139 之间的遗传距离最近为 0.12；玉龙和太姥山野茶间的遗传距离最远，为 0.692 31，平均遗传距离 0.367 09。聚类分析将 17 个品种聚为两大类，凤凰黄枝香单枞、白样观音、鸿雁 1 号、优 4、丹桂、浙农 117、茂绿、浙农 139、春兰、白毛 2 号、太姥山野茶、鸿雁 9 号、武义早聚为一类，鸿雁 7 号、尧山秀绿、玉龙、福鼎大白茶聚为一类。前一大类中白毛 2 号、太姥山野茶、鸿雁 9 号、武义早聚为一类，其他 9 个品种聚为一类。

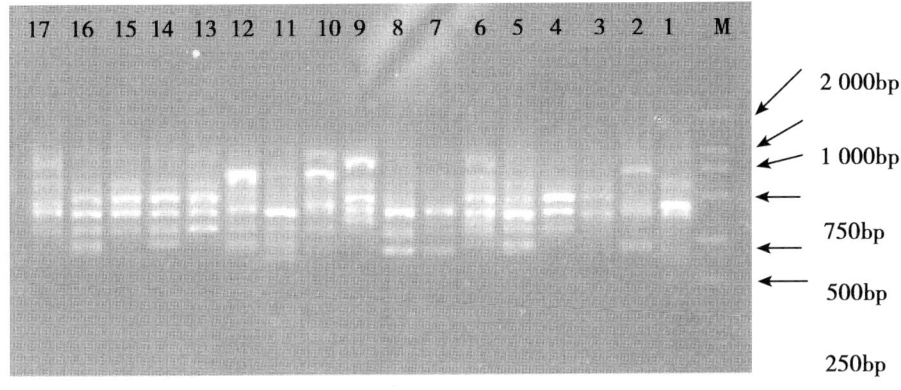

图 2 引物 818 对茶树基因组 DNA 的 ISSR－PCR 扩增结果

注：M 为 Takara 公司的 DL2000；1～17 代表的品种名与表 1 一致

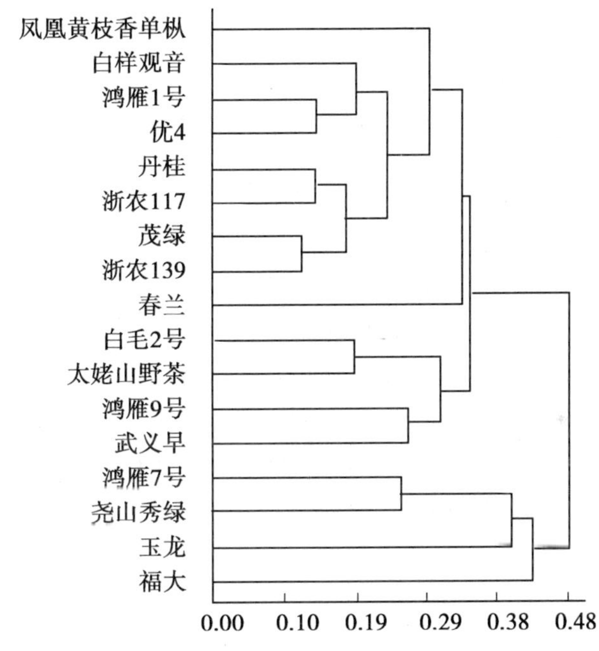

图 3 供试品种遗传关系树状图

3 讨论

由于茶树叶片富含茶多酚、多糖等物质，DNA 的提取和纯化相对比较困难，可能影响 PCR 扩增。本研究采用改良的 CTAB 法提取茶树基因组 DNA，在提取前加入提取预处理液，整个提取过程中提取液均保持原来的绿色，无褐变现象发生，并且得到的 DNA 经电泳检测显示条带整齐，无 RNA 或者多糖等杂质污染，无论从纯度还是浓度均符合试验要求，效果比较理想。

多态位点百分率是衡量物种遗传变异水平高低的一个重要指标，是度量遗传多样性的重要参数。Harmrick 和 Godt[23]用等位酶对 449 种植物进行遗传变异研究，揭示种的多态位点平均水平为 50.5%，种群多态位点平均水平为 34.2%。本研究 ISSR 分析的 17 个茶树品种的平均多态性比率达到了 87.08%，这一结果表明茶树具有丰富的遗传多样性，遗传基础比较广泛。如此高的多态性与我国茶树种质资源丰富，茶树分布地区广泛，不同茶树产区各有特定的生态环境，所栽培的品种一般具有明显的区域适应性以及茶树长期的异花授粉造成的遗传背景高度复杂等因素有关。

ISSR 由于具有操作简单，重复性好，效率高的特点，相对其他几种标记有着明显的优越性。何予卿等[24]用 ISSR 分子标记研究了 37 份栽培稻和野生稻的亲缘关系。结果 38 个 ISSR 引物共扩增出 133 个多态性条带，每个引物平均扩增多态性条带 7.4 个。李进波等[25]用 ISSR 和 SSR 标记建立了 24 个水稻光温敏核不育系的 DNA 指纹图谱，利用 13 个 ISSR 引物和 20 对 SSR 引物，分别获得 174 个多态性片段和 62 个多态性片段，平均每个 ISSR 引物检测到 13.38 个多态性片段，远远高于 SSR 引物的检测率。本研究表明，ISSR 标记在揭示茶树品种遗传关系和遗传多态性方面是一种高效的分子标记，因此，在茶树的遗传育种中，通过 ISSR 标记更好地了解茶树品种资源、开展茶树品种资源鉴定，必将为提高育种效率提供了一种科学、快捷的技术手段。

参考文献

[1] Wachira F N, Waugh R, Hackett C et al. Detection of genetic diversity in tea (C sinensis) using RAPD markers [J]. Genome, 1995, 38: 201 - 210

[2] Wachira F N. Characterization and estimation of genetic relatedness among heterogeneous population of relatedness among heterogeneous population of commercial tea clones by random amplification of genomic DNA samples [J]. Tea, 1997, 18 (1): 11 - 20

[3] Wachira F N . Genetic diversity in tea revealed by randomly amplified polymorphic DNA markers [J]. Tea, 1996, 17 (2): 60 - 68

[4] 罗军武，施兆鹏，李家贤等 . RAPD 分子标记技术在茶树亲子鉴定中的应用 [J]. 湖南农业大学学报（自然科学版），2002，28 (6): 502 - 505

[5] 梁月荣，田中淳一，武田善行. 应用分子标记分析“晚绿”品种的杂交亲本 [J]. 茶叶科学，2000，20 (1): 22 - 26

[6] 罗军武，施兆鹏，沈程文等. 茶树种质资源遗传多样性的 RAPD 分析 [J]. 作物学报，2004，30 (3): 266 - 269

[7] 韩文炎译 . Horticultural Abstracts，2003，73 (1)，117，765，中国茶叶 . 2003，6: 38

[8] 谢国禄摘译 . Breeding science 54 (3) . 2004，技术与方法: 18

[9] 陈宗懋译 . Horticultural Abstract，2002，72 (11)，1511，10416，1 中国茶叶 . 2003，5: 37

[10] T. Balasaravanan, P. K. Pius R. Raj Kumar, N. Muraleedharan, A. K. Shasany Genetic Camellia diversity among south Indian tea germplasm camellia sinensis,

C. assamica and C. assamica spp. lasiocalyx) using AFLP markers [J]. Plant Science 165 (2003) 365 -372

[11] Paul S W, achira F N, Powell W and Waugh R. Diversity and genetic differentiation among populations of Indian and Kenyan tea revealed by AFLP markers [J]. Theor Appl Genet, 1997, (94): 255 -263

[12] Wachira F N , et al. Genetic variation and differentiation in tea (*Camellia sinensis*) germplasm revealed by RAPD and AFLP variation [J]. Journal of Horticultural Science and Biotechnology, 2001, 76 (5): 557 -563

[13] 黄福平，梁月荣，陆建良等．乌龙茶种质资源种群遗传多样性 AFLP 评价 [J]. 茶叶科学 2004，24 (3): 183 -189

[14] Zietkiewicz E, Rafalski A, Labuda D. Genome fingerprinting by simple sequence repeat (SSR) 2anchored polymerase chain reaction amplification [J]. *Genomics*, 1994, 20 (2) : 176 -183

[15] Jou Ann Lai, Wei-Chen Yang and Ju-Ying Hsiao. An assessment of genetic relationships in cultivated tea clones and native wild tea in Taiwan using RAPD and ISSR markers [J]. Bot BuU Acad Sin. 2001. 42: 93 -100

[16] Hu C Y, Tsai Y Z and Lin S F. Using ISSR DNAmarkers to evaluate genetic diversity of tea germplasm in Taiwan. [J]. Agri. Assoc. China. 2005, 6 (5): 463 -480

[17] 姚明哲，黄海涛，余继忠等．ISSR 在茶树品种分子鉴别和亲缘关系研究中的适用性分析 [J]. 茶叶科学．2005，25 (2): 153 -157

[18] 侯渝嘉，何桥，李品武等．川渝茶树种质资源遗传多样性 ISSR 分析 [J]. 第四届海峡两岸茶业学术研讨会论文集，2006，85 -89

[19] 谭和平，徐利远，余桂蓉等．茶树种质资源 ISSR 分子标记初步研究 [J]. 核农学报 2006，20 (2): 113 -115

[20] 姚明哲，王新超，陈亮等．茶树 ISSR-PCR 反应体系的建立 [J]，茶叶科学 .2004，24 (3): 172 -176

[21] 罗军武，沈程文，施兆鹏．茶树基因组 DNA 提取纯化技术研究 [J]. 茶叶通讯，2002，(4): 20 -24

[22] Nei M, Li W H. Mathematical model for studying genetic variation in terms of restriction endonucleases [J]. PNAS USA, 1979, 76: 5 269 -5 273

[23] Harmrick J L, Godt M J W. Alloayme diversity in plant species. Plant Population Genetics, Breeding and Genetic Resources [M]. Sunderland Mass: Sinauer. 1989, 43 -46

[24] 何予卿，张宇，孙梅等．利用 ISSR 分子标记研究栽培稻和野生稻亲缘关系 [J]. 农业生物技术学报，2001，9 (2): 123 -127

[25] 李进波，江良容，李春海等．水稻光温敏核不育系 ISSR 和 SSR 遗传分析比较 [J]. 分子植物育种，2003，1 (1): 42 -47

Application of ISSR Markers in Polymorphism of 17 Tea (*Camellia sinensis*) Cultivars

TANG Yu-hai　CUI Xiang-ju　DONG Mei-hua　HAN Jin-hong

(*Weifang University of Science and Technology*, *Shouguang* 262700)

Abstract: Inter-simple sequence repeat (ISSR) is a recently developed molecular technology. In this study, the Applicability of ISSR on relationship analysis of tea cultivars was carried out. 61 bands were amplified by 12 primers, of which 53 was polymorphic. The average polymorphism was 87. 08% and each primer combination amplified 5. 08 bands averagely. The results of this study indicate that ISSR is a high efficiency molecular markers with good repeatability, it is a useful tool for relationship analysis of tea cultivars.

Key words: ISSR; Tea (*Camelliasinensis*); Phylogenic analysis; Molecular markers

不同基因型桃枝条的解剖特征与树体矮化的关系

王成霞[①] 孙 虎

（潍坊科技学院，寿光 262700）

摘 要： 以普通型品种——春艳、短枝型品种——超红短枝和极矮化型桃——寿星桃3种生长类型桃树的一年生新梢为试材，对其节间长度和部分解剖结构指标的相关性进行了分析研究。结果表明，不同生长类型桃各解剖结构指标存在显著和极显著差异。韧皮部面积/横断面积比值和筛管密度与节间长度分别呈极显著负相关和正相关；维管束的数量、枝导管密度和面积、枝导管总面积/木质部面积比值、枝木质部面积/横断面面积比值与节间长度呈显著正相关；枝皮率与节间长度呈负相关，但相关性不显著。

关键词： 桃；解剖结构；矮化；相关性

普通桃品种普遍表现生长过旺，树势难控制，管理难度大，树冠易郁闭，结果部位外移快，结果年限缩短等缺点。因此，生产上多用化学药物控制，这既增加了劳动量，也不符合绿色食品的生产要求。所以，对桃树的矮化机制进行研究，选择有效的矮化预选指标，尽快的选育矮化和短枝型品种用于生产，是桃树生产上亟待解决的重要问题。有关果树根枝的解剖结构与树体矮化关系的研究，以前很多学者多以苹果、柑橘、梨等树种为试材，研究也较深入[1~7]。由于桃树的生物学特性与其他树种相比，存在较大的差别，故对桃树各生长类型方面的研究甚少。本试验以普通型、半矮化型和极矮化型桃品种的新梢为试材，研究了部分解剖学指标与树体矮化的关系，并将部分指标与其相对应的新梢节间长度进行了相关性分析，以探讨桃树的解剖学矮化机理，为矮化、短枝型品种选育找出科学的预选指标，为桃树矮化密植、丰产优质栽培和优良矮化、短枝型品种选育提供理论依据。

1 材料与方法

试验于2005－2006年在潍坊科技职业学院实验站进行。试验材料为普通型桃品种春艳（*Prunus persica* Stoke）、短枝型品种超红短枝（*P. persica* var. *nectarina* Maxim.）和

① 王成霞，女，硕士，潍坊科技学院讲师。研究方向：果树矮化机理。E－mail：412178377@qq. com

极矮化型桃寿星桃（*P. persica* var. *densa* Mak.），其基砧均为青州蜜桃（*Prunus persica* Stoke）。随机区组设计，每一类型桃均4株为一小区，重复3次。树龄2～3年生，株行距2m×1m，并设置保护行。

取各品种树冠外围发育正常，粗度0.3～0.5cm的新梢，每株10个。测量完整新梢的节间长度；用游标卡尺测量新梢距基部10cm处的皮层厚度、木质部厚度，计算枝皮率；切取新梢距基部10～15cm处的材料，用FAA液固定，采用石蜡切片法，切取厚度10μm的横切片制成永久切片，在Olympus生物显微镜下观察，每个类型选10～20个样片，每片镜检3个视野观测。统计分析横切面上导管、筛管的密度、孔径大小，木质部、韧皮部的面积及其与横切面总面积的比值。用Duncan's新复极差法对不同生长类型桃间新梢解剖结构指标进行差异显著性检验，并用Excel对新梢解剖结构各指标与对应品种节间长度间的相关性进行分析。

2 结果与分析

2.1 不同生长类型桃新梢节间长度间的差异分析

同龄树3个生长类型桃树体矮化程度，从大到小依次为寿星桃、超红短枝和春艳。这3种类型桃新梢节间长度的测量、分析结果见表1。

从表1可以看出，新梢的节间长度随矮化程度的增强，逐渐降低。并且3个品种间的差异均达到了极显著水平。最大的是春艳，为2.07cm，最小的是寿星桃，只有0.63cm。春艳新梢的节间长度是寿星桃的3.3倍，是超红短枝的近1.5倍。

表1 三种类型桃新梢的节间长度比较

品种	春艳	超红短枝	寿星桃
节间长（cm）	2.074 92Aa	1.397 62Bb	0.634 51Cc

注：小写和大写字母分别表示达到5%显著和1%极显著水平，以下同

2.2 不同生长类型桃新梢解剖结构与树体矮化的关系

枝皮率是预测树体矮化与否的一个重要指标。从表2可以看出枝皮率与树体的矮化程度呈正相关，即枝皮率越大，树体越矮化。枝皮率最大的是寿星桃为0.484，比春艳的高33.7%。但与超红短枝的差异不显著。春艳与超红短枝及寿星桃间枝皮率的差异均达到了极显著水平。

从表2还可以看出，新梢维管束的数量与树体的矮化程度呈负相关。随乔化程度的增强，新梢维管束加粗，数量增多。且维管束的数量在3个品种间差异均达到了极显著水平。春艳的维管束数量为28.6个，比寿星桃的高74.4%。在维管束的面积方面，春艳与超红短枝间的差异不显著，而这两个品种与寿星桃间的差异达到了极显著水平。说明茎部维管束发达，更有利于水分、无机盐、养分等的运输，这与普通品种桃树生长势强相吻合。所以，维管束的数量和面积可作为预测树体矮化的一个重要指标。

新梢导管密度和面积与树体矮化程度呈显著负相关，随新梢导管密度和面积的减小，树体的矮化程度变大。导管密度和面积在各品种之间的差异均达到了极显著水平。导管密度和面积最大的是春艳，分别为 77 个/mm^2 和 0. 000 76mm^2，最小的是寿星桃，仅为 54. 54 个/mm^2 和 0. 000 33mm^2，春艳的导管平均面积为寿星桃的 2. 3 倍。这表明，导管变少、变窄，使矮化型品种的输导效率在一定程度上受限，枝条吸收的养分消耗少，积累多，植株营养生长弱、树体矮化[8,9]。试验结果为解释短枝型品种矮化、早果的生理机制提供了细胞解剖学依据。

导管总面积占木质部面积和木质部平均面积占横断面面积之比在各品种之间的差异均极显著，寿星桃最小，其值分别为 2. 63% 和 25. 67%，最大的是春艳，分别为 4. 07% 和 35. 37%，超红短枝居中，且与矮化程度呈显著负相关。说明在桃树上此测定值能准确反映品种的矮化特性。

韧皮部中筛管密度在 3 个品种间的差异极显著，且与生长势呈显著正相关。春艳韧皮部中筛管的平均密度为 5. 17 个/mm^2，而寿星桃的为 3. 46 个/mm^2。在筛管面积方面，3 个品种间的差异达到了显著水平，春艳和超红短枝及寿星桃间的差异极显著。筛管总面积与韧皮部面积之比在 3 个品种间的差异不显著。韧皮部面积与横断面积之比在 3 个品种间的差异均达到了极显著水平。最大的是寿星桃，为 27. 1%，比超红短枝大 4. 4%，最小的是春艳，只有 16. 6%。

表 2 三种类型桃新梢解剖结构

品种	春艳	超红短枝	寿星桃
枝皮率（%）	0. 362 00Bb	0. 461 00Aa	0. 484 00Aa
横断面维管束平均数量（个）	28. 600 0Aa	24. 600 0Bb	16. 40 00Cc
维管束平均面积（mm^2）	0. 155 30Aa	0. 154 70Aa	0. 120 30Bb
木质部中导管平均密度（个/mm^2）	77. 000 0Aa	60. 770 0Bb	54. 540 0Cc
导管平均面积（mm^2）	0. 000 76Aa	0. 000 51Bb	0. 000 33Cc
导管总面积/木质部面积（%）	4. 070 00Aa	3. 070 00Bb	2. 630 00Cc
木质部平均面积/横断平均面积（%）	35. 370 0Aa	28. 600 0Bb	25. 670 0Cc
韧皮部中筛管平均密度（个/mm^2）	5. 170 00Aa	4. 250 00Bb	3. 460 00Cc
筛管平均面积（mm^2）	0. 000 09Aa	0. 000 07Bb	0. 000 06Bc
筛管总面积/韧皮部面积（%）	0. 035 00Aa	0. 032 00Aa	0. 024 00Aa
韧皮部平均面积/横断平均面积（%）	16. 600 0Cc	22. 700 0Bb	27. 100 0Aa

2. 3 不同生长类型桃新梢解剖结构与节间长度的相关性分析

枝条长度是树体生长习性的重要组成部分，也是生长速率、节间长度等的最终体现，节间长度则与枝条长度直接相关，也在很大程度上影响树体的高度。分析节间长短与相对应的不同生长类型桃树新梢的解剖结构指标的相关性，即可判断树体矮化性与这些指标间的关系。

由表 3 得出，新梢节间长度与筛管平均密度存在极显著正相关性，相关系数达

0.996 9，这说明，筛管密度越大，对应品种新梢的节间长度越长，表现出生长势越强；节间长度与韧皮部平均面积/横断面平均面积的比值存在极显著负相关性，相关系数为 -0.991 9，也就是说，随着韧皮部平均面积/横断面平均面积的比值的增大，对应品种新梢的节间长度变短，树体矮化性越强。

节间长度与维管束数量、导管密度、导管面积、导管总面积/木质部面积、木质部面积/横断面面积、筛管面积呈显著正相关，相关系数分别为 0.986 9、0.959 4、0.988 1、0.967 5、0.966 6、0.974 9，即维管束越多、导管越粗越多、筛管越粗，对应品种新梢的节间长度越长，表现出生长势越强。

节间长度与枝皮率呈负相关，相关系数为 -0.928 8，但相关性没有达到显著水平。

相关系数的绝对值越大，说明其相关性越强。从表 3 得出，新梢解剖结构各指标与节间长度的相关系数的绝对值按大小排序得：筛管密度 > 韧皮部面积/横断面面积 > 维管束数量 > 导管面积 > 筛管面积 > 导管面积/木质部面积 > 木质部面积/横断面面积 > 导管密度 > 枝皮率，这说明，筛管密度的大小与树体矮化程度的相关性最强；其次为韧皮部面积/横断面面积、维管束数量 > 导管面积、筛管面积、导管面积/木质部面积、木质部面积/横断面面积、导管密度，以上指标可作为桃树矮化性的预选指标；而枝皮率与节间长度的负相关性不显著，可作为矮化预选时的参考指标。

表 3 新梢解剖部分指标与节间长度的相关系数（r）和回归方程（y = a + bx）

新梢解剖部分指标		节间长度
枝皮率	r	-0.928 8
	y = a + bx	y = -10.325x + 5.867 3
横断面维管束平均数量	r	0.986 9*
	y = a + bx	y = 0.114 4x - 1.284
木质部中导管平均密度	r	0.959 4*
	y = a + bx	y = 0.059 6 - 2.453 2
导管平均面积	r	0.988 1*
	y = a + bx	y = 3 287.9x - 0.373 5
导管总面积/木质部面积	r	0.967 5*
	y = a + bx	y = 0.944 9x - 1.708 3
木质部平均面积/横断面平均面积	r	0.966 6*
	y = a + bx	y = 0.14x - 2.816 4
韧皮部中筛管平均密度	r	0.996 9**
	y = a + bx	y = 0.839 5x - 2.235
筛管平均面积	r	0.974 9*
	y = a + bx	y = 459 92x - 2.003 8
韧皮部平均面积/横断面平均面积	r	-0.991 9**
	y = a + bx	y = -0.135 6x + 4.369 3

注：*、** 分别表示达到显著和极显著水平，$r_{0.05} = 0.950$，$r_{0.01} = 0.990$，df = 2

3 讨论

前人在苹果、柑橘砧木上的研究结果表明砧木枝皮率可以用来预测砧木的矮化性[4,7]。枝条导管密度越大，导管总面积占木质部面积百分率越大，生长势越强[3]。但本研究统计结果发现，在桃树各生长类型之间的枝皮率差异极显著，其与节间长度呈负相关，相关性却不显著。

营养物质运输是决定植物长势和品质好坏的一个重要因素，而植物体内养分和水分的运转主要是靠维管束进行的[10]，所以维管束越粗、数量越多，养分供应越好，生长势越强[9]。本研究结果认为维管束的数量和面积与生长势呈正相关。维管束的数量在3个品种间的差异极显著，与节间长度呈显著正相关。

导管的主要作用是输导水分并且把随水分运输而来的矿质营养传输到各个营养器官。根据本试验来看，枝条导管密度和面积在3个品种间的差异显著性达到极显著水平，与节间长度呈显著相关，所以，枝条导管密度和面积可以有效的反映导管水分传输及矿质营养的供给能力，平均值越大，说明树体运输营养的能力越强，容易导致树体乔化。枝条导管总面积/木质部面积和木质部面积/横断面面积比值可以有效的区分生长势不同品种之间的区别，且本研究结果认为，两者比值与节间长度呈显著正相关。

筛管的主要作用是将地上部合成的同化产物运输到地下部，筛管密度和面积越大，其运输同化产物的能力愈强，促进了地下部的生长，反过来又增强了生长势。本试验结果表明，筛管密度和面积在3个品种间的差异均达到了极显著水平，且筛管密度与节间长度呈极显著正相关，与张玉兰[3]在山楂上的的研究结果一致。筛管面积/韧皮部面积的比值与生长势无相关性。韧皮部面积与横断面积之比与节间长度呈极显著负相关，在3个品种间的差异极显著。

参 考 文 献

[1] 王中英，解思敏，杨佩芳等．苹果矮砧解剖构造研究［J］．果树科学，1988，5（1）：6－10

[2] F. Loreti，R MassaiF. cinelli，et al. Evaluation of eleven dwarfing apple rootstocks：preliminary results［J］．Acta Hort，2001，557：155－157

[3] 张玉兰，杨焕芝．枝、叶解剖构造、过氧化物酶活性与山楂属种、株型生长势的关系［J］．内蒙古农牧学院学报，1999，20（1）：46－51

[4] 赵大中，陈民，罗先实等．柑桔砧木矮化特性分类研究［J］．西北植物学报，1999，19（1）：46－50

[5] 陈长兰，贾敬贤，侯潇等．梨树矮化中间砧嫁接树的解剖及酶活性测定．中国农学通报，2000，16（3）：20－21

[6] 王宏伟，张连忠等．甜樱桃矮化砧木矮化机理解剖学研究．山东农业大学学报（自然科学版），2004，35（2）：298－300

[7] 史宝胜，徐继忠等．几种苹果矮化砧木枝条与叶片的解剖结构研究．河北林果研

究，2000，15（4）：334－338
[8] Aloni，R. Differentiation of vasculartissues. Annu，Rev. PlantPhysiol. 987，38：1 175－178
[9] 秦巧平．短枝型苹果不同枝类木质部细胞解剖构造及枝条矿质养分含量的相关性研究．山西农业大学硕士学位论文，2001
[10] 赵燕，洪亚辉，刘清波等．菊花辐射后代部分器官维管束与气孔的解剖观察．湖南农业大学学报（自然科学版），2003，29（6）：468－470

Studies on the Correlation of Anatomical Structure and Dwarf of Peach Branches

WANG Cheng-xia　SUN Hu
(*Weifang University of Science and Technology*, *Shouguang* 262700)

Abstract: The general type of peach "Chunyan", spur type "Super red spur" and dwarf type "Shouxing" were used to study the correlation of the anatomical structure indexes and length of internodes in different type peaches. The results showed that every anatomical structure index had significant or fearfully significant differences among dwarfing peaches of different types. They had fearfully marked negative correlation between the ratio of phloem area / transect area and length of node; fearfully marked positive correlation between sieve tube density and length of node; marked positive correlation between fascicular number、vessel density and area of shoot、vessel area/xylem area of shoot、xylem area/ transect area and length of node respectively; negative correlation between the ratio of wood to bark of shoot and the length of twig, but the correlation was not marked.

Key words: Peach; Anatomic structure; Dwarf; Correlation

贝类细胞培养的应用研究进展*

李云玲① 韩金宏 孙 虎

（潍坊科技学院，寿光 262700）

摘 要： 从病毒病的研究、体外珍珠的培育、毒理学、细胞生物学及活性物质生产等几个方面综述了贝类细胞培养的研究现状及在实际应用方面所取得的成果，提出了存在的一些问题及下一步的研究方向。

关键词： 贝类；细胞培养；染色体

近几年，国内外关于贝类细胞培养或组织培养的研究很多，国外如 Buchanan（1999）[1]、Chen and Wang（1999）[2]、Le Marrec-Croq（1999）[3]、Odintsova（1999）[4]、Faucet（2003）[5]对牡蛎或者贻贝进行了细胞培养，Sud（2001）[6]对鲍进行了细胞培养，但是仅有 Chen and Wang（1999）对太平洋牡蛎和硬壳蛤的心脏细胞进行培养以建立细胞系，但最后只成功建立了原代培养体系，其中，硬壳蛤心脏细胞生存时间最长可达 5 个月。国内有石安静、王爱民、李霞、崔龙波等人对河蚌、三角帆蚌、珠母贝、鲍及牡蛎作过许多研究，但基本都是局限于原代培养，也有的进行了传代，但传代后细胞活力不好，最终死亡。

到现在为止，贝类也没有建立细胞系，但是可以应用这一技术作为基础手段进行多方面的研究。总结贝类的细胞培养的研究，归纳起来主要集中在以下几个方面。

1 病毒病的研究

近年来，由于水产动物病毒病的流行，在世界范围内对水产养殖业带来了严重的危害。按照传统方法辨其外形及病理形态，即使有很多的经验，有时会出现谬误；而且病毒病发病快、传播广，这样极有可能会造成病情的加重，延误了治疗。为了解决这一难题，有两条思路可以思考：一是将病毒分离，鉴定其种类，从而根据病毒的特性采取合适的治疗措施；二是在饵料或者生长环境方面提供合适的条件，从根本上提高贝类的免疫机能，增强其抗病毒能力。

细胞培养技术可以产生大量增殖的细胞或者获得某一细胞系，而这些细胞具备供病

---

* 基金项目：山东省自然科学基金项目资助（编号：Y2002D12）

① 李云玲，女，硕士，潍坊科技学院讲师。研究方向：动物学。E－mail：liyunling82@126.com

毒增殖的全部条件，这样就可以分离、鉴定、研究病毒的感染、复制、形态发生、遗传变异和测定病毒的效价。所以，这一技术可以为贝类病毒学的研究提供支持和基础。迄今为止，已报道的海洋贝类病毒有几十种，有疱疹病毒（Herpesviridae）、虹彩病毒（Iridoviridae）、呼肠弧病毒（Reoviridae）及乳多空病毒（Papoviridae）等。这些病毒引发了贝类的多种病症。如文蛤的“红肉病”；牡蛎爆发的鳃部变黑，卵巢囊肿；皱纹盘鲍的“裂壳病”[7]。

细胞培养作为一种潜在的工具，在贝类病毒病的诊断及探针技术的应用方面已日益受到广泛地关注，迫切需要建立它们的细胞系或细胞株，以供病毒的分离、纯化、鉴定及病理学研究，同时，为口岸检疫病毒性贝类提供必要的条件（Toullec et al.，1999）。

对于贝类的病毒病害目前尚无特别有效的治疗方法，以防为主是最根本的。要避免病害的发生，首先要保持良好的养殖环境；其次就是要使用优质的合适的饵料或营养物质，增强贝类体质。通过培养贝类的免疫细胞，可以在培养基中加入一些生长因子或者营养物质，看这些物质对培养细胞的影响，从而筛选增强免疫机能的活性物质或者药物，提高贝类的生活力和抗病能力，尽量减少病毒病的感染率，为病毒病的治疗赢得时间，减少损失。柏鸣等[8]在不同浓度的 $CuSO_4$ 和不同梯度的酸碱度下对椭圆背角无齿蚌进行了杀菌能力检测的 NBT 试验．结果表明，较低浓度的 $CuSO_4$ 和弱酸性水体可刺激河蚌的免疫系统，使血细胞吞噬杀菌能力增强；而较高浓度的 $CuSO_4$ 和较低 pH 值的水体则会对蚌的免疫系统造成不可逆的伤害。

同时，免疫细胞的培养还可能为贝类免疫机制的研究提供一定的支持。Canesi L 利用培养的牡蛎血细胞进行了防御机制的研究，这个结果同时能对一些药物或污染物对贝类免疫的影响提供支持[9]。Novelli A 对贻贝小脑颗粒细胞进行了原代培养，这为进行贻贝提取物主要是氨基酸类物质的毒性试验提供了一个有价值的模型[10]。

2 体外珍珠的培育研究

珍珠贝外套膜的分泌能形成贝壳和珍珠，现代人工海水珍珠的培育技术就是通过人工手术，将供体珠贝的外套膜组织块同珠核一道移植到受体珍珠贝的体内，被移植的外套膜组织块的上皮细胞经移行增殖，包裹珠核形成珍珠囊，珍珠囊上皮细胞在珠表面分泌珍珠质，最后形成人工有核珍珠。

目前，珍珠养殖业已在我国得到了极大的普及和发展，但传统的外套膜植片法对育珠贝的损伤较严重，增加了植核后育珠贝的死亡率和吐核率，从而影响珍珠的质量和产量。通过组织细胞培养技术、体外培育有核珍珠囊，再进行插囊育珠，有可能建立一种新的珍珠培育模式。

鉴于珍珠贝外套膜在珍珠形成中的重要作用，国内外学者对珠贝外套膜的组织学，组织化学以及珍珠囊的形成过程进行了大量的研究，但对珍珠贝外套膜的组织培养研究较少，国内主要有四川大学石安静等对淡水蚌外套膜组织培养及分泌物性质的研究[11]，海南大学王爱民等从 20 世纪 90 年代中期一直坚持对我国沿海重要经济珍珠贝—马氏珠母贝（Pinctada martensii D）外套膜组织培养的研究，建立了一套较完善的培养条件和方法，成功地培养了外套膜组织，使外套膜上皮细胞分泌珍珠质[12]；并且应用培育的体外珍珠囊进插囊育珠移植试验培养出海水珍珠[13]。国外的主要有日本学者町井昭（Machii）对日本产的马氏珠母贝外套膜组织培养的研究，Barik S[14]对淡水珍珠贝的外套膜进行了42～45d的培养，在培养12h后表皮细胞开始迁出，到12～15d时，细胞形成单层，当培养到38d时，细胞开始表现特异的生活能力，可以观察到细胞分泌的$CaCO_3$霰石结晶物。Suja等通过对多变鲍（Haliotis varia）的外套膜组织培养，也为体外培育鲍珠打下了基础（Suja and Dharmaraj，2005）。

3 毒理学的研究

在过去的30年中，海洋无脊椎动物的生长情况常被用来反映生长环境是否良好及预测可能出现的污染。此时，通常检查的是动物整体或某种器官的生长情况。到了近几年，随着体外细胞培养技术的发展，体外建立合适的细胞系进行毒理学实验来对环境进行监控已成为一种优秀而简便的方法。Le Pennec等[15]（2003）进行了扇贝消化腺的细胞培养，观察了一些化学物质对GST（glutathione-S-transferase，谷光甘肽转硫酶）的诱导情况，进行了为期一年的监测。这种模型可以为日后的一些污染物的影响提供一种可能的解决方法。

4 遗传学和细胞生物学等方面的研究

细胞培养技术还为遗传学和细胞生物学的研究提供了便利。制备贝类染色体的材料，大多采用繁殖期的精巢、卵裂或囊胚阶段的早期胚胎、孵化的担轮幼虫及成贝的鳃组织，此外，也可利用成贝的外套膜、触手等，这些细胞具有分裂旺盛、容易观察到分裂相的优点，但是很多组织的取材都受季节限制。用培养的组织或者细胞就可以获得大量增殖的细胞，解决这个难题。

在培养前，对贝类注射一定剂量的分裂素如PHA、ConA等，在培养结束前几个小时加入一定剂量的秋水仙素中止分裂，使其停留在中期阶段，此时，染色体清晰可辨，适合进行制片研究。

哺乳动物染色体研究多利用血淋巴细胞培养技术，但由于大多数贝类的血液系统为开管式循环，加之贝类个体小，血液量少，采血不便，且易污染，所以，贝类血细胞培养技术一直进展缓慢。但可见培养贝类别的组织进行染色体研究。Cornet M（1995）[16]首先对贻贝的外套膜和足肌进行了6～7d的培养，为进行染色体研究做准备。在随后的研究中进行了一些改变，对成熟雌性贻贝的外套膜组织进行了培养，在培养时加入了鸡胚提取物，采用挤压过滤法获得大量单细胞，培养后的细胞进行了染色体分析。据实验报道，要尽量避免采用雄性的外套膜，因为极有可能沾染成熟的精子，这样会对最后结果的分析造成麻烦，雌性卵母细胞会有特定的中期分裂相，则不会有影响。石安静等[17]培养了圆背角无齿蚌的血细胞，在活体内注射或在培养基上加入PHA和ConA，作染色体观察，但未观察到转化细胞和有丝分裂相，指出贝类的血细胞分化程度较高，即使培养后也很难分裂。王立新等（2001）对青蛤的鳃和外套膜进行组织培养后制备染色体，却取得了成功。贾志良也曾经对牡蛎的鳃组织进行短期培养，获得了大量清晰的染色体分裂相。以上实验得出的结果并不尽相同，可能是因为材料不同所致，也有可能是所用培养条件并不适合所用材料的生长。

5 活性物质的生成

Cao 等（2003）[18]在进行贻贝血细胞原代培养时发现，细胞的活化与细胞膜上白介素 2 受体的 α 亚基（IL-2 Rα）数目的增加有关，而且在培养基中添加脂多糖（LPS）的情况下，LPS 对 IL-2Rα 的诱导效果要比 IL-2 效果好。为研究产珠鲍外套膜分泌珍珠质的机理，龚由彬等[19]研究了河蚌外套膜组织培养细胞分泌珍珠质的药理作用。组织培养后的培养液，能缩短小白鼠出血时间，对大鼠离体子宫及蟾蜍离体心脏收缩有增强作用，对兔离体小肠有抑制作用。这些药理作用与培养液中牛磺酸含量变化一致。实验结果表明，河蚌分泌珍珠质的细胞，在离体人工培养条件下，能旺盛地分泌珍珠质，分泌的珍珠质具有天然珍珠相同的一些药理作用。石安静等[20]以淡水珍珠蚌为材料，观察组织培养的外套膜的分泌物的形成和变化及分泌物的性质，结果表明；离体培养的外套膜细胞不仅能产生活体细胞相同的分泌物，而且分泌物还能在培养过程中形成结晶，并逐渐生长。其中珍珠所含的各种氨基酸均增加，尤其是珍珠中含量最高的丙氨酸、甘氨酸和谷氨酸增加最多；珍珠药用有效成分之一的牛磺酸，随组织培养时间的延长而逐渐增加；用等离子光谱测定培养组织匀浆液与未培养比较，钙的含量也大为增加。结果表明；离体组织培养分泌的珍珠质的化学成分和性质与活体基本相同。这些研究表明可以用细胞培养的方法生产大量珍珠质。

由于贝类的细胞培养起步较晚，同时受到许多因素的制约，培养比较困难，至今尚未得到连续性细胞系。贝类细胞培养较之哺乳动物困难，除了两者的细胞生长特性不同之外，影响贝类细胞培养的关键因素，诸如适宜的培养基和培养环境等问题尚未完全搞清，特别应当指出的是，贝类等水生无脊椎动物细胞培养至今仍沿用着经典的陆生哺乳动物的细胞培养基，由于水生无脊椎动物与哺乳动物的代谢途径有很大差异，对各种营养因子的需求也不同，因此，对虾贝类细胞的适宜培养基及其添加成分，有必要从细胞基础代谢的角度深入研究，筛选适合贝类的培养基为建立细胞系奠定基础。

参 考 文 献

[1] Buchanan J T, La Peyre J F, Cooper R K, Tiersch T R. Improved attachment and spreading in primary cell cultures of the eastern oyster, Crassostrea virginica [J]. In Vitro Cell Dev Biol Anim, 1999, 35 (10): 593 - 598

[2] Chen S N, Wang C S. Establishment of cell lines derived from oyster, Crassostrea gigas Thunberg and hard clam, Meretrix lusoria Roding [J]. Methods Cell Sci, 1999, 21 (4): 183 - 192

[3] Le Marrec-Croq F, Glaise D, Guguen-Guillouzo C, Chesne C, Guillouzo A, Boulo V,

Dorange G. Primary cultures of heart cells from the scallop Pecten maximus (mollusca-bivalvia) [J]. In Vitro Cell Dev Biol Anim, 1999, 35 (5): 289 -295

[4] Odintsova N A, Belogortseva N I, Ermak A V, Molchanova V I, Luk, rsquo, yanov P A. Adhesive and growth properties of lectin from the ascidian Didemnum ternatanum on cultivated marine invertebrate cells [J]. Biochimica et Biophysica Acta (BBA) - Molecular Cell Research, 1999, 1448 (3): 381 -389

[5] Faucet J, Maurice M, Gagnaire B, Renault T, Burgeot T. Isolation and primary culture of gill and digestive gland cells from the common mussel Mytilus edulis [J]. Methods Cell Sci, 2003, 25 (3-4): 177 -184

[6] Sud D, Doumenc D, Lopez E, Milet C. Role of water-soluble matrix fraction, extracted from the nacre of Pinctada maxima, in the regulation of cell activity in abalone mantle cell culture (Haliotis tuberculata) [J]. Tissue Cell, 2001, 33 (2): 154 -160

[7] 李霞，王斌，刘淑范等. 皱纹盘鲍“裂壳病”的病原及组织病理研究 [J]. 水产学报，1998，22 (1): 61 -66

[8] 柏鸣，石安静. 硫酸铜和酸碱度对河蚌血细胞免疫功能影响的研究 [J]. 四川大学学报 (自然科学版)，1999，36 (6): 1 116 -1 119

[9] Canesi L, Scarpato A, Betti M, Ciacci C, Pruzzo C, Gallo G. Bacterial killing by Mytilus hemocyte monolayers as a model for investigating the signaling pathways involved in mussel immune defence [J]. Mar Environ Res, 2002, 54 (3-5): 547 -551

[10] Novelli A, Kispert J, Reilly A, Zitko V. Excitatory amino acids toxicity in cerebellar granule cells in primary culture [J]. Can Dis Wkly Rep, 1990, 16 Suppl 1E (83 -8; discussion 88 -89

[11] 邱安东，石安静. 三角帆蚌珍珠囊细胞的分泌活动 [J]. 水产学报，1999，23 (2): 115 -121

[12] 王爱民，苏琼，阎冰等. 马氏珠母贝外套膜组织培养 [J]. 广西科学，2000，7 (2): 135 -139

[13] 王爱民，阎冰，苏琼等. 马氏珠母贝珍珠囊体外培养及插囊育珠 [J]. 广西科学，2000，7 (1): 70 -74

[14] Barik S K, Jena J K, Janaki K R. In vitro explant culture of mantle epithelium of freshwater pearl mussel [J]. Indian J Exp Biol, 2004, 42 (12): 1 235 -1 238

[15] Le Pennec G, Le Pennec M. Induction of glutathione-S-transferases in primary cultured digestive gland acini from the mollusk bivalve Pecten maximus (L.): application of a new cellular model in biomonitoring studies [J]. Aquat Toxicol, 2003, 64 (2): 131 -142

[16] Cornet M. Description of a tissue culture technique using tissue from mussel (Mytilus edulis) for the preparation of chromosomes [J]. C R Acad Sci III, 1992, 315 (1): 7 -12

[17] 石安静，邱安东，唐敏等. 圆背角无齿蚌血细胞培养 [J]. 水生生物学报，

2001, 25 (2): 116-122
[18] Cao A, Mercado L, Ramos-Martinez J I, Barcia R. Primary cultures of hemocytes from Mytilus galloprovincialis Lmk.: expression of IL-2R [alpha] subunit [J]. Aquaculture, 2003, 216 (1-4): 1-8
[19] 龚由彬，石安静，张烘渊. 河蚌外套膜组织培养细胞分泌的珍珠质的药理作用 [J]. 水生生物学报，1994，18 (4): 327-333
[20] 石安静，陈蜀娜. 褶纹冠蚌外套膜组织培养的分泌物的偏光显微镜观察 [J]. 动物学报，1995，41 (1): 35-42

Application of Cell Culture for Shellfish

LI Yun-ling　HAN Jin-hong　SUN Hu
(*Weifang University of Science and Tecnology*, *Shouguang*　262700)

Abstract: Theoretical research and Practical application were summarized from virus disease research, pearl culture in vitro, toxicology and activity of material production etc. And finally the report proposed next step in the direction of the research.
Key words: Shellfish; Cell culture; Chromosome

盐·寿光·历史

赵守祥[①]

（寿光市委党史研究室，寿光 262700）

摘　要： 盐是在人类生命发展和社会发展中起着特殊作用的物质，盐是人类生命发展和社会发展中特别重要、非常奇特的现象，盐中折射着人类智慧的灵光。中国最早的海盐产地在寿光。海盐生产技术由寿光扩展至整个环渤海地区，又随着历史发展传至南方。盐在整个中国文明史中扮演着“口粮”的角色，在寿光的发展史上更是如此。海和盐与寿光人血脉相连。寿光文化、寿光人的性格都深深地透露着海和盐的底色。

关键词： 盐；寿光；历史

自2003年南水北调工程支线西水东调沿线文物普查发现寿光双王城大型制盐遗址以来，山东省考古研究所、北京大学文博学院已累计投资100多万元，连续进行了5年发掘和考古研究，在双王城水库附近40km^{2}范围内发现上迄商周时期的大型制盐遗址和陶窑群遗址100多处，其中，商周时期的76处，为环渤海地区时代最早，也是世界范围内商周时期最大的制盐遗址，明确了这一带是中国商王朝制盐中心的考古结论。遗址群已被国家文物局确定为一类保护区，中央电视台《新闻联播》节目做了报道。考古组还告诉笔者，山东省政府近期将专门举行新闻发布会，向全世界宣布这一重大考古发现。

盐是在人类生命发展和社会发展中起着特殊作用的物质，盐是人类生命发展和社会发展中特别重要、非常奇特的现象，盐中折射着人类文明人类智慧的灵光。自古以来，寿光北部就是一片盐碱和盐田，这是寿光特有的风光特点、人文特点和经济地理特点，是寿光人性格中具有典型意义的一部分。寿光的文化，寿光人的性格，无不深深的渗透着海的风韵、盐的味道。正是基于此，笔者作成此文，与邑人品享之。

1　盐的概念及储量

盐在现代社会，按照用途分为食用盐和工业用盐。化学成分是氯化钠（NaCl），是

① 赵守祥，男，寿光市委党史研究室主任，潍坊市政协委员，潍坊市社会科学联合会委员，寿光市《齐民要术》研究会秘书长。研究方向：中共党史、中国历史及文化。E－mail：baobao126sg@126.com

金属钠离子（Na^{-}）与酸根氯离子（Cl^{-}）的化合物，按照重量，钠占 39.34%，氯占 60.66%。

人类知道盐很早，但知道钠却很晚。英国人弗莱·戴维 1907 年用电解方式分离出钠，他的电解实验为他赢得了永久声誉。

钠是地球上第七大元素，是一种性质不稳定的白色金属元素，与味臭的毒气氯结合成氯化钠。酸碱之间有天然的吸引力，结合而成为性状非常平衡的物质，这就是盐。氯化钠晶体是由 6 个晶面、8 个角顶、12 条晶棱构成的正方体。同冬天的雪花一样，盐结晶是大自然的艺术杰作。有人说，盐是大自然和宇宙的缩影，至为完美。

盐能与许多物质发生化学反应，产生多种钠化合物和氯化合物。通过电解还原能够产生金属钠和气体氯，电解可生成烧碱、氯气、氯酸钠，与氨、二氧化碳反应可生成纯碱和氯化铵，与硫酸镁在 0℃以下反应，可生成水硫酸钠和氯化镁，在电解槽中电解并通入二氧化碳，可生成纯碱、氯气、氢气等等。世界上的盐及衍生物总数达 15 000种之多。盐与煤炭、石油、石灰、硫磺合称为五大基本工业原料，被称为“化学工业之母”。

盐与土壤、空气、水、火一起构成人类生存的五大要素。盐对人类的生命学意义是盐与血浆共同制造维持生命的养分。盐在人体细胞中起着维持正常渗透压的作用，维持向细胞正常输水的过程，使体液保持中性功能。盐在人体内起着兴奋神经的作用，是制造胃液、胆汁的重要原料，人体缺盐就会疲劳、食欲下降，消化不良，神经失常甚至死亡。钠对人体蛋白质和碳水化合物的代谢起着重要作用，氯则用来保持人体酸的平衡。调节人体盐分平衡的器官是肾脏，人体 200 万个汗腺分泌的汗液含有 0.35% ~0.7% 的盐，人体大量排汗不能补充盐分就会发生热痉挛。0.9% 的氯化钠溶液中钠离子与人体血浆的钠离子浓度相当，合乎生理要求而称为生理盐水。较浓的盐溶液使水分从细胞中渗出，使蛋白质凝固而产生杀菌作用。盐在人体内正常含有量为 0.66%，百毫升血液含盐 0.89g，一个体重 75kg 的人体内含盐 0.5kg。

全世界盐的总储量为 6.4×10^{8} 亿 t，其中，矿盐 2.1×10^{8} 亿 t，海盐为 4.3×10^{8} 亿 t，海盐是矿盐的两倍多。每年从陆地流入海洋的盐有 39 亿 t。有的地质学家即以海水中盐的多少来计算地球的年龄。全球海洋含盐总量 4 500亿 t。如果把海水中的盐全部提取出来，铺在陆地上可得到 153m 厚的盐层，如果全部铺在中国陆地上，可使地面平均多出海面 2 400 m。中国盐产量以海盐为大宗，其次是湖盐、井矿盐。中国海岸线 18 000km，现在海盐年产量 2 000万 t，居世界第一位。

2 盐在人类发展中的地位

中国文化主要源于中原文化和东夷文化。中国历史记载中最早的盐神，也是东夷族最早“煮海为盐”的是宿（夙）沙氏。而中原先民用盐是从古羌人那里学来的。中原黄帝族源于古羌族。汉代以前，陇西地区吃的是西海盐池（今青海省都兰的茶卡盐池）的羌盐，黄帝族入中原定居后才发现和食用运城盐池的盐。西周文字中还无盐字，却有卤字。盐从古声，与卤一声之转，即卤是早时盐的称谓。在金文中，“卤”与“西”为一字，即中原之盐来自西方之意。《说文解字》释盬（gu，音鼓）：指河东（运城）盐池。盐池的盐微苦，专称盬（盬即苦音），而海盐则微咸而称盐。咸字，从戈，与人、口，示盐之味具刺激性。咸加心，为感觉之“感”。加水则味减，故为减退之减。箴、鍼（针）都是取盐味刺激之意为字。咸字也是古代表示食盐之字。

古代临字也指盐。临的原始写法为“臨”，其象形意义为人眼注视三口锅察看火候，是在煮盐实践中形成的字，商周时期即以临指盐。初煮盐是一口锅，发展为看三口锅，说明煮盐技术的进步，到西汉后期就不用临字示盐了。鹾（cuo，音措）字也指盐，是羌语察的译音字（说明秦汉时羌盐还行销中原）。盐字在历史典籍中第一次出现是在《周礼》中，盐古字为鹽，“盐人，掌盐之政令”。监是因临产生的另一个与盐有关的字，其意为皿盛临（盐），表示盐已煮成，放在器皿中，有人守护。商周甲骨文和金文，監都是临与皿的合体字，只是省去三锅而代之一点，一点即表示盐的意思。

盐在中国历史上诗词歌赋中被称为“玄滋素液”，“玉洁冰鲜”。盐在人类饮食文化中被称为“上味”“百味之主”，有“盐调百味”之称。如今在台湾还有一俗语：“吃尽滋味盐好，走遍天下娘好”。四川人重盐味，说人有情有义为“有盐有味”，把人质很差者称为“没盐淡味”。

地球上最大的盐矿是海洋。生命科学揭示出地球上生命最初来自于海洋。人的生命起源也来自于海洋。人与海洋有着一种天然联系。盐作为物质世界的一部分，是世界的存在形式之一，人也是物质世界的一部分，也是世界的存在形式之一。由于人与海洋的天然联系，人在生命成长和进化过程中，人体内一开始就含有盐，盐从一开始就是人体生命的有机组成部分。随着人类前期生命的进化旅程，他们走上陆地，逐步进化为灵长类、类人猿及原始人类，人类早期生命从生活在由盐分包围的海洋液体中到生活在不含盐分的空气中，人类生命发展需要的盐分需要以专门精力去寻找。由于人与海洋的天然联系，或许人类很早即到海边舔食海水和盐碱。这是与自然变迁和人类进化繁衍的进程相伴随的。在人们从高山森林向陆地平原迁徙过程中，人体所需要盐分有的是从植物与动物体中补充来的，动物的血液含有较多盐分，正是古史上所说的“茹毛饮血”时代。

人是大自然进化出的精灵。人的智慧最初首先来源于人对外界的感知力。味觉当是推动人智力发展的重要助推力之一。而咸味因为人的生命发展对于盐分的特殊需要，可能是推动人智力发展、促进人的进化发展的最主要味素。其他一些低等动物也同样需要盐分，然而在寻求盐的嗅觉上可能又是人所不及的，最早的路即是人类沿着动物脚印寻找盐而形成的。历史发展科学研究已经将盐与人类的发展做出一个描述，适当的足量的盐的摄入，是推动人类进化发展的加速器。学者告诉我们，人类社会之所以经过漫长的旧石器时代，而在进入新石器时代后有飞快发展，是与人类成功地认识和规模化地开发大自然中的盐资源直接相关的。

人类最早食用的盐来自于海洋。人类在伴随着对盐的认识的自身发展过程中，由于所处自然环境的不同，他们创造了不同的获取盐的渠道和方法。生活在远离海洋的内地的最早人类，发现了不用特别煮制就能够直接取用且量大无比的天赐之盐——盐湖。盐湖，位于今山西省南部运城市，这是一座中国历史上因盐湖产盐运盐而最早兴起的城市（初名潞村，因之所产之盐又称潞盐，因湖在黄河东又称河东盐，盐湖又称盐池，故又称池盐）。盐池是太行山支脉中条山在地壳运动中山体断裂带形成的湖泊，经亿万年沉积蒸发而形成的自然结晶盐湖，总面积 130km²。自从人类意识到盐是生活必需品，盐就成为人类不同族群、不同集团攫取、追杀、拼争、聚敛的对象，成为最重要的交易品和财富的象征，并由此演绎出人类漫长而辉煌的发展史和文明史，成为迄今为止人类文明社会大部分时间前进的重要物质基础之一。

中国境内最早与盐有关的故事，是与中华文明起源直接相关的。因为盐湖的发现，在盐湖周围爆发了中华民族历史上著名的炎帝、黄帝、蚩尤大战。这一大战的结果，是山东一带先民东夷族首领蚩尤（长期统治东夷族的少昊氏鸟官中“五鸠”之音转，鸟官中的玄鸟氏即源于寿光以燕子象形为图腾的益族，薄姑氏即鹁鸪氏，在今寿光青州交界处）被杀，身首相分。《孔子三朝记》载：“黄帝杀之于中冀，蚩尤股体身首异处，而其血化为卤，则解之盐池也。因其尸解，故名其地为解”。因为这一事件，诞生了盐池边上的地名解梁，古为朝廷盐运使驻地，称解州（解州治所在地），即今运城市解镇，因之盐湖产盐又称“解盐”。正因此，“三皇五帝”时代，尧、舜、禹都建都于盐湖附近，尧都平阳（盐湖北，今山西襄汾陶寺镇）、舜都蒲坂（盐湖西，今山西永济县境内），禹都安邑（盐湖东，今山西夏县境内）。

3 煮盐业的发展

中国历史记载中最早的煮制海盐者，也是最早制盐人是宿沙氏。宿沙氏，传为炎帝时人。炎帝、黄帝时代距今约 5 000年，炎帝早于黄帝，又说炎帝即神农氏。而炎帝、黄帝时代，今山东一代东夷族的代表人物是太皋（太皋即伏羲）、少昊，太皋早于少昊，后少昊氏族取代太皋氏族而成为统治者。历史记载比较清楚的太皋后裔有宿，在今山东。《中国历史地名大辞典》载：“宿沙，亦作夙沙。炎帝时诸侯国，在今山东滨海之地。”《太平御览·世本》载：“宋衷曰，宿沙卫，灵公臣，齐滨海，故卫为鱼盐之利”。中国历史典籍中有关盐事的最早记载是《尚书·禹贡》中所记“厥贡盐絺”，即夏禹时青州一带的贡品第一就是盐。宿字的本意是盖下窝中席上有人息（正在发掘的双王城商周制盐遗址中就发掘出一具躺在地窝中的骸骨），而古时宿、夙、肃通用，夙的本意为月下（天未明）有人做事，肃为肃杀严急（冷），三字统起来，正是滨海煮盐人生活环境的写照。既然太皋后裔有宿，又太皋早于少昊，又早于炎帝，而少昊氏是大汶口文化的创造者，距今6 000年前后，是宿为太皋后裔或太昊传至少昊时。至战国时代的齐国，宿沙卫地在齐国滨海，有鱼盐之利，说明宿沙卫在古青州和古齐国的沿海。山东地区较早的文化是北辛文化，距今7 000年前后，在今寿光南部边线王村西就发现面积60 000m² 的北辛文化遗址（中期北辛文化遗址山东省仅有 10 处），又于边线王村北发现总面积5 7 000m² 的龙山文化城堡（是山东地区建国后发现的第一座龙山文化城堡），龙山文化的上限距今 4 600年。从边线王村（这一带为寿光最南部也是寿光海拔最高点）向北到羊口镇渤海边纵跨 60km，从边线王城堡开始，到最北边的郭井子村，均发现龙山文化遗址，并且均出土了煮盐工具陶器——盔形器。无独有偶，寿光边线王村到羊口郭井子村（在双王城商周制盐遗址发现了用于提取地下卤水的盐井）之间就有多个村庄以沙为名，如沙窝、沙埠屯等，沙埠屯村是一个古老的村庄，村周围布有多处龙山文化遗址。而寿光双王城制盐遗址发掘报告关于遗址土壤的描述也是“粉沙淤泥土质”。这是山东渤海沿岸发现最早最密集的海盐生产遗址。这说明，从北辛文化始，经大汶口文化、龙山文化，至夏商时期，这一带先民很早就开始食海盐、煮海盐的历史，至商代出现和形成了大规模海盐制作作坊、海盐制作工场、海盐制作中心，而留在今天的见证，就是几乎遍布寿光全境大量存在的煮盐工具盔形器。

中国历史记载中最早的盐官是《周礼·天官》中的“盐人”，掌百事所需之盐，且盐人以奄二人为之。而奄则是源于寿光的伯益之嬴姓后裔，在商时期为奄国，居今曲阜市。

自炎帝时的古国时代，炎帝族、黄帝族和以蚩尤（五鸠）为代表的东夷族即展开了争河东（运城）盐池的搏斗。随着东夷先民与中原先民的交流与融合，居于中原地区的先民开始尝到不同于池盐（味苦）的海盐（味咸），或者海盐味优于池盐，至商朝时，东进强度加大了，其势力一直达到今潍河以西地区，并在今寿光北部双王城附近建立起庞大的海盐制作中心以支撑和维持商王朝巨大的经济开支。或许正因为海盐的开发，商王朝才强大起来，开创了辉煌的商文化。商王朝著名贤王武丁，用傅说为相，他赞美傅说：“若作酒醴，尔惟曲蘖，若作和羹，尔惟盐梅”，把治国的大道理寓于饮食调味之中。

随着商王朝在今寿光北部双王城附近大规模海盐开发和历史演进，海盐生产技术在环渤海地区渐渐普及开来，至西周和春秋战国时期，环渤海的齐国、燕国成为主要海盐产地，史称齐有“山海之利”，人民多“布帛鱼盐”，燕有“鱼盐枣栗之饶”。

春秋战国时期，齐桓公所以能够“一匡天下，九合诸侯”，成为首霸，最重要原因是他任用管仲为相，进行了一系列改革。其中重要的一项，也是在中国经济史上具有重要意义的是确立了国家统制盐业的管理模式。管仲提出“官山海”的盐法，由国家垄断盐资源，实行国家专卖，即不管官煮民煮一律官收官运官销，用经济手段增加财政收入。方法是：官民并煮，官煮为主，每年10月至正月共4个月（草木燃料丰足）为官煮时间，这个时间及其后的春季不许百姓煮盐，借以提高盐差（盐价常升至4～10倍以上）。在管仲主持下，齐国盐业经济得到迅速发展，由此建立起国家强大的物质基础。管仲创造的“官山海”盐法，成为后世各朝各代沿用至今的不变之法，管仲因创制这样的盐法也被誉为最早的盐神之一。

继齐桓公成为春秋首霸之后，晋文公又成霸主，这不仅与晋文公一系列改革有关，还与晋国拥有盐湖有直接关系。《左传》记晋侯与韩献子对话，韩献子说：“山泽林盬，国之宝也”。后晋为韩、赵、魏分，盐池为魏据有，韩无盐而早亡，后魏据盐池又为秦夺得，魏从此不振，直至被秦消灭。

战国的频繁战争导致许多国家盐政松弛，盐商趁机大发盐财，有的富可敌国，秦孝公用商鞅，最先改变这种状况。商鞅提出“壹山泽”之法，即国家“专山泽之利，管山泽之饶”，在盐区设置盐官，统管生产和流通，禁止私煮私销（少数商人经许可也可从国家取得分销权，但需交纳极重的专卖说）。秦国实行商鞅变法，增加了国家财政收入，增强了国力，为秦最终统一中国打下坚实的经济基础。

在中国古代，可谓没有盐无以立国，盐为国之命脉。

煮盐、冶铁、铸钱在中国古代被称之为“三大利”。自战国以降，著名大商贾，多营盐铁业，在各地都是第一等大富豪。1981 年，于寿光纪台镇吕家村前发现一处汉代大型冶铁遗址，出土铁器碎片达 1.5t，遗址内共分布炼铁炉 8 座，炉内径 52cm，炉壁分 4 层筑成。碎铁件中有犁铧、镢、锄、刀、矛、戈等。1985 年 5 月，又在寿光孙家集街道西侯村出土一组汉代完好的锐角大铁犁。汉时山东大铁商孔仅家值千金，邴氏则值亿金。贝益 为益的古文，贝益 币产于益地，历史记载中益为“聚贝益 之都”，即今寿光古城是很早时候的造钱（贝币）、铸钱（金属币）之都。《古城乡志》载，1943 年古城村民挖土中挖出了石钱范、铜钱范，1958 年学生掘得莽币 100 多斤，1966 年又挖出大布黄币（俗称叉子钱）一宗 14 枚，出土的其他铜器铁器不计其数。镒为古货币单位，一镒相当于今 20 两或 24 两。考古学专家孙敬明在认真研究 1983 年 12 月于寿光古城村出土的 64 件商己国青铜礼器后提出：“齐刀币铭文及其形制皆源于土著，或即源于商周时期弥水流域的‘己’文化”。

秦朝在所有产地都设置盐官。汉高帝曾向豪强让步，三大利均允许民营，盐铁商积财多至万金。公元前 119 年，一代大帝汉武帝擢用桑弘羊、孔仅、东郭咸阳 3 个大盐商做理财官，召开历史上著名的盐铁会议，御史大夫桑弘羊全面阐述了盐铁官卖对国家强盛的重要意义（宫中郎官桓宽根据会议中桑弘羊等的言论集为《盐铁论》）。汉武帝采纳桑弘羊建议，实行盐铁官营的国策，由政府募民煮盐，同时实行官收、官运、官销，宣布有私自煮盐铸铁者以砍其左脚趾为刑。至西汉末，全国设有盐官的郡国和县共 37 处，布于 27 个郡国，从此盐铁官营成为定制。盐铁专营国策的实行，为朝廷增加巨大财政收入，为长达 400 多年的大汉王朝和大汉文化的繁荣奠定了重要物质基础。

中华民族历史上由于商、周、秦、汉几代王朝的统一和拓展，来自北方中原地区先进生产技术随着人民流动，而渐渐传播到江南，江南最早的海盐生产记载是战国时期吴“东有海盐之饶”的记载。总体上到唐朝时期全国海盐产量超过池盐。之后，在中国从北到南 18 000km 海岸线上，形成中国四大海盐产区，即复州湾盐区（辽宁省）、长芦盐区（河北省、天津市）、莱州湾盐区（山东省）、淮盐产区（江苏省）。由于江苏海岸带有全国最广阔的沿海滩涂和四季分明的气候条件，随着南方开发，至元朝时期，江苏全省盐场发展到 30 个，海盐规模居全国之首。唐宋以来盐税占国家财政收入的 1/3 到 1/2，其中来自淮盐的盐税最多。淮盐行销 10 个省、270 县，供 2 亿人口食用。

以寿光为代表的山东海盐产区，有海岸线 3 024km，海盐生产能力达 1 000万 t，占全国总产量的 1/3 以上。其中食盐生产能力 100 万 t，莱州湾畔、鲁北地区的大粒盐（含寿光）、寿光、青岛两地生产的海精盐驰誉海内外。

4 寿光盐业从古至今的发展

寿光作为最早的海盐生产地和海盐工场生产技术发源地，由于煮海盐历史悠久，寿光很早即设立了盐官。秦孝公用商鞅“壹山泽”之法，在盐区设置盐官管理盐政。清康熙《寿光县志》载：“秦之郡县，汉初因之，汉县即秦县，寿光之为县当在秦时”。清嘉庆《寿光县志》载：“盐城在（今）县城西北六十里，清水泊侧，俗名霜雪城，以寿光故城也”。清光绪《寿光乡土志》载：“古城在清水泊侧，汉寿光故城也”。《汉书》载：“寿光有盐官”，今尚有官台，今官台村北明万历年间台上的灶志碑、灶学碑尚在。北魏郦道元著《水经注》载：“巨羊水（弥河）东北经益县（今圣城街道益城村）故城，又东北而为潭（即临泽洼，今古城街道临泽村南），枝津出焉，谓之百尺沟，又北流经北益都城（今古城村），又东北经县故城（即秦之寿光城）西，又西北流注入巨淀矣”。明嘉靖时期这一带仍称秦城乡。《汉书·武帝记》载：“征和四年（公元前 89 年）三月，上（汉武帝）耕于巨淀”，即在盐城（古寿光城）附近。《山东盐业》2005 年第二期载《商周大型制盐遗址惊现寿光双王城》载：记者随寿光博物馆人员在双王城水库西侧的双王城（即盐城、霜雪城、双王城）遗址的排水沟中发现大量古代陶片，经鉴定最早的是夏代的，然后是商周的。民国《寿光县志》载：官台村北“元初有盐官，名官台场，大德十一年，台上建孔子庙，后废。清初时官台盐场大使署在此。乾隆三十四年，潮漫溢，始徙于侯镇。”由于秦王朝建立后仍行商鞅之法，于盐区设置盐官，而寿光是东部沿海最重要的海盐产地，所以秦朝在双王城盐区旧（盐）城上设置了寿光县，并设盐官在此。只是由于海水漫溢，寿光县治才渐渐南徙。

至清朝时期，盐制仍沿旧制，由户部管理全国盐务，宣统二年（1910 年）由户部尚书兼任督办盐政大臣总摄。产盐地区设都转运使司，或以盐法道、盐粮道兼理，使司以下设分司机构以事。当时全国 40 省共有 178 场（县、井、池），山东共设 8 场，供 4 省销用。

寿光自秦汉时设置盐官以来，根据已有的记载，东晋时期（安帝隆安年间，即 397—401 年），南燕慕容德在乌常泽（今营里镇黑冢子村，秦始皇东巡筑台观海即在此）附近设置盐官。元朝时期（元世祖至元年间，即 1264—1294 年），寿光设有官台场，为当时山东 19 场之一。清雍正年间（1730 年）潍县固堤场并入寿光官台场。清宣统年间（1896 年）利津县永阜场被黄河决口淹没，山东巡抚李秉衡奏准在官台场大量辟滩，且允许商人建滩，5 年内辟滩 348 副。1914 年，广饶县的王家岗场并入官台场，称官岗场，场署驻侯镇（1945 年原国务院总理李鹏由延安转赴东北途中即在此驻地休息。寿光重镇侯镇的兴起与政府盐署机关设在侯镇、这里集有众多盐商、是盐的集散地有重大关系。侯镇曾有 20 余家酒坊，是山东四大酒镇之一，也是这个原因。贵为国酒的茅台酒也是盐商华联锋建厂酿制并获得巴拿马世博会金奖），其时官岗场辖有盐滩 1062 副。1918 年，更名为王官场，场署移驻羊角沟。

寿光境内盐业史上的一件大事，是光绪十三年（1887 年）登莱青州道烟台海关监督盛宣怀奏请朝廷疏浚小清河以通盐运，方便寿光官台场原盐的运出。该工程采用以工代赈方法，集款百万银元，自济南黄台桥至寿光羊角沟海口，全长 250km，于 1890 年完成。这是山东历史上最大的盐运工程，为寿光官台场原盐在商埠重镇济南集散开辟一条空前的通航水道，羊口镇也成为著名的鱼盐重镇。1945 年 7 月，因其有特殊重要性而设立了羊口特别市，是今潍坊市境内设立最早的市。

国家关于环渤海地区地下卤矿勘测的权威著作《中国北方沿海第四纪地下卤水》一书载：“环绕现在滨海地带分布有一条连续的巨大地下卤水矿带，东起莱州沙河，西至黄河三角洲平原，东西长 120km 以上，矿带宽度受第四纪古地理环境制约，一般

10～20km，最大宽度达30km，最大面积2 500km^2”。其中“东起莱州市沙河西至寿光市小清河口，面积约1 500km^2 的地区内，卤水浓度常出现大于12～15Be′（波美度即俗称卤度）的高浓度富集区域，成为一个个小型聚卤盆地”。20世纪80年代，权威机构测得寿光羊口盐田的平均浓度为13.13°Be′，岔河盐区则达到17Be′，为环渤海、黄海地区卤度最高值。这一得天独厚的资源优势正可以解释为什么寿光北部沿海能够成为中国最早的海盐生产地和海盐制作中心、海盐生产技术中心。而双王城商周时期大型制盐遗址揭示出来的生产工艺，正是采用掘井汲取地下卤水经晒池蒸发最后火煎成盐，代表了当时最先进的海盐生产工艺和技术。

1904年，盐商肖锡纶在大家洼刘家呈子村北建滩110副，同时铺设通往羊角沟的“寿羊铁路”，长40华里，是寿光境内第一次出现铁路。

1939年1月，日军侵占羊角沟和侯镇，占据王官场公署，日伪军（盐警）分别达到200多人，为日军在寿光境内最大据点，日军配备了汽车，专事从盐区至昌乐火车站运盐，大量掠夺寿光所产原盐。产于侯镇郭家滩的大粒盐因其味美成为在日本倍受尊崇的腌菜专用盐。

1949年春，中共领导下的渤海行署在侯镇西河南村成立莱州盐务分局。山东省盐警部队第二大队在寿光成立，共400余人，驻今营里镇益隆道口村，防区辖广饶、寿光、潍县、昌邑、掖县等。

1956年4月，莱州盐务分局裁撤，成立山东省羊口盐场管理处（县级），驻羊角沟。10月，山东省盐务局在对寿光北部沿海勘查基础上，提出“关于在山东新建盐场的初步建议”（即筹建山东羊口盐场）。同月，国家食品工业部和国家盐务总局成立“山东羊口盐场勘察委员会”，国家食品工业部部长李烛尘率队到羊口实地勘察。

1956年，成立山东省盐业科学研究所（1998年更名为山东省海洋化工科学研究院），是全国继中国盐业总公司制盐工程技术研究院（成立于1955年）之后成立的第一个省级盐业科学研究机构。

1957年，羊角沟、岔河盐场扩建，新建成“地方国营寿光县盐场”，建成新盐田22副，6 600公亩。1959年在场西建成“寿光县化工厂”，为寿光历史上第一个盐化工企业。

1958年春，国家计委正式批准建设“山东羊口盐场”，总投资4 200万元，年原盐生产能力130万t（分多期建设）。12月，除主体劳力由寿光组织外，潍坊专署还从辖县调民工13 000人赴羊口开工建设羊口盐场。1959年，继续采取这个方法进行盐场续建。岔河盐场新建盐田10副，3 000公亩。

1959年，安徽省政府投资在寿光菜央子村北建设“国营安徽菜央子盐场”，建成盐田51副，面积2 300公亩。1975年，菜央子盐场建成氯化钾厂，总投资868万元，年产氯化钾1 500t，溴素150t，氯化镁15 000t，为20世纪70年代寿光境内最大的盐化工企业。

1960年，羊口盐场自备电厂建成投产，为寿光地域内第一个电力生产企业，1975年，扩建至1×3 000kW机组，增加投资211万元。同年，山东省盐业学校由青岛市迁至羊口盐场。

1964年，羊口盐场建成厂内轻轨铁路14.7km，为寿光境内建成的第二条铁路。1968年，又建成羊口盐场化工厂，为寿光境内第二处盐化工企业，当年生产氯化钾35t。1971年，又建成羊口盐场吹溴厂，年产溴素100t，为寿光境内第三处盐化工企业。1978年，羊口盐场又建成洗盐厂，年产粉碎洗涤盐7 300t。

1966年，寿光、广饶两县盐务局合并，成立"山东羊角沟盐务管理局"，驻寿光菜央子盐场，隶属中国盐业公司。同年，昌乐盐业运销站成立，归羊口盐场管理。

1977年，寿光在原有9个公社建有盐场的基础上，又有18个公社建立盐场，全县21个公社全部建成盐场，社队盐场至1980年总面积达到17.7万亩。

1978年，成立昌潍地区盐务局，驻寿光大家洼村。

进入改革开放时期后，寿光市党组织和人民，乘借着寿光深厚的盐文化底蕴，他们的智慧和创造力有两次惊人爆发，铸就中国盐业史上两次令人目眩的精彩华章。

1982年9月，党的十二大胜利召开，提出建设社会主义现代化的宏伟目标。新一届寿光市委、寿光市政府建立后，科学分析寿光面临的形势。当时摆在寿光发展面前的一个突出问题是，由于寿光原盐产大于销，且由于交通、加工等方面问题，原盐积压严重。40岁以上到过寿北的人脑子里都会留下一副景象：寿光北部除了大片盐碱地，望不到边的盐田和布满盐田中堆如山头的巨大盐坨，总积压量有300万t之多，由于积压严重，曾进行过多次限产，甚至毁滩。带着这一问题，寿光市政府分管工业生产的副市长王明新代表市委、市政府多次到山东省化工厅寻策，并提出建设纯碱厂的设想，与省化工厅取得共识。在山东省化工厅大力支持下，寿光县政府委托化工部第一研究设计院（又称天津设计院）、省化工厅设计院联合进行各项勘探勘查，进行可行性论证，制订年产60万t纯碱生产项目的设计方案。这其中尤为艰苦的是前期长达几年的各种生产条件勘查论证，仅供水条件一项，即在原寒桥镇营子村、建桥乡马疃村打群井进行抽水试验三个月。年产60万t纯碱除每天几十吨的水源供应、年消耗原盐90万t外，还要消耗90万t石灰石、90万t煤。为了解决石、煤运输问题，寿光市委、市政府又会同山东省盐业公司积极向国家计委争取益羊铁路建设项目，最后各项生产要件逐一攻破。期间时任国家化学工业部部长秦仲达、山东副省长谭庆琏多次为该项目带队到寿光进行考察论证，同时也引起昌潍地委、行署的重视，省政府专门成立以宋一民副省长为首的项目建设领导小组。经过艰苦细致坚持不懈的攻坚、拼搏、努力，终于取得上下各方面对该项目的一致意见。在1985年6月国家计委召开投标会议前，由省化工厅举行定标会议，厅长贺国强主持会议，标书将该项目定名为"山东寿光纯碱厂"，项目负责人为姜万喜（化工厅办公室主任），项目总投资5.8亿元，全部由国家投资。"寿光纯碱厂"项目投标组一行旋即赴京，参加为期13d的投标会议。会议由化工部、国家计委联合举行。在参加投标的3个单位中，江苏省长顾秀莲、河北省长高扬亲自坐镇，山东省仅去两名副厅长，但寿光却在竞标中奇迹般地夺得第一名，寿光市副市长王明新自始至终参加会议，并在后来项目建设中担任副指挥。化工部部长秦仲达在投标会议结束的讲话中，特别对寿光纯碱厂项目提出三个要求，要求寿光项目要做到工程开工第一、项目投产第一、建设质量第一。寿光纯碱厂作为我国第一个动工兴建的年产60万t纯碱项目于1986年4月1日开工建设，1989年4月建成并一次投料试车成功，全部实现了秦仲达部长提出的要求（项目于建设过程中改名为潍坊纯碱厂）。

如今纯碱项目已经过多次扩产，今天已成为年产 200 万 t 的世界最大合成碱生产企业。1995 年，企业更名为山东潍坊海洋化工集团总公司，1996 年，更名为山东海化集团有限公司。1998 年，企业又以母公司独家发起人身份发起募集股份成立山东海化股份有限公司。2007 年，企业完成营业收入 220 亿元，实现利税 24 亿元，企业累计上交税金 40 亿元（税收直接上交潍坊市，寿光并未获益）。2008 年 7 月 11 日，于上海举行中国化工行业 500 强发布会，山东海化集团有限公司名列第一名。

寿光（潍坊）纯碱厂项目的成功建成和企业的发展，是寿光党组织和寿光人民创造力与奉献精神的集中展现。

随着“寿光纯碱厂”项目的落实，进一步打开了寿光党组织的思路。他们意识到，随着碱厂的建成投产，寿光生产的盐再也不会积压，寿光巨大的卤储量，巨大的盐生产能力很快就会变成滚滚财富，风吹卤苦的北部碱滩很快就会变成全市人民的聚宝盆。乘借这样一个历史机遇，寿光市委市政府高瞻远瞩，毅然决然，决定开发大寿北，把聚宝盆的潜在财富变成事实。从 1986 年 11 月，寿光市组织 560 人的规划设计队伍对寿北盐碱滩进行勘探规划，设计出年产 35 万 t 的盐田建设规划（同时规划设计了 10 万亩农田，3 万亩虾池）方案。从 1987 年 10 月 8 日，全市 34 处乡镇，组成 20 万人的施工大军，在东起丹河、西至塌河、南至咸淡水分界线、北至渤海岸方圆 1 200km^2 的大地上展开了中国有史以来一次性最大规模的盐田、台田、虾池开发大会战。40 天的背负、40 天的战斗、40 天的风寒、40 天的骇浪，寿光党组织、寿光人民以他们的英雄气概，把寿北荒滩变成一望无际的盐田（台田、虾池）美景。经过这一役，寿光境内盐田总面积达到 280 万公亩，至 2000 年，寿光境内原盐产量达到 700 万 t，仅盐一项，一年给国家和寿光人民创造的财富就达 3.5 亿元。

寿光盐田大开发，是中国历史中盐业开发史上的一次壮举，是宿沙氏“煮海为盐”创造精神在历经几千年沉积后在寿光土地上的又一次大绽放，是寿光党组织、寿光人民智慧、意志与创造力的一次集中展现，是寿光历史上一座泽惠人民的高大丰碑。

2010 年是改革开放 30 年。在中共中央政策研究室、中共中央财经领导小组办公室围绕 30 年改革开放总结的 18 个典型中，关于寿光经验的概括是：“山东省寿光市，发挥初始的农业比较优势，由农业起步，创新农业生产方式，以农业培养工业，以工业提升经济，靠农业富民，靠工业强市，实现了工农互助，城乡互动，工业和农业共同繁荣，城市和农村协调发展”。但是，这个概括并没有道出一个秘密：寿光有着优质的巨大的盐业资源。在整个 20 世纪 80、90 年代，寿光市财政比较宽松，因为寿光有数额巨大的盐业收入，地方财政的 70% 来自于盐业，由于这个原因，寿光没有给其他企业增加负担，得以实施放水养鱼的政策，没有给群众增加负担，得以藏富于民。由于寿光对其他市属企业实行放水养鱼的政策，这些企业顺利完成原始资本积累，使他们在进入新的发展阶段后得以迅速发展，成为寿光经济的支柱。由于藏富于民，才使寿光人民得以进行太阳能蔬菜高温大棚建设这样的高农业投入，使寿光农村经济得以持续高速的发展。正是由于寿光巨大的盐业资源这一“物阜”特点，才最终形成了寿光的“民丰”，这是寿光经济社会建设能够发展到今天的经济方面的原因。显然，盐是 30 年来寿光发展的真正“口粮”，是寿光发展最初最重要的经济基础。

盐在寿光历史发展中的作用是扮演“口粮”角色，在中国迄今为止的大部分历史上，盐同样扮演这样的角色。唐宋以来，盐税始终占国家财政收入的1/2～1/3，汉武帝（公元前119年）在江苏产盐地建立盐渎县，东晋时（公元411年）改为盐城县，因“环城皆盐场”而得名，有盐亭123所，唐王朝的“边饷半数出于兹”，成为中国东南盐业中心。至清朝，“天下税赋盐税居半，天下盐税两淮居半”，江苏扬州因此成为当时中国最大金融中心。俄罗斯学者库兰斯基说：“从人类文明开始直到大约100年前，盐都是人类历史上搜寻频率最高的一种商品”。正是靠着盐这样一种普通而又奇特的物质和商品，支撑起了中国秦、汉、隋、唐、宋、元、明、清的盛世王朝。而立朝160多年的元朝的灭亡，竟然是由盐而引起的。元代全国有盐场160余处，年产盐达到256万引（每引400斤），灶户等盐业劳动者超过5万人，其规模与产量远远超过宋代。元代卖盐实行盐引法，户部印引，盐产区都转运使司卖引，同时实行“计口摊课”，即由官府强行抑配食盐收取盐课，盐司又将卖不出去的盐强摊百姓以征盐课，农民终岁之粮，不足一引盐值，元惠宗年间（公元1341年），盐贩张士诚、方国珍与其他农民揭竿而起，元朝灭亡，史者称“元朝亡于盐政之乱”。

盐在中华民族历史上是如此重要，它也就成了祖国经济文化的“酵母基”。由此衍生出来的景象说不清、道不完。有日本学者提出，中国文字中当商人讲的贾（gǔ，音鼓）即出于盬字，盬即山西运城盐池之盐。由此可以看出，中国最早最重要的商品就是盐。《史记·货殖列传》记载战国时代的大商人：白圭、猗顿、郭纵、乌倮氏、寡妇清先世、蜀卓氏、梁宛氏。除去白圭、乌倮氏，其余5人均是营盐铁而富之。战国期间最有名的商人为猗（益）顿，是古代第一个以盐生意而著名的盐商，原是齐国境内一个小贵族，后去山西南部经营盐业和畜牧起家。历史上的“陶朱、猗顿之富”说，陶朱即居于山东定陶的范蠡，他助越王勾践灭吴后，以为勾践不可共安乐而弃官到定陶，成富商后称“陶朱公”。猗顿即求教于陶朱公，依其指点远行至郇（即盐池地河东），在此营盐十年成巨富，《史记》形容他为“赞拟王公，驰名天下”。齐人成为晋商之祖。扬州瘦西湖，六朝以来即是风景胜地，至清康乾年间，更是盛极一时，为扬州雍容华贵的象征，然而瘦西湖就是扬州众盐商为求乾隆帝减免贩盐课税而将护城河改造而成，成为“两堤花柳全依水，一路楼台直到山”的美景。大盐商江春竟用白盐一夜之间将北京白塔重建于瘦西湖上，获得乾隆称赞。曾任密州、登州知府的苏轼，在登州任上仅有5d，即为民请命，就盐制改革向宋朝廷提出了《乞罢登莱榷盐状》，提出莱州近海，地瘠民穷，官府专卖，加重百姓困苦，不利于增加财政收入，要求罢榷盐，令灶户卖盐与百姓，官收盐税。曾任（1051年）青州知府的范仲淹，仁宗年间曾任今江苏西溪盐仓监，负责管理5个盐场的生产和储运，他向泰州知府张纶提出修建捍海堰保护堤西盐田的建议被采纳，共修海坝近百公里，人称“范公堤”，为民景仰，后成为北宋王朝丞相。他在做盐仓监期间，留下一首《至西溪感赋》的诗：

谁道西溪小，西溪出大才。

参知两丞相，曾向此间来。

（连范仲淹在内，连续三任西溪盐仓监均升至丞相）。

清康熙年间青州（其时清山东提督府驻今青州市）一代文豪安志远写下著名的赞美家乡的诗作《寿光疆域赞》：

寿为岩邑兮逼处海澨，（岩：险要，澨：shi，水涯）
东界潍而西抵淄兮南尽于纪。
横则约而纵则侈兮幅员百里，
猗堂皇之巍峨兮伟东秦之侯国。
威行则万民知惧兮惠怀则四方咸喜，
伊任性以逞欲兮恐威惠之倒置。
待士如宾兮抚民如子，
谁为良牧兮挥弦而理？

公元1698年（康熙37年）安志远、安真父子受知县刘有成重托，纾家修志，编成清康熙《寿光县志》。其子安真在志后序中称寿光佳句有“北海名城，东秦壮县”、“浪莽效原，人物辐辏”、“衣冠文采，标盛东齐”、“桑枣渔盐，称雄左辅”、“瀛带洪川，民物交错”、“背临少海，鱼龙出没”，最后说“请询耆旧，海国名贤”。他们用“海澨”“北海”“少海”“海国”这样的词语来说寿光，“海滨广斥，厥土白坟”（《禹贡》语。意思为沿海一带是一片盐碱地，这里的土壤又白又肥），这是寿光的地貌特点，而这片土地上，正有天赐地赐神赐的晶莹之物——盐。

前边提到秦时寿光治设在双王城附近的盐城，盐城后为海水漫没，寿光县治才渐往南迁。而发生于北宋仁宗皇祐年间（1049年）的大海潮却被一个名叫黄庶的诗人记载下来：

盐民没利家海隅，奔走末业田荒芜。
天意似遣阳侯驱，卷水沃杀煎海炉。
怒涛百尺不及逋，老幼十五其为鱼。

而安真（1698）在编著《寿光县志》而走“耆旧”寻访中到了寿北盐场，亲眼目睹了煮盐人的劳苦，作下《煮海叹》一诗：

煮海成盐属官家，豪狡盘踞为生涯。
白镪千亿归囊橐，隐如大吏坐排衙。
编氓不敢挟升台，私贩罪重遭箠挞。
安得百川化为卤，万民负载无忧嗟。

历史发展到中国北魏时期，生活在寿光的一位大学问家贾思勰写出一部著作《齐民要术》，这是世界历史上现存最早最全面最系统的百科全书性质的科学著作。它集中反映了北魏时期中国先进的经济、文化和科学技术，是了解中国古代史、中国科技史、中国经济史、中国社会史不可多得的一部著作。著作开端，在申明写这部著作宗旨的《序》中，贾思勰就提到在中国盐业史上有重要地位的桑弘羊，提到姜太公封齐后在齐国盐碱地上种出谷子的业绩，提到他记录的范围是自耕田务农到酿造酱醋全过程的生产技术。在《齐民要术》第8卷第二节（总第69节）专门记述了常满盐、花盐、印盐的生产技术。常满盐、花盐、印盐相当于我们今天的精制盐。他描述生产出来的花盐“厚薄和光泽很像钟乳石”，他描述生产出的印盐“像豆粒一样大小，呈四方形，全都一个样子”，他赞美花盐、印盐，说“都像玉石、雪一样洁白，味道也特别鲜美”。在其第 8、第 9 两卷中，他记载达 209 种食品（不含酒类）的制作加工方法，其中需要用盐加工的 103 种。堪称世界历史上第一部盐与饮食的技术大全。

寿光盛产盐，寿光历史上也有不少盐官，在明清之际寿光第一名门望族斟灌李氏落地寿光 600 年间，共出了大小 100 多位朝廷命官，其中就有多位出任过盐官。最著名的是湖北巡抚李封，他与刘镛、纪晓岚等同科考中进士后，先做翰林庶吉士，后任职刑部，又任庐州知府，旋迁江西盐法道，续升浙江按察使。当他从江西盐法道位上谢职即将升迁浙江时，江西盐商感念他的惠德惠政，赠他 8 000 两纹银作程仪，被他严拒。他一生为官清廉，离职返家时“宦橐萧然”。他逝世后，嘉庆帝派出太监 11 人，带御祭 8 担亲往吊祭，当朝第一大学士纪晓岚亲自为他提撰墓志铭，对他为政清廉的一生给予高度评价。铭曰：“人以官富，公以官贫，贫则贫矣，而秋水无尘。”

其美其赞，无以复加！

寿光人血脉里与海与盐相联。历史到了 20 世纪 40 年代，当抗日烽火骤起之时，寿光有两支抗日队伍揭竿而起，一支是共产党领导的八支队以及其后的八路军寿光地方部队，一支是国民党员张景月领导的十五旅。这两支队伍起义后都迅速发展，相继与日寇开战。八支队起义后奉命东征，杀七支队中的叛逆张洪礼，救胶东抗日武装于危急，旋赴鲁中成山东纵队第一支队。国民党十五旅，盘踞寿光，兴学治乡，为国民党政府所欣赏。国民党山东省长何思远自重庆领命来鲁，即首至昌乐（由寿光田马官村人张天佐为县长，兴办昌乐中学，在校生达 2000 人，治为国民党统治中“模范县”），再至寿光在张景月部队护送下至济上任（抗日战争时期，震惊世界的亚洲最大集中营“潍县集中营”2400 名同盟国侨民生命难继之时即由寿光黄家庄人黄乐德赖张天佐、张景月等资助十几万美元而得以存活。黄乐德是寿光不为世人所知的第二次世界大战中的“辛德勒”）。这两部分队伍在寿光均未给群众造成大负担，且发展迅速，其中重要原因是寿光北部有拉不完的盐。盐是滋养这两部分队伍的重要经济来源。

盐对于寿光和寿光人，说不尽，道不完。寿光北部商周时期大型制盐遗址的发现，引起了有心人、有心地方的注意。遗址考古负责人燕生东对笔者说，一个同在渤海边，汉时在那里设过盐官的地方，正在积极争取中国盐文化博物馆项目，并且为此悄悄地到寿光商周制盐遗址探视多次。我们该做些什么呢？

血脉总要流传。用一位盐民后代的心声来结束这番言语吧：

我感到，盐在我体内的血管中，
伴随着脉搏的跳动一阵一阵地激荡。
当大海的潮汐慢慢地退去，
就把几千年里的滩涂留在岁月的空旷里。
日月在盐田上静静地轮回，
盐工在盐田里默默地劳作，
盐粒不仅是海水的结晶，
也是汗水和智慧的结晶。

盐田积满了海水和阳光，
也积满了岁月和苦难，
盐田是大海的缩影，
也是日子的沉淀。
咸涩的海风，
总是吹向盐田深处。
在盐田的深处，
有我祖辈生活的家园。

参 考 文 献

[1] 范文澜，蔡美彪. 中国通史 [M]. 北京：人民出版社，1992
[2] 贾效孔. 寿光考古与文物 [M]. 中国文史出版社，2001
[3] 王仁湘，张征雁. 盐与文明 [M]. 辽宁人民出版社，2007
[4] 魏道揆. 安静子诗词选注 [M]. 中国文联出版公司，2002
[5] 张学海. 考古学反映的山东古史演进 [M]. 山东文联出版社，2004
[6] 山东省寿光县地方史志编纂委员会. 寿光县志 [M]. 上海. 中国大百科全书出版社，1992
[7] 吴晓东，袁萍. 双王城商周制盐中心何以炼就，寿光日报 [M]. 寿光：寿光日报社，2008，9：22

Salt, Shouguang City and its History

ZHAO Shou-xiang
(*Party History Research Center of CPC Shouguang Municipal Committee*, *Shouguang* 262700)

Abstract: Salt material is playing important role in the development of human life and the society and, it is extremely unusual phenomenon in the development of human life and the society. The wisdom of human is able to be refracted from the salt. Shouguang is the Chinese earliest habitat of sea salt. The sea salt production technology has expanded from Shouguang to the entire areas surrounding Bohai Sea, and also passed on along with the history to South of China. Salt is acting as "grain ration" in the entire history of China civilization, and so is in Shouguang's history. The sea and the salt are sharing the same roots with Shouguang people. The Shouguang culture, the Shouguang people's personality can be disclosed deeply in the impression of sea and the salt.

Key words: Salt; Shouguang city; History